Emery Walker ph.sc.

Wm Osler

The young Professor at McGill

THE LIFE OF
SIR WILLIAM OSLER

BY

HARVEY CUSHING

VOL. I

'Thus there are two books from whence I collect my divinity: besides that written one of God, another of his servant nature, that universal and public manuscript, that lies expansed unto the eyes of all; those that never saw him in the one, have discovered him in the other.'
Religio Medici.

Second Impression

OXFORD
AT THE CLARENDON PRESS
1925

Printed in England

TO MEDICAL STUDENTS

IN THE HOPE THAT SOMETHING OF OSLER'S SPIRIT MAY BE CONVEYED TO THOSE OF A GENERATION THAT HAS NOT KNOWN HIM; AND PARTICULARLY TO THOSE IN AMERICA, LEST IT BE FORGOTTEN WHO IT WAS THAT MADE IT POSSIBLE FOR THEM TO WORK AT THE BEDSIDE IN THE WARDS

BECAUSE of Osler's interest in the history of his profession the effort has been made in these volumes to bring him into proper alignment with that most remarkable period in the annals of Medicine through which he lived and of which he was part.

Those who knew him best will appreciate the difficulties of compiling these present records, which are *mémoires pour servir.* Little pretence is made in them to do much more than let his story so far as possible tell itself through what he puts on paper.

His rare personality, spirit, and character stand out in his recovered letters, brief though they are. An appraisal of his professional accomplishments need not at present be attempted. Here are merely the outlines for the final portrait, to be painted out when the colours, lights, and shadows come in time to be added—colours and lights chiefly, for only one heavy shadow is cast, just before the end.

The author herewith expresses his deep gratitude to the many whose names occur in the following pages, and to a still larger number whose names do not, yet who have equally lightened his labour of love by innumerable kindnesses.

OXFORD,
August 1924.

CONTENTS OF VOLUME I

PART I

THE CANADIAN PERIOD, 1849–1884

Bond Head and Dundas.

Toronto.

Montreal.

PART II

THE UNITED STATES, 1884–1905

Philadelphia.

Baltimore.

ILLUSTRATIONS IN VOLUME I

LIST OF ABBREVIATIONS IN VOL. I

A. A. P.	Association of American Physicians.
A. M. A.	American Medical Association.
B. A. A. S.	British Association for the Advancement of Science.
B. C. H.	Boston City Hospital.
B. M. A.	British Medical Association.
B. M. J.	British Medical Journal.
C. M. A.	Canadian Medical Association.
D. N. B.	Dictionary of National Biography.
E. Y. D.	Egerton Yorrick Davis.
F.R.C.P.	Fellow of the Royal College of Physicians.
H. M. S.	Harvard Medical School.
J. H. H.	Johns Hopkins Hospital.
J. H. U.	" " University.
M. G. H.	{ Montreal General Hospital. { Massachusetts General Hospital.
'Medico-Chi.'	Medico-Chirurgical Society (Montreal).
M.R.C.P.	Member of Royal College of Physicians.
N.A.S.P.T.	National Association for the Study and Prevention of Tuberculosis.
R. C. P.	Royal College of Physicians.
R. P. M.	Regius Professor of Medicine.
R. V. H.	Royal Victoria Hospital (Montreal).
S. G. L.	Surgeon-General's Library (Washington).
S. G. O.	" " Office.
T. B.	{ Tubercle Bacillus. { Tuberculosis.
U. C.	University College (London).
U. P.	" of Pennsylvania.

PART I
THE CANADIAN PERIOD

'Those who have written about him from later impressions than those of which I speak, seem to me to give insufficient prominence to his gaiety. It was his cardinal quality in those early days. A childlike mirth leaped and danced from him; he seemed to skip upon the hills of life. He was simply bubbling with quips and jests; his inherent earnestness or passion about abstract things was incessantly relieved by jocosity; and when he had built one of his intellectual castles in the sand a wave of humour was certain to sweep in and destroy it. I cannot, for the life of me, recall any of his jokes; and written down in cold blood they might not be funny if I did. They were not wit so much as humanity, the many-sided outlook upon life. I am anxious that his laughter-loving mood should not be forgotten, because later on it was partly, but I should think never wholly, quenched.'

Edmund Gosse on Robert Louis Stevenson.

CHAPTER I

BOND HEAD AND DUNDAS

William Osler, the youngest son in a family of nine, was born July 12, 1849, in a parsonage at Bond Head, Tecumseth County, near the edge of the wilderness in what was Upper Canada. How this came about, as to place, time, and circumstance, needs telling from the very beginning.

One of the old Canadian trails used by voyageur, missionary, and Indian led from 'Muddy York' (Toronto) on Lake Ontario to a landing on the south-eastern end of Georgian Bay bearing the name of Penetanguishene. This was a matter of some seventy miles as the crow flies, but by stream and portage—up the Humber, the long carry across the low ridges, down the Holland, across Lac aux Claies (Simcoe), and finally by the Severn River to 'Penetang' [1]—it must have been so devious as to make the longer way round, by Niagara and Detroit to Lake Huron and the Sault, seem the shortest way across this upper-river portion of the original Province of Quebec.

Geographical obstacles, however, can be energetically attacked when a military objective is in view: and so when Upper Canada was partitioned off from the Old Province in 1791 and General John G. Simcoe, who had commanded a Loyalist corps under Cornwallis during the Revolutionary War, came to be its first Governor, with the aid of his soldiers, the 'Queen's Rangers', he built a strategic road, or, more properly speaking, broke trail through forest and swamp for such a road, in direct line the thirty-eight miles from York to Holland Landing near the southern arm of what came to be called Lake Simcoe. This road is now the celebrated Yonge Street, said to be the longest 'street' in

[1] According to Parkman it was the route to Lake Huron and Michilimackinac followed in 1680 by La Salle in his expedition to relieve Henri de Tonty, whom he had left the year before at Fort Crèvecœur on the Illinois.

the world, though for many years after it was projected it scarcely deserved even the name of trail.[1]

But Governor Simcoe wisely devoted himself to other things than the mere military defence of his province. A thorough surveyal and the promise of 100-acre grants to settlers greatly encouraged immigration, particularly on the part of the United Empire Loyalists who had flocked into all parts of Canada after the revolt of the colonies. Concessions were also made in course of time for the British half-pay officers and pensioners, veterans of the Colonial and Napoleonic wars, so that the fertile province began to be settled by a loyal stock, people in many instances of birth and education. They adapted themselves to the life of frontier farmers, whose chief enemy was the forest and whose main outlet for their simple produce was along Yonge Street, the straight road to Toronto, the growing capital of the Province.

These early settlers and concessionaires, being law-abiding and God-fearing people, felt the want of ministers

[1] 'Lieut.-Governor Simcoe's route on foot and in canoes to explore a way which might afford communication for the fur-traders to the Great Portage, without passing Detroit in case that place were given up to the United States. The march was attended with some difficulties, but was quite satisfactory; an excellent harbour at Penetanguishene; returned to York, 1793.' (Note on contemporary map.)

'*Monday, Dec.* 28, 1795. A party began to cut a road from hence [York] to the Pine Fort at Holland River near Lake Simcoe. Mr. Jones the Surveyor says the Indians killed over 500 deer in a month.' (Mrs. Simcoe's diary.)

It was along this narrow trail behind nine yoke of oxen, with the naval base at Penetang as his destination, that Pierre le Pelletier (Peter Pilky) of Scarboro Township, one time baker to the garrison at York, dragged a two-ton anchor as far as Holland Landing, where it was abandoned in the bush when the belated news finally reached him that the war of 1812–15 was ended.

Along the same trail at the close of the war Lord Selkirk's last expedition, representing the Hudson Bay Company interests, passed on their way to the Georgian Bay, the Sault, and Fort William (the 'Northwest Fur Company's' stronghold), and finally the next year (1817) pushed on to the Red River Settlement.

During the war of 1812, on land purchased from the Indians, a rough forest road had been cut through from Kempenfelt to Penetanguishene. Lake Simcoe remained the connecting link between the two highways until 1827, when 'Yonge Street' and this northern segment were connected by a track through the wilderness to the west of the lake with its northern terminus at Barrie on Kempenfelt Bay.

of the Gospel and accessible places of worship, and as many of them were members of the Anglican Church, urgent calls as time went on were forwarded through the colonial bishops, to the Society for the Propagation of the Gospel in Foreign Parts [1] for young clergymen who were unafraid of the rigours of frontier and wilderness.

There was need of one of these to cover the townships of Tecumseth and West Gwillimbury, half-way between Toronto and 'Penetang', and thus it came about that in the early summer of 1837 Featherstone Lake Osler and his young bride Ellen Free Pickton with all their earthly goods, including a tin box of home-made Cornish gingerbread, found their way north along Yonge Street as far as Holland Landing, and thence the following day, as will be told, to a hamlet or cross-roads subsequently known as Bond Head.[2]

This young couple who hailed from Cornwall were representatives of very different ethnic types—Anglo-Saxon and Celt. The clergyman, whose readiness for a service spiced with adventure may have resulted from several years of apprenticeship in the Royal Navy, was reserved in temperament, stocky, fair, grey-eyed, and broad-headed. His wife, a native of London, adopted by an uncle in Falmouth, though blessed like her husband with a good mind in a sound body, was, however, of short and slender build, and of so dark a complexion that in later years many who did not know her ancestry assumed that Indian blood flowed in her veins. But these small, olive-complexioned English people, sometimes called 'black Celts', are thought to be remainders of the original Briton driven by successive invasions into the inaccessible parts of Argyllshire, of mountainous Wales, of Western Ireland,

[1] The original Society, founded in 1649 with the Hon. Robert Boyle as its first Governor, had as its avowed object, until the separation of the colonies, 'the propagation of the Gospel in New England and the adjoining parts of America.'

[2] From the celebrated Sir Francis Bond Head, then Lieutenant-Governor, who quelled the insurrection of 1837. Yonge Street was named after Sir George Yonge, Secretary for War in 1791. Bond Head lay a few miles off the direct overland route to 'Penetang', representing the extension of Yonge Street across the great swamp and through the wilderness of Innisfil to the west of Lake Simcoe.

and of Cornwall and Brittany[1]—the regions of Gaelic speech and crosses.

Another tradition, as old as Tacitus, ascribes this brunette type to an Iberian infusion, and it is not inconceivable that the Mediterranean folk who for centuries came for trade, if not for conquest, mayhap left behind them, in exchange for Cornish tin, darker skins, and livelier dispositions quite foreign at least to anything donated to the British character by Angles or Saxons. However this may be, known to her schoolmates as 'Little Pick', old friends in Falmouth spoke of Ellen Pickton as 'a very pretty girl, clever, witty, and lively, with a power of quick repartee, wilful but good-tempered, not easily influenced, very faithful in her friendships, and of strong religious principle'. In these traits as well as in their personal appearance two of her sons, Britton and William, closely resembled her.

The Oslers had lived for long in Cornwall, a race of successful merchants and shipowners for the most part, and the family was strong in traditions of the sea. In a fragment of autobiography left by Featherstone Osler, he says: 'My grandfather Osler died in the West Indies from the effects of a wound. One uncle was killed in action with a French privateer. Another was drowned in Swan Pool near Falmouth, and a cousin a lieutenant in the Royal Navy died of yellow fever in the West Indies.' The 'Grandfather Osler' here mentioned was Edward, who had married Joan Drew, the sister of Samuel the Cornish metaphysician; and it is not unlikely that from this source there came into the Osler line a strain which modified the strongly developed family trait which went to the making of hard-headed men of business and venturesome merchants. This Edward and Joan left six children, only two of whom had issue, Edward the father of Featherstone, progenitor of the Canadian branch of the family, and Benjamin, whose descendants are now scattered in the United States, South Africa, and Australia.[2]

[1] According to W. Z. Ripley's 'Races of Europe', 1899, a trace of them remains in the fen district of East Anglia.

[2] The writer has met a member of the Australian branch, whose likeness to Sir William Osler in figure, stature, gesture, feature, and shape of head

This second Edward became a Falmouth merchant, and in 1795 married Mary Paddy, who lived to be ninety-nine, and was herself the daughter of a shipowner. Of their nine children there were three particularly notable sons, all of whom showed outstanding ability coupled with strongly developed religious tendencies. Edward the eldest son, of dark complexion and short stature, after a period at Guy's Hospital became a member of the Royal College of Surgeons, a surgeon in the navy, a Fellow of the Linnean Society, a writer of poems, psalms, and hymns, and a newspaper editor, who despite all this practised medicine long years in Truro, Cornwall. If one may judge from the titles of his three best-known publications,[1] his heart wavered between the navy, the Church, and natural history; and in him as physician, naturalist, and author may be recognized many marks of resemblance, mental and physical, to those possessed by the nephew with whose traits this memoir is primarily concerned.

Featherstone Lake, the third son, has just been left with his bride in Upper Canada, where five years later he is to be joined by his younger brother Henry Bath, Edward's fifth son. For he, also, became a missionary clergyman, who after a residence of thirty-two years in Lloydtown, not far from Bond Head, was transferred to York Mills on Yonge Street north of Toronto. There he continued as rector for another twenty-eight years, until his death in 1902 in his eighty-eighth year.[2] Thus, for the most part, an enviable longevity has characterized the Osler family.

Probably all Falmouth boys brought up within the sight and smell of the sea come to feel its lure, and so it was with Featherstone Osler, a reckless and daring boy, who

was so striking that he might have passed as a younger brother, though as a matter of fact their common ancestors were this gentleman's great-great-grandfather and grandmother—Edward Osler and Joan Drew. Hence, though Sir William's resemblance to his mother was striking, it is evident that his physical type cannot be laid entirely at her door in view of the close resemblance between such distant cousins.

1 'The Life of Admiral Viscount Exmouth'; 'Church and King'; 'Burrowing and Boring Marine Animals', &c. Cf. *Dict. Nat. Biography*.

2 He was made Canon of St. Alban's, Toronto; and Rural Dean of York.

when very young had been sent inland to a boarding-school lest he should be drowned. But the appeal was irresistible, and in his teens he was at sea on a schooner, the *Sappho*, bound for the Mediterranean. A dreadful voyage it was, with storms, a near shipwreck and starvation, adrift for weeks on the ocean. Undaunted by this experience he later joined the Royal Navy and went to sea as a cadet. This time his brig-of-war was wrecked in earnest near the Barbadoes, and there followed yellow fever and a pest ship on the way home to face a court-martial, as is the custom when a ship-of-war is lost, from whatever cause. Then to sea again as sub-lieutenant on a 'crack' frigate, the *Tribune*; and four full years of cruising in remote seas ensued, with much of interest and excitement that might be quoted from the journals which, sailor-fashion, he kept during this period. At the end of this long absence, when word came that his father was in poor health and wished to see him before he died, he threw up his prospects in the navy despite a tempting offer from the Admiralty to remain in service, and in 1832 left his ship at Rio and returned to Falmouth. Shelved from the navy by his decision, and having often entertained the thought of taking Holy Orders, after some preliminary studying of Latin and Greek he entered St. Catherine's Hall, Cambridge, in October 1833, and was elected Mathematical Scholar of the college at the first examination. Here, he says, he 'read very hard and looked forward to the prospect of obtaining a high degree and settling down in England in a quiet parish'—with Ellen Pickton as his wife, it may be added, for they had become engaged not long after his return. But this was not to be: it was made clear that his duty lay elsewhere and he could not refuse the call:

It was desired that I should go to Canada early in the spring. Before doing so I had to pass the University Examinations, take my degree, pass the examination for Holy Orders, be ordained, get married and make all necessary preparations for leaving England. This I was enabled to do by the University allowing me to pass my examinations a term before the usual time, though by so doing my name would not appear on the Honour List. The Bishop of London also kindly admitted me to examination two months before the ordinary time, and gave me letters dismissory to the Archbishop

LOWER CANADA
L. Nipissing
CHIPPEWA HUNTING COUNTRY
Immense Forests
LAKE HURON
Black River
Penetanguishene
Kempenfelt Bay
Lake Simcoe
Barrie
Great Tract of Woodland
UPPER CANADA
Newmarket
Bond Head
Yonge Street
York Mills
Weston
Toronto
LAKE ONTARIO
Hamilton
Burlington Bay
Dundas
Niagara Harbour
Niagara Falls
Gennessee R.
NEW YORK
UPPER
CANADA
1837
From a map compiled by David William Smyth Esq.
R.R.C. Davis

of Canterbury by whom I was ordained in Lambeth Palace early in March 1837.

I had been married early in the previous month, and made arrangements to sail in the barque *Bragila* some time during April, Henry Scadding (then a Divinity student) to be our fellow-passenger. On April 6, 1837, we sailed from Falmouth for Quebec, and after a tedious passage of seven weeks and a half, having narrowly escaped shipwreck on Egg Island, in the Gulf of St. Lawrence, landed in Quebec, and were warmly received by Bishop Mountain . . .

After a stay of eight days in Quebec we proceeded on our journey towards Toronto, and, that we might not lose sight of our luggage, took the route from Montreal and via the Rideau Canal to Kingston, thence by steamer to Toronto. Here we were cordially welcomed by the Archdeacon who informed us that the Rev. H. O'Neil had made all necessary arrangements as to our future residence. We remained four days in Toronto, then resuming our journey northward reached Holland Landing late that same evening, slept there, and the afternoon of the following day arrived at Tecumseth in safety, after driving over roads such as we had never seen before. So bad were they that the driver, with a pair of strong horses, after driving us ten miles to what was then called the Corners (afterwards Bond Head) positively refused to take us the remaining two or three miles, declaring it would kill his horses to do so. Here, after procuring refreshments we got fresh horses and drove to the residence of a farmer named Mairs, where Mr. O'Neil had secured for us the only accommodation to be had in the parish. It consisted of a tiny sitting-room and an apology for a bedroom. Our entire luggage had to be stored in a barn. Poor as was our accommodation, we were thankful to have reached our journey's end.

Bond Head

For the first few months, indeed for the first few years, these young people endured a life of actual hardship. The nearest post-office was at Holland Landing twelve miles away; the nearest doctor fifteen miles away at Newmarket; the nearest blacksmith six miles away, and the roads permitting access to them were much of the time wellnigh impassable. The two townships were sparsely settled, and it was a most difficult matter for the young clergyman to carry out what he regarded as the duties of his pastorate.

The white settlers in Simcoe County at this time were of many sorts, though the Indians possibly still outnumbered them.[1] Among the 'U. E. Loyalists' there was a body of Quaker settlers from Pennsylvania who had taken up grants on the northern slopes of the Ridges, and around Holland Landing was a smattering of Lord Selkirk's colonists, mostly Sutherlandshire Highlanders, who in canoes had despairingly made their way back from the Red River country, when lawlessness reigned during the struggle between the Great Companies for supremacy in the fur trade.[2] There were, too, a few French Canadians, but perhaps the majority of the more recent colonists, from 1830 on, were Irish, with a predominance of ardent Orangemen from Ulster, who will be heard of again.

But in a new country a minister, whatever his denomination, is welcome, and in the County of Simcoe—where many of the settlers had not seen a Protestant clergyman for years, their children remaining unbaptized and uninstructed—whenever Featherstone Osler appeared all within reach for miles around attended service; none the less eagerly that the setting must be in some farmer's unchinked log barn. A better place of worship was an outstanding need, and he set to work with his accustomed energy to erect a church before considering what would seem to be still more essential, a dwelling for himself. However, the people were poor, money was scarce, and building materials impossible to get, for as there were no saw-mills near dry lumber was not to be had; and, what is more, 1837, as it may be remembered, was the year of the disorder associated with the abortive rebellion engineered by William L. MacKenzie, the first mayor of Toronto. Nevertheless, somehow a church for each township was finally got under cover, and as they were only seven miles apart, the young clergyman could manage a Sunday sermon in each place, as well as

[1] These were mostly Chippewas (Ojibways). The Hurons whom Champlain found in this country the century before had been exterminated. The counties adjacent to York and Simcoe contained many Iroquois, particularly Mohawks from New York, whose chief, Joseph Brant, under the influence of Sir William Johnson, had sided with the British on the revolt of the colonies.

[2] Many years later Sir William Osler purchased and sent to the library at Winnipeg some of Lord Selkirk's journals, which he had picked up at a sale in London.

an afternoon service in a stable at Bond Head, which lay half-way between.

Meanwhile, their own living conditions were nearly intolerable, even for two stout-hearted young people, and Ellen Osler years later as a grandmother would tell how her husband was 'away from Tuesday till Friday each week as a general thing, riding on horseback through the woods and swamps, over trails and corduroy roads, the bridges over the wetter parts of the swamps, where there was no footing, being made of floating logs fastened together—this floating road at one place being two miles long and very insecure it was, for the logs dipped and shifted'.

The clergyman himself has left a vivid account of these days, not only in a journal he kept as an aid in preparing his regular reports for his superiors, but in a fragmentary autobiographical sketch [1] which states:

At the expiration of our three months we found we had to leave our quarters, and where to go we knew not. At length a hut was found, in which cattle had been kept. Several women of the parish met together and cleaned it as far as it was possible, and into this we moved for the winter, our clothing, trunks, &c., having to be kept in a barn three-quarters of a mile off. The hut was surrounded by dead trees, and, with the exception of wolves, no living creatures were within a third of a mile from us. Part of the winter my good wife spent at Newmarket where our first son, Featherston, was born, during which time I lived alone, chinking up the holes in the hut with snow and cooking my own food. It was so lonely that no servant would live there.

When the spring opened even this poor accommodation had to be given up, a farmer needing it for his cattle. After much search a log house about twelve feet square with loose boards as flooring was found at West Gwillimbury. A stable three-quarters of a mile from it was secured, and all our luggage, beyond absolute necessaries, was stored in a barn three miles distant. The utter discomfort to which we were subjected began to affect our health. The hut in which we were living was on the roadside, far from any house, and we had to depend upon the parishioners to bring us wood for fuel. This they would occasionally forget to do, and we had at times to go to bed in the day to keep ourselves warm.

---

[1] These journals have been privately printed by his sons—'Records of the Lives of Ellen Free Pickton and Featherstone Lake Osler.' The Oxford University Press, 1919, 4to, 257 pp.

The next spring an acre of ground was given and money subscribed for a parsonage, 'a cottage 30 × 40, the people engaging to erect a stable'. Here on the crest of a low hill by the roadside, a long mile to the north of Bond Head Corners, they finally took up their residence, and ere long Trinity Church was built near by on the lower slope of the hill. So they may be pictured, he at home with his family and local parish from Friday to Tuesday, but away on the other days on horseback and alone, with the baptismal register[1] in his saddle-bag, covering a huge territory to the north as far as Penetanguishene and as far south as Thornhill, establishing congregations and opening Sunday-schools. His ministrations often took him into districts so remote he could only reach them twice a year, and as there were few post-offices he would have to announce the day of the subsequent visit three to six months hence as the case might be, 'and without any other notice the congregation would be waiting at the time specified'.

Ellen Osler, meanwhile, not only had the responsibility of a rapidly accumulating flock of her own, but conducted a famed Sunday-school to which children came from miles around. She also established a celebrated sewing-school, for:

> . . . Observing how ignorant the girls were and how untidily they dressed, she proposed to give instruction in cutting out and making their clothes every Tuesday and Friday in the afternoon. Soon a class of twenty-eight girls and young women were gathered together, who instead of coming in the afternoon would come in the morning, remaining the whole day, anxious for instruction. That school did more towards elevating the tone of the people than almost anything else, and to this day many of the women of Tecumseth, now mothers and grandmothers, speak of it as one of the greatest blessings of their lives.

The low one-story parsonage with such a couple in residence naturally became in time the social as well as

[1] This register of marriages, baptisms, and births is still preserved in the parish church, Bond Head, and contains entries of christenings not infrequently as many as fifteen a day. Among them is that of William Osler, and on the same page that of the father of Dr. Banting, the recent discoverer of Insulin. The church contains the white-oak benches from the original building that stood by the Osler parsonage, but of which no trace now remains.

the religious centre of the region. The neighbouring farms, mostly 200-acre grants, began to be taken up by those who became intimates and friends of parents and offspring, for children were born to those early settlers in generous numbers. In the parsonage itself in the course of the first fourteen years all but two of the nine Osler children came into the world. As his father's journal relates, Featherston [1] the eldest was born in Newmarket during the first winter, and the second son, Britton,[2] known in the family as 'B. B.', the following year in Bond Head.

The year 1841 found the father somewhat broken in health, with a bad cough and an abscess in the back caused by the continuous riding on horseback, necessitating a rest and change. A much-needed vacation with a sojourn in England was therefore taken, and on their return some months later, with their Falmouth-born daughter, Ellen Mary, they found 'upwards of sixty wagon-loads of people' gathered at Holland Landing to escort them the twelve miles to the rectory. In renewed vigour the active life of a frontier parson was again resumed. The church was enlarged with funds donated at home, and the business ability of his merchant forebears began to show itself in his relations to his parishioners in matters temporal as well as spiritual. He taught them farming, and how to make husbandry pay, lent them money, drew up wills for them, dispensed spectacles, and in countless other ways tended to their material and physical as well as spiritual needs.

In a country with an almost unbroken primeval forest, clearing the land for farming is a slow process, and Bond

[1] The Hon. Featherston Osler (*b.* Jan. 4, 1838) entered the law, practising in Toronto (1860–79) until appointed Justice of the Court of Appeal for Ontario (1879–1910). On his retirement from the bench he was chosen President of the Toronto General Trusts Corporation and served in that capacity until his death in 1924 at 86 years of age.

[2] Britton Bath Osler (*b.* June 19, 1839; *d.* Feb. 5, 1901). Graduating in Toronto in 1862, he entered the law, and as Queen's Counsel and the leading figure at the Canadian bar his name became a household word in Canada, where he was called 'the thirteenth juryman'. He is said to have been the most brilliant of all the brothers. Physically he bore a close resemblance to his brother William.

Head, largely surrounded by 'stump farms', was still on the edge of the wilderness. The elder children well remember migratory visits of Chippewa Indians to the parsonage, numbers of whom, indeed, were drawn by curiosity to attend the Sunday services; and it is related that one of them, pointing at a child, as dark of complexion as his mother, who lay in a cradle on the parsonage verandah, grunted, 'Papoose, papoose', which aroused a fear that some day they might run away with him. In 1842, the year after their return from England, the third son, Edward Lake, was born, and three years later Edmund.[1] In 1847 came twins, Charlotte (the 'Chattie' of subsequent letters) and Francis, who had a roving disposition, and like his father went off to sea in his early years. The son William was born as stated on July 12, 1849, and two years later a daughter Emma, who died in her third year. Walter Farquhar rather than William was to have been this last son's name, presumably in honour of the patron of the Upper Canada Clergy Society, but pressure of an unexpected sort was brought to bear on this subject.

Bond Head was by this time a growing village of some two hundred souls, and boasted not only of a doctor, Orlando Orr, who officiated at the births of the younger Osler children, but of a school-house, a blacksmith-shop, a tavern, and a lodge. For some years it had been the custom of the Orangemen of the district to gather here for their annual fête-day on July 12th; and adorned with sashes, rosettes, and yellow lilies it was part of their programme to march, to the tune of 'Teeter Tawter Holy Water', behind their cockaded leader on his white horse, from the Corners the mile or so to Mr. Osler's parsonage, where speeches were made and felicitations offered in return. In view of this well-established custom, it was

[1] Sir Edmund Boyd Osler, *b.* Nov. 20, 1845; *d.* Aug. 4, 1924, inherited through his father the business ability for which his ancestors were renowned. As a financier he had been for years an important figure in Canadian affairs, being the head of one of the most important brokerage houses in Canada, President of the Dominion Bank, Director of the Canadian Pacific Railway and many other companies; he was a member of the Canadian House of Commons for many years. In physical type he closely resembled his father. Edward Lake also became a barrister, and practised in the North West.

inevitable that on their annual visit in 1849 they should insist that the newcomer, of whose arrival they were made aware by his being brought out in his father's arms, should be 'William'. He was promptly dubbed the 'young Prince of Orange', and an anti-popish acrostic on his name was composed, in the last line of which he is bade to 'Remember all thy Fathers bled to gain'. Hence William he came to be christened, and decked out in appropriate colours with a broad sash of orange and blue he was brought out on the parsonage verandah on his later birthdays to greet the procession which the other children came to regard as arranged solely in his honour.

Without any written record, the early life may be pictured of these eight children, the youngest of whom was often referred to by his mother as 'Benjamin', and by his father in babyhood, owing to his complexion and black eyes, as 'Little burnt-holes-in-a-blanket'. The earliest recollection of this particular boy, as he used to recount years later, was of being nearly drowned the day his younger sister was born, though as he was only two at the time it may have been a figment of his imagination. Both he and a calf had been tethered in the field adjoining the parsonage. There was a pail of milk near by, which on hands and knees he proceeded to investigate. At a critical moment of unbalance he was toppled head first into the pail by the calf, who shared his interest in the contents. Another story he was wont to tell in after years was of his once meeting a bear in a raspberry patch, but this, too, may have been apocryphal.

It was an old-fashioned household in which regulations were strict and promptitude was expected, beginning with early morning prayers and ending at bed-time. The most difficult problem concerned the children's education. At first a log school-house near by, where one of the neighbouring family of Gavillers taught the rudiments of the 'three R's', was all that the vicinity afforded. Then a Mrs. Hill started a school near Bradford some miles away, which the elder boys attended, and finally a school was opened in Bond Head by a Mr. Marling, to which in due course the children trudged. But between the hours dedicated to school and the many chores of farm and household there was abundant time for such play as healthy youngsters enjoy in the open, unhampered by organized sports—coasting and skating and snowballing in the winter, fishing and swimming in the pond by the saw-mill at the foot of the hill, frolicking with Rover the Newfoundland dog, who was trained to go to Bond Head for the mail; playing Indians in what remained of the great forest of hardwood—white oak and maple, basswood, elm and beech, with spruce and pine and beautiful red cedar which was split and used for the miles of snake fences.

In spite of their hours passed on Mr. Marling's benches, doubtless most of the instruction of these children took place at their mother's knee, and with the Bible as the main source of it. Theological books naturally predominated in the parsonage, for Featherstone Osler, in the absence of a provincial school of divinity, prepared a number of young men, his brother included, for their ordination. There was Hooker's 'Ecclesiastical Polity', Butler's 'Analogy', Bishop Burnet's 'Lives', Bishop Taylor's and Isaac Barrow's works, the Parker Society publications (Reformation), Bunyan's works, 1771, with the terrifying illustrations to the 'Pilgrim's Progress'. There were indeed, as one of the sons recalls, 'solid and indestructible blocks of divinity of all kinds'. The writings of his brother Edward Osler, the naturalist-doctor, were also well represented, as told in this pencilled note found among Sir William's papers some seventy years later:

> As a boy in a backwoods settlement in Upper Canada, the English post would bring letters from an Uncle Edward for whom we cherished an amazing veneration; for on the shelves in Father's little study were there not actually books written by him, and poems, and mysterious big articles with drawings about shells, and now and again did we not sing in church one of his hymns? The reputation of the family seemed to circle about this uncle whose letters were always so welcome and so full of news of the old home and so cheery. We boys could read the difference in our father's face when the post brought a letter from Uncle Sam, the black sheep of the family.

Then there was, of course, Locke on the Understanding, Josephus's 'History of the Jews', Hone's 'Everyday Book' with its fine wood-cuts; and other volumes whose backs and titles were familiar to children of the 1850's. A Macaulay, too, is remembered, and a 1721 Addison; 'Sandford and Merton'; 'The Fairchild Family'; an early copy of Tennyson; and an occasional pious novel like Hannah More's 'Cœlebs in Search of a Wife' was probably sent out from England in the missionary boxes by 'the S.P.G.' or by friends in Cornwall. There came also stray copies of Sharp's *London Magazine of Entertainment and Instruction*, the forerunner of *Cornhill*, and perhaps there may have been odd numbers of 'Sketches by Boz', for one of the children remembers his father 'roaring over Pickwick', though this must have been exceptional, for he is described by another of them as 'a reticent sort of a man, English to the backbone, who seldom let himself go'.

Then there was George Borrow, who as a missionary of Cornish ancestry could not have written hurtful books; so 'The Bible in Spain' and even 'Lavengro' were not taboo even on Sunday. Still, as Osler confessed long after, though Sunday reading was remembered as a trial, yet to see a person with a novel on the Sabbath gave him to the end of his life a reflex shock reminiscent of his early training. Copies of the *Illustrated London News* are also remembered, partly for its pictures of the Crimean War, but largely because this remote episode put up the price of Canadian wheat to $2.00 a bushel. In consequence of this and owing to the fact that the farm manager inconsiderately died in the summer of 1855, Edmund and Britton under their father's direction had to run the partly cleared 100-acre farm, get in the harvest, store the hay and dispose of the turnips, potatoes, and wheat. One of them to-day, sixty-nine years later, recalls vividly the feeling of the straw scratching his bare legs, and the delight of a swim in the pond two or three times a day.

On farms in the vicinity there were many families of gentlefolk: the Williamses, the Gavillers, the Tyrwhitts, the Perrins, the Caswells, and others, who became intimates, and there were assuredly many picnics and parties for the children. Mr. Perrin, their nearest neighbour, used to dabble in chemistry and physics, and another avocation was the new art of amateur photography. To this, posterity is indebted for a chance picture of some of these children dressed in their homespuns, with a restless child, William, at the end of the line. A few years later another incident occurred at a picnic in the Gavillers' woods. The children were gathering firewood, and Willie, armed with a hatchet, was engaged in chopping the faggots into lengths on a stump. His sister 'Chattie' to tease him would put her small hand on the stump, and finally he said he would count three, and if she didn't take it off she would lose a finger. She lost it, fortunately only a tip, and brother Willie disappeared to the hay-loft—from which he was extracted some hours later—to escape the punishment to which he was entitled, on the appeal of his still devoted sister and playmate.

The elders, strict as they may have been with their children, were not given to corporal punishment, and this boy in particular, impulsive and full of mischief as he continually was, was so forgiving and affectionate that he probably escaped many a deserved wigging. His elder brother Frank relates that the onus for many of his own escapades was apt to be voluntarily shouldered by Willie, and that the younger brother once deservedly gave him a black eye for some offence, but subsequently shielded him before their parents and took the blame himself for the quarrel. In a family of children essentially unselfish and generous with their small possessions, Willie even as a boy was quick to give the last penny of his scant pocket-money to another who might be hard up.

In an address given in Glasgow fifty years later,[1] Sir William drew upon his early memories of these days for this following comparison:

> The most vivid recollections of my boyhood in Canada cluster about the happy spring days when we went off to the bush to make maple sugar—the bright sunny days, the delicious cold nights, the camp-fires, the log cabins, and the fascinating work tapping the trees, putting in the birch-bark spouts, arranging the troughs, and then going from tree to tree, collecting in pails the clear sweet sap.

---

1 'Pathological Institute of a General Hospital.' *Glasgow Medical Journal*, Nov. 1911, p. 15.

One memory stands out above all others, the astonishment that so little sugar was left after boiling down so great a cauldron of liquid. And yet the sap was so abundant and so sweet. The workers of my generation in the bush of science have collected a vaster quantity of sap than ever before known ; much has already been boiled down, and it is for you of the younger generation while completing the job to tap your own trees.

In the years since 1837 great changes had taken place in Tecumseth and its adjoining townships, as well as elsewhere in Upper Canada, but the region about Lake Simcoe, nevertheless, was lacking in much that was desirable for the upbringing of a large family of children. Hence in September of 1854 Featherstone Osler felt impelled to write Bishop Strachan of Toronto to request that he be transferred, partly on the basis of indifferent health, which was affected by the necessity of constant travel, but more particularly on the grounds of his children's education. The elder boys had already been sent away to school in Barrie, and were preparing to enter college, but there were six younger children in need of more than Bond Head offered and the purse of a frontier parson could afford.

Two years later the rectorship of Ancaster and Dundas became vacant, and the Bishop on January 1, 1857, ordered his transfer to those parishes. But a transplantation is no easy thing, and they found it a hard wrench to leave Bond Head, despite its shortcomings, as is evident from this passage in Canon Osler's diary :

It was one of the hardest trials of my life to leave the place where I had lived happily nineteen and a half years, and the people with whom I had lived without a jar or discord during the whole period, but I felt that the Church would not suffer by my leaving it. In the neighbouring townships many churches had been built, and in Tecumseth and West Gwillimbury, my specially licensed charge, where there had been neither church, parsonage, nor glebe, there were now six churches, two parsonages, and two glebes ; the one in Tecumseth being especially valuable, consisting of 200 acres. I had 160 acres cleared.

So it came about that the Bond Head farm was sold and the family was moved to a more self-contained community where conditions of life were far less primitive and arduous. For Dundas at the time, situated most picturesquely at the very western tip of Lake Ontario, half-way between Toronto and Niagara, promised, owing to its favourable position, to become the metropolis of the new province.

Two of the boys had already gone to a boarding-school in Dundas, and fortune favoured the transfer of the remaining family in a curious way, for having journeyed safely by the recently opened Northern Railway from Bradford to Toronto and having made arrangements to go from there by rail the following day to Dundas, the boy Willie, as is related, came down unexpectedly with the croup, and the second stage of the journey was deferred. The train they were to have taken on the Great Western Railway became derailed as it was approaching Hamilton, and the coaches plunged through the viaduct into the canal forty feet below, with great loss of life—the Desjardin catastrophe of March 12, 1857.

Dundas

Here in the prosperous and fertile river-valley at the head of the lake there began an entirely new life. With Dundas in the centre of his parish, with good roads making travel comparatively easy, with accessible schools for the children, and cultivated people as neighbours, Canon Osler spent his next twenty-five years. A temporary residence in the centre of the town situated in the valley was soon given up and a permanent move of the rectory was made to the southern heights overlooking the valley towards its still higher northern escarpment called the Mountain—a panorama of rare beauty. There are indeed few more picturesque spots on the Great Lakes, and in a comfortable home in these charming surroundings with an intimate group of ideal neighbours and friends the years passed happily by for parents and children.

There was an Episcopal boarding-school for girls in Dundas at the time, and one of the pupils, then fourteen, vividly recalls even at this day Canon Osler and his wife, to whom the tradition still clung that she was of Indian ancestry:

I can see the little Episcopal Church with the sunshine filtering through the coloured windows. One of our teachers was organist,

FEATHERSTONE LAKE OSLER

Taken circa 1870 in Dundas

ELLEN FREE PICKTON OSLER

Taken circa 1870 in Dundas

two others sang in the choir and we were all required to attend services, Lenten too, and often Matins, and early Communion—we were really part of the church. The Rector as I remember him was a good-looking, rather short ‘roly-poly’ man with blue eyes, bushy whiskers and heavy eyebrows, intoning the service and rows and rows of girls repeating at intervals, ‘Lord, have mercy upon us, and incline our hearts to keep this law.’ He was a fine character, though quite unlike his brilliant sons, but we all loved him though we called him in private ‘Sneezer’ (this is of course *entre nous*). Then those Saturday, Easter, and Christmas parties! The romantic tales we wove around Mrs. Osler! Of course in our minds she was directly descended from Pocahontas, and a beautiful chief wanted to marry her but her father chose the Englishman! How disappointed we would have been had we known the truth.

There was every prospect that Dundas, then a town of some 3,000 souls, possessing a daily newspaper! and seven churches!! was destined to become the chief city at the western end of the lake. The great highway, Governor's Road or Dundas Street, passed through it to the west; it had a splendid water power, and the Desjardin Canal, cut through the marshes for a distance of five miles, connected it with the ideal land-locked harbour made by Burlington Bay. All this bid fair at the time to ensure its future growth and prosperity. One of the most attractive features of the lower valley was the huge marsh, long called ‘Coote's Paradise’, after an early sportsman of Governor Simcoe's time, who spent much of his leisure in shooting game there; and in the course of years, as will be seen, this same marsh became the hunting-ground for zoological specimens by a young naturalist and his preceptor.

The younger boys, promptly dubbed by their new playmates ‘Tecumseth cabbages’, in view of their rural place of origin, were sent to the local grammar-school, conducted first by a classical scholar, a Mr. John King of Trinity College, Dublin, who had come out to Canada in 1854, and subsequently by another Irishman, a Mr. J. J. Flynn, as principal. This grammar-school occupied quarters upstairs in a building which also housed a common-school on the ground floor, a situation almost certain to lead to trouble, particularly as the head master of the common-school was a despot who disliked boys as a class, but particularly grammar-school boys. Doubtless Mr. Flynn himself was the victim of many pranks on the part of his own irrepressible pupils, than whom there was probably none more notorious than a rollicking boy named Willie Osler, who though adored by all was particularly ingenious in evolving and perpetrating practical jokes of an elaborate and unusual sort, in which as a rule he took the leadership.

Which one of many escapades led to his final dismissal makes little difference—whether it was the flock of geese found one morning locked in the room of the common-school, or the discovery on a Monday morning of a school without furniture, the desks and benches all having been unscrewed from the floor and laboriously hoisted up through a trap-door into the garret the Saturday afternoon before; or whether it was some disparaging remarks concerning the head master of the common-school shouted through a keyhole.[1] At all events, expelled he was, with his four accomplices.

His sister recalls meeting him on the way home that eventful day. He was riding bareback on the Canon's horse, picked up at the shop of his friend and confidant, Pat O'Connor the blacksmith, on whom he had called to impart the news; waving his hand he shouted, gleefully, 'Chattie, I've got the sack!'

[1] An account of the episode with the altercation which followed it may be found in the local news-sheet, *The Banner*, June 2, 1864, et seq.

CHAPTER II

1864–7

BOARDING-SCHOOL DAYS

Barrie

THUS Willie Osler came to be sent away the next autumn to a boarding-school, and following the footsteps of his brothers was entered in the grammar-school at Barrie, a town on the western arm of Lake Simcoe, half-way between his old home at Bond Head and Penetanguishene. The Rev. W. F. Checkley, a famous schoolmaster of the day and a friend of the boys' father, was principal, and under him many sons of the early settlers in Upper Canada spent their first year away from home, though by this particular time the school's reputation had somewhat waned and its numbers dwindled. Of the mischievous boy who had come from Dundas there is little but hearsay record, for the school no longer exists, and the old brick building after many vicissitudes has been demolished. One may gather from his mother's weekly chronicle of home news that his wants were few, and it is hoped that he secured some slippery 'elem' in Barrie, and that brother Frank, who had been rusticated, got his skates by Christmas:

From his mother to W. O. Dundas. October [1864].

My dear Willie,—I can excuse you if you begin to think of yourself in a small degree slighted, for I ought to have written last week but could not manage it and we were for some days expecting a letter from you before it came. I am sorry to find you had such a bad cold but hope it will not wind up with another attack of Intermittent; we too all of us have or have had colds indeed who has not during this changeable weather. Charlotte has written you all the news of the day and the Pater told you how well the Ancastrians did at their Bazaar—$400 was more than any of us expected to make. . . . I bought a winter necktie for you which I will try to enclose in this letter but both Papa and I think it will be useless to send up a box, as apples are scarcely to be had and Frank's expedition for nuts the other day was only productive of *one quart* so if Papa sends you up a dollar it must do instead and I dare say you could get a tooth brush and a packet of slippery Elm (not Elem) bark at Barrie nor can we find your 'Horace' in the study to send up. I am glad your clothes suit. Frank went down by Boat last week to Toronto and got a suit of clothes at Walkers and Felt hat; they make him look quite the young man; nothing yet has turned up for him to do, but all are looking out for him. . . . Papa is going to take this down town to get a dollar note and a stamp to enclose, if we can find the 'Horace' we will send it up by post next week. Give my kind regards to Mrs. Checkley and love to Mrs. Stewart when you see her and with my best love to you hoping that you are on terms of love and friendship with your books I am ever

Your affectionate Mother

ELLEN OSLER.

Frank left his skates at Barrie. Mind you take care of them to bring home at Christmas.

The school was divided into day-pupils and boarders, the latter living with Mr. Checkley, who does not seem to have left any deep and lasting impression, upon one of them at least. But no matter how slack his observance of regulations, a boy who is affectionate, chivalrous, and generous, who has no difficulties with scholarship and at the same time excels in sports—such a boy becomes a leader wherever he may be put to school, and makes fast friends. Indeed, one of Osler's outstanding characteristics was his tenacity for friendships, which once made were never forgotten, and with his particular friends of this early school period he kept up a running correspondence during his subsequent migratory life and even till his last days, never failing to send messages of greeting on holidays and birthdays, nor to hold out a helping hand when they or their families were in trouble or want.

The mere transfer from one institution to another does not suffice to subdue the effervescent spirits of a fun-loving boy, and there were three youngsters among the fourteen or more in the school who earned the appellation of 'Barrie's Bad Boys'—Ned Milburn, Charlie Locke, and Willie Osler—and the last-mentioned, in his later years, used to recount with glee to his special children-friends the pranks of these Barrie days. One of them writes:

Sir William used to tell me stories of his boyhood as I sat on the floor at his knees by the library fire, but I am afraid they were all either lacking in details of time or place. . . . I was in the garden with

THE FORMER PARSONAGE AT BOND HEAD

Circa 1875

THE OLD BARRIE GRAMMAR SCHOOL

Circa 1870

him one day and dared him to throw a stone and hit something that was a long way off, and he hit it *true* with the first stone, and told me that on his way to school one day with three other small boys Ned Milburn dared him to hit a pig with a stone. The pig was a long way off, but with the first stone he hit it directly behind the ear and to his chagrin killed it instantly. He would always laugh till the tears came into his eyes at the thought of how 'that old pig looked as he rolled over on his back with his four legs stiff in the air,' and of how the farmer came out and took him by the scruff of his neck straight home; and his father had to pay eight dollars for the pig. . . . During those last sad years I never saw him laugh so heartily or look so happy as when he forgot the present and lived again his old pranks.

Mr. Milburn, who of these three boys alone survives, writes as follows of those days, passing over in a few words, as taken for granted, that owing to his remarkably retentive memory and exceptional powers of concentration, 'Osler easily ranked first in the whole school'; also, that even when at Barrie he was notably proficient 'in that greatest of books, the Bible'.

. . . The spirit of fun was well marked in him—real fun that hurt nobody but sometimes caused a little annoyance to the victims of the joke. The fact is we were often blamed for the misdoings of ill-conditioned boys belonging to the town, even though we could prove a perfectly good alibi. At times a zeal for study would seize us, especially when exams were imminent, and as our study-hours ended at 9.30 at which time all lamps were taken away, we would jump out of our dormitory window some six feet above the ground and study our Xenophon, Virgil or Caesar by the light of the full moon, then we would go down to the Bay distant a little over 100 yards and disport ourselves an hour or two in the cool water. . . .

Not far from the school was a large cottage, the residence of Sheriff Smith, with a fine garden in which the gardener took great pride. In it was a fine melon-patch. We determined to have a melon, so taking advantage of the absence of the household we secured each a melon, but just as we came to the road, up came the gardener. As the Sheriff insisted on our punishment the result was we were gated for a week and had to write out the text of Virgil, Bk. I. O. said little, but watching his chance he got on the roof and put a board over the chimney—soon the excitement began. The Barrie Hook and Ladder Co. with what we called 'Cataract No. I' came tearing along—only to find no fire—only smoke. This was our reprisal, so to speak. . . .

One of the last tricks, indeed the last, I think, that we played, was on an American who had advertised for a wife. In our Toronto papers O. noticed the advertisement and suggested the following plan—to answer the advertisement describing ourselves as a brunette and a blonde respectively—so that he could make choice according to his fancy. We had some trouble in fitting ourselves out with girls' clothes, but with my sister's help we developed into pretty fair specimens of the genus girl.

In due time the farmer arrived at the Grand Trunk Station where we had agreed to meet him, for the station we knew was badly lighted, which would be of advantage to us. All went well—we resisted his request for another meeting by daylight and asked him to make his choice then and there. He did so, and as he rather liked blondes his choice fell on me. I wonder at it, for O. made a beautiful girl with his clear-cut features and olive complexion. We never knew what became of the farmer—he left us, promising to return in a month, as this would give him time to fix up his house. I hope he got a blonde.

As mentioned above, Osler possessed a remarkably supple body which enabled him to excel in all youthful sports; and the elastic swinging step of a boy characterized him to his last days. He at one time won a school prize for kicking the football, and after leaving school and when in college played in matches with the Hamilton cricket team during his summer vacations. Mr. Milburn continues:

We were all very fond of athletics and were big boys for our age. . . . Nothing could tire us. We were all bone with steel bands for muscles. On one occasion we three essayed to swim across Kempenfelt Bay, there (at Barrie) I fancy about a mile-and-a-half wide. Accompanied by a boat we started on the trip. I managed to cover about a mile when my fingers began to cramp and I climbed into the boat. O. and Locke kept on and accomplished the feat, a very difficult one due to the many cold springs in the Bay. He was also good at cricket. On one occasion I saw him throw a cricket-ball 115 yards, a throw never beaten I think, at least by an amateur.

Weston

The reputation of the Barrie school being at this time on the wane, this, together with its distance from Dundas, must have influenced the boy's parents in favour of a change. A circular had been received by them describing a new school recently opened at Weston, a town on the Humber, a few miles west of Toronto, and a paragraph in the circular stated that senior boys would go into the drawing-room in the evening and be taught music, dancing, and painting. If this was the lure, it seems to have been a vain one, for in the capacity to learn such arts William Osler was by nature deficient; but to the school he was sent, and here something not advertised, but far more important than these parlour accomplishments, was found —namely, a real master, ' who knew nature and how to get boys interested in it '.

The Rev. William Arthur Johnson was born in 1816, in Bombay. His father, then Quartermaster-General to the Bombay forces, was an engineer officer, who not only had a distinguished military career in India but had served earlier as aide-de-camp to Arthur Wellesley (first Duke of Wellington) from whom this his second son received the name Arthur. On retiring with the rank of Colonel he returned to England and lived at Down House, where later Darwin lived and died; and he became a friend of Turner and of Landseer, and was ' no mean artist himself '.

The son William Arthur for whom Wellington had stood as godfather had been sent to the military school at Addiscombe,[1] and it is said was later offered a commission by the Duke. But, disliking the army, he abandoned that career and with the Jukes family migrated to Upper Canada in 1831, where his father soon followed him, to take up one of the land grants for retired officers near Port Maitland. Johnson subsequently entered the Church, and became curate under Archdeacon Bethune (subsequently Bishop of Toronto) then at Cobourg. From the first he was apparently influenced by the Oxford Tractarians, and had he been in England instead of Canada in 1851, the year he was ordained, he might have joined forces with Newman. Some of his ' low church ' parishioners both at Cobourg and at his subsequent parish of St. Paul's, Yorkville, made trouble for him on these grounds. Bishop Strachan exonerated but did not support him, and he was finally inducted as the rector at St. Philip's, Etobicoke, a remote hamlet across the river from Weston.

[1] His elder brother had been there before him; had gone into the army; seen service in Arabia; been advanced to Captain, and was drowned at Surat in his twenty-seventh year.

In this parish he became much beloved, though he remained to the end more or less of a thorn in the flesh to his bishop on account of his ritualistic proclivities, which he defended both in pulpit and press. Having a family of three boys of his own to educate and there being no distinctly church school in Toronto at the time, he determined to start one himself. Accordingly, at his own expense and on his own responsibility, a school known as 'Weston' was opened in a small building on the west bank of the Humber, overlooking the ruins of an old mill, traces of which still stand in the lowlands of the picturesque river valley.

The project thrived, and in 1864 Johnson proposed to the governing body of Trinity University that the school come under their supervision, that it be called the Trinity College School, and serve to prepare boys for Trinity University. For himself he proposed that as a master, he should teach French, drawing, and water-colour painting, without remuneration, and, what is more, would make himself responsible for the expenses of the establishment, provided he might use the name of Trinity College in the circular of announcement, to which reference has just been made.

There were many pourparlers, and it may be assumed that Bishop Strachan had some misgivings regarding the unruly priest he had been disposed to discipline. However, the corporation on the 8th November 1864 sanctioned the arrangement, and the school formally opened the next May with about a dozen boys, a greater number than had been expected or could well be cared for. As there was no room for them available in the village, the pupils, soon twenty-five in number, were somehow accommodated in the parsonage, the half-basement of which was fitted out with rude desks, a large upper room being converted into a dormitory. In this school Willie Osler was entered on January 18, 1866. 'I can see him now', writes one of his mates, 'soon after he arrived at the rectory—with a red pocket-handkerchief round his neck and a sling in his hand taking a survey of any chance birds in the garden.' This occupation must have been more to his liking than practising scales indoors, for his mother writes at the expiration of a few weeks: 'Papa I dare say will be at Weston next week and then will give you the V for the quarters music if it is still your mind to learn.' But it was not to be through his advertised courses that Johnson came to mould and influence the thoughts and subsequent career of his young pupil, in whose attitude towards life a great change took place in the short space of the next eighteen months. But years are longer at seventeen than later in life, and fortunate the schoolboy who at this impressionable age makes contact with such a guide, philosopher, and friend as the Rev. W. A. Johnson proved to be. It was an association never forgotten, and to his indebtedness the pupil in after years made repeated reference in his writings and addresses.

'Father' Johnson,[1] though the founder and Warden of the school, and its real influence among the boys, was not the Head Master. This position, filled by the Corporation of Trinity, was occupied by a tall, austere young man with 'long black whiskers and a very decided mouth', a classical scholar and recent graduate of Trinity College who had learned during a subsequent sojourn in England, it is said, how a good Church School should be conducted on the long-established traditions of the great English Public Schools. Being a martinet and addicted to the birch, believing that the way to reach a boy was through his hide, the Head Master was as unpopular as the Warden was otherwise. He lived in rooms built off the parsonage, and from them could see the windows of the schoolroom in the half-basement, which put the boys to the great disadvantage of never knowing when his eye was on them. The consequences of any misbehaviour has been so vividly recalled in an article written by one of the boys [2] that one feels he may have had experience with 'caning which was one of the strong points of the school':

> The canes, too, were peculiar. They were made of beautifully polished, round strips of what was known as second-growth Walpole

[1] The appellation 'Father' Johnson, as his friends loved to address him, was one which in those days a Protestant might have regarded as a term of reproach—a reproach in which Johnson, however, would have gloried.

[2] Arthur Jukes Johnson. *Trinity College School Record*, 1915, p. 57.

hickory. They were practically unbreakable, and would bend like a bit of India rubber, warranted to be felt over every spot they touched. There was a decided advantage to the culprit in his being sent for the cane: in the first place it gave the master, supposing that he had been somewhat ruffled, time to get thorough command of himself, and it also gave the boy an opportunity of preparing for the ordeal. Having to go through a long passage outside the house before he reached the Head Master's room, opportunities might occur to his mind of so arranging matters that the caning was not so hard to bear. . . .

With the object, it may be, of escaping from such tyranny Osler and one of his mates early in his Weston career contrived an ingenious and effective method of enjoying a sojourn at home, by deliberately exposing themselves to a boy who was in quarantine with chicken-pox—a fact now made public for the first time, as the one surviving member of the conspiracy no longer feels bound by their oath of secrecy.

The school gradually increased its numbers until it was no longer possible even for an elastic parsonage to encompass it all. Hence a new building had been secured some little distance away, for classrooms and dormitory, where the Head Master reigned supreme. He had engaged a housekeeper, an old woman, and her buxom daughter, both of whom came to be heartily disliked, and thereby hangs a tale, for to be disliked in a boys' school is to invite molestation. The story can be found in the county court records of the *Toronto Globe* for April 8–13, 1866, under the caption, '*School Row at Weston. Pupils Turned Outlaws. They Fumigate the Matron with Sulphur.*' A mild rendering of the episode has been printed elsewhere [1] by the Warden's eldest son, one of the culprits, but a somewhat more lively version comes from the little girl to whom stories of his boyhood used to be told by Sir William before the library fire in Oxford. In this rendering the assault was in revenge for a specified offence, the despised female the day before having upset a pail of slops on the stairs, which soused one of the boys. Hence, on the day in question, the coast being clear and at Osler's instigation, they barricaded 'the old girl' in her sitting-room and made a paste of molasses,

[1] *Trinity College School Record*, Jubilee Number, 1915, xvii, 63.

THE WESTON SCHOOL IN THE EARLY DAYS

From a sketch by W. A. Johnson

mustard, and pepper, which they put on the schoolroom stove, so that the fumes rose to her room through the stovepipe hole. The prisoner stuffed the hole with some clothes, which the boys pushed back with pointers. Being resourceful and to avoid suffocation, she sat on the register and screamed for help, while the boys poked at her from below as they had done to the clothes. Ultimately she was rescued by the Head Master, and the boys, as can be imagined, duly experienced the effects of the Walpole hickory strips. But this did not satisfy the Matron, who demanded their arrest for assault and battery. Unable to get a warrant issued in Weston, she finally secured one in Toronto, so that the nine boys, including the Warden's two sons, passed a few days in the Toronto jail, and were defended by the young Osler's elder brother, Featherston, before the magistrate in the county council-chamber, with the result of a reprimand and payment of a dollar and costs. At all events, they had effectually 'smoked the old girl out', for she refused to stay longer at the school. 'It was an unfortunate affair', wrote his mother on April 19th, 'that of all you boys being brought into public notice in such a disreputable manner, and although I do not think it was meant to be more than a mere schoolboy prank, such things often tell against a person long after, and I hear many say they think it will injure the reputation of the school.' With which mild reprimand his 'ever loving Mother' ended by enclosing two dollars and a postage stamp.

It was a humble setting at Weston, a square, two-storied, plastered house which served as parsonage as well as school, in which Johnson, his wife, and three children lived, together with as many boys as could be crowded in; and their names to-day can be seen scratched with some one's diamond on the low windows. In addition to the Warden's family was the Head Master, and he in turn had an assistant, and a Mr. Sefton came out for the week-ends and gave music lessons. There was also a Mr. Carter, who, when not engaged in the classics, taught cricket and football; and a 'Captain' Goodwin, an old Waterloo veteran and great favourite with the boys, not only drilled them every Saturday afternoon, but taught them the manly art of self-defence with fist and cudgel. There was a playground near by, and also the Warden's private chapel, while the woods on one side and the little town on the other stretched along the bluff overlooking the river valley. In this setting the effort was being made by the Head Master to reproduce on a small scale something of Eton, Harrow, or Rugby, by transplanting to new soil the traditions of these and similar foundations as little modified as possible, to make them fit in with or to neutralize the democratic ideas which were beginning to take hold of the country. Though 'fagging' had not been introduced, the school discipline was maintained by the 'prefect' system, whereby the boys were placed on their honour and practically governed themselves under the supervision of four prefects chosen from their own number. The prefects, of whom Osler was soon made head, held their positions as long as they could retain the boys' confidence, and there were ways of superseding a prefect if he showed himself unworthy of his position. They exercised large authority in the school, and dealt with all such petty incidents as squabbling, Billingsgate exchanges, bullying, and so on—occurrences which may make the life of an unprotected small boy in a school utterly wretched. As one of Osler's mates recalls:

> The process was simple. A sharp voice would ring out: 'Stop that, you muckers.' If *that* wasn't stopped—'Well, we must settle this business at once.' If the lads were evenly matched, well and good; if not, the heavyweight must submit to some handicap, or the lightweight might call upon his particular pal and the thing would be fought out—'Queensberry rules—shake hands—now to it.' The prefect would see fair play and when in his opinion enough punishment had been given the fray must cease, the warriors shake hands and as a rule be fast friends—for a time at least. Sometimes two rooms of boys would have to settle their difference in this way, but the general engagements of this kind were frowned upon by the Head Master.

The boys were garbed in a sort of Eton attire, and were expected to appear in public wearing top-hats. This must have been particularly tantalizing for the town boys of this small country village; and to wear a top-hat certainly puts one at a great disadvantage in a snowball battle. Christian

THE FOUR PREFECTS AT WESTON
WILSON, OSLER, JONES AND HELLIWELL
Toronto. 1867

names, of course, were ignored and nicknames discouraged. Jones was 'Jones' in classroom, on cricket-field, or at roll-call, and this last was a duty which devolved upon the prefect, who had to recite from memory the list of names at fixed hours, even during play-time, to ascertain whether any boy was out of bounds without leave of absence. As one of the surviving prefects of Osler's day recalls, this was easy enough if there was only one Jones, but otherwise the senior Jones would be 'Jones max.'; and after fifty-five years he recalls like an old tune the roster of his time: 'Anderson max., Anderson major, Anderson minor, Beck, Boulton, etc., etc.'

But as a man is more important than his workshop, so the Warden was more important than his school, and it is to him that this story must return. For the Rev. W. A. Johnson's conception of education did not lie in the greatest number of facts which could be drilled into his boys, but in the ideas which centrifugally would radiate from them under varied stimuli not necessarily confined to the schoolroom. He must have been the despair of his Head Master. He was an artist, among other things, and sketched well; he was a wood-carver, and the products of his chisel, some of which still adorn the parish church at Weston, can perhaps be best seen on the carved altar table of St. Matthew's, Toronto. He was a nature-lover, not in the casual sense of admiring her beauties from afar, but in the sense of the scientist who thinks nature even more beautiful and thrilling if seen close at hand under the microscope. With all this he was an ardent high-churchman, given to genuflexions, to prayer and meditation in his private chapel adjoining the school,[1] and was such a punctilious observer of high-church ritual that it kept him in more or less hot water. The head prefect of these Weston days, nearly fifty years later in an address [2] dealing with science in the public schools, expressed himself as follows:

As a boy I had the common experience of fifty years ago—teachers whose sole object was to spoonfeed classes, not with the classics but

[1] This chapel (St. John's), removed from its former site beside the old rectory, now stands encased in brick on the north side of Main Street, Weston.

[2] *The School World*, London, 1916, pp. 41–4.

with syntax and prosody, forcing our empty wits, as Milton says, to compose 'Theams, Verses and Orations', wrung from poor striplings like blood from the nose, with the result that we loathed Xenophon and his ten thousand, Homer was an abomination, while Livy and Cicero were names and tasks. Ten years with really able Trinity College, Dublin, and Oxford teachers left me with no more real knowledge of Greek and Latin than of Chinese, and without the free use of the languages as keys to great literatures. Imagine the delight of a boy of an inquisitive nature to meet a man who cared nothing about words, but who knew about things—who knew the stars in their courses and could tell us their names, who delighted in the woods in springtime, and told us about the frog-spawn and the caddis worms, and who read us in the evenings Gilbert White and Kingsley's 'Glaucus', who showed us with the microscope the marvels in a drop of dirty pond water, and who on Saturday excursions up the river could talk of the Trilobites and the Orthoceratites and explain the formation of the earth's crust. No more dry husks for me after such a diet, and early in my college life I kicked over the traces and exchanged the classics with 'divvers' as represented by Pearson, Browne and Hooker, for Hunter, Lyell and Huxley. From the study of nature to the study of man was an easy step. My experience was that of thousands, yet, as I remember, we were athirst for good literature. What a delight it would have been to have had Chapman's 'Odyssey' read to us, or Plato's 'Phaedo' on a Sunday evening, or the 'Vera Historia'. What a tragedy to climb Parnassus in a fog! How I have cursed the memory of Protagoras since finding that he introduced grammar into the curriculum, and forged the fetters which chained generations of schoolboys in the cold formalism of words. How different now that Montaigne and Milton and Locke and Petty have come into their own, and are recognized as men of sense in the matter of training youth.

So the interests of these days come to a focus in W. A. Johnson and his microscope in so far as they relate to a boy who was expected to follow his father's footsteps and enter the ministry. Two months after entering the school he had been prepared by the Warden for confirmation at St. Philip's; and that he had strong leanings towards the Church is apparent from one of his mother's letters written towards the end of the spring term:

From his mother to W. O. Dundas, May 30th, 1866.

My dear Willie,— . . . Papa had your letter a day or two ago and will probably write to you soon and as well to Mr. Badgely about your remaining another year at school. And now my dear boy let me have a little serious chat with you about entering the Church which you say you have made up your mind to do. My first impulse was to thank God that he had heard my prayer and inclined one of my six boys to make choice of that as his path in life. It is a matter not to be decided on hastily any more than is any other profession—take your time for consideration and above all search your heart for the motives inducing your decision, for remember that God always judges of us by our motives while man can only judge of our actions. . . . I send you a *volume of good advice* which was given many years ago by a good man to his son at Shrewsbury School it is good for boys in all ages and at all schools *read it carefully and follow it fully* and in the *Book of Proverbs* which the wisest of fathers wrote for the benefit of his son and which is meant for you as well as for him you will find far better advice than I can give. May God incline your heart to love and serve Him through His beloved Son is the prayer of your loving Mother,

ELLEN OSLER.

[PS.] I see your name flourishing in the Games of Monday, it was a bad day, nevertheless I hope you all enjoyed the fun.

[PPS.] My dear Willie,—I must just scribble another line to tell you how proud we all were to see 'Osler 1st' so many times in the paper to-day and I was so sorry to see the rain yesterday, but it does not seem to have made much difference; we hope to have a long account of the day's proceedings from you soon; the notice in the Leader was very short. You will have a long letter from me as soon as I can find time for such a proceeding. Bye-bye.

His name indeed 'flourished', for according to the *Toronto Leader* he came out number one in the majority of the athletic contests which had been staged for the preceding Monday—the hurdle race, the 200- and 400-yard flat races; the 100-yard hop race, the mile steeplechase, and throwing the cricket ball, though there seems, from the following recollection of one of his schoolmates, some doubt about its having been a record throw:

Physically Osler was rather undersized but extremely wiry and well proportioned, a fine all-round athlete, without being a champion in any particular line. I believe though, he did break the record for throwing the cricket ball at one of our term-end sports. Unfortunately, however, the Campus (if we may use a word I don't like, which our college athletes have to-day taken over from the Yankee vocabulary) proved too restricted for his prowess, and the ball hit the high fence near the top. Such a throw was never dreamed of. But Professor Jones, of Trinity, possibly not an unprejudiced referee, came to the rescue, and by the aid of most compelling mathematical calculations—no doubt they were absolutely accurate as became the dictum of an exact science—demonstrated to our entire satisfaction that if the wretched fence had not been in the way the ball would have hit the sod at a distance that neither Rugby nor Eton had ever achieved. Anyhow, it is not on record that our English schools yielded their claim to the championship on the strength of Professor Jones's verdict.

But the excursions on week-ends in the beautiful valley through which the Humber flows, and the expeditions to more distant places during vacation time in company with the nineteenth-century edition of the Sage of Selborne, who had a like taste for observing and for recording natural phenomena, served to deflect him from his drift towards the Church. One of his boyhood companions, the Rev. Arthur Jarvis of Toronto, in some reminiscences of their school-days at Weston, says:

It was our greatest treat when 'Old Johnson' could be led to take a squad out for a field day, hunting fossils, and he did not need much persuasion. I can still see the Warden wielding an old prospector's pick, and Osler the most eager boy of the lot to secure a perfect orthoceratite or whatever Lower Silurian relic the soft stone about Weston might yield. Some of us were keen to retrieve a few good sections of orthoceras to be diligently polished and converted into prodigious sleeve-links at 'Kent's store' in Yonge Street.

Osler, however, was the scientist of the expedition. To him was entrusted the delicate work of grinding down and mounting specimens for microscope slides. Sometimes he might graciously, after the manner of Tom Sawyer, delegate some of this protracted mechanical grinding on the Water-of-Ayre stone to our less skilled hands—it wasn't every day that a boy had a chance to help in the construction of valuable scientific exhibits! Nevertheless experts pronounced them exceptionally fine—after Osler had put the finishing touches.

W. A. Johnson was an omnivorous naturalist, ranging widely with no attempt at specialization. Everything interested him, the structure of the hair of different animals from the caribou to the flying squirrel, the structure and growth of wood, the study of fossils and minerals, the finer anatomy of moths and butterflies and insects of every kind, some of which he unblushingly transferred from his own person or bed to the stage of the microscope; seeds and shells, ferns and mosses, bones and teeth of vertebrates from those of a thirty-pound 'Masquenonge', caught by his son-in-law, to the molar of an old cow killed on the railway track. He was an amateur, it is true, and dabbled in many fields, but the flame nevertheless burned brightly, and he knew how to transmit it to others. His field note-book with the tabulation of his microscopic slides all carefully enumerated and indexed, tells the story better than words, and it is a pity that it cannot be quoted in full, particularly during the year when the young Osler begins to appear on its pages. He took the *Microscopical Journal*, and consulted other books of reference, as can be seen by some of these illustrative entries:

§ 493. 16/i/67. *Aspidiotus conchiformis*, or 'oyster shell bark louse'. For a description of this little destructive thing see Harris pg. 254 & Practical Entomologist at pg. 31 of Vol. ii, where there is a good drawing & description.

§ 733. 12/xii/67. Fossil wood. On the 8th Nov./67, Mr. W. Grubb gave me a roughly ground seal wh. he said was fossil wood, an oak? tree from Craigleigh Quarry nr. Edinburgh, Scotland, at about 100 ft. below the surface: he got the bit of stone himself. See pg. 40, and pg. 375, Lyell's Elementary Geology, 6th edition, 1837.

§ 749. 7/i/68. Larva (aquatic) *Palpicornes Hydrophilus*, with curious head, tripartite shovel on head. Taken in July, 67, in W. Holley's pond on G. T. Railway Weston. See Animal Kingdom, by I. R. Jones, p. 125.

§ 1430. 15/ii/71. Leg bone of a Crane, Hern or Heron shot Sept. 28, 1867. *Note* these two are ground on glass with pumic[e] stone wetted and put up with Balsam. See Qua^{ly} Journal microscopical science.

§ 1488. 15/i/73. Insects in a book—In the first page of Carpenter's Comparative Physiology. This intensely cold weather seems a strange time for them to be about. Unknown to me at this date, except by sight. This stellate form, wh is often so plentiful in watery collections, is from the seeds of the Mullein collected about Oct. 1st.

Accordingly, though Johnson's library of five or six hundred volumes was chiefly ecclesiastical, the boys in the parsonage had access to Lyell and Dana, to Gray, Harris, Hogg, and Carpenter, which in the hands of the Warden probably interested them more than did the *Principia*

Latina, Arnold, Anthon, and Todhunter in the hands of the Head Master, whose tasks consisted largely in the committing to memory of countless lines of Homer and Virgil, read with the aid of Schrevelius' lexicon and Ross's grammar, in which the definitions were in Greek and Latin respectively. How Osler's powers of concentration, that stood him in such good stead in later years, came to be so highly developed is indicated by this recollection of one of his schoolmates :

> Imagine a room full of IV-Form *enfants terribles* at ' prep.' where the prefect's ideal of discipline was to limit noisy demonstration so that the sound waves shall in no wise break upon the ear of the Head Master. Then maybe a few moments of intense application to the work of the hour, a little surreptitious scribbling of imposition lines, a generous exchange of tips as to the translation of a ' rotten ' line, or the solution of a ' beastly rider '. Such serious toil produced a demand for relaxation, taking the form of practical jokes played by the shirkers upon those, especially, making some effort at a semblance of study. In the pandemonium Osler might be seen grasping his head, with thumbs in his ears, oblivious to everything but his book ; till perhaps a paper dart, with or without inked point, roused him to a consciousness of outward things. Retaliation followed as a matter of course, but the *deaf adder* pose would be resumed so soon as circumstances might permit. After one or two such experiences the *pose* was likely to be treated with due respect.

The much-dreaded Head Master established a rule that roll-call would be held every two hours on holidays, but nevertheless the boys on these days would take to the woods for bird-nesting or hunting chipmunks, and one of them recalls the chance discovery in the late autumn of a nest of hibernating chipmunks which were slipped into his shirt and carried to chapel, whereupon they revived and raced around his anatomy. This must have kept him awake, but doubtless took his attention from the lesson.

Among some of the early entries in Johnson's field notebook there is found a name which will frequently recur in this story :

> 1859. Vine : transverse section, given me by Dr. Bovell.
> 1864. Part of scale of dog-fish, given me by Dr. Bovell.
> 1865. Fossil chalk from Barbadoes, given me by Dr. Bovell.

And in the summer of 1866, when he seems to have become

engrossed in mosses, there is this: '§ 384. 18/6/66. Leaf of moss (Dr. Bovell took it)'—and it is probable from what is known of him that he forgot to return it; but these entries will suffice to introduce another character whose influence upon Osler came in time to be even greater than that of 'Father' Johnson himself. One of the Warden's sons writes:

> . . . One thing I remember vividly—Old Bovell and my father were (as usual, on days Bovell spent at the rectory) working at the microscope case which had many tempting little drawers in it and I (boylike) opened one of these drawers and seeing a small bone took it out—when Old Bovell said in his fash, impetuous yet loving manner: 'Don't take that—that is one of the bones of Nebuchadnezzar's *Cat* and you *must* not have it.' It made an everlasting impression on my boyish mind. That probably occurred on one of those days when Osler and myself were rewarded by being allowed in my father's study for bringing home a good haul of frogs—used by Bovell and my father for studying the circulation of blood in the frog's foot.

Doubtless drawn together by their mutual interests in natural science, as biology was called in the days before Huxley, Dr. James Bovell and the Rev. W. A. Johnson had been acquainted for several years, and when the school at Weston was projected and became accepted as the Trinity College School under the authority of the Bishop, Bovell was appointed its medical director. Though in practice in Toronto and a teacher in the medical college, it was his habit to spend a part of each week-end in Weston, quite forgetful of his patients in all likelihood, absorbed with Johnson in collecting, staining, and mounting specimens for microscopical study. In this pursuit he must first have encountered the dark-eyed enthusiastic head prefect who used to accompany the Warden on his collecting expeditions.

Though a high-spirited boy and the ringleader in many escapades, Osler is said by his contemporaries to have been so straightforward, manly, and clean—'unobtrusively good without sanctimonious pretence'—that he exerted a splendid influence on the morale of the school. Moreover, at the end of the spring term as head of his class he had received the Chancellor's Prize, and it is not to be wondered at that Johnson had set his heart on having him, as well as another of the prefects—'Jones max.' of the roll-call—return for an extra year, although both had passed the subjects necessary for college. Osler had returned to Dundas for the summer, and apparently it was during this vacation, possibly as a by-play in connexion with the excitement caused by the Fenian Raid, that he is supposed to have drilled a company of youngsters for military service. He may have volunteered for this task under the influence of 'Captain' Goodwin's tutelage; and Dundas, it may be recalled, was not far distant from Fort Erie, which in June 1866 had been captured by O'Neil's band. However this may be, of another episode of the summer there exists written record. For there were a number of attractive cousins, both Canadian and English, who were visiting at the parsonage, and with each of them, as is the way with seventeen, he probably fell successively in love. This at least is to be gathered from letters of warning against entanglements, which he received from his elder sister after his return to school.

Meanwhile, during this summer vacation of 1866, 'Father' Johnson returns to his collecting, and the entries begin with '*June* 20. Diatomes, desmids and congregating algae put up in glycerine, water & spirit and fastened immediately.' Although he turns aside to examine the stomachs of the katydid and dragonfly, and to investigate butterfly eggs, the spores of rust, and much else besides, by the time school reopened the Diatomaceae, Algae, and Polyzoa seem to have become the dominant interest.[1] In this new subject, as would appear, the head prefect on the reopening of school was quickly fired in turn, and the valley of the Humber on many a half-holiday afternoon doubtless saw the two together in quest of specimens, in the collection of which the younger was the more persistent, as time will show.

The home letters of the period (unfortunately none of his own have been preserved) indicate that there are cricket

[1] 'A History of the British Fresh-water Algae.' By A. H. Hassall, London, 1857, is still among Johnson's books, and probably was the source of this new interest.

matches, visits from the cousins, and a 'Grand Shine', regarding which his mother writes a breathless sentence on October 29th:

I do not know whether I can send you the wished for Dimes because Papa is not home and I have no notes in the house, however, if he comes in time I will enclose it as I suppose you want it before the grand day of Games. And now what will you say when I tell you that *Marianne, Jennette, Ellen Mary and Charlotte* are to be with you on that day—and if you can escape from the Games to meet them at the Station they will be glad to see you there, they are (if all be well) to *leave here by the morning train*, lunch at the Toronto Station, and on to Weston, and *if they should get an invitation to remain the evening at the Grand Shine* they would sleep at the Hotel at Weston, returning to Toronto next morning, if not they will return to Toronto and mean to stay there till Saturday or perhaps Monday, if it is possible I would like you to write directly you get this, so that we might get it by Wednesday evening, telling us if the Games are really to come off and at what time, in fact tell us all about it and if it will be possible for the girls to put up comfortably in case they stay the night, they anticipate quite a pleasure trip and are anxious to see their cousin Willie. I think you'll like them, we all do.

It was this autumn that in a rugby football scrimmage he injured his shin so badly that he was laid up for some weeks with what evidently was a severe osteomyelitis. Affectionate and unbosoming letters which have been preserved were received from many of his old schoolmates—from Ned Milburn, one of the 'Barrie Bad Boys', who was already in his first year at Trinity, and from 'Jemmy' Morgan, another intimate of the Barrie days, who being a few years his senior, was at this time teaching school in Oakville, half-way between Toronto and Dundas. 'Father' Johnson rigged up for his damaged leg 'a common kind of rest, such as is used in England largely by men who suffer from the gout—a thing you could put your foot on and it changes its position with your position in the chair'. During these weeks of enforced inactivity he sat much of the time in the Warden's study where the microscopical specimens were prepared, and it is probable that the man and boy had long talks together, and that the boy's interest in the microscope and what it might reveal was further aroused at this time. It is probable, too, that being his patient he came more intimately at this time in contact with Bovell during the latter's week-end visits at the school.

But troubles meanwhile were brewing for 'Father' Johnson. The daily control of the school was naturally in the hands of the Head Master, but a number of the boys still lived with the Warden at the rectory, and so came under the Head Master's eye during school hours only. This division of authority was an inevitable source of friction, for it is quite probable that some of the school regulations were disregarded by the Warden, and as time went on relations became strained. It was a case of incompatibility of temperaments. One can easily appreciate the lack of sympathy or understanding on the part of a classicist for a clergyman who was in a position to engage the attention of his pupils in such occupations as grinding bones and teeth, the structure of which seems to have aroused Johnson's enthusiasm early in 1867.[1] The first entry in his specimen-book which mentions the name of his favourite pupil was on January 22nd, and on the same day the relic of 'Nebuchadnezzar's Cat' seems to have been mounted for study:

§ 505. 22/i/67. Crocodile scale ground by Osler, ground through (dry).

§ 506. 22/i/67. Longitudinal sections of bone of a cat, brought from the Pyramids of Goya (dry). Supposed to be 4000 years old. The bone was given me by Dr. Bovell.

§ 511. 28/i/67. Tooth of Bear, transverse, this had lain a long time in an Indian mound near Lambton, C.W. Turpentine and Balsam.

§ 524. 29/i/67. Transverse section, half of palatal tooth of fish. Given me by Dr. Bovell. Extremely hard. In the sac.

§ 530. 7/ii/67. Dentine & enamel of beaver incisor tooth, dry.

§ 540. 11/ii/67. Longitudinal section, leg bone of wild swan

---

[1] Presumably Johnson's interest in bones and teeth must have been awakened either by the 'Odontography' (1840–5) of Sir Richard Owen, or his 'Anatomy and Physiology of the Vertebrates' which had just appeared, though it is doubtful if he could have afforded to possess such expensive volumes; but his note-book shows that he had access to the *Quarterly Journal of Microscopical Science*, London, the official organ of the Royal Microscopical Society of which Owen was the first President and of which William Osler subsequently became a Fellow. Very probably they knew also of the Micrographic Dictionary of Griffith and Henfrey, 2 vols., 2nd ed., 1860.

having a small portion of the hard part of the cuticle. Dry. The bone is more brittle, & the haversians are more regular than in the Goose.

§ 550. 12/ii/67. Trans^e section, Human Fibula. This bone must have lain many years in the ground; it was taken from an Indian burying mound at Woodbridge, C.W. Put up in inspissated Balsam (changed to Balsam, *pure*).

§ 566. 28/ii/67. Transverse section leg bone of a cat, very thin, dry. Cat was killed on the railway track during the winter. Very pretty. Ground & finished by Jimmy.

The 'Jimmy' of these notes was the Rector's second son, James Bovell's namesake, who living in the parsonage far from the Head Master's reach could be called upon to grind bones and teeth for his father at irregular hours without fear of a birching. His elder brother Jukes had already gone up to Trinity College for a course preliminary to medicine, where appeals from Osler apparently reached him for bones of a variety Weston did not afford. During these winter months of 1867 a goodly number of teeth, it may be assumed, were also being ground in the irascible Head Master's room, though they did not come to be listed among W. A. Johnson's specimens. Far from it, for the unsuspecting Warden ere long had his school taken away from him by the machinations of others and transferred elsewhere; but this is perhaps another story.[1] By spring the head prefect's much discussed lame leg had so far recovered that it no longer kept him from his favourite expeditions, nor from engaging in cricket matches, to judge from this letter to his cousin:

To Miss Jennette Osler from W. O. [no date]

. . . I have splendid times with Mr. Johnson out after specimens of all sorts. I wish you had been with us last Tuesday down at the Peat Swamp, there are such splendid flowers down there and the Moss is so nice and springy one would like to make a bed of it. We got the smallest and rarest variety of Ladies Slipper or Indian Moccasin plant. I would so like you to see them they are the most beautiful of all Canadian wild flowers there are none about Dundas

---

[1] The school was finally removed from the auspices of its founder and established at Port Hope. Johnson was encouraged by his many supporters to organize another school at Weston, and this he attempted, with the Rev. Mr. Checkley, formerly of Barrie, as Head Master. The venture was unsuccessful and was abandoned after a year or two.

not being the right sort of soil for them to grow in. And if you could only see the Algae, that green stuff that you see on ponds and stagnant water, it is so beautiful, the thousands upon thousands of small animals all alive and kicking that are in it. We get some dirty looking brown stuff that at this time covers all the stones of the river and we found that on every pins point there were one hundred of the small creatures, fancy what there would be on a square inch and on a square mile. But I suppose you will think this sort of thing rather dry so I will stop it and turn to something perhaps nicer. We are having such a splendid run of Cricket Matches this term. We played Toronto yesterday and gave them such a thrashing, you will see it in Mondays Leader. Frank played with the Toronto fellows. Jemmy Morgan came out with them to see us all. We play Trinity on Thursday but I am afraid we will be badly beaten as they have the best Club in Toronto, but we have such a jolly player here, a regular old Englishman called Mr. Carter, he has been out here for about ten years roughing it in the backwoods ; he is at present our third Master . . . Believe me ever your affec cousin,

WILLIE.

So though working hard for a scholarship, sports and natural history had their due share of his time, and in conjunction with ' Father ' Johnson he began during May and June to tabulate and study his collection of the Diatomaceae which ere long constituted the basis of his first scientific publications. In furtherance of this quest, after the close of school the Warden paid a visit to Dundas, where he and his disciple frequented the Desjardin marshes and the adjacent waterways in search of specimens, the number of which increased by leaps and bounds. They may be pictured setting out on their daily expeditions with their nets and old-fashioned tin candle-boxes as specimen-containers slung over their shoulders ; and ere long their attention was drawn to a still more engrossing topic—the fresh-water polyzoa. In a paper on this subject, which was put together ten years later,[1] Osler drew upon his note-books for the following description, which manifests the flame of a youthful naturalist :

. . . The specimens on the table show well the hyaline gelatinous nature of the *cœnæcium* and the arrangement of the Polyps upon the surface. This is perhaps the most abundant fresh-water Polyzoon in the country, being found in the quiet waters about the mouths

[1] Cf. p. 151.

of the numerous streams, and in the small lakes. It is not very abundant in Quebec, but it has been found near St. Andrews, and I obtained a beautiful specimen from Lake Memphremagog. I have not seen it in the neighbourhood of Montreal. This species prefers quiet, still waters, not too much exposed, nor of large extent and subject to commotion from waves. Thus I have never found it in Lake Ontario itself, but always in little sheltered marshy bays, where it is found encrusting long, upright sticks, and the stems of rushes. My attention was early directed to this form as it exists in extraordinary profusion in the Desjardin Canal, which leads from Burlington Bay to my native town of Dundas. The wooden sides of the canal basin in the months of July and August are almost uniformly covered with this magnificent species. The growth begins about 1½ to 2 feet below the surface and extends in depth for the same distance or even further, rarely, however, deeper than six feet. The masses form extensive sheets usually a few inches in thickness, or else beautiful symmetrical projections, 6–12 inches in thickness, which spring either from a bed of the Polyps or are isolated. In the summer of 1867, during a visit of my friend, the Rev. W. A. Johnson of Weston, I showed him the masses and we agreed to submit them to examination with the microscope, not having any idea as to their real nature. Judge of our delight when we found the whole surface of the jelly was composed of a collection of tiny animals of surpassing beauty, each of which thrust out to our view in the zoophyte trough a crescent-shaped crown of tentacles. Recognizing it as a Polyp we were greatly exercised as to its position, presenting as it did in the method of growth such variation from the ordinary species described in our zoological text-books. Happily in the *American Naturalist* for that year we met with Mr. Alpheus Hyatt's papers on the Fresh-water Polyzoa, then in course of publication, and obtained full information therefrom . . . In some seasons the luxuriousness of the growth of these creatures is extraordinary. In the still, quiet water in the marsh on either side of Desjardin Canal, just before it passes through the Burlington heights, I have met with masses which would not go into a pail. The largest I have ever seen lay at the bottom in about nine feet of water. I could hardly believe it was a mass of Polyps, but to satisfy my curiosity I stripped and went in for it. With the greatest difficulty I brought it up in my arms, but could not get it out of the water for the weight, which must have been close upon 25 lb. It resembled in form one of those beautiful masses known as brain coral . . .

The end of July found master and pupil once more together in Weston, where doubtless collecting, 'in spite of his poor leg', was again so ardently resumed that letters home appear to have been somewhat slighted, if one may judge from his mother's gentle hints. During their rambles he and 'Father' Johnson must have talked freely about his future, and it was decided apparently that he should go up to Trinity College, with the expectation of entering the ministry. Another of the school prefects, L. K. Jones, had made a similar choice of career, and they determined to go to Oakville together and read up for the matriculation examinations. The remainder of the summer, therefore, was passed at the house of the Rev. Mr. Fletcher on the lake shore at Oakville, where they enjoyed the companionship of 'Jemmy' Morgan, who recalls that after lessons they would all sit up till midnight watching under a microscope, borrowed from Dr. Bovell, the activities of fresh-water algae.

Meanwhile in this year of 1867 the Canadian Confederation came into being, and ere long Ontario and Quebec came, in the people's minds, to take the place of Upper and Lower Canada, and a sense of national life began for the first time to be felt even in the smallest of communities in the Dominion.

CHAPTER III

1867–70

TRINITY COLLEGE AND THE TORONTO MEDICAL SCHOOL

OSLER went up to Trinity in the autumn of 1867, having in his possession one of the Dixon Prize Scholarships which he had well earned at Weston. Moreover, he apparently had theology still in the back of his mind. Trinity College,[1] it may suffice to say, was naturally enough regarded as a nursery for the divinity faculty and most of the teachers in the Arts course were clergymen, from among whom, as has been seen, the visiting board for the school of Weston were chosen. But not a few of these clergymen, like their more famous prototypes Stephen Hales, Gilbert White, and Joseph Priestley, were inclined to dabble in science and, no less than W. A. Johnson, felt a consuming interest in the phenomena of nature. One of them indeed, the Rev. John Ambrey, Professor of Classics, was the donor of a school prize for the best collection of geological and entomological specimens. Ministers with an interest in the natural sciences, particularly in those days when Wilberforce and Huxley represented the antipodes of thought and men's minds were greatly unsettled over original sin and Darwinism and Man's Place in Nature, made dangerous teachers for youths whom they expected to induct into the Church. To them science was a pastime; but the

[1] The all-influential Bishop Strachan, acting upon an old Royal Charter, had established a Church College—King's—in 1842, to which a medical department was attached. The Provincial Legislature in 1849 repealed the earlier charter and designated the institution The University of Toronto. A firm believer in the union of Church and State, with the Church in control of education, Strachan had long been the uncompromising centre of the fierce battles which had raged over the university question and the clergy reserves. Undaunted by the action of the legislature, he secured in 1850 another Royal Charter for a Church of England University, which became the University of Trinity College. The situation had its counterpart in London, for King's College was founded as an offset to the non-sectarian University College where, as the Established Church claimed, no moral or religious care was exercised over the students.

pleasant avocation of one generation easily becomes the vocation of the next, and his introduction to zoology must already have done much to deflect the impressionable mind of Osler from the very calling his revered preceptor expected him to follow. It is quite certain, however, that the boy's mind was not fully made up until a year later, and it is probable that his decision in favour of science became fixed through the unconscious influence of James Bovell, who himself, curiously enough, was in the process of changing in the reverse direction from Medicine to the Church. If Johnson's influence over the schoolboy had been considerable, that of Bovell was to become far more so, and to be more enduring.

James Bovell was born in the Barbadoes in 1817, where his father, an English banker, had long been resident. Possessed of ample means, he went to England in 1834, and after a short stay at Cambridge determined to study medicine, entering Guy's Hospital, where he became one of Astley Cooper's dressers and enjoyed the friendship of Bright and Addison. His London University degree could not be granted as he was two years under age, and to pass the time he repaired to Edinburgh to study pathology under Dr. Craigie and subsequently took his first doctor's degree in Glasgow. The next few years were passed in Dublin under Stokes and Graves, who were at the height of their fame. While there he was stricken with typhus, and on his recovery instead of acting on the advice of Stokes, who predicted a brilliant career for him in Great Britain, he returned home to take up practice at Antigua, whence in 1848 he was one of many who migrated from the West Indies to Canada. He settled in Toronto, and two years later with Dr. Hodder helped to organize a medical department for Trinity College—the Upper Canada School of Medicine.[1] In this school, which for the times was an excellent one, requiring an arts degree for entrance, Bovell acted both as Dean and as Professor of

[1] The history of the medical schools of Upper Canada is a long and complicated one, with a succession of institutions which flourished, languished, and died. The story up to 1850 is told in Wm. Canniff's 'The Medical Profession in Upper Canada, 1783–1850'.

the Institutes of Medicine: but the school had a short life, and though Bovell subsequently joined the Toronto Medical School Faculty, he retained the Chair of Natural Theology in Trinity, where until 1875 he lectured on physiology and pathology.[1] His particular and favourite course was on the subject of 'physiology as related to theological conceptions'!

With his four daughters Bovell lived on Spadina Avenue, and the young Osler soon after his entrance to Trinity began to frequent the place 'to keep the aquaria stocked with pond material likely to contain good specimens of algae'; and also to gather and study a variety of animals which shortly overflowed to 112 St. Patrick Street after one of the daughters married a Mr. Barwick and moved there to live. Besides this, what engaged him as a first-year student at the university, if it was other than what engages most young men, is not recorded, though it is evident that he repaired to Weston as often as week-ends and vacations permitted, in order to go over with Johnson the accessions to his zoological collection.

A few classroom note-books of the period have been preserved. One of them starts out bravely, under the date 21/10/67, with '*Latin Prose Composition*', and after the first exercise there is written in the teacher's hand, 'Very good indeed my boy.' But after November the exercises cease to be copied out and the remainder of the book is filled with notes regarding his fresh-water polyzoa: '*Genus I Epithemia*: adherent, quadrilateral; valves circinate furnished with transverse canaliculi, &c., &c.' and there follows a list of elaborately described specimens taken from Humber Bay, Grenadier Pond, the Thames, London [Ontario of course], Desjardin Canal, Burlington Bay, Sandy Cove, together with other genera and species from the same and other places; from the sunken boat in the mouth of the Humber often mentioned in W. A. Johnson's note-book; *Cyclotella Kützingiana* of which there are myriads in the river at London; from the Northern Railway wharf where *Navicula tumida* are common; from the Don River,

[1] Cf. Arthur Jukes Johnson on 'The Founder of the Medical Faculty'. *Trinity University Review*, Jubilee No., June–July 1902, p. 104.

Cedar Swamp, Weston; and finally from Buckley's water-trough, Dundas, which evidently found him at home for Christmas.

It was Johnson's custom to read aloud to the boys in the parsonage, and for this purpose, as Osler recalled in later years, he often selected extracts from such works as the 'Religio Medici' 'in illustration of the beauty of the English language'. But it must have been more than this. That a high-churchman should have cared particularly for Sir Thomas Browne is remarkable enough, but that he should have been able to transmit this appreciation to a boy of seventeen is truly amazing. It moreover is an important thread which from this point weaves its way through Osler's story to the end; and the 1862 edition of the 'Religio', his second book purchase,[1] to which he referred more than once in his published addresses, was the very volume which lay on his coffin fifty-two years later. In Osler's library alongside this particular book, handsomely rebound and evidently much read despite the few marks it contains, there always stood another volume in its original covers entitled 'Varia: Readings from Rare Books', by J. Hain Friswell, London, 1866, which is inscribed in his eldest brother's hand: 'Wm Osler from F. O. Xmas 1867.' One of the best of the charming essays this volume contains is upon Sir Thomas Browne, and one may imagine a young man destined for the ministry reading during his Christmas holidays about 'The Religion of a Physician', and how few people there are who know its author, mistaking him either for the facetious writer of 'Laconics' or the Tom Brown of Mr. Hughes's imagination; how he came to practise in Norwich and to write his books; how 'Sir Thomas grew pleasantly old, and died as we have seen, boldly and manfully when his time came'; how he came to be buried there in St. Peter Mancroft in 1682; how in 1840 his grave was despoiled

[1] Osler has given the date of this purchase as 1867, but there are reasons to believe that this was a slip of memory. The first book he bought was the Globe Shakespeare which he said was afterwards stolen, and he often invoked 'the curses of Bishop Ernulphus on the son of Belial who took it.' His favourite copy of the 'Religio' was probably purchased in 1868.

and his skull, rescued from private hands, came to adorn the museum of surgery in Norwich, rendering prophetic certain passages in his 'Urn Burial'.

It must have been shortly after this Christmas vacation that the 1862 Ticknor and Fields (second) edition of the Completed Works, dedicated to the authors of 'The Autocrat of the Breakfast Table' and of 'Rab and his Friends', was purchased at W. C. Chitwell's bookstore in Toronto. There is written, at least, on the fly-leaf 'W. Osler. Coll. S.S. Trin. Lent Term 28/2/'68'. In the book itself there are but three marked passages.[1] Few marks were needed, for only one other book, the Bible, did he come to know more nearly by heart. One note is dated Dec. 6, 1919, and will come later in these annals. Two passages of the 'Religio' are marked by stars—one of them the paragraph (p. 10) beginning 'Holy-water and crucifix deceive not my judgement . . .', the other the great paragraph with which the essay opens:

> For my religion, though there be several circumstances that might persuade the world I have none at all, as the general scandal of my profession, the natural course of my studies, the indifferency of my behaviour and discourse in matters of religion, neither violently defending one, nor with that common ardour and contention opposing another; yet in despite hereof I dare, without usurpation, assume the honourable style of a Christian.

The spring term of 1868 passed by without any definite decision as to his future, though there are abundant straws to indicate the direction in which he was tending. Early in the year he had written his cousin Jennette: 'I attend the Medical School every afternoon and I have been grinding at Lyell's "Principles of Geology" in vacation, hoping to get through it before term begins. I am at Dr. Bovell's every Saturday and we put up preparations for the microscope . . . Mrs. W. was here this morning and told me about a stratum in the mountain which was full of fossils; but for the deep snow I would go up and get

[1] There are one or two corrections. Thus on p. 317 of 'Urn Burial' where Browne says 'Plato's historian of the other world lies twelve days uncorrupted', &c., W. O. has changed 'twelve' to 'ten', with marginal reference to the 'Republic', Bk. X.

some for I have none from Dundas and they are difficult to find.' Moreover he had begun to make a collection of entozoa, the earliest entry in the list bearing the date 'Feb'y 7th, 1868', and on these matters he probably consulted Father Johnson, doubtless taking advantage of these Weston visits to engage in the school sports. As Mr. E. Douglas Armour of Toronto recalls :

He had left school in the summer of 1867, and I went there in the autumn term. When the cricket season opened in 1868, he used to come out to Weston where the school was then situate, to play cricket with us, and that was when I first saw him. He was a lithe, swarthy, athletic, keen-eyed boy. I don't think I ever saw anyone with such piercing black eyes. He deserved the encomium bestowed by Horace on Lycus in Book I, Ode xxxii, both for his jet-black hair and beautiful black eyes. He had a peculiar forward inclination of the body as he walked, which caused his arms to hang slightly forward and gave them an appearance of being always ready to use. He was an excellent round-arm bowler, and a batter became distinctly conscious of the strength of the lithe arm, which seemed to acquire a great part of it from his determined and piercing glance as he delivered the ball. You may think it strange that I should enlarge upon this, but the fact that it is as distinctly impressed upon my mind after a lapse of fifty-three years as if I had seen it yesterday will indicate the strong personality that a boy of eighteen or nineteen possessed.

Whether his college standing suffered because of these pastimes does not appear ; probably not, for he acquired knowledge readily. The examination papers of the next June are preserved, and very stiff examinations they were, held on successive days in *Algebra*, *Euclid*, *Greek* (Medea and Hippolytus), the *Catechism*, *Trigonometry*, *Latin Prose*, *Roman History*, *Pass Latin* (Terence), *Classics* (Honours). How he got through the trigonometry with his dislike for mathematics is difficult to conceive. And certainly the Catechism test was searching enough without the enchantment of the polyzoa to have affected his choice of a career. There were eighteen questions, such as these :

Show that the Holy Spirit is both a person and divine.

Eternal life is distinguished as being initial, partial, and perfectional. Explain and illustrate under each head from Scripture.

It is difficult for those of a later generation to imagine

the struggle and turmoil which in those days engaged men's minds. Following Cuvier and Owen, the doctrines and theories of Lyell, Darwin, Wallace, and Huxley threatened to split the very Church asunder. Some, like Wilberforce in the Church, attacked them ; some, like Gosse in science, did likewise, and one may imagine, it being but nine years since 'The Origin of Species', that in discussion with his favourite pupil Johnson faced the controversy fearlessly, and that his attitude was not an ambiguous one. In those days, moreover, it was still expected that the Anglican Church would absorb one at least of a family of children, but the youth of the day were graduating from Butler's 'Analogy', which failed to satisfy them as it had satisfied Newman. Subjects more appetizing than theological revelation they were eagerly lapping up in an anonymous volume, 'Vestiges of Creation', in Lyell's 'Antiquity of Man', in Herbert Spencer's 'First Principles' and in Huxley's 'Lay Sermons and Addresses' which appeared anti-theological to a degree.

The Toronto Medical School

The summer of 1868 evidently was passed in gathering further samples of algae from the waterways in and about Dundas. Concerning one of these specimens—a mass of Pectinatella found in an old submerged barge near the mouth of the Humber—he consulted his botany teacher, father of the Rev. Thomas Hincks, F.R.S., the authority on the British polyzoa, into whose hands this rare finding seems thereby to have fallen.[1] He returned to Trinity for his second year in Arts, but after enduring it for a few days announced to his parents and to the Provost his determination to go into Medicine. He had come to learn his own mind and it appears to have been the only momentous decision of his life—and there were many to make—over which he long wavered. It must have caused some disappointment at home, but if so his parents were not of a sort to bring undue pressure to bear in influencing the

[1] Cf. foot-note to Osler's 'Canadian Fresh-water Polyzoa'. *Canadian Naturalist*, 1883, new series, x, 406.

choice of a career for one of their sons. Even had they been so inclined, Johnson and Bovell unconsciously drew him in another direction. Another environment, an earlier decade, would almost certainly have seen him enter the Church.

And what of his friends and preceptors? Johnson had left the Army for the Church. His two sons chose for Medicine, though one of them subsequently took Holy Orders. And Bovell in a few years came to do likewise; but at this time as soon as he heard of his young friend's decision he exclaimed: 'That 's splendid, come along with me.' This the boy literally did, and during the next two years the two lived more like father and son than as teacher and pupil. From the first he evidently entered into his medical studies with the industry and enthusiasm which characterized his relation to his choice of profession to the end. A number of letters from his surviving class-mates are unanimous in stating that he was exceptionally studious and faithful in attendance at lectures; that he spent most of his hours in the dissecting-room and when not so engaged was 'always to be found looking through a microscope at Bovell's cells'; that he was a general favourite not only with the class but with their preceptors, of whom Hodder, Richardson, H. H. Wright, and of course Bovell, are chiefly mentioned; and that, when 'grinding' the class, the teachers were apt to turn to Osler when others could not answer their questions. These letters, too, uniformly testify to his companionableness, and state that he was always ready for a frolic and bit of fun.

> One of the sports indulged in to a very limited extent was boxing, the champion being big John Standish who could box all day. He had the strength of a giant with a kindly gentle heart and took care never to hurt anyone. The students were amused one day to see little Osler tackle the giant, and quite surprised to find that the little one was almost the only member of the crowd who could strike Standish.

Of Bovell, likewise, many tales survive—tales which emphasize his absent-mindedness—of his putting some blisters on a patient and forgetting them until three weeks later; of losing his horse and buggy, which were found standing before a house where he had called the previous day. Dr. R. H. Robinson, a fellow student of Osler's, writes that on one occasion he felt ill, and having consulted Bovell at the Medical Building, was told to go to bed in his boarding-house, and to remain there until Bovell called the next morning. Bovell forgot about it until the third day and then took Osler with him, to look for the patient somewhere on Grosvenor Street at a number he could not remember. Robinson, who meanwhile had recovered, was out walking and saw Bovell standing in the street in evident distress while Osler was running from door to door inquiring whether there was a sick man in the house.

It is not easy to trace the activities of a medical student of fifty years ago, particularly of one who was habitually reticent about himself, so that even were the letters of the time preserved they would tell little. A visit must have been made to Weston both at the beginning and end of the Christmas recess, for under the dates '19/xii/68' and '9/i/69' Johnson records a number of microscopic specimens such as: 'Trachea of a mouse given me by W. Osler. Gly. beautifully stained.' Inasmuch as there was no course in histology in those days these specimens evidently were prepared on his own initiative by Osler himself; and Johnson in return inscribed to him as a Christmas gift Alpheus Hyatt's 'Observations on Polyzoa, Suborder Phylactolæmata' which had just appeared in the Proceedings of the Essex Institute. Osler's first appearance in print describes an episode of this particular holiday season, possibly under the influence of a morning's perusal of Johnson's present. It was a short sketch entitled 'Christmas and the Microscope' which he sent to a semi-popular and now extinct English journal devoted to nature study.[1] As he said years later, this was the beginning of his inkpot career and showed his 'fondness, even at the very start, for tags of quotations; this one from Horace then a familiar friend.'

Nec iam sustineant onus,
Sylvae laborantes, geluque
Flumina constiterint acuto,

might well be said of the Canadian woods and streams at this season of the year. The earth has put on her winter robes, and under them

[1] *Hardwicke's Science-Gossip*, Lond., 1870, v. 44 (Feb. 1, 1869). Edited by M. C. Cooke.

she hides most of those objects which in summer please and delight us so much. A cheerless prospect for microscopists, one would think. So I thought, as on Christmas I sallied forth with bottles and stick in search of diatoms, infusoria, snow-peas, &c., though I did not expect to be very successful. After wandering about for some time, searching vainly for an unfrozen stream, I was about to return home with empty bottles, when I suddenly bethought myself of an old spring which supplied several families with water, and which I knew therefore would be unfrozen. In this country, wherever there is a good spring some kind individual sinks a barrel for the benefit of the community at large, and thereby benefits microscopists in no small degree, for in these you are generally sure to find a good supply of microscopic objects. When I got to the spring the first thing that greeted my sight was a piece of algae floating on the top of the water, and on a closer examination of the barrel I saw that the sides had a dark-brown coating, in which I knew diatoms and infusoria would be found. Scraping some of this off, I placed it in a bottle and retraced my steps homeward, well satisfied with my afternoon's walk. Getting home at that unfavourable time for working, just as the light is beginning to fail, I had to exercise my patience and wait till evening to see what my bottle contained. I had not long to wait, as darkness soon succeeds the light here; so when I had got a lamp lighted I proceeded to examine my spoils. A short account of the things I found may not be uninteresting to English readers of the *Science-Gossip* as it will give them some idea of what lovers of science meet with in this country. . . .

And the young microscopist of nineteen goes on to enumerate the living 'things' he was able to identify in his bottle of water. Thus his holidays were passed, and the Easter recess likewise found him collecting specimens in the region around Lake Simcoe, a goodly number of which he forwarded to Johnson from Sandy Cove and Kempenfelt Bay; and a week later on his way home, this from a horse-trough:

28/iv/69. Alga? Tindyredia &c. in gathering from a horse-trough on the road and hillside between Hamilton and Dundas, sent me by post from W. Osler to see water bears; did not find any. In Hantz fluid and sealed immediately.

In spare hours during all this first year he and Bovell were doubtless much together, and the latter's granddaughter writes:

He was about twenty in those days and literally lived at our house. He adored Grandfather and the latter loved him like a son—and they were both crazy about the microscope. Mother [Mrs. Barwick] says her life was a perfect burden to her with weird parcels arriving which might contain a rattlesnake, a few frogs, toads or dormice. She found quite a large snake meandering around the study one afternoon, and when she protested violently, the two told her she should not have been in there. . . .

The summer vacation was largely passed at home and he must have attached himself to the family physician, Dr. A. Holford Walker, for in a paper on appendicitis written twenty years later, shortly after this malady received its baptism, he recalls having seen with Dr. Walker during this year of 1869 two cases in which the abscess had formed and discharged in the groin. But he devoted himself chiefly to his zoological collection, and from time to time forwarded to Weston some new species from Niagara Falls and elsewhere. Not only does Johnson's familiar specimen-book duly record their receipt, but it makes clear also that he again joined his disciple in Dundas during September for a series of excursions in and about their favourite hunting-grounds, which evidently supplied the Warden with material for study for some months to come.

Among Osler's several student blank-books that have been preserved is one bearing the date October 1, 1869, which is of no great significance except for one thing. It contains a few pages of notes on chemistry and materia medica (Nov. 3, '69 to Feb. 9, '70), but it is largely filled with the next year's lectures on obstetrics, chemistry, and pathology taken at McGill. In pencil on the fly-leaf in W. O.'s hand is: '*James Bovell, M.D., M.R.C.P. Prof. Nat. Theology in Trinity College Toronto. Lecturer on Institutes of Medicine, Toronto School of Med. Consulting Physician to Toronto General Hospital. Physician to Lying-in Hospital. Lay Secretary to Provincial Synod. Author of Outline of Natural Theology, &c. &c. &c. James Bovell.*' And through the book the name is scribbled whenever a lapse appears to have occurred in the lecture, or the student's mind wandered—'*James Bovell M.D. M.R.C.P.*'; '*James Bovell M.D.*' The man must have come to exercise an extraordinary influence over the boy, and to his last days, as will be seen, in moments of absent-mindedness or when trying a pen it was the name of James Bovell that came first to paper, not his own.

In those days, before the multitudinous special subdivisions of medicine which have bid fair to crowd the fundamentals out of the curriculum, the course of anatomy extended over two years, and as the dissecting-room represented the only laboratory to which a student had access the abler ones revelled in it. The teachers of the pre-clinical branches, moreover, were at the same time practitioners; and in a lecture on aneurysm [1] delivered years later Osler wrote:

> When a student in Toronto I occasionally visited the jail with our teacher of Anatomy, Dr. J. H. Richardson, and among the prisoners was an old soldier who had been discharged from the army after the Crimean War for aneurysm of the aorta, so his papers said, and, considering the large experience of the army surgeons with the disease, it is not likely there could have been any mistake.[2]

He goes on to say that the old man died in 1885, thirty years after the Crimean War, and Dr. J. E. Graham gave him the specimen to be drawn and described—a healed saccular aneurysm at the junction of the arch and descending aorta. It is quite likely that these visits with his teacher of anatomy aroused the inquisitive boy's special interest in aneurysm, so evident in his Montreal days; but this is anticipating. As has been stated, the outstanding recollection of him on the part of his surviving fellow students is that he was always dissecting. Dr. Albert MacDonald, who was prosector in anatomy, recalls that he 'spent more time in the dissecting-room than any other student, frequently bringing his lunch with him in order to get some extra time there. He did much of this work alone, working out problems of his own in his own way, without the aid of a demonstrator. Thus he pointed out the presence of

[1] *International Clinics*, Phila., 1903.

[2] James Henry Richardson was Professor of Anatomy in the Toronto schools from 1850 to 1902, and for the same period Surgeon to the Toronto Jail. He was a famous rifle-shot and fisherman, and is said to have chosen the maple-leaf as the national emblem of Canada. To Richardson as well as his other teachers in the school Osler paid tribute in his address, 'The Master Word in Medicine', given in 1903, on the occasion of the amalgamation of the Toronto and Trinity Schools of Medicine.

the *Trichina spiralis* in the muscles of one of the bodies, which no one else had observed.' This episode of the winter of 1870 sufficiently illustrates his characteristics, not so much in that it shows unusually acute powers of observation for a student, but rather in giving evidence of his wide-awakeness and his ability to use acquired knowledge, for he had already seen the trichina under the microscope, as is apparent from two sources—from Johnson's specimen-book as well as from a remarkable note-book of this period kept by Osler himself, in which occur lists of entozoa from all possible sources. Of this more will be said in its proper sequence.

Another event, in this first year's study, which had some influence on my later life, was the discovery of the *Trichina spiralis.* Dr. Cobbold has told the story of the several steps leading to the discovery and following it, in his latest work on the Entozoa. My share was the detection of the 'worm' in its capsule; and I may justly ascribe it to the habit of looking-out, and observing, and wishing to find new things, which I had acquired in my previous studies of botany. All the men in the dissecting-rooms, teachers included, 'saw' the little specks in the muscles: but I believe that I alone 'looked-at' them and observed them: no one trained in natural history could have failed to do so.

This paragraph was not written by William Osler, but occurs in the short autobiography of Sir James Paget.[1] The circumstances, however, were much the same, and Osler with his instincts as a naturalist also 'looked-at' as well as 'saw' the specks in his own turn. Literally, thousands of sections were cut and studied; specimens were sent to Father Johnson; Bovell doubtless became interested; innumerable feeding experiments were performed in the attempt to infect other animals, for at the time but little was known of the disease in America. Some six years later, in his first paper on the subject, Osler wrote:

When a student with Prof. Bovell of Toronto I had several opportunities of studying these parasites. In the month of February 1870 while dissecting a subject with Dr. Zimmerman in the Toronto School of Medicine, we discovered numerous trichinae thoughout the whole muscular system, all of which were densely encysted, many

[1] The discovery was made in 1835. Cf. 'Memoirs and Letters of Sir James Paget'. Longman & Co., Lond., 1901, p. 95.

having become calcified. From a single drachm of one of the muscles of the arm I obtained 159 cysts, the greater number of which enclosed healthy-looking worms. This man was a German, and had been janitor at the hospital, where I had known him for over two years.[1]

It is interesting that he says 'a student with Prof. Bovell', rather than a student at the Toronto Medical School, and it is characteristic also that he links the name of his schoolmate with the discovery, for it is evident from the personal notes accompanying his list of entozoa that it was his own.

This new and consuming interest in the entozoa had been awakened some time before—indeed, when he was still at Trinity, the earliest specimen which he records being under the date '7/ii/68'; but it was not until January 1st of 1870 that he began systematically to make a list of his specimens in a blank-book and to give detailed explanatory notes. It was quite consistent with what was still under way in his study of the Diatomaceae and fresh-water polyzoa, but it illustrates the formative stage of his habit of observing, collecting, recording, and tabulating specimens of cases, and thus preparing material for future publications. Many of the specimens are evidently carried or sent to Johnson, who duly makes such entries as this: '§ 1315. Entozoa from the mucous stomach of a bat, given me by W. Osler and put up by him.' Johnson's interest in this new subject is obviously aroused, though the preparations all appear to have been mounted by his young friend, who is rapidly forging ahead of him. Even when Osler's name is not mentioned, the source of many of Johnson's specimens may be easily traced. Thus:

> 22/iv/70. § 1388. Parasites on fins, body, &c., of little fish in my aquarium. They seem to have a chitinous horseshoe-shaped piece inside, & are large brown-looking things with powers of locomotion & short cells all round the edges. . . .

Whereas in Osler's records occur three corresponding entries, the first of which reads:

> 21/iv/70. On the fins of chub in the Rev. W. A. Johnson's

---

[1] 'Trichina Spiralis.' *Canadian Journal of Medical Science*, May 1876, i. 175.

> aquarium were noticed several round white spots. These on examination proved to be some sort of Entozoa. In addition to these, some yellow spots were seen which seem to be a more advanced condition of the parasite. (See slide . . .)

Another entry the following day records the catching of a pike 2 ft. 7 in. long, from which he obtained '68 specimens of Taenia and two or three small Ascaridae', the microscopical characteristics of which he proceeds to describe in detail. In no sense a Waltonian, as his son came to be, Osler nevertheless could endure fishing when it furnished side-interests of this sort, though it was easier for him on the whole, as his note-book shows, to get his specimens from the fish-market.

There can be little doubt that had William Osler at this time come under the influence of Leidy or Agassiz or possibly of Huxley, he would have gone on with his biological studies and abandoned medicine; for aside from his opportunities in the dissecting-room it would appear that the school was not proving a great success, and his lecture notes, with their 'James Bovell M.R.C.P.' scribblings, would indicate that his mind was not captured by the lectures. There is possibly one thing that might have deterred him, his ineffectiveness with his pencil, for though many of the sketches of his specimens are probably accurate enough they are lacking in any artistic quality—the only accomplishment in which the Rev. W. A. Johnson excelled his pupil. However this may be, he persisted in sketching as best he could what he saw under the microscope, and his copious notes with their accompanying illustrations of diatoms, polyzoa, and entozoa are comparable to those accompanying the notes made later on in Montreal and London when he was poring over blood specimens; those made in Philadelphia when absorbed in the malarial parasite; and those made during the first year in Baltimore on the amoebae of dysentery, which practically ended his days with the microscope. The method of the pursuit in each instance was the same, and though occasionally he ventured to reproduce some of his own sketches in his early papers, the art of illustration was not his best card. In all these extra-curricular pursuits, though his name appears less frequently than that of Johnson, Bovell probably figured largely, for they were much together. Nearly fifty years later Osler wrote:

It has been remarked that for a young man the privilege of browsing in a large and varied library is the best introduction to a general education. My opportunity came in the winter of '69–'70. Having sent his family to the West Indies, Dr. Bovell took consulting rooms in Spadina Avenue not far away from his daughter Mrs. Barwick, with whom he lived. He gave me a bedroom in the house, and my duties were to help to keep appointments—an impossible job!—and to cut sections and prepare specimens. Having catholic and extravagant tastes he had filled the rooms with a choice and varied collection of books. After a review of the work of the day came the long evening for browsing, and that winter [1869–70] gave me a good first-hand acquaintance with the original works of many of the great masters. After fifty years the position in those rooms of special books is fixed in my mind. Morton's 'Crania Americana', Annesley's 'Diseases of India' with the fine plates, the three volumes of Bright, the big folios of Dana, the monographs of Agassiz. Dr. Bovell had a passion for the great physician-naturalists, and it was difficult for him to give a lecture without a reference to John Hunter. The diet was too rich and varied, and contributed possibly to the development of my somewhat 'splintery' and illogical mind; but the experience was valuable and aroused an enduring interest in books. In such a decade of mental tumult as the '60's, really devout students, of whom Dr. Bovell was one, were sore let and hindered, not to say bewildered, in attempts to reconcile Genesis and Geology. It seems scarcely credible, but I heard a long debate on Philip Henry Gosse's (of, to me, blessed memory) 'Omphalos, an Attempt to Untie the Geological Knot'. A dear old parson, Canon Read, stoutly maintained the possibility of the truth of Gosse's view that the strata and the fossils had been created by the Almighty to test our faith! A few years ago, reading 'Father and Son' which appeared anonymously, the mention of this extraordinary 'Omphalos' work revealed the identity and, alas! to my intense regret, the personality of the father as Philip Henry Gosse.

Of this mental struggle the students reaped the benefit—for Dr. Bovell was much more likely to lecture on what was in his mind than on the schedule, and a new monograph on Darwin or a recent controversial pamphlet would occupy the allotted hour. One corner of the library was avoided. With an extraordinary affection for mental and moral philosophy he had collected the works of Locke and Berkeley, Kant and Hegel, Spinoza, and Descartes, as well as those of the moderns. He would joke upon the impossibility of getting me to read any of the works of these men, but at Trinity, in '67–'68, I attended his lectures on Natural Theology, and he really did get us interested in Cousin and Jouffroy and others of the French School. Three years of association with Dr. Bovell were most helpful. Books and the Man!—the best the human mind has afforded was on his shelves, and in him all that one could desire in a teacher—a clear head and a loving heart. Infected with the Æsculapian spirit he made me realize the truth of those memorable words in the Hippocratic oath, 'I will honour as my father the man who teaches me the Art.'[1]

In regard to the 'consulting rooms' referred to in the foregoing, tradition has it that the venture was entered upon at Osler's suggestion, with the object of starting a consulting practice for Bovell and of obliging him thereby to collect his fees. The partnership is said to have continued for about a year, and apparently the business methods, or lack of them, of the senior partner, in the end prevailed. Dr. R. B. Nevitt, who entered Trinity as one of Osler's contemporaries, writes that 'he brought there no marked reputation except that he was a good fellow and held the distance record for throwing a cricket-ball'. He says further:

One afternoon I had some engagement with W. O. and called for him at Bovell's office. The room was large and bare with a few chairs and a small deal table—like a kitchen table. Osler opened the drawer of the table—Dr. B. had gone out—and said: 'Look here! This drawer has been filled to overflowing with bills two or three times this afternoon and now look.' One solitary bill lay in the drawer. As the patients paid their fees Osler placed them in the drawer. A needy patient came along, and Dr. B. reversed the process and handed money out so that the sick man might get his medicine and the food and other things required.

Many other stories of Bovell could be told—many of them probably true and many of them having Osler as an appendage. The older man was adored by all the students, though it could never be told whether the topic of his lecture was going to be medical or theological, or indeed whether he would remember to come at all; and on occasions, both at Trinity and the medical school, it devolved upon Osler to give his lecture for him. It was during the spring of 1870, despite all of his accumulating

[1] Introduction to 'Bibliotheca Osleriana' (in the press).

interests, that Osler began visiting the veterinary hospital, possibly drawn there in the first place by his interest in comparative parasitology and in the expectation of adding to his growing collection of entozoa—an expectation fully realized.[1] Nevertheless he found time to prepare for publication the results of his studies on the Diatomaceae and to forward the manuscript to Principal Dawson of McGill, who was at the same time President of the Natural History Society of Montreal.[2] This, his second appearance in print, Osler introduced with this paragraph :

> Among the many beautiful objects which the microscope has revealed to us, none, perhaps, are such general favourites (especially with the younger microscopists) as the Diatomaceae. Their almost universal distribution—the number of species—and above all, the singular beauty and regularity of their markings—have all tended to make them objects of special interest and study. In the following paper I propose to give briefly the principal points connected with their life, history and structure, together with a list of those species I have met with in Canada . . .

The article, as W. T. Councilman has said,[3] contains 'an admirable description of the structure, mode of division, and propagation of the diatom, evidently based on personal observation'. There is mention of a 'diatom-prism', which he has been enabled to use through the kindness of Professor Bovell ; due acknowledgement of his obligations to the Rev. W. A. Johnson is made ; and he proceeds to enumerate 110 species in 31 genera collected from the haunts with which the reader has become familiar—the Don River, the cedar swamp of Weston, the wharves at Toronto, the sunken boat at the mouth of the Humber, Lake Simcoe, the Welland Canal, Coote's Paradise, the Niagara River, and so on—and he adds : 'Many more no doubt will be found as the number of practical microscopists increases in the country.' One or another of these familiar haunts finds him at the close of school adding to

[1] Quite consistent with this were his subsequent associations with the veterinarians at McGill.

[2] The paper was not presented before the Society until the October meeting, though it was published in the June volume of the Transactions.

[3] 'Some of the Early Medical Work of Sir William Osler.' *Johns Hopkins Hospital Bulletin*, July 1919.

the collection of entozoa obtained from a variety of creatures which were hooked, trapped, or shot—including a large male skunk! And later on at Dundas he continues through July, August, and September with this same exciting quest of the parasites in beast, bird, and fish:

> 13/viii/70. Shot a kingfisher. A few small Diatoms were found in the liver. The small fish which constitute the food of this bird seem not to share in the common fate of fish, inasmuch as few or immature entozoons were found in them, &c., &c.

On other days he shoots a hawk, or hooks a large black bass in Burlington Bay, or examines ten sunfish caught in the canal, and so on—a combination of sport and science, with the chief emphasis on science, to judge from the elaborate notes on his pathological findings and the scant reference to their source. Johnson must have paid another visit to Dundas early in August, for on the 16th he wrote an amusing bread-and-butter letter which Osler had preserved, and a few days later sent the following remarkable note, doubtless believing that the young student of entozoa was capable of an investigation which might have anticipated Theobald Smith:

To W. O. from Rev. W. A. Johnson. The Parsonage, Weston, Ont. 23 Aug[t] 1870.

My dear Osler,—The cows &c. round us are all afflicted & several dying from what appears to be the bite of the little fly that teazes horses so much just now. I went out yesterday & captured 8 or 10 on the fences & sides of an old horse & by the time I got into the house from Holley's field there were 8 small maggots in the clean bit of paper. These were extruded from one of the flies. Question, Is this little fly known to be a vivipositor? If so, are these Maggots adapted to live in the skin of a living animal? The sores on the cows legs bags, &c., would show this. Could not you inspect them. The country would be benefited by knowing, because the papers are writing about a *disease?* Come over & have a look. In the mean time I will drop a line to Bethune & Hincks & find out (if they can tell me) whether said fly is a vivipositor.

Yours sincerely

W. A. Johnson.

During this summer vacation, if not before, Osler had determined, in all probability on Bovell's advice, to leave the Toronto School for McGill, for it must have been apparent to both of them that the clinical opportunities in the Montreal hospitals, which were more open to students, far exceeded those which Toronto then offered. Bovell had gone to the West Indies for the summer, and before leaving must have known of his pupil's decision, and have given him a letter to Palmer Howard, then Professor of Medicine at McGill. But at the time Bovell seems to have given no intimation that he himself might not return, and though rumours to this effect had reached Osler during the summer through letters both from Johnson and from his son, Bovell's namesake, the following from Bovell himself made the matter final, and must have reconciled Osler to his own first migration.

To W. O. from James Bovell. Spring-Well near Charles Town
Nevis West Indies.
August 11th [1870].

My dear Osler,—My last will have given you some general idea of the outline of Nevis and its gorges. This will not add much local news as I am not yet settled and cant yet get myself used to the idea that I may not get back to Canada this year. I now write to beg you to see that all my Microscopical Apparatus is very carefully packed—all the things being taken out of the very large binocular case and made to fit the smaller binocular. All the object glasses carefully put in the cases and a case made for the instrument in the Cabinet—The Specimens looked over and packed. You are to have my surgical instruments and Stethoscopes but send my Clinical Thermometer. I dont want to keep the monster Microscope stand and Eye pieces so if you like to pack carefully all the rest of the apparatus up, you can have as a present the stand and Eye-pieces. I will next mail write you the name of the Merchant at Halifax who ships goods out to this place and if the Express will take the things down to Halifax they can come out here to me—but any thing must be put up and packed in book-binders shavings papers. I am going into the large Star-fishes of which there are many to be had out here and I am watching repair in Lizards and tubercle in Guinea pigs the last are only now breeding so I shall not have enough to begin with before October, but it is an advantage to have them. The Lizards here are very large and I hope for some good results. The [Toronto] School paid very little this year so I am not sorry to leave it although I do care a great deal leaving Richardson and my old friends of years—I cant think of Johnson without a choking for we are brothers of years affection and not even you can know how deeply I love him. I am however not acting from choice but from necessity and duty. I have made a purchase which if watched and cared will be a fortune to my children and however little I may benefit it is to them every thing that I should be here to see after its development. I hope to be in Toronto in June unless Mrs Barwick comes this way to avoid a Canadian summer. I have not a bit of thin glass to see anything with. The 1/8th was done for by its fall and Gannot could do nothing with it. It got a crack right through it—I do hope you will work on for I have quite made up my mind that you are to get a first Class for the East India Comp^y. Write me all the news and fully—Do look after my Microscopes and see to them—Give my love to your good Father and to all who ask for me. I write you again by next mail—Love for you dear boy.

Y^rs affect^y

J. Bovell.

It has been said of Bovell, perhaps by Osler himself,[1] that in spite of his rich mental endowment there was, from attempting too many things, 'a want of that dogged persistency of purpose without which a great work can scarcely be accomplished', and he adds: 'It may be well for a physician to have pursuits outside his profession, but it is dangerous to let them become too absorbing.' It was perhaps just as well that Osler at this time was destined to come under the steadying influence of a less brilliant personality. Nevertheless, in spite of, or because of, Bovell, it is apparent that in this last year at Toronto Osler laid the foundations of what were to be his subsequent habits of life. The cornerstone of the foundation was work and the finding of this a pleasure. To this were added three qualities, of which he speaks in a later address [2] to medical students: the Art of Detachment, the Virtue of Method, the Quality of Thoroughness; and to these he adds a fourth as essential to permanence—the Grace of Humility. He commends to them what obviously he had by this time learned himself:

In the first place, acquire early the *Art of Detachment*, by which I mean the faculty of isolating yourselves from the pursuits and pleasures incident to youth. By nature man is the incarnation of idleness, which quality alone, amid the ruined remnants of Edenic

[1] Cf. an unsigned obituary notice in the *Canadian Journal of Medical Science*, 1880, v. 114.

[2] 'Teacher and Student.' 1893.

characters, remains in all its primitive intensity. Occasionally we do find an individual who takes to toil as others to pleasure, but the majority of us have to wrestle hard with the original Adam, and find it no easy matter to scorn delights and live laborious days. Of special importance is this gift to those of you who reside for the first time in a large city, the many attractions of which offer a serious obstacle to its acquisition. The discipline necessary to secure this art brings in its train habits of self-control and forms a valuable introduction to the sterner realities of life.

Twenty-three years later in an address[1] given in Toronto on the occasion of the amalgamation of the Toronto and the Trinity Schools of Medicine, Osler paid the following 'tribute of filial affection' to the man from whom he was now in this summer of 1870 to become separated:

There are men here to-day who feel as I do about Dr. James Bovell—that he was of those finer spirits, not uncommon in life, touched to finer issues only in a suitable environment. Would the Paul of evolution have been Thomas Henry Huxley had the Senate elected the young naturalist to a chair in this university in 1851? Only men of a certain metal rise superior to their surroundings, and while Dr. Bovell had that all-important combination of boundless ambition with energy and industry, he had that fatal fault of diffuseness, in which even genius is strangled. With a quadrilateral mind, which he kept spinning like a teetotum, one side was never kept uppermost for long at a time. Caught in a storm which shook the scientific world with the publication of the 'Origin of Species', instead of sailing before the wind, even were it with bare poles, he put about and sought a harbour of refuge in writing a work on Natural Theology which you will find on the shelves of second-hand bookshops in a company made respectable at least by the presence of Paley. He was an omnivorous reader and transmuter, he could talk pleasantly, even at times transcendentally, upon anything in the science of the day, from protoplasm to evolution; but he lacked concentration and that scientific accuracy which only comes with a long training (sometimes, indeed, never comes) and which is the ballast of the boat. But the bent of his mind was devotional, and, early swept into the Tractarian movement he became an advanced Churchman, a good Anglican Catholic. As he chaffingly remarked one day to his friend the Rev. Mr. Darling, he was like the waterman in 'Pilgrim's Progress', rowing one way, towards Rome, but looking steadfastly in the other direction, towards Lambeth. His 'Steps to the Altar' and his 'Lectures on the Advent' attest the earnestness of his convictions; and later in life, following the example of Linacre,

[1] 'The Master Word in Medicine', 1903.

W. A. Johnson

James Bovell

R. Palmer Howard

OSLER'S THREE TEACHERS

he took orders and became another illustration of what Cotton Mather calls the angelical conjunction of medicine with divinity. Then, how well I recall the keen love with which he would engage in metaphysical discussions, and the ardour with which he studied Kant, Hamilton, Reid and Mill. At that day, to the Rev. Prof. Bevan was intrusted the rare privilege of directing the minds of the thinking youths at the Provincial University into proper philosophical channels. It was rumoured that the hungry sheep looked up and were not fed. I thought so at least, for certain of them, led by T. Wesley Mills, came over daily after Dr. Bovell's four o'clock lecture to reason high and long with him

On Providence, Foreknowledge, Will and Fate,
Fixed Fate, Freewill, Foreknowledge absolute.

Yet withal his main business in life was as a physician, much sought after for his skill in diagnosis, and much beloved for his loving heart. . . . When in September 1870 he wrote to me that he did not intend to return from the West Indies I felt that I had lost a father and a friend; but in Robert Palmer Howard, of Montreal, I found a noble step-father, and to these two men, and to my first teacher, the Rev. W. A. Johnson, of Weston, I owe my success in life—if success means getting what you want and being satisfied with it.

CHAPTER IV

1870–2

THE McGILL MEDICAL STUDENT

In a later address [1] Osler gave the following thumbnail account of his two years in the McGill Medical School:

When I began clinical work in 1870, the Montreal General Hospital was an old coccus- and rat-ridden [2] building, but with two valuable assets for the student—much acute disease and a group of keen teachers. Pneumonia, phthisis, sepsis and dysentery were rife. The 'services' were not separated, and a man for three months looked after medical and surgical patients, jumbled together in the same wards. The physic of the men who were really surgeons was better than the surgery of the men who were really physicians, which is the best that can be said of a very bad arrangement. . . . Scottish and English methods prevailed, and we had to serve our time as dressers and clerks, and, indeed, in serious cases we very often at night took our share in the nursing. There were four first-rate teachers of medicine on the staff—Howard, Wright, MacCallum and Drake—three of whom had learned at first hand the great language of Graves and of Stokes. The bedside instruction was excellent and the clerking a serious business. I spent the greater part of the summer of 1871 at the hospital, and we had admirable out-patient clinics from Dr. Howard, and a small group worked in the wards under Dr. MacCallum. An excellent plan, copied from an old custom of the *Lancet*, was for the clinical clerk to report the cases of special interest under *Hospital Practice* in the local medical monthly. My first appearance in print is in the *Canadian Medical and Surgical Journal*, reporting cases from Dr. MacCallum's wards. Our teachers were men in whose busy lives in large general practice the hospital work was a pleasant and a profitable incident. A man like Palmer Howard got all that was possible out of the position, working hard at the hospital, studying the literature, writing excellent papers, and teaching with extraordinary care and accuracy; naturally such a man exercised a wide influence, lay and medical. I left the old General Hospital with a good deal of practical experience to my credit and with warm friends among the members of the staff.

On his way to Montreal Osler appears to have stopped at Weston, and while there must have been consulted regarding 'Jimmie' Johnson's choice of a career: 'Father' Johnson at least sent after him post-haste a letter on the

[1] 'The Medical Clinic': *British Medical Journal*, Jan. 3, 1914.
[2] Rat-riddled? 'At the foot of your rotten-runged, rat-riddled stairs'.

subject, though a scoop from the Grenadier Pond was evidently a matter of greater concern at the moment, and 'Jim' must wait. His English cousins, Marian and Jennette, the former now Mrs. Francis, had returned to Canada two years previously, and had settled at Montreal. Featherstone Osler in a letter to his sister Elizabeth in Cornwall mentions that 'Willie has gone to McGill College where the hospital advantages are greater than at Toronto. I wish to give him every advantage in my power though it is very expensive. Chattie went with him for a visit to Marian. She has not been very well lately and we thought a change would do her good.'

Montreal in the '70's and for some years to come had unquestionably the best medical school in Canada, and the opportunities offered to students were possibly rivalled by those in only one city in the States—namely, in Philadelphia. The McGill school, founded by Scotchmen, had from its inception closely followed the educational methods in vogue at Edinburgh, where only the year before, a young man named Joseph Lister had been called from Glasgow to succeed Syme as Professor of Surgery. The school, moreover, was in the process of being moved from its old site on Coté Street to the university grounds, where a new building, whose foundations were laid in 1869, had just been completed. The 'hospital advantages' spoken of by Osler's father were those at the Montreal General, which like the Edinburgh hospitals was in close affiliation with the school, and students were given a degree of freedom in the wards such as existed in no other large hospital on the continent. In the Upper Canada schools at Toronto and Kingston, on the other hand, traditions of the great London hospitals largely prevailed—traditions in themselves as worthy of emulation as those of Edinburgh, but one only needs to consult the Canadian medical journals of the late '60's and early '70's to learn that in Toronto much dissatisfaction was rife, and that the staff and the trustees of the Toronto General Hospital were at loggerheads over matters relating to medical instruction.[1]

[1] In September of 1869 the Canadian Medical Association had met in Toronto, at which time Palmer Howard, the Professor of Medicine at McGill

A number of students had already gravitated to Montreal from Toronto, and among those living on Lower St. Urbain Street were six of Osler's particularly intimate friends: 'Charlie' Locke and Clarkson McConkey, former schoolmates at Barrie, Thomas Johnson of Sarnia, Keefer, later of the Indian Army, Arthur Browne of Montreal, and Harry P. Wright of Ottawa. They were a youthful group, most of them graduating before they were of sufficient age to receive their diplomas, but they were of robust appearance, and this 'St. Urbain clique' came to be known as the 'bearded infants'. Harry Wright, who became Osler's room-mate, is said always to have laughed in later years when Osler's name was mentioned, and one may imagine that his love of innocent fun and addiction to surprising pranks was rampant at this time, though a greater love of serious work was becoming deeply ingrained. These two, Harry Wright and Osler, were taken up by Palmer Howard, and came to be constant visitors in his household, where Sunday dinner always found them.

To judge from Osler's student note-books, Howard must have been a systematic teacher of the old school, one who presented his topic under headings in a way very gratifying to students, '*Zymotic diseases*: due to a specific poison. They have been called miasmatic and the poison which produces them has been called morbid, etc.', and there is a good deal of stress laid on therapeutic measures, all of which sounds rather old-fashioned—this presentation of medicine of fifty years ago. Throughout, the young student is evidently very attentive and has less temptation, or less opportunity perhaps, to scribble his favourite preceptor's

and President of the Association, had read two notable reports on preliminary and on professional education in medicine. He had recommended not only a high standard for matriculation with examination requirements, but a four-years' professional course of nine instead of the usual six months and no diploma to be given before the age of twenty-one was attained. It is of interest that Dr. Davis, of Chicago, the founder of the American Medical Association, was present at the meeting and urged the Canadians to adhere to these high standards as the example would be an influence in the establishment of something comparable to them in the States. There was much discussion over these matters which must have reached the ears of the students.

name on the pages, as he comes later to do while taking lecture-notes on mental diseases, medical jurisprudence, materia medica, and chemistry, fragments of which are in these same student volumes.

From W. A. Johnson to W. O. The Parsonage, St. Philip's, Weston. 20th Octb 1870.

My dear Osler,—Your kind letter was duly received and gave me much pleasure. I hope your connection with McGill will prove an advantage to you in many ways. The size of the city and its various opportunities may prove of service alone, and the change of ideas together with seeing and knowing different persons ought to be of great service too. Jimmy tried the examination and failed not in things of any importance, but as the examination was suited chiefly for aged school masters and such like [etc.]. . . . I send you by this mail a little bottle which you will easily get at by picking away the corks with your pen knife at both ends and the bottle will drop out. It contains specimens of my stranger. Vaginicola? I suppose but can not find anything in my illustrations like it. The two that are attached, one to a green leaf, the other a dry, were free when I put them into a saucer. No doubt some naturalist will tell you the name. If so let me know. The tentacles are very like those of Hydra. . . . I send you also a copy of Taylor's Holy Living. I have returned to my habit as a boy of reading a few lines of it every morning before going downstairs, and am not a little pleased to see in it the origin of all my religious that is practically religious ideals. It is a little book well worth using as a friend. Its teaching is higher than any High Churchism of the present day and in many things more plainly to the point. Liking Sir T. Browne as you do, you will be pleased with it and I trust and pray it may long be your friend and companion. We have not anything new doing here. The Dr [Bovell] is not likely to return this year. . . . Remember me very kindly to your Sister and tell me who you find in Montreal to talk to about religious or Church matters, as well as scientific. Let me hear from you frequently. It is a sort of duty I would like to exact from you, as well as a great pleasure to me. Hoping it will please God to bless you with health of mind and body and a strong zeal for others welfare believe me Very faithfully yours

W. A. Johnson.

The young Osler must have pondered considerably over this letter, for 'James Bovell, M.D., M.R.C.P.' is written meditatively on its margins. 'Father' Johnson, apparently somewhat upset by his son's failure to meet the matriculation requirements, expresses relief at his entering Trinity, and quickly passes on to more agreeable subjects—to things put up in balsam and glycerine, and to matters of religion. He makes no mention of his own troubles, which must have been acute at this time, for he was in open opposition to his bishop, and the school he had founded was taken away from him in this year of 1870, and moved to its present home at Port Hope. Johnson, alas, was in matters of theology a born controversialist, and it is not unlikely that this may have reacted upon his most famous pupil, for Osler either had a native aversion to, or in some way acquired the happy gift of avoiding, what his first preceptor seemed destined to fall into—controversies. And in the end, as Dr. Garrison says:

> What made him, in a very real sense, the ideal physician, the essential humanist of modern medicine, was his wonderful genius for friendship toward all and sundry; and, consequent upon this trait, his large, cosmopolitan spirit, his power of composing disputes and differences, of making peace upon the high places, of bringing about 'Unity, Peace and Concord' among his professional colleagues. 'Wherever Osler went', says one of his best pupils, 'the charm of his personality brought men together; for the good in all men he saw, and as friends of Osler, all men met in peace.' [1]

But Johnson need have had little worry for his young friend's spiritual welfare at this time, nor lest Taylor's 'Holy Living' be not read like the 'Religio Medici', a few lines a day. For during his medical-school period he was a regular attendant at early service at the then little Chapel of St. John the Evangelist near where he lived, and it was not until several years later that he became a casual church-goer.[2] One would be interested to know the tenor of his

[1] From the Foreword in 'A Physician's Anthology of English and American Poetry'. Oxford University Press, 1920. Selected and arranged by Casey A. Wood and Fielding H. Garrison.

[2] His copy of 'Hymns Ancient and Modern' is preserved. On the fly-leaf he has written '*W. Osler, Easter 1871*', and below there follows '*Holy Trinity Toronto. St. John the Evangelist's Montreal. All Saints, Margaret Street, London.*' All Saints is near Portland Place, and while in London in 1872–4 he and Arthur Browne lived not far away in Gower Street. The Rev. Arthur French has sent this note of Osler's relation to St. John's during his student days:

'This "little church round the corner" was greatly valued by many of the Montreal medical men at that time; it was not only situated near

Christmas letter to Johnson which brought forth this reply :

From W. A. Johnson to W. O. The Parsonage, Weston, Ont.
25 Decbr 1870.

My dear Osler,—Your very affectionate and thoughtful gift and letter are both at hand. The Photo. is very good, and I am delighted to have it. Montreal has surely agreed with you. I could not ask a greater treat than such a work as 'Preparation for Death' by Alfonso, Bp. of Agatha. The subject is one of all others that I like best : really believing as I do that, 'better is the day of a man's death, than the day of his birth', and it is divided into short meditations just suited to my time early in the morning, when I can generally make 1/2 of an hour before I go down to Chapel. Talking of the Chapel almost everyone feels it is a success. One thing seems pretty clear, that almost any thing would be admitted now in the way of adornment. The cross stands out or peeps through at every arch and every window and we had two vases of flowers on the altar tonight and up at the Church the girls have made crosses between

---

the old Medical School on Coté Street, and very near the General Hospital, but it was under the spiritual direction of the Rev. Edmund Wood, nephew of Aston Key the once well-known surgeon at Guy's. Mr. Wood had won the affectionate regard of the medical faculty generally, and of the students, by his faithful ministrations to the patients in the hospital, and to the poor who were numerous in the district where the medical students then lived.

'The periods of the lenten season and of the final medical examinations often synchronized, as it did in, I think, the year in which Sir William took his medical degree and greatly distinguished himself. The pressure on the time of this industrious and methodical student did not lessen his regular attendance at the daily service, even at the time, so important to him, of his examination.

'Though with succeeding years there was modification of the manner of showing his appreciation and attachment to "the practice of religion", there were throughout his life signs, though latent, that it always existed. He not only was a personal supporter for a considerable time of the work of St. John's, but to the last it was his custom, in many of his frequent visits to Montreal in later years, to call upon his friend and rector, Mr. Wood. His last visit to him was shortly before the latter's death and was marked by Sir William's suggestion that he should collect a fund, among former colleagues, to erect a memorial in the church to Dr. Wright. The latter had been Professor of Materia Medica at McGill, in both the student and professional days of Sir William, and also subsequently being ordained, joined the staff of clergy of the church. Notwithstanding the death of Mr. Wood, the memorial was erected and stands to-day not only as a mark of appreciation of one who was both his instructor and colleague, but also of the attachment Sir William had to his old friend and rector, Mr. Wood, and also to the church which as a student he was accustomed regularly to attend.'

each window and even unhappy Couron begins to fancy he can permit them and still worship.[1] These little things are an advance to a certain extent, but still it is humiliating to see how little we accomplish. Surely one might expect that at this season of Advent a few would try to examine their ways and seek counsel and advice at the mouth of God's ambassadors. Among the papists there seems to be a general waking up during advent. In the city and here they are thronging daily to confession before Xmas. Possibly they may err greatly in this, but do not we err in totally neglecting it? . . . I am glad you saw Prof^r Dawson. You know all I have of the Polyzoa and anything you want I will gladly draw write or send. Profr Hincks hopes to give me the name of that (larva?) with such beautiful tentacles. Shew it to Prof Dawson and see if he knows anything of it. Hoping you may live to be blessed in fulfilling all your hopes and expectations believe me very affectionately yours

W. A. Johnson.

These 'hopes and expectations' of which he was writing to Johnson must have concerned an elaboration of his entozoan collection, for preserved with Johnson's epistle is a fragment in Osler's hand, evidently the first draft of a letter to some authority recommended by Principal Dawson. For he says under the date 'Jan'y 4th 1871':

I have been engaged for a short time in the study of entozoa and find great difficulty in getting the species described. On consulting Prof. Dawson as to who would be the most likely person to aid me, he referred me to you. I subjoin a list of those I have met with and the creatures in which they are found; hoping you will be able to either name them or refer me to papers in which they have been described, etc.

J. W. (later Sir William) Dawson, F.R.S., at this time Principal of McGill, was largely responsible, with the financial backing of Sir William MacDonald, for the building up of a real university out of what before 1870 had been little more than a flourishing medical department. Primarily a geologist and a follower of Lyell, he was much interested in the theory of evolution, about which he had his own ideas: 'The egg grows into the animal and the organism produces the egg again. This is revolution, not evolution.' But he was not only Principal: he held the Chair of Botany

[1] Johnson's efforts to adorn his chancel with the customary symbols of the Christian belief had been regarded as popish if not idolatrous by many of his parishioners, who on more than one occasion had broken into the church and demolished them.

and Zoology, subjects covered in the primary medical courses, and was at the same time President of the Montreal Natural History Society before which Osler's paper on the Canadian Diatomaceae had been presented on October 31st of 1870. This may have served to draw his favourable attention to the young medical student who had come up from Toronto for his final clinical years ; and that he was duly impressed will appear from a later episode. Osler, indeed, had already begun to make his mark in the school, and though doubtless a prejudiced witness, his cousin Jennette writes in January to his mother : 'Willie has shed the light of his countenance upon us this evening. I cannot tell you what a pleasure it is to us to have the dear, merry fellow coming in and out and to look forward to our Sunday treat. We hear his praises on all sides and from those whose good opinion is hard to win and well worth having. He is pronounced "thoroughly reliable", "as good as he is clever", "the most promising student of the year", and finally from a learned professor, slow to praise, "a splendid fellow".'

Despite his prescribed hospital 'clerking' referred to as 'a serious business', Osler not only found time for some outside reading, but as the interview with Principal Dawson showed, was still engaged with his entozoan collection. Specimens were obtained from many sources, as his notes indicate—from the Montreal fish-market, from the Natural History Society through whom he secures a dead lynx for study ; '8/3/71. From a rat at Montreal General Hospital I obtained 5 Taeniae from low down in intestine—a small fine species with motor-vascular system very distinct', etc., etc. Certainly not the usual pursuits of a medical student of the '70's. Whether he never heard from the parasitologist to whom he wrote early in the year, or whether he became so engrossed in the clinical studies, to be his life's chief interest, that his further pursuit of entozoa was necessarily side-tracked, is impossible to tell. For one reason or another he never worked up his collection of specimens for publication, though he always retained a live interest in the subject.[1]

[1] His early studies had possibly been stimulated by Casimir Davaine's book (1860) on 'Entozoa in Man and Animals', or more probably by

Occupied as he had been with these extra-curricular studies, the brief Franco-Prussian War of the preceding months, now coming to a settlement, does not appear to have touched very deeply if at all the young student whose medical career spanned the two great European wars of his generation, in the last of which the heart-breaking tragedy of his life was to occur. In the family letters of this time sent to the Cornwall relatives there are, to be sure, occasional references to 'the horrors of war raging', but home news is of greatest interest, and of her son's progress Ellen Osler writes: 'I will send one of Willie's photos as soon as I can get them from Montreal where he is going on in a very satisfactory manner a great favourite with every one, with the leading medical men especially, so I ought to be thankful, indeed I have been very lovingly dealt with in every way all the past years of my life, and only wish I had a more grateful heart.'

Word had come early in the year, that Bovell had decided to take Holy Orders in the West Indies (this despite the rumour that he was one of the organizers of the new Trinity College Medical School just projected), and two days after his ordination, it being Johnson's birthday, he sends this letter which Johnson evidently forwarded to Osler, among whose very scant residue of old letters it has been found:

Rev. W. A. Johnson from James Bovell. Clare-Hall, St. John's,
Antigua, W. I.
June 27th 1871.

My dear Johnson,—As you may fancy my thoughts to-day went by telegraph to Weston, and I am spending a deal of time in the old arm chair with you. The worst part of the business is, that although you are visible to me, you are as dumb and silent as ghosts who come to earth. The paper cutter is in your hand and the Church Times is being opened and you are grumbling about Bennett

---

Thomas Spencer Cobbold's 'Entozoa' (1864). He probably did not know Rudolph Leuckart's 'Die Parasiten', recently translated (1867), though it was with Leuckart that he subsequently studied in Leipzig. Chiefly through his active support a special course in parasitology was given to the Johns Hopkins students during his period there, and years later he was instrumental in securing for McGill a professorship in Parasitology whose first incumbent was Dr. John Todd.

and Purchas, but hang it all you wont converse. Well then I will come back from reverie to earth and take to writing. Here I am in the good Bishops house; over an examination and waiting to go down to Nevis to take up, as Rector, the United Parishes of St George and St John. It seems very wonderful, very mysterious. . . . On Saturday the 25th in the Cathedral I was called to the holy order of Priest and now here I am flesh and blood set to do God's work. The time is short and there is a deal to do, but having stood so long in the Market Place idle and no man having hired me, now that I have found a Master let me go in too for the [illegible]. The Work is very severe and the area comparatively large and populous but still I can do a great deal. I intend to keep up my four services those on Sunday and on Wednesdays and Fridays; and I have just got our school going with 115 children. In St John's Parish, I have been bundling out a Three-decker and Kitchen Table, and have got in a neat Chancel, proper altar, Lectern Prayer desk and 10 new sittings round the Chancel. By degrees things will go well. I wish you would send me the address of the man who sent you the paper for the Church. I want to get as much as will do the Chancel Walls of both Churches. How I wish I was near you now. I dont despair. Some day when I have set the two old decayed parishes up and made the work easy, I will run back to the old place and end my days in the snow. . . . I am trying to get you a collection of ferns which I hope to find an opportunity of sending through Halifax. I have not looked at an object since I left Toronto, and I dare not even think for five Minutes of any work that is past. We wont talk about it. I long to hear from the Provost for he does give one such good advice and useful hints. . . . Now my reading for examinations is over I will have more leisure for writing and dear Osler shall have a scrawl. Tell Jim I will send him a letter about the Medical Books. Osler can help him select them. Love for all. Farewell old fellow.

Yr affect

J. Bovell.

One of the few of Osler's early letters which have come to light dates from this period. That there are not more of them is lamentable, in spite of his sharing the strong family characteristic of reticence regarding his personal doings. It makes clear that even in his youth words so ran from his pen that it was left for others to dot the i's and cross the t's for him:

To his sister Charlotte from W. O. Montreal, July 6th [1871].

My dear Chattie, First and foremost you may mention casually that though I am 'too proud to beg too honest to steal' yet I shall be reduced to one or other remedy before long unless a check arrive soon. Lazarus was nothing compared to what I have been for nearly three weeks. Drat the dimes. I wish we could get along without them. I got your letter to-day, after being five weeks from home & thought it time. Marian's baby was baptized on Tuesday afternoon & was honoured by me standing Godfather. I am so glad poor Frank has got home safe & sound, give him my love. Tell Molly to take her boy if he is a good one & not likely to take to drink & abuse her. If he does I will be down on him. Poor Hal! wonder he did not break his neck, he may yet. I am up to my eyes in work, but keep healthy & as we have had no very hot weather it has been quite endurable. Such a nice fellow is boarding here now called Henderson. I knew his Sisters when I was at Weston. He is a St Johnsite & a high 'un and good 'un too. There has been a jolly flare up at St Johns. Deacon Prime circulated two copies of an extreme sheet called the 'Rule of Life'. Mr Wood & Mr Norman were accused of it at the Synod & both declined to answer then but would answer their Bishop. Luckily they knew nothing about it, but poor Prime has had his license taken away. On Sunday last Mr Wood preached a Sermon on it & acknowledged that though he could not hold it all himself he would not quarrel with any of his Parishioners if they did. He took exception principally to 'prayers for the dead'. It was a regular 'Confession of Faith' on his part & was splendidly given. I will send you a copy of the Rule &c. when I get some surplus cash, but *dont* you circulate it (on the Guv's account) as it is strong meat not fit for Protestant babes to chew. I am glad Dr Locke progresses, tell him my letter is coming & hint that his has most probably been detained at the Dundas P. Office. Ask him to hunt it up. How does your lad get along in England. Tell him not to forget to hunt me up when he is on his way back. 48 St Urbain St is my number yet. Our Dutch is progressing but not as rapidly as I would wish. I have so little time to spare for it. Forgive this scrawl, you dot the I^s^ and cross the T^s^ for me. Love to Mammy, aunt & all Yours

BENJ.

As will be seen, being hard up was no uncommon thing for one who habitually behaved with his own meagre resources as Bovell did with his patients' fees, which went out as fast as they came in. The 'Rule of Life', the 'extreme sheet' which raised such a rumpus at St. John's, must have been similar to some of the tracts often found in Rev. W. A. Johnson's possession, to the consternation of some of his parishioners, being strong meat, not fit for the orthodox like Canon Osler.

The summer of 1871 was spent largely in Montreal,

according to his own statement in one of his later lay sermons,[1] and it was at this time that he came into particularly filial relationship with Palmer Howard, whose library was put at his disposal. He was probably clerking in the General Hospital, and attending the post-mortem examinations there, and he confesses that 'much worried as to the future, partly about the final examination, partly as to what I should do afterwards, I picked up a volume of Carlyle . . .', and in it read the familiar sentence, 'Our main business is not to see what lies dimly at a distance but to do what lies clearly at hand'—the conscious starting-point of a habit that enabled him to utilize to the full the single talent with which he often said he had been entrusted. It was, in his estimation, one of the two trifling circumstances by which his life had been influenced, the first having been the paragraph in 'Father' Johnson's circular of announcement stating that boys would learn to sing and dance ('vocal and pedal accomplishments' for which he was never designed)—a paragraph which diverted him to Johnson's school in Weston. The other trifling circumstance was the line from Carlyle. Thirty years later in an impromptu talk[2] to the students of the Albany Medical College, he is reported to have said:

I started in life—I may as well own up and admit—with just an ordinary everyday stock of brains. In my schooldays I was much more bent upon mischief than upon books—I say it with regret now—but as soon as I got interested in medicine I had only a single idea and I do believe that if I have had any measure of success at all, it has been solely because of doing the day's work that was before me just as faithfully and honestly and energetically as was in my power.

How he found time to acquire his familiarity with general literature has always been a source of mystery to Osler's many friends. Probably it was at this early period that he began his life-long habit of a half-hour's reading in bed before putting out his light. Most medical students, alas, are too engrossed with their work for such literary pursuits, desirable though they may be. But he never ceased to

[1] 'A Way of Life.' An address to Yale students, 1913.

[2] Delivered Feb. 1, 1899. Cf. *The Albany Medical Annals*, June 1899, xx. 307–9.

encourage the habit, and the books he recommended [1] as a student's bedside library in all likelihood represent those with which he himself became acquainted in this way.

Until 1870 the McGill Medical School had been run on a proprietary basis, and the teaching was almost entirely in lecture form and given by general practitioners. The Chair of Materia Medica, for example, fully stuffed with time-honoured drugs, was occupied by William Wright, who incidentally had considerable repute as a surgeon, and subsequently became a preacher. Robert Craik held the Chair in Chemistry and later became the Dean of the Faculty. Lectures on the Institutes of Medicine, which comprised what is now recognized as physiology and pathology, were given by William Fraser, a graduate of Glasgow, though there was no semblance of a laboratory until Osler himself in 1875 succeeded to the chair. A bluff Englishman named William Scott was Professor of Anatomy, who rarely if ever was known to enter the dissecting-room, this disagreeable duty being left to his demonstrator; and the material is said to have been obtained from convenient cemeteries by the French students, who thereby paid their school fees. All this, which resembled the Edinburgh programme of an earlier day, was soon to be revolutionized by Francis J. Shepherd, one of Osler's contemporaries and intimates.[2] Indeed, as will be seen, there were a number of youngsters among the students of the day, who in the course of a few years were destined to take over and instil a modern spirit into the pre-clinical years of the old school. Of the clinical teachers whom Osler came under, there was Duncan MacCallum in midwifery, who leaned heavily, in his meticulous lectures, on the traditions of the Dublin Rotunda, but otherwise was chiefly occupied with a lucrative practice, so that the senior students were largely left to their own resources at the Lying-in Hospital. Another was George W. Campbell, Dean of the Faculty and Professor of Surgery, a vigorous and confident operator trained

1 'A Bedside Library for Medical Students.' Appended to 'Aequanimitas and other Addresses'. 1904.

2 Cf. Dr. Shepherd's privately printed 'Reminiscences of Student Days and Dissecting Room'. Montreal, 1919; written at Osler's solicitation.

in pre-antiseptic days, for Lister at this time was little more than a rumour in Canada, if even that, and the surgeon of the day operated in his ordinary clothes, collar, cuffs and all, the more particular ones, indeed, in a frock-coat. There was a short course, too, in medical jurisprudence, and the clinics at the old General Hospital were conducted by George E. Fenwick in surgery and J. Morley Drake in medicine. Fenwick was a bold operator of pre-Listerian type, his house surgeons at the time being George Ross and Thomas G. Roddick, of whom more will subsequently be heard; and Roddick a few years later brought back from Edinburgh the 'Lister ritual' which was to transform surgery. J. Morley Drake soon succeeded Professor Fraser in the so-called Institutes of Medicine, though he gave up the post two years later, when it became filled by a new type chosen from the younger generation.

But the member of this faculty to whom Osler was chiefly indebted was R. Palmer Howard—a courtly gentleman, scholarly, industrious, stimulating as a teacher; and though the students of the day felt that he was devoid of humour, he nevertheless was popular with them, and even at this time was one of the chief figures in the school of which in 1882 he became Dean. Like his colleagues he, too, was a general practitioner of surgery as well as physic, but where he perhaps differed chiefly from them was through his interest in morbid anatomy, an interest with which he succeeded in inoculating some of his pupils. In a later address Osler gave this picture of him:

In my early days I came under the influence of an ideal student-teacher, the late Palmer Howard of Montreal. If you ask what manner of man he was, read Matthew Arnold's noble tribute to his father in his well-known poem, 'Rugby Chapel'. When young, Dr. Howard had chosen a path—'path to a clear-purposed goal'—and he pursued it with unswerving devotion. With him the study and the teaching of medicine were an absorbing passion, the ardour of which neither the incessant and ever-increasing demands upon his time nor the growing years could quench. When I first, as a senior student, came into intimate contact with him in the summer of 1871, the problem of tuberculosis was under discussion, stirred up by the epoch-making work of Villemin and the radical views of Niemeyer. Every lung lesion at the Montreal General Hospital had to be shown to him, and I got my first-hand introduction to Laennec, to Graves, and to Stokes, and became familiar with their works. No matter what the hour, and it usually was after 10 p.m., I was welcome with my bag, and if Wilks and Moxon, Virchow or Rokitanski gave us no help, there were the Transactions of the Pathological Society and the big *Dictionnaire* of Dechambre. An ideal teacher because a student, ever alert to the new problems, an indomitable energy enabled him in the midst of an exacting practice to maintain an ardent enthusiasm, still to keep bright the fires which he had lighted in his youth. Since those days I have seen many teachers, and have had many colleagues, but I have never known one in whom was more happily combined a stern sense of duty with the mental freshness of youth.[1]

It has been said that the school borrowed its traditions largely from Edinburgh. These were a mixture of work and hilarity, and though there were no rival political parties such as Edinburgh sees engaged in active warfare in connexion with its rectorial elections, there was gaiety enough, and what were in the day called 'footing sprees' were bibulous affairs, for the expense of which the seniors were privileged to tax the freshmen. The annual 'Founders' Festival' was another occasion in which the students took untold liberties with their seniors and played practical jokes of a kind it has long been the tradition of unbridled students the world over to play. Though at the time he was a 'teetotaller', Osler doubtless entered into all these pranks with as much spirit as any, for there are certain dispositions which do not require any adventitious stimulus to enliven them. But though among the gayest when occasion offered, better than most young men he had learned to conserve his time, and though not a gold-medallist of his class he received at the end of the term an honourable mention of unusual sort. The prizes announced at the annual convocation of 1872 were as follows:

(1) The Holmes Gold Medal awarded to the graduate receiving the highest aggregate number of marks for all examinations, including primary, final and thesis. [Awarded to Hamilton Allen.]

(2) A prize in Books, for the best examination—written and oral, in the Final branches. The Gold Medallist is not permitted to compete for this prize. [Awarded to George A. Stark.]

---

1 'The Student Life.' 1905. Cf. 'Aequanimitas and other Addresses'.

(3) A prize in Books, for the best examination written and oral, in the Primary branches. [Awarded to Francis J. Shepherd.]

(4) The Faculty has in addition this session awarded a special prize to the Thesis of William Osler, Dundas, O., which was greatly distinguished for originality and research, and was accompanied by 33 microscopic and other preparations of morbid structure, kindly presented by the author to the museum of the Faculty.

The gentlemen in order of merit who deserve mention :—In the Final examination, Messrs. Osler, Browne, Waugh, Marceau, Hebert, Pegg, St. John, and Morrison. In the Primary examination, Messrs. Alguire, Hill, Carmichael, McConnel, Ward, Kitson and Osler.

Osler's thesis was never published, and only a fragment of it remains—the introduction, couched in rather flowery and figurative language. As it is one of his youthful productions, and his first essay in studies from the pathological laboratory where he was to spend so many years, a paragraph or two may be quoted, misspelling and all :

In that Trinity of being—of body mind and soul—which so marvellously make up the Man, each one has its own special ills and diseases. With the first of these—the body—have we here anything to do, leaving the second to be attended to by that class of men whose duty it is, ' to minister to minds diseased ', i. e. the Psycologists, while those of the third class beyond a Physician's skill seek aid elsewhere. Few indeed are permitted to end their days in a natural manner, by a gradual decline of the vital powers, till that point reached, where nutrition failing to supply the fuel, necessary to keep the lamp of life alight, leaves decay to drag back the fabric to the dust. . . . The number of avenues through which death may reach us, the natural fraility of our bodies the delicate and intricate machinery which maintains us in a condition of health may well make us exclaim with the Poet

Strange that a harp of thousand strings
Should keep in tune so long.

To investigate the causes of death, to examine carefully the condition of organs, after such changes have gone on in them as to render existence impossible and to apply such Knowledge to the prevention and treatment of disease, is one of the highest objects of the Physician. . . .

CHAPTER V

1872–4

STUDENT DAYS ABROAD

A voluminous letter from 'Father' Johnson addressed to Osler in Dundas after his graduation, indicates that his departure for a period of study abroad—the natural goal of every newly-fledged Canadian M.D.—was impending. Johnson lamented that he was tied down and would be unable to meet him in Toronto to see about Bovell's microscope,[1] and enclosed 'a copy of Devout Life for your dear Sister God bless and protect her'. Canon Osler could scarcely have afforded to send a son to Europe for the proposed two years' absence, even though the elder children were by this time married and living away from home. But one of his sons came to the rescue, for Edmund, who was engaged to a Scotch lady, a Miss Cochran of Balfour, was on the point of paying a timely visit to his future relations and was glad to have the lively companionship of his younger brother—indeed furnished the $1,000 necessary to see him through his prolonged stay.

They sailed on one of the Allan Line steamers, on July 3rd, and landing in the north of Ireland visited the Giant's Causeway and the Lakes of Killarney. From there W. O. must have gone on to London, for in a pocket note-book of the period is written: '*William Osler, M.D. London July 1872. Cash Account. Be frugal: pay as you go.*' It seems to have been one of the few periods of his life in which he kept an account of his expenditures, and cab fares and tips and tea are all duly recorded. In later years after beginning his consulting practice he methodically entered all items of his professional income in a small account-book for physicians such as are put out

[1] The Rev. James Bovell Johnson writes that 'when Bovell's personal belongings were sold in Toronto I can remember being with Osler at the sale, and Osler then bought-in certain family treasures for Mrs. Barwick, Bovell's daughter, then living in Toronto'.

each year by some of the various medical publishers.[1] The items, to be sure, for many years were few and far between, but after this first sojourn abroad he apparently kept no record of his outgoings, and was in consequence continually hard up. Like Bovell he responded to every appeal, indeed often before the appeal was made, with a generosity which was apt to be beyond his means. It was not until August that he rejoined his brother in the Highlands, as told in the following letter—one of the few home letters which escaped a subsequent conflagration :

From W. O. to his mother. Balfour, Aug 14th [1872].

My dear Mother, Up here in this far north region, I had forgotten the distance from Liverpool and so let Canadian mail day pass, this however will reach you via New York. Since I last wrote, I have visited many new places & met many new people. I left London on Thursday evening for Edinboro' by the London & North Western via Carlisle. I was fortunate in having a nice travelling companion and one who knew something of old friends ; it was a gentleman from the West Indies who knew Dr. Bovell intimately & had seen him within the last few months. He gave a very nice account of him and his doings which naturally interested me very much. I managed to sleep pretty fairly, though not as I would have in a Pullman. We arrived in Edinboro at 9.30 a.m. on Friday morning, too late to take the through train to Aberdeen so that left me four hours to examine the city. I was much struck with its beauty ; it exceeds anything in cities I have yet seen. I found out young Grasett (of Toronto) who is studying medicine at the University, and under his guidance *did* the wards of the Royal Infirmary (the chief hospital of the city) a queer rambling old place, as you may imagine as it was built in the beginning of last century. . . . At Aberdeen I was met by Mr. Alex. Cochran who took me to his house, where I slept that night. In the morning I had a few hours to spy out the 'Granite City'. It is very regularly built, somewhat too uniform but has a delightful cleanliness about it which to a Londoner like myself was very refreshing. I left at noon for Glenninan, Mr. D. R. Smith's place, where Edmund was staying ; it is a nice spot & he has recently rebuilt his house, in grand style. Both he and his wife seem very delicate, but probably his trip to Canada with Edmund will do him good. In the evening we went on to Balfour,

[1] These account-books from 1872 to 1919 have all been carefully preserved and Osler had them rebound. He evidently felt that the professional income of a consultant in his position and of his day might some time be a matter of historical interest.

the Cochrans' place, and there received a hearty welcome. The trip up the Deeside as far as Aboyne is very lovely, but up towards Balmoral it is still more so. I will have to postpone the account of my journey to the Aberdeen Highlands as I wish this to catch the Friday mail via New York. We go down to Edinboro again and from thence to Glasgow and the Western Highlands, but more of all this by the Cunard. I hope all are well. Much love.

Yours in haste,

WILLIE.

One incident of the hearty Scotch welcome has been gathered from other sources, indicative of his teetotalism as a young man: for Mrs. Cochran is said to have remarked to her prospective son-in-law that it was sad one so young as his brother should have to refrain. Otherwise there is scant record of this sojourn in the Highlands, which in after years he came to know so well, though in one of his later addresses [1] he refers to the visit in Glasgow where he first met Joseph Coats the pathologist and Sir William Macewen. In another place also [2] he gave a brief summary of the professional occurrences of the next year or more:

In the summer of 1872 after a short *Rundreise*, Dublin, Glasgow and Edinburgh, I settled at the Physiology Laboratory, University College, with Professor Burdon Sanderson, where I spent about fifteen months working at histology and physiology. At the hospital across the way I saw in full swing the admirable English system, with the ward work done by the student himself the essential feature. I was not a regular student of the hospital, but through the kind introduction of Dr. Burdon Sanderson and of Dr. Charlton Bastian, an old family friend, I had many opportunities of seeing Jenner and Wilson Fox, and my note-books contain many precepts of these model clinicians. From Ringer, Bastian and Tilbury Fox, I learned too, how attractive out-patient teaching could be made. Ringer I always felt missed his generation, and suffered from living in advance of it.

From W. O. to his sister Charlotte (now Mrs. Gwyn). Sept. 24th.

My dear Elizabeth, I dated this letter last night, and had I gone on with it would have given you all a good wigging, most unjustly, for I thought the Canadian mail had been delivered & there were no letters. However, in the morning on going to the Hospital

---

[1] 'The Pathological Institute of a General Hospital.' *Glasgow Medical Journal*, Nov. 1911, lxxvi. 321.

[2] At St. Bartholomew's Hospital, Dec. 1913: cf. 'The Medical Clinic: a Retrospect and a Forecast.' *British Medical Journal*, Jan. 3, 1914.

I received yours of the—I don't know. Why can't you date your letters?—and Jennette's of the 8th Sept. which amply made up for the brevity of yours. The man at the letter box always has such a knowing smirk on his face when he hands me my letters on a Wednesday morning, the looney must think they come from my girl, whoever she may be. I am sure that any one reading yours & Jennette letters of this morning might suppose that they came from Utah and I was a young Mormon in embryo, so feelingly do each of you allude to two separate girls as *mine*. . . . We have had it wretchedly cold for the last week and several typical London days have been interspersed. I went to the Harrisons' one day last week and after dinner accompanied them to Mr. West's church which is rapidly being repaired after the fire. On Sunday I took a trip out to Putney to dine at Atwell Francis's. I got there early and went to St. John's Church, moderately high and very well filled. The Francises do not trouble Church much, I do not think it runs in the family. Mrs. Francis is very pleasant and they have a brace of fine boys. I went with Atwell in the afternoon to Kew and pulled down the river in the evening over the course of the Intervarsity boat-race. Next Sunday I shall probably go to the Boyds' [family friends in England who used to send missionary boxes to Bond Head, and one of whom he was subsequently to meet in Oxford days] and take with me your wedding cake as an introduction to the sisters. . . . They had a grand commemoration service at All Saints Lambeth on the Anniversary of the S.P.U.C. (I am afraid those initials are incorrect, it is the Christian Unity Society). I did not go, but regretted it after reading the description. The Williamsons I suppose are just now in the agony of moving as I saw in the Banner that the sale was to take place on the 20th. Edmund by this time has been with you or ought to have been. Love to Mother & all the Rectory folk.

Yours affectionately,

WILLIE.

As is characteristic, he says very little about his own plans for the future, though others are concerned about them, as this letter from the West Indies indicates:

From James Bovell to W. O. The Farm, St. John's, Nevis, Sept. 27th, 1872.

My dear Boy,—I have no one whom I love better than yourself, and altho' I have been careless in writing it has been caused by my hard work and ever increasing trouble. However I need not burden you with my griefs, which my sisters will tell you of when you call on them. Find them at 193 Hampstead Road, Regents Park, N.W., tell them I asked you to call to introduce you to Stuart. I more than rejoice at your success and if you will only go on as you have been doing the end is clear. I am at a loss what to say about your settlement. I still cling to the notion of India as I know that no such field for fortune and fame is open to man elsewhere. Canada for some time to come must be limited in resources sufficiently remunerative, whereas India with its teeming population and immense wealth in Native Princes and Merchants affords all a professional man can desire. The Church here is in an awful state, it is being disestablished and disendowed and the negroid life is a very sorry one to work upon. Methodism has eaten Christianity out of them and in place of it they have an emotional system which employs the phrases and language of Christians which is entirely void of life or principle.

I would give anything if Johnson could be induced to come here, there is a vacant Parish, £130 sure for a time and £130 more, easily made up. Of course with a good but *low*-church Bishop we can't have Vestments but I take care to have all I can in order. I have just finished a reredos the centre panel of which has a Cross 18 inches high. The new altar is quite correct and altho' I am not permitted to stand in the middle front, I do for primary consecration stand at the North W. corner, but kneel in front at receiving, and saying the service. I have sent home to my sister a Manuscript of all Hooker has said on the Eucharist. It is now lawful so I think if it was published separately it would do good. He is plain. . . . I will write next Mail,—Post time up. Yrs. ever

J. Bovell.

The project of taking up his work in India, where in Bovell's estimation was offered the greatest 'field for fortune and fame', was evidently very seriously considered at this time, and apparently roused some consternation among his relatives and friends at home, for it was not until early in the following year that he wrote to his cousin Jennette to quiet her soul about his India schemes. Whether there was any influence other than the advice of Bovell is not apparent, but the India Medical Service had always attracted a goodly number of the very best of the British medical students, and it was well known that it was a corps with the highest *esprit*, and that the opportunities for work as well as for 'fortune and fame' were great. Many years later in an address before the members of the first graduating class of the newly established Army Medical School in Washington,[1] he said: 'As I write, an inspiration of the past occurs, bringing me, it seems, closer to you than any of the points just mentioned, a recollection of the days

[1] 'The Army Surgeon.' Feb. 28, 1894.

when the desire of my life was to enter the India Medical Service, a dream of youth, dim now and almost forgotten —a dream of "Vishnu land, what Avatar!"' But this was a short-lived aspiration, for he appears to have set his heart on a career in ophthalmology. Various reasons must have led him to this decision, and it was undoubtedly a bitter disappointment when the project was finally relinquished. Specialization in medicine was just coming to the fore, and in Montreal as yet there was no one who limited his work to the diseases of the eye. Realizing that in the absence of financial backing, and with existing conditions of medicine in Canada, he would have to enter practice for a living, he decided upon a speciality which would permit him in his spare hours to pursue science rather than to have practice pursue him, as would be the case were he to succeed as a general practitioner. Moreover, he was evidently influenced by the career of the most eminent eye-specialist of the day, who though chiefly identified with the Royal Ophthalmic Hospital at Moorfields, had formerly been Professor of Ophthalmology at King's College. His deep admiration for Bowman as the type of man who, because of a thorough grounding in science, could subsequently rise high in a speciality, was expressed years later in an address to a body of specialists in another field.[1] But Bowman still retained his enthusiasm for physiology, and he advised the young man, whatever he was to do in the future, to begin by a period of work at University College Hospital[2] with John Burdon Sanderson. The advice was taken, and a profitable and happy seventeen months was passed in Sanderson's laboratory. It was a curious trick of fortune that he should have come to work under the man whom thirty-four years later he was destined to succeed as Regius Professor of Medicine at Oxford.

[1] 'Remarks on Specialism.' *Archives of Pediatrics*, Phila., 1892, ix. 481.

[2] University College was born in 1828 of an effort to establish what was to be a non-sectarian University in London, a project which was thwarted by the establishment of a rival institution, King's College, backed by the Anglican Church, which was jealous of any loss of its hold on national education. In consequence of this split the University of London long remained a name only, and functioned chiefly as an examining board.

Osler's laboratory note-book of the time is preserved,[1] showing that the course began on October 7th with the examination of the inflamed anterior chamber of the eye of a frog and of an inflamed lymph sac experimentally produced, with subsequent microscopical study of the tissues. It was actually a course in what to-day we would call experimental pathology, for physiology and pathology were not divorced as they have since become, to the harm of each and to the considerable neglect of their offspring histology, which concerns the microscopical examination of the tissues in health and disease. The '70's, as may be recalled, saw the dawn of a most important period for medicine, which had awakened with the new learning relating to the microscopical sources of disease following upon the cellular doctrine of Virchow, and leading up to the bacteriological discoveries of Pasteur and Koch, and the adaptation of them by Lister to surgery.

Interesting as it might be, this is no place to do more than hint at the story of the gradual separation of structure and function. Earlier anatomists like the Hunters and their associates of the Windmill Street School were as much concerned with the one as the other. But in a progressive school like that at University College a curious situation arose, there being one Professor of Anatomy and another Professor of Anatomy and Physiology. The subject of anatomy had become little more than a weary descriptive science, and remained so until it was revivified in course of time by Professor His and his pupils. Meanwhile its one-time handmaiden physiology was pressing for a separation, and when this was accomplished the clever child took with her the microscope and the finer study of structure, leaving nothing but the cadaver for anatomy. Thus it came about that histology, in which lay the chief promise of future reward from research, has to this day in English schools been part and parcel of physiology rather than of anatomy.[2] It was

[1] 'Short Notes on a Course of Practical Physiology by Burdon Sanderson at University College. London, 1872–3.'

[2] The *Chair in Anatomy* at University College has been held successively by J. R. Bennett, Richard Quain, G. V. Ellis, and G. D. Thane. The *Chair of Anatomy and Physiology* was held first by Jones Quain, then by the famous

into this situation, with its spirit of revival of physiological investigation for which Burdon Sanderson, Michael Foster, Lauder Brunton, and E. Klein were chiefly responsible, that Osler was introduced, and it was one of which his early familiarity with the microscope and his growing taste for experimental pathology particularly qualified him to take advantage. The situation, too, explains in a measure his peculiar fitness, despite his youth, for the position offered him two years later at McGill as Professor of the Institutes of Medicine, then comprising physiology, histology, and pathology. Unless perhaps with Cohnheim in Germany, no more stimulating group could possibly have been found than those who were at work in the '70's in Burdon Sanderson's laboratory. Sanderson's great desire was to make experimental physiology pre-eminent in the teaching, and this part of the work he reserved for himself, while to Edward Schäfer, a young man of Osler's age, was delegated the practical histology, to T. J. M. Page the teaching of physiological chemistry, and to Klein, who had come over from Vienna, was given the histological pathology.

To W. O. from R. Palmer Howard. Montreal, 25 Oct. 72.

My dear Osler,— . . . You have by this time well settled down to y^r work in the Metropolis, I doubt not, and are picking up much that will be useful to you hereafter. Touching your prospects as

---

William Sharpey whose pupil and successor was Burdon Sanderson. With this chair there was established a separate *Lectureship of Practical Physiology* which was held in turn by Sharpey's two most distinguished pupils. The first of them, Michael Foster, was captured in 1870 for Trinity College, Cambridge, where he started the modern science movement, Burdon Sanderson having been appointed to succeed him at University College. This lectureship was finally changed into a separate *Chair of Practical Physiology and Histology*, and Sanderson, after succeeding Foster, occupied it until Sharpey's retirement from the Chair of Anatomy and Physiology, at which time the *Jodrell Chair of Physiology* was established to include physiology and histology. The Jodrell Chair has been occupied in succession by Burdon Sanderson, by Edward A. Schäfer, and by E. H. Starling. Burdon Sanderson's withdrawal was in 1882, when he accepted the Waynflete Professorship of Physiology at Oxford. This appointment was the first movement towards the revival of what had been termed 'the lost School of Medicine of Oxford', and it is noteworthy that the proposed grant of £10,000 to build Sanderson a laboratory met with organized opposition on the part of the antivivisection societies—an opposition which was overcome at Convocation by the small margin of 188 to 149 votes.

Oculist, you will have much more to contend with than we ever thought of when we spoke together on the subject. In July or August last Mr. Morgan, resident Surgeon at Moorfields, and formerly in charge of the eye-wards at Netley, wrote to me informing me that he purposed coming to Montreal as an Oculist. We had known each other six years before at Moorfields during a short visit I made at that time. . . . Of course were he to come, it would seriously affect your hopes as to making eye dis. a speciality. As between you and Dr. Buller I may safely say, you would have the countenance and support of your old teachers. But here the plot thickens. . . .

And Howard went on at length to say that there were indeed three candidates in the Montreal field with better chances than Osler, so that his advice would be to abandon ophthalmology and 'to cultivate the whole field of Med. and Surg. paying especial attention to practical physiology', which in his opinion was destined to become one of the most popular departments of medical teaching. He closed by announcing that Dean Campbell had requested him 'to present an order from Dr. Wright upon Nock, the medical bookseller for your books—which you will select yourself and have printed upon them: "Graduation Prize Awarded to William Osler, etc."' With Howard's letter the rough draft of Osler's reply has been preserved. It says:

. . . As you may imagine I was not a little disappointed at the blighting of my prospects as an ophthalmic surgeon, but I accept the inevitable with a good grace. I spoke to Morgan yesterday and he tells me as follows: that he purposes going out early in the spring stopping until August, when he has to return on business, and then going back if the place suits him. He is a very practical man and one of great experience, so much so that there is no surgeon connected with Moorfields who does not listen with deference to his opinion. He might be younger and in better health, but it is difficult to procure an article absolutely perfect. I now have to look forward to a general practice and I confess to you it is not with the greatest amount of pleasure. I had hoped in an ophthalmic practice to have a considerable amount of time at my disposal, and a fair return in a shorter time, but in a general practice which will be much slower to obtain (if it becomes of any size) what ever time you may have is always liable to be broken in upon. Now Practical Physiology—setting aside anything like original work—and considering merely the teaching, requires much time and will need, to be done properly, some outlay on the part of the College or myself. The upshot of all this is, that I want something definite stated as regards my future connection with McGill College and I have written the Dean to that effect. It simply will not pay me to go on here spending quite half my time working at a subject [physiology] which may eventually become popular with the students, but the fees from which in Canada will never alone repay either the outlay required to qualify myself or the time spent over it. I am sorry to have to appear so mercenary, but the recollection of my old friend Dr. Bovell, who tried to work at Physiology and Practice both and failed in both, is too green in my memory to allow me to take any other course. My ambition is in time to work up a good Laboratory in connection with the College, and if I get a favourable answer from Dr. Campbell, with that object in view I will continue my Physiological studies after this winter, but if not, I must turn my attention more fully to those branches which will enable me to engage in a general practice most successfully. . . . I am very busy at present in the Laboratory, spending four or five hours in it every day. I commenced as a green hand *ab initio*, in order that I might miss no little details. I have a little private work going on under Dr. Sanderson's superintendence connected with the antagonistic action of Atropin and Physostigmin on the white corpuscles, but whether it will come to anything or not remains to be seen, however in any case the practice is helpful. I purpose after Xmas taking a thorough course in Practical Chemistry on your advice, for of course that is the basis of many Physiological investigations. I get some good P.M.'s at Univ. Coll. and the remarks made by some of the men especially Drs. James Barlow and Ringer are very valuable. I have made a good many useful friends at Moorfields among the Surgeons and as they are nearly all connected with General Hospitals one can go about with less restraint always feeling sure of a personal welcome. Browne and I are together which makes it very pleasant. . . .

He and Arthur Browne shared a room somewhere in Gower Street, and there were a number of other young Canadian students of their acquaintance in London. Zimmerman, who had entered the Toronto school with him, was at St. Thomas's, and Buller, who ere long returned to Montreal, where he took up the practice of ophthalmology and rented an upstairs room to Osler, was now house surgeon at Moorfields. However great may have been Osler's disappointment in regard to his pet project, it was borne in a cheerful spirit, and the preceding exchange of letters indicates that before he left Montreal there must have been some movement on foot to create a position for him in the school. His reply to Palmer Howard evidently was transmitted to Principal Dawson, who shortly after made a new proposal: in effect, that he was shortly to retire from the Chair of Botany; that a new lectureship was to be created to embrace the faculties both of Medicine and the Arts; that the incumbent should be proficient in structural and economic botany, including the use of the microscope; that botanical science held out a good chance for scientific reputation, though from a pecuniary point of view—well, the fees from the medical classes alone amounted to $200 and might increase. With Principal Dawson's letter was enclosed one from Dean Campbell, which enlarged on the subject as follows:

The enclosed note from Principal Dawson anticipates much of what I have to state upon the subject. A three months' course of Pathology with the use of the Microscope might be added to the Botany course. It is not compulsory with us, but it is among the requirements of the Medical Council of Ontario, and I have no doubt would be well attended. We have the advantage of now being able to offer you first rate accommodation, probably as good as any in America, but our chairs are not endowed, and the Professor depends upon his class fees for the remuneration, so that you must take your chance as all of us have done, and look chiefly to private practice for a *living*.

We all as a Faculty will be most happy to have you associated with us, and the fact that we entertain such a high opinion of your acquirements and character, as to offer you the Chair of Botany, will give you, a comparative stranger in Montreal, a Great Advantage in commencing practice. I was most thankful in my early career here, to obtain such a connection, with precious little in the way of emolument.

I am not authorized to make any definite offer of a separate Chair of Pathology, at present that branch is included in the Institutes course, and taught by Dr. Drake, who might or might not be willing to confine his instructions exclusively to Physiology, I merely speak of the possibility of such a decision being at some future period considered advisable. You should certainly devote the chief share of your attention to Medicine and Surgery. A young married couple might as reasonably expect to live upon love as a medical man to live upon pure science in this most practical country. Let me know when you have Maturely considered the subject, whether you will accept Principal Dawson's proposal, and qualify yourself to teach Botany in the way in which he points out, or whether we are to look elsewhere for some one to relieve him from that portion of his labours. . . .

This proposal was followed in the next mail by a long and friendly letter from Palmer Howard, who hopes that he 'will feel the College is doing what it can towards advancing your interests and securing for you some official connexion with the University', and expresses the belief that Principal Dawson might in time turn over to him not only the medical but the arts course in Botany as well, and some day might also entrust him with Zoology. However, the university being poor and needy and in no position to establish lectures in practical physiology at present, he advises his young friend to qualify himself for general practice, and if he would 'spare the time and money to run up to Edinbro. for the F.R.C.S.—which will cost only £5, and coming back here it will do you no harm to have a diploma from the "Old Country" although not intrinsically worth more than if fairly obtained here.'

Osler's replies were frank and straightforward refusals of the offer, on the grounds of his absolute unfitness for the position. The rough drafts of his answers to all three of these letters have been preserved; it may suffice to quote one of them:

My dear Dr. Howard, I have written to Dr. Dawson refusing the kind offer made me of the lectureship in Botany. I am afraid you will not be pleased at it, but I really can not do otherwise. If I knew anything of Botany at present; if I had nothing else left to do for two or three years it might be thought of; but as matters stand now I would only make a fool of myself in accepting such a position. I would feel far too keenly the anomalous situation of holding a chair in Botany & knowing absolutely nothing of the Flora of my native land. I am afraid the offer was made more from personal feelings than any fitness for the Post. I can assure you I appreciate highly the compliment paid me & consider that McGill has more than fulfilled any obligation she may have considered herself under. I hope nothing was said about it for I should not like it to come to the ears of my people, they would be vexed at me, not knowing the ins & outs of the case. I continue my work at U. C. Laboratory & am satisfied so far with my progress....

It was unquestionably the right decision, though the offer was one that might easily have tempted a young man of twenty-three who knew his mind less well. This exchange of letters has been a chance finding: Osler himself, so far as is known, never referred to the matter again. It is a somewhat curious coincidence that this, his first offer, was a post in Botany, and that almost the last position he accepted, though an honorary one, was the Presidency of the Botanical Society of the British Isles.

To his sister Mrs. Gwyn from W. O. December [1872].

My dear Chattie, Though I wrote you last week I cannot help writing again and wishing you—though late—'Many happy returns of the day'. Also it will be Christmas time when you get this; and it is but brotherly to write and wish you at this the first Christmas of your married life, both a happy one and a merry New Year. There goes. I have reversed matters but you must overlook all mistakes as I have a host of letters this week, one of which already written, you will blow me up for. The Canadian mail is very late this week, but we must expect that as the winter comes on. Nothing much has been going on. I am very busy but shall slacken a little at Christmas.

Wednesday. I had intended on Sunday to go up and see the Pellatts, but Canon Liddon was preaching at St. Pauls and I could not resist the temptation of hearing him again. He is very long (i. e. his sermons), nearly an hour; we did not get out till after five o'clock. I went to All Saints both morning and evening. As I came up from church in the morning I went into a very dour looking edifice about five minutes walk from our lodgings and to my surprise I found it another High Church. I could not see any name to it, but I will find out and go there occasionally. Christ Church, Albany Street which is almost within a stones throw, is not nearly so high, no vestments, incense or the like, but I do not want to become enamoured of those as I will not get them in Montreal nor can I quite forego the notion that they are not at all orthodox. [Johnson and Bovell to the contrary.] To-day has been glorious, blue sky and no rain. Canadian steamer is telegraphed so that letters will be at the Hospital in the morning after reading which I may add a postscript. Much love. Got your letter this morning.

Yours,

WILLIE.

Meanwhile very little is said of the work which has been going on since October 7th over the microscope in Burdon Sanderson's laboratory, or who were his fellow-workers, though for a time Francis Darwin had a table near by, and several times spoke of taking him for a week-end at 'Down', but did not do so as his father was not well. A letter from 'Down' to W. A. Johnson, telling him of such a meeting in the old home of the Johnsons, would have been interesting, to say the least. Sanderson's course ended on January 24th with an exercise on the physiology of secretion, and Osler's last note reads:

On the propriety of using the lower animals for the purpose of experimentation Dr. Sanderson said 1st, we are at liberty to use them on the same ground as we do for food: 2nd for scientific investigation are justified in giving pain: 3rd for mere demonstration we are not justified in giving pain. Hence all experiments are omitted which cannot be performed on anaesthetized animals.[1]

To W. O. from W. A. Johnson. The Parsonage, Weston,
Jany 9th 1873.

My dear Osler,—Yours of the 8th Ult° is at hand, & it is the third you have very kindly and thoughtfully written without an answer from me. . . . Reasoning on general principles, no doubt your friend Dr Howard's advice to devote yourself to general medicine is good. I can not be expected to even offer an opinion on a thing I know nothing of. . . . I think I was turned from Botany as a specialty early in life, by some old medical man who lived near those steps wh go down from Oxford Street by his saying, 'don't you think of a specialty until you are forty', or some such words. I really must not write so much on a thing I know nothing about. Is it likely that the faculty of McGill College can afford to answer you distinctly in writing, concerning your future position with them? I do not see how they can, because you would have a claim upon them. Perhaps they will; but if they do, they surely rate you very high. It is quite likely they will extend the offer, but not definitely, & it will be for you to consider what it may lead to eventually; provided there is a reasonable remuneration for the present. If you are obtaining a present remuneration (i. e.) if you are in a position where you are regularly paid, though it be only a small amount, look well before you leave it for future increased salary, or something indefinite; for one bird in the hand is better than two in the bush. I am very glad you got comfortably settled in London. I envy you your Church privileges. Do not be afraid to use them freely & lovingly. Many Churches in London, from what I hear & read must be doing a good work. I suppose many of them freely & openly admit every sensible usage of the Roman Churches without any reference to papal authority, or to the errors wh have grown up from it. It is just what I could enjoy, &

---

[1] In the early '70's, as may be recalled, the antivivisection controversy in which Huxley was so actively engaged as protagonist for the scientists, was the subject of much discussion. It, however, was not until 1876 that in spite of the protests by Huxley, Darwin, Burdon Sanderson and others, the drastic act was passed which has so hampered medical research in the British Isles.

seems to me right. A return to the old paths. Tell me all you can about these matters when you write, but remember dear fellow I do not expect a letter. . . .

This very long letter contained a deal of excellent advice, which need not be quoted save for one question Johnson asked: 'May you not lessen your usefulness and knowledge in passing by general information to pursue a specialty?' This, too, had been Howard's suggestion, and accordingly the next ten months were given over very largely to 'walking the hospitals' in the old signification of the term; and in doing so he was particularly impressed by Murchison at St. Thomas's, and by the clinics given by Sir William Jenner and Wilson Fox[1] at University College. There he also followed Ringer, as well as H. C. Bastian, who lectured on nervous diseases though he was chiefly engrossed at the time by his theories regarding spontaneous generation. Early in the year he took a course of lectures on embryology given by E. Klein at the Brown Institution, and must have been interested, for '*James Bovell, M.D., M.R.C.P.*' appears only once on the pages of a full note-book; and at this time he evidently started some experiments on the blood of guinea-pigs, which, however, do not seem to have come to much. He even attended surgical operations, for Browne, his room-mate, who regularly sent medical letters home for publication in the journals, acknowledges his indebtedness to Dr. Osler for notes of surgical cases at the University Hospital, where Mr. Erichsen was then in attendance. The two friends during this time had been making a desperate struggle to master German, but one of them at least had little gift for speech in foreign tongues, possibly

[1] Wilson Fox was not well at the time, and when he died some years later Osler wrote: 'When I look back, through the mist, to 1872–3 and try to recall specific days and hours, there are few which will return with greater distinctness than those in which I see Wilson Fox standing at the head of a bed at University College Hospital, unravelling for the class the complicated symptoms of some chest case. He had a refinement and charm of manner particularly attractive. Something of the gentle spirit of the great Friend, whose name he bore, and into whose Society he was born, pervaded his nature, and there was a kindliness in his manner which won the hearts alike of student and of patient.' [In 'Notes and Comments', *Canada Medical and Surgical Journal*, June 1887, xv. 702–3.]

owing to his unmusical ear. They evidently got greater satisfaction out of their general reading, and to his ' much-loved Arthur Browne ', himself devoted to English literature, Osler ascribes his introduction to Lamb and Coleridge. Together they must have begun to frequent the antiquarian book-stands ; and as Osler had the prize money for his treatise, in the shape of an order for books on S. & J. Nock of Hart Street, Bloomsbury, he proceeded there, and in after years recalled the place as ' an indescribable clutter of books, whereas the brothers Nock, far advanced in years, were weird and desiccated specimens of humanity '.

To Miss Jennette Osler from W. O. January 16th 1873.

. . . I hope they have sent down my last two or three letters as they tell of my Xmas visit in Norfolk.[1] I spent a very happy ten days in spite of a rather severe cold which kept me in doors for nearly a week. I did not get to church on Xmas day even ; I was going to say for the first time in my life, but probably my first two Xmas days were spent in a very similar manner, eating & sleeping forming the chief part. Books, Music and cats are the chief features in Witton vicarage. The former I read, the second I listened to, & tried to understand, while the third I teased unmercifully. The girls are accomplished, good musicians, &c., but are lacking in looks which in spite of all else are very requisite. At Norwich I visited the Cathedral & saw what I could of the relics of my favourite Sir T. Browne. His skull & a good painting were in the Infirmary ; his tomb in the church of St. Peter Mancroft. I could not resist the temptation of seeing Ely and so stopped there on my way up. It is a wonderful building, the restoration making it look almost perfect. I was there for the morning service, forming in fact with a couple of kids, the congregation. I am very sure that after a months residence in this moist Isle you would pine for the land of your adoption. It only needs the ' fountains of the great deep ' to break up and then in many parts the deluge would be complete. For a few days the rain has ceased, but the clouds only permit an occasional gleam of sunlight. . . . I went to Drury Lane the other evening & saw the Xmas Pantomime. It was very grand & nice but oh ! so long. I left long before it was over. Napoleon's death has caused such a sensation ; he was buried yesterday. I will try & get a paper with full particulars in it though of course the news will be stale enough by the time you get this letter. You may quiet your soul about my India schemes. I shall *not* go there. Canada's my destination. . . . Kisses to all the kids. Yours

WILLIE.

---

[1] To visit relatives of his new brother-in-law, Colonel Gwyn.

This sojourn on the East Coast gave him his first opportunity to visit Norwich, and while there he was much moved by the sight of Sir Thomas Browne's skull, which many years afterwards he was instrumental in having placed in a proper receptacle. In a later address he thus refers to this visit:

The tender sympathy with the poor relics of humanity which Browne expresses so beautifully in these two meditations [' Urn Burial' and ' A Letter to a Friend '] has not been meted to his own. ' Who knows the fate of his bones or how often he is to be buried?' he asks. In 1840, while workmen were repairing the chancel of St. Peter Mancroft, the coffin of Sir Thomas was accidentally opened, and one of the workmen took the skull, which afterwards came into the possession of Dr. Edward Lubbock, who deposited it in the Museum of the Norfolk and Norwich Infirmary. When I first saw it there in 1872 there was on it a printed slip with these lines from the ' Hydriotaphia ': ' To be knaved out of our graves, to have our skulls made drinking-bowls, and our bones turned into pipes, to delight and sport our enemies, are tragical abominations escaped in burning burials.'[1]

He must have written promptly to W. A. Johnson, who replied on February 5th, saying:

. . . I would have liked to have been beside you while examining what remains of old Sir Thos. Browne. How markedly England does differ in that particular from this Country. Though we could put the whole Island into one of our Lakes yet there is more local interest in any one parish than there is in the whole of our Dominion. Say what people will about pictures, emblems, relics & the like, they have ever been and ever will be the most delightful & I think reasonable means of raising the thoughts to higher & holier hopes. The more I use them the more I delight in them. Word painting according to some eminent men in England is all that is needed but I think they must mean '*needed*' for wiser heads than mine. These things do help meditation so much, even if they do not actually create it. For instance, how difficult it is to *recall* the warmth of feelings we experience when actually in sight of relics connected with great names or events. Such I suppose is the legitimate use of the crucifix. It certainly is a lively incentive to meditation & a wonderful help to it. We protestants do not know half enough of these things, or how to use them.

From W. O. to his mother. February 12th [1873].

My dear Mother, Last weeks letter sent to you ' did not count', it was but a scrap; so that this one goes to you by proper turn.

[1] The ' Religio Medici'. An address delivered at Guy's Hospital. London, Chiswick Press, 1906, 31 pp. 8vo.

A mail arrived to-day with one letter from Chattie of Jan. 3rd & some papers. . . . I finished the afternoon by going to the Misses Bovell and had a long chat with them about West Indian friends. They hear from the Doctor very regularly and report him very busy, having three Parishes to attend and four Sunday Services. I did intend to go out to Putney on Sunday to see the Atwell Francis's but it was such a dreary bleak day that I postponed it, Browne and I spending a quiet Sunday together. I went to Christ Church and after dinner took a long walk around Primrose Hill returning through the Park. The snow has quite disappeared but an occasional flurry with a lowering of the Thermometer remind me that it is winter time. London is much agitated just now over the coal question, the prices having got up last week to 53s. per ton & a still further advance is talked of. As we only have our fire in the morning and evening it does not fall so heavily but what the poor will do if the weather gets much colder it is difficult to say. To-day has been remarkably clear and fine and as it was one of my days at the Brown Institution, I enjoyed the bright view—not often seen—on the river; going up on one of the Boats. . . . I send the 'John Bull' of this week to the Pater. Ask him to pass it on to J. Babington. I got it thinking it would contain a full account of the Athanasian Creed defence meeting, but you will see all about that in last week's Guardian. I am glad you have a 'slavey' that promises well; Even in England they are not immaculate judging from the complaints one hears. . . . Your most affectionate Son

WILLIE.

So the winter passed, by no means always with 'clear and fine' days, for he wrote to his sister a few weeks later: 'My cold is much better but I cannot dispense with "wipes" yet. We have had three or four days of cold yellow fog, not very thick, but horribly stuffy and it penetrates into all the rooms, chilling ones vitals'; and he adds in a postscript: 'I send B. B. a "Telegraph" with Gladstones speech in it. Tell him to excuse the dirty condition but I rescued it from the pile which the slavey collects to light fires', &c.

A paper on the results of some experimental studies undertaken earlier in the winter was read, as he later confessed, 'in a state of Falstaffian dissolution and thaw', on May 16th before the Royal Microscopical Society, and subsequently reported and published in its journal.[1] It

[1] 'On the Action of Certain Reagents—Atropia, Physostigma, and Curare—on the Colourless Blood-corpuscles.' *Quarterly Journal of the Microscopical Society*, 1873, xiii. 307.

represented an effort to determine whether the antagonism between atropin and physostigmin could be demonstrated by the behaviour of colourless corpuscles under the microscope; and though the findings were negative they served to arouse an interest in studies of the blood, which was to bring results later on. Incidentally the paper led to his election as a member of the Society. His laboratory notebook indicates that in June he had started on a new quest, for beginning with the date 14/6/73 the entries are accompanied by drawings labelled 'Colourless elements of my blood'. In the course of this investigation he very soon ran across some peculiar globoid bodies which he attempted to illustrate, and on certain days he found them 'very plentiful'.

> 10/6/73. After fasting 15 hours examined 3 preparations of my blood. Granular white corpuscles were found; 2 in two of the slides, none in the third. Fig. 5 represents the appearance of one which looks degenerated.

The blood of other people in the laboratory was also examined, and of various animals—modified by feeding, by fasting, &c.:

> On the 21st from Mr. Schäfer's blood one or two masses like Fig. 1 above seen [sketch]. The mass under observation on a warm stage was at first rounded in outline and distinctly corpuscular. Within two hours it had become more irregular in shape, while about it were several bacteria in active movement; connected with it were small filaments. Unfortunately as a higher power was being adapted it was lost.

He continued to describe and picture what he thought to be bacteria developing from these masses; and later on many patients were examined—cases of Addison's disease, malaria, diabetes—and he succeeded in demonstrating the masses he had discovered in many different conditions. These studies occupied his time from June to October, and this summer's work was the basis of his first and possibly his most important contribution to knowledge. Though a few previous investigators had observed these bodies, which came to be called blood platelets, or the third element of the blood, and which play an important rôle in the phenomenon of clotting, they had never before been

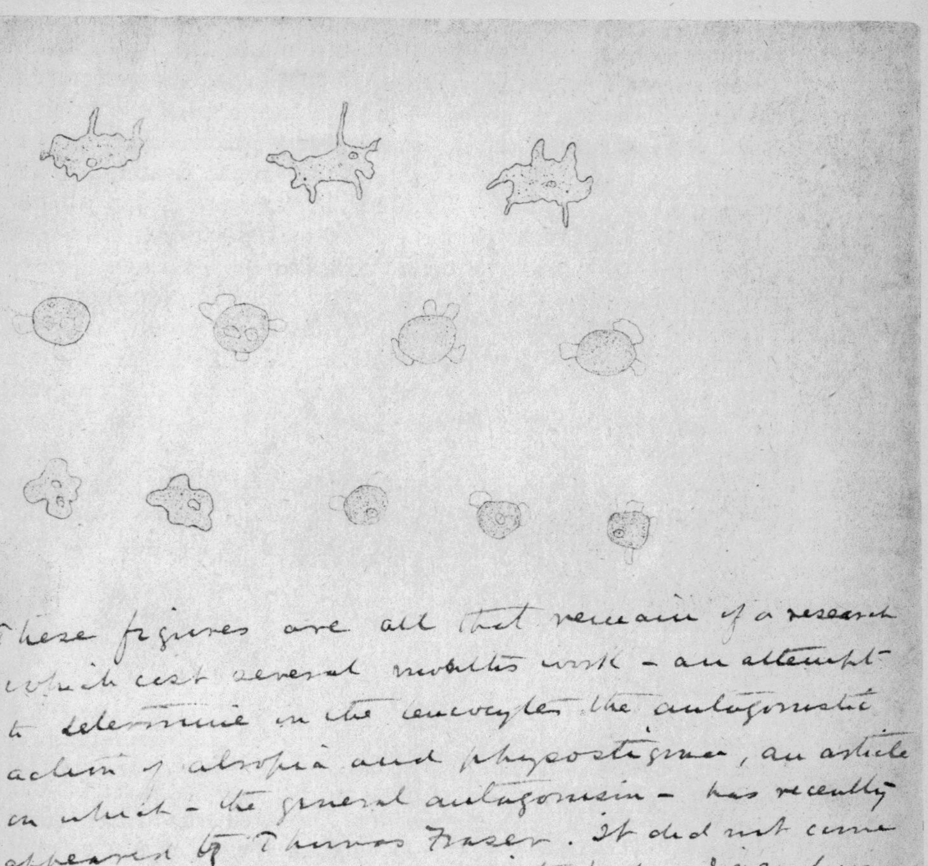

These figures are all that remain of a research which cost several months work — an attempt to determine in the leucocytes the antagonistic action of atropia and physostigma, an article on which — the general antagonism — has recently appeared by Thomas Fraser. It did not come to very much but the first paper I read was before the Medical Microscopical Society in May 1874 (in a state I remember of Falstaffian "dis-solution & thaw") There is a note upon it in the Quarterly Jr. Micros. science . The curious hyaline processes ~~which~~ thrown out by the leucocytes ... these figures represent probably physical effects. It was while working at this subject that my attention was called to the Schultze's granule masses & the blood platelets.

W. O.

SOME SKETCHES OF LEUCOCYTES WITH A LATER NOTE

so thoroughly studied, and none of his predecessors had actually seen them in the circulating blood. The observations, which had been conducted with great originality and been carefully described, were assembled the next spring on his return from the Continent, when Sanderson presented them before the Royal Society. News of this discovery must have reached Montreal, for in his introductory lecture on the opening of McGill in October, Palmer Howard spoke as follows in the course of his address :

> In connection with this new subject of scientific interest, the older students present, as well as my colleagues, will be pleased to hear that Dr. Osler, who graduated here in 1872, has just made a discovery of great interest, and that promises well for the future of our young countryman. . . . I wish that some friend of this University would endow a Chair of Physiological and Pathological Histology, and that our young friend might be invited to accept the appointment and devote himself solely to the cultivation of his favourite subject, and at the same time bring honour to himself and to Canada.[1]

Before leaving England for the Continent, Osler evidently struggled over the preparation of a letter to one of the Canadian medical journals, a rough draft of which is preserved. It contains an apology for not having followed the example set by Arthur Browne in sending a monthly letter, and ends with an expostulation regarding the waste of time and money spent by most of his young countrymen in 'grinding' to pass the English qualification examinations: these he calls neither degrees nor honours, and advises young Canadians to devote themselves to hospital work rather than to waste their substance in this way. This has a familiar sound to those who know of his later feelings regarding these examinations. Despite these unpublished expostulations, he nevertheless succumbed to the usual custom and not only became a Licentiate of the College in this year, but in 1878 took the examination for and was given his M.R.C.P.

To his sister, Mrs. Gwyn, from W. O. October 8th [1873].

My dear Chattie, How good I am to you—so undeserving—is evidenced by the enclosed. It differs from the Mothers so if she likes yours best—(which I dont) give it her. Folks here think it good

---

[1] *Canada Medical and Surgical Journal* 1873–4, ii. 208.

but it is too stern to please me. I bid goodbye to London next Wednesday. Address me till you hear further 'Poste Restante, Königs Strasse, Berlin'. I dare say there will often be slight irregularities but I will write some one weekly. I took your boys Photo down to the Boyds last week. They did make a row over it. The servants had it in the Kitchen & all decided it was like its dear Grandfather [Osler]. Thats one on the Governor—wont he be flattered. By this time Edmund has I hope arrived & you have got that Service book at last. I dine at the Sheppards tomorrow—have my hands full in that line for the week. Tell Jennette she shall have the first Berlin letter or Hamburg probably as I shall be there on the mail day, though it is not unlikely I may miss next weeks post, but I will try not to. I am rather sorry to say goodbye to London; it is not a bad place to spend a year in & have picked up a wrinkle or two which will I trust be useful. With benedictions, Yours

WILLIE.

Berlin

In a fragment of what appears to be a journalesque home-letter written during his early days in Berlin, he states: 'The politeness here is overwhelming, they bow you in and out and seem in agony till you are seated, while in meeting hats come wholly off. In rising from a table a man will stand and make a bow to every individual he has addressed and even to a perfect stranger if he has been alone in a room with him. It looks well and I like to see it'—and he goes on to tell of his old landlady, and getting settled, and the picture-galleries, and a visit to Charlottenburg on a Sunday afternoon. It became his established habit in later years to send, for the home consumption of his fellows, an open letter to the editor of some medical journal, wherein his impressions of the foreign clinics he visited were picturesquely jotted down. And though dissatisfied with his effort to compose a letter from London, he managed to write one from Berlin dated November 9th [1] in which he gives an account of the men he had seen in the clinics and elsewhere, and of the life which he and Stephen Mackenzie, his new friend, were leading. He comments also on matters of domestic economy which struck him as strange, particularly the breakfasts, and the beds—'wretched agglomeration of feathers—no sheets, no blankets, no

[1] *Canada Medical and Surgical Journal*, 1873–4, ii. 231.

quilts—but two feather beds, between which you must sleep and stew, but I am now reconciled'.

From W. O. to his sister, Mrs. Gwyn. 44 Louisen Str. N. [Berlin], November 23rd, 1873.

My dear Chattie, Your letter of last week was very acceptable, for home news still comes in a jerky, erratic manner very different to the regularity of the mail in London. Dont address any more letters to Berlin but to the 'Allgemeines Krankenhaus', Vienna, indeed I should have told you before, for I go on there about the end of next month. This ought to reach you about the 10th of December, just too late to offer 'many happy returns of the day'. How old we are getting! Even I am nearly a quarter of a century old and not on my own legs yet. . . . Thanks for the offer of hair but I prefer to cut locks for myself—from heads, also, of my own choosing. Talking about hair, it is a pity you cannot see my progressing imperial, with which I look like a cross between a Frenchman & an American. I am usually taken for the former, and to my disgust get 'Monsieured' or else asked interrogatively 'französisch?' and when I answer 'englisch' I can see it sometimes shakes the faith of an individual in his notions of national physiognomy. My friend Mackenzie is one of those red faced, stout, sandy-haired Englishmen whom no one could mistake, so that we are rather a contrast. In other respects also we are opposites, for he is an out and out Radical in Politics, Religion, & every thing else so that we are constantly at logger heads. However he is a hard working chap and we have but little time to dispute about our differences & get on very well together, with the exception of a rub now & then. Three Edinburgh graduates turned up, nice fellows, but we do not see much of them. The weather has been unpleasant for the past week & yesterday we had our first snowstorm, which lasted all morning, while to-day—Sunday—it has rained incessantly. On Thursday night I had a great treat in the way of Music, & I suppose it would have been a still greater one if I had had a more educated ear. It was at one of a series of nine concerts given annually by the Emperor's Orchestra in the Royal Concert room of the Opera house. I went with my friend Dr. Gutterböck who had tickets for the series. There were over a hundred performers all of whom are paid by the old Kaiser and many among them are well known composers. The Music was strictly classical, Beethoven & the like, somewhat over my head but very grand. I was as much interested in the people as anything for the elite of Berlin chiefly composed the audience. Dr. G. pointed out most of the swells all with outlandish names, with which I will not trouble you. Undoubtedly the women are far from good looking yet trim & neat withal. Why don't you girls do your back hair in a Christian style? it looks so much better plainly braided without all that horsehair padding, &c. The old ladies were even worse in point of features than their daughters. Four within my immediate ken could with a slight alteration in dress have sat for 'Sairy Gamp'. The audience was evidently a most appreciative one and knew what good Music was. I varied my programme this morning by going to the American chapel, where they have not any fixed person to officiate but depend on chance for some one. It is a dissenting service, not at all bad of its kind, and the young man—a theological student—who preached was an improvement on our steady-going old black-gowner at the English chapel. The congregation was not very large but thoroughly American. Usually on a Sunday we dine out as it were, i. e. we do not go to our accustomed place, but to some Restaurant in the Linden and then adjourn to some Conditorei to see the Papers. Our favourite one is Spalangani's, but it is so much frequented by Englishmen that it is often difficult to obtain a paper. I take my news 'weekly', generally through the illustrated. . . . My old woman has just been in and on a Sunday night usually gets very communicative, entering fully into family history, &c. Her Mother was the chief theme this evening and she seemed very proud to be one of fifteen children which that remarkable woman presented to her unhappy Fritz—she laid particular stress on this point—with praiseworthy regularity. . . .

25th. Have you heard or seen anything lately of Mr. Johnson? You should pay him a visit and take the lad along. . . . Dont let your heart be troubled about German Theology. I dont want it, though some of it may be good enough, even if a little unorthodox. My hands are full without anything else outside ordinary Medical subjects. Love to all

Yours, &c.

WILLIE.

Another long letter was sent off at this time,[1] evidently written before the sanitary reforms instituted by Virchow came to transform Berlin:

Berlin, Nov. 25th [1873].

Nature could hardly do less for a place than she has done for this. A barren, sandy plain surrounding it on all sides without a vestige of anything that might be called a hill; and the muddy, sluggish Spree, just deep enough to float barges, flowing through it towards the Baltic, form the sole natural features. Being a modern city it is well laid out, with wide but wretchedly paved streets; while the houses, though of brick, are stucco-covered and uniform, so that the general appearance of the place is clean. Unfortunately the cleanliness goes no farther than looks, being the very opposite in reality. The drainage is everywhere deficient, and in the greater part of the

[1] To the *Canada Medical and Surgical Journal*, 1873–4, ii. 308.

city the sewers are not even covered but skirt the pavement on each side, sending up a constant odour, which until one gets acclimatized is peculiarly disgusting. The Berlinese have, however, at last roused themselves, and the council has voted two millions sterling for sanitary purposes, so that a striking reduction in the present high death-rate from Typhoid and kindred diseases may be shortly expected.

It would be superfluous to speak of the advantages here offered for medical studies, the name of Virchow, Traube, and Frerichs in medicine and pathology; of Langenbeck and Bardleben in surgery, of DuBois-Reymond and Helmholtz in Physiology and Physics are sufficient guarantees; all of these men, who though they have been prominent figures in the medical world for a long time, are still in their prime as teachers and workers. In contrast to London, where the teaching is spread over some twelve schools, it is here centralized and confined to the Royal Charité,—for though there are several smaller hospitals in the city, yet they have no schools in connection with them, but are used chiefly for training nurses. . . . There are only three or four Americans here, and the same number of Englishmen. They go chiefly to Vienna, where greater advantages are offered in all the specialties. The native students seem a hard-working set, much given to long hair and slouched hats, and a remarkable number of them wear glasses. They possess the virtue, quite unknown as far as my experience goes, among their English or Canadian brethren, of remaining quiet while waiting for a lecture, or in the operating-theatre. There is never the slightest disturbance, though most of the lecturers give what is called 'The Academical quarter', that is they do not begin till fifteen minutes past the appointed hour. At Langenbeck's Clinique only, are students allowed to smoke, and often by the time a patient is brought in the condition of the atmosphere is such that as you look across the large theatre from the top, the men on the opposite side are seen through a blue haze. Quite a number of the students, more than I expected, are badly marked with sword-cuts received in duels. One hopeful young Spanish-American of my acquaintance has one half of his face—they are usually on the left half—laid out in the most irregular manner, the cicatrices running in all directions, enclosing areas of all shapes—the relics of fourteen duels! The custom has decreased very much of late, and is now confined to a few of the smaller university towns. A great diminution has taken place in the attendance here within the last few years, and I am told it is greater than ever this session, due to the increased cost of living. Speaking from a six weeks' experience, I find it quite as dear as London. Field-sports, such as cricket and football are entirely unknown among the students; but they have a curious habit of forming small societies of ten or twelve, who have a room at some restaurant where they meet to drink beer, smoke, and discuss various topics. If tobacco and beer have such a deteriorating effect on mind and body, as some of our advanced teetotallers affirm, we ought to see signs of it here; but the sturdy Teuton, judging from the events of the past few years has not degenerated physically, at any rate, while intellectually he is still to the fore in most scientific subjects; whether, however, in spite of—or with the aid of—the 'fragrant weed' and the 'flowing bowl' could hardly be decided. Drunkenness is not common, at least not obtrusively so, but they appear to get a fair number of cases of delirium tremens in the Charité. . . .

From this he went on to describe in what way the method of clinical instruction differed from the English and Scotch schools, and the methods of those two great teachers, Traube and Frerichs, particularly appealed to him:

But it is the master mind of Virchow, and the splendid Pathological Institute which rises like a branch hospital in the grounds of the Charité, that specially attract foreign students to Berlin. This most remarkable man is yet in his prime, (52 years of age), and the small, wiry, active figure, looks good for another twenty years of hard work; when one knows that in addition to the work at the Institute, given below, he is an ardent politician, evidently the leader of the Prussian Opposition, and a member on whom a large share of the work of the budget falls; an active citizen, member of the Council, and the moving spirit in the new canalization or sewerage system; an enthusiastic anthropologist as well as a working member in several smaller affairs, some idea may be formed of the comprehensive intellect and untiring energy of the man. On Monday, Wednesday and Friday from 8.30 to 11 he holds his demonstrative course on pathology, the other mornings of the week the course on pathological histology, while on the fourth day at one o'clock he lectures on general pathology. Virchow himself performs a post-mortem on Monday morning, making it with such care and minuteness that three or four hours may elapse before it is finished. The very first morning of my attendance he spent exactly half an hour in the description of the skull-cap!

On Wednesday and Saturday the demonstrations take place in a large lecture-room accommodating about 140 students, and with the tables so arranged that microscopes can circulate continuously on a small tramway let into them. Generally the material from 10 to 12 post-mortems is demonstrated, the lecturer taking up any special group and enlarging on it with the aid of sketches on the blackboard, and microscopical specimens, while the organs are passed round on wooden platters for inspection. A well provided laboratory for physiological and pathological chemistry also exists as well as rooms where men may carry on private investigations; and a library and reading-room is now being fitted up. A description of some of the other classes and things of interest must be reserved for another time.

The contents of this long letter were built up from the careful notes kept in a *Tages-Kalender* with such care as his difficulties with the language permitted: but his detailed notes of what he was seeing of the clinics and above all of Virchow's painstaking autopsies, were to stand him in great stead on his return. Later on, this same *Tages-Kalender* contains some daily entries regarding a brief illness which sounds like influenza, the last of which reads: '*Dec.* 13, *Saturday*. Much better, up most of the day, ate a good dinner; finished "Adam Bede". Evening no headache nor any pains but felt a little weak.'

Throughout his life Osler always took sufficient interest in his own maladies to make notes upon them, usually entered in his account-books, and, what is more, always took advantage of being laid up in bed to surround himself with books and to catch up on outside reading. It was in this way that he came invariably to 'enjoy' one of his recurring attacks of bronchitis in later years. The last of the Berlin entries was made on December 18th, but the subsequent pages of the *Kalender* contain many quotations from books he had been reading—from Tyndall, from Poincaré, from 'The Two Gentlemen of Verona', &c.

On the 24th of this same December there died in Baltimore a wealthy merchant, Johns Hopkins, who bequeathed his property 'to foster higher education'. Little did the young student, just completing a short three-months' sojourn in Berlin, realize the part he was to play, sixteen years later, in the establishment of a medical department provided for under this great foundation.

Vienna

Such daily entries as any young man of good intentions, in a foreign country and with a new note-book in his pocket, might undertake to write and soon abandon, appear in a *Geschäfts-Taschenbuch* for 1874:

January 1. Arrived at Vienna last night, put up at Hotel Hammerand, explored the city in the morning and in the afternoon.

With Schlofer's aid went in search of lodging-house, deciding finally on a room at Herr von Schultenkopf, No. 5 Reitergasse, Josefstadt, Thur. xiii.

January 2, Fr. Continued the survey of the city. Saw St. Stephen's Church and the chief business localities. Visited the Allgemeines Krankenhaus with Schlofer and tried to get some idea of its topography—rather difficult matter.

January 3. Visited the Krankenhaus again and made further exploration in the city.

4th, Sunday. Tried to find the English Church, but failed. Spent the rest of the day with Schlofer and his friend Herr B.

5th, Monday. Went to meet Hutchinson at the Nordwestbahnhof. Had the felicity of going to 5 of the 7 stations in the city in search of his trunk.

6th, Tuesday. Went to the Krankenhaus and afterwards walked round the Ring.

7th, Wednes'y. Commenced work with Bamberger at 8.30. Neumann at 10. Wiederhoffer at 11, and Braun from 12 to 2. Much pleased with this my first introduction to Vienna teachers and material.

For the five months in Vienna he must have worked assiduously and have filled up his time with all the courses he could squeeze in, as the following account he sends home to the Canadian journal [1] makes evident :

March 1st, 1874.
'Allgemeines Krankenhaus'.

. . . I left Berlin on the 29th of December, and stopped at Dresden for a few days, to see the galleries there, which pleased me very much, and then continuing my journey I arrived here on New Year's day. With the aid of a Yankee friend, I soon obtained a room in Reitergasse, close to the Krankenhaus. The Krankenhaus is arranged in nine courts, occupying a whole district in the city, and accommodating more than two thousand patients. We were not long in getting to work, and our daily programme is as follows :

At about half-past eight we go to Hebra, who visits his wards at this hour, and at nine we go to his lecture-room. Undoubtedly he is *the* lecturer of the Vienna School, and he combines the humorous and instructive in a delightful way. I generally go every other morning to Bamberger, who lectures at the same hour, on General Medicine. He is a splendid diagnostician, but is, I think, inferior to those Berlin giants, Traube and Frerichs. At ten we have another hour on the skin, from Neumann who has the run of Hebra's wards, and an out-patient department of his own. He enters more par-

---

[1] The *Canada Medical and Surgical Journal*, 1873-4, ii. 451.

ticularly into individual cases than Hebra and gives us more differential diagnosis. At eleven, we go to Wiederhoffer the professor in the children's department, and have there in the first half-hour a series of selected cases, and in the second a lecture. There are not many in his class, so that one has a good chance to examine the children oneself. At twelve I attend a course on ear diseases with Politzer, not that I am going to make a specialty of them but I thought it well worth while, when an opportunity occurred, to make their acquaintance. Politzer is good, and shows us a great many cases, and makes us pass the Eustachian Catheter daily. At one, Braun the Professor of Obstetrics, lectures, but more of the Clinique shortly. Between two and four we dine, and take our constitutional, and at four we have a class on the laryngoscope. This is a six weeks' course, and I am just beginning another and take kindly to the larynx. At five we have one of our very best classes, viz: obstetric operations, with Bandl, Braun's first assistant, in which after as much theory as is needful, work begins on the cadaver. I begin next week to go on duty about every fifth or sixth day and hope to get three or four forceps cases before leaving. Altogether, midwifery and skin diseases are the specialties in Vienna, while in general medicine and pathology it is infinitely below Berlin. . . .

After having seen Virchow it is absolutely painful to attend post-mortems here, they are performed in so slovenly a manner, and so little use is made of the material. Professor Rokitansky lectures at twelve, but usually to less than a dozen men. Most of the six or eight weeks' courses, for which the school is so famous, are £2, but the ordinary university ones only £1, so that it quickly mounts up, especially if one takes second courses. I do not attend any surgical classes, having as you see my hands full, but we go to Billroth occasionally, and I shall take a course of operations from his assistant before I leave.

Americans swarm here, there are fifty or sixty of them at least, and Great Britain is represented by five or six Edinburgh men and a couple of Londoners. The city itself is very beautiful, having a splendid wide street, like the Thames embankment, surrounding the inner town, and occupying the position of the old wall and moat. I expect to leave about the end of April, and shall touch at Paris on my way home, to see the city. . .

And he went on to give a long account of a seventieth-birthday celebration in honour of Carl Rokitansky, which 'the city, university and students all combined to celebrate in true German fashion and in a manner worthy of themselves and of the distinguished man who has so long shed lustre on their school'.

Osler was evidently aiming to get the broadest possible

grounding in general medicine and the specialties. He even took sufficient interest in obstetrics to translate an article—possibly also to improve his German—from Virchow's *Archiv*, which was sent home to Fenwick for the Montreal Journal.[1] His chief interest, nevertheless, lay in pathology, and despite the proverbial wealth of material, perhaps because of it, he found Vienna to be behind Berlin. Carl Rokitansky, at his best merely a descriptive pathologist, was at this time near the end of his career, and indeed the group of other Bohemians, the great masters who had made the 'new Vienna School' and turned the eyes of the medical world towards Austria, had most of them, with the exception of Billroth, been born in the first decade of the century. The Berlin School, with Virchow as its chief figure, represented a group fifteen years younger.

He had scant funds at his disposal, and in one of his notes written years later, Osler says: 'There were cobwebs in my pockets in Berlin and Vienna, and only the most necessary text-books were bought. On leaving Vienna, however, I could not resist Billroth's "Coccobacteria Septica" an expensive quarto, with beautiful plates—a curious pre-Kochian attempt to associate bacteria with disease, and now of value only as illustrating the futility of brains without technique.' This was one of Billroth's early works, published in this same year, and what may have been in Osler's mind when the paragraph quoted above was written, was the fact that Billroth, though even at that day by far the most distinguished Austrian surgeon, had failed to appreciate the relation of bacteria to suppuration, a matter which since the autumn of 1872 had received the unstinted support of other German surgeons, notably Karl Thiersch and Richard von Volkmann. Whether his expectation of taking a course in surgery was fulfilled is not apparent. It is, however, hardly conceivable that the discussions Lister's work had aroused should not have come to his ears while at University College, for his sojourn practically coincided with this great revolution in surgery, which must

1 'Uterine Thermometry.' *Canada Medical and Surgical Journal*, Dec. 1874, iii. 294.

have been freely talked of in laboratory circles, even though London operating rooms were admittedly slow to adopt Lister's principles.

To Miss Jennette Osler from W. O. Vienna, March 22nd.

My dear Jennette, . . . I trust this week to begin my homeward progress and will probably get as far as Paris by Saturday. It is a matter of some forty hours by rail and I shall probably break the journey either at Munich or Strassburg, the galleries attracting at the former, the laboratories at the latter. A good deal will depend on how I feel on getting to Munich after a night on the train. My friend Hutchinson is still in Paris & will act as guide there. I expect to be in London for Easter Sunday. As a pleasing change we had our proper Parson at the chapel to-day, in whose place a converted Native has been officiating for some time. Anything—High—Low—Broad—will do for me after six months on the Continent. The chaplain here, a Mr. Johnson, is a remarkably fine looking old man, with long white hair & a face which reminds me of the portraits of the old Musicians. There is a dash of sadness also about it as though he was one of those who did not 'take the current when it served', and hence the consequence—a chaplaincy abroad, instead of a Bishopric at home. You see I am rather Shakespearian tonight. Shakespeare has been my light literature for some time: that accounts for it. We—Stephen [Mackenzie] & I—went for a long walk this afternoon to the Prater Park & the new Danube Channel in process of making. This latter is a wonderful work of engineering. . . . I am going to do the Royal Treasury and Stables, with one or two other little things this week, & then shall have pretty well finished the Vienna sights. My next will probably be dated Paris. Love to all

Yours

WILLIE.

It was not until 1908 that Osler revisited Vienna. He sent home a letter at the time, intended for the American medical profession.[1] The paragraphs which describe the influence of the Vienna School on American medicine deserve reprinting:

I spent the first few months of 1874 here. I came from Berlin with Hutchinson, an Edinburgh man (Sir Charles F., who has recently died), and we lived together near the Allgemeines Krankenhaus. As illustrating the total blotting out of certain memories, particularly for places, I may mention that strolling to-day up the Alserstrasse I could not recall the street, much less the house, where we had lived

[1] 'Vienna after Thirty-four Years.' *Journal of the American Medical Association*, May 9, 1908, l. 1523.

for the four months. I found my way readily enough to the Riedhof, where we were in the habit of dining, and where I first met my old friends, Fred Shattuck, E. H. Bradford, E. G. Cutler, and Sabine of Boston. An extraordinary development has taken place in the city within thirty years, and I scarcely recognized the Ringstrasse. Then, only the foundations of the new university buildings and of the Rathaus had been begun. Now these, with the parliament house, the courts of justice, the twin museums of art and natural history, and the new Bourg Theatre, form a group of buildings unrivalled in any city. . . . As a medical centre, Vienna has had a remarkable career, and her influence particularly on American medicine has been very great. What was known as the first Vienna School in the eighteenth century was really a transference by van Swieten of the School of Boerhaave from Leyden. The new Vienna School, which we know, dates from Rokitansky and Skoda, who really made Vienna the successor of the great Paris School of the early days of the nineteenth century. But Vienna's influence on American medicine has not been so much through Skoda and Rokitansky as through the group of brilliant specialists—Hebra, Sigmund and Neumann in dermatology; Arlt and Jaegar in ophthalmology; Schnitzler and von Schrötter in laryngology; Gruber and Politzer in otology. These are the men who have been more than others responsible for the successful development of these specialties in the United States. Austria may well be proud of what Vienna's school has done for the world, and she still maintains a great reputation, though it cannot be denied, I think, that the Æsculapian centre has moved from the Danube to the Spree. But this is what has happened in all ages. Minerva Medica has never had her chief temples in any one country for more than a generation or two. For a long period at the Renaissance she dwelt in northern Italy, and from all parts of the world men flocked to Padua and to Bologna. Then for some reason of her own she went to Holland, where she set up her chief temple at Leyden with Boerhaave as her high priest. Uncertain for a time, she flitted here with Boerhaave's pupils, van Swieten and de Haen; and could she have come to terms about a temple she doubtless would have stayed permanently in London where she found in John Hunter a great high priest. In the first four decades of the nineteenth century she lived in France, where she built a glorious temple to which all flocked. Why she left Paris, who can say? but suddenly she appeared here, and Rokitansky and Skoda rebuilt for her the temple of the new Vienna School, but she did not stay long. She had never settled in Northern Germany, for though she loves art and science she hates with a deadly hatred philosophy and all philosophical systems applied to her favourite study. Her stately German shrines, her beautiful Alexandrian home, her noble temples, were destroyed by philosophy. Not until she saw in Johannes Müller and in Rudolph Virchow true and loyal disciples did she move to Germany, where she stays in spite of the tempting offers from France, from Italy, from England, and from Austria.

In an interview most graciously granted to me, as a votary of long standing, she expressed herself very well satisfied with her present home where she has much honour and is much appreciated. I boldly suggested that it was perhaps time to think of crossing the Atlantic and setting up her temple in the new world for a generation or two. I spoke of the many advantages, of the absence of tradition—here she visibly weakened, as she has suffered so much from this poison—the greater freedom, the enthusiasm, and then I spoke of missionary work. At these words she turned on me sharply and said: 'That is not for me. We Gods have but one motto—those that honour us we honour. Give me the temples, give me the priests, give me the true worship, the old Hippocratic service of the art and of the science of ministering to man, and I will come. By the eternal law under which we Gods live I would have to come. I did not wish to leave Paris, where I was so happy and where I was served so faithfully by Bichat, by Laennec and by Louis'—and the tears filled her eyes and her voice trembled with emotion—'but where the worshippers are the most devoted, not, mark you, where they are the most numerous; where the clouds of incense rise highest, there must my chief temple be, and to it from all quarters will the faithful flock. As it was in Greece, in Alexandria, in Rome, in Northern Italy, in France, so it is now in Germany, and so it *may be* in the new world I long to see.' Doubtless she will come, but not till the present crude organization of our medical clinics is changed, not until there is a fuller realization of internal medicine as a science as well as an art.

Early in April he returned to London to complete the paper dealing with his researches in Sanderson's laboratory, and to revisit his friends and relatives before his departure to Canada.

To his sister from W. O. Thursday, April 16th.

My dear Chattie, Your letter addressed U.C.H. arrived all right to-day. I am still in London having postponed my Cornwall visit till next week. I had intended to go down on Saturday but Prof. Sharpey the Vice-President of the Royal Society most kindly gave me an introduction to their Soirée which comes off next Wednesday & as it is a very swell affair—swell in my line—I shall wait for it. I have been very busy since my return, spending the whole day at the Laboratory from 9 a.m. to five. I am glad to hear such good news of the Staplehurst people & I suppose by the time I get home they will look themselves again. I leave from London somewhere about the 20th May so that early in June you may be on the look out. I heard Canon Liddon last Sunday afternoon at St. Pauls; he is as good as ever. I have got very low-church lately & am afraid Fathers Johnson and Wood will be horrified. . . . I am scrawling away in the Library of the Coll of Surgeons where I have been hunting up some references and had almost forgotten about the Canadian mail. Another budget of letters were forwarded from Vienna a few days ago. I dined last evening with the Schäfers at Highgate. The son is Sanderson's Assistant in the laboratory and has been very kind, assisting me in many ways. They are nice people, & such *nice girls.* I did not know who Sophie was engaged to until yesterday when on calling at the Sheppards they told me all about it. Goodbye old girl pro tem. Love to all Yours

WILLIE.

Reminders of the affair which was 'swell in my line' are to be found in two of the books in Osler's library. In one of them he mentions having met Charles Darwin at this soirée, and of the pleasure it gave him to have the kindly old man with bushy eyebrows speak pleasantly of Principal Dawson of McGill. And it is quite probable that it was at a dinner beforehand that Sharpey gave him as a memento the volume in which he subsequently made the following note:

Professor Sharpey had resigned the previous year but was much about the laboratory and often came to my desk in a friendly way to see the progress of my blood studies. One evening he asked me to dinner; Kölliker, Allen Thompson and Dohrn were there. When saying goodbye he gave me Davy's *Researches* with an autograph inscription.

It must have been a treat for the young man to meet these distinguished anatomists and friends of Sharpey's in this intimate way. Kölliker, a Swiss of the highest distinction, was at the time Professor in Würzburg, while Anton Dohrn was Director of the Naples Zoological Station. Like Sharpey himself, they were anatomists of the physiological school.

His 'scrawling in the library' was probably in completion of his paper submitted on May 6th, and presented by Burdon Sanderson on June 18th before the Royal Society after he had sailed for home.[1] The title was not particularly

[1] 'An Account of Certain Organisms Occurring in the Liquor Sanguinis. *Proceedings of the Royal Society*, 1874, xxii. 391–8.

fortunate, and the paper contains a hint as to the possible relation to bacteria of the masses of blood platelets which others had seen before him. This can only be accounted for by the influence of H. C. Bastian, whose 'The Beginnings of Life' had just appeared, and whose views on spontaneous generation may have permeated even into his colleague Sanderson's laboratory at University College. The most important fact brought out by the study, and which was quite novel, was that these 'elementary particles' as they were called, are discrete in the circulating blood and never clumped, as is always the case after blood is drawn; and Osler's figure showing them within a small vein is still in use in text-books of histology.[1]

[1] The importance of this study has been fully commented upon by W. T. Councilman ('Some of the Early Medical Work of William Osler', *Johns Hopkins Hosp. Bulletin*, July 1919, xxx. 193–7). There were three subsequent papers in which he added still further to the knowledge of these platelets: viz. 'Infectious Endocarditis', *Archives of Medicine*, N. Y., 1881, v. 44, in which he discussed the newly accepted view of their relation to thrombus formation. This was further elaborated in an article, 'Ueber den dritten Formbestandteil des Blutes', *Centralblatt für d. med. Wissenschaften*, 1882, xx. 529. Again in a final article 'On the Third Corpuscle of the Blood', *Medical News*, Phila., 1883, xliii. 701, he gave a general presentation of the subject.

CHAPTER VI

1874–5

THE YOUNG PROFESSOR AT McGILL

After his long absence Osler had returned to Canada with empty pockets, and naturally anxious for a job. It is recorded that for a time he took over the work of a local practitioner in Dundas, and the first fee as a practising physician entered in his account-book reads, 'Speck in cornea . . . 50¢'—an entry he was known to point out to aspiring young M.D.'s in later years with a twinkle in his eye. He also served for a month as *locum tenens* for Dr. Charles O'Reilly, a McGill graduate who had long been Resident Physician at the City Hospital in Hamilton, and tradition relates that he took the post 'for the consideration of $25 and a pair of old-fashioned elastic-sided boots which had proved too small for Charlie O'Reilly'. However this may be, he was not long left in uncertainty as to his future:

To W. O. from Palmer Howard. 47 Union Avenue, Montreal, July 6th, '74.

My dear Osler,—I have just ret[d] from a Meeting of the Med[l] Faculty of the College at which I am happy to be able to inform you it was agreed to recommend you to the Governor of the College for the office of Lecturer upon Institutes in the room of Dr. Drake who resigns on account of ill health. You have not been spending your time in vain in working at practical physiology and I must heartily congratulate you upon this fine prospect that has opened before you. The fees of the students will at least meet your actual expenses for board, clothes, etc., and the position in the college will afford the strongest proof to the public that you are at least a well qualified physician and that experience is all that you require to merit their patronage. I would advise you to come down at once, hang out your shingle, and set actively to work upon your *lectures*—you will find the time short enough. Drake can be of much assistance and is willing to be; and he has a fine collection of diagrams which will be of use and which he will no doubt dispose of to you very reasonably. You will receive an official letter from the Dean no doubt by the same mail that conveys this—answer it at once. The time is a favourable one moreover at which to enter upon practice—for although you will have to wait for that like others—labour will procure its reward in that field also. Please present my congratulations to y[r] father upon this gratifying recognition of y[r] merits by the oldest medical school in Canada. All y[r] friends here will be much pleased on your account. I regretted to have missed you on your arrival from Europe as you must have had lots of recent information to impart and as I wanted to hear of your doings—but you know what I was about and no doubt will forgive me. I hope soon to see you here and 'to hear of y[r] affairs'. Till then I remain Very sincerely yours

R. P. Howard.

Preserved with this letter is the fragmentary draft of Osler's reply, which says:

. . . I do not accept without some diffidence, still I hope to be able to work up a decent set of Lectures. I am glad it is only a Lectureship. It not only sounds better (as I am so young), but to my English friends Sanderson, Sharpey, Klein, &c., it will seem more in keeping with what they know of my attainments. It now remains to be seen whether with teaching & [private practice] I can follow up any original work. Of course I shall try hard.

Meanwhile, during his few weeks in Dundas and Hamilton he had cemented friendships with members of the local profession. Indeed he never failed to ingratiate himself, wherever he might be, with the older practitioners in particular, towards whom he always felt especially drawn. So an enduring attachment was established at this time with two Hamiltonians of an older generation, themselves intimate friends: Dr. John A. Mullin and Dr. Archibald Malloch, a fine Scot, one of Lister's pupils and the leading surgeon of the region. Evidence of his affection for and interest in the 'doctors of the old school'—men like James Hamilton, who practised sixty years in West Flamboro—crops out in many of his writings. There was, for example, a Dr. Case, who in 1809, when four years of age, had been brought from Pennsylvania to Upper Canada by his U. E. loyalist father. For fully forty years he had occupied a house in Hamilton, on the corner of King and Walnut Streets, and long after he had given up practice he was wont to sit in the window and nod to his numerous acquaintances, or reminisce with those who would drop in and pass the time of day with him. This Osler never failed to do when in Hamilton, and some years later in an editorial entitled 'Doctors' Signs', in which he poked fun at this questionable form of advertising, he ends with this paragraph:

> Happy the man whose reputation is such or whose local habitation is so well known that he needs no sign! This is sometimes the case in country places and small towns, not often in cities. We know of one such in a prosperous Canadian city. Grandfather, father and son have been in 'the old stand' so long that to the inhabitants of the locality the doctor's house is amongst the things which have always been. The patients' entrance is in a side street and a small porch protects the visitor. The steps are well worn and the native grain is everywhere visible in the wooden surroundings. There is neither bell nor knocker and the door presents interesting and, so far as we know, unique evidences that votaries to this Æsculapian shrine have not been lacking. On the panels at different heights are three well-worn places where the knuckles of successive generations of callers have rapped and rapped and rapped. The lowest of the three, about three feet from the floor, represents the work of 'tiny Tim' and 'little Nell', so often the messengers in poorer families. Higher up and of less extent is a second depression where 'Bub' and 'Sis' have pounded, and highest of all, in the upper panel a wider area where the firmer fists of the fathers and brothers have as the years rolled on worn away the wood to nearly half its thickness. Such a testimony to the esteem and faithfulness of successive generations of patients is worthy of preservation.[1]

He must have proceeded to Montreal about the first of August, to judge from an account-book of this period—almost the last in which he took the trouble to itemize his expenditures. It begins: 'Fare, Hamilton to Montreal, $12.50'; and his first entries after his arrival are:

Fees for Desk and Chair on acct.	12.25
Book case, on account	12.35
Ton of coal	8.00
Subscription to 'Churchman'	3.00
Book bill Dawsons	20.00
Rent of room $10 per month	

He thus with a desk, a chair, a bookcase, and a ton of coal furnished a room at 20 Radegonde Street, below Beaver Hall Hill, in the lower part of Montreal, and there he hung out

[1] *Canada Medical and Surgical Journal*, Dec. 1883, xii. 312. When the old house was finally demolished in 1894 the door was saved and is now in the Hamilton museum in Dundurn Park.

his 'shingle', though it does not appear that any patients were ever attracted thereby, nor, had they been, that he would have been found at home. His first task, for which he had little taste, was to prepare the formal lectures for the year, and, as he later confessed, he groaned heavily over the obligation: 'When I returned to Montreal in September 1874 the Professor of the Institutes of Medicine had had to retire on account of heart disease, and instead of getting, as I had hoped, a position as his demonstrator the Faculty appointed me lecturer with the ghastly task of delivering four systematic lectures a week for the winter session, from which period dates my ingrained hostility to this type of teaching.' One of the pupils in his first class, Dr. Beaumont Small of Ottawa, thus writes of his impressions:

I saw him first as he entered the lecture-room to open his course on the Institutes of Medicine. Quick and active, yet deliberate in his walk and manner, with a serious and earnest expression, it was evident that he looked upon his lectures as serious, and at once imparted the same feeling to others. In a very few words he welcomed his class, stated what he hoped to do and what he expected in return, concluding with a gentle warning that he expected attendance and attention from all. We succumbed to that genial and kindly manner which has been so characteristic throughout his life, and I doubt if any professor had more carefully studied lectures, or better attention than was given to him.

The lecture began with an explanation of the old Edinburgh term of Institutes of Medicine. Then in bold outline he sketched inorganic and organic matter, vegetable and organic life, vital force, and closed with a description of cellular life and an outline of future lectures. From that hour physiology was an attractive study and the lectures like unto the Gods.

When I look back upon that period it is evident that 1876–7 was the beginning of a period of *renaissance* for McGill, and Osler the moving spirit, but it would not be right to impart to him all the credit. The recent appointments to the Faculty of Ross, Roddick, Shepherd and Gardner, all young and energetic, of the highest type of professional standing, was not without design. These supported by the mature wisdom of Dean Campbell, R. P. Howard and Craik could mean only progress and resulted in the reputation that McGill achieved during the succeeding decade.

The period, as Dr. Small says, was truly one of a new birth for McGill, and though by no means due to Osler entirely, his personality nevertheless—there as in other places during his subsequent migrations—proved to be the leaven which raised the loaf, as shown by the flattening-out which always followed his departure.

'Jimmie' Johnson had entered the school, and for various reasons Osler's advances in the way of giving him financial aid and of taking him as a boarder were rejected. Father Johnson, if one may judge from his letters to his son, undoubtedly felt that the unorthodox and non-sectarian environment of University College had had a demoralizing effect upon his former pupil: he could not stomach the fact that Osler had gone to an institution where youths on their admission were not obliged to sign the Thirty-nine Articles, and which revered the secular Jeremy Bentham to the extent of preserving in its museum his clothed skeleton —for he had left his body to be dissected at University College. One of the letters is particularly severe—to the effect that Osler's power of application was the single characteristic worthy of imitation. But this after all was what Osler often said of himself—that he had but a single talent—a capacity for industry. Osler, however, could apply himself not to work alone, but to play as well, and always knew where to find children with whom he could frolic. His cousin writes: 'Willie dropped in four times on Saturday; he stole the new kitten, and now the old kitten, and the children are wondering where she is. He has just come in to tea.'

During these years in Montreal chance brought him into frequent contact with a group of men who were enriching Canada and incidentally themselves by transactions concerned with the opening up of the great West. He often recalled in later years how at this time his brother, 'E. B.', then chairman of the Temiskaming or some other railway, used to come down to Montreal nearly every week, and how on his return from the college or hospital he would find a note from Donald A. Smith (afterwards Lord Strathcona), saying: 'At 7.00 as your brother is down.' R. B. Angus, McIntyre, George Stephen, and others would be likely to be there also; and after the meal, in spite of Osler's presence, the talk would be on matters foreign to his taste and understanding—of finance and the affairs of the C. P. R., which was going through a period of hard sledding. Far more to his taste was the monthly dinner club formed by a group of the younger members of the Faculty—a club famous for the pranks and practical jokes its members played on one another. In this coterie, Osler's chief intimates, with the possible exception of Arthur Browne, were George Ross and Francis J. Shepherd, and such outings as he permitted himself to engage in were usually taken 'up country' in company with these two.[1]

He went home to Dundas for the Christmas recess, stopping off for a visit with the Toronto relatives; and while there, as was characteristic of him, he dropped in to introduce himself and to give a welcome to the newly appointed Professor of Biology in the Toronto School, who had come from Edinburgh. Ramsay Wright had recently arrived in Toronto to take this post, and he recalls that Osler, behaving like an old acquaintance, and stating that he had borrowed his brother Edmund's carriage for the purpose of driving out to see his old preceptor in Weston, asked if he would not go along. They found Johnson wearing cassock and cross, and living alone in the old rectory, for his wife before this had left him, to go and live with one of their sons. They shared a frugal meal prepared by Johnson and laid out on a plain deal table, beside which they sat on a pine board seat. But there was talk of natural history, particularly of animal parasites and of some of the entozoa they had found and observed but were unable to identify. One of these in particular, a trematode worm found in the gills of a newt, Professor Wright subsequently became sufficiently interested in to describe in full in his first paper published in Toronto. In view of the source of his primary introduction to Canadian helminthology at the time of this Christmas visit to Weston, he named this particular species *Sphyranura Osleri*.[2]

[1] Dr. F. J. Shepherd relates that in 1874 Osler examined both him and Ross for life insurance, he being rejected owing to a valvular lesion of the heart. Of the three he alone survives.

[2] R. Ramsay Wright: 'Contributions to American Helminthology', *Proceedings of the Canadian Institute*, new series, Vol. I, No. 1, 1879. *Sphyranura Osleri, nov. gen. et spec.* 'I have lately received [he wrote]

To F. J. Shepherd from W. O. No. 20 Radegonde St., Montreal, January 1st, 1875.

My dear Shepherd, I was so glad to get your note from Marburg. You did nicely to go to a small University town where English Students are scarce. One sees more of German life in that way & picks up the language in half the time. When do you go on to Wien? I shall call on your people this afternoon and find out where I am to address this letter. I am glad you saw Philpot in London: he is a first rate fellow & his introductions will be useful. The 'Riedhof' Restaurant you will no doubt patronize in Vienna. It is about the best and you are sure of meeting other English fellows there. When do you return? & are you going to settle in Montreal? There is a talk of the Dean resigning in the spring and of course there will be a vacancy in consequence. Or in any case there must be a vacancy before long and the Demonstratorship will be open. The question is: why should not you get it? Cameron of course will be in the field; but I am sure if a vacancy occurs in the spring & Chipman goes out of the Hospital leaving Cameron full Surgeon, there will be opposition to his holding both appointments; and you would have backers for the Demonstratorship among the Faculty. Remember this comes solely from me. I have heard no other opinions on the subject. I think however you would be wise in paying some attention to practical anatomy in Vienna and attend the lectures of Hyrtl's successor—whoever he is. The courses on operative surgery by Billroth's assistant are also splendid. I am working away at my lectures and so far have got on fairly well. Do you return by way of Paris? If so I would like you to execute a little commission for me there; and I may also trouble you to bring a few little things from Germany. I will send a list & place the dimes to your credit at—where? Bk. of Montreal here or London?

Yours very sincerely

Wm Osler.

Preparing for these formal old-time lectures, such as were expected of a teacher in the '70's, must have been a torment to him. The portfolio, ' tanned with exposure and chapped

from my friend Professor Osler, of Montreal, several specimens of a worm taken from the gills and cavity of the mouth of our common lake-lizard (*Necturus lateralis*, Raf.). These had been preserved for eight years in Goadby's fluid, and proved to be comparatively useless for further examination, having become quite opaque and black in colour. From some specimens, in a good state of preservation, mounted by Dr. Osler for microscopical examination, and also from his notes and sketches made on observation of the fresh specimen, I am able to communicate the following. The only specimen of Necturus which I have had the opportunity of examining since receiving these did not yield any of the worms . . .'

with rough handling', in which he carried them, holds to-day a few yellow, much-foxed sheets with the students' names, and this note written in a later hand:

This is my lecture portfolio with the list of students in the last class (1883–4) to which I lectured at McGill. The rule was to call the roll once a week, but as the list shows this was not always carried out. For the first few years I wrote out and read my lectures. I am sorry no copy has been kept for I destroyed them all on leaving Montreal. Then I got into the habit of lecturing from slips, two of which are here preserved, one on the skin and the other on glycogen.

To W. O. from W. A. Johnson. The Parsonage, Weston, March 4th, 1875.

My dear Osler,—I suppose you are getting to the close of a first term now & are getting a little breathing time. I never seem to forget you. . . . There are few, very few conditions in this world, in w[h] men may not, and do not jostle one another, cross one another's path, get into one another's way, so to speak. Friendships may be formed, but circumstances interfere with them. The nearer our calling or occupation or profession is alike, the more likely to cross one another. I always had, & have still the highest esteem for our mutual friend D[r] Bovell as a D[r] but I do not know how to address him as a Priest. With his medical opinions I could not differ; only do as he told me to: it is not so with religious opinions, there might be different opinions leading to different ends or doctrines, & demanding diverging or crossing courses of action. It is pleasant to have a friend in whose case these things can not occur. It is pleasant to feel that what your friend is doing, is right (for you can not even surmise it is wrong) & ask a blessing on it. This is the kind of spot left in my memory of yourself. . . . Are you working *especially* at any one point this winter? I look for a specimen or two: anything; it will be interesting, & always serve as a remembrancer. How is Jimmie doing? . . . He has twice or thrice mentioned, when sending an a/c of fees paid or unpaid, that you had given him his ticket; & intimated or said, it was not necessary to pay for it. I know your kindness would suggest this, but you are not indebted to me in any way to warrant such a deprivation. . . .

I suppose you must have noticed that, to all appearance, I did not do the kind thing to your dear Father & others on the Com[n] w[h] the Bp. [Bishop] appointed to find charges against me. Whether you thought so or not, there was good reason from all the *public* has seen, to think so. I was very peculiarly placed, and saw no way but irony to meet it. I am waiting the Bp's decision before writing a last letter, apologizing for seeming rude, & showing why that was the only course open to me. Two most important principles were assailed. I told the Bp. I dare not be a party to the proceedings. He tried to force me. I could not submit. I must meet the Com^{n} or my case would go by default: I could not appear or the principle was compromised: I could not touch the subject by way of evidence, or reason upon it, because it had not been heard: & having assured the Bp. he had no authority whatever to create the commission, irony was the only way to show I meant all I said, & defy further proceedings. I know irony & sarcasm drive away one's friends, therefore you had better never attempt to use them: but they have their time & place, & looking at it now with calm & unbiased view I still think I did well, & if the same causes arose would treat them as I did then. The private correspondence between the Bp. & myself is the only means of understanding the matter, but this shall never be made public with my consent alone. The poor Bp. whose kindness to me is unwearied and real, expressive of high praise also, is really in a 'tight' place. I have promised to *obey his orders* immediately & without a murmur, but neither to gainsay or accept his *opinions*. I have removed every obstacle to his decision that I know of, & I hope daily to receive it.

Is there any chance of your coming up this way after Easter? I suppose the smallpox hospital keeps you more or less busy; but the number of patients decreases a good deal towards spring & summer, so you might get away for a trip to see, & gladden old faces again. Everything much as usual here. I have not paid the Humber Ponds a single visit this winter, & now we are snowed in in every direction. With my best wishes for your success, health & happiness, & hoping to have a line, when you have time & inclination believe me, as ever Your sincere and affect^{e} friend,

W. A. Johnson.

It was a dictum of Southey's that 'a man's character can more surely be judged by those letters which his friends addressed to him than by those he himself penned, for they are apt to reveal with unconscious faithfulness the regard held for him by those who knew him best'. And there might be added to this statement—particularly if they were letters which the recipient saw fit to preserve. There need be no other excuse for the inclusion in this story of these several epistles from Johnson, much as one might prefer to see those passing in the other direction. They were among the few old letters found among Osler's papers, for it was not his habit to preserve correspondence. Poor Johnson! It was a needless warning to his favourite pupil that he should be a stranger to irony and sarcasm. Abandoned by his wife, it is said that Johnson never again locked the door of the rectory; but though a lonesome old man he did not live in the past alone, as this note by Miss Kathleen Lizars of Toronto indicates:

> When I was eleven and twelve years old I spent many week-ends with the Rev. Mr. Johnson. The picture of him is in my mind quite clearly, even across this space of time. Tall, spare, his hair brushed straight back in the style now affected by young men, austere and lovable in combination; always in his cassock, and the cross hanging unostentatiously, always with his house half full of people and most of them young. He often talked of his boys, but I did not take it in then what he meant. The school had gone long before I knew him. His ritualistic practices (very ordinary for nowadays) earned the enmity of the villagers—we were always awestruck at the signs of broken windows and marks of stones or hatchets on the altar.

On March 31st Osler gave the valedictory address to the graduating class at the annual convocation. It was his first effort in this direction, and though he probably agonized over it as most young men would under the circumstances, it shows little of the literary quality which gave the charm to his later addresses. They were often better in the material than in the manner of delivery, for he never possessed those oratorical gifts not uncommon among medical teachers which make possible the impressive presentation of material that proves to be shadowy in substance on later perusal. One finds in this brief address, nevertheless, many hints of the professional points of view he came to acquire. It is therefore an epitome of things he continued to dwell upon more and more emphatically as the years progressed. After pointing out that their training was incomplete, that they must be students always, since medicine, unlike law and theology, is a progressive science, he urges them to keep up with their reading, to cultivate books, to get in the habit of attending societies and reporting experiences, thus co-operating with the journals. He points out that behaviour is more certain to bring success than 'a string of diplomas'; quotes Sir Thomas Browne to the effect that 'No one should approach the temple of science with the soul of a money-changer'; touches on their obligations to the poor, on the question of livelihood, on the relationship between doctors, and ends with an appeal for sobriety, more needed happily by students of those days than of the present. Still a total abstainer himself, some of his more intimate young friends, men of the greatest promise in the profession, were already going to the ground, despite his personal efforts to help them, of which there are many stories.

At the end of the semester Osler was officially appointed to Dr. Drake's chair as Professor.[1] He had distinctly made good during his year as Lecturer. His industry, to which, as already told, he often referred as his single talent, was prodigious. He was not content merely with the mapping out of his new course and preparing the necessary lectures, a task arduous enough in itself. Having no hospital position and being eager for opportunities in the pathological laboratory, he volunteered for this work, and though it was the custom at the time for the visiting physicians and surgeons at the Montreal General to perform their own autopsies, they came more and more to lean upon Osler for this purpose, and it was inevitable that in time the position of Pathologist should be created for him.

Nor did he fail even in these early days to prod others. Some one once said in after years that it was always a pleasure to receive even a postcard from Osler, in spite of the drawback that it often suggested a lot of work. The following hint to Shepherd to send an open letter to Fenwick, who was editor of the local journal, has therefore what comes to be a familiar ring:

To F. J. Shepherd from W. O. April 6th, 1875.

My dear Shepherd,—I am delighted to be able to inform you that at a meeting of the Faculty last evening you were appointed Demonstrator of Anatomy, & allow me to offer you my sincere congratulations on the occasion. An official letter from Craik will either accompany or follow this, and containing also a recommendation to take advantage of the remaining time at your disposal to

---

[1] Dr. Maude Abbott relates that in 1908, when Sir William paid one of his periodical visits to the Pathological Museum at McGill, she showed him a heart among the specimens in the collection, in a jar which had lost its label, and asked if he could identify it. He made the enigmatical remark: 'If that heart had not petered out when it did, in all probability I would not be where I am now.' It was Drake's.

work up as far as possible the subject in its practical bearing, injecting, &c. I should think any of the Demonstrators at Wien would be only too glad for a 'consideration' to put you up to all the latest methods and old Hyrtl's museum would be worth going over carefully. Could you not send Fenwick a paper—or letter—on 'Anatomy at Vienna'. It would take well if you did. You are lucky in having had warning and time to prepare, & not taken short as I was. . . . I called at your house this morning to tell the news, but only found your sisters at home, & they as you may suppose were very glad to hear it. It seems to give very general satisfaction to all and no doubt it will to you for of course it is only a stepping stone to other appointments. I am going to pickle some brains for my own use this Summer & will try to get some for you also. It would come useful if you had a course on the Microscope as well & if you return to London by the end of June, Klein of the Brown Institution is the man to go to, but I dare say one of Brücke's assistants in Vienna has good courses always in progress. Have you seen Hyrtl's 'Handbuch der praktischen Zergliederungs Kunst'? Dr. Campbell has resigned the chair of Surgery but remains as Dean of the Faculty. Fenwick succeeds him and Roddick gets Clinical Surgery. The Dean still retains active connection with the school and will preside at meetings, &c. He goes home to Europe for next Winter. Browne has taken Ross's house (Craik's old one) & should do well at the corner. I do not know where to go; rooms are so difficult to get. . . .

Though Joseph Hyrtl was, and will always remain, one of the brilliant figures of medical history, and though his manual of dissection was a classic to put in a class with Virchow's post-mortem manual, it is nevertheless interesting at this early day to find Osler referring others to important books, even to those which did not happen to be in his special field. He not only read widely and voraciously, but had already started at this time a Journal Club for the purchase and distribution of periodicals to which he could ill afford to subscribe as an individual. Into this club were drawn Buller, Shepherd, Fenwick, Drake, Howard, Ross, Cline, MacDonnell, and Godfrey, each of whom 'chipped-in' ten dollars for the purchase particularly of the French and German journals. The first instalment was ordered on April 13, 1875, and Osler kept a list of their reception and distribution. Most of the excellent abstracts, contributed to the local medical journal of which Fenwick and Ross were editors, were doubtless supplied by the members of this club, the pen of the secretary-and-treasurer being probably the busiest.

These were happy though penurious days: for to teach physiology and histology, the subjects comprised by the 'Institutes of Medicine', as he thought they should be taught, meant drawing heavily on his small income. 'The students', as he subsequently wrote, 'paid fees directly to the instructors, who provided equipment and material and lived on the balance. I did more of the former and less of the latter. The supply of microscopes was meagre, and after remedying this defect there was little left in my pockets.' Indeed he had often to go to Palmer Howard to borrow cash to meet his day's expenses, and as he quaintly expressed it in later years: 'I suffered at that time from an acute attack of chronic impecuniosity.'

To F. J. Shepherd from W. O. No. 20 Radegonde St., May 28th [1875].

My dear Shepherd, Your letter came to hand yesterday. I can very well understand your hesitation in accepting the Demonstratorship for I have felt the same thing myself. You will get over that, and should too, for remember what advantages you have had and are having. You will come to your work better prepared than any Demonstrator McGill has had for many a year. When had Roddick dissected last on his accepting it? probably in his third year. I wish I was with you in Wien just now. Everybody says it is so enjoyable there in the spring months. I suppose you will bring a Hartnack microscope out with you when you come; it will be useful. Do you return by way of Paris? If so I wish you would call at his place No. 1 Rue Bonaparte and see what condition the Microscopes I have ordered are in. I ordered 12 & want them out before the session begins so that you may perhaps hurry him up a little. I want you to get me the Photos of the following men—that place in the Graben is the best. Hyrtl, Hebra, Bamberger, Skoda, Oppolzer —(dead but photo extant), Jäger, Billroth, Stricker, Rokitansky—(who is his successor, by the way? Is it Recklinghausen, if so one of his also)—one in any case, no matter who—Carl Braun, Brücke (2). Also a set of those cheap photos of the City (Cartes). Could you also get a Strickers *simple* warm stage. They are made by Kuntz, I believe, but Schenck could tell you about them. They are about 6–8 guelden. I want badly some back numbers of the Arch. für Heilk. but it will pay me better to go to Boston and consult them than buy the whole set. I have a number of cases of purpura in smallpox & am preparing a paper on the subject. Take a note of anything you may hear or see upon the subject. I may want a treatise or two, but if so will write you by next mail. I shall deposit some cash to your credit at your brothers office. We are getting a little nice weather at last, but things as yet are very backward. Browne is doing very well in his large house. Practice is dull—never has been brisk. O.C.E. is in much the same state, but unfortunately has not a College and Hospital to butter his bread. Your people have been very kind indeed to me. I was at Como on the 24th with your brother & spent a very pleasant day. Let me know when you are to be in London.

The twelve microscopes which he had ordered for his class were made possible, as will be seen, by a small salary which he was given for undertaking a disagreeable and, it may be added, a dangerous task. It was, however, an entering wedge to get clinical opportunities, which he promptly drove home. For it is evident from the letter of March 4th from Johnson, as well as from this one to Shepherd, that he was already at work in the smallpox wards, and it is characteristic of him that he immediately began to make profit out of the clinical and pathological material the position offered for purposes of publication. The Montreal General in the 1870's was a modest institution of only about 150 beds, ill-lighted and ill-ventilated. The mob-capped nurses were then of the Sarah Gamp type, who, as Dr. Shepherd recalls, were not strangers to the cup that more than cheers, and it was long before modern wards and the modern type of nurse came to supplant the old order. Attached to the hospital, with quarters worst of all, was an isolated smallpox ward, in which it was the custom, apparently, for members of the attending staff to serve successively for periods of three months. In this year of 1875 smallpox of a particularly malignant form was rife, and early in the year Osler's offer to take the service had been accepted, though at the time he was merely a volunteer worker in the dead-house, and not a member of the hospital staff.

Smallpox, at this period more or less epidemic everywhere, was particularly severe in most seaport towns. Vaccination was not compulsory, revaccination was rare, and quarantine most infrequent. There had been a succession of editorials and protests in the Montreal journals over the existing conditions; and the 'M. G. H.' had long made efforts to have revoked the existing law which obligated all hospitals receiving grants from the legislature to accept smallpox patients.[1] The contagion on several occasions had spread from the isolation ward to other parts of the hospital, with the forfeiture of the lives of people who had been admitted for minor complaints ; and finally, Peter Redpath, then President of the Hospital Board, made an appeal through the lay press in which he quoted from the Report of the Boston City Hospital to the effect that not a single case of smallpox had appeared in Boston during the preceding twelve months owing to their proper city care, whereas in the poorly segregated wards at the Montreal General Hospital there were always more than one hundred cases at a time.

It is quite possible that one influence which led Osler to volunteer for the position was his interest in skin diseases, which during his sojourn in London had been aroused by Tilbury Fox, for otherwise it certainly was not a service which he would have courted. However, it was his first chance to have hospital patients under his control, and we may imagine with what enthusiasm he went to work. His first publication from these wards was the report in July 1875 of a case of scarlatina which had appeared in a woman convalescing from smallpox, and at the end of the report he admits with frankness that he might possibly have conveyed the contagion himself.[2] If he had wished for an active service, as he probably did, he could not have struck a better time, for the epidemic, though not so severe as that of 1885–6, was at its height during this summer. In August another editorial appeared in the local journal, which stated : 'The smallpox wards of the Montreal General Hospital must be removed or else the hospital will be ruined as a general hospital.' And in September of this year there was an anti-vaccination riot, during which the house of one of the medical health officers was gutted. Meanwhile, undistracted by all this agitation, Osler was using his opportunities to the full, for the service put

[1] Cf. the *Canada Medical and Surgical Journal* for 1873–4.

[2] 'Case of Scarlatina Miliaris.' *Canada Medical and Surgical Journal*, July 1, 1875, iv. 49.

post-mortem material under his control, and from this source were drawn several of the reports, like that 'On the Pathology of Miner's Lung', presented during the subsequent months before the Medico-Chirurgical Society. This particular report [1] was an admirable article dealing with the experimental pathology of anthracosis, in which he became greatly interested, and for which he made the drawings accompanying the text. Other papers, of less moment, followed during the course of the year—on the pathology of smallpox; on the development of vaccine pustules—but more important were his two articles on the initial rashes and on the haemorrhagic form of smallpox, the most virulent type of the disease known since the beginning of the century. In this latter article he says:

> The epidemic which has raged in this city for the past five years has been remarkable for the prevalence of this variety of the disease; and the present paper is based on 27 cases, 14 of which came under my own observation, chiefly at the General Hospital, while the remaining 13 were under the care of my predecessor, Dr. Simpson, to whose kindness I am indebted for permission to utilize them. . . . In the smallpox department of the Montreal General Hospital there were admitted from Dec. 14, 1873, to July 21, 1875, one year and seven months, 260 cases. Of these 24 died of the variety under discussion, or 9·23 per cent.[2]

As an example not only of his kindness of heart but also of how strangely people's paths may cross in this world, a story of this period may be told. He had joined his first club this autumn of 1875, the Metropolitan, where he was accustomed to dine, and as he was often alone he occasionally sat with an attractive young Englishman who chanced to be in Montreal on business and who had been put up at the club. One evening, observing that he appeared ill, Osler questioned him, and suspicious of the symptoms, got him to his rooms and to bed, where it was soon evident that he had malignant smallpox. The disease proved fatal after an illness of three days, and having learned the young

[1] *Canada Medical and Surgical Journal*, 1876, iv. 145.

[2] 'Haemorrhagic Smallpox.' *Canada Medical and Surgical Journal*, Jan. 1877, v. 288, 301.

man's name and the address of his father in England, he wrote:

To Mr. N—— from W. O. 20 Radegonde St., Montreal.

My dear Sir,—No doubt before this, the sorrowful intelligence of your son's death has reached you, and now, when the first shock has perhaps to a slight extent passed away, some further particulars of his last illness may be satisfactory. On the evening of Thursday 22nd, & on the following day, I discovered unmistakable evidence of the nature of his disease. On Saturday in consultation with Dr. Howard—the leading practitioner of our city, his removal to the smallpox Hospital was decided upon. I secured a private ward & took him there in the evening.

Even at this date was seen the serious nature of the case, & I sent for Mr. Wood at his request. At 10 p.m. I found him with your son, & we left him tolerably comfortable for the night. He was easier on Sunday morning, but well aware of his dangerous state. He spoke to me of his home, & his mother, and asked me to read the 43rd chapter of Isaiah, which she had marked in his Bible. I spent the greater part of the morning talking and reading with him. Mr. Wood called in 3 or 4 times during the day, & at 9.30 p.m. I found him there again. Mr. Norman had also been in just previously. He was still sensible & requested to see Dr. Howard again, in consultation with Dr. Simpson, the attending Physician to the smallpox Hospital. After 11 o'clock he began to sink rapidly, & asked me not to leave him. He did not speak much, but turned round at intervals to see if I were still by him. About 12 o'clock I heard him muttering some prayers, but could not catch distinctly what they were—'God the Father, Son and Spirit.' Shortly after this he turned round and held out his hand, which I took, & he said quite plainly, 'Oh thanks'. These were the last words the poor fellow spoke. From 12.30 he was unconscious, and at 1.25 a.m. passed away, without a groan or struggle. As the son of a clergyman & knowing well what it is to be a 'stranger in a strange land' I performed the last office of Christian friendship I could, & read the Commendatory Prayer at his departure.

Such my dear sir, as briefly as I can give them are the facts relating to your son's death.

Thirty years almost to the day after this letter was written, the newly appointed Regius Professor of Medicine in Oxford chanced to meet at dinner a Lady S——, who, attracted by his name, said that she once had a young brother who had gone out to Montreal and been cared for during a fatal illness by a doctor named Osler, who had sent a sympathetic letter that had been the greatest possible solace to her parents: that her mother, who was still living in the south of England, had always hoped she might see and talk with the man who had written it. Later, on his way to Cornwall, Osler paid a visit to this bereaved mother, taking with him a photograph of her boy's grave, which he had sent to Montreal to obtain.

School had opened the first of October, with many changes in the Faculty, and the 'Introductory Remarks' of the newly appointed Professor of the Institutes of Medicine were duly published.[1] He said in part:

> . . . In this spirit [of reforms in medical teaching] the course you are about to begin has been inaugurated. An opportunity will henceforth be afforded to the students attending this School of becoming practically acquainted with the use of the microscope in physiology and pathology; and I may venture to congratulate McGill College as the first in this country to offer such a course, and in so doing to be the first to conform in all respects to the requirements of the College of Surgeons of England which demand that such shall be provided. . . . The first essential in a course like this is a proper supply of good microscopes, every student must be furnished with one to enable him to follow out the demonstrations with any degree of satisfaction. These have been obtained from Dr. Hartnack of Paris and Potsdam, and are the same as are in use in the chief laboratories of Europe. . . .

He concluded with the hope that the course, thus newly inaugurated, contained merely a promise of still better things—a properly equipped physiological laboratory to be under the superintendence of a well-trained assistant. One thing he failed to mention, namely from what windfall Dr. Hartnack of Paris and Potsdam was some day to receive payment for the instruments ordered the preceding April. Apparently in this same month Osler changed his rooms from Radegonde Street, opposite the old Haymarket, and moved up to 26 Beaver Hall Hill, where he took quarters from a man who from his looks was known on the streets as 'Don Quixote', but with whom he had some common interest, and of whom he has left this story:

> On leaving Berlin, December 1873, while ordering Virchow's *Archiv* at Reimers I saw on the desk the prospectus of Schmidt's Shakespeare-Lexicon, which I asked to be sent to me as soon as

[1] *Canada Medical and Surgical Journal*, Oct. 1875, iv. 202.

published. In October 1875 I moved from Victoria Square up Beaver Hall Hill to rooms with Mr. King an Englishman, employed in the Custom House, who had but one thought in life—Shakespeare. He had an excellent library in which I very often spent a pleasant hour. He was a dear old man, much esteemed, and always ready to spend more than he could afford on his hobby. One afternoon at the College, just before my lecture, the postman left on the table a parcel from Reimers and to my delight it was Schmidt's Concordance, which had really been forgotten. My first thought was: 'How happy Mr. King will be to see it.' I looked at it hurriedly, but with much anticipatory pleasure. On my return to the house, Mr. King who had just come in, was sitting by the fire and greeted me in his cheery way with: 'What 's that you've got?' 'Something that will rejoice your heart,' I said, and deposited the work in his lap. The shock of the realization of a life-long dream—a complete concordance of Shakespeare, seemed to daze the old man. He had no further interest in me and not a word did he say. I never again saw my Schmidt's Concordance! For months he avoided me, but helping him one day on the stairs, my manner showed that Schmidt was forgotten, and he never referred to it again. The work went to McGill College with his Shakespeare collection. When in the Library in 1912 I asked for the first edition of Schmidt and was glad to see my book again after nearly forty years. This story is written on the fly-leaf as a warning to bibliomaniacs! [1]

In October Father Johnson paid to Osler a long-deferred visit, which must have served to clear up some of his misgivings regarding his favourite pupil's supposed unorthodoxy. However, a subsequent letter to his son shows that Principal Dawson's views on life, past, present, and future, had at least been too much for him. He evidently stayed with the Francis cousins, at whose house Osler and his friends were constant visitors; and he appears to have carried home with him from Montreal one of the precious Hartnack microscopes.

From W. A. Johnson to W. O. The Parsonage, Weston, 19 Oct. 1875.

My dear Osler,—I enclose my cheque. My bad business habits made me delay longer than I ought. I find the instrument all I could wish. Have not adjusted the polarizing prism yet, but when Potter receives his consignment in all probability he will have one to imitate, & then I will send mine. My thoughts often return to you & your surroundings. I am very glad I went to Montreal. I enjoy a capa-

[1] Introduction to 'Bibliotheca Osleriana'.

bility of thinking of you all and understanding what you are doing, which I could not before. Moreover I added greatly to my friends. Your cousin Mrs. F. is a good soul: fortunate for you young man to have such a relation. 'Her hints shew meaning, her allusions care.' . . . Do, if you think of it some day, tell her how much I esteem her kind hospitality. I shall long remember it. I did not go to Montreal expecting acceptance of my person in any way. Accustomed to be looked upon as an extreme man such kindness confused me, rather than otherwise. It has taught me a lesson, which I am always practising, but have still been erring in (viz) not to judge of other people at all. Mr. Wood, too, I remember with much pleasure and can communicate freely with now if necessary. The scientific men also. Principal Dawson and Mr. Whiteve [?]. Could you not beg a bit of Eozoon Cana^e^ from him for me to grind. Might I venture to write him a line. I want to know about his sporangites, they are very curious. Your high power shews spines on them clearly. I want to know if he has written anything 'in re' & where. I am ashamed to trouble him and ashamed also to remain in ignorance. The specimens you gave me are quite a treat. They got home all right. If you are acquainted with a botanist in M. ask him to name the three ferns we found on the mountain, the small one, the middle sized (both left with Mrs F.) and the large one. You will be glad to hear I am much better of my trip. I was not well all summer before I went away. My love to Jimmie when you see him. Remember me most kindly & thankfully to Mrs F., & with best wishes for yourself spiritually & temporally, believe me,

Ever your very affectionate friend,
W. A. Johnson.

However much Johnson may have longed to get at Principal Dawson's sporangites, in a letter written a few days later to his son he expresses little regard for his writings, particularly his 'Earth and Man'. 'Doubtless he is a good geologist [he adds] and knows fossils, but his reasonings, particularly his religious interminglings, are worse than useless. It is to be lamented that all Geologists do not at once give up observations on Theology.' There was much more of this; but what is of greater importance just now is a fact mentioned in the letter, that his recent hostess, Mrs. Francis, had come down with a prolonged febrile attack. Of this illness Osler keeps her sister informed:

To Miss Jennette Osler from W. O. Tuesday.

Dear Janet, Marian continues but poorly, but nothing definite can yet be said of the nature of her illness. Fever is the chief symptom, though it has never yet been high. She is easier than she was & takes plenty of beef-tea and milk. Her spirits are good. If it is to be Typhoid it will in all likelihood be a very mild case. Howard is looking after her with me & tomorrow if any decision is arrived at & you are wanted I shall telegraph. The children keep well. Beelzebub is Beelzebub, and if for nothing else than to restrain his iniquities your presence would be acceptable. Gwyn is beginning to talk quite nicely and says 'Ope' 'Yes' and 'More', the latter word especially; the daughter of the horseleech could not have been more insatiable. I look after Marian at night, running up & down at intervals, & taking a nap on the chair or couch. She is a good patient and no trouble. . . . I hope you received my letter of Sunday. I should have written yesterday, but had a hard day and neglected it till too late. Love to all. Yours &c WILLIE.

The recipient of this note, Osler's favourite cousin, was not a person to hesitate on receiving such news, and on hearing that her sister Marian was really ill, and realizing that she could be of use, she packed up instanter and left Toronto to join the Francis household, where, as she adds, she stayed for the next sixteen years. She has given this note of W. O.'s relation to the household:

While we were living in Montreal Willie was a frequent visitor, especially during his later student years and his professorship. We were then living on McGill College Avenue and he would look in almost every afternoon for 5 o'clock tea with Marian and the baby and dowager baby—successively Brick, Willie, Gwen and Bea—this explains the interest and affection he has always shown for them—not so much for Brick who was always my special boy and who usually preferred to stay with me and the other elder children. He was like a breezy boy when not at work, would leap over the dining-table, dance, play tricks on the elder children, join in the rough-and-tumble pranks of the boys, sing, toss the babies (of which there was an unfailing supply) and pet and comfort the little girls and any small invalid. He was my dearest friend as well as cousin; we studied German together for a time, but the children left me little leisure or quiet and he very soon distanced me. He was the Well-beloved of the whole family and Willie F. adored him from his babyhood. He went regularly to church (St. John the Evangelist) and spoke of things religious with unfailing reverence.

Reference has been made to his interest in old people, but this was more than equalled by his devotion to children, with whom he had the rare gift of putting himself immediately on terms of intimate familiarity. On first acquaintance he would coin unforgettable nicknames for them : one with curly hair and another with wide-open eyes remained always as ' Bedsprings ' and ' Owl's Eyes '. He appreciated, too, a child's delight in repetition, so that vaulting the dining-room table at the Francis's was always demanded of him ; and his pranks with children, some of which became proverbial, will in time be referred to. But all his life he was a great hand to drop in upon people informally for brief visits—all too brief for their recipients. In an article written long afterwards, in which he had occasion to speak of the malady that affected his friend and colleague, George Ross, he says : ' As a young man in Montreal there were two doors I never passed—47 and 49 Union Avenue : going up I called on Dr. Palmer Howard, and if he was not in or was engaged I called on Dr. George Ross; going down, the reverse. Any growth in virtue as a practical clinician I owe to an intimate association with these two men, in whom were combined in rare measure enthusiasm and clear vision.'[1]

With his advent successively in Montreal, Philadelphia, Baltimore, and Oxford, a period of unusual activity of medical societies, of student gatherings, and of literary production immediately set in, largely from the example of his own whole-hearted participation and his unusual popularity. Soon after his return to Montreal in 1874 he had taken an active part in revivifying the old Medico-Chirurgical Society ; was immediately put on the Programme Committee with Roddick and Gardner ; and for the succeeding ten years was a regular attendant at the monthly meetings. Most of the clinical papers emanating from the Montreal General were first presented before this society, and there was hardly a meeting[2] in which he did not participate in some way or another. Until the time of his own appointment on the hospital staff, even the brief clinical papers, medical or surgical, written by others, were usually supplemented by a pathological note, ' By Dr. Wm. Osler ', describing the tissues—a note which often contained, it may be added, the only portion of the communication at all original. It was a new thing for the profession to

[1] *Canadian Medical Association Journal*, Oct. 1911, i. 919.

[2] Cf. records of these meetings in the *Canada Medical and Surgical Journal*, 1874–84.

have a histological pathologist in their midst. Easily enthused himself by every novel condition, he infected all others with whom he came in contact with something of the same spirit, and as he worked for work's sake alone and cared more for giving others credit than for what he might gain, his reputation spread widely, and soon went beyond his own community.

Another trait which had much to do with his development was his utter lack of Chauvinism. Though at this time there was much less inter-communication between men of different schools in different localities, he took an early opportunity to run down to Boston and to familiarize himself with its medical traditions. There he not only looked up all his old Vienna friends, but invaded the Boston Medical Library, then in its original humble quarters, where he found a hard-working librarian, Dr. Brigham, little accustomed to have this kind of sunshine invade his seclusion. The charm of the visitor was never forgotten, nor did Osler on his part fail, as will be seen, to remember this chance acquaintance in the years to follow. He must have paid a call also at this time on Henry I. Bowditch, the leader of the Boston profession, whom with reason he greatly admired. There remains a bound pamphlet in Osler's library (Bowditch's 'Consumption in New England', 1862) in which he has written: 'Henry I. Bowditch was one of the finest characters I have ever met in the profession, with the true fire. I valued his friendship highly. I met him in 1875, and he introduced me to his nephew H.P.B. who became one of my dearest friends.'[1]

But with all this, it must not be forgotten that he had been hard at work in the smallpox wards, supposedly an immune, for though repeatedly vaccinated he had never had a successful 'take', and it is evident that meanwhile he mingled freely with friends and relatives. It was in this month of December, as near as can be told, that he came down with the disease himself, and in years to come he always cited his own case to illustrate the fallacy of the 'non-take' belief as an evidence of immunity which prevailed at that time.

[1] Cf. foot-note, Vol. II, p. 133.

CHAPTER VII

1876–7

THE PATHOLOGIST

After prolonged agitation a community smallpox hospital was finally provided for Montreal early in 1876, and it is probable that Osler was the last to take charge of this dangerous service at the Montreal General. His own attack, contracted the preceding month, proved luckily to be a mild one, as shown by the following note to Arthur Jarvis, one of his old schoolmates:

Jan [1876].

My dear Arthur, I have just received your very kind letter and am happy to be able to write in return that I am completely convalescent. My attack was a wonderfully light one the pustules numbering sixteen, all told, and of these only two located themselves on my face; so that 'my beauty has not consumed away'. I have been out of Hospital now a week and am regaining my strength rapidly. The disease has been and is very bad. You need not be afraid of this letter. I will disinfect it before sending. Ever your aff. friend W. O.

The smallpox ward, nevertheless, not only had given him a chance to show his worth as a hospital attendant, but the remuneration of $600 for his services proved a boon which enabled him to meet the obligation entered into the preceding April—'In account with Hartnack, Paris. A batch of 15 microscopes. Net price frs. 2107.50.' His 1876 account-book shows a scarcity of entries: consultations, few and far between, and an occasional group of house visits are noted, with 'Howard laid up' written opposite them as an apologia. He was still in his small room on Beaver Hall Hill at a rent of $10 a month, boarding meanwhile elsewhere at another $20, with the occasional variation of a dinner with Arthur Browne at 'the Terrapin' on St. James Street. His income for the year, of $1178, including his professorial salary, tells its own story.

In February of this year he gave the Somerville Lecture before the Natural History Society, on 'Animal Parasites and their Relation to Public Health',[1] a topic which indicates two other sources of his activity in Montreal—his naturalistic and his public-health interests. This lecture also serves to illustrate his accumulative method of assembling material for the purpose of publication, for the subject of trichinosis on which he chiefly dwelt dates back, as has been seen, to notes and experiments made while a student in the dissecting-room in Toronto. In the 1873 note-book kept in Berlin, where he had seen a case in Traube's clinic, he had jotted down: 'So far as I can learn only four or five cases of Trichinosis have occurred in Canada, one in Montreal, three in Hamilton, and two cases in which I discovered the parasite post-mortem in Toronto. Others may and probably have occurred, but have been mistaken for something else.' The disease at this time was little known in spite of Owen's and of Paget's early descriptions of the parasite; and in his paper which he sent to Toronto for publication by his friend Zimmerman, then corresponding editor of the *Canadian Journal of Medical Science*, he reviewed the subject in general, gave his own experiences, and recorded the experiments he had performed in Toronto, to which reference has already been made.

He had been elected a member of the Natural History Society, on October 26, 1874, had been put on the Library Committee in the following May, and had just been chosen as a member of the Council. Moreover, it is apparent that at this time he looked upon his medical work more or less from the standpoint of a naturalist, with the microscope always ready at hand; and some younger members of the society soon formed a junior body of a combined scientific and social character—the Microscopical Club, whose meetings were held at the residences of the members in turn. Of this he was made the first President. The Natural History Society itself was an active body whose transactions and papers appeared in a quarterly journal of science, *The Canadian Naturalist*. Principal Dawson, as previously stated, was for some years its President, and though papers presented before it represented work in many different

[1] 'Trichina Spiralis.' *Canadian Journal of Medical Science*, 1876, i. 134 et seq.

fields into which natural science has since become greatly subdivided through specialization, there must nevertheless have been much to interest Osler, and it is probable that with regularity he attended the meetings. Though one might have thought that his early biological pursuits would have been superseded by this time, they continued to occupy some of his working hours throughout his Montreal period.

Though Osler's specimens treasured in the McGill Pathological Museum testify to his industry as a collector, it does not appear that he was particularly interested in the Museum of the Natural History Society itself, which Samuel Butler, who visited Montreal at this time, described in his famous 'Psalm of Montreal'. This place, indeed, one may assume to have been not unlike those in which most natural-history collections of the period were housed, Butler having found the custodian engaged in stuffing an owl in a room to which the Discobolus had been banished:

And I turned to the man of skins and said unto him, 'O thou man of skins,
Wherefore hast thou done thus to shame the beauty of the Discobolus?'
But the Lord had hardened the heart of the man of skins
And he answered, 'My brother-in-law is haberdasher to Mr. Spurgeon.'
O God! O Montreal!

'The Discobolus is put here because he is vulgar,
He has neither vest nor pants with which to cover his limbs;
I, Sir, am a person of most respectable connections—
My brother-in-law is haberdasher to Mr. Spurgeon.'
O God! O Montreal!

It had been a time-honoured custom at the Montreal General Hospital for each member of the medical staff to make the post-mortem examinations on his own patients, but on May 1st of this year a new position of Pathologist to the hospital was created, as far as can be judged, to make proper use of William Osler, and in the autopsy-room of that institution he laid the foundation of his subsequent brilliant career as a clinician. A three-months' summer session for students was offered this year, beginning the first of May, 'with opportunities afforded in the M. G. H. wards', and the prospectus, after stating that Ross, Roddick, Gardner, Buller, and Girdwood were to be the participants, goes on to say: 'And last, though not least, we have Dr. Osler who is an enthusiast in his department, who will give a course of twenty-five lessons in Practical Histology, and also a course of Practical Pathological Demonstrations in the post-mortem room.'

It was during this summer, therefore, that he began his more serious studies as a morbid anatomist, which were to continue almost without interruption for the next thirteen years—until he went to the Johns Hopkins. He had, of course, been greatly influenced by Howard, who fully realized the importance for the successful clinician of making his own post-mortem examinations; he had been still more influenced during his brief sojourn in Berlin by Virchow; and his familiarity with the microscope, unusual for the time, made him easily excel his fellows in modern methods, permitting the minute study of the processes of disease. But aside from all this, in unravelling the mysteries of a fatal malady he felt the same profound fascination that had kept Bichat, Laennec, and many other brilliant and industrious young men for years at the autopsy-table.

His industry became proverbial. Though he went through the form of dictating notes to student assistants in his course, when it came to completing the report it was set down in detail in his own hand. The three large quarto volumes in Montreal of these manuscript notes, with the cases numbered and fully indexed, remain a monument to his genius—his capacity for work. During the succeeding year, from May 1, 1876, to May 1, 1877, there were 100 autopsies, fully worked up. Many of the more interesting observations were from time to time reported at the meetings of the Medico-Chirurgical Society, and at the end of the year they were assembled and printed in book form, representing the first serious report of the kind from any hospital on the continent. Many of the more interesting specimens were preserved, and form the basis of the pathological collection in McGill, of which Dr. Maude Abbott has written so fully; and he came to know the material which passed through his hands during this and succeeding years so well that he constantly drew upon it for his later writings.

It is doubtful whether anything more than a great love of the work led him to study this material in such detail; he could hardly have realized until his later years that a long apprenticeship in the pathological laboratory always has been and always will be the only way to reach the very top either for surgeon or physician—the way followed by Addison, Bright, Stokes, Paget, Fitz, and a host of others. He had, moreover, the imaginative type of mind which made him prompt to grasp the problem laid bare by whatever he touched, and with this visualization came the desire to make some record thereof. It was this characteristic, handed on in goodly measure to his pupils, that made him (and them in turn) so prolific; and in the end, owing to his abundant and well chosen general reading, he acquired a literary style admirably suited to his purposes.

It is not surprising therefore to find him reading a book so unrelated to his subject as St. George Mivart's 'Lessons from Nature'. Apparently he lent his own copy of this book to Henry Howard,[1] and sent another to the Parsonage at Weston. Father Johnson in acknowledgement of its receipt sent off a long letter, dated September 2nd, in which he says that: 'After much effort (for I fear I am very obtuse) I have managed the two first chapters. I wanted to make myself master of them, but it has all ended in a conviction that there is something which fits in uncommonly with what I "feel" I cannot say "know" to be right.' That Mivart's book was making an impression is evident from a letter written a month later by Father Johnson to his son 'Jimmie', who having graduated from McGill in the spring, was now abroad and about to take the same dangerous step Osler had taken. The letter explains his misgivings, to put it mildly, regarding his former head prefect:

. . . *For my part* I am glad you went to London University, though it is manifestly & I believe most intentionally an *infidel* foundation.

---

[1] Cf. Henry Howard's 'Remarks on Haeckel, &c.' before the Medico-Chirurgical Society, Jan. 21, 1881. *Canada Medical and Surgical Journal*, Mar. 1881, ix. 153.

It was begun (I watched it), is continued, & is intended to prosper solely by man's ingenuity, knowledge & skill. Like the rods of the magicians before Moses it will do great things, but in the end will not succeed. . . . Suffice it to say if you go there you will find many excellent opportunities you can not find elsewhere most particularly *infidel* ideas. What would I give to be well versed in such ideas: but only to disprove them in other people. Probably it is a dangerous school for you my son. Unquestionably W. Osler shews it was so to him: but there is no good without its evil, 'no rose without a thorn'. When you know this much go, & go freely, only do not accept as *true* what seems on every side to be so. Would that you had time to read Mivarts 'Lessons from Nature' & you would say 'woe to Darwin Huxley & Co.' I must close. . . .

With the opening of the autumn term Osler's course in physiology was resumed, and he threw open to the class the privilege of attending autopsies at the Montreal General where his appointment now gave him a foothold. One of his students, Dr. Beaumont Small, has given these recollections of the methods he pursued:

His demonstration course in pathology was modelled upon that of Virchow in Berlin with whom he had recently worked. The course being optional and not yet in the curriculum it was nominally for his class in physiology, but many of the seniors took advantage of an opportunity that had been lacking in former years. This class met for an hour on Saturday mornings in his lecture-room in the college. His method was to select three or four of his class to perform the autopsies during the week in the Montreal General Hospital; from these autopsies a certain number of specimens were selected for the Saturday clinic. Before the class met, the specimens were all arranged on separate trays and carefully labelled. Each specimen in turn was carefully discussed and all the important points clearly indicated. At the close of each case, questions were asked for and answered, the whole being most informal and conversational. The facts elicited in the autopsies were carefully correlated with the clinical histories and notes of the cases as taken in the wards. In order that his teaching should be of the greatest value to those in attendance he furnished each one with a written description of each specimen, and with an epitome of the remarks which he had prepared. There were always four pages and at times eight pages of large letter size, written by himself and copied by means of a copying machine; there were from 30 to 40 copies required each Saturday, so that the demand such a task made on his time must have been heavy.

Meanwhile the 'Lessons from Nature' had been finished by Father Johnson, and if he had come to read the

'Genesis of Species' by the same author, one wonders whether his reaction after all would not have been the same as Huxley's.[1]

From W. A. Johnson to W. O. The Parsonage, Weston,
19. 10. 76.

My dear Osler,—At last I have got through Mivart. I have been strongly tempted to put other things aside to enjoy his thoughts. My first feeling now is thankfulness to you for thinking of me at all, then for the kind of book you selected, what it is & what it leads to & what it has done respecting my former ideas. . . . I must read his 'Genesis of Species' if I can find it some day. Everything I see attests to evolution in some sense, but surely not *chiefly* by natural selection. The last chapter I would rather had never been added. Mivart's reverence for the Church makes him claim too much for it, at least so it seems to me. I can believe that *devout unbiased monobibliological* students from St. Aug. to Suarez & to this day if they stated a formula of creation would be compelled so to word it as to include evolution: but I do not at present believe what Mivart seems to, that the Ch. is divinely appointed or called to formulate truth, & science is to work up to it. He may not mean this. I may misunderstand him; but it seems like it. Believing as I do, what I mean is that the book of Nature & the book of Revelation are alike God's books. . . . I do not want to deny him. He may be quite right; but it does not follow as I think Mivart tries to shew, that every formula enunciated by a Pope must be correct because the Pope is divinely appointed for that purpose. I wish that the last chapter had been left out.

---

[1] 'For Mr. Mivart, while twitting the generality of men of science with their ignorance of the real doctrines of his church, gave a reference to the Jesuit theologian Suarez, the latest great representative of scholasticism, as following St. Augustine in asserting, not direct, but derivative creation, that is to say, evolution from primordial matter endued with certain powers. Startled by this statement, Huxley investigated the works of the learned Jesuits and found not only that Mr. Mivart's reference to the Metaphysical Disputations was not to the point, but that in the "Tractatus de opere sex Dierum," Suarez expressly and emphatically rejects this doctrine and reprehends Augustine for asserting it. By great good luck (he [Huxley] writes to Darwin from St. Andrews) there is an excellent library here, with a good copy of Suarez, in a dozen big folios. Among these I dived, to the great astonishment of the librarian, and looking into them as "the careful robin eyes the delver's toil" (*vide Idylls*), I carried off the two venerable clasped volumes which were most promising. So I have come out in the new character of defender of Catholic orthodoxy, and upset Mivart out of the mouth of his own prophet.' ('Life and Letters of Thomas H. Huxley, by his son Leonard Huxley.' 1900, vol. i, p. 392.)

Do like a good fellow try to make my peace with kind Mrs Francis. I longed to be down and tried to get down to Montreal but really it was too expensive. . . . Everything flat & calm here, from the weather to the Village. If anyone is coming up send me something interesting for the microscope. I am all alone as usual but have an invaluable woman keeping house for me. Yours very affectionately,

W. A. Johnson.

A tell-tale of where Osler spent his Christmas holidays appears in an obituary note[1] concerning one of his old doctor friends who died a few months later. What others would regard as needlessly taking trouble he made into a pleasure, and a volume could be written on the subject alone of unexpected but cherished visits when he brought cheer and comfort to some physician who was in trouble or laid low by illness or advancing years. In a war-time address delivered more than forty years later he recalled the day, and the scene, and its lesson, for the benefit of the young Canadian medical officers—his hearers—as follows:

On Xmas afternoon, 1876, I walked up the Galt road along the north side of the valley, and at the summit of what we called the Mountain, turned into a beautiful oak grove, in the centre of which, overlooking the valley was a comfortable old frame house with a wide verandah. Here in an armchair, wrapped in his furs, was the Nestor of the profession of the district, Dr. James Hamilton, who through me as a conductor greets you across a century this evening. In 1818, fresh from Edinboro, he had settled in this district, at first at Ancaster and in 1820 in West Flamboro, on this beautiful site overlooking the valley. To the Grand River on the south and for twenty miles on either side of the lake extended the area of his practice. And he had had a singularly successful life, for he was a hard-headed, good-hearted Scot, equally careful of his patients and of his pockets. On the visits to my home, both as a student and a young doctor, I had been in the habit of calling on the dear old man—I have always loved old men!—and I enjoyed hearing his anecdotes about Edinboro in the palmy days of Monro secundus and of his early struggles as the pioneer practitioner of the place. This time I saw that he was hard hit, with the broad arrow on his forehead. He spoke pathetically of his recent losses, of which I had not heard, and quoted the well known verse beginning, 'Naked came I, &c.' The scene made an enduring impression. The veteran after sixty years of devoted work, beaten at last by a cruel fate. Call no man happy till he is dead! He had been an exceptionally prosperous

[1] *Canada Medical and Surgical Journal*, 1877, v. 478.

man. One of the founders of the Canada Life, Surgeon for years, and afterwards one of the Directors of the Great Western Railway. The savings of a lifetime had gone in *mills*! He died in March 1877.[1]

Whenever possible during all this time he made what progress he could with his zoological studies, and on January 29th his long-deferred paper on the 'Canadian Fresh-water Polyzoa' was read before the Natural History Society.[2] He refers therein, as already stated, to his researches with Johnson in 1867, and to those a year later when a student of botany with Professor Hincks at Trinity. He apparently had given the paper scant preparation, for the next day he wrote his cousin Jennette: 'I have been suffering from the dire effects of procrastination and in consequence have determined to eschew that vice forever and aye. I had a lecture to give on Entozoa at the Veterinary School on Saturday evening, which was not begun on Friday morning. Last night I read a paper on the Fresh-water Polyzoa at the Natural History Society, which was prepared—well, between Saturday evening and Monday at 7 p.m.' One might assume that he had already spread himself thin enough, but this letter to his cousin gives occasion to refer to still another contact he had made. It will be recalled that while in Toronto he was wont to visit veterinarians in connexion with his study and tabulation of animal parasites, and it is evident from the titles he first uses at this time ('Professor of Physiology in the Veterinary College, Montreal' and 'Vice-President of the Montreal Veterinary Medical Association') that his interest in comparative pathology was still sufficiently alive to have induced him to ally himself with this other school.[3] Accordingly on January 27th he had lectured at the

[1] 'The Future of the Medical Profession in Canada.' 1918 (unpublished).

[2] This paper for some unaccountable reason was not published till five years later in the *Canadian Naturalist*, 1883, x. 399–405.

[3] The veterinary students attended the lectures of Dawson on botany, Girdwood on chemistry, and Osler on the 'institutes'. Subsequently the Veterinary College, which had been purely a private venture, became officially a faculty of McGill and on Osler's suggestion was named 'The Faculty of Comparative Medicine'.

Montreal Veterinary College and was somewhat apologetic for his lack of preparation, though the subject was at his tongue's end.

Several papers on comparative pathology were published during the next few years. In the first of them,[1] read before the Veterinarian Association on March 29th, he described a form of bronchopneumonia in dogs due to a previously unknown parasitic nematode. This he incorrectly named, having mistaken its generic identity, and it was subsequently renamed by Cobbold in 1879 the *Filaria Osleri*.[2] He theorized regarding the mode of infection, and probably lack of time prevented him from subjecting his view to the experimental test. Of his other papers on comparative pathology, the more important dealt with hog cholera, echinococcus, bovine tuberculosis, and the parasites in the Montreal pork supply. Until his last days Osler kept in touch with Duncan McEachran, even though their lines of work greatly diverged; and it is perhaps noteworthy that only a year before his death he wrote a review of General Mennessier de la Lance's 'Essai de Bibliographie Hippique', a volume which had come to his attention. In the last paragraph of the article which appeared in the *London Veterinary Review*, he refers to the fact that he had been a 'former teacher in a Veterinary College' and therefore felt permitted to offer the author on behalf of the profession in Great Britain congratulations on the completion of his great work.

As in the preceding spring, so again this year he spent a week during the April recess in Boston, familiarizing himself with the Harvard Medical School, where, through

[1] 'Verminous Bronchitis in Dogs with Description of a New Parasite.' The *Veterinarian*, Lond., June 1877, i. 387. His introductory paragraph begins: 'Early in the month of January I was asked by Principal McEachran, F.R.C.V.S., to aid him in the investigation of a disease which had broken out among the pups at the kennels of the Montreal Hunt Club, and which was believed to be of a pneumonic nature.'

[2] Osler's original designation was *Strongylus canis bronchialis*, but the nematode has none of the characters of Strongylus. Indeed, despite Cobbold, it has so little in common with Filaria that recently a new genus, Oslerus, has been proposed for it. Cf. 'Two new Genera of Nematodes, &c.', Maurice C. Hall. *Proceedings of the U.S. National Museum, Washington*, 1921.

the influence of Charles Eliot in the face of strong opposition, sweeping changes in the matriculation requirements and in methods of teaching were under way in the effort to 'fix a standard of general education for the men who aspire to be her graduates'. He was accompanied this time by Ross and Shepherd, and they devoted themselves largely to a detailed study of the methods of instruction in vogue in the school. H. P. Bowditch's course in practical physiology, Wood's method of teaching chemistry, the course in pathology given by J. B. S. Jackson and his then assistant Fitz, a demonstration in surgical anatomy by David Cheever, sr., and a recitation in anatomy by O. W. Holmes were all attended and commented upon in an account of the visit subsequently written by Osler and published by his friend Zimmerman.[1] He concluded the account with the following paragraph, and it is not without portent that at this early age he had begun to show such an interest in medical education and to urge its improvement:

> It is a matter for surprise that some of the leading colleges in the United States have not followed the good example of Harvard. No doubt it would be accompanied for the first few years by a great falling off in the number of students, and consequent diminution in income, and this in many instances is avowedly the chief obstacle to so desirable a step. One or two of the smaller schools have adopted the graded system and I see by a recent American journal that the University of Pennsylvania has decided to pursue it, though in a modified and curtailed way. These are indications that the medical schools in the United States are being stirred up to some sense of the requirements and dignity of the profession they teach. It is high time. The fact that a Canadian student after completing his second winter session (not even passing his primary) can go to the University of Vermont, and I doubt not to many other institutions, spend ten weeks and graduate, speaks for itself and shows the need of a sweeping reform.

He must have been well aware, though he seems nowhere to have made written reference to the fact, that at this time elaborate plans were on foot for the establishment of a large hospital and medical school under the provisions of the Johns Hopkins Trust in Baltimore. Indeed two years before,

[1] 'The Harvard School of Medicine.' *Canada Journal of Medical Science*, Toronto, Aug. 1877, ii. 274.

an elaborate volume containing the plans and specifications of the buildings which were to be erected had already been published by John S. Billings, in which statements had been made to the effect that this future school was to aim at quality and not quantity, and that the 'seal of its diploma should be a guarantee that its possessor is not only a well-educated physician in the fullest sense of the word but that he has learned to think and investigate for himself, and is therefore prepared to undertake, without danger of failure from not knowing how to begin, the study of some of the many problems still awaiting solution'. Thus was a new note sounded which could hardly have failed to reach Montreal even had not this same Dr. Billings pursued the subject by many subsequent published notes and addresses which were so numerous and which were sent out so broadcast that many people during the next few years must have believed that the Johns Hopkins Medical School and Hospital were already in full operation.

We have seen that Osler, soon after becoming established in Montreal, started among his colleagues a Journal Club for the circulation of foreign periodicals, and it was in this spring of 1877 that through his influence the McGill Medical Society was organized for the special benefit of the undergraduate students. Both of these organizations were of the same type as those he so successfully supported later on in Baltimore. Of the students' society Dr. Beaumont Small has written:

> Its object, as defined by himself in his opening remarks at the first meeting on April 23, 1877, was to 'afford opportunities, which after graduating you never obtain, of learning how to prepare papers and to express your ideas correctly, while your meetings will also secure for you a training in the difficult science of debate'. Osler was its first President, but all the other officers were undergraduates and the whole proceedings were in the hands of the members. Osler, however, never missed a meeting; he joined in all discussions and customarily closed each meeting with a general review in which he combined much criticism and suggestion. A literary character was often imparted to the meetings by the reading of short selections from notable authors ranging from Shakespeare to Dickens.

During the summer session, up to July 17th, weekly meetings of this novel society were held and on the reopening of the school in the autumn they were resumed with a fortnightly interval. Indeed during the short summer session from May to July there were a number of supplementary and extra-curricular courses offered to the students which were entered into with vigour and enthusiasm by the younger members of the Faculty: one of them, Osler's special course on 'The Microscope in Medicine', which grew in later years into the regular prescribed course in clinical microscopy now adopted by all schools, was the most popular of all and the fee of $15 from each student doubtless added considerably to his meagre income.

A month's vacation later in the summer was passed at Tadousac at the mouth of the Saguenay, where he acted as the hotel physician, taking the place of Arthur Browne, who having served in this capacity the year before had expected until the last moment to return. The Governor-General, Lord Dufferin, had his summer residence there, and as the Government wished to have a dependable doctor near by, one or another of the younger McGill Faculty members volunteered for the position. The incumbent was given his board, picked up what practice he could in the summer colony, attended the Governor's family in case of need, and incidentally made pleasant acquaintances.

From W. O. to his cousin, Mrs. Francis. Friday, 9 a.m.

My dear Marian, I am rapidly getting too stout for my clothes and by the time my two weeks are out I expect to be of the build of a friend at—n.s.w. There is absolutely nothing to do here but loaf and eat and sleep. I have had no fishing yet but Robt. Shepherd is coming this evening and we will go up the Saguenay together trout-fishing. Yesterday morning was close & hot, but in the evening a cold fog came up, making such a change. Mrs. Ogilvie I find a pleasant little woman. I went for her last evening to the Urquharts who have a nice house here. Mrs. Howard and her bairns keep well, though little Muriel is rather cross & shy among the other children. Two very agreeable American girls—Bostonians—arrived yesterday and we have struck an acquaintance. One of them in particular is very jolly. I had to lie, in my usual accomplished style, when she asked me if she spoke like an American. I replied unblushingly that her accent was rather like the Midland counties, and delightfully English. The 'vurries' betray her, more than anything else. The only patient I have had was a poor French child with inf. of lungs following whooping cough—which is very prevalent among the natives. There are not many people at the Hotel. Monsig. Conroy [?] arrived last night creating quite a sensation in the village. It turns out that the Rev. Mr. Higginson—Lord Dufferin's Tutor, was curate at West Flamboro some 18 years ago. He saw my name in the book and called. I have a faint recollection of him. I have got one or two nice things for the Microscope, but there are not many animals about. The water is fearfully cold. I made up my mind for a dip this a.m. but the tide was out too far. I wish you and Jack were here & the other chickabids. It is such a nice place for children. . . . Love to Jennette & the chicks. Your affec coz

WILLIE

On the memory of an American girl whose 'vurries' betrayed her is left a lively recollection of a young man of rare charm and gaiety, which however is not particularly apparent in a rather devout note which she has tenderly preserved, and which announces the sending of a little volume to recall the pleasant memories of Tadousac, which 'should have been sent before, but there has been an unavoidable delay in getting a copy, as our "Proper Lessons" differ from those in use in the Protestant Episcopal Church in the United States'.

The annual meeting of the Canadian Medical Association was held this year in Montreal, September 12th–13th, and as Chairman of the Committee of Arrangements he had much on his hands. Nevertheless he took an active part in its proceedings, gave the report on necrology, participated in a paper on Addison's disease with George Ross, in another with John Bell on pernicious anaemia, and responded at the dinner to the toast of the local profession. With the view of assuring an annual report of the society's activities, he provoked a discussion which had the customary sequel of such a suggestion, for he was promptly appointed Secretary of a Publication Committee and in this capacity edited the volume of 'Transactions' which appeared the following year. As in most thankless tasks of this kind, things get done in direct ratio to the activity of the Secretary, which in this case amounted to being Chairman as well, and on Osler's withdrawal the next year the 'Transactions' promptly lapsed. He had likewise been appointed Registrar of the McGill School, and in this capacity, on October 1st at the opening of the session of 1877–8, he delivered before the assembled students the customary 'Introductory Lecture'.[1] It was a serious and somewhat laboured effort and, for him, a long address; for to each class of students in turn he must needs explain the several changes which had been made in the curriculum with their purport and the advantages to be derived. He bade them banish the future and live for the hour and its allotted work, quoting again his favourite line from Carlyle.

In this autumn of 1877 he abandoned his bookish landlord, the Shakespearian Mr. King, and moved into the second-floor front room at 1351 St. Catherine Street, in the house occupied by his colleague, Dr. Frank Buller, who had established himself in the ophthalmological practice to which Osler had once aspired. They were soon joined by two students. The first of them, E. J. A. Rogers, had been a Weston schoolmate of Osler's ten years before, and had made this late resolution to study medicine. He has written an engaging description, not only of Osler's recognition and reception of him after the delivery of his introductory lecture, but also of his own personal feelings, a mixture of 'resolute curiosity and suppressed horror' in being made to participate immediately afterwards at an autopsy:

Leaving the hospital we walked back to his rooms, which I was told were from that time on to be my headquarters. He was living with Dr. Buller in an ordinary built-in city house with a front and back room on each of three floors, the back parlour on the first floor being Buller's consulting-room, the front room a waiting-room, used in the morning as a breakfast-room. The second-floor front room was Osler's; the other rooms were used as bedrooms. Osler said I was to become the third member of the family. Buller acted more deliberately, and it was some little time before these latter rooms were rearranged and I was given the third-floor front as my bedroom and study. Here, until I left Montreal after my graduation, I lived all through my studentship.

Osler never did anything by halves. From those who were willing and ready to work with him his demands were unlimited, but for this he more than repaid in the opportunities and good-fellowship that he returned. I thus had every opportunity for the most intimate knowledge of all his mental and physical activities. Soon I found that through his whole-heartedness his friends had become my friends, but not, of course, through any virtue of mine: his pleasures

---

[1] *Canada Medical and Surgical Journal*, 1877, vi. 204–10.

and joys he shared with all those about him, talking freely of all that he had on hand, for in his ebullient enthusiasm he was still a schoolboy. In his course of life he was more regular and systematic than words can tell; in fact, it was hardly necessary, living in the house with him, to have a timepiece of one's own. One could tell the time exactly by his movements from the hour of his rising at seven-thirty until he turned out his light at eleven o'clock after an hour in bed devoted to the reading of non-medical classics.

His cheerfulness and equanimity were surprising. He never lost an opportunity of saying a word of cheerful encouragement. Nothing ruffled his wonderful temper. We three had breakfast together at eight o'clock. The only impatience I can recollect his ever showing was when the housekeeper was a little tardy in putting our breakfast on the table. . . .[1]

This 'housekeeper', it may be interpolated, was an elderly Englishwoman named Cook whose husband was a labourer of sorts. The janitor of the medical school, who as curator of the dissecting-room came closely in contact with the medical students, was also named Cook. This Cook a few years later disappeared through natural causes or otherwise, and Osler as Registrar of the school promptly substituted the other Cook—nicknamed 'Damphino' Cook by the students—in his stead. He, and his wife who had been housekeeper at the St. Catherine Street abode, became well-known characters at McGill for the next two decades, and they did much to perpetuate Oslerian traditions among the successive generations of medical students. All medical schools appear to have 'trusties' of this kind, who more often than not are characters of real merit and wield actual power, of which Cook's familiar reference to 'Me and the Dean' was significant.

Dr. Rogers has written further regarding Osler's room and habits:

He used the upstairs front room as his study, library, sitting-room and consultation room. Here he did practically all of his reading and writing. The desk, a flat office one, stood in the middle of the room and he sat with his back towards the two windows in front. The desk and the floor about it and also an occasional chair or stand were always piled in apparent confusion with books and papers. It was his habit to bring in volumes from the library and elsewhere for

---

1 'Personal Reminiscences of the Earlier Years of Sir William Osler.' *Colorado Medicine*, April 1920.

reference upon the subject at which he was working and they usually remained convenient until the subject was disposed of. The college library at that time had a considerable number of current books and many bound volumes of old journals and he had taken complete charge of it all.

This room was not arranged for, or inviting to, patients; indeed very few patients ever came to it. He had little desire that they should come, for he seemed to have no inclination to take charge of any patient. He at that time occasionally saw patients outside in consultation with Dr. Howard and other physicians, but always as a consultant. He had no desire for a private practice and was amply satisfied for the time being with his income through the college.

Patients were a secondary consideration. A consulting practice could wait, and when access to him was finally forced as in the later days in Baltimore, they came in such shoals as finally to drive him away. But he was certainly having enough to do, so much indeed as to make a necessity of the regular habits which his house-mate Rogers has pictured. Registrar of the school; pathologist to the hospital; on the Council of the Natural History Society; participating in the clinical reports of many of his colleagues by adding a pathological note usually the most important feature of the conjoint paper; writing papers of his own; the activating spirit of the Medico-Chirurgical Society; translating foreign medical articles for Fenwick's journal; editing the *Transactions of the Canadian Medical Association*; preparing for his elaborate pathological report; and with all this he not only kept up with his studies on the polyzoa but, as Dr. Rogers has stated, acted as voluntary Librarian for the medical school, as an advertisement of the time in the *McGill University Gazette* indicates.[1]

---

[1] As Osler from this time until his death continued to be actively interested in one or more libraries besides his own this advertisement from the *McGill University Gazette*, 1877, lii. 49, deserves quoting. It reads as follows: 'A circular has been issued by the Graduates' Society calling attention to the smallness of the library fund, and requesting subscriptions from graduates, for the purpose of increasing the revenue of this most important adjunct to an Institution like McGill. The annual revenue of the library is now, the circular states, about $600, and with the exception of the Redpath and Alexander collections, the books are of a miscellaneous character. We sincerely trust that the appeal of the Society will meet with a generous response from all interested in the college. It would not be

But Osler was far from being a literary and laboratory recluse, and at the proper time was as ready for play and relaxation as any other. One opportunity for diversion was at the gatherings of the Dinner Club which has been mentioned. He always took a more or less detached and non-gastronomic interest in the various dining clubs to which he belonged, and many years later he scribbled in pencil on the blank leaves of the publisher's 'dummy' of some collected addresses a list of his several 'Clubs and Dining Clubs' to which is appended this note:

Though not a Club man in the usual sense of the term, many of my happiest recollections are associated with Clubs. Not a drinker, not a billiard player, and slow to make friends, the Club served as an hotel. In '74–'76 I dined (usually with Arthur Browne) at the *Terrapin*, St. James' Street or at the Ottawa Hotel; afterwards I joined the Metropolitan Club in Beaver Hall and dined there for five or six years. We had a social club of twelve—Ross, Roddick, Rodger, Gardner, Alloway, Buller, Browne, Blackader, Pettigrew, Molson, and Shepherd—and dined once a month through the winter. There are Apician memories like those of the old surveyor in the introduction to the Scarlet Letter—mine, I confess, rarely last from one day to another. The calendar of my life is not rubricated with dinners, the sweet savour of which returns to tickle my third ventricle. Indeed only two do so with faithful regularity whenever I see anything specially tempting, as currant dumplings or an old-fashioned suet pudding. One Saturday morning in the mid sixties a long, lank parson arrived at the Rectory and announced to father, the Rural Dean of the district, that he had come as Incumbent of Watertown which he thought was a couple of miles away. In reality it was twelve or fourteen and I had to 'hitch up' the buggy and take him to the village. It was in the spring, the roads were awful, it was cold and raining, and he was a hungry Evangelical who persisted in bothering me about my soul. At that stage of boyhood I had not acquired a soul, and I was scared by the very unpleasant questions he asked. I had never had anyone attack me in this way before, and my parents were not the type of Xtian that could worry a growing boy with such problems. I was in

---

a bad idea to have every future graduate pledge himself to subscribe fifty or one hundred dollars, within four or five years after graduation, to the library fund. Almost every one could afford such a sum, and though inconsiderable when viewed separately, the contributions would make a handsome total. Let the Class of '77, which has inaugurated so many reforms in colleges, take the lead in this matter! Graduates who have not received the circular may obtain copies by addressing Dr. Osler, 26 Beaver Hall Hill, Montreal.

despair as he had reached the stage of wishing to pray for me when I saw a wayside tavern—clapboard, desolate-looking, but it had the cheery sign—I see it now—*John Rieman: Accommodation for Man and Beast.* It was half-past two and with the sensations of that hour much intensified. A nice warm kitchen, and in less than 15 minutes a meal fit for the gods!—ham and eggs, a big loaf of home-made bread—hot!—a pat of butter and a pot of green tea. The parson had a change of heart. The frying-pan was still on the stove, and the kitchen was still hazy with the ambrosial atmosphere. We could not resist the offer of more eggs. After more than 50 years stomach and brain combine to remember *that* as the very best dinner in their record. I delivered the Incumbent to his churchwardens and to my great relief was not billeted that night in the same house.

The other occasion recurs neither so often nor so acutely. One day Dr. Buller with whom I lived in St. Catherine Street said: 'I am not going to have an ordinary dinner at the Club—we shall have an oyster supper here instead.' It was the middle of November and the faithful Cook—remembered as 'me and the Dean' by three generations of McGill medical students—was sent to the dock for three barrels of Caraquet oysters, which in those happy days sold at about $1 (4*s.*) a barrel—

Here the note abruptly ends. One could wish he had continued, but the memory of the occasion may have overcome him, for this particular club-meeting is recorded as having been a rarely festive affair. The note will serve to explain, to those who knew Osler at the table, his sentimental devotion to currant dumplings and a stodgy suet pudding, on the appearance of which he invariably burst into a Gregorian chant of exultation, keeping as nearly on the key as his unmusical ear permitted. It is perhaps worth noting that servants always adored him, nor did he ever forget them: so it was to the last, and to this day the servants at Christ Church and the Oxford Museum speak of him with moist eyes but with a smile on their lips. His cousin Jennette of the letters—the 'little Auntie' of the Francis children—writes:

My remembrance of him as a student and a young professor is of one gifted with abounding vitality; hard-working for the love of work; prompt, alert, always cheery and always kind; thinking no evil of anyone and refusing to listen to ill-natured gossip and censoriousness. Of self-conceit or boastfulness he had not a trace; he thought for others and seemed to forget himself. The servants would gladly do anything possible for him; he had the happy knack of friendliness to rich and poor, young and old, learned and ignorant; and what he was in character as a boy and young man he continued to be throughout his life: an out-giving, expressing nature, sympathetic and true.

The volume of pathological reports[1] representing his first year's work as Pathologist to the 'M. G. H.' up to May 1, 1877, was apparently completed for the press on December 10, 1877—at least his preface is so dated from 1351 St. Catherine Street. The bulk of the report had appeared serially during the course of the year in the local journal,[2] and a large number of the more important observations and rare cases had been reported before the Medico-Chirurgical Society or at some other meeting, in conjunction with the clinician who had the case in charge.[3] On the title-page he quotes Wilks's statement: 'Pathology is the basis of all true instruction in practical medicine'; and the volume bore this dedication:

To my Teacher
James Bovell M.D.
Emeritus Professor in Pathology in the Toronto Medical School
This first pathological report from a
Canadian Hospital
is gratefully and affectionately dedicated.

---

1 'Montreal General Hospital Pathological Reports.' Montreal, Dawson Bros., 1878, 97 pp.

2 *Canada Medical and Surgical Journal*, July 1877, vi. 12 et seq.

3 It is largely due to this fact that such an amazing number of titles appear for the years 1877 and 1878 in Miss M. W. Blogg's enlarged 'Bibliography' of his writings, issued in Baltimore 1921. A bibliographer is interested chiefly in dates and places of publication, whereas a biographer's concern lies with the purpose of the writing, the date and place of preparation, and delivery (a bio-bibliography); and during 1877 there were no less than forty-nine entries on this basis in his bibliography. It is impossible to give more than a general idea regarding the character of most of these contributions. Their chief value, as is true of the writings of most young men, lay in the personal training which the author received thereby, and throughout the rest of his life he continued to draw upon, and to make reference to, his pathological observations of these early years. Some of the studies were unquestionably important, and some of the observations original, but he was a person who always took the greatest pains to point out priority of observation on the part of others and rarely if ever made any claim in this respect for himself. The more important of the studies were doubtless those upon the anaemias, those upon aneurysms, and those on endocarditis and valvular diseases of the heart. These three topics were ones which he subsequently developed and wrote upon in detail.

While at home for the Christmas holidays he paid his usual visit to Father Johnson, who was in somewhat broken health owing to an infection received during a smallpox epidemic in Weston. Johnson, missing Bovell greatly, had written earlier in the year :

. . . you observe about my Lenten Services. They were more than I can manage again. The additional work in consequence of not having a Dr to attend to small-pox cases made it necessary for me to be on the go incessantly, so many saying 'we will not keep you a moment, but do call & tell us if so & so has small-pox,' & of course everyone thought they had it. I am still overdone but getting well, and all you Drs could say of me is, Oh, he is tough, he will be well if he rests awhile, but somehow that rest awhile does not come. I am netted up, or webbed up with these poor people, & they are my children in some sense, & without knowing it they depend upon me for more than they know, & my constant habit of being found in the Vestry leads more and more to come to me about some trifle or other. The absence of a medical man with a little common sense & fellow feeling increases my work too. There is nothing noticeable hereabout. Prices high, war prospects increasing. An occasional cracked skull from too much whiskey, & on the other hand some one failing for want of a little. It is hard to hit the happy medium. . . .

CHAPTER VIII

1878–80

PHYSICIAN TO THE MONTREAL GENERAL

On January 23rd, before the Pathological Society in New York, Osler presented the results of one of his more important studies in the domain of comparative pathology.[1] He had chanced to hit upon a most baffling epidemic disease affecting hogs, knowledge of which at the time was most meagre and for that matter still remains so, for it appears to be one of those infectious disorders due to what is called a filterable virus, that is, an organism too small for microscopic observation. A trained microscopist, a keen observer and ardent pathologist, had Osler undertaken as Pasteur did just at this time (1877) the study of a simpler disease such as anthrax, the causative agent of which even unstained is easily seen in the blood when examined under the microscope, he might in all possibility have been led to make equally important discoveries. But he had come under Bastian's rather than Pasteur's influence: he never really became an adept in bacteriological technique; and, by the time Pasteur's views had become accepted, had moved on to other fields than experimental medicine and comparative pathology—fields moreover which engrossed him completely.

Pasteur had written to Bastian in July 1877: 'Do you know why I desire so much to fight and conquer you? It is because you are one of the principal adepts of a medical doctrine which I believe to be fatal to progress in the art of healing—the doctrine of the spontaneity of all diseases.' Naturally enough the younger generation sat back and watched the tilting of these giants, and, until Tyndall entered the lists on Pasteur's side and finally Lister, English-trained youths were naturally imbued with the ideas of spontaneous generation, as Osler seems to have been when he saw the blood platelets apparently transform into bacteria.

1 'On the Pathology of so-called Pig Typhoid.' *Veterinary Journal and Annals of Comparative Pathology*, Lond., 1878, vi. 385. Instead of his actual title, viz. 'Professor of the Institutes of Medicine', he gives 'Professor of Physiology and Pathology in McGill University and the Veterinary College, Montreal.'

This particular epidemic among hogs, which Osler undertook to study, had originally been regarded as a form of anthrax, though latterly the view prevailed that it was the counterpart in hogs of typhoid fever in man, the bacterial origin of which was of course as yet unknown. 'Having in the course of my reading become acquainted with this unsettled state of the matter,' Osler wrote, 'I gladly at Principal McEachran's suggestion investigated a local epizoöty which had broken out near Quebec in a drove of 300 hogs, hoping that by a series of independent observations the truth of one or the other of these views might be confirmed.' And in the course of his inquiry he not only studied the post-mortem appearances of the disease, but performed a few successful experiments by transfer inoculation, drawing the conclusion that the disease bore no relation to typhoid or anthrax, but that it was dysenteric in character though without parallel in human dysentery—a view sustained to-day, the term 'hog cholera' having been substituted for 'pig-typhoid'.

At this time he was still on the council which arranged for the meetings of the Natural History Society, and on February 25th under the auspices of the Microscopical Club a students' meeting was held at which he demonstrated the newer methods of microscopical illumination—a further evidence of his persistence in emphasizing the importance of the microscope in the study of disease, though this instrument unfortunately had not helped him greatly in his studies of hog cholera. However, it was well suited for investigations of the blood. So among the many pathological specimens exhibited during the spring was one on May 18th before the McGill students' society whose weekly meetings he continued to sponsor—a section of bone from a case of pernicious anaemia with the marrow showing nucleated red-blood corpuscles.[1]

[1] His studies of this case formed the basis of one of his more important contributions to the subject of the blood and concerned its formation from the bone marrow. It was subsequently published *in extenso* in German (*Centralblatt f. d. med. Wissenschaften*, Berlin, June 29, 1878, xvi. 465), and was widely commented upon. (Cf. editorial, *Lancet*, Lond., Aug. 3, 1878, ii. 162.)

He had been engaged during the early spring campaigning for a clinical appointment in succession to Dr. Drake at the Montreal General—and in his account-book there occurs a long list of names and addresses of people whose support he might count upon, for this is the custom when applicants seek positions in British or in Canadian institutions. It was a distasteful procedure—this solicitation of testimonials—and it is little wonder that thirty years later, on his call to Edinburgh, he flatly refused to repeat the process, contrary to all precedent. The Board must have felt sure of their man, for it was an appointment which not only required vision but a certain degree of courage, qualities in which trustees are sometimes wanting. In the first place he was thoroughly identified as a laboratory worker in physiology and pathology, though, to be sure, with pronounced clinical interests and capabilities as shown during his period in the smallpox ward. Moreover, like many other pathologists, he was so imbued with the futility of most of the drugs in common use that later on he came to be termed a therapeutic nihilist ; and fifty years ago one holding such views was far less likely to be regarded as a suitable candidate for a clinical position. Furthermore, he had not gone through the usual apprenticeship as physician to out-patients as some of the rival candidates had done. But outweighing all this, what must have influenced the Board of Governors was a petition from the students, who, having taken part in the campaign, Edinburgh-fashion, warmly favoured his candidacy. Long afterwards in his address at St. Bartholomew's Hospital in 1914 he reminisced as follows concerning this period :

> Four years in the post-mortem room of the general hospital, with clinical work during the smallpox epidemic, seemed to warrant the Governors of the general hospital in appointing me, in 1878, full physician, over the heads—it seems scandalous to me now—of the assistant physicians. The day of the election I left (with my friend George Ross) for London to take my Membership of the College of Physicians and to work at clinical medicine. For three months we had a delightful experience. Murchison, whom I had seen before in 1873, was most kind and I do not think we missed one of his hospital visits. He was a model bedside teacher—so clear in his expositions, so thorough and painstaking with the students. My

old friend Luther Holden introduced us to Gee, in whom were combined the spirit of Hippocrates and the method of Sydenham. Fred. Roberts at University College Hospital showed us how physical diagnosis could be taught. We rarely missed a visit with Bastian and Ringer, and at Queen Square I began a long friendship with that brilliant ornament of British Medicine, Gowers. With my old comrade Stephen Mackenzie we went to Sutton's Sunday-morning class at the London—his 'Sunday School' as it was called—and we learned to have deep respect for his clinical and pathological skill. I mention these trivial details to indicate that before beginning work as clinic teacher I had at least seen some of the best men of the day.[1]

The object of the trip, as he explains, was primarily to pass his M.R.C.P. examination, and incidentally he wished to brush up on his clinical work before assuming his new position in the autumn. This 'quinquennial brain-dusting' became a habit with him and in later years similar visits had no little influence in keeping him always in the front rank. They visited Edinburgh, where the new Royal Infirmary was just approaching completion, and they felt while there that what had come to be called 'Listerism' was not making great headway even in this northern metropolis. They attended the *conversazione* of the Royal College of Physicians, and heard Burdon Sanderson's Harveian Oration (June 26th) in which he urged young men to devote themselves to research despite the promise of no immediate reward. It was at this time that Osler first made acquaintance with two of his lifelong friends, Seymour J. Sharkey and George Savage. Sharkey had just returned from a long period of study on the Continent and, having been appointed Resident Assistant Physician at St. Thomas's Hospital, the position gave him practical control of the wards during the summer months. On finding in Sharkey a physician of their own kind, Osler and Ross took full advantage of this opportunity.

It was in '78 when Osler was studying in London, that I first made his acquaintance [writes Sir George Savage]. I was then Physician to Bethlem Royal Hospital, and I had classes for post-graduates and for other members of the profession who were not

---

[1] An address on 'The Medical Clinic, &c.' *British Medical Journal*, 1914, i. 10.

ordinary medical students: in fact I used to have men belonging to various professions. I used to have literary men and actors as well as doctors, who came to study what might be called the psychological side to mental disorders. Among them was Osler. I admit I did not at that time appreciate the strong individuality of the man, yet I was drawn to him at once. We also were members of the Savile Club, which was and is a London centre for scientific and literary men. At this club there was a regular table d'hôte and men talked freely to their casual neighbours and associates. There was a constant literary give-and-take which suited Osler very well. The talks in the smoking-room after dinner were eminently interesting and very far-ranging. Osler did not pretend to make any special study of mental disorder, but in after-life he used to chaffingly say that from my clinics he learned all that he knew on the subject, and that in Canada he got a reputation which he did not deserve. Then, as ever, he was bright and friendly with anyone and I never heard of a man who spoke ill or unkindly of him. Years passed and we kept up occasional correspondence, but I never found Osler to be what might be called a good general letter-writer: he would in a few words convey his meaning and did not give way to sentiment. He was, in some respects, rather like Gladstone in that he communicated his wishes or his intentions by means of postcard. . . .

Osler himself mentioned the Savile Club in connexion with the malady that carried off his dear friend Ross, the premonitory symptoms of which first showed themselves at this time;[1] and to another incident of this summer's visit in London, he referred in an address many years after when portraying the two types of students—the owl and the lark; he himself throughout his life managed to keep a very happy mean between these two extremes, though he does not say so:

One day, going with George Ross through Bedlam, Dr. Savage, at that time the physician in charge, remarked upon two great groups of patients—those who were depressed in the morning and those who were cheerful; and he suggested that the spirits rose and

[1] 'Transient Attacks of Aphasia and Paralyses in States of High Blood Pressure and Arteriosclerosis.' *Canadian Medical Association Journal*, Oct. 1911, i. 919. It was Osler's first experience with the condition which came to be called Cerebral Angiospasm, and though Dr. George Peabody was the first to call attention to the condition in a formal paper on the subject, Osler describes it in all the editions of his Text-book; and in a letter of November 17, 1912, to the *Lancet*, Lond., says: 'My knowledge of transient aphasia and monoplegia in arteriosclerosis dated from the early '80's when a dear friend and colleague had scores of attacks.'

fell with the bodily temperature—those with very low morning temperatures were depressed, and vice versa. This, I believe, expresses a truth which may explain the extraordinary difference in the habits of students in this matter of the time at which the best work can be done. Outside of the asylum there are also the two great types, the student-lark who loves to see the sun rise, who comes to breakfast with a cheerful morning face, never so 'fit' as at 6 a.m. We all know the type. What a contrast to the student-owl with his saturnine morning face, thoroughly unhappy, cheated by the wretched breakfast-bell of the two best hours of the day for sleep; no appetite, and permeated with an unspeakable hostility to his vis-à-vis, whose morning garrulity and good humour are equally offensive. Only gradually, as the day wears on and his temperature rises does he become endurable to himself and to others. But see him really awake at 10 p.m.! While the plethoric lark is in hopeless coma over his books, from which it is hard to rouse him sufficiently to get his boots off for bed, our lean owl-friend, Saturn no longer in the ascendant, with bright eyes and cheery face, is ready for four hours of anything you wish—deep study, or 'Heart affluence in discursive talk', and by 2 a.m. he will undertake to unsphere the spirit of Plato. In neither a virtue, in neither a fault; we must recognize these two types of students, differently constituted owing possibly —though I have but little evidence for the belief—to thermal peculiarities.[1]

They attended the meeting of the British Medical Association, held this year at Bath, August 6th–9th, where possibly Osler first encountered Grainger Stewart, Jonathan Hutchinson, Clifford Allbutt, Gairdner, and William Broadbent, who were coming to be the outstanding figures in British medicine and who subsequently became his staunch friends. An account of the proceedings, forwarded by Ross for publication in Fenwick's journal, of which he was soon to become co-editor, was dated August 12th from Paris, where they must also have gone for a short time, possibly to attend the first International Congress of Hygiene, held there during the summer. It was the year, as may be recalled, of the yellow-fever epidemic in the States and Osler's public-health activities in Montreal must have made him deeply interested. They did not get back to Canada until too late in September to attend the annual meeting of the 'Canadian Medical' held in Hamilton earlier

[1] 'The Student Life', in 'Aequanimitas, &c.', 2nd ed., 1906.

in the month. Osler was still a member of the Publication Committee, and despite his labours of the previous year in editing the Transactions, no one, in his absence, had sufficient influence to win support for their continuance; nor did his attempt to revive the project by a circularized letter calling upon the 'co-operation of every intelligent practitioner' bring in enough voluntary subscribers to justify further publication.

His position as Registrar of the Medical School necessitated his being early on his job; and though a time-consuming duty it brought him in contact with the entire student body, and his unusual memory for names and faces specially qualified him for the post. Fortunate the school that could have such a one the first to meet its candidates for admission, and there is hardly a McGill student of the day who does not vividly recall his first interview. Dr. William M. Donald writes:

When I, a raw stripling, marched into his office to register in my Freshman year, he greeted my answer to his query regarding my residence with the question: 'What has become of Ephraim ——?' naming a student who lived in a small village in Ontario, which was my home. I replied that he was not coming back to college, and that unfortunately he had fallen into evil ways, and was drinking somewhat heavily. Immediately he retorted: 'Ah, Ephraim is joined to his idols.' I smiled, remembering my reading of the prophet Hosea, and came back at him with the quotation from the Second Epistle of Peter: 'The dog has returned to his vomit and the sow that was washed, to her wallowing in the mire.' Osler smiled and replied: 'Good Scripture, Donald, but rough Anglo-Saxon.' I always felt that there was a somewhat closer bond between us after this on account of our mutual knowledge of the Book of Books.

Another student of the day has written:

. . . There was, too, a most engaging lightness and aliveness about him, and a friendliness that we undergraduates rather took for granted, not realizing at the time how virtually unique it was, in sincerity, helpfulness and lastingness. His very walk, 'light-hearted, spring-heeled' (that 's R.L.S., isn't it?) showed both the temperament and the youth. One often met him walking with books or papers under his arm, and with him, generally foreshadowed in a smile, came the greeting, always cheery and always the right one for the occasion, the place and the persons. This was entirely instinctive and yet so noticeable that more than once it provoked the remark that he was 'among us but not of us'. Beyond that no one in Montreal, at least no one of us students in medicine, ever had so much as a glimpse of W. O.'s bright and shining place in the future medical world.

In his introductory lecture to the students on the re-opening of the school, October 1st,[1] William Gardner made the following statement:

I have to announce to you that this Faculty congratulate themselves on a most important step they have taken, in providing the means for the practical teaching of an all-important subject. For some years the Faculty have contemplated establishing a Physiological Laboratory. To-day I am proud to announce to you that that Laboratory is an accomplished fact. Under the able direction of my friend Prof. Osler we expect that this very laboratory shall be the scene of many original researches by present and future students of McGill in the unexplored fields of physiology.

Despite this 'important step' which for the first time gave the budding Department of Physiology an opportunity for development, it was not as an experimental biologist that Osler's particular bent showed itself. Of this he made repeated confessions in years to follow. But it was quite another matter when he came to enter the hospital wards as an attending physician, as he did this autumn. His belief that over-treatment with drugs was one of the medical errors of the day has been hinted at, and it was always one of his favourite axioms that no one individual had done more good to the medical profession than Hahnemann, whose therapeutic methods had demonstrated that the natural tendency of disease was toward recovery, provided that the patient was decently cared for, properly nursed, and not over-dosed. This, it is true, had been emphasized among others by Jacob Bigelow in his essay, remarkable for the time (1835), on 'Self-limited Disease'; but it was

---

[1] On this same date Osler was giving the opening lecture before the students of the Montreal Veterinary College under the title, 'Comparative Pathology', a report of his remarks *in extenso* being given in the *Veterinary Journal*, Lond., 1878, vii. 405. After defining pathology as the physiology and microscopical anatomy of disease, he referred to the Contagious Diseases (animals) Act of 1878 as unjust to the cattle trade and warmly advocated inspection as a protection against hog cholera, Texas fever, and so on.

the therapeutic cult of homoeopathy, contrary to its intent, that had given the actual proof. Dr. Rogers thus speaks of Osler's advent as physician in the 'M. G. H.':

When therefore his time came to take charge of a section of the hospital, older doctors looked on with bated breath, expecting disastrous consequences. He began by clearing up his ward completely. All the unnecessary semblances of sickness and treatment were removed; it was turned from a sick-room into a bright, cheerful room of repose. Then he started in with his patients. Very little medicine was given. To the astonishment of everyone, the chronic beds, instead of being emptied by disaster were emptied rapidly through recovery; under his stimulating and encouraging influence the old cases nearly all disappeared, the new cases stayed but a short time. The revolution was wonderful. It was one of the most forceful lessons in treatment that had ever been demonstrated. . . .

During this autumn, winter, and spring, the usual succession of brief reports before the Medico-Chirurgical Society continued. There are eighteen separate titles given in the full bibliography of the period, which would seem to represent more presentations than could have been thoroughly prepared for; but his painstaking methods are sufficiently well illustrated by the report upon two examples of rare kidney tumour,[1] as an appendix to which he gave a long translation on the subject of tumours from Cohnheim's celebrated 'Vorlesungen über allgemeine Pathologie' which had just appeared (1877). So one may easily dog the trail of what Osler called his inkpot career. He was the activating spirit of the 'Medico-Chi.', and should any one wish to know how his contemporaries felt towards him, the remarks made by Henry Howard, the distinguished Canadian alienist and criminologist, on retiring as President for the year, may be consulted. For Osler, in Hunterian fashion and with an enthusiasm which was infectious, appears to have given demonstrations on topics as diverse as 'Giacomini's Method of Preserving the Brain' and 'The Heart of the Swordfish with an Explanation of the Comparative Anatomy of its Circulation'.

During all this time, lest James Bovell be forgotten, there are letters to his namesake which show not only that Father

[1] *Journal of Anatomy and Physiology*, Lond., Jan. 1880, xiv. 229.

Johnson is far from well ' because of the poison inhaled from that unfortunate small pox ', but also that the church is not occupying Bovell's attention to the exclusion of medicine.

I am a most miserable recluse [he wrote], and rarely see any but the members of my own family. I am not idle but have collected a good deal towards a little Class Book on Germs in relation to Disease. But I am kept back from want of a high objective. I had just written to Beck about his 1/20th when your letter comes. Becks is $85 so I felt quite dispirited. Have a talk with Fred, and see if he can squeeze out 65 for Spencers Professional 1/4 which must be a wonderful Glass. I am very poor it is true, but my goodness anything to relieve this cruel monotony. As soon as the Manuscript is ready I will send it with Drawings and most of the Specimens. You see my clothing is Brian O'Lyng's, ' for I have no breeches to wear ' and altho' I am obliged to Knock under to Granny and let her keep the purse I do hope somehow to contrive to get the 1/4 out of saved clothes. We have had a terrible time of it.

Bovell had become enthusiastic over the new views regarding the bacterial causation of infectious diseases, and from another of his letters it is evident that he had actually observed anthrax bacilli in the organs of animals affected with ' cattle plague '. He could hardly have known of Robert Koch's epochal paper of the year before, identifying the bacilli as the cause of the disease, but he writes to Arthur Jukes Johnson : ' Go quietly to work and without letting anybody know what you are doing examine the blood in every case of fever and pyaemia and also the matter adhering to the ligatures when you draw them out. You must get at least a 1/16th or a 1/20th Hartnack. Don't sink into a hum-drum sort of life.' Such was James Bovell, ' kept back from want of a high objective '.

From May to July of this year Osler had his first taste of instructing students at the bedside in the wards of the Montreal General ; and during the next five years his teaching-time was divided between the prescribed courses in physiology and pathology during the winter session, and clinical medicine in the summer.

We worked together [he subsequently wrote [1]] through Gee's ' Auscultation and Percussion ', and in the ward visit, physical-

[1] ' The Medical Clinic ; a Retrospect and a Forecast.' *British Medical Journal*, Jan. 3, 1914.

diagnosis exercises, and in a clinical microscopy class the greater part of the morning was spent. I came across the other day the clinical note-book I had prepared for the students, with a motto from Froude, ' the knowledge which a man can use is the only real knowledge, the only knowledge which has life and growth in it, and converts itself into practical power. The rest hangs like dust about the brain, or dries like raindrops off the stones.'

In August, Ross and Molson took over from Fenwick the editorship of the *Canada Medical and Surgical Journal*, in which so many of Osler's brief papers during these past years had been published, and he soon sent to them an account of the meeting of the American Association for the Advancement of Science held on August 27th at Saratoga.[1] This he had attended in view of a circular letter issued by the General Secretary to the effect that a subsection of Physiology and Anatomy would be established at the meeting, and he must have foregathered with his future Baltimore colleague Remsen, as well as Michelson and C. S. Minot. He speaks also of Edison as the ' bogie of gas companies ', and says that Edison told him in conversation that ' he believed it would be possible to illumine the interior of the body by passing a small electric burner into the stomach '. It appears that after this meeting Osler paid his first visit to Beede's, the famous Adirondack camp of his Boston friends, H. P. Bowditch, Charles and James Putnam, and William James, who ' had adapted the little story-and-a-half dwelling to their own purposes and converted its surrounding sheds and pens into habitable shanties of the simplest kind. So they established a sort of camp, with the mountains for their climbing, the brook to bathe in, and the primeval forest fragrant about them.' [2]

The annual meeting of the Canadian Medical Association held in London, Ontario, soon followed, and there he made a report for the Publication Committee in regard to the second volume of Transactions, stating that the Association evidently was not sufficiently advanced to justify the continuance of the effort. The project, therefore, was abandoned, but with Mullin and Sloan he was appointed

[1] *Canada Medical and Surgical Journal*, Sept. 1879, viii. 63.
[2] ' The Letters of William James.' Boston, 1920.

to a committee to look into the Association's financial affairs, a post for which he was far less well fitted. The minutes of the meeting state that: 'On the morning of September 11th, Dr. Osler of Montreal gave a description of the anatomy of the brain, illustrating his remarks by specimens preserved by Giacomini's new process.' This Giacomini whose methods he had adopted, a most extraordinary man, was Professor of Anatomy at Turin, where in his laboratory he literally lived, died, and was buried, in the midst of an amazing collection of brains. One of his paramount interests was in cerebral topography, and being a colleague of the famous criminologist Lombroso [1] it was natural that he should have made a special study of the brains of criminals, an occupation in which Osler likewise became engaged, as will appear.

There followed a visit to Hamilton, where he saw for the last time his old Barrie school friend 'Charlie' Locke, for Locke died the next spring,[2] leaving scant funds for his family to live upon, like many another doctor; and the burden of the education of his three children was subsequently assumed by Osler, who put one of them through the medical school. Then Dundas, Toronto, and Weston for the extensive round of visits it was his habit to make on all old acquaintances; and particularly when there were children in the house one may be sure that there was a frolic with considerable disarrangement of the nursery. The pictures would have their faces to the wall, or a pillow-fight would be promptly organized and in brief time an untidy but happy child would be abruptly left with its delighted but hysterical nurse. Dr. Adam Wright relates that Osler called at his house one morning, and finding Mrs. Wright telephoning the butcher, took the instrument from her and most violently but amusingly berated the surprised person at the other end for sending such an outrageously tough steak the day before.

Another student, on Osler's appeal, was added this autumn to the establishment at 1351 St. Catherine Street.

[1] Lombroso's 'L'Uomo delinquente' had been recently published, 1876.

[2] 'Charles F. A. Locke, M.D., C.M.' Obituary notice by W. O. *Canada Medical and Surgical Journal*, 1880, viii. 379.

Henry V. Ogden, a Southerner whose parents had gone to Canada after the Civil War, had been at Bishop's College School at Lennoxville near the lakes Magog and Memphremagog in Southern Quebec. He was a tall youth, therefore with schoolboy quickness of wit called 'Og, Rex Basan', and there was a school jingle concerning 'Og, Gog, and Memphremagog' which might mystify boys less familiar with the Scriptures than those attending a church school. As a first-year student in medicine, Ogden had been attending Osler's lectures, and on learning from Rogers that he was living in a forlorn boarding-house in a cheap part of the town, Buller was persuaded by Osler to have him taken in.

... I can, and do [writes Ogden], see him perfectly as he came up to my room on the third floor of 1351 St. Catherine Street, the second or third night after I moved in. I happened to be sitting up in bed reading at physiology. He broke out at once in praise of the habit of reading in bed, but heartily disapproved the physiology —only literature, never medicine. He walked across the room standing with his back to me, his hands in his trousers' pockets, tilting up and down on his toes, and inspecting the little collection of about twenty or thirty books I had ranged on two small hanging shelves; and taking down the 'Golden Treasury' came over, sat on the foot of the bed, and half-recited, half-read, interjecting a running comment, a number of the poems. Then tossing the book to me he said: 'You'll find that much better stuff than physiology for reading in bed.' That same evening, too, he spoke of Sir Thomas Browne and the 'Religio', and probably for the first time, for I don't remember his making any reference to the subject in the lectures at the college. His enthusiasm rose as he spoke, and running downstairs he brought up his copy, pointed out and read several passages and then left me. . . .

The whole incident—W. O.'s coming up to my room, I mean—made a tremendous impression, for I had never before met a professor who struck one as so completely human, who actually liked some of the same things you did, and above all talked about them with you as an elder equal, so to speak. As you can imagine, it started my relations with him on a pleasant footing and in a pleasant direction, and naturally I have blessed my friend Rogers a thousand times for getting me into 1351.

The three upstairs tenants breakfasted with Dr. Buller, familiarly known as the 'Landlord', but otherwise they lived a life apart—a young professor and two students who became friends and intimates. Incidentally the students were used by the professor from time to time for his own dire purposes, and Ogden one day was sent to perform an autopsy on a horse that had died from some mysterious nervous ailment. It necessitated the removal ' intact and in one piece ' of the animal's brain and spinal cord, a difficult enough procedure even for one more experienced, and it took Ogden nearly all day. Not knowing how to dispose of the trophy, it being late afternoon, he took it home and proudly laid it out full-length in the family bath-tub, where it unfortunately was first discovered by Buller, who was furiously angry. Osler luckily came in in time to save from harm both specimen and student, and pacified the ' landlord ' by agreeing to take the first bath.

In his reminiscences Dr. Rogers has stated that ' Osler's charity reached everyone in whom he could find some measure of sincerity and application ' ; that ' he had the greatest contempt for the doctor who made financial gain the first object of his work ' ; and ' even seemed to go as far as to think that a man could not make more than a bare living and still be an honest and competent physician '. His student house-mates remember only three consultations in his office, which indeed was hardly suited for this purpose, being usually littered with untidy evidence of literary activity. One of these consultations, however, was such an important one that preparations had to be made for it and Ogden was requisitioned as an assistant, for the patient was none other than old Peter Redpath, the wealthy Montreal sugar-refiner, who being on the ' M. G. H.' Board had hopes that the newly appointed physician might be able to cure him of an intractable lumbago. He arrived exhausted after mounting the stairs, and in due course they proceeded to treat him by acupuncture, a popular procedure of the day, which consists in thrusting a long needle into the muscles of the small of the back. At each jab the old gentleman is said to have ripped out a string of oaths, and in the end got up and hobbled out, no better of his pain, this to Osler's great distress, for he had expected to give him immediate relief which, as he said, ' meant a million for McGill '.

The first glimmering of Osler's subsequent deep interest

in matters relating to medical history and biography dates from this time, in connexion with an aged French-Canadian, a one-time *voyageur* in the service of the American Fur Company who had been accidentally wounded in the side by the discharge of a musket on the 6th of June 1822 at Michilimacinac. This accident and its consequences, and the fact that the victim came under the care of William Beaumont, a United States Army surgeon stationed at the time in this frontier post, led to the most important contributions to the physiology of digestion made during the century. Fifty-seven years had elapsed, but, according to a note in the *Montreal Medical Journal* for August of this year, Alexis St. Martin, father of twenty children, still with the hole in his stomach, was living at St. Thomas, Joliette County, Province of Quebec. It is not improbable that this note may have been inserted by Osler himself, for it was his invariable custom to tell the story of Beaumont and St. Martin when taking up the subject of digestion in his course in physiology. After doing so he usually asked the class where St. Martin's stomach should finally be deposited. A student of the time recalls that, in his year, some one shouted: 'The McGill Museum!' Osler said: 'No'. Another then volunteered, 'Ottawa', and again, 'No', when a third suggested, 'The Hunterian Museum'; whereupon Osler said: 'Can't you use your heads? The United States Army Museum in Washington, of course', and at this juncture a red-headed Irish student asked 'Why?'

This had gone on with successive classes for a number of years and it became generally known that Osler expected to hold a post-mortem examination after old St. Martin's demise. So in this spring of 1880 Ogden was told that he might have to go out to Joliette County at a minute's notice, for it was learned that St. Martin's end was near. Knowledge of Osler's intent had reached the community, which had apparently been aroused in opposition, and on the day of St. Martin's death a warning telegram came from the local doctor, saying: 'Don't come for autopsy; will be killed', and this was followed by the announcement that the grave was being guarded every night by French Canadians armed with rifles; but it was a great disappointment to Osler, who 'had offered to pay a fair sum in case the relatives would agree to deposit the stomach in the Army Medical Museum in Washington '.[1]

During this academic year of 1879–80 he had prevailed upon his colleagues at the Montreal General to issue a volume of Clinical Reports, of which he was the voluntary editor. Though customary in British hospitals, this was the first publication of the kind to be issued from a Canadian institution,[2] and its perusal shows that he was not only the prime mover but the chief contributor; for two of the sixteen original papers were written by him, his name appears as participant in several of the others,[3] and the volume also contains a long detailed account of his second series of autopsies. These were subsequently extracted from the volume and separately published as his 'Pathological Report No. II', which contains a preliminary note stating that it 'comprises a selection from 225 post-mortems performed between October 1877 and October 1879'. Though he credits the students with much of the labour, as a matter of fact the actual autopsy records were written out in long-hand in detail by himself, possibly from the notes given to the students as bare memoranda. In the printed report, however, the autopsy note is invariably preceded by a brief account of the patient's condition during life. Many of the cases of more particular interest had from time to time been presented at one of the meetings of the 'Medico-Chi.' Society, and for this purpose probably put into some sort

[1] Osler's own brief account of the episode was given in his well-known address, 'William Beaumont. A pioneer American Physiologist', before the St. Louis Medical Society in 1902. Cf. p. 590.

[2] 'Montreal General Hospital: Reports Clinical and Pathological. Ed. by William Osler, M.D., M.R.C.P., Lond.' Montreal, Dawson Bros., 1880, 369 pp.

[3] Thus R. P. Howard, who has the leading article, an important one on 'Cases of Leucocythaemia', states in his preamble that: 'An additional gratification is derived from the reflection that several contributions to the condition of the bone medulla in pernicious anaemia have been made within the last two years by my friend Professor Osler of this city, and it is owing to his ability, industry, and zeal, that the writer of this paper is in a condition to record the histological conditions of the bone-marrow and blood in the following examples of that interesting and obscure affection, leucocythaemia.'

of shape for ultimate publication, but the mere transcription of such a record as this in the days before the typewriter shows a prodigious energy.

During this academic year also, in addition to his physiological course, his pathological demonstrations, his hospital duties, and these two large Reports, he had published five papers in conjunction with his colleagues, three original independent papers, seven in conjunction with his students, and before the 'Medico-Chi.' had exhibited and recorded at the successive meetings which he invariably attended, thirty-five different specimens of sufficient rarity in most cases to justify their preservation in the McGill Museum of Pathology.[1] There was one noteworthy thing about Osler's career as a pathologist, both in Montreal and Philadelphia, vividly recalled and commented upon by many who then stood as students at his elbow. This was his frankness over his own diagnostic errors, for if anything was disclosed which had been overlooked or misinterpreted he particularly dwelt upon it and called every one to see. Then as regards the mistakes of others he had none of the sly delight which many pathologists have evidenced in 'showing-up' at the autopsy table the opinions of their clinical colleagues. A remarkable story is told, indeed, of how, to spare a surgeon's feelings, he concealed the truth regarding a bad operative error. When this incident was recalled by some one in his presence many years later, Osler hesitated and then said: 'He never asked me for a definite written report. In fact, no one but you and I ever knew of the unfortunate circumstance—and we have both forgotten it.'

But with all this serious attention to his real work in life, it must not be forgotten that Osler was always ready for a frolic and was fond of a jest, whether at his own expense

[1] It had been Osler's intention to issue a third volume of these Reports, as subsequent notes will show. Though he was never actually appointed Pathologist (so it is stated) at the 'M.G.H.', his official successors in the position were in turn Wyatt Johnston, John McCrae the soldier-poet, B. D. Gillies, C. W. Duval, S. B. Wolbach, and Lawrence J. Rhea. In 1895 Wyatt Johnston issued a third volume of Reports consisting largely of a bare statistical study. He states that since Osler's day there had been fifteen complete changes of management in the laboratory.

or at that of another. In 1880, shortly after Ross and Molson had taken over from Fenwick the *Canada Medical and Surgical Journal*, there appeared on the scene a creature named Egerton Yorrick Davis, soon recognized as a pathological fabricator of ill repute, whose name became coupled with that of William Osler. Among the manuscripts preserved in the Osler library there are eight sheets of note-paper containing an article which starts off as follows :

Professional Notes among the Indian Tribes
about Gt. Slave Lake, N.W.T.
by
Egerton Y. Davis, M.D. Late U. S. Army Surgeon.

The following notes may be of interest to the readers of your local journal, though bearing as much upon social as upon medical subjects. They are the outcome of many years' intercourse among the natives in the above-mentioned locality. . . .

The article, purporting to deal with some ancient tribal rites observed by the Indians of the Northwest and written in a pseudo-serious and somewhat Rabelaisian vein, had been mailed to the journal office during the absence from town of Ross, the senior editor, and soon after Molson's appointment as co-editor. Accepted by Molson as an authentic communication, it was forwarded to the Gazette Printing Company to be set up for publication. This printing office used to be frequented by Osler, who scribbled across the manuscript on its being returned with the galley-proof to the journal office : 'Joke on Molson. W. O.' Molson had his revenge a year later.

This man E. Y. Davis, who was first heard of at Fort Desolation in the Great Slave Lake district and subsequently moved down to Caughnawauga, a hamlet across the river from Montreal, had an interesting and somewhat varied life ; and so far as is known he was the only one of Osler's early Montreal acquaintances who in later years he deliberately endeavoured to avoid. There are many stories about him, some of them probably apocryphal, and from time to time he had a way of unexpectedly bobbing up without proper introduction, to the mystification of the uninitiated.

Doctors as a class are notably gregarious, but perhaps none

of his kind were ever more faithful in their attendance upon medical meetings, local or national, general or special, than Osler. To follow his footsteps ere long inevitably leads to one somewhere, and this June he was found in New York for the annual session of the American Medical Association. He wrote an open letter, for Ross to publish, describing the occasion for the benefit of his Canadian colleagues not in the habit of attending American—scarcely their own—society meetings; and though it is hardly in his best vein he mentions the registration of 800 members, then regarded as phenomenal, and also the organization under Abraham Jacobi's leadership of a new Section to deal with the diseases of children.

After the close of the summer session, August was passed in an excursion for his almost-forgotten fresh-water polyzoa, and together with Ross he probably spent some time at the Shepherds' summer place at Como on the Ottawa, for the three were not often long separated. Osler was a lean and somewhat shadowy person at this period, but full of fun as usual, and it was his delight to abuse an old Irish housekeeper of Shepherd's by calling her the 'hypotenuse of a right-angled triangle' and using similar terrifying epithets until she had retreated to her proper regions, audibly chuckling that 'that skinny yaller Doctor Rosler would be the death of her yet'.

Early in September came a meeting in Ottawa of the Canadian Medical Association, of which at the time Palmer Howard was President, and Osler as usual took an active part in the proceedings. He read an important paper on spastic spinal paralysis, gave a report on the progress in pathology, and it is characteristic to find him proposing at the business session: 'that the time devoted to the reading of any paper, except addresses on special subjects which at a previous meeting had been assigned to a member, shall not exceed thirty minutes'. There were two human frailties which perhaps irritated him as much as any others—one of them was unpunctuality, the other was garrulousness; and it was one of his common sayings to students that punctuality and brevity were primary requisitions of a physician and might ensure success even with other qualities lacking.

THE YOUNG PROFESSORS
WILLIAM OSLER, F. J. SHEPHERD AND GEORGE ROSS
Montreal, circa 1878

The new physiological laboratory of which Gardner had given promise to the students the year before was ready for occupancy in the autumn, and Osler in describing it[1] could hardly have failed to have uppermost in mind Bowditch's ample space and abundant apparatus at Harvard. It was merely the conversion into a laboratory of three small lecture-rooms of the medical building; but it was a forward step, for he confesses that for six years he had used 'the practical chemistry laboratory for the Saturday demonstrations and the students' waiting-room in the summer session for the histology classes'. He enumerated, piece by piece, the equipment he had been able to gather together, including, besides his eleven Hartnack microscopes (the twelfth appears to have gone to Johnson) and three microtomes, a kymograph and other things commonly found in a physiological laboratory of the Ludwig-Kronecker type with the use of which he was less adept. He was unskilled in the setting-up of apparatus, his physiological training with Sanderson having been of a different sort from that received by Bowditch and the innumerable other pupils of the Leipzig School under Carl Ludwig. For in Germany the microscope was primarily the research instrument of the anatomist and pathologist rather than of the physiologist as in England; and years later in a letter to W. G. MacCallum he confessed:

> . . . I followed the line of least resistance. There was always technique enough to do a good p.m., but never enough to handle complicated apparatus. I never could get my drums and needles and tambours to work in harmony. After all, it makes a good basis for the hard work and for the teaching of bread-and-butter medicine to medical students.

More to his taste were medical and public-health questions, and in December of this year he was made a member of a committee, together with two others from the Faculty of Medicine of Bishop's College, to investigate an outbreak of typhoid fever which had occurred at Bishop's College School, Lennoxville.[2] It may be recalled that in 1880 Eberth had

[1] *Canada Medical and Surgical Journal*, Nov. 1880, ix. 198.

[2] This led to an elaborate report, signed Jan. 21, 1881, dealing with the sanitary conditions at the school, which were far from the best. Cf. the *Canada Medical and Surgical Journal*, Feb. 1881, ix. 433.

only just isolated the typhoid bacillus, and the methods of its cultivation had not as yet been perfected, so that had the discovery been known and the relation of the bacillus to the disease been widely accepted it could hardly have been utilized at this time. In conjunction with the committee's report, an editorial appeared in the local journal, entitled 'Does Typhoid Arise Spontaneously?' And it is not unlikely that Osler, too, may have been influenced at this time by the opinion of Murchison, Flint, Pepper, and others who believed that the poison might be generated independently and not merely passed on from a previous case. The chief interest, however, in this episode lies in the fact that Osler was chosen to serve on a committee with members of the faculty of a school which, having a medical department of its own, regarded itself as a rival of McGill; and to pass judgement on a public-health question which chiefly concerned a dependency of this other institution.

This year of 1880 bridged the last days of the two men whose influence on Osler's life had been greatest. For a year or more Bovell's concern about Johnson's health had been expressed in numerous letters, but Bovell himself was first to go—on January 15th in his seventy-fourth year, a few days after a paralytic stroke. On December 29, 1880, the Rev. W. A. Johnson died, in his sixty-fifth year—much beloved despite his faults. Not long before, he had written to his son, Bovell's namesake, these words of his boyhood in England:

> . . . I remember Greenwich & Lewisham well. Bromley Hays Common & a little bit further to a village called 'Down'. You may go & see my old home. It was then called 'Down House'. *The* House of the neighbourhood in those days. Some of the oldest crones in the Village would soon tell you all about Col^{n} Johnson &^{c}. These English peasants do not move much: & that village is so situated as not to be cut up by Railways. You had better take a horse and ride over there some day. Tell me how the old Ch. is. Drummond was the Priest in my time the lowest of the low. The Hendersons are at Seal too I believe. See the old Roman trenches at M^{r}. Wards park & on Hays Common. The ponds called 'ravensbourne' said to be so called because a raven was seen drinking there w^{h} led to the discovery of water for Caesar's men. Those chalk hills are interesting as well as magnificent.

I expect a long account one of these days. Lewisham is no longer long, lazy, lousy Lewisham as Geo. IV called it, I suppose. I remember a very nice stream running through it on the left hand as you go from Bromley to London. Hundreds of times have I ridden and driven through it. Further down near Chiselhurst and Farnboro & over the hills to Seven Oaks is the beautiful country. Said to be the Garden of Eng. How I have made the horse hoofs patter over those hills as a boy. Fine hunting in those days, they used to throw off at Farnboro: and a stag has been known to run for the coast from there. O how I would like to set foot on those pleasure spots of my youth once again but cui bono? It is only the natural man & the less he has that gratifies & indulges him the better. Still methinks it would cause my heart to bound with thankfulness but there is plenty here to be thankful for. Write long descriptions like a good fellow when you get time. . . . The Lord prosper you. . . .

For four years ' Father ' Johnson had been far from well—ever since a serious smallpox epidemic in Weston during which he had volunteered as a public vaccinator, having, it is said, on one day alone vaccinated the two-hundred employees of the Weston Woollen Mills. It is not clear whether he actually contracted a mild form of the disease himself, but if so he was less fortunate than Osler had been. The coroner's statement reads as follows:

County of York: Division Yorkville.

Death Certificate of W. A. Johnson.

Septicaemic Lymphadenitis contracted in Weston in handling a dead body infected with Black Small Pox and which all but himself and his clerk refused to touch.

CORNELIUS JAMES PHILBRICK.
Dec. 29, 1880.

Johnson lies buried in the churchyard of St. Philip's, Weston; Bovell in that of his parish, St. Paul's, in Nevis, British West Indies.

CHAPTER IX

1881–3

LAST YEARS IN MONTREAL

It is possible that the death of his two old friends and preceptors spurred Osler to put in print the results of some of the zoological studies with which they had been so intimately associated. At the January meeting of the Natural History Society he presented some notes supplementary to his paper on the fresh-water polyzoa, read before the same society just four years before. He mentioned a species of Cristatella as having been found in abundance and described what he regarded as a new species of Pectinatella—evidently the one already mentioned which had fallen into the hands of the Rev. Thomas Hincks, F.R.S., of London, by way of his father, whose class in botany had been attended at Trinity. Moreover, during the next summer, as will appear, he returned to his old—and to some new—hunting-grounds for further specimens.

Osler frequently referred to himself as a note-book man—for he read pen in hand and was in the habit of jotting down a quotation which had struck his fancy or a thought which had come to his mind in relation to something he was composing. It was not uncommon for him, at least in later years, to write fragments of papers or addresses on a stray piece of paper or on the blank fly-leaves of a book he might happen at the time to be reading. Many of these fragments are still to be found scattered among the volumes of his library. In the copy of Alpheus Hyatt's 'Observations on Polyzoa', which W. A. Johnson had given him for Christmas 1868, occur some random notes which probably formed the basis of this paper read before the Natural History Society. The first of them tells how he found the Cristatellae the summer before during a stay of two weeks at the country residence of Mr. G. W. Stephens at Lac à l'Eau Claire, about 35 miles north of Three Rivers. He identified them with the *Cristatella ophidioidea* of Hyatt.

He read by invitation on January 26th an important

paper before the New York Pathological Society, an organization which since its foundation in 1844 had comprised among its members the most active and influential of the local profession. His topic was Ulcerative Endocarditis,[1] and he described the presence of what he took to be micrococci in the vegetations of the valves of the heart, a finding which was received with some scepticism. So the year was punctuated with meetings in various places; with papers on most varied topics. For his second Somerville Lecture, given in March under the auspices of the Natural History Society, he spoke 'On the Brain as a Thinking Organ', suggesting a flight into psychology, with the results of which it would seem he was not sufficiently satisfied to put anything into print. Later in the same month he was delegated to attend the Cincinnati meeting of the American Association for the Advancement of Science, and the association accepted a pressing invitation to hold its next meeting in Montreal under Dawson's presidency. Nor was there any let-up in the succession of communications to the local societies—sometimes a few unusual autopsy specimens were shown; occasionally some original contributions or a partly worked-up subject was presented; and later on during the summer session a few of his more carefully prepared clinical lectures, after a personal revision, were reported by students. Whatever his other interests, the welfare of his pupils invariably came first, and just at this time the Faculty of Medicine announced that a clinical prize of a fifty-dollar microscope had been offered by Dr. Osler for the student who should pass with highest marks a special examination to be held at the end of the course.[2]

[1] This article was published a month later (Archives of Med., N.Y., Feb. 1881, v. 44) under the changed title of 'Infectious (so-called ulcerative) Endocarditis'. Though the observations were largely confirmatory of the work of Klebs and others, it was the first important paper on the subject in American literature.

[2] Osler and Ross were the examiners, and 'Mr. R. J. B. Howard [Palmer Howard's son Jared] was the successful candidate, obtaining 322 out of the possible 350 marks'. It was an exceedingly thorough test, comprising: (1) a written paper; (2) a practical examination of a patient necessitating the use of the ophthalmoscope and laryngoscope; and (3) microscopical

A recently formed provincial society, the Ontario Medical Association, held its first meeting early in June. It was a movement Osler warmly supported, and an open letter sent to Ross, containing an account of the proceedings, began with the following emphatic expression of his feelings :

> Sir,—That the majority of the members of the medical profession in Canada take no interest other than pecuniary in their calling, would appear evident from the half-hearted way in which the societies and associations are kept up. It seems impossible to get more than about 100 men together for any common object, and for the discussion of questions relating to the welfare of their profession or the advancement of science. Many of the men who should set a good example in this respect persistently ignore both local and general societies. Where are many of the teachers at our medical schools on the occasion of these meetings? Too often conspicuous by their absence. Not a school in the country is free from these professional drones who ought to be thoroughly ashamed of themselves. The ears of many of them must tingle if there is any truth in the old adage. When men in their position systematically neglect such plain duties how can fault be found with the overworked country practitioners who have to make much greater sacrifices in order to attend. . . .[1]

It cannot be unduly emphasized that Osler throughout his life practised what he preached in this respect, and regarded the attendance at medical meetings as one of his professional obligations, an obligation, moreover, of which he made a pleasure. In later years, when he could not go himself, which was unusual, he would send some of his assistants and pay their way in order that his department or school should be represented on the programme at least of the more important gatherings. So at this time his name appears with regularity among those present each week at the students' society ; at the fortnightly meetings of the 'Medico-Chi.' ; at those held monthly by the Natural History Society and by the Microscopical Club ; at the Provincial meetings ; at the annual gatherings of the profession of the Dominion ; and finally at the international assemblies staged at longer intervals.

examination of various specimens. Cf. *Canadian Journal of Medical Science*, 1881, vi. 258.

[1] *Canada Medical and Surgical Journal*, June 1881, ix. 662.

One of the most notable of the succession of great international medical congresses was that of 1881 held in London under the presidency of Sir James Paget. Osler and R. Palmer Howard went to this meeting together, sailing on the Allan Line s.s. *Parisian* for Liverpool some time in June,[1] and at the close of the congress he sent a long account of the proceedings in the form of a letter (dated August 10) for Ross to publish.[2] As he said, 'the sight of above 3,000 medical men from all parts of the world, drawn together for one common purpose, and animated by one spirit was enough to quicken the pulse and to rouse enthusiasm to a high pitch, whereas the presence of the Prince of Wales and Crown Prince of Prussia added a flavour of Royal patronage which even science—republican though it be—seemed thoroughly to enjoy'. The event of the meeting was unquestionably Paget's opening address—high praise, considering the names of those who spoke at the subsequent general meetings: Virchow 'On the Value of Pathological Experiment'; John S. Billings of Washington 'On Medical Literature'; Huxley 'On the Connexion of the Biological Sciences with Medicine'; and finally Pasteur, who at the special request of the President described his recent experiments, which showed that animals could be protected 'against certain scourges' by vaccination.

Osler evidently heard these addresses, but his time was spent elsewhere: in the Physiological Section, where an animated discussion on Cerebral Localization took place in which Goltz of Strasbourg, Brown-Séquard, Ferrier, and others participated; in the Pathological Section presided over by Wilks, where the discussions on tubercle (Koch's discovery of the bacillus was not reported until the next year), on germs, on cardiac and renal disease chiefly interested him;

[1] Shortly before, at a meeting of the 'Medico.-Chi.' Society on June 10, a paper was read by Dr. Armstrong on 'Perityphlitis' describing a case in which the autopsy by Osler had shown an abscess at the head of the caecum. In the discussion, 'Dr. Osler referred to the fact that no part of the body varied so much as the appendix vermiformis. It coils in various directions and owing to its changed situations may get inflamed.' He evidently was very near to an understanding of appendicular disease. This was five years before Fitz gave his classic paper on perforative appendicitis.

[2] *Canada Medical and Surgical Journal*, Sept. 1881, x. 121–5.

and in the Medical Section under Sir William Gull's chairmanship, where neurological papers were read by Hughlings Jackson, Brown-Séquard, Buzzard, Erb and others. He even gave an account of the excursions, one of which was to Folkestone, where the memorial statue of Harvey was unveiled and an address given by Professor Owen.[1] All told, it was a remarkable meeting, participated in by many whose names will always occupy a high rank in medical history, the outstanding figures being Pasteur, Lister, Virchow, Huxley, Paget, Hughlings Jackson, and Charcot. But there was also a younger group forging to the front, among them a Hanoverian named Robert Koch, appointed the year before to the Imperial Health Department in Berlin.

It is apparent that Osler, like many other physicians, did not appear at this time fully to grasp as Lister did the significance of Pasteur's work, or to show great interest in Koch's remarkable contributions; and in his letter he dismissed the subject with the mere statement that 'there was an abundant discussion on germs' in the Pathological Section. Indeed the editorials in most of the British and Canadian journals of the time intimate that M. Pasteur saw germs everywhere, and his views regarding their prevalence as a cause of disease were regarded as rather horrible, if not mirth-provoking. Osler's suggestions in his paper on Endocarditis, that there might be a bacterial origin for the vegetations, was based purely on microscopical studies, for he had had no bacteriological training, and indeed the cultivation of organisms was at the time in its infancy, requiring a special technique known to but few.

At the first meeting of the 'Medico-Chi.' held after their return to Montreal, Palmer Howard went into further details regarding the lively discussion which had taken place upon 'the subject of micro-organisms and their relations to specific diseases, and especially to unhealthy processes

[1] He fails, however, to mention his own important paper before the Pathological Section, on Endocarditis, a subject he was still pursuing; nor does he speak of the sessions on comparative pathology and the fact that he was a delegate of the Montreal Veterinary Association to the British National Veterinary Congress, whose session he attended on July 20th and of whose proceedings on his return to Montreal he gave a *résumé* on October 27th at one of the fortnightly meetings of the Montreal association.

arising in wounds '. This discussion had been participated in by Lister, by Virchow, and by Bastian, to whose views on spontaneous generation reference has already been made; and finally as Howard said:[1]

> The great Pasteur produced a sensation by first confessing that his ignorance of English and German had prevented his following the arguments of the previous speakers; and then by exclaiming in reply to Dr. Bastian, who, he was told, held that micro-organisms may be formed by heterogenesis of the tissues: '*Mais, mon Dieu, ce n'est pas possible*,' and without advancing any argument then sat down. The eminent man for the moment seemed unable to realize the possibility of intelligent dissent from his assertion. However, in his address on the germ theory, delivered subsequently, he vindicated his reputation as the 'father' of living fungologists.[2]

One incident of this congress may be mentioned as it introduces a name, or names, to appear in a later chapter. Dr. S. D. Gross of Philadelphia, regarded as the dean of American surgery, who had been President of the International Congress held in 1876, had been prevented from attending in person, but sent in his stead his son, who had recently married Miss Grace Linzee Revere of Boston. They visited the Regius Professor of Medicine in Oxford, Sir Henry Acland, in whose house Mrs. Gross first saw the panel of Linacre, Harvey, and Sydenham over his mantel, a copy of which she was destined to live with for many years. She recalls that on their return Dr. Gross, sr., asked his son to give his impressions of the men he had seen, and he replied that he had heard a swarthy young

[1] Howard, R. P.: 'Some Observations upon the International Congress.' *Canada Medical and Surgical Journal*, Oct. 1881, x. 144–54.

[2] Possibly the most important session of this famous Congress was not attended either by Howard or Osler, viz. when so-called 'Listerism' was discussed at the Surgical Section by Spencer Wells, Marion Sims, and Volkmann the eminent German surgeon (the Richard Leander of German poetry). Lister was beginning to feel that wound-contamination by the air was less important than he had believed, and he was on the eve of abandoning the 'carbolic spray'—a step the profession could not understand, for he was too far ahead for others fully to grasp his views. Much merriment was provoked in the lay press at the expense of microbes in general. Cf. 'The Ballad of the Bacillus' in *Punch*:

> Oh merry Bacillus, no wonder you lay
> Quiescent and calm when at home in your hay, etc.

Canadian named Osler give one of the best papers of the congress, and that he hoped some day they might get him in Philadelphia. This same swarthy young Canadian had returned home too late to attend another meeting, namely of the Canadian Medical Association held at Halifax early in August, and was penalized for his absence by an election to the onerous position of General Secretary to succeed Dr. A. H. David, Dean of the Medical Faculty of Bishop's College, who having held the post for many years wished to retire because of ill health and advancing age.

The Francis cousins spent this summer at Lake Memphremagog in Southern Quebec, and one may be sure, despite all these medical meetings, that the children were not forgotten by their devoted playmate. Before going abroad he had run down for a brief visit, and on his return joined them again at the lake, adorned, as a contemporary letter says: 'with an awful beard and whiskers ultimately removed because of protestations of horror on the part of the medical faculty'. He was apparently accompanied by Ogden, with whom he evidently renewed his zoological studies, as is apparent from some notes read at the November meeting of the Natural History Society,[1] one of which 'On a Remarkable Vital Phenomenon observed at Lake Memphremagog' begins as follows:

During the first week in September 1881, the water of the lake presented a peculiar appearance, owing to a number of minute green particles floating in it. In places they were so thickly crowded together that the water was of a deep green colour. Except near shore they did not float on the surface but were diffused through the water to the depth of several feet. It was suggested to me by a friend that they were pollen grains, but their diffusion through the water and the season of the year seemed against this. They looked not unlike *Volvox globator*, but I have never seen this alga in such profusion. Fortunately, I had my microscope with me and the question was soon settled. Each little green mass formed a gelatinous ball, about one-thirtieth of an inch in diameter, and enclosed numerous unbranched beaded filaments, and proved to be a Nostoc—*Nostoc minutissimum*—a minute confervoid alga met with in water and in

---

1 These were read Nov. 7, 1881, 'to be published in a future number', which possibly refers to the 'Biology Notes' in the *Canadian Naturalist*, 1883, x. 251.

moist places. It is not a very uncommon species in our ponds, the remarkable point is the extraordinary profusion in which it occurred. The *Nostoc commune* is plentiful in the ponds at the Mile End, forming irregular balls the size of a horse-chestnut. . . .

On the reopening of the school in the autumn he enjoyed for the first time the luxury of an assistant—T. Wesley Mills, a promising young physiologist who had been for a year at University College and had subsequently worked under Newell Martin for a time in the Johns Hopkins Biological Laboratory. The course in physiology and practical histology was gradually being perfected, and Osler had prepared an admirable laboratory manual[1] which is prefaced by an appeal 'To the Student' to familiarize himself with the use of the microscope.

As a practical introduction to his subject in hand this concise students' manual could hardly have been bettered. In those early days when the clinical use of the microscope was less familiar than now, the course Osler developed represented a great advance. Histology, as has been pointed out, in the sense he used it really covered the study of structure in the broadest possible manner, with enough physiology and pathology thrown in to give these subjects their proper bearing upon the understanding of disease at the bedside. In later years his laboratory assistants were often astonished by his familiarity with the problems in their particular field, for though fully aware of his unusual experience as a gross pathologist they were apt to forget that the fundamental principles of physiology had been almost as thoroughly mastered during his early years of teaching.[2]

[1] 'Students' Notes: Normal Histology for Laboratory and Class Use.' Montreal, Dawson Bros., 1882.

[2] He was giving at this time four separate courses: *Practical Physiology* every Saturday afternoon from two to four during the winter session; *Normal Histology* bi-weekly throughout the year; *Morbid Anatomy* every Saturday morning; and his favourite course in *Clinical Microscopy*, 'especially designed to meet the requirements of a practitioner', bi-weekly during the summer session. An account of one of the Saturday-morning exercises which gives an idea of their character was reported by Palmer Howard's son, then one of the students, in the *Canadian Journal of Medical Science*, 1881, vi. 350, under the title: 'Notes of the Second Demonstration in the Morbid Anatomy Course in McGill College.'

Such communications as appeared under his name from the physiological laboratory during the next three years were purely observational, not experimental, and dealt chiefly with studies on the blood which continued to hold his interest. One of these papers, 'On Certain Parasites in the Blood of the Frog',[1] began as follows:

> In my Practical Histology class, during the winter of 1881–2, while the students were working at the blood of the frog (*Rana mugiens*) I noticed in one of the slides a remarkable body like a flagellate infusorian. I thought that it was one which had got into the blood, at the time of withdrawal, from the water on the web of the foot. Meeting with examples in the slides of several other students my attention was again directed to it and I made several sketches and wrote down the following description. . . .

The parasites proved to be varieties of *Trypanosoma sanguinis*, and though the observation, as he found, was not original, for Ray Lankester had previously described them, he gave an account of the behaviour of these bodies within the blood cells in a way which indicates his alert powers of observation.[2]

There were few important discoveries or trends in medical science which did not at one time or another engage his attention. In all probability his interest in heredity and especially in the inheritance of disease had been aroused by Francis Galton's writings on the subject which had begun in the '70's. This had already manifested itself by the publication two years before of the first of his several papers on these topics, when he described a hereditary nervous malady occurring in the Farr family in

[1] *Canadian Naturalist*, 1883, x. 406–10.

[2] His three other papers on the blood which may be regarded as contributions to physiology were as follows: one of them entitled 'Cells containing Red Blood-corpuscles' (*Lancet*, Lond., Feb. 4, 1882, i. 181) dealt with the taking up of red blood-cells by leukocytes and he speaks of examining the bone-marrow of over seventy-five persons in making the studies. The term phagocytosis was not introduced until four years later by Metchnikoff, who used it in relation to the engulfing of bacteria by white blood-corpuscles. Osler had evidently observed the same physiological phenomenon. Another paper dealt with the development of the blood-corpuscles in the bone-marrow; and the third was a note on the origin of the microcytes which he had seen separating off from the ordinary red blood-corpuscles.

Vermont.[1] In the early '80's, moreover, following the discovery by Fritsch and Hitzig of the electrical excitability of the brain there was a great wave of interest in localization of cerebral function which had encouraged many to undertake a more detailed study, of the form and volume of the brain as well as the topography of its surface, than had previously been made. Osler's interest in Giacomini's method of preserving the brain has been mentioned, as well as his flight into psychology in one of his Somerville Lectures; and he was now aroused by a recent paper (1879) by Moritz Benedikt of Vienna who had stated that 'the brains of criminals exhibit a deviation from the normal type, and criminals are to be viewed as an anthropological variety of their species, at least among the cultured races'.

Fortune favoured him, for he succeeded in coming into possession of the brains of two notorious criminals who had been executed after trials, famous in Canadian medico-legal annals, reports of which occur in the medical journals of the day. One of these individuals was Hugh Hayvern, who despite the plea of insanity was hanged for a brutal murder he had committed; the other, a poor half-witted Frenchman named Moreau, was executed on January 13, at Rimouski in Lower Canada. Osler had secured permission from the Dominion Government to attend the execution and perform the autopsy, and H. V. Ogden was sent by him as his representative with the admonition that he was to secure the brain without fail—an unpleasant task, as he recalls, for a raw young medical student speaking French imperfectly, who never having performed a human autopsy in his life was therefore in a desperate 'funk', in an out-of-the-way place and in the dead of a Canadian winter with the temperature 10° below zero.

In his paper Professor Benedikt had made certain statements regarding the prevalence of convolutional peculiarities in the brains of criminals. This finding Osler not only failed to support, but pointed out that the supposed anomalies in question were frequent in the general run of human brains. The article represented a careful topo-

[1] 'On Heredity in Progressive Muscular Atrophy.' *Archives of Medicine*, N.Y., 1880, iv. 316.

graphical study of the brains of the two homicides, but it otherwise is, for him, somewhat sarcastic.[1] He closed by saying, as 'B. B.' Osler might have done: 'One thing is certain: that, as society is at present constituted it cannot afford to have a class of criminal automata, and to have every rascal pleading faulty grey-matter in extenuation of some crime. The law should continue to be a "terror to evil-doers", and to let this anthropological variety (as Benedikt calls criminals) know positively that punishment will follow the commission of certain acts, should prove an effectual deterrent in many cases.' Subsequently an editorial appeared in the London *Lancet* taking him to task for being too severe with Professor Benedikt, and to this he replied,[2] clearly setting forth the reasons on which he had based his own conclusions. The entire episode is important only in showing Osler's eagerness in the pursuit of knowledge and his outspokenness of opinion. It has a bearing, too, upon some subsequent events, for it was not his last paper on cerebral topography; and when some years later the Wistar Institute came to be established in Philadelphia, he with a number of others (F. X. Dercum, Harrison Allen, Joseph Leidy, William Pepper, and E. C. Spitzka) formed what was called the Anthropological Society and agreed to bequeath their own brains for study.

Lest the recital of all these academic pursuits leave an impression of drab scholarly life without relaxation, it should be said that there was undoubtedly time for play, though of this there are fewer documentary records. Innumerable stories of the famous Dinner Club still continue to be handed down in Montreal; and at the monthly meetings which took place at the homes of the various members in succession there was great skylarking. They are mostly tales of Osler's pranks, many of which were perpetrated at Molson's expense. They are not much in the telling: at the first meeting, for example, after Molson's

[1] 'On the Brains of Criminals.' *Canada Medical and Surgical Journal*, 1882, x. 385–98. A year later he made a report on the brains of two other notorious criminals: *ibid.*, xi. 461–6. In this he adds nothing new, and merely dismisses Benedikt's conclusions as unwarranted.

[2] *Lancet*, Lond., 1882, ii. 38.

marriage, Osler going somewhat late to the club stopped at Molson's house and asked Mrs. Molson for a latchkey, remarking that it might be needed; they usually had some trouble in getting 'Billy' home, and as he might have to be carried in it would be convenient to have a key. An abstainer himself at this period, no stimulant was needed to make Osler the gayest of a dinner-party.

His interest in parasitology, which, as the natural outcome of his early microscopic studies with Johnson and Bovell, had led him to study and tabulate all the parasites he could identify in man and animals, was still in evidence. He rarely failed to report before one of the societies any chance post-mortem finding which had some bearing on the general subject. Thus on February 17th before the 'Medico-Chi.' he showed an example of bronchiectasis in the lung of a calf, a case of glanders, also a rare specimen of verminous aneurysm from a horse's aorta; and later in the year an example of *Amphistoma conicum* from the paunch of a cow. All this merely serves to indicate his great interest in the study of animal diseases, to satisfy which he continued to hold his position with the Veterinary School.

Throughout this year, in conjunction with one of the veterinary students, A. W. Clement, he was engaged in an exhaustive study of the parasites of the pork supply of Montreal. In their report,[1] ultimately presented before the Board of Health, January 12, 1883, they emphasized the necessity of strict governmental supervision over the sources of food supply, and of meat inspection in particular. They dealt particularly with the three more common parasites transmissible to man—trichina, cysticercus, and echinococcus—and the amount of labour expended on their studies is indicated by the statement that 1,037 hogs were examined, chiefly at the Dominion abattoir, during a period of six to eight months. When this is gauged with what was said in the section on Trichina, namely that in his human autopsies numbering between 800 and 900 Osler had found four cases, it can be seen that their material and experience, enabling them to draw comparisons between

[1] *Canada Medical and Surgical Journal*, Jan. 1883, xi. 325–36.

animals and man, was large. This timely investigation was of great public service and was a contribution to the health and hygiene of the community which probably had more weight as coming from a physician holding no political office than had it originated from some other source. As a by-product of this study he took up, as he had already done with trichinosis, the subject of echinococcus infections in man, this being a parasitic disease transferred more commonly from the dog to man, and a rare condition except in Iceland and Australia. On this quest he visited the museums of New York, Philadelphia, and Washington [1] in the search for specimens.

He was engaged at this same time in another piece of work of similar nature, though it pertained to a purely animal disease produced by a parasite, namely, cestode tuberculosis.[2] This study was also carried out in conjunction with Mr. A. W. Clement, and they recorded a successful feeding experiment with the production of the disease in the calf—an experiment undertaken to afford the students of the Veterinary College an opportunity of studying the development of the symptoms.

One of the most important discoveries bearing upon the relation of micro-organisms to disease, a subject which made this particular decade stand out above all others in the

[1] 'In 1881 I paid my first visit to the great library of the Surgeon-General's Office, Washington, to look up the literature of echinococcus disease in America, a subject in which I had become interested. At that date the Library had not yet moved from the old Pension Office and the books had far outgrown the capacity of the building. It was my first introduction to Dr. John S. Billings, at present the head of the Public Library, New York, to whose energy and perseverance the profession of the United States is indebted for one of the greatest collections of medical books in the world. He handed me over to the care of an elderly gentleman who very quickly put at my disposal the resources of the library and for two days did everything in his power to further my wishes. This was the beginning of a warm friendship with Dr. Robert Fletcher, and during the thirty years which have since passed I always found him a kindly, wise and generous adviser in all matters relating to medical bibliography. Probably few men in the profession owe a deeper debt of gratitude to the Surgeon-General's Library than I.' ('Robert Fletcher. 1823–1912.' *Bristol Medico-Chirurgical Journal*, Dec. 1912.)

[2] Presented before the Montreal Veterinary Association, Jan. 19, 1882. *American Veterinary Review*, Apr. 1882, vi. 6–10.

history of medicine, was announced this same year—Koch's discovery of the tubercle bacillus. It is difficult to realize to-day, in view of our familiarity with these matters, what a stir this must have made; for though tuberculosis, despite its protean manifestations in the different organs of the body, was beginning to be understood with the aid of the microscope, without the discovery of the bacterial agent the 'tubercle' apparent to the naked eye would have remained as the characteristic lesion of 'consumption' of tissue, whether of the lungs, bones, joints, or glands.

That a young English chemist, William Henry Perkin, in 1856 had become interested in the by-products of coal-tar and discovered 'mauve', the first of the aniline dyes; that German chemists had enormously developed these dyes; that a particular one should have been found to have an affinity for the tubercle bacillus, a hitherto unknown and unsuspected organism; that Koch had the imagination to devise the necessary combination of dyes, the intelligence to realize the significance of his discovery, and the genius which enabled him subsequently to cultivate the minute rods shorter than the diameter of a red blood-corpuscle—all this is a serial story well known, and the world looks forward with expectancy to the final chapter, the practical eradication of the 'white plague', one of its greatest scourges.

Koch's celebrated address in which he first gave proof that tuberculosis was a highly infectious bacterial disease affecting both man and animals, was delivered before the Physiological Society in Berlin on March 24th.[1] It was reported in full in the June issue of Ross's journal, and in the July number there occurs a note to the effect that at the McGill Physiological Laboratory Professor Osler before the class of senior students successfully demonstrated the presence of the organism in the lung of a man who had died of rapid general tuberculosis.

Osler's microscopic leanings, as has been indicated, were chiefly towards the morphological elements of the blood; his studies of communicable diseases were chiefly devoted to those due to animal parasites, of a far higher order than the bacteria; and though his interest in bacteriology was

[1] *Berliner klinische Wochenschrift*, 1882, xix. 221–30.

sufficiently acute to make him quick to confirm Koch's discovery, his inexperience with bacteriological technique rendered him incapable of pursuing the subject farther.

Koch's celebrated address ended with the statement that when the idea of the infectious nature of tuberculosis had taken root among physicians the means of warfare suited to contend with this enemy would be elaborated. It was along these lines that Osler's subsequent work in connexion with tuberculosis mainly lay, and in later years he became one of the chief leaders in the antituberculosis crusade. But even prior to Koch's pronouncement he had seen the light. For as Dr. Duncan McEachran recalls,[1] at one of the early meetings of the 'Medico-Chi.' after he had given an address on the contagious character of bovine tuberculosis, Osler expressed the opinion that tuberculosis was spread by contagion in the human species also and advocated a campaign to popularize this view. But it was urged by others that this would merely cause public alarm and that the apparent hereditary character of the disease could sufficiently well account for its occurrence in the several members of a family.[2]

In August the American Association for the Advancement of Science, as prearranged, met in Montreal under the presidency of Principal Dawson. Since Osler was on one of the local committees of arrangement he must have been kept busy, the more so as he was on the programme to give certain demonstrations and to read, before the Section on Histology, three short papers which contained an account of some of his original observations on the blood. On the heels of this gathering, the Canadian Medical Association, of which he was still the General Secretary, held its annual meeting in Toronto, where he not only read his paper on Echinococcus Disease,[3] but also gave a demonstration of the

[1] 'Osler and the Montreal Veterinary College.' *Journal of the Canadian Medical Association*, 1920.

[2] The idea of contagion did not reach the public for another twenty years, not until after the Tuberculosis Congress in London in 1901, on which occasion McEachran was the representative of Canada, and Osler of the United States.

[3] This paper, 'On Echinococcus Disease in America', was a statistical study of sixty-one cases gathered from various sources, together with his own

newly discovered bacilli of anthrax and tuberculosis; and one may feel sure that the spirit of James Bovell hovered over the microscopes through which they were shown. It was said to have been the most successful gathering in the history of the Association, the chief credit of which the official accounts of the meeting ascribed to the activities of the General Secretary, for the membership had more than doubled since he had taken the position.

The semi-centennial of the McGill Medical School fell in this year of 1882, and Palmer Howard, who had recently succeeded to the position of Dean on the death of Dr. G. W. Campbell, arranged to recognize the occasion suitably, invitations being issued to all graduates. On the evening of October 4th the assembly gathered in the large lecture-room of the new Peter Redpath Museum—he of the acupuncture episode. There were the usual receptions and dinners customary at such celebrations, and Howard made the announcement of a promise from an anonymous donor, who proved to be Donald A. Smith (later Lord Strathcona), of $50,000 for an endowment, provided a like amount could be raised by August 1883. Osler promptly wrote an enthusiastic letter to H. V. Ogden, saying that 'the Festival was a grand success—and prospects are good of the 100,000.' Ogden had graduated in the spring, and though Rogers had a successor, a Mr. Cantlie, the household at 1351 St. Catherine Street ultimately broke up a short time before Buller's marriage. For a time Osler lived on Dorchester Street with Arthur Browne (by now Professor of Midwifery in the School) and temporarily also with the cousins on McGill College Avenue. He was apparently paying court at this time to a young lady, whose father is said to have objected to a son-in-law with agnostic leanings and no visible means of support. However this may be, letters from the cousins to Ogden say that 'he is most scrupulous in his get-up, a beaver hat on all occasions and an extremely fashionable London importation for particular ones! The important question of "to be or not to be" is not settled yet, *so don't congratulate him.*' It was not to be.

personal observations. He signs himself as 'Lecturer on Helminthology, Montreal Veterinary College'. Cf. *American Journal of the Medical Sciences*, Oct. 1882, lxxxiv. 475–80.

In January 1883 a firm of medical publishers in Philadelphia, Henry C. Lea's Son & Co., transformed the old *Medical News*, a monthly publication which had been going for forty years, into a weekly paper in the quarto format of the *Lancet*. Dr. Minis Hays continued to be the Editor and he made it a feature of the journal to give abstracts of the proceedings of the more important medical societies: the New York Pathological Society, the Philadelphia Academy, the New York Academy of Medicine, the Medico-Chirurgical Society of Montreal, and so on, being included. Osler was asked to be the Montreal correspondent, so that during the next two years the frequent 'Montreal Notes' and the abstracts of the proceedings of the local society were written by him. His connexion with the *Medical News* in this capacity had some bearing on his subsequent call to Philadelphia.[1]

He had expected to go abroad for another period of study on the Continent in 1883, but for some reason, possibly because of difficulties which had arisen between the students and the teacher of materia medica whose resignation they demanded, this trip was postponed. His assistant, who does not appear to have made himself very popular with the students, was sent in his stead. Another trouble which the school faced at this time was due to the custom of 'body-snatching' for anatomical material, and it was not until Shepherd succeeded in getting a proper anatomical law through the Quebec Legislature that this practice and the disturbances it occasioned abated. It must have seemed to Osler, with the multitude of local activities with which he had become connected, that he was likely to become more and more firmly anchored as time went on.

In June he was elected a Fellow of the Royal College of Physicians of London, an honour which he mentions off-hand in this letter to Ogden:

To H. V. Ogden from W. O. 30/6/83.

Dear Ogden, Very glad to get your letter and to hear that you are progressing. Oddly enough I was on the Mountain this after-

[1] Osler was not unknown to Philadelphia, for he had been there in 1881 on one of his periodic tours 'to look over the museums and hospitals'; had met, and been impressed by, Pepper; and had visited Tyson. Cf. *Philadelphia Medical Journal*, 1899, iii. 607–11.

noon and met Mrs Barnard with a troop of friends and among them the lady you mentioned. I shall call tomorrow or the day after. Things here are pretty quiet, but the changes, as you will see by the announcement—to be mailed on Tuesday—have been numerous, and I hope for the improvement of the teaching in the school. Stewart will be a great acquisition. He is still in Vienna but will return in time. A. A. Browne and Gardner will make a good pair for Obst. & Gynecology. Penhallow, Asa Gray's assistant, takes Dr D's botany lectures this winter. Dr D. goes abroad for a year. That blooming Y.C.M.R.D. is in Winnipeg looking after Convention practice. We are joyful in the prospect of the $100,000 endowment. We have $40,000 of the $50,000 necessary to secure the equivalent sum from our anonymous friend. Buller keeps well: he has moved to a mansion on Dorchester St. I am next door, i.e. in Browne's, until his return and then I dont know where I shall go—perhaps with Stewart. R. J. B. H[oward] comes out in Oct. to take the Jr. Dem. of Anatomy. He has passed the Primary of the F.R.C.S. Did you hear that the R.C.P. Lond. had honoured me by electing me a Fellow? I feel very grateful, as my period of probation as a member (5 years) had scarcely expired. All are well at No. 66. The children are very jolly and often talk of you. Willie, only this evening, was laughing at the remembrance of giving you the mumps. Tell Dorland I will send him a formal invitation to the C.M.A. meeting—also the other Dr. The papers will be most acceptable. Write again soon.

The Royal College of Physicians—'R.C.P. Lond.'—of which he had already become a member by taking the examinations in 1878, is probably the most ancient society of physicians in Europe, its charter having been granted by Henry VIII in 1518. It was founded by the king's three physicians, the leader of whom, Linacre, 'a disciple of the new learning brought from Italy', was one of Osler's chief heroes of medicine. The reaction which this election had upon his Canadian colleagues is reflected in many fulsome notes which appeared in all the journals of the Dominion containing felicitations on 'a distinction which few men of Dr. Osler's age attain and which is now held by only two resident Canadians of any age'.[1]

As usual, the early summer was punctuated with medical

[1] By a coincidence another F.R.C.P. elected at this time was a physician of Leeds, Clifford Allbutt, a man several years Osler's senior. In course of time the two came to be the Regius Professors of Medicine, respectively, of Cambridge and Oxford.

gatherings. Thus July 11th finds him at Quebec with Ross for the triennial meeting of the College of Physicians and Surgeons of the Province, held at Laval University; and as he says in one of his 'Montreal Notes' to the *Medical News*, 'no little excitement at the time prevailed among the French-Canadian members of the profession regarding the disestablishment of the Montreal branch of this college which finally had been settled by a Papal decree' in favour of Montreal. Later in the summer he was again with H. P. Bowditch at the Adirondack camp, and a letter of August 29th tells of a 'scramble to the top of Beede's Falls, and along the cliffs towards the Washbowl'. It may have been during this outing that he read with unconcealed delight the third volume of John Brown's 'Spare Hours', and immediately set himself to write a review of the essays for the *Medical News*. To hand on a book he had enjoyed, either as the volume itself or through a review calling attention to it, became a fixed habit with him, and as this appears to have been his first published book-review it deserves passing attention:

Its American title [he said] is a rather unhappy translation of the author's *Horae Subsecivae*, but the 'pith and marrow' is just as good under one name as another. The general popularity of the first two volumes is such that 'Rab and his Friends' is now an English classic, and few of our readers, we trust, are not friends of 'Marjorie Fleming', with her 'Newgate calendar of all the criminals as ever was hung', or are ignorant of the 'Mystery of Black and Tan', or the splendid description of Chalmers, or the loving tribute to his father. The present recent volume—and we must add the last we shall ever have from his accomplished pen, now, alas! laid aside for ever—contains mostly purely professional papers, and as such will interest us all as physicians. Most of us would take exception to the genial doctor's conviction 'that a mediciner should be as free to exercise his gifts as an architect or a mole-catcher', but all surely will be with him in his plea for 'the cultivation and concentration of the unassisted senses'. This phrase is the key-note, indeed, to most of the volume. We are apt, amidst our learning and our scientific observations, to forget that the ear, the eye, and the hand are after all the chief avenues of knowledge, and to neglect their finer cultivation in our eagerness to learn the mysteries of all our 'scopes' and our reagents. We need the *experientia* as well as the *experimenta*. And it comes with peculiar force from one who is such an exuberant classical scholar that his Latin and his quotations from the older English classics overflow on almost every page. . . .[1]

What John Brown had written of Dr. Adams of Banchory, and of Locke, and of Sydenham 'the Prince of English Physicians, at the mention of whose name Boerhaave invariably removed his hat' may have been still in his mind when in September he attended the annual meeting of the C.M.A. in Kingston. For an episode occurred there during one of the sessions, which concerned the 'General Secretary', who made clear what were his feelings regarding the proper relations of one physician to another. The official report of the meeting states that a certain Dr. D—— read a paper on 'The Conduct of Medical Men towards each other and towards each other's Patients', in which he scoffed at the custom requiring a new-comer to call on those already settled in the place; claimed it was perfectly justifiable to report one's cases of operation or extraordinary cures in the papers; and went on to say: 'Take all the cases you can get, and keep them if you can without reference to the previous attendant.'[2] There were a few occasions, some of which will be referred to later, when Osler became, for righteous reasons, greatly worked up, and this was one of them. It is said that on the conclusion of this amazing paper he arose and, to the consternation of his fellows, waved a copy of the Code of Ethics in the reader's face and publicly denounced him.

Meanwhile, during this summer the trouble with the McGill students over the professorship of Materia Medica had been settled largely through Osler's intermediation, by the resignation of the former incumbent and the appointment of Dr. James Stewart in his place.[3] On Stewart's return from a sojourn in Vienna he and Osler lived together

[1] *Medical News*, Phila., Sept. 8, 1883, xliii. 273. Arthur Browne had given Osler a copy of the 'Horae Subsecivae' in London in 1872. Cf. 'Bibliotheca Osleriana' (in press).

[2] Cf. *Canada Medical and Surgical Journal*, 1883–4, xii. 107.

[3] An amusing account of this student protest against an incompetent teacher occurs in an undergraduate publication, the *McGill University Gazette* (May 1, 1883, vi. 7). It contains a note about a 'scribe short of stature but of a mighty understanding' evidently meaning the Registrar. The article purports to have been found by 'Damphino Cook, B.S., Zn Cl_2 + H_2S', the efficient Janitor of McGill College Medical School.

in T. G. Roddick's house during a European trip Roddick had taken in his turn. Stewart, though an able and industrious colleague, was a most silent man, of whom his house-mate was accustomed to say that he never could tell whether 'Jim' Stewart had the gift or the infirmity of reticence; but it was a pleasanter home and better quarters than Osler's previous ones. Roddick had recently become co-editor with Ross of the *Canada Medical and Surgical Journal*, and during his absence Osler evidently took over for him the task of preparing the editorials, for some of them, like that on 'Doctors' Signs' already quoted, are unmistakably his.

With Palmer Howard and F. W. Campbell he attended the centennial celebration of the Harvard Medical School on October 17th, at which time Oliver Wendell Holmes gave the memorable address [1] in which, when speaking of the three founders of the school, John Warren, Waterhouse, and Aaron Dexter who was Professor of Chemistry, he mentioned the 'Settee of Professorships'. He told the following story of Dexter which must have amused Osler, who himself was conscious of the difficulties in making a class experiment do what it should:

> It is sad to think that professors honoured in their day and generation should often be preserved only by such poor accidents as a sophomore's jest or a graduate's anecdote. The apparatus of illustration was doubtless very imperfect in Dr. Dexter's time, compared to what is seen in all the laboratories of to-day. We may admire his philosophy and equanimity therefore, in recalling the story I used to hear about him. 'This experiment, gentlemen', he is represented as saying, 'is one of remarkable brilliancy. As I touch the powder you see before me, with a drop of this fluid, it bursts into a sudden and brilliant flame', which it most emphatically does *not* do as he makes the contact. 'Gentlemen', he says, with a serene smile, 'the experiment has failed; but the principle, gentlemen,—the principle remains firm as the everlasting hills.' [2]

---

[1] 'The New Century and the New Building of the Medical School of Harvard University.' *Medical News*, Phila., Oct. 20, 1883, xliii. 421.

[2] In an unsigned article ('The Harvard Centennial.' *Canada Medical and Surgical Journal*, 1883–4, xii. 251) obviously from Osler's pen, he speaks of the stand which Harvard, under the leadership of Charles W. Eliot, had taken in reforming 'the lax and imperfect system of medical education which prevails in the States'.

During this autumn and the winter of 1883–4 the usual miscellany of case reports was read before the 'Medico-Chi.', including the exhibition of further post-mortem specimens from the Veterinary College. Before the naturalists, too, on October 29th, he gave a paper on the comparative anatomy of 'The Brain of the Seal', illustrated by many prepared specimens of the brains of various animals.[1] But aside from these diversions he was industriously at work all this time over his endocarditis preparations, and a note-book of the period contains innumerable drawings of his histological preparations of the diseased valves showing the vegetations and their bacterial content, accompanied by pages of written description in pencil, now almost illegible. He had come to believe that this serious disease of the heart-valves was invariably bacterial in origin; and it was this clinical and pathological material which formed the basis of his Goulstonian Lectures in 1885. He made a few inoculation experiments and stained the organisms in the tissues; but his real contribution lay in the assembly of facts and in his graphic picture of the disease, which made it understandable and recognizable by the general profession. It must be recalled that secondary endocarditis may occur in a number of diseases and he had attacked an experimental problem far more complicated even than that concerned with the bacterial origin of pneumonia, the relation of which to a specific organism, despite Fränkel's and Friedlander's descriptions, had not as yet been fully established.

Osler's parents by this time, owing to Canon Osler's retirement, had moved from Dundas to Toronto, where their elder children had settled, and it was there he joined them for the holidays. Otherwise Christmas dinner would have found him at the Howards', where his special friends of the younger generation were 'growing like gossip', as his cousin Jennette is quoted as saying. For gossip, however, we must have recourse to letters other than those signed 'W. O.', and his house-mate Cantlie sends Ogden a long account of this particular Christmas dinner, which says that 'Mrs. Howard, excepting perhaps Miss Jennette Osler and

[1] Cf. Proceedings of the Natural History Society. *Canada Record of Science*, 1884, i. 64.

Mrs. Francis, is the cleverest and most brilliant woman I have met, nor have I ever seen a little girl of such delightful manners as little Muriel'. And he adds: 'Dr. Osler is as usual at home at this season—but returns next week. I do wish he would marry some wealthy woman—'twould be a great boon to him.' Though from hearsay there was ample opportunity, Osler apparently had no intention of immediately following the example of 'the Landlord'.

CHAPTER X

1884

EUROPE; AND THE PHILADELPHIA CALL

In January there appeared an unsigned editorial in Ross's journal, 'On the University Question', unmistakably from Osler's pen, in which he urges increased efficiency, better laboratories, better-paid professors and assistants in all medical schools—'men placed above the worries and vexations of practice, whose time will be devoted solely to investigating the subjects they profess'. The following paragraph from this editorial has a very prophetic ring:

It is one thing to know thoroughly and be able to teach well any given subject in a college, it is quite another thing to be able to take up that subject and by original work and investigation add to our stock of knowledge concerning it, or throw light upon the dark problems which may surround it. Many a man, pitchforked, so to speak, by local exigencies into a professional position has done the former well, but unless a man of extraordinary force he cannot break the invidious bar of defective training which effectually shuts him off from the latter and higher duties of his position. We have, however, many men in our colleges with good records as investigators, and we hear from them but seldom on account of the excessive drudgery of teaching which the restricted means of their college compel them to undertake. The instances are few indeed in our universities in which a professor has but a single subject to deal with, and those which do exist are in subjects of great extent and often subdivided in other colleges. In looking over the list of branches taught by a single professor in some of our colleges, we may indeed say with Dr. O. W. Holmes that he does not occupy a *chair* but an entire *settee*. If Canadian scholarship is to be fostered, if progress in science is to be made, this condition of things must be remedied, and we may confidently hope will be, as years roll on. . . . But unless the liberality of individuals is manifested in the manner of the late Mr. Johns Hopkins of Baltimore, we shall have to wait long for a *fully equipped* Canadian university. The Government of Ontario, however, has now the opportunity to put Toronto University on a proper basis, and do a great work for the intellectual life of this country. And it can consistently do so, as the Institution is a State foundation and is under State control, and the condition of the local Exchequer is plethoric. . . .[1]

[1] *Canada Medical and Surgical Journal*, Jan. 1884, xii. 373.

'Pitchforked by local exigencies', as he himself had been, into the 'settee' of the Institutes of Medicine at McGill, Osler was doubtless fully conscious of his handicap. A well-endowed chair with the single subject of pathology to deal with would unquestionably have kept him in Montreal or taken him to Toronto or anywhere else just at this time—*Dis aliter visum;* and it was probably the better for medicine that it was so willed.

In a letter written to E. A. Schäfer early in the preceding autumn, stating that 'a barrel of apples (*var.* Northern Spy) left to-day per SS. *Polynesian* for Liverpool', he made known his intention to spend the coming summer in Europe. It was to be one of his periodic breaks 'from the excessive drudgery of teaching'. His plans by early spring had matured, and he writes of them again to Schäfer, who evidently was expecting to attend the coming meeting in Montreal of the British Association for the Advancement of Science. Of this body Osler seems to have been the local representative, for he says: 'Please send me within a few weeks the names of those members of the profession—so far as you know—who intend coming to Canada in August. I should like to arrange for their proper accommodation'; and he goes on to give details of railway arrangements, with trips to the Rockies and elsewhere. 'I am afraid we shall not have much to show you here. You will be interested in Bowditch's and Warthin's laboratories, the only good ones on the continent.' And in a postcript he adds: 'I was nearly forgetting the most important point. I am breaking-up home and my arrangements for the autumn are as yet uncertain.' Little did he realize how uncertain they actually were. In company with Palmer Howard's son Jared, who had recently been made a demonstrator in anatomy in Shepherd's department, he sailed on March 26th for Bremen, where apparently his first act was to buy the Tauchnitz edition of 'The Autocrat'; and the copy, still in his library, thoroughly perused and annotated, saw them through to Berlin. It is possible to trace their footsteps by the series of medical and surgical letters (most of them unsigned) sent back to Ross for publication. In April he wrote from Berlin his

'Instalment No. I',[1] in which he comments on the transformation of Berlin during the ten years since his last visit, on the new drainage system, the changes in the Faculty, the new hospitals, and the 'palatial' laboratory buildings on Dorotheen Strasse which he could see from his windows.

To E. A. Schäfer from W. O. 2 Neue Wilhelm Strasse, May 1st [1884].

Dear Schäfer,— . . . I shall be very glad to go to Elstree for a short time but I must go first to some friends in Russell Sq. for a week. I am afraid my lawn tennis days are over but you may tell Mrs. Schäfer that I am susceptible as ever—therein lies my safety—and shall be delighted to meet the young lady. I have seen Kronecker several times and he has showed me one or two very interesting things—particularly the experiment of permanently arresting the *ventricular* action by puncture of a small spot in the upper part of the septum vent. Mills is here working with him and also with Hoffmann and Salkowski. He is delighted with Strassburg. I hope in October to hand him over the Physiology and to another the Histology and have only the Pathology. I shall leave here about the first of July—possibly to go to Leipzig for a few days.

On this same day (May 1st) he got off his second open letter, describing the German Surgical Congress at which he heard Theodor Kocher's paper on cachexia strumapriva —in other words on the peculiar symptoms which may occasionally follow the operative removal of goitre. In solving the mysteries of the disorder known as myxoedema, this represented the first forward step to be taken since Ord's demonstration, which Osler had also attended in London three years before. But aside from this, the fact that he should have been sufficiently interested in a congress of surgeons to attend the meetings and describe what he had seen and heard is of no little significance.[2] The follow-

[1] *Canada Medical and Surgical Journal*, May 1884, xii. 582.

[2] There can be little doubt but that the sound surgical judgement, unusual for a physician and for which he was justly celebrated, was due to his early habit of attending surgical as well as medical meetings, and of reporting them in full. In his accounts not only of the Medico-Chirurgical Society for the *Medical News*, but also of the Dominion association meetings of which he was recorder, his abstracts of the surgical papers and discussions were apt to be as thorough and full as were those in his own subjects.

ing characteristic scribble on a postcard, which chance has preserved, was soon forwarded to George Ross:

16th [May 1884, Berlin].

How are you off for letters? You have one for the June No. perhaps 2—as No. 1 probably did not get out in time for the May Journal tho' I sent it on the 15th April. I [shall] send on the 18th a description of the Koch dinner which might perhaps go after the Surg. Congress letter as it would be rather stale to keep for July No. Why the d. have you not written. What a slovenly careless forgetting unconscionable set of brutes you are—Have not had the Journal yet. If the Koch dinner cannot go in, do not keep it until July, send it to A H Wright, Toronto, as I shall have a good letter for the July No. Hope everything is flourishing. Yours &c., W. O.

The third letter, sent two days later as promised, describes the official dinner in honour of Robert Koch, whose party had just returned from the expedition sent out to India to investigate the bacterial origin of cholera:

It must, indeed, have been a proud moment for the whilom district physician, Robert Koch, on the evening of the 13th inst., when some 500 of his brethren met to do him honour on his return from India and Egypt. The reception was, as remarked to me by one of the privat-docents, unprecedented, and unparalleled in Berlin. It was, indeed, a gay festival. . . . Prof. Bergmann, after greeting the guest of the evening, and congratulating the commission on its safe return, referred to the pride which all felt, from the Kaiser to the lowest citizen, at the fresh honours to German science which had resulted from Koch's labours. 'It was not', he said, 'the courage with which you went forth to investigate the fatal plague which we admire. Many of those about me have done the same thing. He [Virchow] who went to Sperrat and Schliessen, to the typhus epidemic, threw his life on the hazard just as much as the man who examined the bodies of cholera patients in the dirty huts by the Ganges. The device of our profession is that of the candle—"*aliis serviens ipse consumor.*" . . . Who does not know how often the spirit of a country physician is broken, and his thinking powers weakened by the endless round of visits. The reality of the wagon-rattle fits badly with the ideal of scientific work. But the district physician of Wollstein knew how to glean some hours from the restless and driving activity of practice, and in the space of ten years has concluded the series of brilliant observations from the discovery of the spores of the bacillus anthracis to that of the bacillus of cholera.'

These extracts will give but a feeble idea of Prof. Bergmann's stirring address. . . . Dr. Koch's reply was extremely modest: he claimed only to have discovered improved methods of observation. He believed that one important result of the commission would be, if the English Government gave proper assistance, the limitation of the cholera to its native place in India. . . . His career is particularly pleasing, and it reminds one of that other country physician who nearly a century ago made the memorable observations on cow-pox.[1]

The 'good letter for the July No.' dealt largely with Virchow, for whom Osler always felt and expressed the most profound admiration. He was unquestionably the outstanding figure in medicine of the day—a man whose interests extended far beyond pathology, in which his first great contributions to medical science had been made; and knowing of his anthropological leanings Osler had taken him as a present some Indian skulls from British Columbia. The letter begins thus:

The central figure of the Berlin Faculty is Virchow. . . . After 20 years of teaching, it is but natural that he should have much of the drudgery done by his able assistants, Drs. Jürgens, Grawitz and Israel, who conduct the autopsies and the courses on pathological histology. Students have, however, still the great privilege of hearing him in three different classes, and at 11 a.m. each day he gives a lecture on special pathology. . . . The other morning I could not but feel what a privilege it was again to listen to the principles of thrombosis and embolism expounded by the great master, to whose researches we owe so much of our knowledge on these subjects.

Politics and anthropology absorb the greater part of his time. He is a member both of the German Parliament and of the Prussian House of Representatives, and I noticed a day or so ago in one of the daily papers an item stating the number of times that each member spoke—I forget in which House—that Virchow had spoken on 38 occasions during the session. It need scarcely be stated that he is an advanced liberal. He is also a member of the City Council—not an idle one either, as the copious literature of the canalization (drainage) system of the city can testify, and I notice that he has been again urging the further extension of the sewers. His archaeological and anthropological studies are at present most extensive, and it is upon these subjects now that he chiefly writes. When one turns to the index of authors in the volumes of Transactions of the Berlin Archaeological Society the figures after his name stand thick and deep, just as they do in a similar index in medical works. He

[1] 'The Koch Dinner.' *Canada Medical and Surgical Journal*, June 1884, xii. 677. Another even more detailed account of the occasion was sent to Minis Hays for the *Medical News*, June 7, 1884, xlv. 687.

has been collaborator with Dr. Schliemann in several of the important works issued on Trojan antiquities. His collection of skulls and skeletons of different races, one of the most important in Europe, will doubtless find an appropriate place in the new Archaeological Museum erected by the Government. At present, his private rooms are a sort of Gehenna, which has laid every quarter of the globe under contribution. The very day on which I gave him four choice skulls of North American Indians from Prof. Bell's collection, two large cases of skeletons of the natives of Madeira were brought in. There are those who grudge him the time which he thus spends on politics and his favourite studies, but surely he has earned a repose from active pathological work, and may well leave section-cutting and bacteria-staining to the smaller fry; and when we consider that in addition to the classes above mentioned he is President of the Berlin Medical Society, and edits his *Archiv*, now a monthly journal, it can scarcely be said that he neglects professional duties. On all questions of general, medical and scientific interest, his utterances are not infrequent, and display a judicious conservatism—as witness his sound position regarding the Darwinian theory as opposed to the vagaries of Haeckel. . . .

The same letter contains an account of Frerichs, who had 'renewed his youth with the recent jubilee and astonished his medical friends by the production of a monograph on Diabetes'; and he goes on to describe Leyden's, Westphal's, and Henoch's clinics at the Charité; nor does he neglect meanwhile his public health interests, for he mentions a visit to the Royal Veterinary College, under Government control where 'there is much better teaching, and altogether a more scientific tone than is the case in English or American institutions of the kind.' The abattoir also was visited and he was 'able to see the admirable system of inspection of flesh, as well as to secure a number of valuable specimens illustrating the commoner morbid and parasitic appearances'.[1] The letter closed with this charitable comment on the Semitic invasion of Berlin:

The modern '*hep, hep, hep*' shrieked in Berlin for some years past has by no means died out, and to judge from the tone of several

[1] Before the Pathological Society of Philadelphia on Sept. 24, 1885, he subsequently alluded to these visits as follows: 'The liver fluke, *Distoma hepaticum*, so common in Europe, is not very often met with in sheep and cattle in this country, and in my experience it is rare to find here the advanced changes described in works on parasites. When in Berlin in 1884 I spent two afternoons of each week at the abattoir, which owing to the elaborate system

of the papers devoted to the Jewish question there are not wanting some who would gladly revert to the plan adopted on the Nile some thousands of years ago for solving the Malthusian problem of Semitic increase. Doubtless there were then, as now, noisy agitators —prototypes of the Parson Stocker—who clamoured for the hard laws which ultimately prevailed, and for the taskmasters whose example so many Gentile generations have willingly followed, of demanding where they safely could, bricks without straw of their Israelitish brethren. Should another Moses arise and preach a Semitic exodus from Germany, and should he prevail, they would leave the land impoverished far more than was ancient Egypt by the loss of the 'jewels of gold and jewels of silver' of which the people were 'spoiled'. To say nothing of the material wealth—enough to buy Palestine over and over again from the Turk—there is not a profession which would not suffer the serious loss of many of its most brilliant ornaments and in none more so than in our own. I hope to be able to get the data with reference to the exact number of professors and docents of Hebrew extraction in the German Medical Faculties. The number is very great, and of those I know their positions have been won by hard and honourable work; but I fear that, as I hear has already been the case, the present agitation will help to make the attainment of university professorships additionally difficult. One cannot but notice here, in any assembly of doctors, the strong Semitic element; at the local societies and at the German Congress of Physicians it was particularly noticeable, and the same holds good in any collection of students. All honour to them![1]

Another long letter, to A. H. Wright for the Toronto journal,[2] was sent the following month from Berlin. In this an account was given of the Congress of German Physicians which opened on May 20th with Frerichs as President, and which drew a distinguished gathering as it coincided with the festival in his honour. There was much, as would be expected, of infectious diseases and their relation to micro-organisms, for new discoveries were being

---

of inspection, both ante- and post-mortem, offers one of the best fields in Europe for the study of comparative pathology and helminthology; and through the kindness of Dr. Hertwig I was enabled to secure a large number of interesting specimens.' (*Transactions of the Pathological Society*, Phila., 1887, xiii. 222–4.)

[1] *Canada Medical and Surgical Journal*, July 1884, xii. 721–8. Following this letter, signed 'W. O.', is another signed 'R. J. B. H.', who writes about von Bergmann's clinic and describes the antiseptic methods in vogue there.

[2] The *Canadian Practitioner*, 1884, ix. 184.

announced like corn popping in a pan. Friedlander was present, and recounted new experiments with pneumonia; Fränkel described the pneumococcus, the relation of which to the disease was not as yet generally accepted; and Loeffler gave a *résumé* of the diphtheria question, with experimental support for the Klebs bacillus as the cause of the disease.[1] However, in spite of Osler's regard for Virchow and all that Berlin offered, the subsequent sojourn in Leipzig aroused his enthusiasm still more, for there he made his début into bacteriology. But the time, alas, was too short, and he was a little late in getting a start in this field which with his early botanical and microscopical training would have fascinated him. Another year in Montreal, particularly if he could have lived 'under the roof of his laboratory', might have seen him an active worker in the aetiology of the infectious diseases.

To George Ross from W. O. Leipzig, Wednesday 10th [June].

Dear Ross, Journal of May & your letter came on Monday—Glad to have them. April No. never turned up. Have written to Bastian. Hope he will come but he wrote to me saying that he could not. Shall be most happy to play distinguished stranger at 49 Union Ave [Ross's address in Montreal]. Came here last—very glad. Wish I had done so at first as everything is most *angenehm* in Cohnheim's[2] Laboratory. Weigert is in charge, C. being ill with gouty nephritis. I go there at 8 a.m. work until 10.30 at Bacteria, then go to Leuckart's[3] laboratory until 1 p.m. when I dine & return to Weigert[4] or go to Zurn's assistant at the Veterinary School. Wagner's[5] Med. Clinic here is good. I have not yet been to Flechsig. The buildings here are very convenient. I am living opposite the *Zoologisches Institut*—very comfortable pension—much more so than the Berlin one & at 2/3s the cost. Lord! dont I wish I could live all the year round for 120 marks a month (beer included). Were it not for books &c. it would be a great economy to live abroad all the year. I have asked Howard to get a little inner room rigged up for the Koch

[1] It may be noted that in Paris on the date of the opening of this Berlin Congress, Pasteur read before the *Académie de Médecine* his paper announcing the discovery of the virus of hydrophobia and a method of protecting against it.

[2] Julius Cohnheim, Prof. of Pathological Anatomy.

[3] Carl Leuckart, Prof. of Zoology and Comparative Anatomy.

[4] Karl Weigert became Cohnheim's successor in 1884.

[5] Ernst Wagner after a training in pathology became Director of the Medical Clinic on Wunderlich's death in 1877.

apparatus which we ought to have so that we could have some cultures under way when the Association is there. I shall try to bring out some cultures wh. will do for stock—The only trouble is that the heat may destroy them. I do hope the Faculty will be able to arrange for Mills & myself to *live* at the College. How I envy some of these men! Leuckart has about $4,000 a year, with a splendid set of apartments on the 3rd floor of the Institut. It seems *comisch* at first to see the upper flats devoted to the families of the professors and assistants but it saves time and money. Perhaps next summer the Governors might put a double mansard on and give me the upper one. Glad to hear from Dick MacDonnell that a telephone has been put in the College. Have a letter half ready—will be out by 1st & a Leipzig one will do for August. Hope the Surg. Congress one & Koch dinner are both in this No. If that letter came too late dont put it in the July No. as it will be very stale. Glad to hear of the preparation for the C.M.A. Lawson Tait will give an address on abd. Surg. & I have asked Sanderson (with Mullin's consent) to give one on Medicine. I have had no word from him yet tho it is some weeks since I wrote. Shall write again. I leave here July 12th. Bk. of Montreal or 25 Russell Sq. will find me in London. Let me know if I can bring out anything. I shall send out a couple of trunks from here. This writing is awful, but the pen is worse.

The last of his series of letters [1] to Ross's journal opens with a description of the medical conditions in Leipzig; of Cohnheim's pathological institute, and the illness of its distinguished chief; and then passes on to his assistant as follows:

The charge of the laboratory is virtually with Professor Weigert to whom medicine is under a deep debt of obligation for the introduction of the use of aniline dyes in histological work, as well as for the unravelling of many knots in pathological histology. He is a model of industry—first at work in the morning, last to leave at night—extremely affable and attentive, qualities which go so far to make one's stay in a laboratory comfortable and agreeable. I know of no place where a man can better work at pathological histology. . . . The medical clinic is in charge of Professor Wagner. . . . His method and manner remind one of Traube, which in my opinion is one of the highest compliments to pay a teacher. From 9.45 to 11 a.m. instruction is given upon cases brought into the theatre, usually three or four each day. At the beginning of the lecture new

[1] *Canada Medical and Surgical Journal,* Aug. 1884, xiii. 18–22. (Signed 'W. O.')

cases are given out to the students, who go to the wards and make out the history, &c., and then, when one of their cases is brought before the class, the student whose case it is goes into the arena and states the prominent features and makes the diagnosis. The physical examination is made by the student, and then a general summary is given to the class, with the necessary explanatory remarks. We all know how apt this method is—in some hands—to be dry and wearisome; details are obtained slowly by the student, and I have seen a class thoroughly tired, the professor irritated, and half-an-hour consumed in getting primary facts. Professor Wagner seems to get the details quickly, and the students appeared to me to be very much brighter than those at Berlin. To students coming to Germany for post-graduate study I would most strongly recommend them to take a semester at this clinic. For the general practice which nine-tenths of doctors ultimately engage in, it is worth any dozen special courses that I know of.... Probably the most notable figure in medical Leipzig is Prof. Ludwig, Director of the Physiological Institute, and the Nestor of German physiologists. Indeed he has a higher claim than this, for when the history of experimental physiology is written his name will stand pre-eminent with those of Magendie and Claude Bernard. He is now an old man, with bodily vigour somewhat abated, but mentally fresh and suggestive as ever. He has the honour of having trained a larger number of physiologists than any other living teacher; his pupils are scattered the world over, and there is scarcely a worker of note in Europe—bar France—who has not spent some time in his laboratory. . . . It is very hard to adjust the two great functions of a university, or a part of it, as represented, say, by such an Institute. The work which shall advance the science, which brings renown to the professor and to the university, is the most attractive and in German laboratories occupies the chief time of the Director. This function is specially exercised, and the consequence is that medical literature teems with articles issued from the various laboratories. On the other hand, the teaching function of an institute is apt to be neglected in the more seductive pursuit of the 'bauble reputation'.

So the letter went on; and after a description of Leuckart's Zoological Institute and of Dr. Zurn, 'one of the leading authorities on the diseases of birds', it concludes with a characteristic note regarding his 'indebtedness to the University Librarian for many acts of politeness'. Thus Virchow, his most distinguished pupil Cohnheim, who died later in this year, Ludwig, Traube, and Ernst Wagner (among others who stood in the front rank of the profession in Germany) all left an indelible mark on Osler's receptive mind in spite of his brief contact with them. Years afterwards in one of his addresses he said:

. . . I was much impressed by a conversation with Professor Ludwig in 1884. Speaking of the state of English physiology, he lamented the lapse of a favourite English pupil from science to practice; but he added: 'While sorry for him, I am glad for the profession in England.' He held that the clinical physicians of that country had received a very positive impress from the work of their early years in physiology and the natural sciences. I was surprised at the list of names which he cited: among them I remember Bowman, Savory and Lister. Ludwig attributed this feature in part to the independent character of the schools in England, to the absence of the university element so important in medical life in Germany, but above all to the practical character of the English mind, the better men preferring an active life in practice to a secluded laboratory career.[1]

His sojourn in Leipzig which so delighted him—'going for the bacteria' as he expressed it in a letter to Ogden—was to have a sudden and unexpected end. On the fly-leaf of his commonplace-book under the date 17/6/84 is the note, 'Telegraphed Tyson from Leipzig that I would accept Professor of Clinical Medicine in the University of Pennsylvania, "Yes".' And in another place occurs the provisional draft of a letter in reply to the one evidently sent by Tyson, May 29th. Two days later came a package of mail from Montreal, and he writes to both Shepherd and Ross in similar vein as follows:

June 19th.

Dear Ross, Shepherd forwarded me a letter this week which played the deuce with my peace of mind. Tyson writes asking me if I would accept the Chair of Clin. Med. in Univ. of Penn. if appointed. His letter is quite unofficial & nothing may come of it, but after much meditation I decided to reply in the affirmative. The temptation is too great, but the prospect of severing my connexion with McGill & Montreal gives me no end of worry. However, it may come to nought, but of course I wrote to H. at once. Now I think, as I told him, it had better be kept quiet—not let a rumour get about if possible. It would stir up another Hospital agitation. Shepherd may possibly have twigged it from the opening sentence of the letter. I sometimes think it may be a hoax but the matter of fact communication—wh. Howard has—does not look like it. 'My heart within me is even like melting wax' at the thought of the possibility of leaving you all.

---

[1] 'British Medicine in Greater Britain.' Cf. p. 458.

Shorn of its details, the story as he recounted it years afterwards may be given in Osler's own words:

I was resting in a German town when I received a cable from friends in Philadelphia, stating that if I would accept a professorship there I should communicate with Dr. S. Weir Mitchell who was in Europe and who had been empowered to arrange the details. I sat up late into the night balancing the pros and cons of Montreal and Philadelphia. In the former I had many friends, I loved the work and the opportunity was great. In the latter the field appeared very attractive, but it meant leaving many dear friends. I finally gave it up as unsolvable and decided to leave it to chance. I flipped a four-mark silver piece into the air. 'Heads I go to Philadelphia; tails I remain at Montreal.' It fell 'heads'. I went to the telegraph-office and wrote the telegram to Dr. Mitchell offering to go to Philadelphia. I reached in my pockets to pay for the wire. They were empty. My only change had been the four-mark piece which I had left as it had fallen on my table. It seemed like an act of Providence directing me to remain in Montreal. I half decided to follow the cue. Finally I concluded that inasmuch as I had placed the decision to chance I ought to abide by the turn of the coin, and returned to my hotel for it and sent the telegram.[1]

Early in May the announcement had been made of the retirement, after twenty years' service, of Alfred Stillé from the senior Chair of Medicine at the University of Pennsylvania, and it was obvious that William Pepper would be his successor. For Pepper's Chair of Clinical Medicine a lively canvass had been in progress and there were two particularly worthy candidates, both of whom from long service and in junior positions well deserved advancement. The following statement of the subsequent events so far as they concerned Osler has been furnished by Dr. Minis Hays:

The Medical Committee of the Trustees recommended to the full Board that a named member of the existing teaching staff should be elected to fill the vacancy. At a weekly meeting of the Editorial Staff of the *Medical News* held shortly afterwards, upon the conclusion of the routine business, the members engaged in general conversation, and the first and uppermost topic naturally was this recent nomination to the Board of Trustees. There were present at the meeting Doctors Hays, Bartholow, S. W. Gross, Parvin and Tyson. Surprise was expressed that the Committee had not gone

[1] Remarks before the American Club (Rhodes Scholars) of Oxford, July 12, 1916; unpublished.

further afield and taken a wider view of the available material before making its recommendation, and Dr. Osler of Montreal was mentioned as one eminently qualified to fill with marked ability the duties of the Chair, but his name, so far as known, had not been even given consideration in connexion with the filling of the vacancy.

Dr. Osler was then known to the gentlemen present only by reputation and by his writings. Dr. Tyson, a prominent member of the University Faculty, while recognizing Dr. Osler's capacity to fill the Chair with conspicuous ability, seemed to think that it was now too late to move in the matter; but in reply it was strongly urged upon him by those present that as the election had not been consummated the situation was not irretrievable. The other members of the staff strenuously concurred in the views expressed, and recognizing their force Dr. Tyson finally said that he would immediately take up the matter with his colleague Dr. Horatio C. Wood, who was then still in town—most of the members of the Medical Faculty being away on their summer holiday. The suggestion appealed very strongly to Dr. Wood, and with his characteristic energy he at once journeyed to Montreal to learn at first hand more concerning Dr. Osler's attainments and qualifications for the position.

All who were familiar with Osler's consulting-room and study in Baltimore, and with his library in Oxford, will recall certain familiar pictures. There was a large photograph, of course, of Bovell, another of Johnson, and another of Howard. Over the mantel was the panel of his three heroes: Linacre, Sydenham, and Harvey, the great triumvirate of British Medicine. Another portrait gave the fine profile of Newman, whom he admired as greatly for his personal characteristics as Johnson did for his religious views; and still another was a large photograph of H. C. Wood wearing a picturesque fur cap such as a distinguished earlier fellow townsman of his, Benjamin Franklin, was wont to wear.

Though they became great friends, he and Wood, as the foregoing statement indicates, were not acquainted at this time, and as the story is told in Montreal: 'some time in the summer of 1884 H. C. Wood suddenly appeared, unannounced, to make inquiries regarding the local feeling about Osler. He went first of all, curiously enough, to the French hospitals, and found that among the French physicians every one spoke of him in the highest terms; he then visited the Montreal General, where he encountered such a degree of enthusiasm for Osler on the part of the young members of the house-staff that he became himself a thorough convert, and returned home without interviewing any of Osler's colleagues on the Faculty.' So it came about that on June 17th a coin was flipped at 14c Terch Strasse, Leipzig, which fell 'heads'. To this episode Osler, with some stretching of the facts, referred at the time of his departure for England fifteen years later, as follows:

I would like to tell you how I came to this country. The men responsible for my arrival were Samuel W. Gross and Minis Hays, of Philadelphia, who concocted the scheme in the *Medical News* office and got James Tyson to write a letter asking if I would be a candidate for the professorship of Clinical Medicine in the University of Pennsylvania. That letter reached me at Leipzig, having been forwarded to me from Montreal by my friend Shepherd. I had played so many pranks on my friends there that when the letter came I felt sure it was all a joke, so little did I think that I was one to be asked to succeed Dr. Pepper. It was several weeks before I ventured to answer that letter, fearing that Dr. Shepherd had perhaps surreptitiously taken a sheet of University of Pennsylvania note-paper on purpose to make the joke more certain. Dr. Mitchell cabled me to meet him in London, as he and his good wife were commissioned to 'look me over', particularly with reference to personal habits. Dr. Mitchell said there was only one way in which the breeding of a man suitable for such a position, in such a city as Philadelphia, could be tested: give him cherry-pie and see how he disposed of the stones. I had read of the trick before, and disposed of them genteelly in my spoon—and got the Chair.[1]

It became necessary for Osler to engage again in the procedure of soliciting testimonials to forward to the University trustees in Philadelphia. It was done in a less distasteful manner than in his enforced campaign in 1878 for the appointment to the Montreal General—merely by asking some of his London friends, Bastian, Gowers, and Burdon Sanderson, to send some word concerning him to Dr. Mitchell if they felt so inclined. These letters were of such an unqualified nature as to leave no doubt in any

[1] 'L'Envoi': Response at farewell dinner, May 2, 1905. *Medical News*, 1905, lxxxvi. 854-60.

one's mind as to Osler's desirability on every possible score. Mitchell meanwhile had gone to Paris, whence he wrote a succession of letters to Tyson urging him to move, for 'unless we are pretty active we shall be saddled with another'; to Joseph Leidy, adding that, 'Osler is socially a man for the Biological Club if by any good luck we can get him'; and to others of the Faculty:

To James C. Wilson from S. Weir Mitchell. Paris, 17th [July].

I send more letters about Osler. He was to write me after hearing from Howard and as he has not done so I wrote him to-day about it, but the testimonials still coming must mean that he, Osler, *has* decided. Pepper has written me at length, and thinks that Bruen has great strength in the Board; I put him last for fitness and am in no doubt that Osler is in all ways the best man. He has every social need; his age is 35. He has won distinction as an investigator and writer, and will therefore add to our illustriousness, and as to competence as a teacher if anyone can be believed he must be a really unusual instructor. I wish you would write to Howard about him. I would vote for Osler with far less doubt in my mind than one usually has and with less than I should have as to any other candidate. Guitéras would be my second choice and Starr my third. If possible I think that the Provost and individual trustees, and *I* would say the faculty, ought to see the testimonials of Osler, and so much of my letters as concern him, and as you might think well to have *copied*. But these are purely suggestions. If you think well of it, Tyson would put together *all* there is in Osler's favour and see that all concerned saw it. . . .

What Osler wrote to Palmer Howard is not apparent, but a fragment has been preserved of a letter which Howard wrote so soon as rumours had reached his ears and a meeting of the Faculty could be called, and which offers too late some counter-proposals:

From Palmer Howard to W. O. The Saint Louis Hotel, Quebec, [no date].

. . . I avail myself of the first opportunity to communicate to you. In the first place, the Faculty is not willing at once to relieve you of the Professorship of Physiology, and to make an appointment to that chair of a Professor. It thinks it wiser to allow some person probably Dr. Mills to *lecture* in the coming session on that subject for you with the view of finding out his adaptation to and fitness for the work of teaching. Altho' they do not question his ability they have some fears of his personal fitness in other respects. Under this feeling and with these views the following resolution has passed unanimously at a large meeting of the Fac.: Moved by Dr. Farnell, seconded by Dr. Roddick, that this Faculty authorizes the Dean to communicate to Prof. Osler as follows: 'That this Faculty undertakes to make arrangements for the establishment of a chair of Pathology and Comparative Pathology at as early a date as possible. That the sum of sixteen hundred dollars be hereby voted to Dr. Osler for this year.'

Now as to the other part of it I don't know how to speak my own sentiments and those of the entire Fac.; the thought of losing you stuns us, and we feel anxious to do all that we can as sensible men to keep you amongst us, not only on account of your abilities as a teacher, your industry and enthusiasm as a worker, your personal qualities as a gentleman, a colleague and a friend; not only on account of the work you have already done in and for the school, but also because of the capabilities we recognize in you for future useful work, both in original investigation which shall add reputation to McGill and in systematic teaching of any of the branches of Medical Science you may care to cultivate; and finally because we have for years felt that vitalizing influence upon us individually exercised by personal contact with you—analogous to that produced by a potent ferment.

At the same time we know nothing of the inducements that may have been held out from other quarters, but hasten to assure you that the above expresses the spirit of our intentions. In any case don't finally decide to go elsewhere before you have either seen or communicated with us.

To H. V. Ogden from W. O. 25 Russell Sq., London, [Aug. 1, 1884].

. . . I have been in England about three weeks and am enjoying London again. It is the world. How I should like to live here! Perhaps you have heard that by Oct. 1st I may have changed my allegiance and joined you as a citizen of the Gt. Republic. I have been asked by some of my Philadelphia friends to be a candidate for the chair of clinical medicine, vacant by the transference of Pepper to the chair of medicine. I have consented and from what Pepper writes me I think they mean to elect me—at any rate I have the strong professional backing of the electionary board. The salary is about what I get at McGill and of course the temptations are the larger centre and the prospects of consulting work. I am grieved at the thought of leaving McGill and Dr. Howard, but they will get along quite well without me—any one man is never essential. . . . I leave on the 7th and take out with me an aunt—a young girl of 84. I wish you could run down to Montreal for the meeting. . . .

He must have seen all his old friends in London, have visited Schäfer at Elstree, and have gone to Cornwall to see the family relations there; and when he sailed on the 7th he brought out with him ' the young girl of 84'—Mary Anne Pickton, his mother's sister, who was henceforth to share the family home in Toronto. On the fly-leaf of John Henry Newman's ' Verses on Various Occasions', a volume still in his library, Osler had written in a later hand:

This copy was given to my Aunt, Miss Pickton, of Edgbaston, Birmingham, by Cardinal Newman, with his photograph. She gave it to me in 1884, the year I brought her out to Canada. She and the Cardinal were exactly the same age. The additional verse to The Pillar of the Cloud [i.e. Lead, Kindly Light] at p. 152 is in her handwriting.

It is probable that during the voyage he found time to write the ' Notes of a Visit to European Medical Centres', which was published shortly after.[1] It is a *résumé* of his impressions, and concludes with this significant paragraph which shows the direction in which his thoughts were leading him—away from the pathological institute and from comparative pathology to the ideal clinic which became his goal:

The custom of placing one or two men in charge of a large hospital seems odd to us and has both advantages and disadvantages. Thus, Dr. Guttmann is responsible to the city authorities for the care of about 350 patients at the Moabit institution and is, of course, allowed a staff of assistants on whom necessarily a large proportion of the work falls, and in some cases the treatment is entirely in their hands. At the city hospitals the rotation of assistants is much more rapid than at the University clinics, where they gladly remain for years at small salaries for the sake of the opportunity of making reputations as clinical workers. At the Charité the wards of Frerichs, Leyden and Westphal are clinical laboratories utilized for the scientific study and treatment of disease, and the assistants under the direction of the Professor carry on investigations and aid in the instruction. The advanced position of German medicine and the reputation of the schools as teaching centres are largely fruits of this system.

It was while he was at sea that the Editorial Board of the *Medical News* saw fit to make an announcement in their

[1] Editorial. *Archives of Medicine*, N.Y., 1884, xii. 170–84.

issue of 9th August of Osler's appointment. This note was promptly quoted broadcast, so that by the time of his landing, the cat was well out of the bag. The Canadian Medical Association met at Toronto, on August 25th to 27th, the most notable feature of the meeting being a long and, be it said, contentious address by Lawson Tait on the subject of abdominal surgery, then in its infancy—and it is over infants that their sponsors become quarrelsome. It may be assumed, however, that Osler at the mercy of his friends was nevertheless the centre of the gathering. The paper he had planned to read on 'Pneumonia as a Contagious Disease' was given only in abstract; and on the last day of the meeting, Roddick, who read the Report of the Nominating Committee, gave the name of Osler as the next President and of James Stewart to be his successor as General Secretary; and it was reported that 'with singular unanimity Dr. Osler was elected'.

It was a lively ten days, for the meeting of the British Association followed immediately after. At this gathering Osler's interests naturally lay with the physiological section, a long report of which he sent off for Minis Hays's columns.[1] The chief participants were Newell Martin and Howell from the Johns Hopkins Biological Laboratory; C. S. Minot and H. P. Bowditch of Boston; his pupil, Wesley Mills, and his old friend Edward Schäfer, who presided and took an active part in the programme, among other things reporting some experiments on cerebral localization carried out with Victor Horsley.[2]

His time of departure was drawing near and he was subjected to the usual series of tributes: appropriate resolutions were passed by the societies of which he was a member; there was a farewell celebration at the Dinner Club; minutes of congratulation were passed by the McGill Faculty upon 'his recognition by a distinguished

[1] *Medical News*, Phila., Sept. 27, 1884, xlv. 360–3.

[2] Among the British visitors were Drs. Struthers and Cunningham, Professors of Anatomy at Aberdeen and Dublin respectively, who subsequently visited the leading schools of Canada and the United States. Dr. Struthers on his return gave a full account of his impressions—a sorry picture of the conditions of medical education then existent in the States—conditions not yet entirely overcome.

foreign university'; and due acknowledgement made of his services as professor and of the 'admirable and efficient manner in which during the past seven years he has performed the important duties of Registrar'. Finally, on the eve of his departure, a large complimentary dinner, at which Palmer Howard presided, was given at the Windsor Hotel. The students themselves, not to be outdone, presented him with a handsome hunting-case watch, suitably inscribed, and they will be glad to know it was the watch he always wore.

So McGill lost what Howard called its 'potent ferment'; and thus closed Osler's Canadian period. He was thirty-five years of age, at the mid-point of his life, as it proved, though his expectancy at that time, in view of his ancestry, was for a longer tenure than is vouchsafed most men. Such a transplantation from one university to another of a clinician at the height of his career, though common enough in Europe, was unusual in America, and it caused a great deal of comment—favourable, be it said—on all sides. Still, even in America, there was ample precedent, as in the case of Nathan Smith, Dunglison, Gibson, Elisha Bartlett, Bartholow, Flint, Gross, and more besides. Nevertheless there was something different about Osler's call, for it represented the choice of a young man, known more for his scientific papers and his interest in research than for any proved clinical ability. Time has shown that such a preparation is often the best, though the appointment of laboratory-trained men to clinical positions often raises an outcry.

Unwilling to let go entirely, and trusting perhaps that the experiment might not succeed, the McGill Faculty at their meeting on September 3rd had voted him a six-months leave of absence, and his resignation was not officially accepted until October 11th, when final resolutions of regret were passed. Their hopes of his return were vain; and though in years to come he was often urged to do so, it was not to be. But he was never forgetful of what he owed to Johnson and Bovell and Howard; to the microscope and the pathological laboratory; to the Montreal General and to his Canadian friends.

What particularly lured him is difficult now to tell. It

may even have been difficult for him to tell. For a person capable of such strong local attachments there is something contradictory about it. A great career was assured in Montreal, whereas Philadelphia was an uncertainty in a land more foreign to him than England. The singularity of the call may have influenced him; and an ancestral impulse which bade him accept. He possibly realized that his bent lay in the study of disease as it was seen at the bedside rather than in the laboratory. As W. T. Councilman has said:[1] 'He could easily have become a great scientist, but he chose the path which led to the formation of the great clinician which he became; a worthy associate of the great men who have made English medicine famous.'

During the short span of years since his McGill appointment he had stirred into activity the slumbering Medico-Chirurgical Society; he had founded and supported a students' medical club; he had brought the Veterinary School into relation with the University; he had introduced the modern methods of teaching physiology; had edited the first clinical and pathological reports of a Canadian hospital; had recorded nearly a thousand autopsies and made innumerable museum preparations of the most important specimens; he had written countless papers, many of them ephemeral it is true, but most of them on topics of live interest for the time, and a few of them epoch-making; he had worked at biology and pathology both human and comparative, as well as at the bedside; he had shown courage in taking the small-pox wards, charity in his dealings with his fellow physicians in and out of his own school, generosity to his students, fidelity to his tasks; and his many uncommon qualities had earned him popularity unsought and of a most unusual degree.

Years later, in an address[2] given at McGill, while admitting that 'the dust of passing time had blurred the details, even in part the general outlines, of the picture', Osler spoke of this formative period of his medical career as one 'during which he had become a pluralist of the most abandoned

[1] *The Johns Hopkins Hospital Bulletin*, July 1919, xxx. 197.
[2] 'After Twenty-five Years.' *Montreal Medical Journal*, 1899, xxviii. 823.

sort', and concluded his interesting and amusing recollections by saying:

> After ten years of hard work I left this city a rich man, not in this world's goods, for such I have the misfortune—or the good fortune—lightly to esteem; but rich in the goods which neither rust nor moth have been able to corrupt, in treasures of friendship and good-fellowship, and in those treasures of widened experience and a fuller knowledge of men and manners which contact with the bright minds in the profession ensures. My heart, or a good bit of it at least, has stayed with those who bestowed on me these treasures. Many a day I have felt it turn towards this city to the dear friends I left there, my college companions, my teachers, my old chums, the men with whom I lived in closest intimacy, and in parting from whom I felt the chordæ tendineæ grow tense.

PART II

THE UNITED STATES, 1884–1905

There are men and classes of men that stand above the common herd : the soldier, the sailor and the shepherd not infrequently ; the artist rarely ; rarelier still, the clergyman ; the physician almost as a rule. He is the flower (such as it is) of our civilization ; and when that stage of man is done with, and only remembered to be marvelled at in history, he will be thought to have shared as little as any in the defects of the period, and most notably exhibited the virtues of the race. Generosity he has, such as is possible to those who practise an art, never to those who drive a trade ; discretion, tested by a hundred secrets ; tact, tried in a thousand embarrassments ; and what are more important, Heraclean cheerfulness and courage. So it is that he brings air and cheer into the sickroom, and often enough, though not so often as he wishes, brings healing.

Dedication to ' Underwoods '.
R. L. S.

CHAPTER XI

1884–5

FIRST YEARS IN PHILADELPHIA

OSLER'S Philadelphia period began with his arrival on Saturday afternoon, October 11th, 1884, at a family hostelry which then and since has enjoyed the bookish appellation of the Aldine Hotel. The name, for obvious reasons, had been given by Mr. Lippincott the publisher, who had purchased what was formerly a residence and transformed it into a lodging-house in 1876 for visitors to the Centennial Exposition. The place had seen better days, days indeed of society and fashion when in the '50's it had been the suburban home of the son of Benjamin Rush; and though residential Philadelphia has long tended to confine itself within much the same boundaries, 20th and Chestnut Streets were in the '80's far from being suburban. It was one of those off-years when even October brings a spell of sultry weather, which must have been an unhappy contrast to the cool Province of Quebec for a lonesome man searching the heart of Philadelphia for a place to reside. In his account-book of the period he has laconically written opposite Tuesday, October 21st: 'Came to 131 S. 15th Street', and there follows a list of what appear to have been the dinner engagements to which custom subjected the new-comer: 'Oct. 28, Sinkler; 30, Musser; 31, Seiler; Nov. 2, Sun., Gross at 2 p.m.; 10, Brinton; 14, Pepper dinner at 7 p.m.; 17, Brinton ditto; 23, Weir Mitchell 7 p.m.; 25, Dinner at Pepper's; 26, Faculty; 27, Thanksgiving Dr. Tyson; 28, Wood; 29, Mrs. Longstreth.' Here the entries end.

No. 131 South 15th Street where he was to live alone for three years was a narrow, fifteen-foot, three-story brick house of the mongrel type of Philadelphia domestic architecture of about 1830, with basement windows on a level with the pavement, a high flight of steps to the front door, and an area-way beneath. It was one of a row of similar houses crowded in the block south of Chestnut Street where the Union League Club now stands. Osler occupied the two ground-floor rooms; an office in front lined with bookshelves, and a waiting-room behind similarly lined. Among them some one remembers Jowett's 'Plato' in gaudy binding, and also that there were many medals and ribbons, relics of his former athletic prowess, that decorated the mantel. It was a wee establishment—probably kept none too tidy by its good-natured owner, Otto Hansen, a caterer, who lived upstairs, got his tenant's breakfast for him and otherwise tended to his simple wants. One of these was that books and papers should be left where deposited, whether on table, chairs, or floor. This must have been easy for Otto.

Though his advent had been much heralded, little was known about him, as is evident from a story told of old Dr. D. H. Agnew, a devout person of Scotch-Irish ancestry, who wrote and asked if Dr. and Mrs. Osler would not share his pew in the Second Presbyterian Church the following Sunday. When Osler was ushered in unaccompanied, Agnew whispered regrets that he was alone, whereupon Osler's mischievous half got the better of him. He merely raised his eyebrows and finger, which was interpreted by Agnew—and circulated—that the new-comer's wife was 'expecting'.

So far as the students were concerned, there can be no doubt that their first impression was one of disappointment. No polished declamations with glowing word-pictures of disease, such as they had listened to from Stillé and Pepper, and for which indeed the Philadelphia school was famed, came from this swarthy person with drooping moustache and informal ways, who instead of arriving in his carriage, jumped off from a street-car, carrying a small black satchel containing his lunch, and with a bundle of books and papers under his arm; who was apt to pop in by the back door instead of by the main entrance; who wore, it is recalled, a frock-coat, top hat, a flowing red necktie, low shoes, and heavy worsted socks which gave him a foreign look; who, far from having the eloquence of his predecessor, was distinctly halting in speech; who always insisted on having actual examples of the disease to illustrate his weekly discourse on Fridays at eleven, and, as likely as not, sat on the edge of the table swinging his feet and twisting his ear instead of behaving like an orator—this at least was not the professor they had expected.

It is said of Pepper that, with great dignity but conveying the impression of having no time to spare, he would enter the classroom while taking off gloves and coat, and immediately begin a brilliant discourse on some topic, not always related to his prescribed subject. Osler, on the other hand, could be dignified enough and serious, but playfulness and gaiety were always ready to break through the mask. Moreover, anything suggesting the *poseur* was foreign to his make-up, and there was no concealment of the fact that he felt the need of elaborate preparations for his more formal student exercises.

But it was a horse of another colour when the students came in contact with Osler in the wards, for the bedside instruction such as he was accustomed to, was an undeveloped feature in the Philadelphia school. He shared with Pepper in the University Hospital the two large medical wards (B and D they still remain), but Pepper, though the head of the medical department and engaged in a large private practice, was Provost of the University as well, actively at work adding to its resources. Hence he rarely appeared except to give his accustomed lectures, so that Osler had these wards almost to himself; and in them, with an increasingly enthusiastic group of students about him, he was to be found the larger part of each morning during this first year and until greater opportunities took him elsewhere for his main bedside visits.

Among the young clinical men at this time, original study or research of any kind was almost unknown, and even had any sign of an investigative spirit been present there were no facilities for its development. For this, Osler's enthusiasm soon made an opening; almost within a month of his arrival he had rigged up a small clinical laboratory under a part of the hospital amphitheatre, and there, amid surroundings as unpromising as the students' cloak-room at McGill, he is said to have soon 'produced an atmosphere so encouraging and helpful that young fellows trooped to his side '. This was a new experience to the senior students, who had previously been fed largely on graceful generalizations concerning disease, delivered from a platform. As one of them has said, it was like ' a breath of fresh air let into a stifling room ', and disappointment soon gave way to devotion. Of this time Howard A. Kelly has written:[1]

I was living in Philadelphia up in the big mill district of Kensington, culling a surgical out of a large general practice, and at the same time keeping in close touch with things at the University of Pennsylvania, for eight years my college, when it became manifest that some fresh and stirring blood had entered the college life. The university, with so many eminent men camping on her very doorstep in Philadelphia, and with that tendency to nepotism—a form of paternal pride seen in all successful institutions—had, as we younger men thought, driven John Guitéras of brilliant promise in general medicine, away from her doors to protect Pepper from rivalry, and now, not without great hesitation as we understood, she had actually broken her shackles, thrown traditions to the winds and pulled William Osler down from McGill. Fresh invigorating currents of life and new activities in our stereotyped medical teachings began at once to manifest themselves, and every sturdy expectant youngster in short order lined himself up as a satellite to the new star. Osler breezes were felt everywhere in the old conservative medical centre, and yet it was not without some difficulties that he securely established himself.

Medical education at the time in the States was undergoing radical changes. After the reforms at Harvard a few years before under the firm hand of President Eliot, the University of Pennsylvania was the next to follow in making a three-year medical course obligatory; and the senior students of 1884 had been the first of whom an entrance examination had been required. Some of the old faculty members, as was natural, had opposed these reforms which the younger generation, represented particularly by Wood and Tyson, warmly upheld; but the result was that there had been a painful controversy in the Faculty. Before Pepper's appointment as Provost in 1881 the medical school had been larger than the academic department; but with the stiffening of the admission requirements its numbers, as was inevitable, fell off, and this was a source of

[1] ' Osler as I knew him in Philadelphia and in the Hopkins.' *Johns Hopkins Hospital Bulletin*, July 1919, xxx. 215.

anxiety to the younger medical teachers who had favoured the change and who feared there would be a lack of financial support, particularly for the development of laboratories. All of the teachers were active in practice, with the exception of Joseph Leidy, an eminent naturalist, who was Professor of Anatomy. Harrison Allen lectured on physiology but practised laryngology for a living ; Tyson, who was Professor of Physiology, taught many other things and was likewise active in practice, which was also true of H. C. Wood, Agnew, Ashurst, Goodell, and the others. A recent graduate of the period, who, though working in the pharmacological laboratory, came under Osler's influence, has since written[1]:

> The remarkable part of Osler's entrance was that while the report of his election raised waves of regret and indignation, his actual plunge in the pond at once had the effect of making its surface placid, and this without there being any manifest effort on his part to ingratiate himself with any one or all of the factions. He entered so gracefully and ably, and so naturally, that he seemed almost at once to be one of us, young and old. He was gracious to his elders, cordial to his contemporaries, encouraging to his juniors, and jovial almost to the point of frivolity with all ; but the dominant factor that made his way successful with all hands was, to use a student phrase, ' he was up '—that is, he knew his subject and how to teach what he knew.

Osler's disinclination for a general practice, for which a university position was coveted as a portal of entry, and his determination to limit himself largely to consultations, was mystifying to his medical colleagues, most of whom were accustomed to hold afternoon office hours and to engage actively in house-to-house practice. His afternoons, on the contrary, usually found him at ' Blockley ', where, as will be learned, after his morning at the University Hospital and some bread-and-milk picked up in the ward, he would betake himself with a group of students to spend the afternoon making post-mortem examinations instead of sitting in his office awaiting patients. Dr. J. C. Wilson years later, in referring to Osler's advent, said : ' First, then, we at once sought to make a practitioner of him. But of that he

[1] H. A. Hare : ' William Osler as a Teacher and Clinician.' *Therapeutic Gazette*, Detroit, Mar. 1920.

would have none. Teacher, clinician, consultant, yes, gladly; but practitioner—no! And that with emphasis.'[1]

Osler's newly and rapidly acquired friends were by no means limited to those of his own school, and the households he came particularly to frequent were those of S. W. Gross, Minis Hays, James Wilson, and Weir Mitchell. He testified to this in a long letter written many years later to the Jefferson medical students, just before the war, regretting that he could not pay them a promised visit:

> . . . I owe much to the men of this school—let me tell you in what way. The winter of 1869–70 I had a bedroom above the office of my preceptor, Dr. James Bovell, of whose library I had the 'run'. In the long winter evenings, instead of reading my text-books, Gray and Fownes and Kirkes, I spent hours browsing among folios and quartos, and the promiscuous literature with which his library was stocked. I date my mental downfall from that winter, upon which, however, I look back with unmixed delight. I became acquainted then with three old 'Jeff' men—Eberle, Dunglison and Samuel D. Gross. The name of the first I had already heard in my physiology lectures in connection with the discovery of cyanide of potassium in the saliva, but in his 'Treatise of the Materia Medica', and in his 'Treatise on the Practice of Medicine' (in the yellow-brown calfskin that characterized Philadelphia medical books of the period) I found all sorts of useless information in therapeutics so dear to the heart of a second-year medical student. Eberle was soon forgotten as the years passed by, but it was far otherwise with Robley Dunglison, a warm friend to generations of American medical students. Thomas Jefferson did a good work when he imported him from London, as Dunglison had all the wisdom of his day and generation combined with a colossal industry. He brought great and well deserved reputation to Jefferson College. After all, there is no such literature as a Dictionary, and the twenty-three editions through which Dunglison passed is a splendid testimony to its usefulness. It was one of my stand-bys, and I still have an affection for the old editions of it, which did such good service. (And by the way, if any of you among your grandfathers' old books find the 1st edition, published in 1833, send it to me, please). But the book of Dunglison full of real joy to the student was the 'Physiology', not so much knowledge: that was all concentrated in Kirkes, but there were so many nice trimmings in the shape of good stories. . . .

In this vein he went on to say that he had really been

[1] Remarks at the farewell dinner to Dr. Osler, May 2, 1905. Privately printed.

brought to Philadelphia through the good offices of Jefferson men. The senior Gross, who had died only the preceding May, had been the outstanding figure of his generation in American surgery; and during his Philadelphia period, from the time he succeeded T. D. Mütter in 1856 until his death, his household was noted for its hospitality. Rarely did any waif visiting the clinics in Philadelphia fail to partake of his abundant table. In this tradition his son Samuel W. Gross had been brought up, and it was what his daughter-in-law too had come to regard as merely the customary cordiality among doctors. It was natural enough, therefore, that this couple should have called promptly on the new-comer on a Saturday evening in his forlorn rooms on South 15th Street, where they found a most homesick person pestered by mosquitoes, sweltering in the heat of a breathless October evening; and the outcome was that he took his Sunday dinner with them the following day.

This was the beginning of a great friendship, and nearly every Sunday found Osler at the Gross's for dinner, where he often brought with him a friend or two who might be visiting Philadelphia; among them later on, Palmer Howard, Ross, and Shepherd. One of the few laments about his new environment was the want of afternoon tea for one accustomed to it, and for whom lunch was a trifling matter to be carried in the pocket or picked up haphazard in a hospital ward. But a cup of tea could be assured at the Gross's, where too, after the doctor's office hours, young people were apt to be found, and where the door would be opened at the first touch of the bell by old Morris, the smiling coloured butler, known to so many of Osler's friends in the Baltimore years to come, who was able to make an afternoon visitor doubly welcome. Moreover, 1112 Walnut Street was conveniently near the *Medical News* office, and not far from the College of Physicians Library, where he usually buried himself from five to six in the afternoon.

Osler's irrepressible tendency to practical jokes was by no means uprooted in consequence of his transplantation to Philadelphia, and it cropped out frequently, particularly as an outgrowth of the 'E. Y. D.' tradition. Sir James Barrie, in his Rectorial Address delivered at St. Andrews in 1922, remarked that his puppets seem more real to him than himself, and that he could get on swimmingly if he could only make one of them deliver the address :

> It is M'Connachie who has brought me to this pass. M'Connachie, I should explain, as I have undertaken to open the innermost doors, is the name I give to the unruly half of myself: the writing half. We are complement and supplement. I am the half that is dour and practical and canny, he is the fanciful half . . . who prefers to fly around on one wing. I should not mind him doing that but he drags me with him.

Egerton Y. Davis was Osler's M'Connachie—his fanciful half, who first and last got him into a good deal of trouble. As may be recalled, he first appeared on the scene with the perpetration of a joke at the expense of one of Osler's Montreal friends. At about this time Theophilus Parvin, one of the collaborators on the anonymous Board editing the *Medical News*, an obstetrician of considerable pomposity and a tempting mark for M'Connachies, wrote an editorial on an obscure topic relating to his special field of work. This was too much for Osler's mischievous half, and a letter postmarked Montreal and signed 'Egerton Y. Davis, Ex-U.S. Army' was soon received by Parvin, commenting favourably on his editorial and citing in full a fictitious case of the sort Parvin had seen fit to discuss. Certain documents relating to a 'MS. of Egerton Yorrick Davis, M.D., late U.S. Army, Caughnawauga, P. Q.' may be found in the Osler library, and in a note prefatory to them occurs the following somewhat mystifying account of how Osler became entangled with this person :

> I never could understand about Egerton Yorrick Davis. He is represented to have practised at Caughnawauga nearly opposite Montreal, where his collections were stored in the Guildhall. Some have said that he was a drunken old reprobate, but the only occasion on which I met him, he seemed a peaceable enough old rascal. One thing is certain, he was drowned in the Lachine Rapids in 1884, and the body was never recovered. He had a varied life—in the U.S. Army; in the North West; among the Indians; as a general practitioner in the north of London. I knew his son well—a nice mild-mannered fellow, devoted to his father.
>
> These notes of customs among the Indian Tribes of the Great

Slave Lake were sent to Dr. Molson just after he had taken over the *Montreal Medical Journal* with Dr. Ross. One day I was in the job-room of the *Gazette* office where the Journal was printed, and Connolly said: 'Oh, there is an awful article for the Journal this month—Peter is in despair about it (P. was the compositor) and says Dr. Ross will never print it.' I went over and found these sheets all set up [cf. p. 181]. I told Connolly that Davis had not a very good reputation and to hold the printing until Dr. Ross saw the article. Of course he saw at once it was not fit to print.

I heard nothing more of Davis until I went to Philadelphia. I was on the staff of the *Medical News*, and Parvin in 1884 and 1885 was very interested in the action of the perinæal muscles. One day I met Minis Hays the Editor, who said: 'By the way, do you know Egerton Y. Davis who lives somewhere near Montreal? Parvin is delighted as he has sent the report of a case just such as he thought possible.' I said: 'Hays, for Heaven's sake! Don't print anything from that man Davis: I know he is not a reputable character. Ross and Roddick know him well.' 'Too late now,' Hays said, 'the journal is printed off.' So the letter appeared. The case has gone into literature and is often quoted. Minis Hays was disgusted, as Ross insisted that Davis was a joke, and he and Roddick hinted that I of all people was the one who knew anything about him. Some went so far as to say that *I* was Davis, and the rumour got about in Philadelphia. I never but once met the man. Afterwards I often used his name when I did not wish to be known. I would sign my name in the Hotel Registers as 'E. Y. Davis, Caughnawauga'. Once at Atlantic City after I had had bronchopneumonia I registered under that name immediately after Mrs. Osler and Revere. I had been there a week when a man came up and said: 'Are you Dr. Osler? I have been looking for you for a week: your secretary said you were away and not to be got at. My son is ill here and I wished you to see him.' He had said to Cadwallader Biddle, 'Who is that fellow Davis all the time with Mrs. Osler?'—and was furious when he found that I had registered under that name. They tell in Montreal many jokes about Davis, and father many of them on me. I am always sorry that I did not see more of him, and that I never visited his collections at the Guildhall, Caughnawauga.

William Osler.[1]

Osler could thoroughly enjoy a practical joke, even when he himself was the victim, and his own pranks which were merely an expression of his lively sense of fun were what

[1] On the margin is written: 'For an excellent variation of this story, containing all the essentials but the truth, see that of "The Relation of Medical Literature to Professional Esteem" by Dr. Bayard Holmes. W. O.' [Editorials in *Lancet-Clinic*, Cincinnati, Aug. 7–Nov. 28, 1915.]

served to make him such a good companion. But it was not often that his M'Connachie got the better of him; most of the work of the *News* office was serious enough and it was no small task for the four anonymous editors, who met every Wednesday noon in Hays's office at 1004 Walnut Street, to run a weekly journal of twenty-eight quarto pages with its four or five editorials in each number. It was here that Osler was of greatest help to the Board, and he appeared to have an inexhaustible supply of material on hand which he could easily put into shape for publication in an emergency.

As has been seen, he was a rapid, methodical reader with an exceptionally retentive memory, but in addition he had formed the habit of jotting down the gist of what he had read so that it could be drawn on when needed, and moreover he would often augment the notes with some reflections of his own. It was due to this habit of writing as he read that he finally acquired the charm of style which characterized his later essays, and which had already begun to show itself. It was due also to this habit that so many brief notes and postcards of comment and commendation were promptly sent off to rejoice the hearts particularly of young writers whose fledgling articles he happened to have read. Owing to his editorial writing on new and important subjects, his ideas came to be so well formulated and his information so exact in many directions, that when he composed his medical masterpiece five years later in Baltimore it was done throughout with such a sureness of touch and with his facts expressed in such readable form that it immediately superseded all other text-books of general medicine and still continues to hold the field.

During this first year in Philadelphia he usually dined alone at the old Colonnade Hotel, diagonally across the street from his rooms, always it is said with books and manuscript on the table, and he was usually to be seen reading and making notes during the course of the meal. But later on he was accustomed to dine at the Rittenhouse or the University Club, and, though essentially sociable, he had the great gift of appearing to be longer in company than he really was; of being able to fraternize briefly and to withdraw without his withdrawal being pointed; and if missed and sought for he was certain to be found in the club library where, as is recalled, 'Osler usually cut the magazines others rarely read, like the *Revue des Deux Mondes* and the *Nineteenth Century*.'

From the note previously quoted, it is evident that he did not regard himself as what is called a club man, in spite of the fact that he was much sought after by the most exclusive of them. Certainly in the sense that he much preferred his own table, library, and fireside, when he came to have a real home, to anything a club could offer, he was not 'clubbable'. However, during his bachelor years he perforce was a frequenter of clubs, and though distinctly companionable he was not one to sit about, to sip and gossip. But with dining clubs it was different, for at those he would let himself go and was usually the bright spot of the party—vivacious, friendly, amusing, and with the gift of stimulating others to their conversational best.

There were three dining clubs in Philadelphia to which he belonged—the Medical Club or 'Club of 19', the Biological Club, and the Mahogany Tree Club. The 'Club of 19' consisted of a group of intimates who held the reins in the University of Pennsylvania School, and who at this time met fortnightly in rotation at one another's houses, where 'a club', as was said, was given. This amounted at first to a simple repast of coffee and biscuit, but such plain living and high thinking has given way in time, as it not infrequently does with such gatherings, to a more formal and largely gastronomic function. The Peppers, George and William, H. C. Wood, Tyson, Harrison Allen, H. A. Hare, S. W. Gross, Herbert and William F. Norris, William Goodell, Wharton Sinkler and others had all been or still were members.

As Weir Mitchell had written to Leidy on August 3rd, Osler was socially 'a man for the Biological Club' if they could get him. This they did, and the meetings of this group of scientists always stood out among the pleasantest recollections of his Philadelphia period. This Club, which had been in existence since 1856, was patterned somewhat on the lines of Huxley's *X* Club which had begun to hold meetings two years before, though it does not appear that the Philadelphia copy of its London prototype ever had excursions or accepted the formula of '*X*'s + *YV*'s'. It met more frequently, however, and dined on the second and fourth Friday of each month, there being two guests permitted on each occasion.

As was said by Huxley of the *X* Club, these friends forgathered with no special object beyond the desire to hold together a group of men with strong personal sympathies and to prevent their drifting apart under the pressure of busy lives; and, as he also said, they probably could have managed among them 'to contribute most of the articles to a scientific encyclopaedia'. As was true also of the *X* Club, no effort was made to perpetuate it, and as the *X* Club died in 1892 with its most devoted supporter, T. A. Hirst the mathematician, so the Biological Club did not survive Joseph Leidy's death in April 1891. Joseph Leidy, at this time sixty-one years of age and at the height of his intellectual powers, was Osler's chief delight at these meetings. For Leidy's accomplishments and particularly for his skill with a pencil he had unbounded admiration, and though they were of different generations there was great similarity between the manner of upbringing and the early interests shown by these two men, both of them having begun their life's work with a study of the parasitic entozoans. Leidy's magnificent monograph on Rhizopods, illustrated by his own exquisite drawings, had been published by the Government shortly before this time.[1] A copy is in Osler's library, its association value enhanced by the insertion of one of Leidy's incomparable microscopic drawings, secured (as the following letter makes clear) years later, at a time when books were his chief solace.

To Joseph Leidy Jr. from W. O. Oxford, 16/vi/15.

Dear Leidy, Oh! I would take the risk. Send those Notes over. I want to have them bound with the 'Flora and Fauna'. The steamers are running regularly and we get about four mails a week from America. Could you not steal me one of the original sketches of the rhizopods? You see what a greedy devil I am! Did you

1 'The Fresh-water Rhizopods of North America.' *Report of the U. S. Geological Survey*, vol. xii, 1879.

find any memoranda in his papers about the Biological Club? He was the life of the club & the member about whom we all used to rotate—Mitchell, Franklin Gowen, Chapman, Hunt, Wistar and Sellers.[1]

As has been seen, Osler had a particularly warm spot in his heart for men of an older generation, whom he always treated like contemporaries; and if in the course of conversation a person's years were in question he was wont to reply: 'Oh, he's just our age.' What he said in a later address,[2] appreciative of Alfred Stillé, expressed the feelings he always held for an aged member of the profession, who had kept up with the stream:

So far as I know, the chapter on the old man in the profession has not yet been written. To-day, as in the sixteenth century, the bitter *mot* of Rabelais is true: 'There be more old drunkards than old physicians.' Take the list of Fellows of our College, look over the names and dates of graduation of the practitioners of this city, and the men above seventy years of age form, indeed, a small remnant. All the more reason that we should cherish and reverence them. It interested me greatly in Dr. Stillé, and I only knew him after he had passed his seventieth year, to note the keenness of his mind on all questions relating to medicine. He had none of those unpleasant senile vagaries, the chief characteristic of which is an intense passion for opposition to everything that is new. He had that delightful equanimity and serenity of mind which is one of the blessed accompaniments of old age. He had none of those irritating features of the old doctor who, having crawled out of the stream about his fortieth year, sits on the bank croaking of misfortunes to come, and with less truth than tongue lamenting the days that have gone, and the men of the past. He was not like the sage of Agrigentum of whom Matthew Arnold sings:

Whose mind was fed on other food, was train'd
By other rules than are in vogue to-day;
Whose habit of thought was fix'd, who will not change
But, in a world he loves not, must subsist
In ceaseless opposition.

---

[1] The sketch forwarded by Leidy's nephew is of a magnified *Menopon perale* drawn on the back of a 'Penn Club' card of invitation. With the possible exception of this single example, the Leidy drawings had all been deposited in the Academy of Natural Sciences of Philadelphia of which the Biological Club was an outgrowth.

[2] *University of Pennsylvania Medical Bulletin*, June 1902.

1885

During all the previous autumn, when time permitted, he had probably been preparing for his Goulstonian Lectures, which were built up from his Montreal material; and, as indicated, he chose as his subject 'Malignant Endocarditis' (acute valvular disease of the heart), on which he was able to speak not only with authority but with considerable originality.

In 1632 a bequest of £200 had been left to the Royal College of Physicians by Dr. Goulston for the maintenance of an annual lectureship, 'to be read by one of the four youngest doctors in physic of the said college . . . between Michaelmas and Easter on three days together both forenoon and afternoon,' for an honorarium of £10. Thus the Goulstonian Lectureship for 250 years had been handed out as a form of compliment to the youngest of the Fellows, reckoned on the basis of their appointment. As has been seen, both Osler and Allbutt were made Fellows in 1883, and though Allbutt in age was several years the senior, his was the last name on the list and hence he was the youngest Fellow in point of duration of his fellowship. For this or some other reason Allbutt had been selected as lecturer in 1884, and as no new Fellows were appointed in that year Osler was given the lectureship for the ensuing one.

Though he had already written a number of occasional papers on the subject of endocarditis, these lectures, which were delivered in London on February 26th, March 3rd and 5th, contained the first comprehensive account in English of the disease, and did much to bring the subject to the attention of clinicians.[1] If one may judge from an enthusiastic account sent home by a quondam pupil,[2] who admits he 'scarcely kept his seat, with emotion', they must have been warmly received. In the intervals between his lectures he probably made a succession of visits, overlooking none

---

[1] Orth's successful experiments in producing valvular endocarditis in animals which Osler made the subject of an editorial (*Medical News*, Oct. 24, 1885) were not known until later in the year. Osler had made a few experimental observations himself which were inconclusive. His contribution was largely clinical and pathological, not experimental.

[2] Letter to the *Canada Medical and Surgical Journal*, Mar. 1885, xiii. 488.

of his old London friends ; and probably, too, was subjected to the usual receptions and entertainments. He evidently visited Horsley, then at work in the Brown Institution on his experimental investigations of myxoedema in monkeys—at least this may be inferred from an editorial on the subject which appeared in the *Medical News* on April 4th soon after Osler's return.[1] It was on this visit also in all probability that Hawksley, the London instrument-maker, perfected for him the type of binaural stethoscope, which replaced the single-tube stethoscopes until then in common use in Philadelphia and known as Pepper's and Da Costa's models. With little variation in its construction, the next generation of medical students everywhere came to utilize this new instrument ; but Osler carefully kept his name out of it.[2]

To F. J. Shepherd from W. O. 131 South 15th St., 27/3/85

So glad to hear from you. Such a budget of Canadian letters came in on Tuesday afternoon and not two minutes after, Sutherland, Mills & Thornton. We had a very pleasant evening together—such fun over the Exam papers in McGill Gazette which also came in at the same time. Mills took them in very good part. Poor devil! I am sorry for him. I doubt if he will ever *assimilate*, and I think some position away from Doctors would be more suitable. Sorry you will not be down this spring. Get Ross to join Gardner ; it will do him good. I wish he would get away to England & drop a great deal of his 2nd year work. As usual, I have been used much better than my deserts. I mean in connection with the [Goulstonian] lectures. It is a pity that I had not the appointment last year but anyone can see they are virtually Montreal lectures. The more I see here the more I think of the great advantages of the M.G.H. and the general condition of things medical. So glad to hear from Howard that there are prospects of an addition this summer. I am well in harness again & can scarcely realize that I have been away. Love to the children. Best regards to the Frau. If you ever come across anything worth while with reference to the general & special

---

[1] He was quick to see that it was the next important step in the untangling of thyroid function since that taken by Kocher ; but it led him to make a poor prophecy regarding the future of the surgery of the gland, though the conclusions were doubtless justified by Horsley's findings, which of course did not take the parathyroids into consideration.

[2] Cf. Wm. A. Edwards : 'A New Binaural Stethoscope'. *Medical News*, Phila., Nov. 7, 1885, xlvii. 527.

evolution of the profession let me know. I am thinking of some such subjects for my address in August.

August and his address as President of the Canadian Association were a long way ahead for one who did things by the day, and he was meanwhile hard at work in other directions. The editorial writing in connexion with the *Medical News* he had assumed in large measure and, as already stated, he was always ready to do more than his share. It was evidently his intention to issue a third Pathological Report from the Montreal General, in which his full series, amounting to nearly 1,000 autopsies, could be recorded. This is apparent from a foot-note to an article on 'The Morbid Anatomy of Pneumonia' read before the Pathological Society of Philadelphia on April 23rd.[1] The article was succeeded by another statistical study on 'The Morbid Anatomy of Typhoid' published in August,[2] but like other good resolutions of the sort he had by this time become so engrossed in new lines of work and was so nearly swamped by undertaking a chapter for Pepper's 'System of Medicine' that the project was abandoned; and Wyatt Johnston's brief list of his later Montreal autopsies is the only printed record that remains.

But he was by no means to be a stranger at the autopsy table, for even without any official appointment he managed to continue with his work in morbid anatomy. He had succeeded in evolving for himself the same sort of existence he had so enjoyed in Montreal—a doctors' dinner club, an association with a group of men interested in medical publications, his bedside hospital clinics, his detailed studies of post-mortem appearances, and the reports of his observations before a local society. The Philadelphia Pathological Society soon came to take the place of the Medico-Chirurgical Society of Montreal of which he had been so devoted and

[1] 'This, with other articles on morbid anatomy which will follow from time to time, will constitute my third and last Pathological Report from the Montreal General Hospital.' The paper was based on a series of 105 post-mortem examinations of cases of lobar pneumonia. (*Canada Medical and Surgical Journal*, Jan. 1885, xiii. 596–605.

[2] This paper gives a study of 56 autopsies on typhoid cases. Its first few pages not only exhibit the extent of his reading but show an historical trend and charm of style beginning to be apparent in his writings.

active a member. Its minute-books show that long before his election to membership, which did not occur until March 12, 1885, Osler had been a frequent guest. The society at this time was a most active one, and it has been stated that those who subsequently gained local eminence in the profession were almost without exception men who were frequent participants in its sessions. In one of his later delightful addresses [1] Osler comments on the purposes and value of medical societies 'to foster professional unity and friendship, to serve as a clearing-house in which every physician of the district should receive his rating and learn his professional assets and liabilities', and so on:

In a city association the demonstration of instructive specimens in morbid anatomy should form a special feature of the work. After all has been done, many cases of great obscurity in our daily rounds remain obscure, and as post-mortems are few and far between, the private practitioner is at a great disadvantage since his mistakes in diagnosis are less often corrected than are those of hospital physicians. No more instructive work is possible than carefully demonstrated specimens illustrating disturbance of function and explanatory of the clinical symptoms. It is hard in this country to have the student see enough morbid anatomy, the aspects of which have such an important bearing upon the mental attitude of the growing doctor. For the crass therapeutic credulity, so widespread to-day, and upon which our manufacturing chemists wax fat, there is no more potent antidote than the healthy scepticism bred of long study in the post-mortem room. The new pathology, so fascinating and so time-absorbing, tends, I fear, to grow away from the old morbid anatomy, a training in which is of such incalculable advantage to the physician. It is a subject which one must learn in the medical school, but the time assigned is rarely sufficient to give the student a proper grasp of the subject. The younger men should be encouraged to make the exhibition of specimens part of the routine work of each meeting. Something may be learned from the most ordinary case if it is presented with the special object of illustrating the relation of disturbed function to altered structure.

Osler's first presentation before the Pathological Society was on April 9th, and Dr. R. M. Landis writes that during the four years of his active membership, in the little first-floor corner room at the old College of Physicians where

[1] 'On the Educational Value of the Medical Society.' Read on the occasion of the centennial celebration of the New Haven Medical Society, Jan. 6, 1903. *Boston Medical and Surgical Journal*, 1903, cxlviii. 275.

the society met, he appeared before it no less than fifty-two times. Just as in Montreal, it was seldom that he did not have some interesting specimen to show, some new technical method to demonstrate, or some subject of interest to present in relation to comparative pathology; for though the opportunity in Philadelphia was less, since the Veterinary Department of the University had only just been established, he took advantage of every possible occasion to pursue his studies of disease in the lower animals. The following letter to H. V. Ogden, written at about this time, shows how he kept abreast of the newer laboratory methods, for Hans Gram's procedure for the differential staining of bacteria had just been published.

131 S 15th St.
Tuesday.

Your very nice sections & photos came safely. That from the tumour of foot is evidently myeloid sarcoma, springing doubtless as they sometimes do, from the periosteum. The other, I am in doubt as to the true nature of & have not yet gone over it very carefully. You will have quite a nice microscopical section. Have you used Gram's method for staining bacilli and micrococci? It is exceptionally good. [He proceeds to fill a page with most minute details.] Do you get good staining fluids in Milwaukee? R. & J. Beck Optic. here (on Chestnut St) keeps good magenta fluid for Bacillus tubercul. rapid method, & Hayes, Chemist, Cor. Broad & Walnut, makes good Gent. and Methyl violet stains & Bis. brown. If you don't get them good in M. let me send you some. I shall send you a copy of my Goulstonian lectures in a day or so. Was in Toronto for Easter. All well. Saw Reynolds in Hamilton. He seems thriving. Do you go to New Orleans? I shall go to Winnipeg by the Lakes. Feel quite at home here now. A few consultations have come in. Finished exams. Methods very much behind McGill. Men are pretty bright. Let me know about the stains. So much depends on getting them well made. If you would like some good slides of T. Bacilli or top covers charged with sputum containing them say the word. Yours ever,

The consultations had been few indeed—not that he much minded. They are noted in his account-book. There were seven in January, and from February to May only two—at least only two from which fees were collected. It is evident that he was keeping up with pathology, and much of his staining and section-cutting, which must have been 'free hand' for the most part, was probably done in his makeshift laboratory at the University Hospital. It is recalled that he always carried in his pockets a small bottle or two containing some tissue fixative, and when the opportunity offered of securing some specimen or piece of tissue that needed study, he would take a fragment away with him for microscopic examination.

Most of these fragments, in all likelihood, came from the 'Blockley' Hospital. This venerable institution, originally the Philadelphia Alms-house, which in 1742 was 'fulfilling a varied routine of beneficent functions', has just claim to be the oldest hospital in the States. Having migrated twice during the growth of the city, it finally in 1834 moved from the 'Bettering House' in what is now the heart of Philadelphia, to a farm in the suburbs in the then township of Blockley on the west side of the Schuylkill. Here, far out in the country, the indigent poor and afflicted, the alcoholic and insane of Philadelphia came to be housed—'went over the hill to the poorhouse'; and in the early days when Alfred Stillé served his six months as Resident Physician, patients were bled wholesale, the place was infested with politics, and had the 'immortal smell of an alms-house'. In those days the medical students visiting Blockley used to cross the Schuylkill by the south ferry to a landing on the alms-house grounds to avoid the longer way round over the Market Street bridge. But Philadelphia was rapidly coming to envelop Blockley Township, and in 1870, a few years after Stillé's brother Charles became Provost of the University, the first group of buildings, chiefly medical ones, encased in the green serpentine stone then so much in fashion, were erected on part of the old Blockley estate which had been lopped off from the dwindling property originally owned by the alms-house. The move had been made with reluctance, for the University thereby lost contact with the old Pennsylvania Hospital; but in a few years a hospital of its own in the same architectural style was erected alongside the original medical building, adjacent to but with its back turned haughtily upon the architecturally unpretentious old Blockley buildings with their quadrangle of some twenty acres.

Owing to the proximity of these institutions, for those accustomed to making short cuts it was possible to leave the University Hospital by the rear entrance and enter the Blockley enclosure by a postern gate in the old wall. The advantage of this lay in the fact that near this gate stood the little two-story red brick building which served in Osler's day as the half-way house to the Potter's Field, and here almost every afternoon he was to be found with the group of students accustomed to camp on his trail.[1] Blockley even then was a huge place, not unlike the Allgemeines Krankenhaus in Vienna, or the Salpêtrière in Paris, with over two thousand inmates, many of them with interesting chronic maladies; and the opportunity for post-mortem studies was unusually good.

There were at this time two officially appointed pathologists—good men too—E. O. Shakespeare and Henry F. Formad, the coroner's physician; but they probably were busy elsewhere or had less insatiable curiosity about disease than had Osler, nor did they have a pack of students at their heels. The old servant in the dead-house quickly saw the difference, and whenever an examination had been waived as without particular interest, since no one had come to conduct it, Osler was certain to be informed and to appear with his followers. This finally reached a point at which regulations had to be made that no one should perform an autopsy without the written consent of the official pathologists; but in time Osler himself received a Blockley appointment.[2]

Many of the labours engaged in by physicians in the dissecting-room are repulsive enough, and those of the dead-house still more so, for there are tasks to perform which a chambermaid or stable-boy would shrink from undertaking; and as O. W. Holmes once said: 'We cannot wonder that the sensitive Rousseau could not endure the

[1] A vivid description of Blockley in the '80's from the standpoint of a student-interne is given in 'Blockley Days' by Arthur Ames Bliss, 1916. Cf. also J. Chalmers Da Costa's 'Old Blockley Hospital', *Journal American Medical Association*, April 11, 1908.

[2] His election occurred at a meeting of the Board of Guardians, December 28, 1885, at which time seven other physicians were appointed, among whom were his friends Tyson, Wilson, and Musser.

atmosphere of the room in which he had begun a course of anatomical study. But we know that the great painters, Michael Angelo, Leonardo, Raphael, must have witnessed many careful dissections, and what they endured for art, our students can endure for science and humanity.' At the present time the Pathological Department at Blockley is housed in a magnificent institute under the direction of a man who values tradition. But in Osler's day there were none of the modern appurtenances one associates with a laboratory—nothing, indeed, but a storage vault and the small room with its stone table on which the examinations were made. That any special post-mortem records whatsoever, under these circumstances, should have been kept is remarkable; and though he never held an appointment as pathologist, the opportunity to perform an autopsy was never lost and the volumes contain 162 of these records in his own unmistakable chirography. No less than forty-eight of these were cases of pulmonary tuberculosis, an evidence of the fact that he felt there was always something to learn from an examination, no matter how familiar the pathological picture was likely to be. Dr. William T. Sharpless, one of the Blockley internes of the time, writes:

I have most distinct recollections of the Sundays when he came early in the morning and spent the whole day in making necropsies, which we saved for him so far as it was possible to do so. I have known him to begin at 8.00 in the morning and continue at this work until evening. He would hunt for hours to find the small artery concerned in a pulmonary haemorrhage or the still smaller one whose rupture produced a hemiplegia. If he found something especially interesting he would send out the runner to get all the boys and show what a wonderful thing he had found and how interesting and instructive it was. Once in the ward class there was a big coloured man whom he demonstrated as showing all the classical symptoms of croupous pneumonia. The man came to autopsy later. He had no pneumonia but a chest full of fluid. Dr. Osler seemed delighted, sent especially for all those in his ward classes, showed them what a mistake he had made, how it might have been avoided and how careful they should be not to repeat it. In thirty years of practice since that time, whenever I have been called upon to decide between these two conditions I remember that case. I am sure that it had the same effect upon the other members of the class that it had on me and was certainly the right sort of medical teaching. . . .

To F. J. Shepherd from W. O. University Club,
Friday [May 1885]

When did you fellows get the notion that I was coming up on the 20th? I cannot possibly. I have been away so much (in Toronto April 5th) and am full of work with our short spring session, having four classes a week. And lastly & most important, I must try to economize this year as I am still in arrears, and expenses here are very heavy, though I am living most quietly. I do hope Campbell will not beat Mac. It will be too bad; still I have but little fear of the result. So glad to hear that the building operations have begun. I have written to Kerr, Sullivan & others about the meeting. If there is any prospect of a failure we had better postpone the Winnipeg meeting & hold the session somewhere in the East. Poor Molson! It would have been a sad thing for the Gunn Artillery [Riel rebellion]; I could not go on to N. Y. to see him. He should have come on here. I am struggling towards a little consultation work. Mitchell is most kind in this matter & I have seen some interesting cases with him. That glanders case will make an interesting communication. I hope Howard has saved some specimens. Love to the chicks.

Campbell did not 'beat Mac' though it was a close contest, for on June 21st the Montreal General Hospital Board announced that Dr. Richard MacDonnell had been appointed to fill the vacancy occasioned by Dr. Osler's resignation, having received 93 votes against the 71 for Dr. F. W. Campbell, the rival candidate, who, however, was made an assistant physician. The 'building operations' are to be explained later in a letter from Palmer Howard.

It was at about this time, in May and June of this year, that two editorials appeared in Ross's journal, possibly only inspired but more probably written by Osler, and telling, as dispassionately as possible for the benefit of his Canadian friends, the story of a lamentable altercation which had arisen among the profession in the States.[1] This episode directly or indirectly affected most of the prominent American physicians, for long disturbed their cordial relations to the American Medical Association, and must have been particularly distressing to one like Osler, whose nature 'sloped towards the sunny side'. The story has

[1] 'The International Medical Congress.' *Canada Medical and Surgical Journal*, June 1885, and July 1885, xiii. 696, 762. Also Feb. 1886, xiv. 437.

been told in sufficient detail in Garrison's 'Life of John S. Billings', whom it chiefly concerned; and the only reason for mentioning Osler's part in it is to show how ready he was to take up cudgels in defence of others when he saw injustice being done. An invitation which originated with the American Medical Association to hold the IXth International Congress in Washington had been accepted, and the energetic Billings, as Chairman of the Committee of Organization, had perfected a programme which would have ensured the success of this formidable undertaking had not certain malcontents, dragging cheap medical politics into an international event, succeeded, at a meeting of the 'A. M. A.' in New Orleans, in repudiating the action of Billings's committee. This involved making charges later on against a number of eminent men included in Billings's provisional list of officers, on the grounds that they were not supporters of the code of ethics adopted by the Association. These were men of unquestioned repute but of independent views, like Jacobi and Loomis of New York, and Henry I. Bowditch of Boston; and Osler was sufficiently aroused to call a meeting of the prominent Philadelphians, who passed resolutions declining to hold any office whatsoever in connexion with the Congress as newly organized. Osler made a copy of these resolutions which he sent the same day to H. P. Bowditch with the following explanatory note:

131 S 15th St. Phila.
29th [June]

I enclose you resolutions of Phila. meeting to-day anent Congress. Have written Chadwick & Warren asking them to call meeting of Boston men to express their views of the situation and if feasible to send a Committee to join ours at Flints & urge upon him the advisability of the old Committee resuming its functions and going ahead in spite of all opposition, or failing this—at any rate to refuse to lend his name to the organization as at present constituted. We all feel very sore about the removal of your dear uncle from the vice-presidency, an insult which all respectable members of the profession must resent and which in itself is sufficient ground for severing connection with the men who have got control at present. . . .

The Philadelphia resolutions were followed by similar ones passed both in Boston and Baltimore. It is quite possible that this action was taken overhastily; quite possible, too, that there was some justification in the umbrage felt in the South and West that the better-known men in the larger cities of the East were unnecessarily well represented on Billings's original committee. However this may be, and it is not very vital to-day, the enlarged original committee withdrew practically in a body, and, instead of eminence, mediocrity came to control the Congress. This unfortunate episode, which for months filled the medical press of America [1] and Europe with public discussion of a petty action, caused a rift in the profession which it took years to smooth over. That Osler felt strongly in the matter is shown by the series of editorials in Ross's journal, but being a man who never harboured a grievance he did not let this controversy affect his subsequent relations with the association. For, with others, he realized that in spite of its having been led astray by designing, ambitious, and selfish men, the A. M. A. would continue to represent the great body of the profession and, with experience, its leaders would come to realize that science recognizes no sectional lines.

During a part of August Osler was evidently in Toronto, dividing his time between his immediate family and the Francis cousins who had left Montreal. He was meanwhile writing editorials, reviews [2] of the books he was reading, and getting his presidential address into shape for the Canadian Medical Association meeting which, on account of the disorders in Manitoba, was to be held in Chatham in Western Ontario. As is shown by the following note from Palmer Howard, he had written for information, for his immediate purposes, regarding the official Acts regulating the practice of medicine in the Province. Moreover,

[1] *The Medical News* and the *Transactions of the American Medical Association* contain full accounts of this historical squabble from opposite points of view. The discussion, reaching Europe, was participated in by Paget, Virchow, and others, to the humiliation of the better element among the profession in America.

[2] One of them dealt with Stillé's 'Treatise on Asiatic Cholera', for this was the summer of the last serious cholera epidemic in Europe and there were fears of its reaching America. Epidemics were rife, with yellow fever on the rampage in Vera Cruz and small-pox again in Montreal.

Howard had evidently booked him for a later address in the autumn:

From Palmer Howard to W. O. Montreal Aug. 24

On the enclosed slip are some statements that may answer your queries. The Act wh. regulated our affairs was that of George the III. Then came the Act—4th & 5th Victoria, providing for reciprocal rights in Upper & Lower Canada. This was succeeded by the Act incorporating the Prof. in this Prov. in 1847—10th year of Victoria—I was writing this letter when yours of the 22nd arrived. We hope to be ready for the 1st but may not be and personally I am so desirous that you should be with us & give *the* address that I feel we ought to postpone the opening till Monday the 5th—That w[d] allow of you delivering y[r] own opening lecture on the 1st & coming up to us for Saturday the 3rd or Monday the 5th. Dawson will not return until the 1st or 2nd of Sept & nothing can or will be settled until after your Chatham meeting. We shall hope to have a meeting of the Faculty on Saturday Ev[ng] the 5th by which time *you*, Ross, Stewart, Shepherd etc. will have arrived. I am greatly pleased that you have consented to come down on the 5th and spend Sunday with me. If you came down with Ross, Stewart & Shepherd you might talk over the affair with them so that at the meeting on Saturday they may have some ideas & views to present of a promising and useful nature.

How would it do to postpone the formal opening till the second or third week in Oct[r]. & begin the ordinary work without an opening address on the 1st? I w[d] prefer the other way, but if it cant be accomplished, why it cant. What Canadian physicians do you think might be asked to attend the ceremony & who w[d] be most eligible to make a short address? Would McD[l] or Mullin or Malloch of Hamilton be likely to come? or who in Toronto or London? Oh for a half hour's chat with you! In the meantime make your calculation that you will have to open the new building with an address from your ever active brain. We are busy vaccinating [1] and

[1] 'The disease [smallpox] smoulders here and there in different localities, and when conditions are favourable becomes epidemic. This was well illustrated by the celebrated Montreal outbreak of 1885. For several years there had been no small-pox in the city, and a large unprotected population grew up among the French-Canadians, many of whom were opposed to vaccination. On February 28th a Pullman-car conductor, who had travelled from Chicago where the disease had been slightly prevalent, was admitted into the Hôtel-Dieu, the civic small-pox hospital being at the time closed. Isolation was not carried out, and on the 1st of April a servant in the hospital died of small-pox. Following her decease, with a negligence absolutely criminal, the authorities of the hospital dismissed all patients presenting no symptoms of contagion who could go home. The disease spread like fire in

nothing more; except fuming at plasterers carpenters etc. Jared desires his kind regards to be added to mine. Yours very truly,

R. P. Howard.

As President of the association, yet able to look upon the situation of the Canadian profession through the eyes of a teacher in another country, Osler's position gave him opportunity for a plain straightforward talk intended for ears other than those of his immediate auditors.[1] He divided his subject, which concerned in general the growth and development of the profession, into three topics: the organized profession, the medical school, and the medical society; and in the address, which was for him a long one, he dwelt seriously for the first time upon a number of topics which throughout his life he continued to harp upon—the preliminary education of a doctor, the regulation of the medical curriculum, the raising of admission-requirements to the schools, the lengthening of the course, the importance of a proper Federal Bureau of Registration which should have the licensing power; the need of supporting the Provincial boards of health; of regular attendance at medical-society meetings to which every one should come, both to learn and bring something he can teach. It was characteristic of him to add:

By no means the smallest advantage of our meetings is the promotion of harmony and good-fellowship. Medical men, particularly in smaller places, live too much apart and do not see enough of each other. In large cities we rub each other's angles down and carom

---

dry grass, and within nine months there died in the city of smallpox 3,164 persons.' (Osler's 'Practice of Medicine'.)

[1] 'The Growth of a Profession.' *Canada Medical and Surgical Journal*, Oct. 1885, xiv. 129.

At this same meeting he was down for a paper on 'The Clinical and Pathological Relations of the Caecum and Appendix', which apparently was read but not published, possibly because the pressure of preparing his more formal address had prevented its completion. Had it been, it would have antedated Fitz's classical paper on the subject by two years; and it has been mentioned that he had presented to the Medico-Chirurgical Society in 1880 a case of perforation of the appendix with circumscribed abscess perforating into the bowel. What probably represented the substance of his remarks was not published until a year or two after the ideas regarding primary appendicular inflammations and perforative appendicitis had been generally ascribed to Fitz, who like Osler had first gained his knowledge of them as a pathologist rather than a clinician.

off each other without feeling the shock very much, but it is an unfortunate circumstance that in many towns, the friction being on a small surface, hurts and mutual misunderstandings arise to the destruction of all harmony. As a result of this may come a professional isolation with a corroding influence of a most disastrous nature, converting a genial, good fellow in a few years into a bitter old Timon, railing against the practice of medicine in general and his colleagues in particular. As a preventive of such a malady, attendance upon our annual gatherings is absolute, as a cure it is specific. But I need not dwell on this point—he must indeed be a stranger in such meetings as ours who has not felt the glow of sympathy and affection as the hand of a brother worker has been grasped in kindly fellowship.

He must have gone on to see Howard immediately after this meeting and then have rushed back to Philadelphia, for he sends word to his sister in Dundas that he is 'treating her shabbily but must be back on Friday'. He could not have been very well, for his mother writes on September 14th and ventures to prescribe for him:

I could not help feeling worried about that horrid carbuncle though I felt you were in the best of hands for treatment and nursing at Dr. Howard's. Being vaccinated while that was going on must have been very sickening; you will need some good attention and I hope will prescribe the best of everything for your dear self so there may be no repetition of those evil things if you were able to leave as intended on Thursday we shall look for a note to-morrow and hope to hear that you are much better—would not preparation of Wyeth's beef, wine and iron, be good for you to take and no trouble if you kept it at hand you know that or good beef tea would be good for others and if you indulge in boils you ought also to take the remedies required to heal them.

And in her chronicles of the family doings of the next week, she hopes his 'boils and blains are clean gone' after a few days at the sea with the Hays, and adds that they had all enjoyed reading the President's address at Chatham and that 'Aunt [Pickton] thought it equal the wisdom of 107 years of experience—sound sense it certainly was'.

It was customary for him to spend a week or two each summer with the Hays at Point Pleasant on the New Jersey coast. He was given a room on the top floor and was accustomed to spend a part of his day writing, a task often interrupted, however, by his unannounced visits to the nursery or the sewing-room, where the Hays children would be found, and where another chapter would be told from the story of Arabella Elizabeth, 'a rude little girl who used to put out her tongue, and one day was struck by a fairy's wand because of this habit and went through the earth all the way to Australia, and when she got there found she could not get her tongue back and had, in consequence, a series of most awful times.'

Quite possibly as an outcome of the squabbles over the International Medical Congress, it had seemed desirable for the leading physicians of the country to organize a society similar to that which had already been formed for the surgeons by the senior Gross some five years before. Accordingly, on October 10, 1885, at the office of Dr. Delafield, Drs. Draper and George L. Peabody of New York, R. T. Edes of Boston, Pepper, Tyson, and Osler of Philadelphia being present, the Association of American Physicians had its birth. Who originally suggested this organization is not recorded, but probably it was Osler, who later on was responsible for similar foundations.[1] A name for the proposed society was decided upon; a committee composed of Edes, Peabody, and Osler was appointed to draw up the necessary plans of organization; and there was a full discussion of the men who were regarded as eligible for such an association as was contemplated.

As indicated in Howard's letter of August 24th, plans were under way for the opening of the new building of the McGill Medical Faculty, which had been made possible by Strathcona's original gift. It is probable that in reply to Howard's inquiry Osler had suggested Pepper's name as the chief speaker on the occasion. At all events they went on

[1] In his memoir of William Pepper (*Philadelphia Medical Journal*, Mar. 18, 1899), Osler says: 'For many years those of us whose work lay in the special field of medicine had felt that a society was needed in which we could meet our fellows in the same line of work. As early as 1881 I had written to Dr. Tyson, shortly after my first visit to Philadelphia, urging the organization of such a body, but it was not until the winter of 1885–6 that the initial steps were taken . . . I remember well in the preliminary meetings how by tacit consent Dr. Pepper assumed the headship, and in formulating the details and in arranging the final organization his executive abilities made the work very easy.'

together from Philadelphia for the ceremonies which had been postponed to October 22nd. There, before a gathering of distinguished guests, of whom the Hon. Donald A. Smith, who made the occasion possible, was naturally the central figure, Osler's appearance was greeted 'with prolonged cheering' on the part of the students; and though he was the first called upon by Howard to speak, his remarks were brief and he gave way promptly to Pepper, who in his usual brilliant style delivered the principal address.

In view of his labours to improve medical standards of education in the States through the example of his own school, Pepper had been a wise choice as speaker. He pleaded for the better endowment of medical schools, 'so as to secure fixed salaries for the professors, who would then cease to have any pecuniary interest in the size of their classes'; and he referred to other munificent gifts to medicine during the past decade—those of Johns Hopkins, of Mrs. John Rhea Barton, of Vanderbilt, and of Carnegie. The customary dinner followed, and 'after the loyal toasts and that of the President of the United States were given', Osler was called upon to speak of medical education in the United States and Canada. This he did in no doubtful terms, and in referring to his brethren 'south of the line', and to the many anomalies of the profession in their country, he is quoted as saying: 'How it is that such a shrewd practical people as those in the United States should have drifted into such a loose, slipshod way of conducting medical schools is unintelligible.'

He must have been somewhat exhausted by all this—what with his 'boils and blains'—for after Sunday supper with Pepper the night of their return he noted in his account-book: 'Weighed on Pepper's scales to-night. 138½ lbs. Thin underclothing, no overcoat, thin frock coat.'[1] This does not sound as though he was particularly fit to start in with his school work; and when one considers the number of his active interests there was perhaps

[1] The 'thin frock coat' betrays the custom of the day, especially for a physician, and even more for a Canadian one. His friend Chadwick of Boston was once called to Montreal in consultation, and appearing in tweeds, was not permitted to see the patient till he had been properly outfitted.

sufficient excuse for him to be somewhat run down. He does not appear, however, to have ever admitted to others such a thing as fatigue—far less to himself. His literary activities during the preceding year, taken alone, must have been a considerable tax on his strength and show his enormous industry; for published in the *Medical News* alone, for the year, thirty of the editorials [1] and nine book-reviews have been traced to him, and there is no telling how many more may have gone to Ross. All this was apart from his less fugitive writings like the Goulstonian Lectures and, above all, the important chapters in Pepper's 'System of Medicine'. These dealt with the diseases of the blood, of the blood-glandular system, and of the heart, constituting an eighty-five-page treatise in itself [2]—one of the most important sections in this encyclopaedic publication of five volumes.

Most of the distinguished men, whose participation in this elaborate 'System' Pepper had secured, were the same as those who came to be the founders of the Association of American Physicians. On December 29th a second meeting was held in Delafield's office, at which Drs. Loomis of New York, R. P. Howard of Montreal, Minot, Fitz, and the two Shattucks of Boston were present, in addition to those who attended the earlier meeting in October. It was decided

[1] Some of them show the wide range of his interests: for example, that on 'Medicine in China', inspired by the Annual Report of the Soochow Hospital and concluding with the statement that 'in the modern crusade the stethoscope has replaced the sword'. Another on 'The Imperial Customs Medical Reports' dwells on the researches of Patrick Manson into the rôle of mosquitoes in human pathology which he had run across in this obscure publication. Many of the editorials, like those on the recent discoveries concerning actinomycosis and hydrophobia, are an indication of his continued interest in the diseases common to man and animals. None of the newer subjects escaped him, and many of the editorials were reviews of the more recent papers in the leading French and German periodicals to which he had access at the College of Physicians. One may identify many of the editorials by internal evidence, as that on the 'Death of Dr. Wm. B. Carpenter' (*Medical News*, Nov. 14, 1885, xlvii. 546), whose name he couples with that of Huxley and Owen and whose works on Comparative Pathology, and the Microscope, were often consulted in his days at Weston with 'Father' Johnson.

[2] The style of these admirable articles is unmistakably that which in fuller development was to make his Text-book of Medicine such a successful work.

that the number of members should be limited to one hundred. Delafield was chosen President, with Tyson as Secretary; and a circular was sent out to the selected candidates with the announcement of the first meeting to be held in Washington the following June. He had been home for his usual Christmas visit before this meeting, but his mother wrote: 'We did not see much of Willie, as he was soon off to New York with Dr. Howard.'

CHAPTER XII

1886–9

PHILADELPHIA: THE LAST YEARS

As can be seen, it had not taken Osler long in his new environment to get into his full stride. Meanwhile, on all sides he had made staunch friends, with many of whom he was on terms of such informal relationship that he came and went as he chose; and if there happened to be children in the household his brief and frequent visits were more often to the nursery than the drawing-room. It is said that one of the places where he was best known in Philadelphia was at the toy-counter in Wanamaker's, and that the sales girls used to draw lots to see who could wait on him the next time, because he invariably bought something, made up his mind quickly, and giving an address to which the contraption was to be sent, would depart leaving the small coins of change behind him. He had the pleasant habit of dropping in on people should he happen to be passing by; and should he have been away for a few days he was apt to make a round of visits, stopping only to leave his card, or a book, some flowers, or for a word of greeting or a brief frolic with some one's child. Whether it would be inconvenient never seemed to enter his head. He always behaved with every one as though he was a member of the family, and under these circumstances a visitor can hardly be an inconvenience.

His reputation as a desirable consultant was spreading, and though hard to find, according to local tradition, when found and an appointment made he was scrupulously punctual; and his visits to patients with other physicians were invariably a solace and comfort to both parties. His unusual gifts of human sympathy and of understanding were such that every one with whom he came in contact retained a vivid picture of him. Nor was Osler himself forgetful. One of his patients was Walt Whitman, of whom he has left these fragmentary reminiscences: [1]

Not long after removing to Philadelphia a telegram came from my friend Dr. Maurice Bucke of London, Ont.: 'Please see Walt and let me know how he is.'—to which I had to answer: 'Who is Walt

---

[1] They were written, as will be seen, in the summer of 1919 when he was recuperating in Jersey.

and where does he live?' It was very stupid of me as I should have remembered that a few years before when Dr. Bucke had been a guest at one of our Club dinners in Montreal he had startled us into doubts of his sanity by extravagant praises of one Walt Whitman, a new seer of a new era, whom he classed with our Saviour, Buddha, and Mahomet. Then I remembered, too, to have seen notices of a book he had written about Whitman; but I had no idea where the prophet lived. The next morning I had the answer: 'Mr. Walter Whitman, 328 Mickle Street, Camden.' In the afternoon I crossed the Delaware River ferry and in a 'clean, quiet democratic street' I found the little, old-fashioned two-story frame house. A pleasant middle-aged woman answered the door, to whom I showed Dr. Bucke's telegram. 'He will be glad to see you—anyone from Dr. Bucke. Mr. Whitman is better to-day and downstairs.' The door opened into what appeared to be a room, but I had no little difficulty at first in getting my bearings. I have seen what the tidy housewife calls a 'clutter', but nothing to compare with the front room, ground floor of No. 328 Mickle Street. At the corner, near the window, the head and upper part of a man were visible—everywhere else, covering the floor, the chairs and the table, were, to use his own description, 'heaps of books, manuscripts, memoranda, scissorings, proof-sheets, pamphlets, newspapers, old and new magazines, mysterious-looking literary bundles tied up with stout strings.' The magazines and newspapers, piled higher than the desk, covered the floor so completely that I had to pick my way by the side of the wall of the room to get to the desk. I thought of Prof. Teufel's room in 'Sartor Resartus'. After a hearty greeting, I had some difficulty in explaining that I did not come directly from Dr. Bucke, but that he had sent me over from Philadelphia to find out how he was. There was nothing serious the matter—a transient indisposition which had passed away. With a large frame, and well-shaped, well poised head, covered with a profusion of snow-white hair, which mingled on the cheeks with a heavy long beard and moustache, Walt Whitman in his 65th year was a fine figure of a man who had aged beautifully, or more properly speaking, majestically. The eyebrows were thick and shaggy, and the man seemed lost in a hirsute canopy. . . . My visit was made without any of that preparation—that expectation, upon which Gideon Harvey dwells as influencing so profoundly our feelings. I knew nothing of Walt Whitman and had never read a line of his poems—a Scythian visitor at Delphi! . . . That evening at the Club after dinner I opened the volume of 'Leaves of Grass' for the first time. Whether the meat was too strong, or whether it was the style of cooking—'twas not for my pampered palate, accustomed to Plato and Shakespeare and Shelley and Keats. This has been a common experience; even Dr. Bucke acknowledging that 'for many months I could see absolutely nothing in the book', and would even 'throw it down in a sort of rage'. Whitman himself has expressed this feeling better than anyone else, speaking of his 'strange voice', and acknowledging that critics and lovers of poetry may well be excused the 'chilly and unpleasant shudders which will assuredly run through them, to their very blood and bones' when they first read him, and exclaim: 'If this is poetry, where must its foregoers stand?' . . . At this time, of the two men Bucke interested me more. Though a hero-worshipper, it was a new experience in my life to witness such an absolute idolatry. Where my blurred vision saw only a fine old man, full of common sense and kindly feelings, Bucke felt himself in the presence of one of the world's great prophets. One evening after dinner at the Rittenhouse Club with Dr. Chapin, Dr. Tyson, Dr. J. K. Mitchell and a few others who I knew would appreciate him, I drew Bucke on to tell the story of Whitman's influence. The perfervid disciple, who talks like [Chaerephon] in the [Apology] is not often met with in these matter-of-fact days. It was an experience to hear an elderly man—looking a venerable seer—with absolute abandonment tell how 'Leaves of Grass' had meant for him spiritual enlightenment, a new power in life, new joys in a new existence on a plane higher than he had ever hoped to reach. All this with the accompanying physical exaltation expressed by dilated pupils and intensity of utterance that were embarrassing to uninitiated friends. This incident illustrates the type of influence exercised by Whitman on his disciples—a cult of a type such as no other literary man of our generation has been the object. . . .

In like vein, through several manuscript pages of what is the first uncorrected draft of an unpublished address, he proceeds to tell of subsequent visits the next year or two, during which time he 'gradually came to realize what Whitman's life and message meant to his followers'.

So there were occasional consultations which gave him contact with interesting people, but it was his students that chiefly occupied his time. His formal exercises as arranged for him in the curriculum could not have represented during this time a particularly satisfactory portion of his week's schedule, and he was at his best with volunteer groups of students in the dispensary or at Blockley. Years later, in 1915, referring in general to the period of medical teaching antedating the new order of things which came about through the example of the Johns Hopkins, he said: [1]

Twenty-five years ago there was not a single medical clinic worth the name in the United States. A most pernicious system prevailed

[1] 'The Coming of Age of Internal Medicine in America.' *International Clinics*, Phila., 1915, iv. 1–5.

—bad for the teacher, worse for the pupils. At the University of Pennsylvania, Pepper held a Saturday clinic and gave two didactic lectures weekly. I gave one clinic, and with Bruen and Fussell and Jack Mitchell held classes in physical diagnosis, which were good enough in their way but the students had no daily personal contact with patients. There was abundant material, and between the University Hospital, Blockley, and the Infirmary for Nervous Diseases, where Henry W. Cattell was my assistant, I was for five years very nearly a 'whole-time' man. There was no clinical laboratory, only an improvised room under the amphitheatre, which was very active the year George Dock was in charge.

He filled his prescribed lecture hours in most unorthodox ways, and often utilized as texts subjects not in the books. For example, the first time he met the class after Austin Flint's death he began:[1] 'Since we met together on Saturday, a veteran of the army of which you are recruits has fallen'; and a large part of the hour was given over to a review of Flint's services to the profession. In the course of these remarks he said:

In the third place, Dr. Flint has done a great work in helping us to arrive at more satisfactory therapeutical laws. In this he no doubt followed the instructions of Jacob Bigelow of Harvard, to whose teaching he probably listened, for he was the author of an essay, one of the most classical in American medical literature, 'On the Self-limitation of Disease.' He laid down there that a cardinal principle in the consideration of the therapeutics of a disease was a knowledge of its natural history; that we had to know the course of a malady left to nature before we could appreciate the action of the medicines given for its cure. At the time that Dr. Flint graduated who would have dared to treat a case of pneumonia from its beginning to its termination without a drop of medicine? No one. The man who would have attempted it would have been looked upon as in the highest degree worthy of blame and censure, and certainly in private practice would not have had the confidence of the family for twenty-four hours.

In this way he chose to mirror in a self-analytical way his own views of therapeutics, and one of the Blockley internes of the day, Dr. Samuel McC. Hamill, writes that:

Osler's rational use of drugs was much too far advanced for staid Philadelphia. Can't you imagine a naturally conservative city to whom the eloquent Wood was extolling the value of drugs and the

[1] 'Remarks to the Class in Clinical Medicine at the University of Pennsylvania.' *Canada Medical and Surgical Journal*, April 1886, xiv. 571.

equally eloquent Pepper recommending a dozen different drugs in the treatment of individual disease, shocked into insensibility by having a young Professor of Medicine, recently come into their midst, go through his wards with his internes and finding nothing definite the matter with his patient say, 'Did we give that last fellow Compound Tincture of Cinchona or Compound Tincture of Gentian?' . . . But in reality Osler was a very good therapeutist as we internes realized, and used drugs not empirically but scientifically, and in his teaching laid great stress upon the general management of the disease. . . .

Late in March he delivered three lectures[1] on the Cartwright Foundation, before the Alumni Association of the College of Physicians and Surgeons in New York. He devoted these lectures to 'certain problems in the physiology of the blood', a subject which was engrossing the attention of many of the leaders of medicine at this time; and in them he incorporated the results of his own detailed microscopic researches which, begun years before in Burdon Sanderson's laboratory, had continued through the Montreal period with the investigation of anaemia, and were soon to merge into his malarial studies.

As April approached, his mother's letters, which had been telling of much sickness in a family whose third generation was rapidly increasing in number, begin to express eagerness for his home-coming after the winter term, for she sees that his father is becoming more and more helpless. He must have been April-fooling his nephew, for she wrote: 'Poor little Billee was highly indignant at your Apl. 1st postal, but B. B. traced out some invisible sentences much to the lad's satisfaction and you were forgiven the insult. We shall be counting the days now till we see you—stay as long as possible when you come.' He divided his Easter recess between Toronto and Montreal, where a cousin was to be married, and this festivity over, it appears that he

[1] *Medical News*, Phila., 1886, xlviii. 365, 393, 421. His three main topics were: (1) the blood platelets; (2) the degeneration and regeneration of the blood corpuscles; and (3) the relation of the corpuscles to the processes of coagulation. The lectures, which were copiously illustrated by original drawings cut from his note-books, give an exact presentation of the existing state of knowledge on topics to which he had made notable contributions, but it is necessary to read between the lines to determine the real significance of his own personal observations and discoveries.

went to Perth on a Sunday to make a post-mortem examination on an old patient, a physician in whose case every one had made a wrong diagnosis, and found to his amazement a rare tumour at the base of the brain which he subsequently reported.[1] So almost everything he did became grist to his literary mill.

The inaugural meeting of the Association of American Physicians, which Osler in an article thirty years later referred to as 'the coming-of-age party of internal medicine in America',[2] was held in Washington on the 17th and 18th of June.

Special societies [he writes] had already been successful, and the idea was in the air, so to speak. The suggestion came, I believe, from Dr. James E. Graham, of Toronto, to Dr. James Tyson. Pepper was actively sympathetic and took a leading part in the organization. From the start it proved a great success. Francis Delafield, the first President, struck the true note when he said : 'We want an association in which there will be no medical politics and no medical ethics : an association in which no one will care who are the officers, and who are not ; in which he will not ask from which part of the country a man came, but whether he has done good work, and will do more ; whether he has something to say worth hearing, and can say it.' The leading clinicians and pathologists of the country were present. One man whom we had all hoped to have with us, the Nestor of clinical medicine in the country, Austin Flint, had recently died, and some seniors who attended this meeting did not care to join the Association. Meredith Clymer an old pupil of Andral and Chomel, was an interesting link with the past. Looking over the list, it is sad to see that only twenty-five of the original seventy-five members survive. . . . The association set a standard, promoted good-fellowship, encouraged research among the younger men, and has led to the formation of many societies dealing with various aspects of medicine and pathology. . . .

His own contribution to the programme of this first meeting was a paper of minor interest dealing with a rare condition of the valves of the heart, but there were many other communications of more than ordinary importance : by William H. Welch of the Johns Hopkins on 'An Experi-

[1] 'A case of Cholesteatoma of Floor of Third Ventricle and of the Infundibulum.' *Journal of Nervous and Mental Diseases*, N.Y., 1887, xiv. 657–73.

[2] *International Clinics*, Phila., 1915, iv. 1.

mental Study of Nephritis'; by F. W. Draper on 'Pancreatic Haemorrhage'; by Reginald H. Fitz of Boston on 'Diseases of the Appendix'; by Weir Mitchell on 'Observations upon the Knee Jerk', for Westphal's recent discovery was coming to be looked upon as an important diagnostic sign in diseases of the nervous system; and particularly one by W. T. Councilman from Welch's laboratory on 'Certain Elements Found in the Blood of Malarial Fever'. Thereby hangs a story, illustrative of Osler's methods of work.

During the year 1880, a French army surgeon, Alphonse Laveran, while stationed in Algiers had discovered certain pigmented bodies in the blood cells in cases of malaria, of which a report was made before the Academy of Science in Paris. Though promptly taken up by the Italians,[1] in America little attention had been paid to this discovery previous to Councilman's work in Welch's laboratory in Baltimore, where malaria at this time was rife. Possibly no member of the association, not even Councilman, had had an experience equal to that of Osler with microscopical studies of the blood; and consequently when Osler arose and expressed scepticism, 'speaking in the fulness of his ignorance', as he said later, regarding Laveran's claims, not all of which Councilman had been able to verify, his remarks must have had considerable weight. Osler stated that he had examined the blood of six cases, in three of which at the time of the chill he had seen the amoeboid bodies, but he was inclined to believe they were nothing more than vacuoles in the cells. Even Councilman was doubtful as to whether they represented the cause or the effect of malaria; but Sternberg, who was present, warmly upheld Laveran's work and both he and Councilman pointed out that if Osler had stained his preparations he would have been convinced that he was dealing with actual organisms.

[1] It is quite probable that the long delay in following up and verifying Laveran's discoveries was due to the claims by Swiss and Italian investigators of the discovery of a bacillus of malaria which proved, as Osler said, 'an *ignis fatuus* which had led many astray'. To arrive at the truth is a long and tedious process, and it may be noted that at this time scepticism was being expressed regarding Pasteur's work on hydrophobia, and even the tubercle bacillus was encountering formidable opposition, for many claimed that it was merely a concomitant of the disease and not its cause.

In the wards at Blockley, to which he now had official access, there had been a good many patients with malaria during the spring, and Osler had made full notes of the cases whose blood he had had an opportunity of examining. In the very first of them, on April 20th, he had unquestionably seen and made drawings of the amoeboid stage of the malarial parasites, though he was evidently uncertain as to their interpretation.[1] Immediately after the meeting he returned to Philadelphia and set to work to satisfy himself as to the truth of the matter. He must have spent countless hours over the microscope, for his note-book, which is extant, contains observations on the blood of seventy cases, with notations and frequent illustrations of what he had observed. It was the beginning of his great interest in malaria, but it was not until his studies were resumed in the autumn that he became fully convinced of the truth of Laveran's claims regarding the protozoal origin of the disease.

He had expected to get away early in July for his holiday and had hopes of a trip to England, though of this he was doubtful, for as he wrote to his sister: 'I may be too hard up, but I should like to attend the British Association Meeting in Dublin and keep up my connexion with English friends.' But his malaria studies kept him in sweltering Philadelphia well on into the month despite appeals from his mother, who in her birthday letter says that 'Toronto is cool', that she is 'dotting off the days till the 21st', and that awaiting him 'there are 14 or 15 children at the Island, who are revelling in the water and escape drowning wonderfully!'

With evident reluctance, particularly after his experience

[1] His scepticism is a little difficult to understand, particularly as the *Medical News* for January 16th contained an account of the researches by Marchiafava and Celli, which had fully corroborated those of Laveran; these Roman investigators had even recorded an instance of the experimental transmission of the disease in man. Malaria was coming to be a topic of great importance, and it was in the course of his celebrated address before the British Medical Association on August 11th of this year, at Brighton, that John S. Billings stated in regard to the malaria-ridden regions of the Southern States, that despite some few exceptions 'malaria and science were antagonistic'.

with 'Case XVII, July 14, 1886', when he saw the plasmodia in abundance, Osler broke off his studies for a brief visit home and a subsequent five weeks' holiday in British Columbia—his first prolonged vacation in many years. This trip, a voyage of inspection, was made over what was then called the Winnipeg Western Railway in company with his brother Edmund and a group of men who were financially interested in the future development of the great country to the north and west. There is little record of this outing[1] beyond some doggerel lines, written by Mr. F. Faithfull Begg, one of the members of the party, which describe 'a man of pills, in medicine learned in human ills', whose every vein 'the milk of human kindness fills'. It was probably an invigorating life in the open, much of it passed in 'bark canoes, with noble red-men for their crews'; and in an address written long afterwards Osler drew upon his memory of the trip for the following figure:

> There are two great types of practitioners—the routinist and the rationalist—neither common in the pure form. Into the clutches of the demon routine the majority of us ultimately come. The mind, like the body, falls only too readily into the rut of oft-repeated experiences. One evening in the far North West, beneath the shadows of the Rocky Mountains we camped beside a small lake from which diverging in all directions were deep furrows, each one as straight as an arrow, as far as the eye could reach. They were the deep ruts or tracks which countless generations of buffalo had worn in the prairie as they followed each other to and from the water. In our minds, countless, oft-repeated experiences wear similar ruts in which we find it easiest to travel, and out of which many of us never dream of straying.[2]

The 1st of September found him back in Philadelphia again interned at Blockley with his microscope, and a few

[1] One incident which W. O. recorded in his 'Notes and Comments' (*Canada Medical and Surgical Journal*, Jan. 1888, xvi. 377 et seq.) was to the effect that a Mr. Fred. Brydges, who had 'kindly met their party at the Portage to escort them over the Manitoba and North Western Road', told a remarkable story of a new-born infant which had fallen from a moving train and survived. Evidently this story was disbelieved by his Montreal friends, for it had an E. Y. D.-ish flavour.

[2] 'The Importance of Post-graduate Study.' *Lancet*, Lond., July 14, 1900, ii. 73.

days later there appeared a long editorial in the *Medical News* on 'The Malarial Germ of Laveran'. He still was hesitant, without further evidence, to accept the bodies he had seen as the causal agent of the disease, despite their constant presence in acute cases. Further confusion had been recently added to the subject by a paper in Virchow's *Archiv*, which described the finding of a micrococcus in the blood of malaria patients, and Osler states that 'the most rigid scrutiny should be exercised in accepting evidence, and it is to be hoped that those who have the opportunities and the necessary technical skill will soon place us in a position to give an opinion upon the *Plasmodium malariae*'. Both opportunity and technical skill were his, and by the end of the month one of the cases 'showed crescentic forms distinct and abundant on several examinations'. It is apparent from his sketches that he had seen and figured Laveran's flagellate forms; and, no longer with any shadow of doubt in his mind, on October 28th, before the Pathological Society, he gave in detail the results of his observations, which were subsequently published.[1]

Osler's Baltimore students in later years, who became accustomed to the tedious search for the malarial parasite in all obscure fevers, can realize what an amount of time the study of his seventy cases entailed, with its effort to determine in each instance what relation the organisms in their various stages bore to the recurrent paroxysms and in what way they were influenced by medicines; for it was then largely new ground, and hourly examinations of the blood were required. He gained the impression that the pigmented bodies in the red corpuscles were more numerous before than during the attack, and the examples which he saw of 'the remarkable segmentation of the parasite resulting in its rosette form' were in each instance observed during a paroxysm. Perhaps the most interesting paragraphs of this important paper, which put Osler in the first rank of the investigators of malaria (with Laveran, Richard,

[1] 'The Haematozoa of Malaria.' *Transactions of the Pathological Society of Philadelphia*, 1887, xiii. 255; also *British Medical Journal*, 1887, i. 556. In this paper he makes a frank acknowledgement of his former incredulity 'that flagellate organisms should occur in the blood'.

Marchiafava and Celli, Golgi and Councilman) were those in which he discussed the nature of the parasites, a topic of particular interest to him in view of his earlier studies on the parasites he had seen in the blood of the frog. Haematozoa had also been seen in fish, in rats, in birds; and he gave an account of Surra, a disease affecting the horses, mules, and camels in India, which his friend Griffith Evans had recently described in the London *Veterinary Journal*, attributing it to a blood parasite.[1] Osler regarded the flagellate form as the adult condition of the malarial plasmodium; but it remained for one of the Johns Hopkins students, W. G. MacCallum, while studying malaria in birds, to first observe the conjugation of the organisms and thus fully to explain their flagellate form.

It is somewhat difficult, in view of the present knowledge of the full life cycle of the malarial parasite, to project oneself back into the obscurities existing in the '80's; and a full decade was to elapse before Ronald Ross in India proved that the mosquito played the part of an intermediary host in the transmission of the disease—a discovery which has led to the practical extermination of malaria from seriously infected regions like the Roman Campagna and the Isthmus of Panama whence, indeed, one of the patients in Osler's series had come. To most people of that day, lay and professional, the shivering ague was caused by a mysterious nocturnal 'miasm', and it took years to introduce into the southern states, where the disease was pandemic, the idea which Osler quickly grasped and adopted, 'that in malarial regions the examination of the blood will prove in skilled hands a most valuable aid in the diagnosis of many

[1] In the copy of Evans's 'Report on "Surra" Disease' (1885) in Osler's library, he has written: 'When I was a student with Bovell at Toronto, 1868–9, Griffith Evans, who was stationed there as veterinary surgeon to the Artillery, was much interested in the microscope and frequently came to Bovell's rooms to help in the preparation of specimens. He had previously been stationed at Montreal, where he had graduated in medicine from McGill in 1864. When serving in India he made the discovery of the parasites in the blood in Surra—the first trypanosome disease to be described. On his retirement he went to Bangor, where he still lives, a hale, hearty octogenarian. He sent this, and a book of photographs of famine scenes in India, 8 Jan., 1918.'

obscure cases'. A few years later in his Baltimore clinic the regulation was put into effect that no diagnosis of malaria be made without a microscopic demonstration of the parasite. It was a most important matter, for nearly every fever in the South at the time was loosely called typho-malaria and treated with quinine.

Obviously he had become so deeply engrossed in his clinical work, now centring itself more and more at Blockley, that there were few occasions for abstraction when he might be found scribbling James Bovell's name on his pad. But he nevertheless had a moment of nostalgia at the thought of the McGill opening session :

To F. J. Shepherd from W. O. 131 South 15th St. Phila.
12th [Oct., 1886].

How are you all? It seems long since I have heard from any of you. I felt very like skipping North on the 1st, for your introductory lecture. I felt rather homesick. I still, at times, feel like a stranger & a pilgrim though everyone is very kind and I have got on better than I could have anticipated. I must arrange to spend some days in Montreal at Xmas, and run up also to the Carnival if you have one this Winter. Everything goes on here as usual. My hospital work at Blockley keeps me very busy as I have 80 patients to look after. I am able however to do much more satisfactory ward teaching than heretofore. Hays asked me the other day about a note of yours in re Canada Med. Association & the Quebec profession. He thought it would rather stir up dust & I agreed with him. . . .

It must have been about this time that he paid his first visit to Baltimore, in view of the following letter postmarked November 8, 1886, to his old friend Dr. John A. Mullin of Hamilton. It is quite possible that he may have gone over for the purpose of checking up his malaria observations with the work which was in progress there :

Sunday.

Your most interesting specimens came to hand on Thursday & I demonstrated them at 11 a.m. to the class as the typical lesions of Addison's disease. The caseo-fibrous changes are most marked & there is very little normal tissue to be seen. Do send me a note of the case. You should report it as cases are so rare, tho' they seem to come in runs as this is the fourth which has come under my notice since May 1st. . . . I would have acknowledged receipt sooner but I have been 2 days in Baltimore seeing Johns Hopkins,

& more than delighted. It is the univ. of the future & when the Med School is organized all others will be distanced in the country. When you come down in May with Malloch we shall go on for a day or two. Goodell was asking for you both. You made quite an impression on him. I am over head & ears in work, among other things studying the Malarial germ which seems a pretty constant body. Kind regards to Mrs Mullin & to Malloch. So glad you have sent the boy to Port Hope.

During all this year, despite his intensive pursuit of the malarial parasite, there was no let-up in his 'inkpot career'. 'Both pen and brain got a deal of practice in Philadelphia', as he admitted in later years. Besides the Cartwright Lectures and the six or eight more serious clinical and pathological papers which were published, he had, as he expressed it, 'devilled for Pepper for his "System of Medicine", writing in addition to my own sections, those of Janeway on certain of the diseases of the heart.' There were also numerous contributions to the Pathological Society and an endless succession of editorials, of notes, and of book reviews for the *Medical News*.[1] In addition to all this he had been persuaded by Minis Hays to take over another task in connexion with the rejuvenation of the *American Journal of the Medical Sciences*, a journal founded in 1827 and so with one or two exceptions (the *Edinburgh Medical Journal*, 1803; the *Lancet*, 1823) the oldest medical periodical in the English language. Its book reviews were to be made a special feature of the rejuvenated journal and its January issue contained two of them from Osler's pen, one signed, the other not. The latter was a review of Pepper's 'System', which pointed out 'an extraordinary mistake' by the author (W. O. himself) of the section on 'Diseases of the Blood and Blood-glandular System': moreover, the review when submitted was signed 'E. Y. D.' but the editors saw fit to omit these initials.[2]

[1] Forty-nine of the editorials during 1886 have been identified as his, and there are probably many more, sometimes two or three appearing in a single issue. They were on a great variety of subjects.

[2] Another feature of the journal in its new form was its 'Summary of the Progress of Medical Science', and in the April issue Osler's name appeared in charge of the section devoted to Medicine. This he attempted to conduct single-handed, though soon (October 1886) the names of J. P. Crozier Griffith,

1887

At the end of his Christmas holidays, spent as usual in Toronto, he visited his friends at McGill, taking Palmer Howard back with him to Philadelphia for the Centennial Exercises of the College of Physicians held on January 3rd in the old home of the College, at 13th and Locust Streets. Ever since his advent in Philadelphia Osler had frequented the College Library, which then boasted some 34,000 volumes. Indeed only a year had elapsed after his election as Fellow on January 7, 1885, before he was put on the Library Committee with Weir Mitchell, Minis Hays, and F. P. Henry—an evidence of his great popularity, for, as the present librarian testifies, such a thing has never occurred before or since. He served on this committee until he left for Baltimore; and to the end of his life retained the liveliest interest in the affairs of the College, to whose library a goodly number of its more precious books were subsequently added under his auspices.[1]

So it is not surprising to find him taking an active part in the celebration of this year at which honorary fellowships were conferred upon distinguished guests, among whom was Palmer Howard. Indeed the occasion brought together an assemblage of men who either were already reckoned among Osler's friends or who subsequently came to be—among them Hunter McGuire of Richmond; Jacobi and Draper of New York; James Chadwick, George B. Shattuck, and H. P. Bowditch of Boston; Sternberg, Edes, and John S.

his assistant, of Walter Mendelsohn of New York, and subsequently of W. S. Thayer and George Dock, appeared as his coadjutors.

[1] His method is illustrated by the following incident related by Dr. Keen: 'No institution in Philadelphia was more cherished by him than the College of Physicians and its splendid library. He was always giving notable books to it. Even after he went to Oxford his benefactions did not cease. Once he wrote to Mitchell that Quaritch had a superb copy—the best he had ever seen except the famous Grolier copy in the British Museum—of the first printed edition of Celsus (1478), beautifully bound, as became its author, which could be had for £80. He wanted the College to have it and wrote: "I'll give $25. Can't you bleed the Fellows for the rest." Mitchell promptly phlebotomized the other Fellows and the book now ornaments our shelves.' He also bequeathed to the College his finest manuscript, Bernard de Gordon's *Lilium Medicinae*, 1348.

Billings of Washington. But the central figure was Weir Mitchell, who had been elected President of the College for this its centennial year, and who gave in a charming commemorative address [1] an historical account of the growth and position of the profession in Philadelphia. This entailed a medical genealogy of the College from the time its thirteen founders—'some in Quaker dress and some in knee-breeches, most of them carrying the gold-headed cane and the meditative snuffbox, some with queues or powdered wigs'—who, probably dominated by Benjamin Rush, first met in the little house on Fifth Street. And Osler, no less interested than Mitchell in local history, subsequently drew upon the same theme to say:

> The College is local, and the property of a local organization, but John Jones, Morgan, Shippen, Rush, Wistar, Dorsey, Dewees, Barton, Chapman, Wood, Hodge, Meigs, Gross and many others whose names we honour, belong now, not to Philadelphia alone, but to the history of the profession of this country. The social force and influence which physicians have always exercised in Philadelphia is not a little peculiar, and there is much truth in the statement that 'he is, and always has been, relatively a more broadly important personage here than elsewhere'. Certainly, physicians have played a large part in our public as well as private history, and they have 'sustained in noble succession the prominence of this city in all that lifts our art and its sister sciences above the common level of applied usefulness.

No one ever entered more whole-heartedly into making a success of celebrations of this sort, but there was other business of a more serious nature in hand, for with the beginning of the year he had resumed his studies of malaria with an attempt to differentiate the organisms of various types of the disease—quotidian, tertian, and quartan, anticipating the observations of Marchiafava and Celli published two years later. He evidently sent his papers to Laveran, who replied enthusiastically, saying: 'J'ai été pendant plusieurs années très embarrassé pour classer mes parasites; la place que vous leur assignez me paraît leur convenir tout à fait.' Osler had written at this time a general summary of the malaria question which appeared in a March issue of the *British Medical Journal*, and from

[1] *Medical News*, Phila., Jan. 8, 1887, l. 29. In this same issue is Osler's editorial on the centennial, from which excerpts have been taken.

now on his particular interests, so far as his publications indicate, lay in the direction of utilizing the information already gained, that is in differentiating cases of malaria from other obscure febrile conditions, rather than in further studies of the parasite.[1] His writings more than those of any other of his contemporaries served to stimulate interest in malaria and to popularize throughout the profession the knowledge necessary for its proper recognition, for it was evident that the diagnosis could no longer remain merely a matter of probability based on recurrent chills and an 'ague cake', but was capable of exactitude with the aid of a microscope. Osler's enthusiasm was contagious, and many of his pupils and assistants got to work on the subject. In this way he fathered some of the important subsequent discoveries which were made in his Philadelphia and Baltimore clinics. Nevertheless, as he subsequently admitted: 'It was a long uphill battle; most sceptical myself at first, there were many of my colleagues at Philadelphia who could not be convinced, and my good friend Dr. Payne of London, pathologist at St. Thomas's, on the appearance of my paper in the B. M. J. of 1887, wrote confidentially urging me to be more careful in the future, as what I had described and figured were evidently artefacts.'

By his own precept and example Osler stimulated his students to observe, record, and publish. He had, as Clifford Allbutt has said, that wonderful power, only possessed by a few great teachers, of 'inseminating other minds'.

Wherever he went [writes W. W. Keen] the wheels began to go 'round', things began to be done, and all for the good of the pro-

[1] This was not entirely so, however, for in the discussion of a second paper by W. T. Councilman before the Philadelphia Pathological Society early in the following year, Osler stated that he had made a series of observations on the blood of fishes and birds, in view of the statement that some of the forms described by Laveran had been found in the blood of carp and some water-fowl. Professor Baird of Woods Hole had offered him facilities for this work and had furnished him with forty-five carp in which he had failed to detect organisms. Nevertheless, in the blood of a goose sent him from Ontario by Dr. G. A. MacCallum (father of his pupil W. G.) with the statement that the bird had malaria, he had found one or two pigmented bodies. They were not numerous, however, nor was the temperature elevated; nor, so far as could be made out, did the goose have chills. (*Medical News*, Phila., Jan. 14, 1888, lii. 54.)

fession and of the community. The dry bones as in Ezekiel's Vision gathered themselves together and became imbued with active life. The diligent were encouraged to become more diligent, the slothful were shamed into activity. He was a fount of inspiration. His personal influence extended more widely and to better purpose than that of almost anyone I have ever known. Weir Mitchell and William Pepper were of the same type, and when this powerful triumvirate were gathered in Philadelphia they had no rival the country or possibly the world over.

His method of 'insemination' took various forms, though it was often merely a hint of a thing worth doing scribbled to some one on a postcard. Dr. George de Schweinitz treasures two brief notes, one of which spurred him to write the text-book which has gradually 'swollen', as he expresses it, through nine subsequent editions. On his appointment as ophthalmic surgeon to Blockley, Osler promptly sent (May 7th) a few lines of congratulation, saying: 'It will give you a splendid field (of vision).' One Sunday evening shortly after this he found Osler reading, as was his custom, in the library of the Rittenhouse Club. Merely a wave of the hand passed between them, but later on when Osler got up to leave he tossed into de Schweinitz's lap a slip of paper on which was written the following: 'A Manual of Ophthalmic Surgery for Students. By G. E. de Schweinitz, &c. &c. &c. Phila. 1889. *A suggestion—Verb. sap.*'

Encouraged by the success of a series of reports on rheumatism which he had sponsored and which the *Medical News* had published the preceding year, he undertook at this time two other therapeutic surveys: the first was on 'Pneumonia in the Philadelphia Hospitals',[1] in which Pepper, Bartholow, Meigs, Tyson, Wilson, and he himself participated. It is interesting to read Osler's brief statement that there were two groups of pneumonia patients—'the alcoholic and the temperate; the majority of the former die in spite of all treatment; the majority of the latter get well with any, or with no, treatment'—and to compare this with the quinine, antimony, alcohol, and antipyretics, to mention but a few of the drugs advocated by his contemporaries. This Philadelphia report was followed by

[1] *Medical News*, Phila., Mar. 5, 1887, l. 260.

others from the leading physicians of the New York and Boston hospitals, and these in turn by Osler's editorial summary in which it was pointed out that 'pneumonia has come to be known as a specific self-limited disease and the only rational treatment is the expectant one'; but he concludes with this hopeful paragraph:

> It may be, however, that to the generation which will follow, at these same hospitals, the men whose practice we have given, the symptomatic and expectant plan at present in vogue will appear as crude and unscientific as does to us the active antiphlogistic treatment, with venesection *coup sur coup* and antimony to repletion.[1]

Later in the year appeared another series of papers, similarly sponsored, on 'The Treatment of Typhoid in the Philadelphia Hospitals', in which the therapeutic fashion in each of them was put on record. This in turn was followed by reports of the routine treatment employed in the New York, Boston, and Montreal hospitals; and in his subsequent editorial, in which the main facts were assembled, Osler said that the reports showed 'a remarkable uniformity of opinion, with hygiene, diet and nursing as the essentials'—a conclusion hardly justified by the evidence, it may be added.[2] In laying before the profession these examples of the inconsistency and fashion displayed in the use of drugs, his purpose was accomplished. The profession could draw its own conclusions and it was not necessary to rub the lesson in. For his own part he became ere long a warm advocate of Brand's system of cold bathing in typhoid—a revival of the Currie method of treating fevers. The students and nurses of the early years of the Johns Hopkins will vividly recall the laborious tubbings of these cases which were then so common. To-day both tubs and typhoid have wellnigh vanished, together with malaria and the mosquito, thanks to the sanitary transformation of Baltimore, in effecting which Osler's voice, so often raised, played no little part.

[1] Osler's unorthodox views on the treatment of pneumonia by no means went unchallenged, for veratrum viride and antimony continued to prevail, as he confessed in 'Notes and Comments', March 1888, *Canada Medical and Surgical Journal*, xvi. 508.

[2] *Medical News*, Phila., Dec. 10, 1887, p. 677; and Dec. 24, p. 739.

The year passed much as the preceding one. He was busily engaged in his clinical teaching, in laboratory studies, attending meetings, and for ever writing. More busy than ever with his pen, nevertheless he took on two additional tasks, one of which was a series of ‘ Notes and Comments ’ which he sent to Ross for the *Canada Medical and Surgical Journal*, to whose pages a few years before he had been such a copious contributor. In these brief essays, consisting of notes on ‘ practice, books and men ’, he let himself out to his Canadian readers in a delightful, semi-serious, and philosophical vein suggesting the literary style of his later essays. The notes cover about four pages in almost every issue of the journal for the next two years, the first instalment beginning with a discussion of Pasteur's work on rabies and the violent attack to which he had been subjected in the Paris Academy ; he then comments on the opposition to Koch which ‘ seems rank heresy in these days of staining fluids and cultures . . . even Dr. Bastian has not said anything since the debate at the International Congress in London.’ And he adds that though there are protests in Germany and France, and a remnant still in this country who stand out against the germ theory, ‘ the younger generation of workers, to a man, have stained fingers ’.

In his ‘ Notes and Comments ’ for May he confessed that ‘ with the return of spring comes the annual worry of examinations. It has never been my good fortune to be connected with an institution which relieved the teachers of the responsibility of examining the students they have taught. I suppose such a duty should not be a worry, but it is in certain ways, particularly if one has both a heart and a conscience.’ His clinical assistant at the time, Dr. Crozier Griffith, recalls telling him one day that the boys were very much afraid of his approaching examination, and he replied : ‘ I mean them to be ; I am examining in the interest of the public, not of the students.’ But this, one fears, was an idle threat, for he could never bring himself to ‘ pluck ’ students whom he had come to know and be fond of, however much he might talk in the open about high standards and rigid tests. The combat which he waged within himself over these matters, for he was continually protesting and writing on the subject, is both tragic and amusing, and after his transfer to England his personal feeling that it was an examiner's duty to dwell upon the student's character and his method of attacking the problem at hand rather than on the number of facts he could retain in his mind, continually ran counter to the prevailing custom; but his criticisms of English Examinations must be deferred to later chapters. Between the lines of this note to Ross's journal the confession of his own weakness stands exposed, for he says: 'To reject a man in his final examination is no light matter. In every Faculty there are one or two members so kind-hearted that they cannot pluck a candidate. Sympathy for the man excludes all sense of justice.' And yet in the next breath he adds: 'A lively sense of responsibility to the public admits of no such sentiment, and if there is an occasion which demands strictness and firmness, it is when we are asked to decide whether or not a man is fit to take charge of the lives of his fellow-creatures.'

A few of Osler's letters of this period have been recovered; and though they hardly deserve this designation they are characteristic of his laconic brevity in correspondence. Being mostly on postcards their chronology can be established, for he rarely took time for such superscriptions as full dates; '18th' or 'Tuesday' or perhaps even 'Oct.' would satisfy him; his i's and t's and punctuation suffered from equal neglect; and for conjunctions he resorted to a peculiar symbol of his own representing an ampersand. But then, many a budding correspondence has been blighted by too much attention to these details, as well as by the search for envelopes and the folding, licking, and stamping to which a postcard rises superior. The notes—and there are many more of the same kind—were to his friend and colleague, J. H. Musser:[1]

[1] Musser and Ogden seem to have been the only ones who preserved their brief messages from Osler during the '80's. It is for this reason that their names appear to dominate his correspondence, though the notes quoted are merely examples of countless ones he must have showered upon other people as well. His postcard habit was doubtless established partly for reasons of economy, partly for convenience, and stamped correspondence cards on which he could quickly scribble a note were always at hand on his desk.

[May 13, 1887.]

Dear M I never thought of it & then we had sat down when you came in I am glad you didnt order anything else Docks address would be Frankfurt on Main care of Prof Weigert I do not see his letter I fear it went into the W P B I see it is Bruce you ask after he is at the Lafayette Bruen is still south somewhere Yours W. O.

Saturday a m [May 23, 1887].

Dear Musser I wrote out the cheque yesterday a m & was interrupted & forgot to tear it off W. O.

29th [May, 1887].

I have just had a note from one of my nephews stating that he was coming to Phila. for his holiday on the 7th As I asked him to come & as his vacation is a fixed time I cannot disappoint the young codger by slipping away wh means I shall not see C. this year.[1] I am very sorry as I feel the honour On your broad shoulders the burden will rest Yours W. O.

The two first notes relate undoubtedly to the equipment for a small clinical laboratory. He and Musser had agreed to contribute $50 each for the purpose, and Dr. George Dock, who since his graduation had been working as a volunteer in the Dispensary with Musser, was to be put in charge. It is difficult, to-day, to realize that up to this time, far from there being a laboratory, there was no microscope, except Osler's, in use in the University Hospital. To be sure, Dr. Fussell, a classmate of Dock's, had been taught to make microscopic examinations of sputum, but up to this time clinical microscopy in the hospital may be regarded as a thing unknown. In all this Pepper had very little interest, though he would occasionally send a specimen to the laboratory before one of his clinics, so that he might mention the findings. To these clinics his colleague, Osler, as a friendly critic, occasionally used to go, but Pepper's was not his method. Osler was particularly prone, in teaching, to draw lessons from his own diagnostic mistakes. Pepper was known on occasion to give a brilliant discourse to the students on Addison's disease, using a patient with ordinary

[1] 'C.' refers to Chicago, where the American Medical Association met the following month. The note suggests that an olive branch had been held out. Musser from the first was an enthusiastic worker in the A. M. A. and became its President.

jaundice for the purpose of the clinic, knowing full well it was a deception. The two men, in fact, were the antipodes of each other, and a community in which Pepper held sway could not possibly hold Osler long. There was never anything, however, in the nature of a misunderstanding between them. As will be seen, Osler had the greatest admiration for many of Pepper's qualities, but it is easily understood why Osler spent so much of his time at work in other hospitals, for the material at the University Hospital at this time was limited and so was the spirit.

His April 'Notes and Comments' wound up with an announcement of the opening of a new building of the 'Orthopedic Hospital',[1] 'probably the most completely equipped special hospital in the country'. At this institution Weir Mitchell was one of the attendants, and becoming aware, in the course of their intimacy, of Osler's great interest in the diseases of the nervous system, he was instrumental in securing an appointment for his friend. This new obligation Osler took up with his usual enthusiasm, and his first papers published from the Hospital[2] represented a series of lectures which were based on an elaborate statistical investigation of the cases of chorea which had been in the clinic during the preceding decade, 410 in all. Of these, 110 were traced and were submitted to a thorough examination, from which he drew the conclusion that there is no known disease in which endocarditis is so constantly found.[3]

The afternoon clinics for nervous diseases between the hours of one and four-thirty were divided between Wharton Sinkler, Weir Mitchell, and himself, and he was also associ-

[1] The Philadelphia Orthopedic Hospital and Infirmary for Nervous Diseases.

[2] *Medical News*, Phila., Oct. 15, 1887, li. 437, and 465. *American Journal of the Medical Sciences*, Oct. 1887, xciv. 371.

[3] During the course of these studies he became interested in hereditary 'chorea', first described by Dr. George Huntington as occurring in families living on the eastern end of Long Island. A long correspondence followed with Dr. Huntington and Dr. Osborn of Easthampton, where Osler planned to make a visit the summer of this year, but was dissuaded owing to the sensitiveness of the afflicted people in regard to their malady. He speaks of this in an 'Historical Note on Hereditary Chorea' published in 1908 in 'The Huntington Number' of *Neurographs*, a series of neurological studies.

ated at the hospital with Keen, Morton, Goodman, Hunt, Agnew, and Morehouse, between all of whom an unusual degree of professional friendship was established. This highly desirable position was time-consuming, but Osler's calendar was like india-rubber and could be thus stretched without apparent loss of time for other things, and meanwhile a series of important articles representing researches in his more special field continued to appear.[1] One of them, on 'Duodenal Ulcer', deserves mention, for it was written when this lesion, now so commonly recognized and operated upon, was regarded as rare, yet he opens his paper [2] with the statement that 'the solitary ulcer occurs more frequently in the duodenum than in any other portion of the intestine, and in its etiology and morbid anatomy is almost identical with the gastric ulcer'. Many years elapsed before the truth of this statement came to be fully appreciated. Another paper was on 'Irritable Heart in Civil Life', which he read before the Toronto Medical Society on April 14th, when at home for his Easter holiday—a topic which the recent war has brought into prominence, though it was scarcely heard of in the '80's. Still another was on 'Thrombosis of the Portal Vein'; and on June 2nd, when the Association of American Physicians met for the second time in Washington, an entire evening session was given over to the subject of 'Haemorrhagic Infarction', Welch covering the pathological and experimental side and Osler its clinical aspects.

His April holiday in Toronto must have been brief, for his mother wrote to Mrs. Gwyn: 'Willie's meteor-like visit was pleasant while it lasted, he left at noon yesterday—he is lamentably thin, I do wish he had a nice wife to attend to little home comforts for him—he hopes to be home again on the 9th of July and spend an idle time which will be good for mind and body.' With the exception of a visit to the Shepherds at Como and the Howards at Cacouna,

[1] His bibliography contains an amazing number of titles for the year, eighty in all, if his minor reports and editorials are included. This would suggest superficiality were it not realized that his remarks at the society meetings he regularly attended were invariably reported.

[2] *Canada Medical and Surgical Journal*, March 1887, xv. 449.

AT THE ORTHOPEDIC HOSPITAL AND INFIRMARY FOR NERVOUS DISEASES

Left to right: J.M.Cattell, Guy Hinsdale, J.P.Willitts, J.K.Mitchell, G.E. de Schweinitz, Miss C. Dalziel, Mrs. Green, Joseph Otto, Miss J. Dalziel

July and August—'the idle time'—were passed largely in Toronto getting his chorea lectures ready for publication. One of them was given August 31st before the Canadian Association in Hamilton, and from there he must have gone on to Washington for the International Congress which opened September 5th. If he did so, he was one of very few of the original (superseded) committee who could bring themselves to attend. As he intimates, there were few foreign guests, and those without special distinction. The reception at the White House given by President and Mrs. Cleveland was a 'crush', and almost the only redeeming feature of the week was the uniformly good weather. It is well to draw a curtain over the IXth International Medical Congress.

To H. V. Ogden from W. O. [*ca.* Sept. 15].

I have had a quiet summer at home—have not seen so much of my relatives for years. My father is pretty shaky. I was very uneasy about him during the hot weather. Mrs. F. and her tribe are well. May has grown a fine girl & the boys are all thriving. I dare say Mrs F. will send you some recent photos. Very sorry to have missed your sisters, I did not go in tho I should have liked very much to see your grandmother. Very few English or Germans at the Congress. Some of the sections were good, others shocking. Glad to hear that you have been busy. I am sure you will capture the town in time. I saw Rogers in Toronto—larger than ever, but unchanged—My love to poor old Cantlie when you see him. I have been working at Chorea. Paper on Heart relations in Am. Jr. October & lectures will appear in early No's of the News. When are you coming on? Take a holiday about Xmas. I am moving to nicer quarters [1502 Walnut St.] near by. Wish indeed we could get Senn here. His stock is away up in the East. He will get a call before long. It would be a mistake for him to go to Rush.

The new quarters, in which he was to live for little more than a year, were far pleasanter than those at his old address, where as a matter of fact from morning till night he was rarely seen, though there are recollections of occasional Saturday afternoon tea-parties held there for the special children of his special friends with games and cakes—he the youngest of all. The new house, which had been Stillé's, an old, narrow, three-story residence of the familiar city type, stood on Walnut near the corner of 15th Street, and in it Osler had the same sort of unadorned office as his previous one, lined with books and strewn with manuscript. He had merely rented the place and had a housekeeper, and though his brother from Toronto, who soon visited him, having an eye for the advance in real-estate values, urged him to purchase the property on a loan, he did not wish to encumber himself with debt. In debt he never was, in spite of the frequent cobwebs in his pockets. But how could pockets be otherwise when their wearer did not wait for change to be put in them? His familiar formula when he bought a paper from a newsboy was: 'Keep the change, sonny; you're raising a large family and I'm not.'

Consistent with his Montreal programme, he had been responsible for getting a group of men to combine in subscribing for foreign publications, chiefly in French and German, which in all probability he utilized more fully than any member of this 'club'. These journals were doubtless the source of many of his editorials, which, on a great variety of subjects, continued to appear in the *Medical News*. One of them mentions the operation on the throat of the German Crown Prince, the progress of whose malady filled the medical journals during the year; and had the outcome of Morell Mackenzie's treatment been more successful and the Emperor Frederick lived—well, there might have been no Great War in 1914. In another place he happened to mention that pestiferous telephones were beginning to be put in doctors' offices, 'for their convenience!' It was an instrument he abhorred. Indeed he was somewhat slow in adopting time-saving devices—not even having a fountain pen in those days before medical secretaries; and no one remembers ever having seen him using a carriage.

With all this incessant literary labour, there is not much to be recorded in the way of relaxation. Stevenson's 'Underwoods' was published this year and a quotation in a letter to Ross gives a clue to his 'bedside' literature at this time. Then the following memorandum, written down on the evening of Dec. 9, may serve to recall his dinner clubs:

I have just walked home with Weir Mitchell from the Biological Club at Wm. Sellers' and he told me on the way of his discovery, if one may so call it, of the rest treatment. About 12–14 years ago a Mrs S. from Bangor Maine came to consult him at the advice of a mutual friend. She was a bright intelligent woman who had as a girl attended in Boston a school in which Agassiz and his wife were interested and had passed through the four years' curriculum in three years. She then had married and within as short a time as was possible had had four children with the result of a total breakdown, body and mind. Boston and New York physicians were tried for a year; then she went abroad and in London and Paris saw the most eminent consultants and spent months at various spas. But in vain; she returned a confirmed invalid . . . full of whims and fancies. Standing at the foot of her bed, M. felt that every suggestion he had to make as to treatment had been forestalled. Every physician had urged her to take exercise, to keep on her feet, to get about, and she felt herself that this was the best. M. on the inspiration of the moment told her to remain in bed. [There follows a long recital of the successful devices Mitchell resorted to leading to recovery and to the patient's return home.] The improvement persisted; she has since borne several more children and has been the soul of many enterprises in her native town. An incident, post-partum so to speak, was a letter from Mrs. S.'s mother a wealthy New England woman, a speaker at temperance meetings, full of 'isms, &c. She wrote to Dr. M. to say that bodily comfort and ease, health and enjoyment might be dearly bought if at the price of eternal peace. For he had recommended her daughter to take champagne and to have a maid to assist her in her toilette. The former she considered not only unnecessary but hurtful, the latter quite superfluous, as any well-instructed New England husband was quite capable of helping his wife in her toilette. W. O.

1888

Residential Philadelphia is not a place of mighty distances, and most of Osler's chief friends were near at hand; but without a carriage daily visits at the University Hospital, the Infirmary for Nervous Diseases, Blockley, and the late afternoon at the College of Physicians, meant considerable gadding even for one with such an active step as his. It is difficult to understand how he found time to read and where he did all his writing, but he knew how to capture the moment, and his 'deaf adder' training at Weston had brought powers of concentration which were serving him well. Never annoyed by interruptions, ready to give freely of his time to another, he was invariably blithe and gay, apparently the most care-free of mortals. A contemporary Toronto letter says: 'Dr. Osler was here last week for a consultation on Mrs. X, so we saw him for two days. He is the same old sixpence and is writing papers on the Nervous Diseases of Children and so has children on the brain. He dances along the street singing as he goes—as of old.'

In his service at the Infirmary for Nervous Diseases (Orthopedic Hospital) as elsewhere he gave of his best, and as he gave so he received. With devoted colleagues and surrounded by a group of enthusiastic juniors, despite his short term of office he left such an unforgettable impression on the place that those who survive his time, even down to the humblest charwoman, recall him almost with tears of pleasure. Very much the same feeling existed for him at Blockley, and for his part he retained an unforgetting memory of those who had shared his labours. 'I had the best and kindest of colleagues,' he wrote in after years to J. W. Croskey, one of his juniors: 'Tyson, Bruen, Musser, Hughes and others. With peculiar pleasure too I look back on my association with a group of keen and intelligent Residents, and with Miss Fisher and Miss Horner, in the recently established training-school for nurses; nor must I forget dear old Owens, on the medical floor, with his Hippocratic gift of prognosis.' One of Osler's characteristics not to be lost sight of was that of getting up complimentary dinners for people on suitable anniversaries, of suggesting a portrait, of subscribing towards a gift for a servant as in the case of this same celebrated Owens, the male 'head nurse' who for thirty years lived in Blockley and died there. So one may understand brief notes like this to his colleague Musser:

> Dear M – Sorry to have overlooked this – I will ask Pepper to move that the Hosp. or the Faculty stand the expense & you will then be re-imbursed – How much shall we need for Owens? Better consult Wilson & Bruen – I wouldnt ask Henry – He does not know him & has not yet been on duty—Yours W. O.

So it was he, rather than some Philadelphian of longer standing, who is found on a committee with James Tyson, J. William White and a student representative of each class, preparing to celebrate the fiftieth anniversary of D. Hayes Agnew's graduation in medicine—a form of jubilee much more common in continental than American faculties. Agnew, then nearing the end of his indefatigable career, was a surgical colleague not only at Blockley and the Orthopedic Hospital but also held a chair at the University, and well deserved the sort of tribute Osler had seen paid to Frerichs and Rokitansky and others during his sojourn in Europe.

1502 Walnut St., Philadelphia,
4/18/88.

Dear Ogden, You must stay a few days on your way to N.Y. I shall have much more of interest to show you than on your last visit. I am very busy at the cerebral palsies of children, working up the Infirmary material. Shall give three lectures this spring. Gowers has rather got ahead of me in his chapters which are the only ones of importance in the language. Curious that the subject should have been so much neglected. I am writing also on epilepsy, chorea & the spastic palsies for K.[1] Will you not report those cases of Polio-encephalitis? I wish you would send your comm. to one of our journals. It helps you & them. Mrs. F. & chicks all well. I shall spend the summer quietly at home. Let me know when to expect you.

Though Gowers had 'rather got ahead of him'[2] he persisted in the preparation of the 'three lectures'—there were really five—based on an analysis of 151 cases of cerebral palsy, from his own, Mitchell's, and Sinkler's clinics.[3] Their

[1] John M. Keating, his colleague at Blockley, who was editor of an Encyclopaedia for the Diseases of Children, in which many participated. Vol. i, 1889, Lippincott.

[2] In a review (sent to Ross's journal) of Gowers's celebrated text-book which had just appeared, Osler said that the volume had placed 'the author at a comparatively early age among the highest living authorities on all matters relating to the nervous system. No school of medicine in Great Britain has produced such good work in this department as University College: Bastian in the higher psychological relations of mind and brain, Schäfer in cerebral localization, Gowers in his numerous monographs and in this large volume, and Horsley in his brilliant work in the field of brain surgery.'

[3] The lectures were delivered during the spring session in the Infirmary for Nervous Diseases; were published in due course in the *Medical News*, and finally gathered the following year into a volume dedicated to S. Weir Mitchell.

final publication a year later, a timely and important one, placed him high in the ranks of American neurologists, already so eminently represented in Philadelphia in the persons of Weir Mitchell and Charles K. Mills. Theirs was a specialty just coming to the fore, with a society to foster it of which Osler soon wrote to Ogden, saying :

> . . . Would you not come on in Sept. to the Meeting of the Assoc. of Am. Phy. in Washington. The neurological Soc. will also meet there & others. Why not prepare a short report of a case for the latter and come up for membership. I would get Mills to propose you. They are anxious for new men from all parts of the country. I will send on the reports of the Nurses Directory. Do write up those polio-encephalitis cases. Let me know when you are coming. Try to arrange about the Washington meeting. It will be a very good one.

During the spring, plans were on foot for the first combined meeting in Washington of the several special societies to which this note refers. It was the first 'Congress of American Physicians and Surgeons', over which Billings was to preside. The Surgeon-General's Library at this time was nearing completion, and Osler and Billings had many common tastes and interests which had drawn them together. This was not the only shadow of a coming event which was cast at the time, though Osler was probably too engrossed in his work to notice that it fell upon him. Dr. Welch had just given his remarkable series of Cartwright Lectures on 'Fever', of which Osler's editorial review concludes with the statement that it is gratifying 'to have so able and comprehensive a study from a member of the Johns Hopkins University, an institution the medical department of which may, we trust, give a stimulus to advanced study in medicine and surgery in this country, such as the sister faculties have already given to literature, history and science.'

Still another event of this spring has a bearing on the Johns Hopkins. For one trained as a physician, Osler had always shown not only an unusual grasp of the problems confronting the surgeon but an unusually keen perception of surgical ability, which he was quick to use when occasion demanded. His attention had been particularly drawn to the originality of a recent university graduate whose name was beginning to appear in the journals, and who was at work in a hospital in Kensington :

3/7/88

Dear Musser, Dont fail to be at the Staff meeting on Saturday & vote for Kelly in poor Goodell's place. J. William White & others are running Davis and the staff must show its hand strongly by placing Kelly at the top of the list of candidates. D. can wait, he has only been here 14 mos, & is not to be named with Kelly. Yours W. O.

One version of this episode in Osler's own words [1] is as follows :

The circumstances were these : Goodell had resigned, and there was no end of discussion as to who should take his place. On several occasions I had gone to Kensington to see Kelly operate, and I happened to mention to Pepper that I had never seen anybody do abdominal work with the same skill. He knew of Kelly, but had not, I believe, seen him operate, which he immediately arranged to do. Then one evening at the Biological Club, Horatio Wood and Mitchell were discussing Goodell's successor, and I said that Pepper and I were backing a dark horse—a Kensington colt. With that, Leidy chipped in with a remark that if it was young Howard Kelly, his former prosector, he would back him heartily. This is how I remember the story.

Early in June the eldest of the Francis children, to Osler's great distress, had died after a long illness, and a few days later he sent this note to Ogden, which is characteristic in the way it drops the sad topic for matters relating to the day's work :

Dear O, Yes, Grant had typhoid with secondary meningitis. I did not go up. Graham did not think it necessary as he seemed doomed from the outset, with most profound cerebral symptoms. It is very sad for them, & the poor fellow was doing very well & had such good prospects.

That case will do splendidly for the thesis. I am reporting one of spinal syphilis. We shall have a good meeting. I am busy at my cerebral palsies of children lectures. They will come out in 7, 14 & 21 of July in News. I have collected a large amount of material at our Infirmary & at the Penn. Inst. for feebleminded children. Shall be so glad to see you in Sept. Send on those encephalitis cases.

[1] Cf. the memorial sketch of William Pepper in 'The Alabama Student and other Essays', 1908.

In the subject of Death in the abstract Osler always had the deepest philosophical interest, and a large section of his library was given over to a diverse selection of works on the subject. Shortly before this time, after first reading Munk's 'Euthanasia', he had written for Ross's journal the following forerunner of his Ingersoll Lecture:

We speak of death as the King of Terrors, yet how rarely does the act of dying appear to be painful, how rarely do we witness AGONY in the last hours. Strict, indeed, is the fell sergeant in his arrest, but few feel the iron grip; the hard process of nature's law is for most of us mercifully effected, and death, like birth, is 'but a sleep and a forgetting.'

I have been much interested recently in the case of a friend who had entered far into the Valley, and who now, in his convalescence, bitterly contrasts the pains and tortures of suppurating hypodermic punctures with the dream-like, delicious sensations of the profound collapse in which he nearly passed away. Shelley's description, [Mild is the slow necessity of death] is truer in the majority of cases than Newman's marvellous picture in 'The Dream of Gerontius' of the act of dissolution, which, more in accord with popular belief, is described as a 'fierce and restless fight', 'a strange innermost abandonment', and sense of ruin, worse than pain.

Dr. William Munk, the accomplished historian of the Royal College of Physicians of London, has recently written a little work on 'Euthanasia: or Mental Treatment in Aid of an Easy Death'. With much of general and scientific interest, it contains also many valuable suggestions to practitioners and sound advice as to the medical management of the dying. The first chapter, 'On Some of the Phenomena of Dying', is full of interesting testimony on the painlessness of death. He quotes William Hunter's words, almost his last ones: 'If I had strength enough to hold a pen I would write how easy and pleasant a thing it is to die.' Dr. Munk urges the free but judicious administration of opium, not so much for the allaying of pain as for the relief of the feeling of exhaustion and sinking—of indescribable distress and anxiety—referred to the heart and stomach. Hufeland declared that opium 'is not only capable of taking away the pangs of death, but it imparts even courage and energy for dying.'[1]

But when death touched him personally, though he suffered deeply he never permitted others to see within, and as in his note to Ogden so even later on in the loss of his

[1] *Canada Medical and Surgical Journal*, March 1888, xvi. 511.

own child, he brushed his sorrow and its emotions aside with some remark which to the unknowing might have seemed almost flippant: 'And if I laugh at any mortal thing, 'tis that I may not weep.' In his account-book of the year there is a brief and unfinished entry which permits one to understand Osler more than had it been completed. It reads: '*June* 3, 12.15 a.m. 1888. I have just left the death-bed of Miss Fisher—a sweet blessed character whose influence upon me and upon others has been great in——' This was all, but a few days later he wrote for the *Medical News*, to say:

> The public of Philadelphia has sustained a severe loss in the death of Miss Alice Fisher, who nearly four years ago was appointed by the Board of Guardians to take charge of the Training School for Nurses at the Philadelphia Hospital. Only those familiar with the inner history of that institution can appreciate the changes which have been effected under her judicious direction. The good work which she has accomplished has stimulated other hospitals of the city, and training-schools have been established at the Pennsylvania, Episcopal, and University Hospitals. By no means the least important lesson of Miss Fisher's too brief life in this community has been the demonstration of the fact that the profession of nursing affords an ample as well as a most suitable field for women of the highest culture and intelligence.

By the end of June his mother had begun to show impatience for his return: 'We are like school-children counting the days to your holiday—within a week we hope you will be with us.' He seems to have remained in Toronto through July, putting the final touches on his five lectures which appeared in successive numbers of the *Medical News*; and there evidently followed a brief sojourn with his McGill friends at Como and Cacouna, for she wrote on August 7th: 'The house has been cruelly dull all the week. We sadly miss your chirpy voice coming in and out one day after another.' While in Montreal he must have encountered Dr. Egerton Y. Davis, for according to a note in Ross's journal that fabulous person is said to have paid a flying call the same week and to have announced that 'before returning to Pentonville it is his intention to revisit the Great Slave Lake in order to study further the remarkable customs of certain Indian tribes frequenting that region'.

So after a romp with the Francis children at Toronto Island, a visit with his kinsfolk in Dundas, an address on 'The Mortality in Pneumonia' given in Hamilton the last day of the month, before the Canadian Medical Association, September 3rd found him once more in Philadelphia showing hospitality to people on their way to the Washington Congress.

This gathering was to have more of the aspect of an International Congress than the official one which had been so badly staged the year before. Among the distinguished foreign guests were William Ord, Pye-Smith, David Ferrier, Victor Horsley, Sir William MacCormac, Sir Spencer Wells, all of London; Thomas Annandale of Edinburgh, and von Esmarch of Kiel. It was the first of the notable triennial meetings, subsequently held, of the various special associations, for it was the beginning of the era of specialties and though called a 'Congress of Physicians and Surgeons', it was a conjoint meeting whose object, as Pepper, speaking for the Executive Committee, stated in his introductory remarks, was to bring together the active workers in allied fields, which in no way conflicted with the objects and purposes of the American Medical Association. John S. Billings, as President and the central figure of the congress, gave a notable address on medical museums with special reference to the Army Medical Museum, where a large reception was given in the building recently erected to house not only this collection but the Surgeon-General's Library as well.

But Billings, as the medical adviser of the Johns Hopkins Trustees, had another piece of business on his hands, and during the congress was seen so often in Osler's company [1] that suspicions of his motives were aroused. It is related that Provost Pepper, knowing how intimate Osler was with the Grosses, went in one morning to see S. W. Gross, and standing with his back before the fireplace, said abruptly: 'We are likely to lose Osler, and what in the world shall we

[1] In his 'Life of John Shaw Billings' F. H. Garrison says: 'That Billings should have chosen Osler, a character so utterly different from his cool, impersonal self, is an index of his rare knowledge of men and his capacity to appreciate traits which lay outside his own personality.'

do? Billings is browsing around all the time and I am sure something is up.' To this Gross replied: 'Well, Pepper, if the position at the Johns Hopkins is offered him what have we got in Philadelphia to compete with it?' This story is hardly in accord with Osler's own brief account of the matter, which would make Billings's advances much more abrupt, but inasmuch as Osler makes a mistake in his date, likely enough he may have been similarly inaccurate in other details. His account occurs in an obituary notice of Billings written in 1913:

> An important interview I had with him illustrates the man and his methods. Early in the spring of 1889 he came to my rooms, Walnut Street, Philadelphia. We had heard a great deal about the Johns Hopkins Hospital, and knowing that he was virtually in charge, it at once flashed across my mind that he had come in connection with it. Without sitting down, he asked me abruptly: 'Will you take charge of the Medical Department of the Johns Hopkins Hospital?' Without a moment's hesitation I answered: 'Yes.' 'See Welch about the details; we are to open very soon. I am very busy to-day, good morning,' and he was off, having been in my room not more than a couple of minutes.

In his desire to illustrate Billings's abrupt business methods Osler may have used some literary licence, and whether this interview actually occurred in this way, and if so just when it occurred, is not certain. The date may be approximately fixed as just before or just after the action of the Johns Hopkins Trustees appointing Osler Physician-in-Chief to the hospital, which according to the minutes of their meetings was taken on September 25th.[1]

The tail-enders of the Congress—the Horsleys, Ferrier, Sir William MacCormac, the von Esmarchs and others, had lingered in Philadelphia, together with his friends the Shepherds of Montreal, according to the following note in

[1] That there had been other preliminaries is indicated by this note from Dr. Welch: 'I met Osler', he says, 'at a dinner which Séguin gave him at Delmonico's in New York not long after my first return from Europe. He was then in Montreal. I was captivated, and I think that he was my choice for the Hopkins from the time I first became connected with it. In 1888 at a meeting of the Association of American Physicians in Washington I was practically assured that if he got the offer he would come to us. Billings up to that time had Lauder Brunton, and a German professor who had been at the German Hospital in London, in mind for the Chair of Medicine.'

which he makes no reference to the Hopkins appointment, evidently wishing to have his family notified first :

To Mrs. F. J. Shepherd from W. O. Oct. 1st.

I hope you have recovered from your Phila. dissipations. I enter to-day upon a sober life again. My last friend, Dr. Goltdammer of Berlin went away to-day. You have won the hearts of all my friends here, particularly the Grosses & the Hays. I hope the old man is feeling better for his trip. I wish we had a Congress every year. I do not know when I have enjoyed myself so much. Love to the chicks & kind regards to 'Cooie' & to the girls & Mrs. Molson. By the way tell the latter that I shall wake up at an early date to the sense of my God-paternal duties.

On the following day he writes to Dr. Ogden who has been ill : 'So sorry for your b.t.m. You must take a good rest at Hamilton. I shall send you C. P. of Ch. when out & T's letter when I find it. I have settled at work—after a long spree. Get well soon.' In this cryptic note the 'Cerebral Palsies of Children' at least can be identified, and though the lectures had already appeared during the summer they were being issued in book form, in an English and American edition.

To William Pepper from W. O. 1502 Walnut St.
Oct. 3rd, 1888.

I have received a definite offer from the J. H. authorities & have determined to accept it. I shall leave you with deep regret. You have been like a good, kind brother. There need be no hurry about any official action, & I only write this so that you may be the first to know of it.

His acceptance must have come as a surprise, for there could have been no intimation of it even among his close friends, to judge from a contemporary letter written by H. P. Bowditch ; 'Osler is going to take a position in the Johns Hopkins University. I don't think this is quite fair of him for we wanted him in Boston you know, but supposed he couldn't be induced to leave Philadelphia.' The appointment created a great stir, and, widely heralded, was accorded universal approbation, for his popularity was already widespread. His mother wrote : 'Thanks for the Baltimore paper. How proud I ought to be of you. I wonder am I, perhaps so—this I do know that my heart is full of love and thankfulness to Him who has showered so many blessings on my life in the matter of dear precious sons and daughters ' : and she changes the topic quickly, to say that she is going to give his father the digitalis again : ' Ten drops I think you said before each meal.'

To H. V. Ogden from W. O. 10/12/88.

Dear old Man, I hope you are all well again—sound at bottom. The die is cast. I go to J. H. in May. You must pay me an annual visit & I hope to be able to treat you better than I did here. Do me two favours.

1. Write me what you know—not more than 1 vol. of the F—— family, good & bad, a private communication which will not be used in any way against the poor fellow. Have you heard how he is getting on?

2. That sporosperm specimen—Have you the rabbit or pieces? Write me a little note of the same des. of the tumours, & send a bit of the muscle if you can.

So he was to have about six months' leeway, and the transition did not disturb him very much, for his possessions as in 1875 and 1884 were chiefly in his head—and heart—and though a move might be painful it was not laborious. President Gilman, who himself was not particularly given to brevity in his expressions of feeling, must have cogitated over the following note from the new appointee, evidently written in reply to his cordial welcome—but what more was there to say?

To D. C. Gilman from W. O. Oct. 30th.

Dear Sir, Many thanks for your kind letter. I look forward with the greatest pleasure to my life in Baltimore and I am sure that I shall be very happy and comfortable. Sincerely yours, Wm Osler. Thanks for the letter.

Much discussion was aroused in University of Pennsylvania circles in regard to his successor, for his departure would necessitate a shift in existing positions in the Faculty, and an active canvass was started in which his support was naturally sought:

Dear Musser, I have got to go out of town at 1 p.m. & cannot go to 4th St. I shall go down certainly on Friday a.m. & enclose the cheque so that you can pay it in at your bank. So sorry for the neglect but I have not been down town since my return. We could go to the U C after the meeting and have a chat. I have not heard anything further save that T. will be a vigorous candidate. If a suitable Patholog. is available he will get it, I think, unless Mitchell opposes the transfer. It would rather relieve the tension of a serious & growing difficulty in Pathology but I do not know of anyone—except Prudden—who would fill the chair. I do wish Dock had gotten out 2 or 3 good papers last winter. Wood seems strongly in favour of Guitéras as he was in 1884. Keep mum & bide your time.

But Osler did not permit himself to be greatly distracted by all of this, and there was no slowing-down in his university and literary work. He had, even at this time, developed to a high degree the ability of getting mental relaxation in his literary work by merely shifting his topic, and throughout the year there had been no pause either in his editorials to help out the *News* Board, in his papers on diverse medical topics, or in the 'Notes and Comments' for Ross's journal.

He left for his Christmas holiday in Toronto a week earlier than usual to give by invitation three lectures on 'Cerebral Localization', and there 'received an enthusiastic welcome—an ovation in fact—from the university in which he began his medical studies'. On the day after Christmas he read another paper, on Appendicitis,[1] before the local Medical Society, a much mooted subject since Fitz three years before had baptized the malady. Two days later, on December 28th, as recorded in an article published some years afterwards, he was in Hamilton with his friend Dr. Malloch to see in consultation a young man with a remarkable form of aneurysm. The story is worth telling, for it illustrates how he utilized for his literary purposes everything which was unusual; how alert he was in pursuing what to-day are called 'end results'; and how he followed and in his later papers referred to cases which had stamped themselves on his memory. At a symposium on the subject of Arteriovenous Aneurysm held at the Radcliffe Infirmary at Oxford during the war, thirty years later, he gave the following brief account of this particular case with its subsequent history:[2]

Case 3.—I reported the case originally in the *Annals of Surgery*, 1893. In 1878 the man, in running down a sloping grass-plot, fell

[1] 'Typhlitis and Appendicitis.' *Canada Lancet*, Jan. 1889, xxi. 193.

[2] 'Remarks on Arteriovenous Aneurysm.' *Lancet*, Lond., May 8, 1915. He had also reported in full the sequel of this case, as one of arteriovenous

and forced a lead-pencil into the armpit; a gush of blood followed and the arm became black-and-blue to the wrist. The aneurysm involved the axillary vessels. He subsequently lived a very athletic life, rowed in the Argonaut Boat Club, and served in the South African War where he came under Sir G. H. Makins' care. He was invalided in consequence of a sudden pain on the left of the head and neck, and the patient was positive that the tumour had enlarged. He wrote me on October 17th, 1904, saying that he had marched 160 miles in 32 days and fought 16 battles, with the result of increasing the aneurysm very materially, particularly at the base of the neck. He died in May, 1909, 31 years after the accident, of gradual heart-failure.

1889

The January issue of the *Montreal Medical Journal* for this year contained about the last of his Addisonian series of 'Notes and Comments'. It was inspired by an account of an ancient Greek hospital recently excavated at Athens; and from this he was led on to speak of the description in 'Marius the Epicurean' of the hospital in the Etrurian hills where Marius had sought relief and been visited by the great Galen. Next he took up Inge's 'Society in Rome under the Caesars', and then 'The Autocrat', saying:

Literature has often been enriched by those who have deserted medicine for the muses. But to drink deep draughts at Pierian springs unfits, and when the thirst is truly divine should unfit, a man for the worrying rounds of practice. It is shocking to think that had Goldsmith secured the confidence of the old women in Bankside, Southwark, we should probably never have known the Vicar, Olivia, or Tony Lumpkin. Still worse, to think of what we should have lost had Keats passed on from a successful career at Guy's to obtain even a distinguished position as a London Surgeon! Happily, such men soon kick free from the traces in which the average doctor trots to success.

The most conspicuous modern example of success in both fields is offered by the Autocrat of the Breakfast Table, who for many years occupied the Chair of Anatomy at Harvard, and who as a young man made permanent contributions to practical medicine. In his last book, 'One Hundred Days in Europe', he mentions having sat next to Mr. Lawson Tait at dinner and he suggests the question, 'Which would give most satisfaction to a thoroughly humane and unselfish being of cultivated intelligence and lively sense—to have

---

aneurysm of the axillary vessels of thirty years' duration, in the *Lancet*, Lond., 1913, ii. 1248.

written all the plays which Shakespeare has left for an inheritance to mankind, or to have snatched from the jaws of death scores of suffering women and restored them to a sound and comfortable existence?' I know of no man who could so well make answer to this question as the Autocrat himself. Would he rather go down to posterity as the man who, in this country at least, first roused the profession to a sense of the perils of puerperal fever as an infectious disease—and who thereby has probably saved more lives than Lawson Tait—and whose essay on the subject—*pace* shades of Meigs and Hodge—is a classic in American literature, or would he choose to be remembered as the author of 'The Pearly Nautilus' and 'The Last Leaf'?

'Pearly' was of course a slip for 'Chambered', but the thought led him to write to the 'Autocrat', from whom he received this reply:

From O. W. Holmes to W. O. Boston, Jan. 21, 1889.

My dear Sir,—I have rarely been more pleased than by your allusions to an old paper of mine. There was a time certainly in which I would have said that the best page of my record was that in which I had fought my battle for the poor poisoned women. I am reminded of that Essay from time to time, but it was published in a periodical which died after one year's life and therefore escaped the wider notice it would have found if printed in the American Journal of the Medical Sciences. A lecturer at one of the great London Hospitals referred to it the other day and coupled it with some fine phrases about myself which made me blush, either with modesty or vanity, I forget which.

I think I will not answer the question you put me. I think oftenest of the 'Chambered Nautilus', which is a favourite poem of mine, though I wrote it myself. The Essay only comes up at long intervals, the poem repeats itself in my memory and is very often spoken of by my correspondents in terms of more than ordinary praise. I had a savage pleasure, I confess, in handling these two Professors—learned men both of them, skilful experts, but babies as it seemed to me in their capacity of reasoning and arguing. But in writing the poem I was filled with a better feeling, the highest state of mental exaltation and the most crystalline clairvoyance, as it seemed to me, that had ever been granted to me. I mean that lucid vision of one's thought and all forms of expression which will be at once precise and musical which is the poet's special gift, however large or small in amount or value. There is some selfish pleasure to be had out of the poem, perhaps a nobler satisfaction from the life-saving labour. . . .

Osler's interest in such a matter at this juncture would make it appear that his coming transplantation was looked upon with composure, though it must inevitably have greatly increased the calls upon his time; for he not only had to participate in the local canvass for his successor, but it was necessary also for him to secure a desirable personnel for the medical clinic to be organized in Baltimore. In spite of all this, such an admission as he makes in the following note was most unusual:

[Jan. 10, 1889].

Dear Musser, Sorry I could not join you last eve. but I was dead beat, having had a most tiring afternoon, & with a—for me unusual thing—splitting headache. So I went to bed at 9.30. I shall certainly do what you suggest. I have with Ps [Pepper's] consent appointed Fred Packard. I have called 3 times on P. since my return & have missed him. I shall try to see him soon & talk about you.

Then too, as his frequent notes to D. C. Gilman show, there were many calls to attend conferences in Baltimore which he somehow managed to work in during his week-ends. One of these notes towards the end of January reads: 'I will join you at the 5th ave. Hotel about noon on Sunday.' There had been a deal of discussion in regard to the future housekeeping arrangements of the new hospital, and, as the time for the opening drew near, Mr. Gilman had decided on a course of which the following account (somewhat inaccurate so far as dates are concerned) was written by Osler many years after:

The opening of the Johns Hopkins Hospital in 1889 marked a new departure in medical education in the United States. It was not the hospital itself, as there were many larger and just as good; it was not the men appointed, as there were others quite as well qualified; it was the organization. For the first time in an English-speaking country a hospital was organized in units, each one in charge of a head or chief. The day after my appointment I had a telegram from Dr. Gilman, President of the university, who had been asked to open the hospital, to meet him at the Fifth Avenue Hotel, New York. He said to Dr. Welch and me: 'I have asked you to come here as the manager is an old friend of mine, and we will spend a couple of days; there is no difference really between a hospital and a hotel.' We saw everything arranged in departments, with responsible heads, and over all a director. 'This', he said, 'is really the hospital, and we shall model ours upon it. The clinical unit of a hospital is the exact counterpart of one of the sub-divisions of any great hotel or department-store.'

Other things, too, at this complicated period must have served to interrupt his usual routine. Requests for consultations, which up to this time had been few and far between, began to pour in so that he must have been hard pressed to meet his fixed obligations as a conscientious teacher and writer. A number of addresses had been promised for April and May, and his valedictory to the Pennsylvania students was ahead of him—enough to stagger any one less capable than he of getting out of each day the best there was in it.[1]

Early in March he had offered the position, as his house physician or assistant in Baltimore, to Dr. H. A. Lafleur of Montreal, a McGill graduate of two years' standing who had been acting as *locum tenens* for Wyatt Johnston in Osler's former post as Pathologist to the Montreal General. And this important point settled, he shortly after writes to Ogden:

> I go to B. in May. We are getting the Hosp in order. If you know of any A.A.1. copper-bottomed young graduate in the West who could serve for a year as Interne I should like one. He must come with your entire approbation. I shall take Lafleur from Montreal as my Chef de Clinique in charge of the Clin. Lab. & general supervisor of the ward work. We shall need 2–5 resident graduates —ultimately 10–20 & they are to be selected from the country at large.

In the midst of all this he was burdened with anxiety over what proved in each case to be a fatal illness from pneumonia of two of his devoted friends. Late in March word had come that Palmer Howard had been taken ill, and Osler left almost immediately for Montreal and was with him until his death, which occurred on Tuesday morning of March 28th. He had remained conscious to the end, and the sad duty devolved upon Osler of taking in turn each of the children by the hand to their father's bedside for his last messages. His affection for Howard had been truly filial,

[1] He was also busy with the chapter on 'Congenital Affections of the Heart' for Keating's monumental Encyclopaedia of the Diseases of Children —an article which remains a classic on the subject, and must have required an immense amount of reading even though he was able to draw largely on his Montreal post-mortem material for many of his illustrations of cardiac anomalies.

and to see him thus overtaken when in the full tide of his professional and collegiate life was a heavy blow. Howard in turn had loved Osler as a son, and the three younger children, who from now on came after a fashion to be regarded as Osler's wards, had always looked upon him from their earliest years as a combination of elder brother, playmate, and father confessor.

Heavy at heart, he had little time to dwell upon his loss, for he was called promptly to Ottawa for an important consultation; and from there, stopping only for a few hours in Toronto—'on Friday morning to leave a bit of sunshine', as his mother wrote—he appeared in New York on April 3rd for his promised address before the Alumni Association of the Bellevue Hospital. His subject was 'Phagocytosis', and he gave a detailed presentation of the theory elaborated by Elie Metchnikoff, who had recently joined the staff of the Pasteur Institute in Paris. The address shows an astonishing degree of familiarity with all the recent literature, mostly in German, pertaining to a complicated subject, which concerns the scavenger-like function of the wandering white blood-corpuscles in picking up and engulfing foreign materials; but it was a topic to which Osler had made significant contributions himself. From the time he first observed the manner in which 'the pond amoebae play among the desmids, diatoms and algae' to his later studies of the fate of the coal-dust particles inhaled into the lungs of miners, he had pursued the subject along his own lines; and he was particularly interested in determining the rôle of the phagocytes during the course of his investigations of malaria. One would have supposed that such a disease as this would offer the best possible means of studying the process in the actual blood current, but it proved otherwise, and Osler's conclusion drawn from his personal observations was that 'while phagocytosis is a widespread and important physiological process throughout the animal kingdom, and while it undoubtedly plays a most important part in many pathological conditions, the question of an active destructive warfare waged by the body cells against the micro-organisms of disease must still be considered an open one.[1]

[1] *New York Medical Journal*, 1889, xlix. 393–400.

Howard's death was not the only blow. Even before his return to Philadelphia news had come of the acute illness of Samuel W. Gross, his friend and colleague of the 'News' Board, who begged to see him. He was found critically ill, and on April 16th, only five years after the death of his distinguished father, he in turn died at his house in Walnut Street where Osler had passed many happy hours. During the remainder of April he must have been at his wits' end. Yet a number of papers were finished and it may be taken for granted that he in no wise neglected his studies and his clinics. For the first time in years, owing to an engagement to give an address in Baltimore, he had to forgo his Easter visit in Toronto, and on April 24th his mother writes:

We are all more than disappointed to find that you cannot come this Easter tide, but will not be selfish for I'm sure just at this time you must be almost dazed and a few days after you have once changed quarters will be more of a rest for your dear old brains, (I won't say bones) though I fancy they are wearied now and then. A postcard and note came for you last week but so far nothing in the shape of a parcel has come except the coat from Ottawa. If it should come in time to forward the trousers they will be sent direct but supposing there is delay send a card to say whether they shall be forwarded to Philadelphia or Baltimore as I suppose you will be there after May 1st. In all your turmoil I do trust you will keep well and find things fit in without much worry—the loss of those two friends has I know been a hard trial for you to bear for your heart is not of stone and you know why all trials are sent—just to make us more like unto our Master and to fit us for the Home which He has gone to prepare for His people. You will be glad to hear that Father keeps fairly well. . . .

She had reason to be concerned for his 'dear old brains', though they seemed to be working smoothly enough for he had managed to prepare an address which was delivered April 23rd in Baltimore at the annual meeting of the state medical association—a body which bears the honoured name of 'The Medical and Chirurgical Faculty of the State of Maryland'. There were at this time five medical schools in Baltimore, in addition to the new one which was in prospect, all but one or two being schools of a very low order. Osler had fearlessly chosen as his subject 'The Licence to

Practise ',[1] and then and there took up the cudgels which he never ceased wielding: for higher standards of medical preparation. In this he was a true disciple of Palmer Howard, for it was the rôle his preceptor had long played in Canada. He handled his subject squarely and without gloves or apology, though it was one which closely touched certain vested rights of the Medical and Chirurgical Faculty. Only a few years before, a bill advocating a State Board of Examiners had been rejected, and the schools of medicine, largely managed in the interests of the professors, were private enterprises whose diplomas carried a qualification for practice after attendance at two sessions without further tests, a condition resulting in a state of things which in Osler's words 'made the American "system" of medical education a byword amongst the nations':

> . . . It makes one's blood boil to think that there are sent out year by year scores of men, called doctors, who have never attended a case of labour, and who are utterly ignorant of the ordinary everyday diseases which they may be called upon to treat; men who may never have seen the inside of a hospital ward and who would not know Scarpa's space from the sole of the foot. Yet, gentlemen, this is the disgraceful condition which some school-men have the audacity to ask you to perpetuate; to continue to entrust interests so sacred to hands so unworthy. Is it to be wondered, considering this shocking laxity, that there is a widespread distrust in the public of professional education, and that quacks, charlatans and impostors possess the land?

The difficulties, as he pointed out, which confronted legislative bodies, lay in the fact that they could not support class legislation which would debar from patients the homoeopaths and eclectics whose curricula differed from that of the regular schools only in the matter of therapeutics.

> We cannot, however, escape from the important fact that in the eyes of the law we all stand equal, and if we wish legislation for the protection of the public we have got to ask for it together, not singly. I know that this is gall and wormwood to many—at the bitterness of it the gorge rises; but it is a question which has to be met fairly and squarely. When we think of the nine or ten subjects which we have in common, we may surely, in the interests of the public, bury animosities, and agree to differ on the question of Therapeutics.

[1] *Maryland Medical Journal*, 1889, xxi. 61.

But it was not all indignation, for he gives a very clear outline of the course which must be pursued, and his prophecy—'It needs not the vision of a son of Beor to advertise that within ten years in scarcely a State in the Union will the degree carry with it the privilege of registration'—was fulfilled. Thus a new, a vigorous, and convincing voice with a real message was raised before the assembled profession of Maryland, with none of the usual amenities and platitudes which might have been expected from a newcomer in their midst, and above all from one who was not even a naturalized citizen. There must have been wagging of heads, but there was no mistaking the fact that a new leader, whose words carried weight, had addressed them.

This incident, so characteristic of Osler's fearlessness of criticism when he felt strongly on any question, is given prominence for another reason. It introduces him in a new rôle, other than that of student and scholar, namely, as the ardent protagonist for the advancement and welfare of the profession as a whole. And the Marylanders whom he had thus addressed came shortly to regard him not only as their accepted leader, but at the same time with no less devotion for his personal qualities than was universally felt for him in Philadelphia.

To President Gilman from W. O. Wednesday [May 1, 1889].

I have been so worried & driven during the past month that I have not had time to go down. I shall be down on Saturday by the 10.20 train & will drive direct to your office.

PS. I enclose a list—I hope not too long—of personal friends to whom I would like invitations to be sent.

On this same morning of May 1st he gave his valedictory address to the Pennsylvania students. He was brief, and chose to consider but two of the score of elements which might contribute to their future success or be of help in days of failure. The first of these was imperturbability, the second equanimity. Of this second quality he said:

Let me recall to your minds an incident of that best of men and wisest of rulers, Antoninus Pius, who as he lay dying in his home at Lorium in Etruria, summed up the philosophy of life in the watchword, *Aequanimitas*. As for him, about to pass *flammantia moenia mundi* (the flaming ramparts of the world), so for you, fresh from

Clotho's spindle, a calm equanimity is the desirable attitude. How difficult to attain, yet how necessary, in success as in failure!

Then in addressing the Faculty, after referring to the recent loss of Edward Bruen; to the loss sustained by their sister college (Jefferson) in the death of S. W. Gross; and of his own personal loss in Palmer Howard, he closed by saying:

While preaching to you a doctrine of equanimity, I am, myself, a castaway. Recking not my own rede, I illustrate the inconsistency which so readily besets us. One might have thought that in the premier school of America, in the *Civitas Hippocratica*, with associations so dear to a lover of his profession, with colleagues so distinguished, and with students so considerate, one might have thought, I say, that the Hercules Pillars of a man's ambition had been reached. But it has not been so ordained, and to-day I sever my connection with this University. More than once, gentlemen, in a life rich in the priceless blessings of friends, I have been placed in positions in which no words could express the feelings of my heart, and so it is with me now. The keenest sentiments of gratitude well up from my innermost being at the thought of the kindliness and goodness which have followed me at every step during the past five years. A stranger—I cannot say an alien—among you, I have been made to feel at home—more you could not have done. Could I say more?

On this same Saturday evening he was subjected to a complimentary dinner. Pepper presided and there were a number of special out-of-town guests, among them Ross from Montreal, Billings from Washington, Draper from New York, and H. P. Bowditch from Boston; and Bowditch wrote to his family: 'Osler's dinner was quite a festival. It is extraordinary what a hold he has on the profession in Philadelphia. He is one of the most popular men I ever knew.' Though he was by no means to lose touch with his many Philadelphia friends of the past five years' making, any more than his first transfer had put him out of touch with his Montreal friends, it was nevertheless an abrupt and clearly marked break in the period of his American life. There was to be only one more, after another fifteen years had elapsed, and when that time came one of his associates and neighbours, James Wilson, recalled this five years' sojourn in the Quaker City in the following words:

What did he do for us? He made himself agreeable to the older men, and demonstrated to the younger men how medicine should be learned and taught. He broadened our conceptions in regard to the inductive method in medicine. Facts, facts, and always the facts. The facts of the ward, of the microscope, of the laboratory, of the post-mortem room. He made it clear to some of the younger men who are now reaping the reward of their work that it is not necessary for every man to be a practitioner in the ordinary sense, but that long years of hospital and laboratory work constitute a better equipment for the teacher and the consultant. He inspired his students with enthusiasm for letters and taught them the rare rewards that come of searching the medical scriptures. He showed that in the democracy of our profession any man is free by a principle of self-election to attain the most coveted post of distinction and honour. He pointed out not only to us, but to all men, how fine and noble the profession of medicine is for those in it who are fine and noble.

He ornamented his discourse with quaint allusions to Holy Writ and the Pilgrim's Progress, but did not in those days say much about Montaigne and the Religio Medici, and rarely alluded to Plato or Marcus Aurelius. Nevertheless, he helped some of us to do a little thinking. At length, after the fashion of the nautilus, he builded a more stately mansion and left us. We would have fain kept him ; but that could not be.[1]

[1] J. C. Wilson : 'Remarks at Farewell Dinner to Dr. Osler, May 2, 1905.' Privately printed.

CHAPTER XIII

1889–90

THE JOHNS HOPKINS HOSPITAL. ORGANIZATION OF A CLINIC

Johns Hopkins, a Baltimore merchant, a bachelor and a Quaker of economical habits, had amassed during and after the Civil War what for the time seemed a princely fortune. Influenced, it is said, by a conversation with his former fellow townsman, the London banker and philanthropist George Peabody, he came to believe that there were two things that were sure to endure—'a university, for there will always be youth to train; and a hospital, for there will always be suffering to relieve.' Consequently, on his death in 1873 he left in the hands of his chosen trustees the sum of seven million dollars to be equally divided between the two institutions which were to perpetuate his name. The two boards of trustees, which were largely interlocking, in the unhurried manner said to have characterized all their actions proceeded to choose a leader, and, with rare wisdom, two years later decided upon Daniel Coit Gilman, then President of the University of California. To the sagacity of this man probably more than to any other single influence, the institution owes its foundation upon 'the idea of a university', to use Cardinal Newman's phrase, as distinct from that of a college.

For twelve years—since 1877—the hospital had been building. Despite an endowment of three and a half million, the hospital Trustees, with a degree of foresight unusual in a lay board unfamiliar with the problems involved, had bided their time and utilized only the accrued income of the large fund at their disposal in constructing the plant. They had been fortunate in the selection of John S. Billings as their medical adviser, and the general plans of the hospital which were the product of his brain, had been erected in the so-called 'pavilion' style, an outgrowth of the system of separated wards with which Billings had been so familiar in the army hospitals during the later years of the Civil

War. The grounds were extensive, comprising four city blocks on the crest of a hill—a superb site which had been selected by Mr. Hopkins himself, on the eastern edge of the city of his day. The university, ‘across-town’, had no such setting—indeed for the casual visitor was hard to find—for Mr. Gilman believed in spending more money on men and their tools than on buildings, and the first group of six professors he had assembled—Gildersleeve, Rowland, Sylvester, Remsen, Morris, and, in biology, Huxley's pupil Newell Martin—fully justified his judgement, for they quickly placed the Johns Hopkins, as a university in fact rather than in name, far in the lead of all other institutions in the land which were endeavouring to establish higher courses for graduates. It was looked upon in educational circles as more or less of an experiment, though one in which all confessedly were deeply interested. From the outset the place had been well advertised—almost too well on its baptismal day in 1876 when Huxley delivered the inaugural discourse without accessories of music, prayer or benediction—a perfectly consistent Quaker procedure. ‘Vain it was to mention the unquestioned orthodoxy of the Trustees and the ecclesiastical ties of those who had been selected to be the professors. Huxley was bad enough: Huxley without a prayer was intolerable.’[1]

Great changes however may occur in thirteen years, and though there was still considerable local hostility towards ‘the Hopkins’, it was beginning to give way under the unquestioned excellence of the university programme and the rapidly growing fame of the institution which made it in the early years a Mecca for the most brilliant of the young

[1] Cf. Daniel Coit Gilman: ‘The Launching of a University.’ N.Y., Dodd, Mead & Co., 1906. To D. C. Gilman, the hospital as well as the university owed much. Andrew Carnegie said that Gilman's special gift was in drawing all men after him by pleasing all and offending none, ‘doing the absolutely necessary ungentle things in a gentle way.’ And Osler in his ‘Fixed Period’ address said his association with him had been an education and a revelation, adding: ‘I had never before been brought into close contact with a man who loved difficulties just for the pleasure of making them disappear. But I am not going to speak of these happy days lest it should forestall the story I have written of the inner history of the first period of the hospital’—a history, be it said, as yet unpublished.

scholars of the land who were looking for inspiration and post-collegiate instruction.

During all this time Billings had been writing and lecturing on the subject of the hospital and the proposed medical school, and meanwhile all the leaders of medicine of two continents had been consulted by Gilman. In 1883 the first step had been taken towards a provisional medical faculty consisting of Ira Remsen in chemistry, Newell Martin in biology, and William H. Welch, who had been called from New York to take a Chair of Pathology—the first time such a post had been established on a full university basis.[1]

On Welch's return from abroad in 1886 something more nearly resembling an institute of experimental medicine than anything the country had seen before was soon in operation in the first building erected on the hospital grounds. Here, from 1886 to 1889, courses in pathology for graduates were given, and around Welch there gathered a group of enthusiastic co-workers, including Franklin P. Mall, the first appointed Fellow, Sternberg, Councilman, Halsted, Abbott, Bolton, Flexner, Booker, and Walter Reed, some of whom were to remain as permanent appointees. As a culmination of all this, the formal opening of the hospital, coinciding as it did with Osler's advent, was widely heralded. Not only the medical but the lay press of the month contained elaborate accounts of the hospital, its plans, specifications, and purposes. No plant certainly was ever dedicated under more favourable circumstances,

[1] 'Matthew Hay [writes Dr. Welch] was appointed to the Chair of Pharmacology in 1884 at the same time that I was elected to the Chair of Pathology. We corresponded about plans for the school, but never met. I see that Hay records this in "Who 's Who". When I was appointed it was intended to proceed with the selection of other members of the medical faculty, so as to be ready to open the school at the same time that the hospital was opened, which it was thought then would be in two or three years. Then came the financial difficulties due to failure of the B. & O. to pay dividends on the stock, and I found myself somewhat stranded as regards medical teaching and human autopsies. If we had been able to proceed, say in 1885 or 1886, with the selection of other members of the Faculty we should probably have missed Mall, Abel, Halsted, Kelly and, above all, Osler, and our fate might have been very different. Martin became incapacitated only just as we were starting the medical school in 1893.'

nor with a more widespread interest in what the future might have in store for it.

On Monday, May 6th, the new hospital buildings were thrown open for public inspection, and on the following day came the formal opening which this time—thanks to the outcry thirteen years before—began with prayer and ended with music.

> . . . It was a brilliant day, and notabilities, medical and otherwise, from Baltimore and the principal medical schools of America were grouped under the vast dome of the administration building to witness the inauguration of what was confidently believed to be the last word in hospital construction and management for the scientific study and treatment of disease. There was a feeling of elation—one might even say of exaltation—that the structure which had taken twenty years to evolve, absorbing the energies and thought of so many able minds, had at last become a *fait accompli*. And to none more than to Dr. Osler was this a red-letter day. To blaze a perfectly new road, untrammelled by tradition, vested interests, or medical ' deadwood '—best of all, backed by a board of management imbued with a fundamental and abiding respect for scientific opinion and commanding an ample budget—what more could the heart of man desire? The days that followed were filled with the many details of organization. There were record-forms and charts of various sorts to be devised, instruments of precision and appliances for diagnosis to be purchased, diet lists to be drawn up and, not least, a clinical laboratory to be furnished and equipped—the latter a temporary affair, as those who had planned the magnificent pile of buildings had omitted to make provision for this essential feature of a medical clinic. With all these matters Dr. Osler busied himself with his usual cheerful and untiring industry, and the thought that was uppermost was to have the best that could be obtained.[1]

The responsibility of organizing the clinic rested primarily on Osler's shoulders and, from what has gone before, the course he would pursue could have been foretold. From the first, he planned to make much of bedside clinical teaching, with chief emphasis on practical instruction to small groups of students; and though this course could not be put into effect until the medical school should be opened, there was meanwhile plenty to do in preparation. Borrowing

[1] H. A. Lafleur: 'Early Days at the Johns Hopkins Hospital with Dr. Osler.' *Canadian Medical Association Journal*, May 1920, Memorial Number, p. 42.

from his knowledge of the German clinics, a hierarchy of long-term hospital residents was established to take the place of the usual brief period of interneship, which had been and still continues to be the custom in most hospitals. He had made a wise choice in Lafleur as his Resident Physician, under whom J. A. Scott and Harry Toulmin, recent Philadelphia graduates, were to be the first Assistant Residents; and with this nucleus there gathered an ever-increasing group of devoted satellites. One of them, H. M. Thomas, a Baltimorean whose father was one of the Quaker members of the original Board of Trustees, has given an account[1] of those thrilling days, when the staff was a closely united body energized by Osler's example, engaging personality, and generosity, for 'he saw to it that the younger men got the whole credit of the work when often it should have gone to himself'.

Five venturesome patients visited the dispensary the morning its doors were thrown open, and a few days later, on May 15th to be exact, the first case, one of aortic aneurysm, was admitted to the single medical ward then ready for occupancy; and from this small beginning things must have moved rapidly, for a fortnight later he scribbled on a card to Musser: ''Spital booming—very busy.'[2] On the 1st of June a public announcement had been made of the provisional staff organization, consisting of Osler as Physician-in-Chief with his three assistants, while Welch as Pathologist-in-Chief was represented by W. T. Councilman and Alexander Abbott in residence. As the ambulatory clinic for out-patients was to be made a feature of the hospital, Halsted, temporarily appointed Acting Surgeon, was put in charge with F. J. Brockway as the first Resident Surgeon, and J. M. T. Finney and G. S. Clarke as his assistants. All these first-comers, with Mr. Gilman as

[1] H. M. Thomas: 'Some Memories of the development of the Medical School, and of Osler's Advent.' *Johns Hopkins Hospital Bulletin*, 1919, xxx. 188.

[2] He was not too busy, however, later in the month to attend the annual meeting, in Newport, of the American Medical Association, where he reported a case of 'Word Blindness with Hemianopsia', published later in the *American Journal of the Medical Sciences* for Mar. 1891, ci. 219.

Acting Director, lived together in the hospital during these first few months while the wards one after another were being opened.

To H. V. Ogden from W. O. Johns Hopkins Hospital, Baltimore, June 26th, 1889.

Dear Ogden, I send my Cerebral Palsies of Kids, & a val. address. Health Boards will save the profession in this country if well organized. Wish you could come down here—bed always at your disposal. We are in full swing—50 patients in wards & averaging 60–80 in Dispensaries daily. I am largely responsible for Kelly who is the highest gynepod & one of the best operators in the country. I know him intimately. He has a bitter enemy in J— P— & I have no doubt some of his friends have been talking. His record is remarkable. His third successful Caesarian—mothers & children—was performed 6 weeks ago. I wish we could have had Senn here. That Washington escapade & those letters killed him in the East. I shall be in Toronto for Aug. 1st. Was there last week—all well. Yours ever, W. O.

Howard A. Kelly, with his former assistant and future Resident Hunter Robb, joined the group later in the summer; and finally, early in August Henry M. Hurd, previously head of the State Hospital for the Insane at Pontiac, Michigan, who had been chosen as the future Superintendent, came to relieve Mr. Gilman from his self-imposed task. Except for the suite of rooms set apart for Dr. Hurd and his family, for he was the only married member of the household, the most desirable rooms in the administration building were given over to the juniors, several of whom rejoiced in a separate study and bedroom—such quarters, indeed, as hospital internes had never before known.

So this original group living intimately together, the chiefs and their juniors, became a closely knit body of friends who knew how to work as well as to play together. One may be sure that much lively banter passed between these active-minded people and that their individual foibles were not spared. The new Superintendent ceased to preface his remarks by: 'I once knew a man in Pontiac, &c.' after he had reprimanded the staff one morning for putting an out-of-town visitor, unable safely to negotiate

THE JOHNS HOPKINS HOSPITAL

THE FIRST GROUP OF HOPKINS INTERNES WITH 'THE CHIEF'

Circa April 1890

Back row: A.A. Ghriskey, J.M.T. Finney, A.C. Abbott, Hunter Robb, G.S. Clarke, W.H. Baltzell.
Second row: H. Toulmin, W. Osler, J.A. Scott, H.A. Lafleur, W.H. Farr.
Below: F.J. Brockway, D.M. Reese.

his way across town, in bed the night before in one of the wards; for he was told 'it was the man from Pontiac'. It was a toss-up as to who would have the upper hand in some practical joke played on one or the other and carried out with solemn face. Osler one Saturday night had been to see Richard Mansfield in 'The Parisian Romance'—a play in which Mansfield dies of a well-simulated stroke of apoplexy. The pathologists of the hospital naturally enough were eager not to lose any opportunity for post-mortem examinations; and on Osler's return, seeing Councilman reading in the common-room, he announced that there had been a fatality—a cerebral haemorrhage—and an immediate autopsy was requested. This hint was promptly taken by Councilman and Abbott, who repaired to the pathological laboratory and made their preparations; but as nothing happened, after a long wait they telephoned the ward and learned the true facts. Osler had long since gone to bed and taken the precaution of locking his door. In some reminiscences of those days, one of the victims of this prank [1] recalls that—

. . . He [Osler] was then not quite forty and looked younger, a well-knit but rather spare figure, of about the average height, a rather long moustache, the position of the ends of which seemed to vary with his mood; hair even then a little spare, a clear but rather sallow complexion, a broad forehead, good eyes and lively expression. I think that any stranger with good knowledge of men would have thought him from appearance interesting and been attracted by him. His clothes were always simple and worn well, and he fancied cravats of rather striking colour. At first, with the exception of Welch and Mall, we all lived in the hospital, our rooms in the main building were capacious, comfortably furnished, and the outlook over the city and harbour was fine. No one of the small group of men who participated in the hospital life at this early period can forget its fascination. . . . We breakfasted together, then each sought his particular duties, to meet again at luncheon. The luncheon hour, at which most of those working at the hospital gathered, was the most delightful of the day. Osler, Welch, Halsted, Mall, Lafleur, and with the usual visiting stranger, sat at a table in the end of the dining-room. The conversation was always lively and interesting: everyone sought to bring something to the feast.

---

[1] W. T. Councilman: 'Osler in the Early Days, &c.' *Boston Medical and Surgical Journal*, April 1920.

There was talk about work; jokes, and laughter. A favourite game in which Osler rather excelled—his early experience with Egerton Y. Davis and the Caughnawauga Indians having given him previous practice—was to relate the impossible and to lead up to this so skilfully that the line between fact and fiction was obscured. It was very well for us who knew the game, but occasionally it would be played when the serious visitor was present and he often carried away with him striking information of new facts in medical science. The exchanges between Osler and Halsted were always a delight, and we all sought to get something on the other. I remember once that I had gone to Philadelphia to read a paper on a subject in which we were all interested, but unfortunately I had mistaken the date by a week, at that time not being accustomed to think of evils long in advance. I was naturally somewhat fearful of the fact being ascertained, and the first thing, the next day, Osler asked me about the paper, how it had been accepted, what was the discussion, etc. I rather welcomed the opportunity to get the matter over with and spoke of the enthusiastic reception accorded the paper and gave at some length the discussion upon it. 'What did Wilson say?' asked Osler, and I thought it well to put Wilson in opposition and gave as well as I could his opposing argument. 'Yes,' said Osler, 'Jim Wilson spent last night with me and said he immensely enjoyed your paper but he could not quite agree with you.'

Two things must not be lost sight of in regard to the chiefs-of-service. Their youth in the first place; for Osler, not quite 40, was the senior in years, with Welch a year younger, Halsted 37, Hurd 36, and Kelly only 31. In the second place, these young men, as had been true of those originally gathered to make the nucleus of the university, had been imported into a conservative community which had its own fine medical traditions, and it is but natural that there must have been some heart-burnings that there was no representative of the Baltimore profession on the new Faculty. On the part of the newcomers, it was a situation requiring a combination of patience, of tact, of good-fellowship, of kindly feeling and, at the same time, evidence of indubitable professional superiority.

Though the nurses' training-school had not as yet been formally opened nor its directress chosen, a number of capable women had been attached from time to time, one of whom, an Englishwoman, graduate of the Florence Nightingale school, a Miss Louisa Parsons, of whose sad death years later the circumstances will be told, was temporarily put in charge. During most of the summer Osler remained at his post, for though Baltimore in midsummer is not an ideal place for sustained work, the hospital is so fortunately situated that life there is comfortable enough.

To President Gilman from W. O. The Johns Hopkins Hospital, July 19th, 1889.

Dear Mr. Gilman,—I dare say you will be glad to have a line or two from me giving an account of my stewardship. The machine works smoothly, thanks to your manipulation. Thanks, also to your arrangements, there has been no trouble so far. The number of patients keeps about the same—forty-seven to-day. The nurses continue satisfactory. I think we have been very fortunate in our selection. I hope that you are enjoying your well earned holiday, and I will be glad if you will give my regards to Mrs. Gilman—our lady visitor. Should I get anywhere near Mt. Desert this summer, I shall assuredly come to Northeast Harbour.

He must have secured a secretary by this time, an unwonted luxury, for this is the first of his recovered letters which was typewritten, all of his previous correspondence and papers having been written out in longhand. He got away by the end of August for a visit in Toronto, and from there in company with his favourite nephew,[1] W. W. Francis, instead of proceeding to Banff, where the Canadian Medical Association was to meet, he for good and sufficient reasons went to pay a visit to a doctor-friend in charge of the leper colony at Tracadie, on the Gulf of St. Lawrence in the very north-eastern corner of the Province of New Brunswick. New Brunswick is not so large but that some Philadelphia friends who were spending the summer on the Island of Grand Manan, off the southwest corner of the Province, joined forces with them as told below:

Visit to the Leper Colony at Tracadie.

W. O. took me along—I was only 11. When we started from Toronto he intended to leave me with some friends in Montreal and to pick me up on his return a week later. But I was too polite to refuse the cheese at dinner—it was very high—and I would not stay in a house where such food was possible. So on I went with him

[1] Osler was 'uncle' by courtesy to all the Francis children, who in reality were his first-cousins-once-removed.

to Portland, Maine, and from there to Eastport where we waited impatiently for a boat from Grand Manan which was bringing two mysterious friends to join us. They were 'the Widow Gross' (the first time I saw her) and Miss Woolley; and the four of us made the rest of the trip together, via St. John, Bathurst, and a funny little railway thence to Caraquet on the Baie de Chaleurs, where we were all put up by a very charming family, with some girls who made a lot of me. Next day, the rest of them drove 30 miles to Tracadie and inspected the colony of 18 lepers. I was left behind with 'cold feet', the result of heat, lobsters and seeing some pictures of the lepers. When we got back to Bathurst and the main line, the train was late, hot and crowded, and the only accommodation left for W. O. and me and an enormously fat R. C. bishop was the smoking-room of the Pullman. The bishop offered to climb up to the upper berth, but we both looked at his girth, and he joined us in the laugh. W. O. and I shared the upper, and the bishop snored horribly. We dropped our companions the next day at Cacouna. Such is my childhood recollection. Boiled down, I fear there is nothing in it but the fact of the visit and that Mrs. Gross accompanied us.

It was a very brief holiday, for September 10th finds him in Washington for a meeting of the Association of Physicians; and a few days later he wrote to Ogden to say that 'the hospital flourishes apace' and that he is tempted to stay on for another year rather than to take up his abode in town. However, he shortly after took up his residence at 209 West Monument Street, where the eldest daughter of his brother Featherston, whom he persisted in introducing as 'Mrs. O.', came to keep house for him. The arrangement gave him the first opportunity he had ever had of entertaining in his own home, and it came to be the exception for him ever to sit at table without having transient visitors or members of the hospital staff as informal guests. 'I am sure', his mother writes, 'you will find the dear Georgie all you could wish, only be careful in having so many young M. D.'s about and treating them so kindly too. It is only a very special specimen of its kind that is to set his affections on your very extra niece.'

On October 9th the Nurses' Home was formally opened, and the Training School for which ample provision had been made was inaugurated with due ceremonies. Isabel A. Hampton, a remarkably capable woman, a Canadian and a graduate of Bellevue Hospital in New York, had been brought from the Illinois Training School in Chicago, of which she was then Superintendent, and under her leadership as Principal the school rapidly came to hold high rank, for it was the first time such a school had been recognized from the outset as an essential part of the hospital foundation. In this same month, the Monday-evening societies which came to play such an important part in the life and work of the hospital staff were organized. The first and third Mondays of each month were to be given over to the presentation of interesting cases, to the reading of papers, and to the discussion of problems in process of solution. The first meeting was held on October 22nd, with Welch presiding and Hunter Robb acting as secretary; and before this group of enthusiastic young people eager to advance knowledge and to control opinions by experimental tests, hardly a subject could be mentioned at one of these gatherings that did not lead to further work in view of the free and suggestive exchange of ideas. In the history of medicine there has never been anything quite like it: there was no need to drum up an audience for these meetings, and it is recalled that Reginald H. Fitz, who at about this time went down from Boston to learn something of the spirit of this new place which already was being so much talked about, likened the life to that of a monastery, with the unusual feature that the monks did not appear to bother their minds about the future.

It has been seen that both in Montreal and Philadelphia Osler had organized a foreign-periodical club; and so here what was called 'The Journal Club' was started, with its first meeting in the library of the hospital on Thursday afternoon of October 29th, when the current literature was reviewed. The recorded purpose of the 'club' was 'to enable all members of the staff to keep fully informed as to what is being accomplished by workers in every branch of medical science with the least expenditure of time'; and many of these reports and book-reviews subsequently found their way into Hays's journal or elsewhere, so that others could get them second hand, though on the printed page the stimulating discussions which took place on the Thursday afternoons was missing. Such things as this must have occurred many times before in other places, but never under more favourable auspices nor with a more enthusiastic group, undistracted by any outside calls upon their time and eager to justify their connexion with a new institution untrammelled by tradition, whose present and future reputation lay entirely in their hands.

D. C. Gilman was a wise propagandist and realized the importance of getting the publications of the workers stamped with the seal of the university,[1] and consequently the hospital trustees were encouraged to provide suitable mediums of publication for the medical group—not only an annual volume on the lines of the famous Reports which had emanated from some of the London hospitals, but a monthly journal as well, to contain the reports of meetings, discussions, and the shorter occasional papers. Thus in December there appeared the first number of the *Johns Hopkins Hospital Bulletin*, which was to play such an important part in bringing the activities of the hospital group before the medical world. The first number contained the preliminary account of Welch's studies on hog cholera, and a further statement from Osler on the value of Laveran's organism in the diagnosis of malaria, a subject in which his juniors had become deeply engrossed, and which in time led to Thayer's comprehensive monograph on the subject. It also contained an announcement of the courses which were to be offered to graduates, for, disappointed as all must have been in the postponement of plans to open a medical school, teaching was nevertheless regarded as an essential stimulus, even for those engaged actively in research.

At the Medical Society meeting of December 16th John S. Billings brought over from the Surgeon-General's Library some forty items—manuscripts, incunabula, and

[1] The *American Journal of Mathematics*, under Simon Newcomb; the *American Chemical Journal*, under Remsen; the *American Journal of Philology*, under Gildersleeve; *Studies from the Biological Laboratory*, under Martin and Brooks; and H. B. Adams's *Studies in Historical and Political Science* had already been launched under the aegis of the university.

rare medical publications—from among the treasures in the growing collection in Washington which his foresight had made possible. An account of the meeting, with a list of the books, was published in the *Bulletin*, and thus interest was started in the bibliography and history of the profession, which has since spread widely and for which Billings primarily, and Osler and Welch in turn, were so largely responsible. An Historical Club was soon established, one Monday evening in each month being given over to its purposes; and unless he were ill or away from home Osler for the fifteen years to follow was unfailing in his attendance at these Monday-evening gatherings, which he regarded as educational agencies of great importance to the hospital and school.

There was a gathering in Toronto late in December to celebrate the opening of the new biological laboratory, erected largely through the energies of Professor Ramsay Wright, on which occasion a number of distinguished men gave addresses, among them Welch, Charles S. Minot of Harvard, Vaughan of Ann Arbor, and 'our own Osler', as the local papers had it. Welch chose as his topic a discussion of 'Pathology in its Relation to General Biology'; and on the evening of the 20th a special meeting of the local Pathological Society was staged, in which all the guests participated. Accustomed to have Osler play the major rôle in Canada as a pathologist, it must have caused some comment among the profession in Toronto to see how completely he had relinquished to his colleague the leadership in a subject which had for so long been the source of his keenest interest.[1] This was inevitable, for Welch's appointment represented the first recognition of pathology as a subject entitled to stand alongside of biology

[1] Before the Johns Hopkins Medical Society, March 17, 1890, Welch exhibited a series of gross and microscopic specimens of entozoa observed in the domestic animals in Baltimore, and stated that 'the interest in animal parasites has been overshadowed of late years by the study of the pathogenic bacteria, but nevertheless the entozoans are of great interest and importance and deserve our careful attention'. As pointed out, Osler had begun his studies of entozoa many years before and to judge from his note-books he had gone into the subject even more thoroughly than Welch. Unfortunately there is no report of any discussion following Welch's paper.

and the other sciences on the university calendar. Nevertheless, for Osler to have given up without question the privilege of conducting the post-mortem studies upon fatal cases from his own service is merely an example of the generosity of spirit which pervaded the Hopkins group in those days. But his long apprenticeship in pathology had been by no means wasted: it was unquestionably an ideal preparation for a clinician and gave him the rare ability to interpret his patients' symptoms in terms of the pictures which his long hours at the autopsy-table had indelibly stamped on his mind. So, in the text-book he finally came to write, his pathological descriptions, drawn from his own experience, were regarded as the best part of his treatise and could have been written by no other clinician of the day, unless possibly by Fitz, who had had a similar training. In his address given on this very occasion Welch stated that 'pathology must constitute the scientific basis of practical medicine'.

1890

There was a widespread epidemic of influenza at the time, almost though not quite so serious as the epidemic of thirty years later during the Great War; and his mother writes in a Christmas letter on his return from Toronto: 'I hope the cold you had did not lay you up on the sick list. This epidemic is everywhere and keeps the poor M. D.'s very busy, or what is worse lays some of them low; every house has its tale to tell.' Whether he escaped is not told, but he probably did not, for whenever there were 'colds' about he was almost certain to be victimized and it became his custom to surrender immediately, to remain in bed for a day or two and to saturate himself with literature in lieu of drugs. As the hospital affairs were flourishing, as there was no immediate prospect of starting the medical school, and inasmuch as the staff was so organized that any one, even 'the Chief', might drop out without affecting the routine work, he made plans to spend a few months in Europe, for he had not been abroad since his Goulstonian Lectures were given five years before. Of these plans he writes to Mr. Gilman, who, needing a well deserved rest after fifteen years at his post, had taken his family first to the Mediterranean for the winter months and then to England, where honorary degrees were bestowed upon him at Oxford and Cambridge:

To Daniel C. Gilman from W. O. 209 W. Monument Street, March 6th

Dear Mr. Gilman, I feel rather conscience-stricken that I have not reported progress to the Ex-Director. Everything works smoothly on the lines laid down by you but a few details will give you an idea of our present conditions. We have now had nearly 1,000 in-patients & over 11,000 out-patients! To-day the ward population is 130 & the income from private patients over $360. The new Director is excellent in all respects & gets on well with everyone. I do not know that he has quite our appreciation of the Training School tho he & Miss Hampton are on the best of terms. Halsted is doing remarkable work in Surgery & I feel that his appointment to the University & the Hospital would be quite safe. Kelly's department is now in full swing. We made a great hit in Sister Rachel [Miss Bonner] who is a bond of peace, but I tell her that she has sadly degenerated, & has so far departed from the faith once delivered to Fox as to frequent playhouses. Miss Hampton has fulfilled Mrs Gilman's prognosis, and she has been most successful in getting probationers of a high class; but unfortunately she selects them altogether for their good looks & the House staff is by this time in a sad state. The chief is, I fear hopeless—you remember Keats—'They could not in the self-same mansion dwell without some stir of heart &c,' but it is *not* the 'gentle Isabel'. Miss Parsons as I dare say you have heard has gone to the Maryland General.

The Bulletin you will have already seen & the first two numbers of the Reports. Both start with firm support but the latter may drag a little as it is so hard to get men to write. I leave April 26th by Etruria & shall be in London about May 6th. My address will be Brown Bros. Do let me know of your whereabouts as I am most anxious to talk over the Medical School & if possible arrange to go to Cambridge with you. I shall spend the great part of May & all of June in a systematic inspection of six or eight of the leading German & French clinics & return to London about July 1st. We follow your progress with great interest & all rejoice that you are having such a good holiday.

The first fasciculus of Volume II of the Hospital Reports for 1890, to which he refers, comprised seven papers from Osler's clinic, and though such publications necessarily have a small circulation, they had been written—and the second volume indeed was completed—long before the papers were all in hand for Volume I, 'as it is hard to get men to write'. They were on a variety of clinical topics, perhaps the most important being those by Osler himself on tuberculous peritonitis and on the intermittent fever associated with gall-stones, for which conditions, even at this early day, he advocated more frequent operative interference.

At one of the January meetings of the hospital society, Osler had presented a case of *Filaria sanguinis hominis*, a parasitic disease of the tropics and sub-tropics, practically unknown in northern latitudes, an example of which, however, had been sent from Charleston to the hospital for study. Though he had written an editorial on the subject for the *Medical News* in 1886, inspired by John Guitéras's discovery of the parasite, he had probably never before seen a case to recognize it, and the incident, trivial enough in itself, is only mentioned to point out again the intense interest which diseases produced by parasites always roused in him. It was an interest easily traced, for it almost certainly began with his observation of the trichinae during his student days in Toronto, and in natural sequence led to his collection of the entozoa, to his early papers on cestode and echinococcal infections, and subsequently in Philadelphia to his malarial studies. So one may imagine his delight when on March 22nd of this year he discovered amoebae in the material secured from an abscess of the liver of a patient with chronic dysentery whom he had seen in consultation with Dr. Friedenwald of Baltimore, and on whom Dr. Tiffany had operated. Not even Leidy 'with one more rhizopod to discover' could have been more elated. In one of his case note-books which has been preserved, he has drawn numerous pictures of the organism, especially of one amoeba which on March 24th was watched for many hours and of which there is a succession of sketches showing its changes in contour. Two days later he wrote enthusiastically to Musser:

> When are you coming down? MacDonald of Montreal will be here towards the end of the week. Could you not come & take dinner with us & stay the night—always a room ready. We have been much excited over Kartulis' amoebae which we have found in a liver abscess from a case of dysentery—a Dr. from Panama. They

are most extraordinary & striking creatures & take one's breath away at first to see these big amoebae—10–20 times the size of a leucocyte—crawling about in the pus. The movements are very active & in one case kept up for 10 hours. I get a fresh stock of pus from the drainage tube every day so if you could run down some eve. we could look for the creatures in the morning. Koch & Kartulis found them constantly in the stools and bases of the ulcers in Egyptian dysentery & the latter in the liver abscesses. Keep an eye on your Blockley dysenteries as it would be most interesting to find similar bodies in our dysenteries. I am off on April 26th by Etruria. Very busy—I go north for Easter—few days.

An account of this observation was promptly written up and appeared in an early number of the *Bulletin*.[1] It was the first confirmation in English-speaking countries of observations made by an Athenian, Kartulis, who had been stimulated to make studies of dysentery in Greece following upon the discovery by Koch during his sojourn in Egypt in 1883 with the Cholera Commission, that amoebae were occasionally to be found in the intestines of persons dead of dysentery. Up to this time a good deal of doubt had been cast upon the conclusions of Kartulis, for many had regarded the amoebae as secondary invaders, so that the discovery of the parasites in the liver abscess Osler regarded as the first important observation made on the medical service. Late in 1913, when preparing for the address, already much quoted from, in which he gave a summary of his life as a clinical teacher,[2] he wrote certain sections not included in the article when printed. One of them refers to this discovery and its sequel, as follows :

Familiar with the various forms of amoebae, the opportunity appeared to be an important one for the study of a disease which was widely prevalent. We very soon had other opportunities, and within a few weeks Dr. Lafleur demonstrated their presence in a local case. In the same year the amoebae were demonstrated by Dr. Charles Simon in a case in the wards, in which the abscess had perforated the lung. The disease was found to be common, and Dr. Councilman in the Pathological Department, and Dr. Lafleur—then first Assistant in the Medical Clinique—issued in Vol. II of the *Johns Hopkins Hospital Reports* for 1890 the monograph on the subject which still remains the most exhaustive contribution in

[1] *Johns Hopkins Hospital Bulletin*, 1890, i. 53.
[2] 'The Medical Clinic.' *British Medical Journal*, Jan. 3, 1914.

English, and at once convinced both pathologists and clinicians of the specific nature of this type of the disease. Many subsequent reports are to be found scattered through the Bulletins, one of the most interesting of which was the disclosure by Dr. Flexner of the presence of the amoebae in an abscess of the jaw. The hepato-pulmonary abscess—of which we had a great many cases—was made the subject of a careful study by Dr. Futcher.

During all this time he had a sufficient reason for running over to Philadelphia when opportunity permitted, even had he not been called there frequently to participate in some function or other. One such occasion took him, a few days before his sailing, to the College of Physicians, where he gave an address [1] in connexion with the presentation to the College of the portrait of Weir Mitchell, its recent President, than whom, as Osler said, no member of the profession in his generation had more pleasurably 'warmed both hands before the fire of life'.

Reference has repeatedly been made to Osler's habit of note-taking, and a number of his pocket commonplace-books filled with abundant jottings on topics of all sorts, written in pencil and now for the most part illegible, are in existence. It was a habit that he strongly recommended to his students as one of the three essentials in their education:

Given the sacred hunger and proper preliminary training, the student-practitioner requires at least three things with which to stimulate and maintain his education, a note-book, a library, and a quinquennial brain-dusting. I wish I had time to speak of the value of note-taking. You can do nothing as a student in practice without it. Carry a small note-book which will fit into your waistcoat pocket, and never ask a new patient a question without note-book and pencil in hand. After the examination of a pneumonia case two minutes will suffice to record the essentials in the daily progress. Routine and system, when once made a habit, facilitate work, and the busier you are the more time you will have to make observations. . . . Begin early to make a three-fold category—clear cases, doubtful cases, mistakes. And learn to play the game fair, no self-deception, no shrinking from the truth; mercy and consideration for the other man, but none for yourself, upon whom you have to keep an incessant watch. You remember Lincoln's famous *mot* about the impossibility of fooling all of the people all of the time. It does

---

[1] Cf. the *Johns Hopkins Hospital Bulletin*, June 1890, i. 64.

not hold good for the individual, who can fool himself to his heart's content all of the time. If necessary, be cruel; use the knife and the cautery to cure the intumescence and moral necrosis which you will feel in the posterior parietal region, in Gall and Spurzheim's centre of self-esteem, where you will find a sore spot after you have made a mistake in diagnosis. It is only by getting your cases grouped in this way that you can make any real progress in your post-collegiate education; only in this way can you gain wisdom with experience. It is a common error to think that the more a doctor sees the greater his experience and the more he knows. No one ever drew a more skilful distinction than Cowper in his oft-quoted lines, which I am never tired of repeating to a medical audience:

> Knowledge and wisdom, far from being one,
> Have oft-times no connexion. Knowledge dwells
> In heads replete with thoughts of other men;
> Wisdom in minds attentive to their own.
> Knowledge is proud that he has learned so much;
> Wisdom is humble that he knows no more.[1]

During the course of the quinquennial brain-dusting which he took this summer, one of these student note-books was kept. It is filled with the usual miscellany, though for the most part with notes such as any careful observer might have made of clinics which he had attended. A typical continental *Studienreise* was taken during which he enjoyed the companionship of Ramsay Wright, whose purpose was to study museum methods, in view of the recent destruction by fire of the University of Toronto Museum. They decided on Freiburg as a starting-point, reached there May 17th, saw the new surgical theatre, visited Weismann and also Wiedersheim the comparative anatomist, spent a pleasant evening with Ziegler, Kahlden and others at a *Kneipe*; and on the next day, a Sunday, they went to Titi-See, climbed the Feldberg and dined on the top, without, alas, the promised view of the Swiss mountains. They went on to Basel and Berne, where Osler was interested in the number of women students attending the classes of Langhans and Sahli. One was discovered to be immersed in a Tauchnitz novel during the lecture, and Osler notes that he did not see one who looked likely to

[1] Osler: 'The Student Life.' No. XX in 'Aequanimitas and other Addresses'.

become the Trotula of the twentieth century. Then Zurich and Munich, where, being Whitsuntide, the university laboratories were deserted; and as every one seemed to be going to Oberammergau for the Passion Play they followed suit and were fortunate to discover a bedroom of sorts in the Wittelsbacher Hof, since tickets for the play —which Osler described as 'frightfully realistic'—were allotted to the beds in the village. From Munich they went to Erlangen, principally to visit Strümpell and Zenker; and Osler notes: 'The university *is* Erlangen—practically there is nothing else in the little Bavarian town, which forcibly illustrates the great truth that *men* make a seat of learning, and if given proper facilities will attract students.' Then Wurzburg, where a visit to Kölliker impressed him so much that he notes: 'The type of a senior Professor which might well be more common,—the intellectual digestion usually gets feeble after the *crise de quarante ans* and new methods are assimilated with difficulty. A man however who has brought out within a month or so the first part of a new edition of his General Embryology 25 years after the last edition cannot be called old, although he may have reached the Psalmist's limit. Nothing is more inspiring than to see a veteran in the van.' *En route* to Heidelberg they had some hours in Frankfurt with Edinger, and with Weigert, whom Osler had known in Leipzig and who was found busy with a new stain for neuroglia. Heidelberg was described as 'too alluring to spend much time in hospitals or laboratories', and yielding to the seduction of the place they spent some days in long walks over the hills, their evenings *zum Perkeo*, &c. Professor Wright recalls that—

W. O. felt the romance of every nook and corner of the place. On one of these outings, Sunday June 1st, a gypsy caravan passed us, and our attention was arrested by the beauty of the young girl who sat on the end of the last van. Later in the day we encountered the caravan in Neckargemünd; the men had been taken in charge by the police for entering the town without permission, the women were protesting noisily, and our sympathies were awakened and our pockets lightened to the extent of a few marks by the tears of the young beauty—Osler left unfinished a most poetical version of this incident, beginning: 'Upon what trifles depend events of the utmost importance to the individual.' He evidently intended his ' philologically-inclined young cousin Egerton Y. Davis Jr., Instructor in English in the University of X ' to join the gypsy band with the object of acquiring Romany !

From Heidelberg they proceeded to Strasburg, where they saw Schwalbe the anatomist ; but visits were also paid to Naunyn's wards and laboratory, as well as to those of von Recklinghausen, Hoppe-Seyler, Schmiedeberg, and Goltz. All this and much more Osler told in a series of ' Letters to my House Physicians ' sent in turn to ' L ' [Lafleur], ' T ' [Toulmin], ' R ' [Reese], ' S ' [Simon] and ' H ' [Hoch], and which were published serially in the New York and also in the Montreal medical journals of that year. These long letters contain delightful pen-pictures of the men and places that were visited, and many of the things he picked out as worthy of comment find their reflection in some of the teaching methods which he subsequently adopted. The last of the letters, written from Strasburg and sent to August Hoch, ends with the following paragraph :

Now, as you are in part a Teuton, it may interest you to know the general impression one gets of the professional work over here. I should say that the characteristic which stands out in bold relief in German scientific life is the paramount importance of knowledge for its own sake. To know certain things thoroughly and to contribute to an increase in our knowledge of them seems to satisfy the ambition of many of the best minds. The presence in every medical centre of a class of men devoted to scientific work gives a totally different aspect to professional aspirations. While with us—and in England—the young man may start with an ardent desire to devote his life to science, he is soon dragged into the mill of practice, and at forty years of age the ' guinea stamp ' is on all his work. His aspirations and his early years of sacrifice have done him good, but we are the losers and we miss sadly the leaven which such a class would bring into our professional life. We need men like Joseph Leidy and the late John C. Dalton, who, with us yet not of us, can look at problems apart from practice and pecuniary considerations. I have said much in my letters of splendid laboratories and costly institutes, but to stand agape before the magnificent structures which adorn so many university towns of Germany and to wonder how many millions of marks they cost and how they ever could be paid for, is the sort of admiration which Caliban yielded to Prospero. Men will pay dear for what they prize dearly, and the true homage must be given to the spirit which makes this vast expenditure a necessity. To that *Geist* the entire world to-day stands debtor, as over every department of practical knowledge has it silently brooded, often unrecognized, sometimes when recognized not thanked. The universities of Germany are her chief glory, and the greatest boon she can give to us in the New World is to return our young men infected with the spirit of earnestness and with the love of thoroughness which characterizes the work done in them.

The last three weeks in June were spent in Paris, and the note-book gives picturesque accounts of their doings there, which began with a visit to Laveran at the Salpêtrière. They saw Déjerine, Debove, Bouchard, Charcot, Hayem, Straus, and Luys ; and Déjerine's lectures he particularly recommended. Hypnotism was very much to the fore at this time, and there is a long account of a clinic before a crowded amphitheatre—described as 'a regular circus'—given by Luys at the Charité. They were living meanwhile near the Pasteur Institute and often attended Pasteur's hydrophobia inoculations which were held in the early afternoons.[1] They met Metchnikoff, Richet, and Cornil and attended some of their lectures, as well as those of other celebrities like Renan, who was lecturing on the Book of Daniel, and Quatrefages, who gave an active and well-studied attack on Darwinism such as might have been expected in the '60's. So the days passed, and in early July after one of the worst possible Channel crossings they parted in England, to meet again later on in Berlin. While in London he saw, of course, all his London friends and spent a promised week-end with the Schäfers, then living at Croxley Green, Hertfordshire. The following incidents, among many others, remain stamped on Sir Edward's memory :

A good many years ago—about 1890—when I was in London, I happened to be walking with Osler in the West End during one of his visits from the other side, and as we were passing a bootmaker's he said : 'Come along in here a moment, I want to see an old friend.' The proprietor, an elderly gentleman, was standing with

[1] In his introduction to the English edition (Constable & Co.) of the 'Life of Pasteur' which Osler wrote at the request of Mr. Phipps in 1911, he refers to these demonstrations by 'the Great Master', though, as often in mentioning dates, he was casual and got them incorrect.

THE BEECH TREE AT LITTLE GILLIANS, CROXLEY GREEN

From a snapshot taken by Dr. H. J. Shirley, 10, *January* 1921

his back to us: Osler went up, slapped him on the back and exclaimed: 'Hullo, old boy, how have you been all this time?' The 'old boy' had been his bootmaker when he first came to work in London in the early '70's—and the meeting was like that of two old friends. . . . It was nearly always fine summer weather when he made his numerous visits to us in one or other of our country houses in Hertfordshire, and we generally lazed away the hours of the Sunday on the grass or in lounge chairs, doing nothing particular and doing that remarkably well. But on one occasion at Croxley Green he had a fit of activity, spending a great part of the afternoon in carving 'W. O.' and the date in large characters on a fine young beech-tree standing in a charming copse close to our house. I expect the inscription is there to this day, but it is many years since we left the neighbourhood. Next time I go I will try and find the tree: no doubt the inscription will be there still.

It still is; but the tree is now a monarch. Much the same boyish impulse had made him scratch his initials on the window-pane of the rectory at Weston. Had he chanced to cut James Bovell's initials instead of his own during this 'fit of activity' Professor Schäfer might well have been mystified. In reality lazing away hours was not Osler's rôle; he had small powers of keeping still and shortly he is found in Birmingham for the annual meeting of the British Medical Association, not a particularly stirring occasion, from all accounts. And a week later—evidently reading a volume of Lamb's poems *en route*—he joined Ramsay Wright again in Berlin for the Xth International Medical Congress, of which Virchow, Bergmann the surgeon, and Waldeyer the anatomist comprised the Committee of Organization. To them, after the fiasco of the IXth Congress in Washington, had been given the task of putting these important gatherings again on their feet.[1] Virchow's name was not only known to science the

[1] Osler's attendance was more or less obligatory, for with Jacobi, Welch, Fitz, Pepper, James Stewart and others he was officially a member of the American Committee. Any one unfamiliar with the workings of these great assemblies can hardly over-estimate the enormous amount of detailed work the Committee of Organization for months ahead was called upon to perform. At this gathering, for example, there were 8,831 registrants, fifty nationalities being represented, and 600 communications from selected readers were given before one or another of the twenty separate sections representing special subdivisions of medicine.

world over, but he was a prophet, of the people at least, in his own country; and the congress had abundant support from the Government, as well as from those who occupied the new palace in Potsdam. Nevertheless, in his opening address he ventured on the subject of militarism, saying that ' the bonds which unite are really stronger than the sentiments which so often divide people ' ; and pointing to the scientific advances of the Fatherland for the benefit of humanity he assured his hearers that ' there can be no real desire for war among a people who so sedulously cultivate the arts of peace '. But even a host of Virchows—and he was never popular with his Emperor, though finally made Rector of the University of Berlin—could not have stemmed the holocaust precipitated twenty-five years later.

It was customary for the Executive Committee of these quadrennial international congresses, which have been interrupted by the Great War, to invite certain prominent individuals to give general addresses, and on this occasion Lord (then Sir Joseph) Lister of London, Robert Koch of Berlin, C. J. Bouchard of Paris, Axel Key of Stockholm, H. C. Wood of Philadelphia, and Theodor Meynert of Vienna had been thus honoured. Of all these addresses, the one that made the greatest stir was by Koch on Bacterial Investigation, for in the course of it he made the startling and, as it proved, unfortunately premature announcement of the discovery of a cure for tuberculosis, the nature of which, however, was not disclosed.[1] The medical world, taking him for more than his word, promptly went mad, and from every side physicians flocked to Berlin to get tidings of tuberculin, for such the substance was called; and saddest of all, innumerable victims of consumption in its last stages did likewise. On his return home, Osler made some clinical tests with tuberculin and, after a few months' trial, issued a report which on the whole was favourable, in spite of this conservative statement:

The extraordinary enthusiasm which has been aroused by the announcement, is a just tribute to the character of Robert Koch,

---

[1] *Lancet*, Lond., Aug. 16, 1890, ii. 335–6. Koch's address at the congress was soon followed by his article, ' A further Communication on a Cure for

who is a model worker of unequalled thoroughness, whose ways and methods have always been those of the patient investigator, well worthy of the confidence which other experts in pathology place in his statements. The cold test of time can alone determine how far the claims which he has now advanced will be justified, and meanwhile the question has been transferred, so far as human medicine is concerned, from the laboratory to the clinical ward, in which the careful observations of the next few months will furnish the necessary data, upon which to found a final judgement.[1]

By this time or soon after, the Hopkins staff had been augmented by the appointment of A. A. Ghriskey, D. Meredith Reese, C. E. Simon, August Hoch, W. H. Baltzell, W. S. Thayer, Simon Flexner, George H. F. Nuttall, W. W. Russell and others; and early the next spring came a young McGill graduate, the much-lamented 'Jack' Hewetson, whom Osler loved as a son. Even Hewetson, however, did not escape from his practical jokes, and not long after his advent Osler sent him over to Philadelphia to look up something in the library of the College of Physicians, saying in an off-hand way as he was leaving: 'Do drop in on my old friends Philip Syng Physick, and Shippen, and give them my love.' Hewetson, who could not have been expected to know much of the worthies of Philadelphia's medical history, nor of the characteristics of his new Chief, spent most of his afternoon in Philadelphia trying to locate Drs. Physick and Shippen, and it was not until his return that he learned they belonged to the past. Poor Hewetson made a long and losing fight against tuberculosis and after his death in 1910 Osler in a memorial notice[2] gave the following picture of these early days:

The men of the first few years of the existence of this hospital formed a very happy band—young and eager, with a great problem before them, too great, indeed, to be fully appreciated by us. It was a motley group that the gift of a new Foundation in medicine had brought together, strangers to each other, strangers in a strange city; yet there was something in the air, and something in the

---

Tuberculosis'. *Deutsche medizinische Wochenschrift*, Nov. 14, 1890. Even in this article he withheld the nature of the substance (tuberculin) which was called Koch's lymph.

[1] *Johns Hopkins Hospital Bulletin*, Dec. 1890, i. 108.

[2] *Ibid.*, 1910, xxi. 357.

spirit of the place, that quickly ripened a mutual trust into good fellowship. The 'lead' already given by that great triumvirate Martin, Remsen and Welch, with Mr. Gilman's strong personality and intense interest in the hospital, made the running comparatively easy. It has often been remarked that the reputation of the Johns Hopkins Medical School has been made by its young men, to which I may note incidentally my shelves bear weighty testimony in the twelve volumes with the 500 papers of the graduates of the school during the first eight years. . . . In 1891 there came to us, probably through the influence of Lafleur, John Hewetson from McGill who had just finished a term of residence at the Montreal General Hospital. I have just had the sad news of his death, and wish to pay a brief tribute to his memory. Long practice has given me a fair control of my vasomotors, but my grip has never been sure when a letter or some incident brought suddenly to my mind the tragedy of the life of 'Jack' Hewetson. As I write there comes the far-away vision of a young face, frank and open, with the grey-blue eyes that looked so true, and a voice to match, with a merry laugh—no wonder that everyone loved him! Three happy years he lived with us, growing into a strong, earnest worker, and contributing with Dr. Thayer an important monograph on malaria, and many minor papers. Frank Smith and Barker, who joined the staff about the same time, became his devoted friends. The controller, Mr. Winder Emery, at once fell under his spell, and it was touching to see the affection with which the stern old martinet regarded the younger man. In 1894 Dr. Hewetson went to Germany, and in Leipzig appeared the signs of pulmonary tuberculosis. He had had a pleurisy in Montreal, and the disease made rapid progress. He returned to California, where his father lived, and began to fight the long and losing battle which has just ended. Brave and cheerful, never repining, even in his broken life, he had much happiness—happiness that comes with a devoted wife and faithful friends. We who loved him in those early days have never recovered from the tragedy of the wreck of a career of such peculiar promise.

An elaborate schedule had been worked out for the winter courses, which attracted a large number of post-graduate students. The Monday-evening meetings were got under way, Osler presiding at the medical meetings and vying with Welch and Kelly in being the moving spirit of the Historical Club. The first meeting, formally to organize this club, at which Osler presided, was held on November 10th, when Welch was elected President for the year. Osler expressed his intention of briefly reviewing at subsequent meetings 'the essays, monographs, and works of American authors which might be called American Medical Classics, and which have influenced most markedly the progress of medicine in this country '—a pursuit which accounts for a series of letters to Dr. Baumgarten of St. Louis, one of his friends in the Association of American Physicians. Thus on September 27th:

I was very sorry to miss you and the meeting at Washington this spring; but I have been on a delightful jaunt to Europe. I want to bother you for a few minutes. Do you know anything about Beaumont, the army surgeon and gastric physiologist, who died in St. Louis in 1853? Has he relatives in the city with whom I could communicate? I want certain details of his life which are not given in St. Louis M. & S. J. 1854, and I want particularly a photograph or portrait. I know they have called a mushroom school after his name & I dare say that without too much trouble you could put me in communication with persons who know all about him. [And again on October 3rd] Thanks very much for your prompt reply. I have written to Mrs. Kaim, asking for details about her father, for whose memory, these many years, I have had the deepest respect. Judge Baby has promised me full details with reference to the last days of St. Martin (Beaumont's subject) who died only a few years ago. I have a photograph of the old sinner, in his eighty-second year, and I shall at an early date make it a text for a short account at our hospital Medical Society, of the life and work of Beaumont. Welch has just returned. Councilman is on the sea. Lafleur is in the woods enjoying a well earned holiday after four months' hard work in my absence. I suppose there is no chance of seeing you before our next meeting; but should you come East remember I always have a room at my house at your disposal or my room at the hospital.

But this sort of thing was purely avocational: what really was occupying his time was the further pursuit of the malarial plasmodium, a form of sport with which not only his residential staff had become infected, but also chance visitors like Joseph Leidy, Jr., to whom he wrote on November 29th:

Dear Leidy, Those cases are most interesting—I am sure Laveran's organisms will be of the greatest benefit for diagnosis. . . . Look at night with the stimulating warmth of an Argand Burner & 1/12 im. at those rounded pigmented bodies & the crescents Ghriskey has been demonstrating with such care—the development of the flagellate forms, such a show as it makes. It takes away one's breath to see from these [drawing inserted] shaped bodies, apparently free, & resembling in general appearance the crescents—long flagella develop *under the eye*. Come down again soon, some Sunday—I shall not be in Philadelphia again until Xmas.

But his evenings were not entirely given over to the stimulating warmth of an Argand burner, for he had again been ' bedevilled ' into the promise of a contribution for Pepper's projected two-volume ' Theory and Practice of Medicine ' [1] at this very time, while he himself was almost persuaded to undertake an even more ambitious task, in which he was to cover single-handed the whole field of medicine.

[1] This was published 1893-4, Osler's chapters being on Organic Diseases of the Brain, Diseases of the Nerves, Diseases of the Muscles, Vasomotor and Trophic Disorders, Diseases of the Blood, and Diseases of the Ductless Glands—187 pages in all.

CHAPTER XIV

1891–2

THE TEXT-BOOK AND AFTER

THE larger part of the year 1891 was given over by Osler to the writing of his magnum opus—The Principles and Practice of Medicine. Whether he would have undertaken the task had he realized what burdens, in the way of successive editions, its extraordinary success would impose upon him for the remainder of his life, is a conjecture not worth wasting time over. It was certainly then or never. The university was in serious financial straits owing to the depreciation of the Baltimore and Ohio Railroad shares with which Mr. Hopkins had endowed it, and though this misfortune did not seriously hamper the hospital it postponed indefinitely any idea of erecting a medical school, which was primarily a university affair. Disappointing to all, as this was, it furnished the necessary freedom for a long consecutive piece of writing. The hospital was in smooth running order and much of the work could be delegated to his capable juniors: furthermore, serious interruptions were unlikely, for consultations were few and general practice forsworn.

There was need of a new students' treatise on general medicine. For nearly forty years Watson's justly celebrated 'Practice', first published in 1843, had successfully held the field against all rivals, and these were many, but the book was now out of date.[1] There had been, to be sure, no lack of competitors, eminent men too, whose volumes Osler had taken pains to review,[2] but all these efforts had

[1] Sir Thomas Watson had recently died at the age of ninety, 'wearing the white flower of a blameless life', as Osler wrote in a characteristic obituary notice sent to the *Canadian Practitioner*. He had succeeded Francis Hawkins as Professor of Medicine in King's College in 1836, and shortly afterwards delivered the immortal 'Lectures on the Principles and Practice of Physic', which made his text-book a classic.

[2] Three of them—by Nathan S. Davis, by Alfred L. Loomis, and by John S. Bristowe—had appeared shortly before Osler's review, entitled 'Recent Works on Practice', in the *American Journal of the Medical Sciences*, 1885, lxxxix. 175.

been short lived. He had, moreover, written chapters for some of the large Systems or Encyclopaedias of Medicine, like those edited by Pepper and by Keating, and was participating in another of the kind, so that he knew what was required ; he had persistently kept up with the current literature of his subject through the agency of the journal clubs which dogged his steps in Montreal and Philadelphia ; and by his constant reviews and editorials he not only had come to possess an unusual familiarity with medical progress in nearly all departments, but had acquired facility and style in the expression of his thoughts. His pathological training had been such as to make possible, from first-hand knowledge, vivid descriptions of the morbid anatomy of disease in a way unusual for a clinician. He had a great fondness for medical history and its heroes, and for the allusions to medicine which occur in general literature. His only weak spot was in therapeutics, if a healthy scepticism concerning drugs may be regarded as a weakness.

He was, all things considered, extraordinarily well equipped to undertake the task. The one 'weakness' which has been mentioned proved in a curious way, as will be seen, an unexpected and most important service to medicine in general. For it led, in an indirect way, to the rescue of the hospital from its financial embarrassment after the Baltimore fire in 1903 ; to the establishment of the Rockefeller Institute a few years later ; and, finally, to the incalculable benefit to humanity which the General Education Board has rendered with Mr. Rockefeller's money, owing to its interest in the prevention and cure of disease. Indeed, the present position of his colleague Welch, as Director of the Institute of Hygiene, is remotely due to the fact that Osler set himself thirty years before to write a text-book of Medicine, and, as Falconer Madan said years later, 'succeeded in making a scientific treatise literature'. On the fly-leaves of the interleaved copy finally sent him by his publishers when the work was finished, Osler penned the following statement of how the book had been written :

On several occasions, in Philadelphia, I was asked by Lea Bros. to prepare a work on Diagnosis, and had half promised one ; indeed

I had prepared a couple of chapters, but continually procrastinated on the plea that up to the 40th year a man was fit for better things than text-books. Time went on and as I crossed this date I began to feel that the energy and persistence necessary for the task were lacking. In September 1890 I returned from a four months' trip in Europe, shook myself, and towards the end of the month began a work on Practice. I had nearly finished the chapter on Typhoid Fever when Dr. Granger, Messrs. Appleton's agent, came from New York to ask me to prepare a Text-book on Medicine. We haggled for a few weeks about terms and finally, selling my brains to the devil, I signed the contract. My intention had been to publish the work myself and have Lippincott or Blakiston (both of whom offered) handle the book, but the bait of a guaranteed circulation of 10,000 copies in two years and fifteen hundred dollars on the date of publication was too glittering, and I was hooked. October, November, and December were not very satisfactory months, and January 1st, 1891, saw the infectious diseases scarcely completed. I then got well into harness. Three mornings of each week I stayed at home and dictated from 8 a.m. to 1 p.m. On the alternate days I dictated after the morning Hospital visit, beginning about 11.30 a.m. The spare hours of the afternoon were devoted to correction and reference work. Early in May I gave up the house, 209 Monument St., and went to my rooms at the Hospital. The routine there was :—8 a.m. to 1 p.m. dictation ; 2 p.m. visit to the private patients and special cases in the wards, after which revision, etc. After 5 p.m. I saw my outside cases ; dinner at the club about 6.30, loafed until 9.30, bed at 10 p.m., up at 7 a.m. I had arranged to send MS. by 1st of July and on that date I forwarded five sections, but the publishers did not begin to print until the middle of August. The first two weeks of August I spent in Toronto, and then with the same routine I practically finished the MS. by about October the 15th. During the summer the entire MS. was carefully revised for the press by Mr. Powell of the English Department of the University. The last three months of 1891 were devoted to proof reading. In January I made out the index, and in the entire work nothing so wearied me as the verifying of every reference. Without the help of Lafleur and Thayer, who took the ward work off my hands, I never could have finished in so short a time. My other assistants also rendered much aid in looking up references and special points. During the writing of the work I lost only one afternoon through transient indisposition, and never a night's rest. Between September, 1890, and January, 1892, I gained nearly eight pounds in weight.

During all these months of composition Osler's clinical duties were by no means neglected. An instalment of Koch's tuberculin had been sent in December to John S.

Billings, who had turned it over to Welch for the hospital use, and, though Osler soon wrote, 'I am afraid that in pulmonary tuberculosis we are going to be disappointed', a full report of the selected cases in which it was being tried under the supervision of Lafleur, Reese, and Hoch was issued in January. On February 22nd, only three days before he 'sold his brains to the devil' and signed the contract with Appleton's agent, the fifteenth anniversary of the university was held, Osler giving the main address, on 'Recent Advances in Medicine'.[1] This being an occasion when local public officials meet with the university, Osler, doubtless with the notoriously unsanitary conditions which then existed in Baltimore in his mind, laid stress on the movement towards the prevention of disease through sanitary science, in which the profession 'requires and can often obtain the intelligent co-operation of city authorities and the public', pointing out that 'clean streets, good drains and pure water have in many towns reduced the mortality from certain diseases fifty per cent.' He dwelt also on the new knowledge relating to the agents producing disease and how it had revolutionized the practice of surgery through the same methods of bacterial cleanliness that should be applied to prevent the infection of cities. He emphasized as a third great advance the diffusion among the public of more rational ideas concerning the treatment of disease, stating as an interesting psychological fact that 'the desire to take medicine is perhaps the greatest feature which distinguishes man from animals'.

Of one thing [he said] I must complain,—that when we of the profession have gradually emancipated ourselves from a routine administration of nauseous mixtures on every possible occasion, and when we are able to say, without fear of dismissal, that a little more exercise, a little less food, and a little less tobacco and alcohol, may possibly meet the indications of the case—I say it is a just cause of complaint that when we, the priests, have left off the worship of Baal, and have deserted the groves and high places, and have sworn allegiance to the true god of science, that you, the people, should wander off after all manner of idols, and delight more and more in patent medicine, and be more than ever in the hands of advertising quacks.

---

[1] Cf. *Science*, N.Y., 1891, xvii. 170.

But for a time it must be so. This is yet the childhood of the world, and a supine credulity is still the most charming characteristic of man.

The weekly Medical Society meetings continued to be held during the year, with Osler in the chair ; and the interesting reports in the hospital *Bulletin* of the proceedings on these Monday evenings, before small groups of some thirty or forty people, members of the house staff and graduate students, furnish most interesting reading. The monthly meetings of the Historical Club, always less well attended, he never missed, and rarely failed to contribute something, though his communications were not always published.[1] Nor was there any neglect of teaching, for it is evident from the elaborate schedule of exercises that the hours were as full as would have been the case had the undergraduate school been in operation. He kept up with his weekly clinics from October to May, gave a prescribed series of afternoon lectures, and meanwhile his output of papers, though fewer in number than in preceding years, was nevertheless considerable.

There was probably no one feature of his life in Philadelphia at first more greatly missed than his intimate relations with the College of Physicians and its superb library. In Baltimore the Medical and Chirurgical Faculty, before which body he had given his 'Licence to Practise' address in 1889, bore the same titular relation to the local profession as did the College of Physicians of Philadelphia ; but it was a dormant body which possessed at this time a few hundred dusty volumes of the mid-century vintage, housed in the basement of the Maryland Historical Society. The rejuvenescence of this respectable and aged society, which to all appearances had passed into a hopeless dotage, is almost wholly attributable to Osler's interest and activity. In this year, 1891, he volunteered to go on the library committee, and continued to serve in this capacity until the

[1] On Jan. 12th he gave abstracts from John Jones's 'Manual of Surgery', 1776, with a review of the life of this interesting Marylander. On Feb. 9th he gave an account of the introduction of Aspiration for Pleurisy. On Oct. 12th his topic was 'Nathan Smith and his Treatment of Typhus (now Typhoid) Fever'.

end of his Baltimore period in 1905, the 'Faculty' during the interval having made two migrations, each time to better quarters, while its library expanded from the original small nucleus to a collection of nearly 15,000 volumes. As an element in this renaissance he succeeded the following year in getting a trained librarian appointed, Miss Marcia C. Noyes, who has given her own account [1] of Osler's great services, behind the scenes as they often were, and which by no means ended with his departure for England. His interest in libraries was cumulative, and a contact once made was never subsequently lost. As will be seen, the library at McGill, that of the Surgeon-General in Washington, of the College of Physicians in Philadelphia, of the Johns Hopkins Hospital, of this Maryland Faculty, and many others which he perhaps knew less intimately, all continued to profit by his unflagging support—moral and often financial. Nor was his interest confined wholly to medical libraries. But not even his supreme delight in the Bodleian, of which he became a Curator in his later years, effaced in the slightest his zeal for the libraries and librarians known to his earlier days. Like others, he realized the desirability of drawing people with common interests together, but few have been gifted with a genius equal to his of bringing about such combinations, and almost wholly through his personal backing the Medical Library Association, which has done such important work for the profession, was founded at about this time. At the opening of the new building of the Boston Medical Library a few years later he made the following confession:

It is hard for me to speak of the value of libraries in terms which would not seem exaggerated. Books have been my delight these thirty years, and from them I have received incalculable benefits. To study the phenomena of disease without books is to sail an uncharted sea, while to study books without patients is not to go to sea at all. Only a maker of books can appreciate the labours of others at their true value. Those of us who have brought forth fat volumes should offer hecatombs at these shrines of Minerva Medica.

---

[1] 'Osler's Influences on the Library of the Medical and Chirurgical Faculty of the State of Maryland.' *Johns Hopkins Hospital Bulletin*, July 1919.

And he continued:

But when one considers the unending making of books, who does not sigh for the happy days of that thrice happy Sir William Browne whose pocket library sufficed for his life's needs; drawing from a Greek Testament his divinity, from the aphorisms of Hippocrates his medicine; and from an Elzevir Horace his good sense and vivacity? There should be in connection with every library a corps of instructors in the art of reading, who would, as a labour of love, teach the young idea how to read. . . . For the general practitioner a well-used library is one of the few correctives of the premature senility which is so apt to overtake him. Self-centred, self-taught, he leads a solitary life, and unless his everyday experience is controlled by careful reading or by the attrition of a medical society it soon ceases to be of the slightest value and becomes a mere accretion of isolated facts, without correlation. It is astonishing with how little reading a doctor can practise medicine, but it is not astonishing how badly he may do it. Not three months ago a physician living within an hour's ride of the Surgeon-General's Library brought his little girl, aged twelve, to me. The diagnosis of infantile myxoedema required only a half-glance. In placid contentment he had been practising twenty years in 'Sleepy Hollow' and not even when his own flesh and blood was touched did he rouse from an apathy deep as Rip Van Winkle's sleep. In reply to questions: No, he had never seen anything in the journals about the thyroid gland; he had seen no pictures of cretinism or myxoedema; in fact his mind was a blank on the whole subject. He had not been a reader, he said, but he was a practical man with very little time. I could not help thinking of John Bunyan's remarks on the elements of success in the practice of medicine. . . .[1]

But Osler's relations to the Maryland Medical and Chirurgical Faculty were by no means restricted to the upbuilding of its library. At the annual meeting on April 30th of this year, in the old Hall at the corner of St. Paul and Saratoga Streets, he gave an address on 'The Healing of Tuberculosis', which may be regarded as the date of his personal enlistment in the crusade against this disease—a crusade which demanded, above all else, the awakening of public opinion from its existing indifference and ignorance.

Though Osler's writings had been on a great diversity of subjects, his bibliography shows a predominance of articles

[1] 'Books and Men', 1901. Reprinted as No. XII in 'Aequanimitas and other Addresses'.

on typhoid fever, on pneumonia, and on tuberculosis. For like Virchow, whom he so much admired, he became the champion of improved public-health measures, national and local; and though unlike Virchow he never held public office, his time, his pen, and his great personal influence had almost as much to do with the modern sanitary improvements which Baltimore has come to enjoy, as Virchow's influence had to do with those instituted during the '80's in Berlin. But his vigorous early participation in what has become a world-wide campaign against tuberculosis must stand in the forefront of the many public services he rendered—services which in large measure have been lost sight of in the maze of his other activities. In spite of Laennec's writings early in the century on the curability of phthisis, it was still a prevalent idea even among the profession that pulmonary consumption was a hopeless malady. Osler had seen enough of tuberculosis on the autopsy tables at the Montreal General as well as at Blockley, where 52 of his 191 post mortems were made on the fatal cases of tuberculosis, to appreciate, perhaps better than any of his contemporaries,[1] the ravages of which the disease was capable.

In spite of this experience, which must have been discouraging enough to breed pessimism in the mind of a less buoyant individual, his duty as a physician was to inspire hope not only in his patients but among the profession and in the community at large. Only a year hence, Meredith Reese, one of his own house staff, was destined to die of consumption at Saranac. There, too late, alas, he had gone to join Trudeau, who for the past fifteen years had been making his own gallant struggle against the disease in the Adirondack forests. Nor was Reese, to Osler's despair, by any means the only one of the younger members of his staff whose career in years to come was cut short by tuberculosis. In his address, after calling attention to the fact that the discovery of the tubercle bacillus and its presence

[1] He had already published occasional papers on certain aspects of the subject, the more important of which, however, before the discovery of the tubercle bacillus, had dealt with a non-infectious form of pulmonary phthisis, the fibroid or so-called 'miner's' variety.

in the sputum had not only made an early diagnosis possible, but had also supplied a proof that many affected individuals recovered from the disease, and after quoting the maxim ascribed to Virchow, that every one shows, at last, some trace of tuberculosis,[1] he went on to say:

My attention was called to the point in 1870 by Palmer Howard of Montreal, who was in the habit of pointing out the great frequency of puckering at the apices of the lungs in elderly persons. Subsequently, when I became Pathologist to the Montreal General Hospital, we often discussed the significance of these changes, whether indicative or not of healed phthisis. . . . I have carefully reviewed the records of 1000 post-mortems, dictated in all instances by myself, with reference to this question. In 216 cases death was caused by pulmonary tuberculosis. Excluding the simple fibroid puckering, the local thickening of the pleura, and the solitary caseous or calcareous mass, there were among the remaining 784 cases, 59, or 5·05 %, in which persons dying of other diseases presented undoubted tuberculous lesions in the lungs. . . . These facts demonstrate, first, the widespread prevalence of tuberculosis; and secondly, the fact as shown by my figures, that at least one-fourth of all infected persons recover spontaneously. In the great majority of these cases the disease is very limited and has made no progress, and in many instances could not have given physical signs. But even in more advanced disease, where the local indications are marked and bacilli and elastic tissue present in the sputum, arrest is by no means infrequent, and although post-mortem evidence shows that we are wrong in speaking of the process as *cured*, yet the condition is consistent with comparatively good health. . . . Once infection has occurred, the chief indication is to place the person in surroundings favourable to the maintenance of the maximum degree of nutrition. The influence of environment has never been better illustrated than by Trudeau's experiment. Inoculated rabbits, confined in a damp dark place rapidly succumbed, whilst others allowed to roam at large either recovered or had slight lesions. It is the same in human

[1] With an unerring eye for historical priorities, Osler pointed out in his essay on Richard Morton read before the Johns Hopkins Historical Club, January 1900 (published 1904), that Morton had a strong belief in the great prevalence of tuberculosis of the lungs, for in his 'Phthisiologia', the first systematic treatise on consumption, published in 1689, Morton says: 'Yea, when I consider with my self how often in one Year there is cause enough ministered for producing these Swellings, even to those that are wont to observe the strictest Rules of Living, I cannot sufficiently admire that any one, at least after he comes to the Flower of his Youth, can dye without a touch of a Consumption.' This antedates by 200 years Cohnheim's and Virchow's dictum.

tuberculosis: a patient confined to the house, living in close, overheated rooms, or in a stuffy, ill-ventilated dwelling of the poor, or treated in a hospital ward, is in a position analogous to the rabbit confined in the cellar; whereas a patient living in fresh air and sunshine for the greater part of the day has a chance comparable to that of the rabbit running wild. The very essence of the climatic treatment of tuberculosis is *improved nutrition* by change of environment. Fresh air and sunshine are the essentials with which, in comparison, altitude is of secondary importance. . . .[1]

Meanwhile he was hard at work on his Text-book, and must have borrowed his old pathological records from the Montreal General, for, as is known, he made repeated reference to them in his writing. Evidently they were inquiring for these records in Montreal, and on April 6th he wrote as follows to Richard MacDonnell, who had a sister in the training-school, and who, poor fellow, died an untimely death from tuberculosis only three months later:

Dear Mac,—To tell you the truth, it would not be very convenient to part with these volumes just at present for the following reason. I have, like an idiot, agreed to write a text-book on medicine, and am about half-way through it. I am drawing a good deal on them for certain statistical material; thus the other day, in writing up mediastinal growths I went over the whole list, looking for my cases of pulmonary and other thoracic tumours, and also when I come to the liver and other organs I shall do the same thing. I am very sorry as I should like to oblige you in this matter, and as I told you, I shall ultimately put the five volumes in the medical library. There are several things I wish to consult you about in the matter of the book. . . . Excuse this miserable typewritten letter. I know you don't like any such novelties; and forgive me also for disappointing you, pro tem. in the matter of hospital reports. I thought you were coming down this spring. We should be so glad to see you and Mrs. MacDonnell, to whom give my kind regards. Your sister keeps well and seems very happy. . . .

He drew a good deal on the Montreal volumes 'for statistical material', but he also drew even more frequently from another source for many allusions, and poor 'Dick'

[1] 'The Healing of Tuberculosis.' *Climatologist*, Phila., 1892, ii. 149–53. 'Osler was perhaps the first to work out the home-treatment of tuberculosis', writes Professor Welch. One of his patients, still living, with whom he kept up a correspondence till his last days, contracted the disease at this time and was encouraged to live an outdoor life in a specially-constructed sleeping-porch.

Parturit Osler Nascitur Liber.

WRITING THE TEXT-BOOK

MacDonnell may have been in his mind, hoping that 'the seed had fallen upon stony ground', when he utilized the Parable of the Sower in this paragraph :

> In all tubercles two processes go on : the one—caseation—destructive and dangerous ; and the other—sclerosis—conservative and healing. The ultimate result in a given case depends upon the capabilities of the body to restrict and limit the growth of the bacilli. There are tissue-soils in which the bacilli are, in all probability, killed at once—*the seed has fallen by the wayside.* There are others in which a lodgement is gained and more or less damage done, but finally the day is with the conservative, protecting forces—*the seed has fallen upon stony ground.* Thirdly, there are tissue-soils in which the bacilli grow luxuriantly, caseation and softening, not limitation and sclerosis, prevail, and the day is with the invaders—*the seed has fallen upon good ground.*

As stated, he moved into the hospital on May 1st, and, except for a brief interim in August, worked consecutively on his task until the middle of October, when the manuscript was finished. The four senior Residents—in medicine, surgery, gynaecology, and pathology—at the Johns Hopkins have from the earliest days enjoyed the luxury of a separate study and bedroom, sparsely furnished though they then were ; and Hunter Robb, Kelly's Resident, happened to be in possession not only of the largest but the quietest suite, situated at the end of the corridor. It was there that Osler camped out for the next six months. As Dr. Robb recalls :

> He asked me if I would loan him the use of my library for an hour or so in the mornings. I of course said, 'Yes, with great pleasure'. The first morning, he appeared with one book under his arm accompanied by his stenographer, Miss Humpton. When the morning's work was over, he left the book on my library desk, wide open with a marker in it. The next morning he brought two books with him, and so on for the next two weeks, so that the table and all the chairs and the sofa and the piano and even the floor was covered with open books. As a consequence I never was able to use the room for fully six months. Oftentimes right in the middle of his dictating, he would stop and rush into my other room, and ask me to match quarters with him, or we would engage in an exchange of yarns. It was a great treat for me, and except when he would court inspiration by kicking my waste-paper basket about the room, I thoroughly enjoyed his visits.

Dr. Robb does not mention how he was cured of the paper-basket habit, by treating it in his usual fashion one day after it had been weighted with concealed bricks ; but the fact merely serves to show the degree of informality that existed between chiefs and residents in those days. There was also much give and take between the chiefs themselves, as the following tale from Dr. Welch indicates :

I have told the story so often that I really believe it. The circumstances were these : It must have been in 1891 or '92, and Osler who was then living on Monument Street had sent to the printer most of the manuscript of the 'Practice', and galley proof was beginning to come in. He was closing his house, his books were packed up or covered or not readily accessible and he was about to leave for the summer, when he came to my room one evening about nine o'clock (I was living on Cathedral Street) and asked if he could look up the subject of ergotism, which he had discovered suddenly that he had forgotten in the 'Practice'. (You recall how he has something to say about everything in the 'Practice'.) I told him not to bother, that I had been looking up ergotism and could give him the latest information. Taking a number of the *Deutsche Med. Wochenschrift* I pretended to read him a wonderful description of the disease with startling statistics of its prevalence in south-eastern Europe and its relation to obscure nervous affections. He took a pad and jotted down the notes which I gave him. I recall that I gave him the figures for Roumania. He became greatly interested, said that he had no doubt that they were overlooking ergotism every day as a cause of obscure nervous diseases and that he would put Harry Thomas to work on it in the dispensary.

Off he went with the material for a beautiful article on ergotism, which would have immortalized the 'Practice'. I did not really expect him to swallow it, but he did ; and thinking it over I became uneasy, and early the next morning I confessed the hoax to him, and took him around a real article on ergotism. He never quite liked reference to the joke. It was not a very good joke and I am rather ashamed of it, but the facts really are as I have stated. Like most practical jokers Osler was easy to fool, or else he was so confiding that he did not think me capable of trying to fool him.

Though the hospital had only been two years in operation, other schools were beginning to look to it as a source of supply for young teachers : Abbott had already received a call to Philadelphia as Director of the new Institute of Hygiene, and Brockway had gone to Columbia. Calls, however, did not come to juniors alone, for their chiefs also were in a sense on the market; and in the midst of his writing Osler must have been disturbed by the receipt of these two letters and the inevitable parleys which go with such matters:

To W. O. from Furman Sheppard. Philadelphia, May 11, 1891.

My dear Sir,—A joint Committee, consisting of Ex-Mayor Fitler, Professor Hobart A. Hare, and the undersigned, has been appointed by the unanimous action of the Board of Trustees, and of the Faculty, of the Jefferson Medical College of this city, to communicate with you with reference to the vacant Chair of Practice of Medicine and Clinical Medicine in that institution. We would be much pleased to have the favour of a personal interview with you, and will gladly come to Baltimore for that purpose. If, however, you are likely to be in Philadelphia within a few days, and will kindly advise us to that effect, we can meet you here if it will be equally convenient and agreeable to you. We will cheerfully consult your wishes in this respect. Very Resp^ly^ Y^r^ Ob^t^ S^vt^.

To W. O. from H. P. Bowditch. Harvard Medical School, Boston, May 15, 1891.

My dear Osler,—Dr. [Francis] Minot has resigned the Chair of Theory and Practice and we are looking around for a successor. I suppose there is no more use in trying to induce you to consider the subject than there was when the Chair of Clinical Medicine was vacant a few years ago, but still I venture to inquire whether there are any circumstances under which you would like to come to Boston and share our work. I think we shall soon adopt a four years' graded course and your assistance in organizing the instruction would be very valuable. There would probably be no difficulty in getting you a service at one of the hospitals, and it is the feeling of the Faculty that the teaching of theory and practice should in the future be much more clinical than it has been in the past. Drop me a line if possible before next Wednesday as there is a committee meeting, then, to consider the question. Yours very sincerely.

But there was another, for him, still more important consideration, beside which university calls and text-book writing seemed of little moment. The decision regarding the calls to Philadelphia and Boston he settled himself; but this other, a matrimonial one, was settled for him. The object of his attentions, aware that he was engaged in writing a book, which he threatened to let 'go hang', advised the shoemaker, in effect, to stick to his last.

On June 4th graduated the first class from the Nurses' Training School, seventeen in all, including a future Superintendent of the school, who was to be Miss Hampton's successor after her marriage with Dr. Robb. Osler gave the graduating address,[1] in which he paid a tribute to the part his hearers were to play in the great drama of human suffering, with its inevitable stage accessories of doctor and nurse :

> In one of the lost books of Solomon, a touching picture is given of Eve, then an early grandmother, bending over the little Enoch, and showing Mahala how to soothe his sufferings and allay his pains. Woman, ' the link among the days ', and so trained in a bitter school, has, in successive generations, played the part of Mahala to the little Enoch; of Elaine to the wounded Lancelot. It seems a far cry from the plain of Mesopotamia and the lists of Camelot to the Johns Hopkins Hospital, but the spirit which makes this scene possible is the same, tempered through the ages by the benign influence of Christianity. . . . Here we learn to scan gently our brother man, and—chief test of charity in your sex—still more gently our sister woman ; judging not, asking no questions, but meting out to all alike a hospitality worthy of the *Hôtel-Dieu*, and deeming ourselves honoured in being allowed to act as its dispensers. Here, too, are daily before our eyes the problems which have ever perplexed the human mind ; problems not presented in the dead abstract of books, but in the living concrete of some poor fellow in his last round, fighting a brave fight, but sadly weighted, and going to his account ' unhousel'd, disappointed, unaneled, no reckoning made '. As we whisper to each other over his bed that the battle is decided and Euthanasia alone remains, have I not heard in reply to that muttered proverb, so often on the lips of the physician, ' the fathers have eaten sour grapes ', your answer, in clear accents,—the comforting words of the prayer of Stephen? . . . Useful your lives shall be, as you will care for those who cannot care for themselves, and who need about them, in the day of tribulation, gentle hands and tender hearts. And happy lives shall be yours, because busy and useful; having been initiated into two of the three mysteries of the Great Secret—that happiness lies in the absorption in some vocation which satisfies the soul; that we are here to add what we can *to*, not to get what we can *from*, Life; and the third,—is still a mystery, which you may or may not learn hereafter.

According to his terms with Appleton he had finished

[1] ' Doctor and Nurse.' No. II in ' Aequanimitas and other Addresses '.

on time the first sections of his book, as is evident from this line scribbled to J. H. Musser :

Maryland Club, Saturday.

Dear John Musser, Sorry to have left yours of ? unanswered but everything goes now-a-days. I am on the last lap with that blooming old book & hope to finish by Aug. 1st. Have sent July 1st first batch to printers—all the fevers and am now finishing the nervous system. How are you? Do come down for a Sunday. You could give me some good advice & help in one or two matters & suggestions why not next Sunday we have a score of interesting cases on the wards.

Word came from Shepherd on July 31st telling of Richard MacDonnell's death—' the seed had fallen on good ground '. It was a sad business and Osler felt the loss deeply, setting himself as usual to the prompt payment of an obituary tribute to his friend of Montreal days. He had promised to attend a meeting there, shortly, of the Canadian Medical Association, but this had been given up ; and though away from time to time, the Text-book held him for the most part at home, whence issued a succession of letters expressing impatience over the vexatious delays in getting his proof. Thus on another Saturday from the Maryland Club, this undated card to Musser :

Dear Old Man, Shall be so glad to see you—looked for you last Sunday. I am still buried in these infernal proofs. They have been cruelly slow—only up to about 700 pages but they keep me very busy. Poor Wilson would have been bitterly disappointed had he not got the [Jefferson] berth—tho it would have been lovely for you. I hope to be in Phila one day this week—if so I will telegraph you & we might have luncheon together Yours ever, W. O.

The triennial Congress of Physicians and Surgeons had its second meeting in Washington, September 22–25, under the presidency of Weir Mitchell, who at this time gave his much-quoted address on ' The History of Instrumental Precision in Medicine '. There were two important combined meetings of the several societies comprising the congress : one of them on the conditions underlying the infection of wounds, at which Welch was referee and Roswell Park co-referee ; the other was on the subject of interstitial scleroses, with Alfred L. Loomis as chief spokesman and Osler co-referee. Though his chief affiliation was with the Association of Physicians,[1] he was a member of several other special societies as well, and at this time read not only a paper on 'Double Athetosis' before the Neurological Association, but presented two others [2] before the American Pediatric Society, of which he was elected President for the ensuing year, to succeed T. M. Rotch of Boston. Probably no one ever attended one of these large meetings who enjoyed himself more than did Osler, for the responsibility of reading papers weighed lightly upon him. His effervescent spirits and good-fellowship were apt to make him the life of the social gatherings and dinners, and the liberties he took with people were so innocent and apt to be so amusing as never to give offence. One of the traditional tales of the Neurological Association, which dates back to the annual dinner of the society at this time, concerns the ceremonies which accompanied the crowning of W. W. Keen, a lifelong teetotaler, as the infant Bacchus while libations were being poured at his feet.

It is doubtful if any physician ever had a wider acquaintance among the profession at large, and he had the rare gift of recalling people's names and remembering his association with them, no matter how brief the previous encounter may have been. His memory for names has been described as positively uncanny and may possibly be ascribed in a measure to his early training at Weston, when as head prefect it was necessary, on the unexpected order from the head-master, to call the roll of the school from memory to see if any boy was truant. One of his old McGill students, who insists that he was an inconspicuous member of a class in which there was another student of the same name, relates that never having seen Osler in the interval, he met him unexpectedly one day in the corridor of the Johns Hopkins, and said: 'Of course you don't remember me.'

[1] Pepper was President of the Association of Physicians for this year, and paid in his address a glowing tribute to the life and character of Joseph Leidy, whose death occurred April 30th, and with it the meetings of the Biological Club ended.

[2] 'The Diagnosis of Bronchopneumonia from Tuberculosis', and 'The Association of Congenital Wry-neck with Marked Facial Asymmetry'.

'Remember you?' said Osler, taking his arm. 'You're *Arthur J.* MacD——, McGill, 1882. Come with me, I've something to show you and then we'll go to lunch.'

On October 13th there was a local celebration in honour of Virchow's seventieth birthday, to coincide with the great festival being held in Berlin; and fragments from Osler's address,[1] reminiscent of his personal association with 'the father of modern pathology' have already been given. Few tributes have ever been paid a member of the medical profession to equal those paid Virchow at this time, when, to use Osler's words: 'as the shadows lengthen, and ere the twilight deepens, it has seemed right to his many pupils and friends the world over, to show their love by a gathering in his honour.' Prophetic words they now seem to be, for Osler was the next, nigh thirty years later, to whom as a septuagenarian perhaps even more beloved than Virchow, an equally world-wide tribute was paid. One great in the Science of Medicine, the other in the Art; but it was for something else they were loved, and the world may wait long for the counterpart of either. The address concluded with the paragraph:

Surely the contemplation of a life so noble in its aims, so notable in its achievements, so varied in its pursuits, may well fill us with admiration for the man and with pride that he is a member of our profession. The influence of his work has been deep and far-reaching, and in one way or another has been felt by each one of us. It is well to acknowledge the debt which we every-day practitioners owe to the great leaders and workers in the scientific branches of our art. We dwell too much in corners, and, consumed with the petty cares of a bread-and-butter struggle, forget that outside our routine lie Elysian Fields into which we may never have wandered, the tillage of which is not done by our hands, but the fruits of which we of the profession (and you of the public) fully and freely enjoy. The lesson which should sink deepest into our hearts is the answer which a life, such as Virchow's, gives to those who to-day as in past generations see only pills and potions in the profession of medicine, and who utilizing the gains of science fail to appreciate the dignity and the worth of the methods by which they are attained. As Pausanias pestered Empedocles, even to the end, for the details of the cure of Pantheia, so there are with us still those who, 'asking not wisdom,

[1] 'Rudolph Virchow: the Man and the Student.' *Boston Medical and Surgical Journal*, Oct. 22, 1891.

but drugs to charm with', are impatient at the slow progress of science, forgetting that the chaos from which order is now appearing has been in great part dispelled by the work of one still living—by the man whom tonight we delight to honour.

During October, November, and December he was much occupied with proof-reading of what he lightly refers to as his 'quiz compend' in this note to Ogden of November 2nd:

You can just tell Appleton's drummer to hand back that subscription, as, for *you*, there is another way to get the volume, and I shall forward you one of the earliest copies with the greatest pleasure. Why don't you send on that paper of yours of Alkaptonuria to the *Medical News*. I have a short note on it. I hope to go abroad myself next spring, and it would be delightful if we could go together. I have to attend the meeting of the Pediatric Society in May, but I hope to have the meeting early, so as to get off about the middle of the month. Should you have to go earlier, we might arrange in any case to join somewhere, and to take a month's tramp would be perfectly delightful. . . . Mercier has a streak of genius. All his books are good. I have no time for anything but this infernal 'quiz compend', the proofs of which I hope to finish by the first of December.

1892

Osler dedicated his magnum opus, the text of which was completed by the end of December, as follows:

To the
Memory of my Teachers:

WILLIAM ARTHUR JOHNSON,
Priest of the Parish of Weston, Ontario.

JAMES BOVELL,
of the Toronto School of Medicine, and of the
University of Trinity College, Toronto.

ROBERT PALMER HOWARD,
Dean of the Medical Faculty and Professor of Medicine,
McGill University, Montreal.

His prefatory note bears the date of January 1st, but the load was not entirely lifted. This is made evident by the following note sent the next evening to Lafleur, who in

September had resigned from his post as Resident Physician and returned to Montreal to enter practice :

Dear L. So sorry the Path scheme has fallen thro. 'Twould have been a great card for the College. Just back from Toronto—very busy 4 days. Index nearly ready—all proofs in—should be out in a few weeks. Reese better—now at spital, very thin—has looked badly, but will improve now I hope. How soon could you leave for abroad? I am warned as to date of the Pediatric Soc.—meeting is some time in May—At the end I fear, which would be too late for me. I should like to get off earlier. We miss you very much. I often wish you were back again with us. I am glad a few patients are dropping in—they will come in time, too many perhaps. Love to Ross & the brethren. Yours as ever, W. O.

A visit to the North-Italian towns was evidently in prospect with Ogden and Lafleur as companions, and they went as far as to book their passages, but it was a plan not to be fulfilled, for good and sufficient reasons. The Text-book at last was finished and ready for distribution, when from the hospital on March 3rd he wrote to Musser :

Dear Johannes, I shall join you late on Saturday eve. I am going over to dine with the Bakers and shall come in about 11. I hope you have had a copy of my compend by this time. I asked the Appletons to send to the teachers first. I am sorry they cut out the Index of Authors which I had prepared with great care. I see about eight references to J. H. M. I have not neglected my Philadelphia friends—of 1049 references to authors 264 are American. I had the 1100-odd references in Fagge[1] overhauled & found 36 American, so that I have a more even division. Yours ever, W. O.

As no copy of the first printing used to stand on the shelves in Osler's library it is presumable that his may have gone to the lady who had told him to 'stick to his last'.[2] She was visiting friends in Baltimore at the time, and he appeared, it is said, with a big red book under his arm, which was tossed in her lap with the words : 'There, take

[1] The third edition of Fagge and Pye-Smith's 'Principles and Practice of Medicine', 2 vols., London, 1892, had just been published.

[2] Grace Linzee Revere, *b.* June 19, 1854, the daughter of John Revere and Susan Tilden (Torrey) Revere, both of Boston; *m.* Dr. S. W. Gross of Phila., Dec. 1876.

the darn thing; now what are you going to do with the man?' The distribution of a few other presentation copies of less moment was doubtless attended to by the publishers, and one of them of course went to Mr. Gilman, who admitted in his letter of acknowledgement that the volume had kept him up late. 'I find the record of all that I have ever felt and of all that I expect to encounter as I walk through life with your *vade mecum* in my overcoat', he wrote; adding, 'When I see the evidences of science and art which are enlisted in the service of the hospital I can hardly be patient with the delays in starting the School of Medicine.' Not until the second printing, which was necessitated within two months by the unprecedented sale of the book, did he have abundant copies to distribute among his friends, as well as an interleaved one to retain himself, on the fly-leaf of which he wrote:

> Received first copy Feb. 24th, 1892. This one—April 16th, 1892. This is the 2nd printing, with some of the errors corrected. The 1st printing of 3,000 copies was distributed by March 17th, on which date I had notice from Appleton & Co. to send corrections for 2nd printing. *Private Copy*. May all the curses of the good Bishop Ernulphus light on the borrower-and-not-returner or upon the stealer of this book.

And in the copy he left in Hunter Robb's room was written:

> N. B. This book was conceived in robbery and brought forth in fraud. In the spring of 1891 I coolly entered in & took possession of the working room of Dr. Hunter Robb—popularly known as the *Robin*. As in the old story of the Cookoo & the hedge sparrow I just turned him out of his comfortable nest, besplattered his floor with pamphlets papers & trash & played the devil generally with his comfort. In spite of the vilest treatment on my part he rarely failed to have oranges in his cupboard, chocolates &c (yum! yum!) on his table & gingerale & 'Old Tom' on the sideboard. In moments of contrition I feel how sadly he has suffered—and as this is one of those rare occasions I have taken advantage of it & make here my public confessions to him. Signed on behalf of the Author
>
> 4/21/92. E. Y. D.

However conceived and brought forth, the book received both in America as well as England the greatest possible approbation even on the part of those who could not fully subscribe to the author's therapeutic views. But even they were for the most part lenient:

> . . . Osler is a therapeutic conservative, a therapeutic sceptic, though by no means a nihilist. 'Many specifics have been vaunted in scarlet fever, but they are all useless.' 'Pneumonia is a self-limited disease, and runs its course uninfluenced in any way by medicine. It can neither be aborted or cut short by any known means at our command.' These are hard words for the neophyte but not for the experienced. Drugs, drugs, is the cry of the average doctor, and of the average patient too. But drugs are not all, and in many cases it is well for us to remember their uselessness as compared with other means. Weir Mitchell, in his little book on Doctor and Patient, admirably puts the fact that, all along the history of medicine, the really great physicians were peculiarly free from the bondage of drugs. . . .

The volume, indeed, was what might be called a practical pathology in which were given the results of modern investigation, microscopical, bacteriological, and chemical. On this foundation was built up the symptomatology and diagnosis of disease, and where a specific form of treatment was known to avail it was given its due prominence. Otherwise there were few recommendations beyond giving a chance to Nature aided by proper nursing and hygiene.

The birth of a successful text-book, like that of a child, may hold its authors in unexpected bondage; and the corrections which the second printing called for, together with the promised chapters for Pepper's projected volumes, forced him into seclusion for another six weeks. This, or possibly a better reason, had led him to write to Ogden on February 29th:

> I have been delaying writing to you until the last possible moment, hoping against hope that I might be able to finish the articles for Pepper's new text-book. I simply cannot before March 12th & shall have to give it up. I have not got more than half through. Yours of 26th just come—your friend could take my bunk. I am very much disappointed as I had set my heart on a 2 mos. trip to Italy, & it would have been so nice to go with you. You will stop in here of course on the way.

He managed to wade through this task on time, though it was a matter necessitating four pages a day; and much excellent writing, particularly his chapters on the diseases of the blood in the second volume, has come to be entombed in Pepper's covers.[1] He had nearly finished by April 15th, when he scribbled to Musser:

> Dear old man, Had I not a letter from you about 10 days ago? It is lost & unanswered. I am finishing my task & reading proofs—pleasant job. Shall be here for 2 weeks yet. Could you not spend a night—come by the 3.50 dine here with me & Welch & come out for a cool eve at St. Johns. Yours W. O.

He had been at home to impart to his family the news which, apparently as an afterthought he adds as a postscript to a letter of April 25th to Lafleur, and of which his mother a few days later writes to her 'dear Chattie', saying: 'He let Father and me into his secret when he was up, but we were not at liberty to make known the fact—these young things always think their love affairs are secrets to the outside world, whereas lookers-on often see plainly enough.' Though the members of his family, Lafleur, and the Gilmans were let into the secret of these 'young things' in their thirties and forties, it remained unannounced 'to the outside world' until the day of the wedding. Meanwhile, on May 2nd his presidential address on the subject of 'Specialism' was given before the fourth annual meeting of the Pediatric Society held in Boston. The diseases of children as a specialty was a new one, and he referred to the paediatrist as the vestigial remnant of what was formerly the general practitioner. 'That which has been is that which shall be', and he reminded his hearers that medicine seemingly began with specialization and that 'the tail of our emblematic snake has returned into its mouth, for at no age has specialism been so rife as at present'. It was a timely address, on an important topic, and he had the courage to say that 'no more dangerous members of our profession exist than those born into it, so to speak, as specialists'. After an acknowledgement of the un-

[1] Though called a text-book, and recommended to students, Pepper's two volumes ('An American Text-book of the Theory and Practice of Medicine.' Phila., 1893), were really an abbreviated form of encyclopaedia with many contributors, and, as a text-book, completely eclipsed by Osler's.

WILLIAM OSLER

Taken at Toronto, July 1896

GRACE REVERE OSLER

Taken at Oxford, August 1894

questioned advantage of the division of labour in the profession, he went on to say:

> Specialism is not, however, without many advantages. A radical error at the outset is the failure to recognize that the results of specialized observation are at best only partial truths, which require to be correlated with facts obtained by wider study. The various organs, the diseases of which are subdivided for treatment, are not isolated, but complex parts of a complex whole, and every day's experience brings home the truth of the saying, 'when one member suffers, all the members suffer with it'. Plato must have discussed this very question with his bright friends in the profession,—Eryximachus, perhaps,—or he never could have put the following words in the mouth of Socrates: 'I dare say that you may have heard eminent physicians say to a patient who comes to them with bad eyes that they cannot cure the eyes by themselves, but that if his eyes are to be cured, his head must be treated; and then again they say that to think of curing the head alone and not the rest of the body also, is the height of folly. And arguing in this way they apply their methods to the whole body, and try to treat and heal the whole and the part together. Did you ever observe that this is what they say?' A sentence which embodies the law and the gospel for specialists.[1]

Three days later, Thursday, May 5th, the Johns Hopkins Hospital Residents held the second of their annual dinners, at which Osler responded to one of the toasts. These gatherings in the early days were apt to be such festive affairs that it was necessary, lest some of the pranks likely to be perpetrated suffer interruption, to include the Superintendent among the guests. Certainly on this occasion none of the company had any suspicion of what was uppermost in the mind of the gayest of the party. The following Saturday morning, which promised a lovely day in May, Osler took an early train to Philadelphia. There was nothing unusual in this, nor in the fact that in the course of the morning he called at 1112 Walnut Street. Here, 'unbeknownst' even to the faithful coloured servants, Morris and Margaret, some trunks had been packed and sent by an express-man to the station at an early hour in the morning. Shortly before lunch, James Wilson dropped in, and finding Mrs. Gross and his former colleague sitting

[1] *Boston Medical and Surgical Journal*, May 12, 1892.

under a tree in the garden, remarked: 'Hullo, Osler, what are you doing over here? Won't you have lunch with me?' 'No', said Osler, 'I'll come in to tea. I'm lunching here. Why don't you stay?' This he did; and Wilson recalls that 'we talked lightly of Grand Manan which they knew; of St. Andrews and the salmon rivers, and moose hunting; of northern New Brunswick of which I had knowledge; and of the charming Canadian doctors, Osler's friends, whom we had met'. This dragged on between the two men, until presently Mrs. Gross asked to be excused, with the statement that she was going out and a hansom was waiting at the door; whereupon Wilson made his manners, pleading an appointment, leaving Osler, who said that Mrs. Gross would give him a lift as she was going in his direction. It was not until then that the devoted Margaret was told by her mistress that she was to be married at 2.30, and, darkey fashion, the faithful girl, overcome by the informal ways of 'white folks', exclaimed: 'My Gawd, Mam, only a hansom! Lemme go and fetch a hack.' Leaving their bags at the station they drove to St. James's Church, where the ceremony was performed, and having walked back to take their train, Osler sent this telegram to Wilson: 'It was awfully kind of you to come to the wedding breakfast.'

All this may not be exactly correct, but it is nearly enough so to show something of Osler's informality and imperturbability on even such a momentous occasion as this. To be sure, they had known each other for a good many years and both had good reason to feel secure—she in spite of the fact that some one had warned her, perhaps Osler himself, that she was going to marry a man who had books all over the floor. He may have had this in mind in speaking a few months later to some medical students on the virtue of method, when he said: 'In one respect, too, the unsystematic physician is absolutely criminal. By the great law of contraries there is sure to be assigned to him to wife some gentle creature to whom order is the supreme law, whose life is rendered miserable by the vagaries of a man, the dining-room table in whose house is never "cleared", and who would an he could "breakfast at five-o'clock tea and dine on the following day".'[1]

They went to New York, and then to Toronto, where on the 16th he was victimized by a public reception given by his professional friends. They presented him with the bronze inkstand that in later years always stood on his desk, and which Osler acknowledged with a few appropriate remarks to the effect that he owed his success in life largely to James Bovell of Toronto, who by his kindly interest and advice had given him the first impetus in his work and had filled him with ambition to do something in his calling. There followed a visit to Montreal, where Mrs. Osler had to be introduced particularly to some Howard children who thought they were going to be very jealous of any one with whom they would have to share their beloved 'Doccie O's' affection, but they were most agreeably disappointed. Then a similar visit in Boston to introduce him to her Revere relatives; and by the 23rd they were back in Philadelphia, whence he wrote Thayer to expect him 'for bkfast at the Hospital on Wednesday'; and he telegraphed Hewetson to bring over some material which he needed in preparing for a paper to be read the next day in Washington before the Association of Physicians.[2] On the 'Wednesday', in Baltimore, he wrote to Lafleur, saying: 'I—we—sail on the Ems on the 28th to Southampton. We shall be in London until the 1st week of July then go to Cornwall & come north to Nottingham for the 28 for the B. M. A. meeting. Let me know your plans—you might get away for a week or so with us for a little trip at any rate after the meeting. You will like Mrs Osler very much. She is an old friend of mine. I feel very safe.'

To W. S. Thayer from W. O. Radley's Hotel, Southampton,
June 6th, 1892.

Dear Thayer, We arrived here last evening after a delightful trip—sunshine all the way & no rough weather until Thursday.

---

1 'Teacher and Student.' 1892. Reprinted in 'Aequanimitas and other Addresses'.

2 On 'The Cold Water Treatment of Typhoid Fever', a topic subsequently (Nov. 9th) used for a clinical lecture before the graduate students in Baltimore (*Medical News*, Phila., Dec. 3, 1892, lxi. 626). In the discussion

I escaped all discomfort and 'hove' but once. We are off to Salisbury for the day and shall spend tomorrow at Netley Hospital. I hope you are not being worried too much by the cranks. Tell Hoch I shall send the introductory note to Hirt next week. I quite forgot about it. Ask H. to keep up those Typhoid blanks as the cases come in it would save time. Love to all.

Taking rooms in Clarges Street they quietly enjoyed London during the first few weeks undiscovered, but soon found it impossible to escape from being dined and wined by their many and cordial English friends.

To H. V. Ogden from W. O. Savile Club, 107, Piccadilly, W., July 1st [1892].

Dear H. V. O. So glad to have your address this a.m. from Batchelor. Mrs. O. (! ! !) has often said to me, where is Dr. Ogden, I should like to meet him to apologize for the theft of his friend. Our programme is as follows—tomorrow to Exeter and Dartmoor, Cornwall until the 25th, eve of that date at the George Hotel Nottingham for the B. M. A. Do come to it if you can. Sunday 31st at Lincoln—why not go with us there? First week in August London (Psychological Congress) then to Gowers for a few days by the sea & sail on N. G. L. from Southampton on the 17th. Let me know your programme.

So July was passed in Devon and Cornwall, with a visit to his Aunt Lizzie Osler in Falmouth; and they subsequently posted along the picturesque Cornish coast to Penzance and Land's End, where he must have indulged his antiquarian interests and partaken of the squab pasties of his ancestors. But even a honeymoon could not keep him away from medical meetings, and together they attended the British Medical Association gathering at Nottingham, an occasion which gave Mrs. Osler such a distaste for these functions that her advice to wives in general was to keep away from them lest they pass their time darning their husband's socks in an hotel bedroom while he gallivants with his male companions. One cannot spend the entire day seeing the Wedgewood in Nottingham Castle.

There were many old friends at the meeting—Roddick

he mentioned that Nathan Smith had used cold bathing in fevers as early as 1798, shortly after its introduction by Currie.

and Alloway from Montreal, Broadbent, Lauder Brunton, Jonathan Hutchinson, A. E. Wright, Sandwith from Cairo, Godlee, D'Arcy Power, and Allbutt, who had just been appointed Regius Professor of Physic at Cambridge. Victor Horsley was President of the pathological section, and possibly the most important communication of the meeting was made by him and his pupil Murray on 'The Pathology and Treatment of Myxoedema', in which an account was given of the first four cases cured with the juice of thyroid glands—a direct outcome of their experimental researches on animals, researches of which Osler had seen the beginnings in 1885 at the Brown Institution.

They took advantage of the place of meeting to visit Chatsworth and Haddon Hall, and the Dukeries of Sherwood Forest near at hand, and later paid a visit to Lincoln, which he had not seen before. As he commonly made reference in his addresses to impressions which were recent and fresh, so, in the first address delivered soon after his return, in speaking of 'the calm life necessary to continuous work for a high purpose', he said:

Sitting in Lincoln Cathedral and gazing at one of the loveliest of human works, as the Angel Choir has been described, there arose within me, obliterating for the moment the thousand heraldries and twilight saints and dim emblazonings, a strong sense of reverence for the minds which had executed such things of beauty. What manner of men were they who could, in those (to us) dark days, build such transcendent monuments? What was the secret of their art? By what spirit were they moved? Absorbed in thought, I did not hear the beginning of the music, and then, as a response to my reverie and arousing me from it, rang out the clear voice of the boy leading the antiphon, 'That thy power, thy glory and mightiness of thy kingdom might be known unto men.' Here was the answer. Moving in a world not realized, these men sought, however feebly, to express in glorious structures their conception of the beauty of holiness, and these works, our wonder, are but the outward and visible signs of the ideals which animated them. Practically to us in very different days life offers the same problems, but the conditions have changed, and, as happened before in the world's history, great material prosperity has weakened the influence of ideals, and blurred the eternal difference between means and end. Still, the ideal State, the ideal Life, the ideal Church—what they are and how best to realize them—such dreams continue to haunt the minds of men, and who can doubt that their contemplation immensely fosters the upward progress of our race?

Before their departure for England they had looked in vain for a suitable residence, and on the return voyage [1] it was learned by mere chance that the Curzon-Hoffmann house on the corner of Charles and Franklin Streets in Baltimore was on the market. Consequently, no sooner had they reached Philadelphia than Osler dashed over to Baltimore, put his head in the front door of No. 1 West Franklin Street, and without further investigation made an immediate offer, which was accepted. He promptly returned, saying he had bought a house merely because it reminded him of 1112 Walnut Street, Philadelphia. With such unhesitating, snap-shot decisions he often transacted business; but this choice proved a fortunate one, and during the succeeding fourteen years No. 1 West Franklin Street remained their home, famous for its hospitality.

They had returned in time to join many Johns Hopkins friends and the large Osler family connexion for the wedding in Toronto, on August 30th, of his niece and former housekeeper, Georgina Osler, to Dr. A. E. Abbott; but apart from this visit they were fully occupied—Mrs. Osler with the preparations incidental to the transfer of her household to the new home, and her husband with his hospital duties—'minding shop while Hurd is away', as he expressed it in a note to Lafleur. As their new house could not be got ready for occupancy till the middle of October, they meanwhile took rooms in the old Mount Vernon Hotel. One would hardly regard these distractions as favourable for composition, yet he had sufficient 'equanimity' to write one of his most effective addresses,

[1] If they had had any intention of so doing it was not a favourable summer for a visit to the Continent, for it was the year of another cholera epidemic. Somewhat casual in recalling dates, Osler's note in the introduction to Mr. Phipps's reprint of 'The Life of Pasteur', in which he says: 'Except at the London Congress [1881] the only occasion on which I saw the great master [Pasteur] was in 1891 or 1892, when he demonstrated at the Institute to a group of us the technique of the procedure [inoculation against hydrophobia] and then superintended the inoculations of the day', refers doubtless to the visit to Paris in 1890 with Ramsay Wright (see p. 332).

No. 1 WEST FRANKLIN STREET, BALTIMORE

'Teacher and Student',[1] which was delivered October 4th in Minneapolis on the occasion of the opening of the new medical buildings of the University of Minnesota.

The occasion offered, as he said at the outset, a chance 'to still a deep autumnal yearning not unnatural in a man the best years of whose life have been passed with undergraduate students, and who has had temporarily to content himself with the dry husks of graduate teaching'. He spoke freely of the new ideas in medical education beginning to supplant an old order which, however admirable in certain respects, in the absence of the sense of responsibility only to be preserved when the teachers of a school have university opportunities, permitted 'a criminal laxity in medical education unknown before in our annals'. And he went on to emphasize what is so often overlooked, even in these later days, namely, that—

> . . . it is a secondary matter, after all, whether a school is under State or University control, whether the endowments are great or small, the equipments palatial or humble; the fate of an institution rests not on these; the inherent, vital element, which transcends all material interests, which may give to a school glory and renown in their absence, and lacking which, all the 'pride, pomp and circumstance' are vain—this vitalizing element, I say, lies in the men who work in its halls, and in the ideals which they cherish and teach.

And turning to the Faculty, he ventured to speak in no uncertain terms of the professor who has outgrown his usefulness, alone unconscious of the fact; and in a way prophetic of his 'Fixed Period' address thirteen years later, he said:

> From one who, like themselves, has passed *la crise de quarante ans*, the seniors present will pardon a few plain remarks upon the disadvantages to a school of having too many men of mature, not to say riper, years. Insensibly, in the fifth and sixth decades, there begins to creep over most of us a change, noted physically among other ways, in the silvering of the hair and that lessening of elasticity, which impels a man to open rather than to vault a five-barred gate. It comes to all sooner or later; to some only too painfully evident,

[1] Reprinted in 'Aequanimitas and other Addresses'. He appears to have been reading Newman and also Jowett's Plato during his honeymoon, and quotations from 'The Idea of a University' and from the 'Republic' IV are used as texts.

to others unconsciously, with no pace perceived. And with most of us this physical change has its mental equivalent, not necessarily accompanied by loss of the powers of application or of judgement; on the contrary, often the mind grows clearer and the memory more retentive, but the change is seen in a weakened receptivity and in an inability to adapt oneself to an altered intellectual environment. . . . The only safeguard in the teacher against this lamentable condition is to live in and with the third decade, in company with the younger, more receptive and progressive minds.

The following day he addressed the Minnesota Academy of Medicine, on a topic [1] he had once before used to drive home certain truths regarding the prevalent laxity in the matter of registration in the United States—'the only country in the world which commits the mistake of thinking that the doctorate should carry with it the licence to practise'. He must have spoken extemporaneously, and held up as a model plan that which had been adopted in Canada—the election of a medical parliament to control medical affairs, to hold examinations, and to set medical standards, rather than to have each individual school enjoy the privilege not only of conferring its degrees but of licensing its graduates as well. This he had fought out in the McGill Faculty, which had, indeed, not been unanimous in its opinion, for Osler and his friend 'Dick' MacDonnell had heartily disagreed.

There had been many changes on the staff in Baltimore, and he had planned to see Ogden in Milwaukee to discuss the possibility of his joining forces with the Hopkins group. Having failed in this purpose, he wrote shortly after his return, offering him 'a berth as Chief of the Medical Dispensary', adding that 'the town is a God-forsaken place but full of very nice people'.

To H. A. Lafleur from W. O. 1 West Franklin Street,
Nov. 11th, 1892.

Dear Laffie, I was very glad to have your letter to-day. Howard, MacDonnell & Ross—all gone since I left. Poor Ross! My thoughts have been much with him. Had we been in any way settled I should have gone up this night last week but we are still camping in two

[1] 'The Licence to Practise.' *Northwestern Lancet*, St. Paul, Nov. 1, 1892, xii. 383.

rooms & I did not care to leave madam (who has by the way a young Professor under contract) in all the wrack and ruin of painters plasterers & paper hangers. Had Ross not had some leaven of the modern spirit I should not have been appointed in '74 and when the ice was once broken between us he was a warm friend and grew year by year in my affections. . . . I am hard at work on two monographs—tasks for the next six months. Tuberculosis of the serous membranes & chorea. I often wish you were back again—the material grows more interesting every year. Hoch goes about Xmas. Billings & Ramsay are new men—both good fellows. I hope you will be able to come for a couple of weeks in the spring. There will be a room here for you & we might go off to Old Point for a few days or to Phila. Is your friend Martin still in Montreal? I want to send him a copy of my Aequanimitas address. You will have read or skimmed by this time my 'Teacher & Student' platitudes. . . . Yours ever, W. O.[1]

As is evident from this letter, Osler had already plunged into work, with two prospective monographs in mind. But no matter how much occupied, he had thoughts for other people and ample time to dash off frivolous notes and to do kind acts. Thus to one of his small nieces:

Dearest Trixie girl, I was very glad to get your letter this week. Please dear lamb, do not get *icelated* yourself, or catch anything horrid. I have been missing you both to-day & said several times to Aunt Grace—I mean Mrs. —— you know!—I want my little girls, but you are very far away & only my thoughts can go to 40 Division St. Too sorry about the pussy. I am writing a letter of condolence to Gwen. Please you black eyed darling measure yourself from the neck to the hem of your skirt & give me your size for a nice new very superior John Wanamaker-ish winter dress—Hurry too as I may go to Phila at the end of the week. I have a cold in my head—but no pain in my pansy. Kiss yourself in the looking-glass for me and give my love to Auntie & the Jim boy. Ask Mr Jim what he wants for Xmas You just find out quietly & tell me . . .

---

[1] The Billings he speaks of as a new member of the staff was the son of John S. Billings; and Ramsay, a recent Toronto graduate, was subsequently transferred from medicine to a place on Kelly's staff. Among Welch's group, George H. F. Nuttall had succeeded Abbott in July of the preceding year; W. S. Thayer had taken Lafleur's place as Resident Physician in September; John Hewetson, F. R. Smith, and L. F. Barker had been made Assistant Resident Physicians; Hunter Robb had been moved to the dispensary; J. Whitridge Williams had been appointed an assistant in gynaecology; and W. W. Russell, T. S. Cullen, Eugene Van Ness, J. C. Bloodgood and others had come into the house.

On November 28th he read a paper before the Philadelphia Neurological Society on the subject of the hereditary form of chorea (Huntington's), examples of which he had observed in two Maryland families. But of greater present interest than this was an address, seemingly the outcome of his non-professional summer's reading, given two weeks later before the Johns Hopkins Historical Club. This club, during the session of 1891–2 with H. M. Hurd presiding, had mapped out for itself a programme which began with a description by Welch of the Æsculapian temples and worship; and there followed a systematic study of the Hippocratic writings in which many of the staff participated. It was intended to devote the 1892–3 sessions to Galen, but Galen almost proved the undoing of the society—he was too colossal—so that after nibbling at him the club again took refuge in such miscellaneous topics as the mood of its members suggested. The Greek Thinkers had long been a source of inspiration to Osler, who shared Sir Henry Maine's belief that 'nothing moves in the world that is not Greek in origin'. When and by whom he was first introduced to Plato is not clear, unless by James Bovell, those evenings when he browsed in Bovell's library; but however this may be, he had come to mention Plato almost as often as Sir Thomas Browne in his more recent addresses, and had used as a motto for his Text-book, Plato's definition of the Art of Medicine. Accordingly, though Plato only twice directly refers to Hippocrates, it was natural that he should choose, as a sequel to the sessions of the club which had been devoted to Hippocrates, the writings of his great contemporary in so far as they cast sidelights on the conditions of medicine in the fourth century B. C. He restricted himself to the 'Dialogues', the third edition of Jowett's translation of which, purchased in London, had in all probability been devoured on the steamer.

The paper entitled 'Physic and Physicians as Depicted in Plato', read at the meeting of December 14th, consists largely of quotations from Jowett, and he gives at length the dialogue between Theaetetus and Socrates, in which Socrates likens his art to that of a midwife in that he looks after the souls of men when they are in labour. There is in fact less of Osler than Jowett in the essay, perhaps the most interesting paragraphs from the standpoint of the former being the introductory one in which he gives reasons for the selection of his topic. He said:

. . . in the Golden Age of Greece, medicine had as to-day a triple relationship, with science, with gymnastics, and with theology. We can imagine an Athenian father of the early fourth century worried about the enfeebled health of one of his growing lads, asking the advice of Hippocrates about a suspicious cough, or sending him to the palaestra of Taureas for a systematic course in gymnastics; or, as Socrates advised, 'when human skill was exhausted', asking the assistance of the divine Apollo, through his son, the 'hero-physician', Æsculapius, at his temple in Epidaurus or at Athens itself. Could the Greek live over his parental troubles at the end of the nineteenth century, he would get a more exact diagnosis and a more rational treatment; but he might travel far to find so eminent a 'professor' of gymnastics as Miccus for his boy, and in Christian Science or faith healing he would find our bastard substitute for the stately and gracious worship of the Æsculapian temple.

From the Hippocratic writings alone we have a very imperfect knowledge of the state of medicine in the most brilliant period of Grecian history; and many details relating to the character and to the life of physicians are gleaned only from secular authors. So much of the daily life of a civilized community relates to problems of health and disease that the great writers of every age of necessity throw an important sidelight not only on the opinions of the people on these questions, but often on the condition of special knowledge in various branches. Thus a considerable literature already illustrates the medical knowledge of Shakespeare, from whose doctors, apothecaries, and mad-folk much may be gathered as to the state of the profession in the latter part of the sixteenth century. So also the satire of Molière, malicious though it be, has preserved for us phases of medical life in the seventeenth century for which we scan in vain the strictly medical writings of that period; and writers of our times, like George Eliot, have told for future generations in a character such as Lydgate, the little everyday details of the struggles and aspirations of the profession of the nineteenth century, of which we find no account whatever in the files of the Lancet.

But there were other pens busy besides Osler's, and it must not be forgotten that his juniors were all successively spurred to engage in more or less ambitious writings of one sort or another. Thayer had begun his monograph on malaria, while F. R. Smith and August Hoch had been translating

Ludwig Hirt's 'Handbuch der Nervenkrankheiten'. This appeared early in the next year with the introduction by Osler referred to in his letter of June 6th—the sort of introduction he often wrote in later years to boost the sale of some volume in whose authorship he was interested. The courses for graduates meanwhile were still kept going with the participation of all the members of the staff, and, in addition, Billings continued to come over from Washington to give lectures on the History of Medicine. But as Osler had confessed in his recent Minnesota address, the dry husks of graduate teaching were beginning to pall on the Johns Hopkins group. There was even danger lest some of them be lured away by calls from other institutions if there was to be much further delay in the opening of the medical school. Even Welch had been strongly tempted by a call from Harvard to take the Chair of Pathology, and it is possible that this may have expedited Mr. Gilman and the University Trustees in a campaign to secure funds sufficient for a building in which an undergraduate school might be started. The name of the university still represented an individual to the generation who had known Johns Hopkins the Quaker merchant, and many years must needs elapse before an institution would come first to mind when the name was mentioned. In spite of this, it was a Baltimore lady who came to the rescue with a generous sum sufficient to erect the building, which finally became Mall's anatomical laboratory, and to justify the organization of a school—the proper link to hold together the hospital and university.

Meanwhile, Welch was not the only one of the Chiefs who was being angled for. The death of George Ross had left vacant once more the chair Palmer Howard had occupied before him, and a concerted effort, which apparently had taken its origin among the McGill men in Ottawa, was being made in Canada to secure Osler for the post at whatever cost. He must have been strongly urged to return by friends and relatives alike, and too much may have been said, for in reply to a letter from his cousin Jennette he gives this modest opinion of his own attainments:

I do wish you would not build upon me for doing anything beyond my fellows; my abilities are but moderate, & I feel bitterly sometimes that deficiencies in early education & a lack of thoroughness may be with me at every step. In addition to this I have to earn my bread, so that general medical studies absorb the time that might be spent in building up a scientific reputation. One thing is certain: the cultivation of science at the expense of paying work is an injustice to one's family.

This call to Montreal, which had been thoroughly ventilated in the lay press, apparently culminated on December 13th when the McGill Faculty were permitted to announce the action of a generous benefactor. This is explained by the following press item:

Montreal, Dec. 13, 1892.—There is important news this evening in university circles, and the members of the Medical Faculty are particularly anxious that the report which has passed from mouth to mouth to-day shall be abundantly fulfilled. For some months past, ardent desire has been expressed by those interested in McGill that every effort should be made by the university authorities to induce Dr. Osler, who has become as famous in the United States since his connection with the Johns Hopkins University as he was in Toronto and Montreal, to return to Montreal. There was, however, a serious difficulty in the road, as all felt that the presence at McGill of a man possessing the abilities of this distinguished medical professor would require a heavier drain upon the finances of the institution than its present position could possibly allow. McGill's friends, however, have never deserted her in the past and it seems that once more a rich and generous benefactor has come forward with an offer to pay down a lump sum of $1,000,000 and guarantee an additional $8,000 annually if the famous Canadian doctor, already mentioned, will once more place his services at the disposition of McGill and his native land. It can be readily imagined, therefore, the interest such a matter has created in the city amongst all classes of our people.

There was certainly need of expedition on the part of those soliciting subscriptions for the $500,000 fund deemed necessary to justify opening the school in Baltimore, only a small portion of which had been raised. On December 22nd Miss Mary E. Garrett addressed a letter[1] to the university officials offering to make up the remainder of the sum with these provisoes: that women be admitted to the school on the same basis as men; that the building be

[1] *Johns Hopkins Hospital Bulletin*, Dec. 1892, iii. 139.

designated the Women's Memorial Fund Building; and that a lay committee of six women be appointed to supervise the extra-curricular affairs of the women students. On December 24th the University Trustees met and accepted the terms of this timely offer; and during the course of a happy dinner-party of house officers invited to celebrate the first Christmas in 1 West Franklin Street a copy of Miss Garrett's note and of the action of the Trustees, left at the door by Mr. Gilman himself, was brought in and read with jubilation.[1]

[1] Accounts of the early days of the Johns Hopkins Hospital to the time of the opening of the school have been recorded by many hands: cf. 'The Launching of a University', by D. C. Gilman, 1906; Fielding H. Garrison's account in his 'Life of John S. Billings'; Abraham Flexner's testimony before the Royal Commission on University Education, London, 1911; 'Some Memories of the Development of the Medical School and of Osler's Advent', by H. M. Thomas, *Johns Hopkins Hospital Bulletin*, July 1919.

CHAPTER XV

1893–4

THE OPENING OF THE MEDICAL SCHOOL

THE promise of an early realization of starting the medical school, so long delayed owing to the diminished income of the university, must have banished any possible thought of accepting the proposals from McGill. In the following letter the matter is frankly dismissed:

To H. A. Lafleur from W. O. 1 West Franklin Street, Baltimore, Jan. 12, 1893.

Dear L.,—Very glad indeed to have your last note. I have, of course, heard all sorts of rumours about Montreal, but I am too comfortable here to think of any change, and I hope to fill out my twenty years and then crawl back to Montreal to worry the boys for a few years. I dare say you would reserve me a chair at your fireside, and we could have many smokes and chats. We are a good deal excited of course about the organization of the school. Miss Garrett has given the $300,000 necessary to complete the half million endowment. We have the Chairs of Anatomy and Pharmacology to fill, and shall need someone in physiological chemistry. We hope to be able to secure Mall in anatomy. The restrictions placed by Miss Garrett as to the preliminary education necessary will limit the number of our students very materially. The matriculation examination of the university is in itself very stiff, and either the preliminary medical course in Arts, or its equivalent, must be passed before admission to the medical school. . . . I am busy with the subjects of tuberculosis of the serous membranes [1] and finishing some work on chorea.[2] The wards are very interesting, the usual number of cases of arteriosclerosis, a good many interesting cases of malaria, and an unusual number of typhoids. I am sorry I did not get reprints of my lecture on the bath treatment. I dare say you saw it in the *Medical News*. Our results for the first century of cases were really very good. You must arrange in the spring to pay us a long visit. Let me know, too, when you think I should write to the members of the Victoria Hospital Board. You should certainly

---

[1] 'Tuberculous Pericarditis.' *American Journal of the Medical Sciences*, Jan. 1893. Cf. also Shattuck Lecture on 'Tuberculous Pleurisy'. (See below, p. 384).

[2] 'Remarks on the Varieties of Chronic Chorea, &c.' *Journal of Nervous and Mental Diseases*, N. Y., Feb. 1893.

make a strong push to go in there on the staff. Councilman was here for two weeks and Ghriskey for a week, so that the boys are rather demoralized. I enclose a little slip which you will please hand to one of the House Surgeons at the M. G. H. I want very much to find the address of the Farr family of progressive muscular atrophy, which I reported many years ago. . . .

PS. Do you think Shepherd would come here in anatomy? There would of course be no hospital appointment. He combines surgical and scientific anatomy as well. Mall has a comfortable berth in Chicago and I doubt if he can come.

Evidently his work as usual was in full swing, and recourse must be had to his mother's letters to learn that anything out of the ordinary was on his mind. On January 24th she wrote to Mrs. Gwyn: 'I had a scrap from Willie this morning—no wonder he has been laid up with a cold, such a freezing time for one who loves warmth as he does; he puts on a good show of spirits but in his heart of hearts I know he must have an anxious time as to the coming event.' And on February 17th: 'You will have written to Baltimore I know and will have shared with us all in the first glow of gladness and then in the deep wave of sorrow.'

To H. A. Lafleur from W. O. Feb. 18, 1893.

Thanks for Peter Ibbetson, which I shall certainly read on your recommendation. I had intended to write to you last evening, to tell you about my domestic troubles . . . the small boy died at the end of a week, very much to our sorrow. Everything goes very smoothly at the hospital. We hope to open our medical school in October. There has been a slight hitch about the terms of admission but they have all been settled. We shall go to Toronto at Easter, and very probably go round to Boston by way of Montreal. Please do not forget that you have promised to spend a week here some time in the spring. Your room will be ready at any time.

They paid a visit later on to their friends the Conynghams in Wilkesbarre, and one morning his wife found on her dressing-table a letter the tenderness and humour of which must have provoked that mixture of tears and laughter which is best for bereaved people. It was postmarked 'Heaven' and was written by Paul Revere Osler to his Dear Mother:

. . . If we are good & get on nicely with our singing & if our earthly parents continue to show an interest in us by remembering us in their prayers, we are allowed to write every three or four tatmas (i.e. month). I got here safely with very little inconvenience. I scarcely knew anything until I awoke in a lovely green spot, with fountains & trees & soft couches & such nice young girls to tend us. You would have been amused to see the hundreds which came the same day. But I must tell you first how we are all arranged; it took me several days to find out about it. Heaven is the exact counterpart of earth so far as its dwellers are concerned, thus all from the U. S. go to one place—all from Maryland to one district & even all from the cities & townships get corresponding places. This enables the guardian angels to keep the lists more carefully & it facilitates communication between relatives. They are most particular in this respect & have a beautifully simple arrangement by which the new arrivals can find out at once whether they have connections in Heaven. I never was more surprised in my time—we say that here, not life & not eternity for that has not started for us—when the day after my arrival Althea brought me two quill feathers on one of which was written Julius Caesar & the other Emma Osler. I knew at once about the former . . . but the latter I did not know at all, but she said she had been father's little sister & she had been sent to make me feel happy & comfortable. . . .

Unlike the real angels we have no fore-knowledge & cannot tell what is to happen to our dear ones on earth. Next to the great feast days, when we sing choruses by divisions in the upper heavens, our chief delight is in watching the soul bodies as they arrive in our divisions & in helping the angels to get them in order and properly trained. In the children's divisions not a friad (i. e. about an hour of earthly time) passes without the excitement of a father or mother, a brother or a sister united to one of us. We know about 1000 of each other so that it is great fun to see our comrades & friends making their relatives feel at home. . . .

Osler's deep interest in the welfare of all his associates and assistants, past and present, is an outstanding feature of his brief letters. There were literally hundreds of them which have been preserved by his pupils first and last—short notes, which show his concern for their work and prospects, after they had gone out from under his wing. Thus from Baltimore on April 19th he sent one of his frequent missives to Lafleur:

It might not do any harm to write to Donald Smith and to Davidson (both of whom I know well) and urge your claims. It would really be most satisfactory for you to get the position. Do come down if you can, even for a few days. It will be delightful to have you. You must of course come and stay with us. I was overjoyed to hear of the extra hundred thousand dollars. It puts the old school in a splendid position. By the time my twenty years here are up I shall enjoy very much going over all the fine departments which McGill will then have. . . .

He began at this time to plan for a comprehensive review of the hospital's experience with typhoid fever, and the series of eight papers, which form the first fasciculus of the 1895 volume of the *Hospital Reports*, were projected. These studies were based on the 229 cases of typhoid which had been treated in the medical wards in the four years since the opening of the hospital, that is, to May 15, 1893. Two of the eight papers were by Thayer and Hewetson, the other six being written by Osler. Typhoid has become such a rare disease through the improved sanitation of cities that it no longer occupies the important position in medicine it held thirty years ago when the disease was so prevalent that Osler had led off with it in his Text-book, on the ground that it was the most important point of departure for students.

Then regarded with civic indifference, the disease to-day is looked upon as a disgrace in any community, and in bringing about this altered attitude Osler played a part far more important than any contribution he may have made to the knowledge of the disease in the way of diagnosis or treatment, or of pointing out some obscure complication like ' typhoid spine '. One reservation to this statement may possibly be made in view of his constant reiteration that the diagnosis, so commonly made in the South, of ' typho-malarial fever '—as though this were a special disease—was unjustified by any known facts and merely served as a cloak in civic health reports to conceal actual typhoid. Largely through the influence of his writings, this hybrid disease disappeared. Ample opportunity had been given at the Hopkins to determine the point, for in contrast to the 229 cases of typhoid there had been 500 of malaria in the wards, all proven beyond doubt by the demonstration of the plasmodium in the blood. There had been only one patient in the four years in whom a definite typhoid was implanted on a co-existing malarial infection.

But, leaving this aside, his main contribution to the subject related to public sanitation, for until the Baltimore authorities began to wake up, and a skilled bacteriologist was added to the Health Board, he never ceased publicly to reiterate statements such as he gives in the opening paragraph of the last of these papers:[1]

Among the cities which still pay an unnecessary Delian tribute of young lives to the Minotaur of infectious diseases, Baltimore holds a high rank. The pity of it is, too, that this annual sacrifice of thousands of lives (2,281 for 1892, not including consumption), is not due to ignorance. For more than fifty years this gospel of preventive medicine has been preached—whether they would hear or whether they would forbear—in the ears of councils and corporations; that *three measures, efficiently designed and efficiently carried out, reduce to a minimum the incidence of infectious diseases: viz., pure water, good drainage, and a proper isolation of the sick.* Of sanitary essentials in a modern town, Baltimore has a well-arranged water supply; still, however, with unprotected sources and constant liability to contamination. It has nothing else—no sewage system, no system of isolation of the sick, no hospital for infectious diseases, no compulsory notification of such a disease as typhoid fever, no disinfecting station, no system of street-watering, no inspection of dairies, no inspection of meat. The streets are cleaned, but so carelessly that for a large part of the year the citizens breathe a mixture of horse-dung and filth of all sorts. Perhaps the best gauge of the sanitary conditions of a city is to be found in the mortality returns from typhoid fever.

Pneumonia, Typhoid, and Tuberculosis—these were the three scourges at which he aimed his shafts—the three diseases an intimate knowledge of which he hammered incessantly into his students. He lived to see one of them, typhoid, nearly abolished, tuberculosis got under control,—and pneumonia was to be his own undoing.[2]

[1] *Johns Hopkins Hospital Reports*, VIII, 'Typhoid Fever in Baltimore.' 1894–5, iv. 159.

[2] The influence which, first and last, Osler exercised as a national and civic sanitary propagandist has been too little emphasized. To-day in our comparative security against serious epidemics it is difficult to realize the annual death-roll of the '90's from diseases now under control. In this summer of 1893 the International Medical Congress which was to have been held in Rome, despite the prevalence of malaria there, was postponed because of a widespread cholera epidemic which had already taken a toll of 10,000 lives in Mecca, whence it had reached Rome, even Paris; and New York was in

Baltimore in the early '90's probably differed little in its external aspects from the post-bellum Baltimore of the late '60's. Environed north and west by the beautiful rolling countryside of Maryland, to whose wooded hillsides the well-to-do moved for the sweltering months of summer, and in whose fertile valleys they rode to hounds, the city itself, sharply demarcated from all of this, was a homely place of architecturally unpretentious block houses on parallel streets —north and south, east and west. The hospital was planted on a hill on the outskirts of the city to the east, and from the upper windows of the administration building the dwellers, back in their rooms at the end of the day's work, looked across a flat sea of roofs to two other low hills in the residential centre of the town. On one of them, silhouetted against the western sky, stood a tall column—the Washington monument; on the other, near by, the low dome of the Catholic cathedral—in Mr. Gilman's happy phrase, the three hills of Charity, Hope, and Faith.

Near the cathedral was No. 1 West Franklin Street, and the palace, so-called, of his Eminence John Cardinal Gibbons, good neighbour and fine citizen that he was, stood just back of the Oslers', a narrow, rat-infested Baltimore alley lying between. A good two miles separated the hospital from this part of the town, and at peculiar and somewhat uncertain hours a 'bobtailed horse-car' made its tortuous way through untidy, cobbled streets, and after crossing an odoriferous stream called Jones's Falls, convenient for the refuse of the decrepit factories, tanneries, and the like which lined its banks, the car would toil slowly up the hill, east or west, with an extra horse attached. In Baltimore of that day, one's bath flowed shamelessly and soapily into the gutters of the cobbled streets over which were stepping-stones such as are preserved to be wondered at in Pompeii. But there was one sanitary rite religiously observed on bended knee—the scrubbing of the front steps of each of the houses by a genus of polite but easy-going coloured gentlemen known as 'waiter-men'—a matutinal

quarantine. Nevertheless, typhus was raging even in New York, small-pox prevailed widely in England and America, and yellow fever continued its devastations—a third year of successive outbreaks.

rite of suds and marble, yet with an abundant opportunity for salutation and gossip. Meanwhile, the mistresses of the several households likewise passed the time of day, provendering in the old-fashioned, buzzing, open markets, which groaned with the produce of the Chesapeake Bay and the farms of its fertile Eastern Shore. Untidy, lethargic, hospitable, well-fed, contented, happy Baltimore. But this Baltimore, alas, for it was picturesque and beloved, is gone. A beautiful suburban Baltimore has arisen, the city's streets have been paved, the newest of sewer systems installed with the vanishing of Jones's Falls into a conduit; and in all this transformation, the influence of the Hopkins is strongly apparent, and Osler himself had no small part in it.

Faithful as he was at attending meetings, there had to be a limit; and so early in May he writes Ogden to explain why he must forgo the A.M.A. meeting to be held in Milwaukee, saying: 'I have the Pediatric Society at West Point on the 23rd, 24th and 25th, the Association of American Physicians at the end of the month in Washington, and the Massachusetts Medical Society at which I have the Shattuck Lecture on the 13th of June.' He was much beset. On May 17th he sends the following to Lafleur, in distress that he had failed to get the appointment at the Royal Victoria:

Dear L., Yesterday was a *dies irae*. Everything went wrong, so when your letter came I would not read it & said to Mrs. Osler 'I just know Lafleur has not got the R V.' The devil take those fellows! It is too bad & I am sorely disappointed. Why not throw up the whole thing & come down here as Associate in Medicine? We could give you from the school $500, I would supplement it for three years with $500, and you could control the dispensary & do some outside practice. I want Thayer to go abroad for Oct. Nov. & Dec. during which mos. you could live in the Hospital & take his duties. The dispensary work, pathological studies &c would keep you busy & your literary ventures would bring you in time a good berth. It was a mistake to have left without a definite call. Do come to the Pediatric Soc. I shall be there Wednesday eve. Leave with me Friday p m & come straight thro. to 1 West Franklin & we can discuss the situation. . . . PS. Aequanimitas is out of print—not a copy left. I send the other.

The meeting of the Pediatric Society to which he

refers was held at West Point under the presidency of his old dinner-club friend of Montreal days, A. D. Blackader. The group of children's specialists was growing and at this time the society had 45 members, most of them, to be sure, men of broad training in general medicine. Osler, one of the appointed participants in a discussion of whooping-cough, was on the programme for two other papers as well. One of them, an important study of a rare disease, acute diffuse scleroderma, though largely written by Osler was presented in the name of one of the assistant residents—Lewellys F. Barker,[1] and it was characteristic that he should have presented this paper in full, whereas that under his own name was read by title only, to appear subsequently in the Society's published Transactions.[2] A few days later the Association of Physicians, coming to be a group of closely knit friends, met as usual in Washington for its annual gathering, at which the chief topic assigned for discussion had been myxoedema.[3] Francis P. Kinnicutt of New York was the referee and gave an historical account

[1] The patient had been under the care of Dr. Ellis of Elkton, Maryland, and Osler had taken Barker, who had recently joined the house staff, down with him to help perform the autopsy. Barker was the first of a succession of Canadians, Toronto graduates, the picked men of their time, who after finishing a service at the Toronto General Hospital gravitated to Baltimore on the recommendation of Osler's friend, Jas. E. Graham, the Professor of Medicine in Toronto. Succeeding Barker during the '90's were Ramsay, Cullen, Parsons, Futcher, and the McCrae brothers. Their first summer before going into the Hopkins was usually spent at the Garrett Hospital for Children at Mt. Airy, Frederick County, Maryland.

[2] This was entitled 'Notes on Tuberculosis in Children' (*Archives of Pediatrics*, N.Y., Dec., 1893, x. 979) and was a side-issue in the preparation of the article on tuberculosis for Starr's 'Handbook of Children's Diseases'.

[3] Unquestionably, however, the most notable communication was that made by Theobald Smith on 'Texas Cattle Fever' in its relation to protozoon diseases. Though his results had previously been published by the Government Bureau of Animal Industry, this was the first time his epochal discovery —a pathogenic micro-organism which could be transmitted only through the agency of an intermediary host (in this case the cattle tick)—was brought before the profession. The paper was briefly discussed by Welch alone, and one wonders whether the great significance of the discovery, which was to be followed by a succession of others—the mosquito in malaria and in yellow fever, the tsetse fly in sleeping-sickness, the flea in plague, the louse in typhus—could then have been fully taken in by the majority of Theobald Smith's auditors.

of the advance in knowledge of the disease and its treatment since 1881, when Ord first gave it its name and showed the convincing group of cases at the International Congress which met that year in London. Subsequent to the report by Horsley and Murray of the summer before, it had been found by Hector MacKenzie that extracts of the gland taken by mouth were as effective as when its juices were injected, and Kinnicutt was able to report a case of his own thus treated with benefit. James J. Putnam followed with a paper on the treatment by sheep's thyroids, but there was still so great confusion between myxoedema, exophthalmic goitre, and acromegaly that in reviewing the situation to-day it hardly seems possible that the snarl of the thyroid diseases could ever have become so far untangled as it has been. Osler followed in turn with a paper on 'Sporadic Cretinism in America', and there are certain noteworthy things about his article. In the first place, when compared with the papers of his colleagues it indicates an extraordinarily clear grasp of the subject, historical as well as clinical, and he strips his facts of all confusing details. In the second place it shows the immense amount of labour which he put into the preparation of his papers, for in this instance he had not only made an exhaustive search for cases in the literature but had sent letters of inquiry broadcast to the superintendents of all the asylums for the insane, and institutions for feeble-minded children, both in the United States and in Canada, as well as to numberless physicians practising in localities where goitre was supposed to prevail. His picture of that 'pariah of Nature', the adult cretin, remains a classic.[1]

As he had written Lafleur early in the year, he was at work on tuberculosis of the serous membranes, for the tendency to regard many of the inflammations of these surfaces as tuberculous was beginning to prevail. Having already dealt with the pericardial infections, he devoted his Shattuck Lecture before the Massachusetts Medical

[1] At this same meeting he gave a report published in the *Canadian Practitioner* upon five cases of subphrenic abscess; and during the year a number of other papers appeared, the titles of which are to be found in his bibliography.

Society, in Boston on June 13th, to 'Tuberculous Pleurisy'.[1] This lectureship had been established through a bequest made by George Cheyne Shattuck, who had died only three months before in his eightieth year. This Shattuck was one of the group of Louis's later American pupils including Henry I. Bowditch, Stillé, Metcalfe, and Gerhard, who were students in Paris in the early part of the century, when French medicine was at its apogee—a group of men whose names were often on Osler's lips. He was the son of another Dr. George Cheyne Shattuck, and he of a Dr. Benjamin Shattuck, near contemporary and admirer of George Cheyne, the famous old London and Bath physician. During this Boston visit Osler stayed with his friend of Vienna days, Dr. F. C. Shattuck, the son of the founder of the lectureship, who himself had a son George Cheever about to enter medicine, and Osler never ceased to harp on the fact that neither of these two had borne the full name of George Cheyne. So in this bread-and-butter note:

To F. C. Shattuck from W. O. 1 West Franklin Street,
Thursday.

Dear Mr. Prof. Dr. F. C. S.—Such a shame you or G should not have been *G. C.* but I suppose it is now too late. Look up for me in a spare moment your father's paper on Typhoid read before the Paris Med. Obser. Soc. It may be among his old papers. Stillé has his in MS. Gerhard & Pennock's is in print. It would be nice to get the Coll of Phy to issue them together. I will talk to S W M [Mitchell] about it. Thanks for a very pleasant visit.

---

[1] His monograph on the subject, first published in the *Boston Medical and Surgical Journal*, contains an analysis of the seventeen cases which had been observed since the opening of the Johns Hopkins Hospital. The paper well illustrates his invariable custom of mentioning the names of all of those who in any way came in contact with the patients whose histories were included; and scattered through the report one finds the names of Flexner, Councilman, Finney, Halsted, Barker, F. R. Smith, Hewetson, Thayer, Rupert Norton, Welch, and other members of the staff, as well as those of the physicians who had referred the patients to the hospital. His feeling in this matter is well expressed in a note scribbled to one of the junior members of the staff who had submitted a paper to him for criticism. It reads as follows: 'A.A.1. report! I have added a brief note about the diagnosis. I would mention in the medical report the name of the House Physician in Ward E & the clin. clerk, & under the surgical report the name of the House Surgeon who had charge. We are not nearly particular enough in this respect & should follow the good old Scotch custom. Yrs W. O.'

In this dry recital of the occurrences incidental to these many meetings, the activities at the hospital with which Osler's brief letters are chiefly concerned must not be forgotten. 1 West Franklin Street meanwhile saw a succession of visitors, whose bare enumeration would read like an hotel register. But while he dispensed hospitality it was to the work of his colleagues that the attention of his guests was chiefly drawn, and to the pathological department first of all. Welch's laboratory, indeed, for a decade had been in active operation and had proved a nursery for many who subsequently made names for themselves. Among the early group of graduate students who had worked there was George M. Sternberg while stationed in Baltimore as examiner of recruits in the late '80's; and at about this time he had been succeeded by Walter Reed, who likewise was given permission by the Washington authorities to take some courses in the Hopkins clinic and laboratories, where were laid the foundations of the training in bacteriology which first set him to work on yellow fever. All of this led, ten years later in Cuba, in connexion with John Guitéras, Carroll, and Lazear, to Reed's epochal discovery of the part played by the mosquito in this once dreaded disease.[1]

To G. M. Sternberg from W. O. June 29, 1893.

Dear Dr. Sternberg, Though late, let me offer you my sincere congratulations on your promotion to the Surgeon-Generalship. I had hoped before this to be able to call and offer them in person. I see by this morning's paper that you have organized your Army Medical School, and I am delighted to see that you have appointed Dr. Reed to one of the Chairs.

Reed had a winning personality which made him so great a favourite with the early group at the Hopkins that any success he might attain in life would be the source of the

[1] It was not until twenty years after Reed's demonstration of the mode of transmission of yellow fever and when the disease had largely come under control through sanitary measures alone, that Noguchi of the Rockefeller Institute discovered the bacterial agent, an organism beyond the power of vision with the methods at their command in the days when Sanarelli, Sternberg, Reed, and others spent much time in a search for the organism.

greatest gratification to them,[1] and this appointment as Director of the Pathological Laboratory of the new Army Medical School was but the forerunner of many others subsequently bestowed upon men who got their training in Welch's laboratory.

The following note to Ogden, written towards the end of August, tells of his summer movements. It was the year of the Columbian Exposition in Chicago, which they had evidently been urged to attend.

'Nobska,' Woods Hole [undated]

Dear H. V. O. Yours of July 12th has been in my handbag too long unanswered. I was very sorry that we could not go to Chicago, particularly as our friends with whom we were to go were very charming & had a delightful home. I will let you know, should we decide & we would, of course, see you. We left Balt on the 14th of July, went to Toronto stayed 10 days & then I was called away to Wilkesbarre Mountains—case of typhoid in a family very near & dear to Mrs Osler. After 10 days there we returned to Toronto, spent a week & then on to Montreal. I took Gwen & Bea for a little trip and last Friday we came on here to the Fays', cousins of Mrs O. We then go to Mrs Chapin's at Falmouth (a sister in law) & I shall return about Sept 3rd. I cannot make up my mind about the Pan-American [Congress]—but I do not like to desert my friends who are in it. You have not been away for six months. Do come & spend a week or ten days in the autumn. There are three spare rooms in the house & I should like you so much to see & know Mrs Osler.

The Pan-American Medical Congress, held in Washington early in September on the invitation of the Government, was elaborately organized under twenty-two sections, and Osler as usual did not 'desert his friends', for William Pepper, it may be added, was President. The Transactions of this congress were subsequently issued by the Government Printing Office in two fat volumes, within whose covers much excellent work has doubtless been entombed. What is of interest, however, is that Section XXI was given over to a discussion of Medical Pedagogics—a novel topic for such a gathering. The question of proper standards of medical education and the essential preparation therefor

[1] Cf. H. A. Kelly's 'Walter Reed and Yellow Fever'. N.Y., McClure, Phillips & Co., 1906.

was, at the time, on every one's tongue, and much of the discussion revolved around the heretofore unheard-of requirements for admission announced by the Johns Hopkins School, to go into effect with their incoming first group of undergraduate students. Unquestionably the medical schools in the United States had been hampered by their low admission requirements, by the absence of close union with the branches of learning comprising the other faculties of a university, by the scant stress laid on the pre-medical sciences, and by the absence of endowment which made the remuneration of the teachers depend wholly on the fees of the students. Even William Pepper had become converted, for in his inaugural address to the students the following month at the University of Pennsylvania, where an obligatory four-year course had just been adopted, he actually referred to the enormity of teaching by lectures, and stated that 'the broad basis of modern medical education is the careful training of the individual student at the bedside and in the laboratory'. Thus Osler's five years in Philadelphia were evidently not in vain. Meanwhile the group of Hopkins people, who by their action had precipitated much of this, were not themselves entirely at ease—particularly in regard to the question of co-education :

Gilman, Osler and I [writes Dr. Welch] were not enthusiastic about the conditions imposed by Miss Garrett and Miss Thomas in the gift of the 'Women's Memorial Fund' which met the announced condition of the Trustees for opening the Medical School. My impression is that neither Osler nor I signed the petition to the Trustees for accepting these conditions, and we sympathized with the fruitless efforts of Mr. Gilman to induce Miss Garrett to make certain comparatively slight, verbal alterations in the terms of the gift, the main change which we desired being the substitution of 'equal' or 'equivalent' for 'same' in specifying the terms for admission and training of women and men students, but she would not budge. Still, we were so eager to start the school that we were glad that the Trustees accepted the gift. As it turned out, the embarrassments and difficulties which we feared in the novel venture of co-education in medicine never materialized. The terms for admission to the medical school were not the invention of Miss Garrett or Miss Thomas, but years before I had set them down in a document which Mr. Gilman and the Trustees asked me to prepare soon after I came to Baltimore. Miss Garrett got this document through her lawyer, Mr. Gwyn, who was an influential Trustee of the university. She naturally supposed that this was exactly what we wanted. It is one thing to build an educational castle in the air at your library table, and another to face its actual appearance under the existing circumstance. We were alarmed, and wondered if any students would come or could meet the conditions, for we knew that we could not. As Osler said: 'Welch, it is lucky that we get in as professors; we never could enter as students.'

Fortunately there were strong men with strong convictions at the helm of the newly launched school, and probably Welch, Osler, and Billings had most to do with the programme which at this time extended little beyond the mere statement of entrance requirements. For, without any definitely prearranged curriculum, the school in a seemingly haphazard and rather Southern fashion was allowed to grow and develop from year to year. The requirements for admission comprised, in addition to a degree of bachelor of arts or of science, a two years' pre-medical training in biology, chemistry, and physics, with a reading knowledge of French and German—requirements which few collegiate institutions other than the Hopkins itself were prepared to meet; and when it became known that the entering class consisted of only eighteen students, whereas the teachers distributed through the hospital and laboratories considerably outnumbered them, there was doubtless much lifting of eyebrows in medical circles elsewhere. But much water had run over the dam since the exercises attending Mr. Gilman's inauguration in 1876, when Huxley had stressed the importance to a medical course of preliminary biological and chemical studies, and the public was becoming adjusted to these ideas and to the necessity, at whatever sacrifice, of a union in spirit as well as in name between medical schools and universities. Welch had emphatically emphasized this in an address given at Yale [1] the year of Osler's appointment. And now John S. Billings, in an article [2] which had just appeared in print, admitted that this higher medical education

[1] 'Some Advantages of the Union of Medical School and University.' *Journal of the American Medical Association*, Mar. 30, 1889.

[2] 'Medicine as a Career.' *Forum*, N.Y., 1893, xiv. 725.

necessitated a long and expensive preparation. In presenting a hypothetical example, he said :

> My young friend whose attention I wish to direct to medicine as a career will have spent five years at a good intermediate school as a preliminary to entering the university, which he does when he is about seventeen years old. He spends three or four years at the university, four years at the medical school, one and one-half years in the hospital, and two years in travel and special studies. When, therefore, he is ready to begin work he will be about twenty-eight years old, and his education, living, books etc., will have cost about eight thousand dollars from the time he entered the university. It can be done for less, but this is a fair average estimate.

To these beginnings may be traced our present educational quandaries, for this programme has widely come into effect, the only difference being that Billings placed the age of entering college lower than the average, so that his hypothetical young friend would be at least thirty when ready to begin the practice of an arduous profession, the first years of which are apt to be years of patient drudgery. Billings and his colleagues, however, had something else in mind than the average medical aspirant, namely, the training of selected men as teachers and investigators. And though they did not come under Osler's immediate influence until two years later, probably no group of medical students ever began their education with more brilliant prospects or had more devoted attention paid to them than the small coterie who entered the Hopkins school in this autumn of 1893. They started in very simply, these first eighteen, three of whom were women ; and were it not too great a digression it would be interesting to learn whence they had come and what happened to them, one and all, during as well as after their four years' course, for several made notable contributions to medicine even before graduation ; and their subsequent careers show what may be done with a small group of students under such favourable circumstances. The unpretentious, factory-like building where their studies began under Mall the anatomist and Abel the pharmacologist,[1] must in

[1] Physiology was then taught in the university laboratory 'across town' by W. H. Howell, one of Newell Martin's pupils, who had been recalled

itself have been a surprise, though a greater shock came later when they found they were no longer to be simply fed with knowledge previously accumulated but, given the opportunity, must do most of the acquiring for themselves. This, however, is a side issue from Osler.

Until it was time for these students to finish their course, the house positions were filled by a picked group of young men, graduates of other schools. It was a happy and intimate family, and by the students the three heads of departments—Welch, Osler, and Halsted—were soon nicknamed 'Popsey', 'The Chief', and 'The Professor'. Outsiders came to complain that the Hopkins group was a 'Society for Mutual Admiration', and if this may be taken to mean that good feeling, friendliness, charitableness, and helpfulness prevailed—enviable qualities enough in schools where they were less in evidence—the epithet was not misplaced. Nor could other than happiness and good feeling have prevailed in a group of which 'The Chief' made one. There is no gainsaying that the university and hospital bearing the name of its none too greatly beloved founder, was looked upon somewhat askance during these early years by the more clannish Baltimoreans who naturally clung to their local medical worthies. The medical profession, perhaps more than others, guards its local prerogatives with jealousy. There were already five medical schools in the city, resulting, as has been said somewhat cynically, 'in the division of the profession into as many hostile camps, all the members of which extended any remaining hostility to the Hopkins institutions'. But largely through Osler's personal charm and likeableness this feeling was entirely overcome, factions were brought together, hostility vanished, all sharing alike in the reputation being built up for Baltimore as a great medical centre; and there is little wonder that his departure twelve years later was looked upon as a civic calamity which roused a wail of lamentation.

Though W. S. Thayer's absence abroad, for a period of study, added to Osler's responsibilities at this time, and though

from Harvard. Poor Martin's scientific career, so full of brilliant promise, ended about this time.

at work on the chapters promised for the second volume of Pepper's Text-book, he nevertheless found time to write for a meeting of the Historical Club a charming appreciation of Charcot, whose sudden death on August 16th had been so universally deplored.[1] Some of the things he said of Charcot were prophetic of the position Osler himself was rapidly coming to hold, for he too 'escaping the thralls of nationalism' was making an enduring impression as a cosmopolitan teacher and leader. During this school session also his six carefully prepared lectures on 'The Diagnosis of Abdominal Tumours', subsequently collected and published (1895) in book form,[2] were delivered before the post-graduate students. For their benefit it was evidently his intent to compare, so far as possible, the provisional clinical diagnoses of the cases with the subsequent findings either at autopsy or at operation; and although the lectures seem admirably composed, and were doubtless delivered with abundant clinical illustrations in Osler's inspiring manner, they are now out of date and of interest chiefly from an historical standpoint. Though many of the conditions with which he dealt had not as yet begun to be turned over to the surgeon, in concluding the last lecture of the series, given in December, he says: 'You will have noticed in how many cases the surgeon made it [the nature of the tumour] a certainty, not, unhappily, in diagnosis only, but also in prognosis. But desperate cases require desperate remedies, and in no single instance were the chances of a patient damaged by the exploratory incision.' One may read between the lines of this quotation something of his relation to surgeons and surgery. At this time appendicitis was still largely regarded as a medical disorder; the surgery of the gall-bladder had scarcely begun; whereas the stomach and the duodenum lay in surgical fields practically unexplored. The paragraphs of his Text-book which deal with therapeutics, critics had regarded as the weakest feature of the volume, and his courageously expressed views upon the futility of many of the drugs in common usage had been termed nihilistic.

[1] 'Jean-Martin Charcot.' *J. H. H. Bulletin*, Sept. 1893, iv. 87–8.
[2] Published also in the *New York Medical Journal*, 1894.

Perhaps because of this, perhaps because of his unusual powers of visualizing disease gained in the post-mortem room, he was far more tolerant than most of his contemporaries with the so-called surgical invasion of the traditional province of internal medicine which took place during the next twenty years. He knew surgeons well, and their particular point of view; and it has been said of him that few physicians have ever shown better surgical judgement or had a more instinctive and certain knowledge of the proper moment for surgical intervention.

1894

There are scraps of letters which permit one to follow his literary and professional activities during this year:

To H. V. Ogden from W. O. 1 West Franklin Street,
Jan. 23, 1894.

Dear Ogden,—I am due in Chicago on Wednesday, February 7th, to attend a committee about the Association of American Medical Colleges. If I gave you Thursday evening in Milwaukee I could get back, I suppose, in time on Friday to take the Limited, as I must be here on Saturday. I should be very glad to meet some of the boys at a quiet little dinner—not too many of them of course; just some of your special friends. When will you have your paper on alkaptonuria ready? Davis I know will be delighted to have it, and carefully studied cases are so rare that it would make a very satisfactory communication. . . .

A constant worker and writer himself, he rarely failed to spur on his friends and pupils into productivity; and he dogged Ogden about this subject of alkaptonuria in letter after letter until it was written up and published. As already stated, however delighted his pupils might be to get a postcard from 'The Chief', it was not an unalloyed pleasure, for the card usually contained a memorandum likely to keep the recipient busy for some time. His own pen, however, set an example, and his juniors needed little prodding to get out their reports.

To H. A. Lafleur from W. O. Feb. 10, 1894.

Dear Lafleur,—The highly-scented second volume of the American Textbook of Medicine [1] is here, and I will take the first opportunity

[1] The articles in this, Pepper's second volume, on which Osler had been working the year before, represented 64 very carefully worked-over

of sending it. You might let me know if you hear of a chance. Things go on much the same here. In a few days you will have our Typhoid Fever Report, in which you will recognize a number of old friends. Hewetson and Thayer are working hard at the malaria material. I send you three tuberculosis pamphlets.[1] In that toxaemia case there was a serious error of omission, as there was no tuberculosis of the cerebrospinal system. Yours &c.

That Osler was coming to be much called upon, not only for his head and heart, but for his willing pen, doubtless explains the character of his correspondence, for, abundant though it was in amount, it grew to be more and more laconic. Thus, a note of February 25th to William Pepper, whose resignation as Provost had been made public the day before in a remarkable letter to the Trustees of the University of Pennsylvania, merely says: 'Glad & sorry that you have resigned, but you have done your share. A thousand congratulations on the splendid work you have accomplished. Yours ever.' Another example of his brevity is given in the appendix of an address delivered by Weir Mitchell in this same year.[2] Dr. Mitchell had sent out a questionnaire to a number of physicians for an expression of opinion on the existing conditions in the asylums for the insane in America —their present faults, and changes to be recommended. Most of the replies covered one or two printed pages. Osler wrote as follows, probably on a postcard, giving in a nutshell all that the others had said at length:

The needs are: (1) Emancipation from politics. (2) Separation of executive and professional functions. (3) A staff of assistants trained in modern psychological and pathological methods. Yours, W. O.

He, however, could get a great deal more than this on a postcard—as could also E. Y. Davis—a favourite, ready-

printed pages. The first section, 'On Diseases of the Suprarenal Capsules and Ductless Glands', compared to its present-day extent represented a very small subject, including only the thymus, thyroid, and adrenals. The second and larger section, on 'Diseases of the Blood', was a subject then being intensively studied, and one which Osler's experience made him particularly fitted to generalize upon.

[1] The 'Typhoid Fever Report' consisted of a collection of eight papers, four of them his own—a matter of ninety printed pages. In the most interesting of the 'three tuberculosis pamphlets' he made a strong plea for the notification of pulmonary tuberculosis.

[2] Cf. *Journal of Nervous and Mental Diseases*, July 1894, xxi. 413.

at-hand medium of correspondence for both of them, as has been pointed out. The following, bearing the stamp of March 27th, was scribbled to H. P. Bowditch, doubtless when E. Y. D. had arisen from breakfast, which he was accustomed to share with a book at 7.30 a.m. Though Osler himself was almost a teetotaler, E. Y. D. perhaps held different views :

Dear Bowditch That Committee of, & on, drink & drinks & particularly that section of it with which you are concerned, viz. on the deaths from much drink, would do well to investigate the effects immediate and remote of the Berlin Congress spree. I am reminded of it this a m at breakfast (Ham & eggs again !) by my friend Mr. Plutarch who in his life of Alexander gives an account of a rattling old drunk in which 'Promachus drunk four measures of wine & carried off the crown but survived it only 3 days.' Forty three of the guests died ! Love to the family all Yours ever

EGERTON Y. DAVIS.

This postcard alludes to the Committee of Fifty which had been organized the year before for the purpose of accumulating some dependable facts, divorced from opinions, regarding the liquor problem. Four sub-committees had been appointed to consider : (1) the physiological ; (2) the legislative ; (3) the economic ; and (4) the ethical side of the question. Of the first of these sub-committees John S. Billings was chairman and H. P. Bowditch one of the members, while Osler, among many others who were not themselves actually members of the original committee, had been called upon frequently for their advice regarding the researches in progress. Osler knew well enough that it was a serious investigation : it was his 'M'Connachie' that made him appear trivial. What he really felt about the use and abuse of alcohol, which as a physician he almost never prescribed, is shown in a note to a friend in the South acknowledging a reprint of a paper which he had received dealing with the evil effects of drink. He wrote on his usual medium : 'That was a good address but you are a little hard on Bacchus who after all is a pretty good fellow—when sober. W. O.'

As stated, he was beginning to suffer the penalty of his position, his popularity, and literary ability, by being called upon for frequent public addresses, which in the midst of his more serious professional work he somehow found time to prepare. Though he at times fretted under these tasks, he found it hard to refuse an appeal. There were four of these addresses during the following twelve months—the first, at the request of Sternberg the Surgeon-General, being given on February 24th before the students of the Army Medical School, in whose laboratories, as has been told, Walter Reed was at work. This may have influenced him, though he was always ready to lend himself when his spoken word was likely to be of help; and the Medical Corps of the army, then as now, needed the moral support of the profession at large. He chose as his title, 'The Army Surgeon',[1] and spoke of the meaning and methods of work—'the value of experience is not in seeing much but in seeing wisely'—and he pointed out wherein existed the opportunities of research for members of the medical corps even though stationed in remote army posts, provided one followed the maxim of the Sage of Chelsea. He pointed out, also, that 'permanence of residence, good undoubtedly for the pocket, is not always best for wide mental vision in the physician', and quoted Sir Thomas Browne's words regarding the nimble and conceited heads that never look beyond their nests, and plume themselves on light attainments:

> Fortunate it is for you [he said] that the service in one place is never long enough to let the roots strike so deeply as to make the process of transplantation too painful. Myself a peripatetic, I know what it is to bear the scars of parting from comrades and friends, scars which sometimes ache as the memories recur of the days which have flown and of the old familiar faces which have gone.

And after much good and stimulating advice he closed with the story of Beaumont so often told to his students—the story of 'a man who amid circumstances the most unfavourable saw his opportunity and was quick to grasp the skirts of happy chance'. In all this he had in mind the army surgeon in times of peace, unconscious that the young men before him were destined twenty years later to be divisional surgeons serving in France, and he himself an honorary

[1] Reprinted as No. IV in 'Aequanimitas and other Addresses'.

Colonel and Consultant in a war undreamed of, in which bullets were to be more numerous than bacilli.

Early in the spring in a letter to Ogden, which mentions their summer plans of a trip abroad, he says: 'I have already made a number of corrections for a new edition of my text-book as my contract calls for a triennial revision. I shall be very glad indeed to have your list of corrections. When is that paper of yours to come out?' But his own work was in arrears, as he indicates in the following of May 17th to Lafleur:

We have postponed our sailing to July 12th, on the *Fürst Bismarck*. We had taken passage for next week, but I have three or four things unfinished that would have spoiled my holiday, so that I decided it would be better to postpone it, and then stay a little later in the autumn. With the exception of a week in June, which I shall spend in Boston, I shall be at home now until we sail, and I wish you would come down and spend a week here. You could run over to Washington every day. Why shouldn't you come to the meeting of the Congress. You will see a number of old friends, and it will be very pleasant.

Among the things unfinished was possibly the address entitled 'The Leaven of Science', delivered four days later, on May 21st, at the opening of the Wistar Institute of Anatomy, in Philadelphia.[1] This institution, since so well known, was founded by General Isaac J. Wistar, a member of the Biological Club, in memory of his grand-uncle Caspar Wistar, one of the most notable of the famous succession of anatomists at the University of Pennsylvania school—Physick, Shippen, Wistar, Dorsey, Horner, Gibson, and Leidy. After a proper eulogium of these men, Osler went on to a discussion of anatomy and its place in medical science, weaving his account around a story ascribed to Barclay the English anatomist, of the reapers, the gleaners, and finally of the geese who still continue to pick up a few scattered grains among the stubble. Then turning to Pepper, who was to lay down his duties a month later after having done so much for the material prosperity of the university, he continued:

Here at last, and largely owing to your indomitable energy, Mr. Provost, are gathered all the externals which make up a *Schola major*

[1] Reprinted as No. V in his collected addresses, 'Aequanimitas [&c.]'.

worthy of this great Commonwealth. What, after all, is education but a subtle, slowly-effected change, due to the action upon us of the Externals; of the written record of the great minds of all ages, of the beautiful and harmonious surroundings of nature and of art, and of the lives, good or ill, of our fellows—these alone educate us, these alone mould the developing minds. Within the bounds of this campus these influences will lead successive generations of youth from matriculation in the college to graduation in the special school, the complex varied influences of Art, of Science, and of Charity; of Art, the highest development of which can only come with that sustaining love for ideals which 'burn bright or dim as each are mirrors of the fire for which all thirst'; of Science, the cold logic of which keeps the mind independent and free from the toils of self-deception and half-knowledge; of Charity, in which we of the medical profession, to walk worthily, must live and move and have our being.

The triennial Congress of American Physicians and Surgeons, to which he referred in the last letter to Lafleur, met in Washington a few days later—May 29th to June 1st. It was not unlike other gatherings of the sort, with addresses and papers before the various special societies, with dinners and receptions, one of them at the White House—it was during Grover Cleveland's term. Washington, like other places, indeed, is at its very best the last week in May, and so it was this spring of 1894, even though its legislative halls were wrangling over the 'trusts' and Coxey's army was threatening to descend upon them. Moreover, there was a doctor in the Senate—at least he had had a course in a homoeopathic medical school—who was on the eve of making trouble for the profession by the introduction of a succession of antivivisection bills. Alfred L. Loomis of New York, who was President of the Congress, made 'animal experimentation' the subject of his presidential address,[1] and a resolution was introduced before the Congress by William H. Welch protesting against any legislation tending to interfere with the advancement of medicine by means of experimentation conducted by properly qualified persons. Welch, indeed, introduced resolutions of this kind before a great number of medical and scientific societies, and when the most serious test came four years later, he bore, as will

[1] 'The Influence of Animal Experimentation on Medical Science.'

be told, the chief burden of so organizing public opinion that Senator Gallinger's bill was defeated. There was one striking argument in favour of animal experimentation that could not be advanced at this time, for it was a year too early for returns. Nevertheless, Behring's successful elaboration of antitoxins against diphtheria and tetanus had been announced and received with great enthusiasm, for diphtheria was prevalent and hopes were raised that a boundless field for serum therapy was about to be opened up. It was recognized as only the beginning of a new era in the treatment of infectious diseases and in the checking of epidemics, one of which, bubonic plague, was raging at this time in Southern China.[1]

This June saw the close of the first year of the Hopkins Medical School, and though another twelve months elapsed before the students came directly under Osler's tutelage, he was prevailed upon by his friend Chadwick of Boston to attend a meeting of the Harvard Medical Alumni Association held towards the end of the month, shortly before his sailing, and to say something regarding their Baltimore programme. His informal remarks, which were taken down and appeared unedited in print,[2] indicate that he made some apologies for the length of course demanded by their entrance requirements. After suggesting that an arrangement might be made similar to that in existence in Cambridge, England, whereby the pre-clinical studies would be regarded as proper subjects counting for an academic degree, he continued in lighter vein to consider another way in which the Johns Hopkins school differed from others. This, his second point, was,——

. . . an extremely delicate one, namely co-education. It has wrung your withers here to some slight extent. When I parted from my preceptor, he gave me a copy of the Apocrypha, on the title-page of which he wrote: 'When a woman woos, what woman's son will sourly leave her till she hath prevailed?' Now, while on principle I am opposed to co-education, guided as I have always

---

[1] It was in connexion with this epidemic, to investigate which Kitasato had been sent by the Japanese Government, that the discovery was made of the specific organism of plague.

[2] *Bulletin of the Harvard Medical Alumni Association*, 1894, No. 7, 39–43.

been by the Apocrypha and my preceptor, I was warmly in favour of it particularly when the ladies came forward with half a million dollars. You know, of course, that this was offered to Harvard Medical School, and that President Eliot and the late Dean struggled over the offer a good deal. We had but one serious opponent in Johns Hopkins,—Dr. Councilman, who, brought up in theological schools, and with a strong theological bias [!], was opposed most thoroughly to co-education, and would have nothing to do with it. Accordingly, we made a bargain with President Eliot and Dr. Bowditch. We took the money, and you took the man. We have co-education without Councilman, and you get Councilman without co-education. All our plans succeeded, and everything went smoothly and nicely and quietly. The Board of Lady Supervisors arranged with President Gilman and Dr. Welch, the Dean, that Minerva Medica should not be the presiding goddess—she was not good enough—but that the elder Aphrodite, the motherless daughter of Uranus, should be installed as the presiding genius of the school. Under her there would be loyal devotion to truth, to science, and to work. The younger Aphrodite, the daughter of Dione and Jupiter, was banished, and ordered not to be seen within the walls. When you go against nature, you fail utterly. I come here to-day with sorrow at my heart to tell you that co-education has proved an absolute failure, from the elder Aphrodite's standpoint. When I tell you that 33⅓ % of the lady students admitted to the first year of the Medical Faculty of the Johns Hopkins University are, at the end of one short session, to be married, then you will understand why I say that co-education is a failure. If we lose 33⅓ % at the end of the first session where will the class of lady students be at the end of the fourth? In all other respects co-education is a great success.[1]

They sailed for England on July 12th; and from London, where rooms were taken at 40 Clarges Street, he wrote to his assistant, Thayer:

24th [July]

I see the Sydenham Soc. has issued the monographs of Marchiafava & Bignami & Mannaberg, with the plates. I will ask about the cost of reproduction. We are comfortably settled & are enjoying London immensely. After all it is the world. We had a delightful voyage, not a moment's uneasiness. The Robin Robbs dined with us on Sunday. They have been honeymooning at Cliveden forsooth! with the Astors. Robin now takes a 7.75 Lincoln & Bennett, has double soles on his shoes & wears an eye glass. They left on Monday

[1] Later, to his great chagrin, one of the survivors—another 33⅓ per cent. (!)—turned Christian Scientist.

for Paris. [Weir] Mitchell is here, & a great success. In the profession I have only seen a few of my friends as we do not wish to begin a round of dinners. I hope you are not burdened with work. Love to all the boys. Tell Billings I have not yet seen the Ords. I shall go there tomorrow. Send me word now & again how everything is progressing. Mrs Osler sends love to all. . . .

And a few days later to the same:

Yours & the book came this a m. Thanks, I will ask for estimates on the plates. We have been enjoying London so much—theatres dinners &c. I have not seen many Drs. except at the Comitia of the R C P and at the dinner in the eve. They put me next to the president who pumped me dry about our work. Dear old Wilks too has a great idea of the future of the Hopkins. I have been at Gowers' for several evenings. He is much better tho still a little excitable. I went with Horsley to a private operation on Friday. He took out a dural sarcoma about the size of his fist which had been growing for 15 years & had caused fits supposed by a long series of neurologists to be truly Epileptic. . . . I am going tomorrow with Blackader, Roddick, Stewart & de Schweinitz to the B. M. A. at Bristol & then on to Falmouth. We go on the 8th to Oxford & after that to the sea for a fortnight. Then to Paris for a week & back here again. Let me know if I can get you anything. . . .

The British Medical Association met in Bristol the first week in August and there Osler with Hale-White and others participated in a symposium on the general subject of pyrexia and its treatment.[1] This meeting was immediately followed by the gathering in Oxford of the British Association for the Advancement of Science. It was a memorable occasion, chiefly because Huxley, who only the year before had given his Romanes Lecture 'On Evolution and Ethics', was again in the Sheldonian Theatre; but the circumstances were very different from those when in 1860, at the last meeting in Oxford of the same Association, he had rebuked Wilberforce. The Marquis of Salisbury, Chancellor of the University, presided, and in his opening address dwelt somewhat sarcastically on the revolt against Aristotle by the growing sciences of observation, and in regard to evolution stated that 'the laity may be excused for returning a verdict of "not proven" upon the wider issues the Darwinian School

[1] Unpublished. It probably formed the basis of his paper, 'Hyperpyrexia in Typhoid Fever', before the Johns Hopkins Medical Society a year later.

has raised '. Huxley, who had been engaged to second the customary vote of thanks for the address, sat through it, it is said, tapping his foot, but, as he subsequently wrote, resisted temptation and 'conveyed criticism in the form of thanks '. As interested spectators, the Oslers sat in a little pulpit-like place in the Sheldonian and listened to these exchanges, little dreaming how familiar the scene was to become some day when instead of being guests in rooms at the Clarendon Hotel they were to become most abundant hosts on similar occasions to many wayfarers, in what came to be known as 'The Open Arms '. Nor could anything have been further from Osler's prognostications than his address, twenty-five years later, here in this home of the classics and as President of the Classical Association, on 'The Old Humanities and the New Science '.

The usual scientific sessions followed, sessions interspersed by the gastronomic festivities customary to such gatherings —a formal public dinner of course, at which Burdon Sanderson appeared, to the amusement of his pupils of former University College days, unconscious that he wore no tie. More informally they lunched with Sir Henry Acland, who owing to the infirmities of age was soon to resign the Regius Professorship. On first entering Acland's library, Osler exclaimed with delight at the panel of three portraits—Linacre, Harvey, and Sydenham—which stood over the mantel. He made such an ado about it that Mrs. Osler subsequently asked Sir Henry if they might not be copied for him as a birthday present. This was done, and in turn the triumvirate came to adorn the mantel of his own library and office at 1 West Franklin Street, a familiar sight to countless students, friends, and patients. This same panel, moreover, was to dominate Osler's library in Oxford, for though his teacher Burdon Sanderson came between, it would almost seem as though Acland had knowingly handed on an emblem of the Regius Professorship to the man destined, in the whirligig of time and place, to become his successor.

On the last day of the meeting, a bust of Thomas Sydenham was unveiled by Salisbury in the Oxford Museum—a science hall which Acland and Ruskin had succeeded in erecting in the very centre of classical Oxford. The address on Sydenham given by Acland on this occasion, is mentioned in the next letter, written from Swansea to W. S. Thayer:

The Langland Bay Hotel, Langland,
Sunday 19th.

We have been here, in a sort of Welsh paradise, since Tuesday. Delightful Hotel—managed in a way that would warm Mr Emery's heart—and as you see a fine beach. But the thermometer has not gone above 65 since Aug 1st so that for my cold marrow bathing is impossible. The walks are good & we spend the mornings on the rocks. Swansea is only six miles away & my niece May Francis, Mrs. Chas Bath, lives just outside the town, & my Father has a whole tribe of cousins here many of whom I have never seen. You would have been astonished to see me at cricket yesterday. I am stiff to-day from the exercise. The Oxford meeting was a great success—socially at any rate & we enjoyed it very much. I dare say Barker showed you the letter I wrote him while there. We go on to St Davids on Tuesday & Tenby & shall return to London about Sept 1st... Send your Typhoid paper to Professor Sherrington, Brown Institution Wandsworth Rd. London S. E. We saw so much of Hans Virchow, who is wildly enthusiastic about America. Hale-White, Pye-Smith, Broadbent & others were at the meeting. I have received some interesting photos from Sir Henry Acland, whose address on Sydenham I have sent to the *News*. Poor Gould has been laid up—was ill in London—also at Bristol, where I had to take his place at the dinner. Fortunately Dawson Williams edited my remarks about Hart & his missionary work, which was evidently taken *au sérieux*, judging from the report in the journal. I am reading proofs of my little monograph on chorea [1]—How is the Malaria? I suppose you are melted & worked to death. Thank Smith for his letter. I am sure the locum tenens is a great success. Miss H. returns Sept 1st and will be at your disposal. I want her tho. to go over all the old cases & add the anatom. Diagnoses. I will send you a memo of what I want her to do so that you may know how much there is. Love to all the boys—Billings, Norton, Oppenheim, Carter, Barker, Flexner & others—not forgetting Mr Emery & Miss Bonner. Yours ever W. O.

Monmouth, 24th [August]

Dear Thayer, I was very glad to have your nice long letter which reached me at Tenby. We were nearly frozen in South Wales—so cold & damp & we came on here yesterday for the Wye valley which is divine. To-day we were rowed 12 miles down to Tintern Abbey.

---

[1] The English edition was dedicated to Gowers and the American one to Weir Mitchell.

We go up the river to Hereford & then to London. I am delighted to hear good accounts of the malaria. I am sure it will be a telling piece of work. Did you do anything about the subcut. fibroid case? Dictate a lecture to Miss H. on it. I am sorry to say we shall not be back until Oct 1st and as I must see you for a couple of days you might postpone the sailing until the 5th. You need not hurry back you will have earned a good six weeks. We shall go directly from N. Y. to Toronto. I have not had very good accounts of my father—the heat has tried him very much. Set Miss H. at the Histories filling in the no. of the autopsy & the anatom. diagnosis in all the fatal cases. She has also the lectures on abd. Tumours to send off, but there is no hurry as I have told her to be primarily at your disposal. . . . Love to all the boys.

On his return to Baltimore for the opening of the school session, he evidently found awaiting him an invitation from R. H. Ruttan, the Professor of Chemistry and University Registrar at McGill, asking him to participate in the ceremonies planned for the dedication of the new medical building whose erection had been warranted by a bequest left by J. H. R. Molson.

To F. J. Shepherd from W. O. Wednesday

Dear Shepherd, Ruttan's note was sent from England and I found it here on Sunday. I sent word at once, that as the time was so short it was quite out of the question. I thought of course the opening was for Oct. 1st. Your letter this a m made me refer again to his & I find it is for Nov. 1. I really could not prepare another lecture this year & in so short a time. I have, as you know, written two within the last six months (the Army Surgeon, & the Leaven of Science) and I do not feel that I could face a third with the amount of necessary work I have on hand. I am very sorry indeed as it would have been a great pleasure to be with you all again. I heard of you from the [Stephen] Mackenzies. You won the hearts of the children. I had a letter from Cunningham this week in which he says they enjoyed your visit very much. We were kept pretty busy in England. I was preparing a little monograph on chorea & doing some reading about Sydenham in the British Museum. I hope we shall see you here before long.

Within the space of twelve months Medicine lost at this time three great figures—distinguished in very different fields—Helmholtz, Holmes, and Huxley. Oliver Wendell Holmes died on October 7th, and at the next meeting (on October 15th) of the hospital medical society, Osler read with deep feeling his much-quoted obituary address.[1] He termed Holmes 'the most successful combination the world has ever seen, of physician and man of letters':

While it is true that since Rabelais and Linacre no generation has lacked a physician to stand unabashed in the temple at Delos, a worshipper of worth and merit amid the votaries of Apollo, I can recall no name in the past three centuries eminent in literature—eminent, I mean, in the sense in which we regard Goldsmith—which is associated in any enduring way with work done in the science and art of medicine. Many physicians, active practitioners—Sir Thomas Browne, for example—have been and are known for the richness and variety of their literary work; but, as a rule, those who have remained in professional life have courted the 'draggle-tailed Muses' as a gentle pastime, 'to interpose a little ease' amid the worries of practice. Few such have risen above mediocrity; fewer still have reached it. We know the names of Garth, of Arbuthnot and of Akenside, but we neither know them nor their works. The list is a long one, for the rites of Apollo have always had a keen attraction for the men of our ranks, but the names fill at best a place in the story of the literature of the country, not a place in the hearts and lives of the people. Far otherwise is it with a select group of men, Goldsmith, Crabbe and Keats, at the outset members of our profession, but who early broke away from its drudgery. In pride we claim them, though in reality no influence of their special studies is to be found in their writings. Two of these, at least, reached the pure empyrean, and, to use Shelley's words, robed in dazzling immortality, sit on thrones

built beyond mortal thought,
Far in the Unapparent.

'It has been on my soul to write to you ever since my return', he says in a letter of the 18th to Lafleur, 'but I have been very busy and have rather more than the usual arrears of work. It is a great disappointment to me not to be able to go up at the opening of the new building, but it will be simply an impossibility with what I have on hand. Moreover, I am pumped out and another address this year would finish me.' He went on to say that Hewetson and Thayer were back; and 'we have an entry of about thirty-two in the first year, which makes fifty undergraduates'. There was always a group from among the junior house staff, perhaps more intimate than others at No. 1 West

[1] *Johns Hopkins Hospital Bulletin*, Oct. 1894, v. 85.

Franklin Street, who were known as the 'latch-keyers', inasmuch as each was given a key and had free access to the house at any time—an evidence of the readiness with which Osler, no matter how busy, brooked interruptions by his friends. It was another custom of the household to give a plain gold ring to each of these 'latch-keyers' to wear as a form of protection against any designing and matrimonially minded Gretel they might encounter while sojourning on the Continent; and it may be presumed that Thayer and Hewetson were so protected on this their first trip of observation abroad.

The projected Montreal ceremonies must have been postponed for his sake, and somewhat to his despair, until the first of the year; and on November 24th, shortly after returning from the autumn meeting of the Maryland 'Faculty' held in Cumberland, he wrote to Lafleur, saying:

We shall be delighted to see you here after Xmas. We shall probably be in Phila. for the 25th & 26th but I will let you know accurately so that you can arrange when to leave. Miss Humpton (who is still with me) has mailed a copy of the Abd. Tumour Lectures to Dr. Campbell. We have our Malaria fasciculus nearly ready. Thayer & Hewetson have an elaborate paper. I am busy with STUFF for Wilson & Dercum—infernal hack work. I hate it. Remember to take back your Vol ii of Peppers Text-book—I send this eve a copy of my remarks on O W Holmes. What the deuce am I to talk about in January at the opening? I am rather exsiccated at present. Remind me also to give you some duplicate works of Charcot. I treated myself to a complete set lately.

'Exsiccated' though he might have thought himself, and busy with the effort to clear his desk of the 'hack work' he had been beguiled into doing for others, he evidently without effective protest had taken on something more of the same kind. He wrote to Ogden on November 29th:

Dear O. Very glad of your letter this morning. You really must come on in the spring. Why not to the Am. Med. Ass? or better to the Ass. of Am. Phy. towards the end of May. Mrs. O says that my friends do not like her—they never come now to stay with me—so mend your ways soon. I shall get Fitzgerald's letters—I peeped into them at the Athenaeum Club this summer. I am very busy on some of the confounded *composite* text-books & systems. J. C.

Wilson's Handbook of Treatment. Dercum's Nervous Diseases. Clifford Allbutt's New System & Loomis' New System—Deuce take them all.[1] I shall look out for your art[icle]. Where?

For reasons which affected injuriously the finances of the university, Baltimore at this time possessed one modernized but little-used railway station. The chief portal of entry, however, from north and south lay through sulphurous tunnels into a rickety station which belied the prosperity of this the rival railway, which indeed, according to rumour, entertained serious thoughts of side-tracking Baltimore in order to shorten the transit from Washington to Philadelphia. Such Baltimoreans as travelled beyond the suburbs were mostly known by name to cordial and well-mannered cabbies and station porters; but there had come to be an increasing influx of strange faces, so many of whom asked to be taken to a certain residence that the following phrase came to be a by-word among them—'Fur caps and square hats to Dr. Osler's'. Accordingly, any one wearing the peculiar flat-crowned derby of a Bostonian of the day, or the cap suited to a Montreal winter, was promptly and cordially greeted by a smiling darkey with: 'A'll take yo' right to 1 Wes' Franklin Street, sah.' 'March, April, May, June or any month will be convenient for us to put you up, and I hope you will be able to pay a nice long visit—you can potter around and be just as independent as you please', is a familiar paragraph in Osler's letters, and his brief notes always contain in a postscript or elsewhere something to the

[1] The 'confounded text-books and systems' of this particular time, with the number of pages he contributed to each of them, are as follows: In J. C. Wilson's 'American Text-book of Applied Therapeutics' (Phila., 1896, pp. 902–7) he discussed the diseases of the blood, and ductless glands.

For F. X. Dercum's 'Text-book on Nervous Diseases, by American Authors' (Phila., 1895, pp. 203–26), he wrote the chapter on infectious diseases.

For vol. i. of 'A System of Practical Medicine', by A. L. Loomis and W. A. Thompson (Phila., 1897, pp. 731–848), he wrote a concise but masterly presentation on the general subject of Tuberculosis.

For the great English 'System of Medicine', edited by T. Clifford Allbutt (vol. iii, 1897, pp. 721–42), he wrote the chapter on malarial fever; stating that 'the introduction of cinchona into Europe two hundred and fifty years ago ranks not only as one of the greatest events in the history of medicine but as one of the great factors in the civilization of the world'.

MENU OF THE AMERICAN PHYSIOLOGICAL SOCIETY DINNER, 1894

CAVIAR, ... *Cocktails*

"As a child of four I can still recall the delight of my first handful of Caviar, filched from a barrel of that delicacy which stood in the stoop of the corner grocery at Forrest Hill; but it was a week or two later, when the barrel was almost empty, that there came to me the inspiration of my great work on Embryology."

Autobiography. CHAS. SEDGWICK MINOT.
Boston, 1920.

BLUE POINTS, ... *Haut Sauterne*

"In conclusion, gentlemen, I can only refer to the studies of Councilman and Lafleur on the association of Arterio-Sclerosis with oyster-eating, as an illustration of that lack of perspicacity and that absence of logical sequence, which has too often I fear, characterized the work of my collegues of the St. Johns Hopkins Hospital."

From the speech of Professor Brooks at the
Oyster League, Oct. 1st, 1894.

CONSOMMÉ ROYAL, ... *Old English brown Sherry*

"Disguise through dilution must be our motto; and as the mystic cult of Nagual strove to guard the pure American spirit from base European contamination, so we, as members of the Physiological Society (that corps d'elite about the Ark of Science) carefully distinguishing between the esotoric and and the exoteric, must cloak in verbiage those stronger truths, the hasty adoption of which might prove disastrous to the race."

W. H. HOWELL. *Prospectus of the American Text Book of Physiology*, 1895.

TERRAPIN, CELERY. . . . . . . *Veuve Cliquot*

"The question of the relation of diet to population has been solved in reality by the researches of Councilman (see his *Malthus redivivus*, 1895), who has shown that in the Terrapin circles of Maryland the birth rate rises and falls with the price of diamond backs."

F. S. LEE, "*Equilibration in population*," 1896.

BREAST OF TURKEY, FRESH MUSHROOMS. . . . . *Ruinart Brut*

"It passes my persimmon to tell why we physiologists are superior in so many respects to the specialists in the other departments of science. I incline however, to the opinion of Mills that, in a study of the evolution of the elaborate differentation of the complex functions of the higher living organisms, our minds, subdued to what they work in, take that fine polish, which is recognized as the distinguishing attribute of the pure physiologist."

JOHN CURTIS, in the *Golden Calf, a novel*, 1894.

Maraschino Punch.

"The most extraordinary fact of the research remains to be noted, viz., that those members only of the Committee of Fifty who

RED HEAD DUCK, HOMINY CAKES. . . . *Chateau Larose*

"Why did she shave his beard also? I had long pondered on this aspect of the story of Delilah, feeling sure that in its depths, could we but fathom them, lay the whole mystery of the sex. The answer as told in these pages reveals, as never before, the inner springs of action in the heart of woman"

From *Women of the Bible*, by JAMES R. CHADWICK.
Boston, 1895.

ARTICHOKES, VINAIGRETTE, ...

"That I should feel as Heracleitos did about his predecessors—that they had much knowledge but no sense, is partly to be explained by a too sudden change in my environment To a man trained in the Psychopannychia, from John Knox to Herbert Spencer is a longer mental journey than from the Greeks to Darwin."

In preface to "*From the Chinese to Pythagoras*,"
by H. F. OSBORN, 1896.

ICES. . . . .

"And amid these surroundings I leave you to join the chorus of the Initiated in the Elysian Meadows; but I leave you in the full assurance that nowhere in my journey, not even in Nephelococcygia, will I see a more stately group of academic buildings than that with which I have adorned Clift n Park."

Valedictory Address, President GILMAN. 1912.

CHEESE. . . . .

"Methinks I see in my mind a great and noble profession rousing herself like a lovely woman after sleep, and gazing horror-stricken at her innumerable journals and books Methinks I see her, as a serpent sloughing its skin, shaking them off and devoting herself exclusively to the study of Titles in the great volumes which I have edited."

The *New Areopagitica*, a plea for the total suppression of printing in the medical profession. By J S. BILLINGS. 1900.

COFEEE. . . . .

"But my studies have a wider significance and a deeper lesson. In every one and at all times—in the sturdy laborer, in the energetic man of affairs, in the ambitious professional man, and in the crafty politician—the K. J. means Life; and paraphrasing a well-known sentence, I may say, *Ohne K. J kein Leben*.

W. P. LOMBARD, *On the Knee Jerk and Public Morality*.
Y. M. C. A., Chicago, 1893.

CIGARS AND CIGARETTES. . . . .

"A tendency in the man is everything and since the attitude can never be fixed, since *panta rei* is the law of the universe, smoke becomes the emblem of existence, and in the contemplation of the clash of its molecules resides the entire philosophy of life"

S. J. MELTZER. *Why I am a Smoker* North American Review,
January, 1895.

LIQUERS. . . . .

"Let me add here one practical observation on this question of normal jejunal microbic proteolysis. Increasing in intensity, it is apt to become excessive, turbulent, Boreal, unless tempered by a strong cordial, administered two or three hours after the beginning of

effect that 'the kettle boils daily at 4·50', or 'there's always an extra place at the table at seven'.

Though being drawn away from the laboratory into wider fields, he was still a member of the Physiological Society, then, as now, a small and select body of pure scientists who met somewhere each year for the last few days of the Christmas recess. On this occasion Osler played the rôle of host rather than participant in the sessions, and he fully enjoyed his houseful of guests. A memorable dinner was held at the Maryland Club, famous for its table—oysters, terrapin, duck, and madeira to make the mouth water—and the menu graced by quotations concocted by Osler and ascribed to imaginary writings of a number of the Society's members was introduced by the following ('the Yle Utopia Revisited') jibe at Weir Mitchell:

> In that land the wise men, known as Siphograuntes, meet in 'sweet societies', and earnestly bestowe their vacuante and spare hours in seeking a knowledg of the perfect liffe, the which they say is to be atchieved in these gatherings, and more hyghelye in certain evening conclaves known as smokers and dynners. For thoughe in these festivities no man be prohibited to dyne at home yet no man doth it willingly, because it is counted a point of smal honestie to be absent. It were a follye, say they, to take the payne to dresse a badde dynner at home when they may be welcome to good and fyne fare so nighe hand at the club. For herein they suppose the felicitie of liffe to consiste.

Occasions of this sort in which Osler participated were invariably enlivened in some such fashion: evidently he had been reading Sir Thomas More and in a subsequent address at Albany in 1900 he gave the long quotation from 'The New Yle Utopia' in which More describes the care of the sick in the Commonwealth.

CHAPTER XVI

1895–6

TEACHING, OBSERVING, AND RECORDING

The dedication of the new buildings in Montreal took place early in January and Osler's presence served to awaken the periodic rumour that he would be recalled to McGill. Somehow during the past month he had managed to prepare an address, suited for the ears of a lay audience, entitled 'Teaching and Thinking—the Two Functions of a Medical School'. In this, with his usual optimism, he answers the 'bitter cry of Isaiah, that with the multiplication of the nations their joys had not been increased', and tells his audience that they 'may now pray the prayer of Hezekiah with a reasonable prospect of its fulfilment'.

> 'Tis no idle challenge which we physicians throw out to the world when we claim that our mission is of the highest and of the noblest kind, not alone in curing disease but in educating the people in the laws of health, and in preventing the spread of plagues and pestilences; nor can it be gainsaid that of late years our record as a body has been more encouraging in its practical results than those of the other learned professions. Not that we all live up to the highest ideals, far from it—we are only men. But we have ideals, which means much, and they are realizable, which means more. Of course there are Gehazis among us who serve for shekels, whose ears hear only the lowing of the oxen and the jingling of the guineas, but these are exceptions; the rank and file labour earnestly for your good, and self-sacrificing devotion to your interests animates our best work.

However, he does not spare the physician 'who without physiology and chemistry flounders along in an aimless fashion, never able to gain any accurate conception of disease, practising a sort of pop-gun pharmacy, hitting now the malady and again the patient, he himself not knowing which'—a contrast to the studious and hard-working men who live in hospitals and dispensaries endeavouring to obtain a wide and philosophical conception of disease and its processes—men 'who form the bulwarks of our ranks and outweigh scores of the voluble Cassios who talk themselves into, and often out of practice'. Nor do the clergy escape, for with the Bible in hand he raps them 'as notorious supporters of all the nostrums and humbuggery with which the daily and religious papers abound', and finds that 'the further away they have wandered from the decrees of the Council of Trent the more apt are they to be steeped in thaumaturgic and Galenical superstition'. As an indication of the direction of his reading he is found quoting from Keats and from Thomas Dover; and he makes an appeal that McGill reach out widely for the best wherever found, else 'an institution which wraps itself in Strabo's cloak and does not look beyond the college gates in selecting professors may get good teachers but rarely good thinkers'. With McGill already liberally endowed, 'there remains now to foster that undefinable something which, for want of a better term, we call the university spirit, a something which a rich institution may not have, and with which a poor one may be saturated, a something which is associated with men and not with money, which cannot be purchased in the market or grown to order, but which comes insensibly with loyal devotion to duty and to high ideals, and without which *Nehushtan* is written on its portals'—all of which has a sound of John Henry Newman.

It would appear that Principal Dawson was about to resign, and in casting about for his successor Osler must have been the first and single choice of the university authorities. That he would accept must have been taken for granted, and an announcement that he would do so went broadcast through the press on January 10th. This met his eye while *en route* for Baltimore from Boston, where he had gone to meet Mrs. Osler, who had been visiting her mother; and on reaching home they found the servants, including the faithful Morris, in tears, and the Hopkins group in a turmoil. 'You are truly a "Wandering Willie",' wrote Pepper, 'but as long as your peregrinations carry you only from one peak on to a higher one your friends and admirers can only rejoice in your continued progress'; and Weir Mitchell: 'If this is true I shall not congratulate myself or the profession, for I think you were made for a doctor not a college president'; and H. C. Wood: 'Have you agreed to take it? Must we soon take off our hats to Sir William, and how much small beer must you imbibe before your lithe swarthy form can grow and swell and swell and grow to the proper dimensions of a Britannic "Sir"? If so, farewell.' He dismissed all this with his usual brevity, as in the following to Lafleur:

> I enclose the copy of Holmes's poem. We returned here to find quite an excitement about the rumoured appointment at McGill. The Associated Press had telegraphed from Montreal that I had been appointed and there was no end of disturbance. I had a delightful visit with you all up there, and it was a great pleasure to see my old friends again.

The call,[1] one may be assured, was not lightly declined, but decisions came quickly to him. 'Executive work has never been in my line,' he wrote to Ogden; and there was much else to occupy his mind and pen. Though pegging away at this time at the first revision of his Text-book, he meanwhile found relaxation in other and more agreeable literary tasks. In this month of January two of his best biographical essays were presented before the Historical Society of the hospital: one on 'Thomas Dover, Physician and Buccaneer'—of Dover's Powder fame; another entitled 'An Alabama Student'; and a third on John Keats was given later in the year at the October meeting of the same club. He had probably encountered Thomas Dover during his summer's quest for records of Sydenham in the British Museum, for Dover before making his fortune in the South Seas [2] had been one of Sydenham's pupils. While browsing around a subject, Osler fairly lapped up information, and there is evidence in the essay to show that in his pursuit of Dover's medical writings, which had made such a great noise in London in their day, he had gone to libraries beyond the British Museum and in his collateral reading had wandered even into Smollett's

[1] Nor was this the only one, for efforts were made the same month to attract him to New York City by the offer of a university post there.

[2] It has been said that the success of this privateering voyage was what led up to the establishment of the South Sea Company, and, before the bubble burst, one Thomas Guy, a heavy participant, had sold his stock, thereby providing himself with the fortune subsequently bequeathed to found Guy's Hospital. This famous institution, therefore, may trace its origin to the sack of Guayaquil, as famed in later days for its yellow fever as in the early eighteenth century for its yellow gold.

'Peregrine Pickle'. It must suffice to quote his introductory paragraph:

As Sir Thomas Browne remarks in the *Hydriotaphia*: 'The iniquity of oblivion blindly scattereth her poppy, and deals with the memory of men without distinction to merit of perpetuity.' Thus it happens that Thomas Dover, the Doctor, has drifted into our modern life on a powder label (to which way of entering the company of posterity, though sanctified by Mithridates, many would prefer oblivion, even to continuous immortality on a powder so potent and palatable as the *Pulvis Ipecacuanhae compositus*); while Thomas Dover, the Buccaneer, third in command, one of the principal owners, and president of the Council of the *Duke* and *Duchess*—privateers of the ancient and honourable city of Bristol—discoverer of Alexander Selkirk (the original Robinson Crusoe), in spite of more enduring claims on our gratitude, has been forgotten. . . .

What led him to become interested in the story of 'An Alabama Student', a mid-century surgeon of the Southern States, was related in the essay in his own words as follows:

When looking over the literature of malarial fevers in the South,[1] chance threw in my way Fenner's *Southern Medical Reports*, Vols. I and II, which were issued in 1849–50 and 1850–1. Among many articles of interest, I was particularly impressed with two by Dr. John Y. Bassett of Huntsville, Alabama, in whom I seemed to recognize a 'likeness to the wise below', a 'kindred with the great of old'. I wrote to Huntsville to ascertain what had become of Dr. Bassett, and my correspondent referred me to his daughter from whom I received a packet of letters written from Paris in 1836. I have her permission to make the extracts which are here given. . . .

He gave a stirring and appreciative account of this unusual man, rescuing his story from among those forgotten and making him for all time one of the heroes of the 'medicine of the Southland', an example to all young students of medicine, of what courage, persistence, and industry may accomplish in the face of difficulties and discouragements. He closes the essay with the following paragraph:

The saddest lament in Oliver Wendell Holmes's poems is for the voiceless—

for those who never sing
But die with all their music in them.

---

[1] Cf. 'The Study of the Fevers of the South.' *Journal of the American Medical Association*, 1896, xxi. 999–1004.

The extracts which I have read show Dr. Bassett to have been a man of more than ordinary gifts, but he was among the voiceless of the profession. Nowadays environment, the opportunity for work, the skirts of happy chance carry men to the summit. To those restless spirits who have had ambition without opportunities, and ideals not realizable in the world in which they move, the story of his life may be a solace. I began by saying that I would tell you of a man of whom you had never heard, of a humble student from a little town in Alabama. What of the men whom he revered, and for whom in 1836 he left wife and children? Are they better known to us? To-day scarcely one of those whom he mentions touches us with any firmness from the past. Of a majority of them it may be said, they are as though they had not been. Velpeau, Andral, Broussais, the great teachers whom Bassett followed, are shadowy forms (almost as indistinct as the pupil), dragged out to daylight by some *laudator temporis acti*, who would learn philosophy in history. To have striven, to have made an effort, to have been true to certain ideals—this alone is worth the struggle. Now and again in a generation one or two snatch something from dull oblivion; but for the rest of us, sixty years—we, too, are with Bassett and his teachers, and

no one asks
Who or what we have been,
More than he asks what waves
In the moonlit solitudes mild
Of the midmost ocean, have swelled,
Foamed for a moment, and gone.

The surviving daughter of the Alabama Student, Miss Laura Bassett, who had solicited a picture of the author of the essay, wrote: 'You have a different look from what I had imagined and I have not done you justice in any respect, except from an intellectual standpoint. The rotund, bald-headed, eagle-eyed and -nosed Dr., with a slightly dictatorial manner now gives way before the real and true picture.' But neither brush nor camera ever caught the real and true Osler, for a mask of imperturbability concealed the real man capable of flashes of gaiety and outrageous pranks, somewhat mystifying to those who were incapable of seeing beneath the surface. Sir Edward Schafer, his old friend of University College days, writes:

Ever since I knew Osler—as quite a young man—he had always the same quiet serious manner, with unperturbed features and dark-complexioned almost expressionless face—so that strangers were entirely unprepared for the humour which would sally forth at the most unexpected times, without any relaxation of countenance or any change in tone of voice: indeed, people sometimes would take a remark which was entirely jocular *au grand sérieux*, and wonder that it should have been made by so sedate and learned a person. . . .

What is more, behind his mask there lay a tender, affectionate, sympathetic, almost sentimental heart, whose emotions he had trained himself to disguise. There is a story told of how he offended some good people in the early days in Baltimore by humming a tune—as near as he could get to one—on leaving the sickroom of a man, evidently near his end, whom he had been asked to see in consultation. His attention was drawn to this lapse by the doctor who had called him in, with the hint that such unheard-of behaviour would make him an undesirable consultant, and he merely replied, in Uncle Toby's words: ''Tis that I may not weep.' It was not for want of thought that he whistled as he went. So in his letters, when mentioning some sorrow, even that of the loss of his son, which, years later, broke him beyond words, whatever his inward feelings, he disguised them outwardly, and with the gesture of putting sorrow behind him he quickly turned to other things. Thus in a note scribbled to Ogden early in March he mentions his father's death:

Delighted! But you must stay a week at least. Plenty of room & a hearty welcome & I want you to meet Mrs. O. My father died two weeks ago—arteriosclerosis. Sorry to hear that you have had a cold—the trip will do you good. If you have any memoranda for 2nd edition of my Quiz Compend—bring them as I am working at it.

The 97th annual session of the Medical and Chirurgical Faculty of Maryland—the last meeting to be held in its old hall on the corner of St. Paul and Saratoga Streets—fell on April 23rd, when a symposium was held at Osler's suggestion on the subject of 'Typhoid Fever in Country Districts'. He opened the session with a paper in which he urged the regular inspection of dairy farms, measures to prevent the contamination of the water supply, and the compulsory notification of every case of typhoid before an official State Board of Health. These were radical recommendations, and in no uncertain terms he gave warning that the Baltimore death-rate from typhoid never would be reduced to the ratio of modern cities until the local cesspool system of drainage was completely abolished and the city took over control of the watersheds of the Gunpowder River and Jones's Falls. He had good reason to enter the lists in favour of these necessary reforms, for at the time Arthur Oppenheim, one of his assistant residents, was lying ill at the hospital with what proved to be a fatal attack of this preventable malady; nor was he to be the only victim of typhoid among the hospital family.[1]

The 'Faculty' meeting was the opening gun of the succession of medical meetings—appalling even in the '90's—which signalize the closing months of the school year. A short-lived body, the American Academy of Medicine, held a session in Baltimore, May 4th–6th, in one of the halls of the University—an occasion which need be noted only in so far as to explain that Osler, who probably dispensed hospitality to the members, was not only elected an honorary member but was penalized by being made President of an affiliated and comparatively new Society—the Association of American Medical Colleges.

On the heels of these preliminaries came the Baltimore meeting of the American Medical Association, a formidable body for any community to entertain. The meeting, or, more properly speaking, one of its business sessions, was noteworthy from the sidelight it casts upon the subject of this memoir. As a rule, if righting wrongs involved other people's feelings, Osler preferred to do these things man to man; but on a few occasions he flared out in public with an expostulation against an obvious wrong. On this particular occasion he was moved to say openly what others felt but dared not express. A worthy but incompetent old man, Dr. W. B. Atkinson, had been Secretary of the Association for thirty-one years and, as had happened several times before, the Committee on Nominations had reported in favour of a successor. According to the constitution, however, the Secretary could only be retired from office by death, resignation, or removal by a two-thirds vote of those present. The Secretary's supporters all spoke

[1] At the McGill Convocation, April 30th, Osler *in absentia* (probably because of Oppenheim's illness) was given his first LL.D.

in his favour and one of them had made a long appeal to the effect that the sentiment of the Association was '*fiat justitia*—exact justice and mercy to every one', urging the assembly to sustain the existing Secretary. The question was to be put, when Osler rose from the floor of the house—indeed, stood on his chair the better to be heard. The Journal of the Association, for May 18, 1895, in its official account of the proceedings, reads as follows:

> The President—Are you ready for the question? (Cries of Question! Question!)
>
> Dr. Osler—*Fiat justitia* for the Association is all right, but let the quality of mercy be not strained. I stand here and say plainly and honestly before Dr. Atkinson what I and many other members have said behind his back, that he is not an efficient Secretary of this Association, and that we have not found him so. (Hisses, followed by applause.) You may hiss if you will, but I unhesitatingly say that no more important step in advance will be taken by this Association than when it changes its Secretary. (Cries of Question! Question!)
>
> President Maclean put the motion that the present incumbent remain in office, and it was carried by a large majority.

This account—a very mild rendering of an episode which stirred the Association to its depths—fails to record what then happened, for Osler left his seat, walked up on to the platform and, shaking Dr. Atkinson's hand, said things to him one would know that he would say.[1]

During all this time, as told in the following letter, he was pegging away at other matters, not the least onerous of which was the first triennial revision of his Text-book. He writes Lafleur on May 21st:

> I have been hard at work this winter on purpura and purpuric affections, for a set of lectures. I have had such an interesting round of cases this year. By the way, I am over head and ears revising my text-book, and nearly finished. Had you not a number of additional corrections? If so, please send them on as soon as possible. I shall be reading proofs all summer—and swearing. My monograph on Chorea was sent you from Blakiston's; at least Miss Humpton has it on her list, but I have ordered another one. There are one or two points of interest in it, particularly the mottoes from the two old sinners [Bouteille and Bernt].

---

[1] Osler's spectacular pronouncement at this time served its purpose. The agitation it provoked only subsided five years later when George H. Simmons was elected Secretary.

Though over head and ears in his revision, he managed to get away for two other meetings near the close of the month. On the 28th he read a paper on a little-understood malady associated with chronic peritonitis, before the American Pediatric Society, which met this year at the Virginia Hot Springs; and two days later he was in Washington for the tenth annual meeting of the Association of American Physicians, over which body he presided. It is not to be wondered at that the presidential address for the year was a rather perfunctory affair; nor was the programme a particularly exciting one,[1] and in all likelihood the presiding officer had abundant occasion to scribble 'James Bovell, MD MRCP' on his pad. So the spring passed, followed by a hot Baltimore June, which saw the completion of the revision. It had necessitated much labour and, as always, abundant rewriting, though in some fashion he managed, in this as in all other revisions, to keep the volume from expanding.

It is probable that a more vivid memoir of William Osler might be written could letters from his wife be recovered. Extracts from one of them written to Ogden on June 14th give a picture from behind the scenes of what had been going on at 1 West Franklin Street since Ogden's long-promised visit of a few weeks before. It says:

. . . You should see him now. He is deep in the new edition. The first package of manuscript has gone and soon the misery of proof reading will begin. The library is a perfect wreck—floor, tables & chairs covered with books & journals. After you left, my mother soon departed, and she was followed by one relation & friend after another and I only had time to catch my breath and be ready for that—(you know) American Med. Asso. Our plans were changed somewhat as Dr. Osler's sister-in-law died very suddenly and we of course did not take part in any of the entertainments—and Dr. Osler recalled his dinner invitations. Dr. Donald Maclean [A. M. A. President for the year] and his wife stayed here, also Dr. and Mrs. McGuire from Richmond. I hesitate to express my opinion about the A. M. A. probably yours is the same. Thank goodness it cannot come here again while we live here. . . . Dr. Osler distinguished

---

[1] Except for Welch's discussion of that recent epochal discovery—the treatment of diphtheria by antitoxin, subsequently much elaborated in the *Johns Hopkins Hospital Bulletin*, 1895, vi. 47.

himself by maligning old Atkinson the Secretary—I was at the meeting and frightened to death when I heard him pronounce the 'Secretary absolutely incompetent'. It was a benefit to the Association I am told, but I fail to see it. We are miserable at remaining in America this summer but proof must be read and some money saved this year. Dr. Osler says he cannot leave until the middle of July.

The summer months—after 'the middle of July' at least—were passed quietly at 'The Glades' on the Scituate shore of Massachusetts Bay, and while there, as the letters scribbled to his Resident Physician indicate, he finished his proof-reading, made plans for other work, and kept his finger on medical affairs at the Hopkins, where preparations were under way for the long-anticipated clinical teaching of the undergraduates just entering their third year:

Sunday [no date].

Dear Thayer, Do what you like about Camac. The question is tho, whether Lazear would have enough to do with the Bacteriology alone—It would do him good to have the ward at the same time, say, & without any Dispensary work. I finished the proofs yesterday [the second edition of the Text-book]. There has been a delay with the new cuts, but I hope to have the index in hand by the 18th and should have the work ready for distribution by Sept. 15th. We leave for Toronto next Sunday, address 83 Wellesley Street. We go to Canton Mass. to Mrs Revere's on Wednesday eve. This is a delightful place, so quiet & secluded & the headers off the rocks into deep water have renewed my youth. Mrs. Osler keeps very well. I hope you are arranging to leave on a fast SS. Sept. 11th. You could have 2 weeks in England & a few days in Cambridge on your return & be back in the hospital by the 12th of October an extra week would do you no harm. I am glad that they are pushing on with the alterations It will be a great comfort to have Futcher in charge & doing special work. I have almost finished the Typhoid histories of the past two years. There will be nearly enough for a serviceable fasciculus with the paper on Neuritis, which I read last winter, Blumer's paper on Pyuria & if I can get Halsted to put Parsons' paper in also. Love to all the boys. Yours W. O.

Osler was forever smoothing the path for others, and few men have been more active in getting up testimonial dinners or in celebrating anniversaries of friends and colleagues in some such way, or by having their portraits painted. He had an unerring flair which enabled him to foresee before others when words of encouragement or appreciation were needed, and when appropriate. It was in this year that the Congressional subsidy was withdrawn from the *Index Medicus*, the great monthly index of the world's medical literature which Dr. Billings had started; and with the object of finding some means of continuance of the publication, Osler had introduced resolutions at the A. M. A. meeting in June, urging the members to subscribe. But this was largely in vain,[1] for, after struggling along with uncertain financial support for a few years, publication was suspended until 1903 when, at Weir Mitchell's insistence, it was resumed under the patronage of the Carnegie Institute, with Dr. Fletcher as editor-in-chief. In this same year, too, was completed the last volume of the first series of the great 'Index Catalogue' of the Surgeon-General's Library, with its author- and subject-titles in excess of a million—one of the world's great indexes and a monument to Billings's imagination and industry. Billings's part in this was not to be forgotten; from the Glades Club, Osler writes to James R. Chadwick:

In what condition is the Billings testimonial? And in what form is the presentation to be made? Possibly you may know—possibly not; but what I feel is that we should have some general gathering on the occasion of the issue of the last volume of the Index Catalogue; a dinner would be best. I think I spoke to you about it last year, but this money testimonial came up & Mitchell had an idea that the College of Physicians, Phila, would give an entertainment & that the presentation might then be made. I shall be in town next week & will call on the chance of finding you.

A short sojourn with Mrs. Osler's mother in Canton, near Boston, was followed by a visit to his own mother in Toronto. He had invited innumerable friends, children of friends, and nephews and nieces to see him there; but the chief responsibility for their entertainment devolved upon his gracious wife, for, as often happened, he unceremoniously slipped away to attend a medical meeting. This time it was to Kingston, where the Canadian Medical Association met on August 27th, and where he read the

[1] According to J. S. Billings's open letter in the autumn, only thirty subscriptions at $25 a year had been received.

paper on cold bathing in typhoid—a portion of the report he had been working over during the summer.

On his return to Baltimore, early in September, he writes to Lafleur: 'Back again with the typhoid & malaria. Wards full. I am just issuing a second report on Typhoid Fever [1] which will contain some interesting papers.' If nothing else had come out of the clinic during the year, this report by itself would have made a most creditable showing. Some of the beautiful lithographic plates illustrating its several articles were signed '*Max Brödel fec.*'—a name which the year before had begun to appear under the illustrations which accompanied articles from the Hopkins clinic. Mr. Brödel had been induced to come to Baltimore from Leipzig, and in the course of the next decade revolutionized the art of medical illustrating. This, however, is another story, and his name is introduced here chiefly to account for the often-reproduced drawing he made showing Osler with halo and wings dominating a cyclone which swept away disease. It bore the legend, '*The Saint—Johns Hopkins Hospital*', a play upon Osler's frequent reference to the hospital as 'the St. Johns'.

Though he responded at times to professional calls which took him out of town—calls which he always enjoyed, for he was a good traveller and could rest, as well as read and compose, on trains almost better than at home, where interruptions were frequent—for the most part his private practice was confined to a few consultations by appointment between 2 and 4.30 p.m. at 1 West Franklin Street. After his tea he occasionally saw a patient or two in company with some Baltimore physician, but more often he repaired to the Medical and Chirurgical Faculty Library for an hour's reading or to engage in some committee work. There were, however, a few people whom he visited

[1] This and the 'Typhoid fasciculus' reference in the last letter to Thayer relate to the ten papers published this year in the last half of vol. v of the *Hospital Reports*—a matter of 200 pages, quarto, 100 of them from Osler's pen. Six of the ten topics he dealt with himself, and the other contributors were George Blumer, Simon Flexner, Walter Reed, and H. C. Parsons. The first half of this volume was given over to the comprehensive study, to which his letters so often refer, by Thayer and Hewetson of the malarial fevers of Baltimore, and to L. F. Barker's report on some of the fatal cases.

at their homes as much a friend as physician. One of them, a near neighbour, confesses that she would venture to summon him only when she had a temperature of 103°, and a conversation somewhat as follows would ensue: 'What's wrong?' 'In bed with a fever.' 'Why don't you open a window?' 'Because then I'd be cold.' 'But you could put on a wrap; what have you got to read?' So for the few precious moments more agreeable things than symptoms would be talked about until, with a wave of the hand he would vanish, to be welcomed with shouts of glee in the nursery, with whose inmates he was sure to frolic for a moment before leaving the house. This autumn a new arrival had come to this particular nursery, for whom he had been asked to suggest a name, and he wrote:

I feel sure that when the little lassie reaches years of discretion the name of Doris will please her greatly. Then it is Greek & the more we can revert, even in nomenclature, to that wonderful people the better for our modern life. The shadow of the Shemite is still upon us. Let us hope that as Doris she may reach the Greek ideal of a fair mind in a fair body, and be, indeed, as the word indicates, a gift. I hope your mother keeps comfortable. Dr. Smith should see her occasionally & I will look in now & again to see that all goes well.

Years later the mother of this child Doris penned these recollections of Osler as a physician—'a giver of life':

To have been a patient of Sir William Osler in your youth was to have obtained an almost impossible ideal of what a physician could be. . . . As he passed about, gallant and debonair, with a whimsical wit that left the air sweet and gay, with an epigram here and a paradox there, tickling the ribs of his colleagues, none felt him frivolous: there was a point to his rapier for all he played with the button on. The deep, sad eyes of his soul watched a little cynically the light humour of his mind. It was not necessary for him to be sensitive to a social atmosphere, because he always made his own atmosphere. In a room full of discordant elements he entered and saw only his patient and only his patient's greatest need, and instantly the atmosphere was charged with kindly vitality, everyone felt that the situation was under control, and all were attention. No circumlocution, no meandering. The moment Sir William gave you was yours. It was hardly ever more than a moment, but there was curiously no abrupt beginning or end to it. With the easy sweep of a great artist's line, beginning in your necessity and ending in your necessity, the precious moment was yours, becoming wholly and entirely a part of the fabric of your life. He made you respect his time, but he also respected yours. If he said: 'I will come at two', and the hands of the clock pointed to ten minutes after, you knew that he could not come. And if that rare thing happened—a broken appointment—he never failed to send a few lines of explanation. He safeguarded his patient from all annoyance. To be sure, you could not luxuriate into floating reminiscences in his company: your expansions about your family and friends and temperament were not for him—that the nurse had to bear. I think he was always a little sorry for the nurse. One other thing he safeguarded, and that was your purse. If a conscientious secretary sent a bill, it had to be a very moderate affair.

With his patients he recognized at once the thing or characteristic that concerned him and them; and for the rest, whatever was uncongenial or unattractive he put from his mind and prevented any expression of it. A pose or an attempt at a serious chatter about unessentials was intolerable to him. But he was as merciful as he was masterful, and from the very poor and the genuinely afflicted he would even have borne being bored.

Such telling love, such perfect confidence were given him that he could do what he liked without causing offence. Three times in my life I have seen him, when in consultation, smash the attending physician's diagnosis and turn the entire sick-room the other way about; but he left the room with his arm about the corrected physician's neck, and they seemed to be having a delightful time. The reason for this was perfectly evident: every physician felt himself safe in Sir William's hands; he knew that he could by no possibility have a better friend in the profession; that if, with the tip of his finger, Sir William gaily knocked down his house of cards, he would see to it that the foundation was left solid; and no one would contribute so many bricks to the new edifice. . . . He was one of those who having great possessions, gave all that he had. For myself, I may say that every moment he gave me shines out, illuminating the long years of my life.

Subtle in temperament, direct in character, the brilliant mind and soaring spirit were unchallenged, because, under the surface of the gay man of the world, lived the Saint. It is when a man touches other people's lives that you know whether he brings life or death or nothing. Where that swift spirit has gone I do not know; but I know that to those he cared for on earth he brought life. They will look back and remember, and will thank God and take courage.

To H. A. Lafleur from W. O. 1 West Franklin Street,
Sunday [Oct. 19, 1895].

I wish you were here this evening. Thayer and little Billie are reading in comfortable chairs & the former has just been reciting

Lowells commemoration ode. We have had a very sad week. Poor Emery went off suddenly in an attack of Angina which began at 3^{50} on Monday, & continued severely thro the night. In the morning he was better & passed the day comfortably. On Wednesday a m a few minutes after I had seen him & while Thayer & the faithful Gus were helping him he fell over on the bed & died in a few minutes. He was buried at Waverley—Barker & I went down to the funeral. We shall all miss him very much—there was a good heart beneath the rough exterior. I hope by this time you have the 2nd edition of my text-book—there was an unfortunate delay in the binding & distributing. Love to all the boys.

Something of the phenomenal success of the Text-book may be gathered from the fact that about 23,000 copies of the first edition had been sold, a remarkable record for a medical publication. From the preface of the new edition in which he makes his many acknowledgements may be gathered how extensive had been the additions and alterations, and on the fly-leaf of his personal interleaved copy of this second edition he pencilled a note giving what he calls his '"Boodle" Account with D. Appleton & Co.' Some one, some day, could well write a volume devoted to a study of the successive editions of this famous work, which continues to exercise an enormous influence on students of medicine—even on those beyond English-reading countries through its many translations.[1] Its influence, indeed, extended far beyond the profession and led to many important side issues which had better be deferred. To one of them, however, reference may be made here, since it concerned the future of one of Welch's assistants. The post of Pathologist at Jefferson had been offered to Flexner, and Osler had advised him to accept on the grounds that 'good billets in this country are so few it might be many years before another so favourable chance offered itself'. It was mistaken advice, for only a few years later another position in Philadelphia was proffered, and ere long the second edition of Osler's 'Practice of Medicine' got in its work in an unexpected quarter, paving the way for something far more important not only to Flexner but to the Johns Hopkins and to American medicine as well —an allusion to matters which had better come in their

[1] French (1908), German (1909), Chinese (1910 and 1921), Spanish (1915).

chronological order: the Baltimore fire, the Rockefeller Institute, and large gifts of money in the cause of public health.

From this digression concerning the Text-book we may turn again to its author who, with his publishers warded off for another three years, was interested in other matters. There was nothing of the single-track nature about Osler's mind, and he was capable of keeping many things moving at the same time towards their objectives. So, during the summer outing he had switched alternately from the slow-moving text-book revision to the typhoid fasciculus and to the more agreeable companionship of 'John Keats: the Apothecary Poet'—one-time surgical 'dresser' in Guy's Hospital under the celebrated Sir Astley Cooper, on which basis the medical profession, with some justification, enrolls him among its own. He had been reading the new edition, by Forman, of Keats's letters, meanwhile saturating himself with the poems, and the details of Keats's life, in full sympathy and understanding with one 'who unhappily had missed the *Spes phthisica* that has carried so many consumptives cheerfully to the very gates of the grave'. So in October on the centenary of Keats's birth, before the Hospital Historical Club he gave his appreciative account [1] of the man who 'is numbered among the inheritors of unfulfilled renown with Catullus and Marlowe, with Chatterton and Shelley, whom we mourn as doubly dead in that they died so young'.

But the many-sided Osler could turn from the sublime to the ridiculous, and though not given to throwing off fugitive verses he was guilty of doing so a month later when with the sonnet on Chapman's 'Homer' in his ears he paraphrased it in describing a well-remembered episode of the time. Politics in Baltimore was then at its very lowest ebb of unrighteousness. Both parties, no doubt, were equally bad and thoroughly boss-ridden, but the Democrats under the notorious Gorman happened to be in control; gangsters and 'repeaters' would invade precincts known to have a Republican majority and would see that sufficient Democratic votes were turned in to defeat their opponents.

[1] *Johns Hopkins Hospital Bulletin*, Jan. 1896.

Accordingly, a good many of the Hopkins men under H. A. Kelly's leadership constituted a reform party which volunteered to police the polls. Kelly himself chose the Marsh Market for his station, the very hot-bed of the troubles; and wearing a long ulster and knickerbockers he appeared, a marked man, amid the roughs and hoodlums of this 17th Ward, who were 'sicked on' by their local boss. A fight ultimately occurred, some one's jaw was fractured—not Dr. Kelly's—and it may suffice to say that the grip of the political ring was also broken; but all of this is merely to explain the following lines sent to the University President:

xi. 6. 95.

Dear Mr. Gilman, The Dean has been distributing these & has had the audacity to use my *nom-de-plume*, E. Y. D., which is copy-righted. Yours sincerely,

Wm Osler.

The Marsh Market

Nov. 5th.

(With apologies to the late Mr. Keats)

Much have I travelled in the realms of toughs,
And many dirty towns and precincts seen;
Round many a ward industrious have I been,
Which bears in fealty to the bosses hold.
Oft of one wide expanse had I been told
That wide-os'd Gorman ruled as his demesne;
Yet did I never breathe its pure serene
Till I heard Abel speak out loud and bold;
Then felt I like some watcher of the polls
When a repeater swims into his ken,
Or like stout Kelly when with eagle eyes
He stared at the Marsh Market—and all his men
Looked at each other with a wild surmise
And said—*Let us, too, vote again!*

E. Y. D.

The testimonial banquet to John S. Billings, referred to in an earlier letter and with which Osler and Weir Mitchell had the most to do, was held the last day of the month at the Hotel Bellevue, Philadelphia. During the course of the dinner, Mitchell, after a witty speech, presented the guest of honour with a silver box containing a cheque for $10,000, 'from 259 physicians of the United States and

Great Britain in grateful recognition of his services to medical scholars'; and after other speeches had been made Osler rose and stated that 'though Dr. Billings had left Washington, his counterfeit presentment would appear on the walls of the Library, for a sufficient fund had been raised for the purpose'.[1]

Many medical papers were published during the year, often on topics previously used for a clinical lecture or for some meeting at the hospital, the Maryland 'Faculty', or elsewhere. They need not be enumerated.[2] He had begun this December to write a number of short notes for the *Montreal Medical Journal*, entitled 'Ephemerides', six monthly instalments of which appeared in the next year.[3] These jottings consisted for the most part of comments on unusual cases which, in increasing numbers, were being brought to him for his opinion. In the introductory note he says:

> . . . A consultant's life is not without unpleasant features, chief among which is the passing of judgement on the unhappy incurables —on the cancerous, ataxics, and paralytics, who wander from one city to another. Few are able to receive the balm of truth, but now and again one meets with a cheery, brave fellow, who insists upon a plain, unvarnished statement of his prospects. Still more distressing are the instances of hopeless illness in which, usually for his friends' sake, the entire 'faculty' is summoned. Can anything be

---

[1] This portrait of Billings in full uniform and wearing the scarlet gown of an Oxford D.C.L. was painted by Miss Cecilia Beaux and hangs in the Surgeon-General's Library.

[2] Perhaps the most important of them was read before the Medical Society of the District of Columbia, entitled 'The Practical Value of Laveran's Discoveries' (*Medical News*, Phila., Nov. 23, 1895), in which he deals with vital statistics, reiterates the necessity of blood examinations, and states that an intermittent fever which resists quinine is not malarial. Another was his article 'On the Visceral Complications of Erythema Exudativum Multiforme' (*American Journal of Medical Sciences*, Dec. 1895, cx. 629–46), also known as Henoch's purpura, the first of a series of papers on the visceral lesions of the erythema group of skin diseases, a subject in which he for long was greatly interested.

[3] *Montreal Medical Journal*, Jan. 1896, xxiv. 518. In the course of these ephemeral notes he touched on a great variety of topics, and in one of them on 'Tobacco Angina' in the April issue he refers to his own indulgence in tobacco, which as a matter of fact was always in great moderation and was for the most part restricted to a post-prandial cigarette or two.

more doleful than a procession of four or five doctors into the sick man's room? Who does not appreciate Matthew Arnold's wish?—

> Nor bring to see me cease to live
> Some doctor full of phrase and fame,
> To shake his sapient head, and give
> The ill he cannot cure, a name.

How often under such circumstances has the bitterness of the last line occurred to me!

Towards the end of the year there had been absurd rumours of war arising from the dispute over the Venezuela-Guiana boundary, Mr. Cleveland at the time in no uncertain terms having called the attention of the British Government to what it regarded as a piece of American impertinence—namely the Monroe Doctrine. Osler, it may be recalled, during his sojourn in the States never became a naturalized citizen, and it is evident from his various letters that he always anticipated ending his days in Montreal. 'It would be an awkward business for me as I am still British to the core', he remarked in one of his letters, and the day after Christmas he wrote to Ogden:

> Dear O. Thanks for the delightful edition of Omar. I had not seen it. The sketch of 'Old Fitz' is charming. Your mother keeps wonderfully well & Bloodgood says the knee could not be better. I will send the Dover shortly—it comes out in the Jan. no of the Bulletin. I will send two or three reprints. Mrs Osler is very well. . . . we had a very quiet Xmas together. Willie went home. May comes out for a visit in January. Damn these politicians: if they raise a war, 'twill play the devil with me. I should go back & stand by the boys. Happy New Year.

But there was a pleasanter end for the year than this rumour of an international misunderstanding, for on December 28th his son Revere was born.

1896

'Mrs. Osler had a small boy last week—both are doing splendidly. We are of course delighted, and he looks a strong and durable specimen.' In this casual fashion, to his old friend of London days, he announced the birth of his son; but Schäfer knew full well how devoted he was to children and must have been able to read between the lines. Something of his feelings may be gathered from a letter of January 3rd from Mrs. Osler to the child's grandmother Osler, who at ninety years of age had had abundant experience with grandchildren—even great-grandchildren:

. . . You must please excuse the proud father if he leaves unsaid what you want to know, for he is really very much excited. On New Year's day he told me in the most solemn manner that he had not kissed the baby yet, but was going to then. Before he left last night he said he had kissed him five times. He brings all his medical friends up to look at him. . . . I hope you will be pleased to hear that we have decided to call him Edward Revere Osler. We were thinking very seriously of it, and Brit [B. B. Osler, who was in Baltimore on a visit] has clinched it by telling me that he knows you will approve. My youngest brother is Edward, and I am particularly attached to him. Willie is very anxious to have Revere in the name, and says it is more important to have a name the child will be satisfied with when he grows up, than to follow any great sentiment. At first I was quite anxious to call him Palmer Howard, but now I am more than content, as I hear that this will be the fifth generation of Edward Oslers, and I know that my brother will be very much pleased. Tell the little Auntie [Miss Jennette Osler] that Willie says she is to feel a particular share in the boy, as he will have her father's name. . . .

For the remainder of Osler's life, this boy, Revere, the source of his greatest happiness—and whose loss was his greatest sorrow—was uppermost in his father's mind, and in writing to his more intimate friends he never failed to make some reference to the child as 'Tommy' or 'Isaac' or 'Ike' or 'Egerton, Jr.'

On January 11th of this year the exercises were held commemorating the opening of the new hall (at 847 North Eutaw Street) of the Medical and Chirurgical Faculty. It was the first migration of the old Society which this comparative new-comer in Maryland medical circles had done so much to revivify. The month before, he had written to Dr. James Chadwick in Boston:

After many struggles the old Medical & Chirurgical Faculty of Maryland has at last secured a local habitation. They have a library of about 10,000 volumes, and we are very anxious to stir up the profession to take an interest in it, and to contribute more largely than they do. We propose to have at some time in January a formal opening, and I have been requested to ask whether you would not give a short address on a library, its use, and development? Any date in January which would be convenient to you we could arrange for the opening. If you come, of course you will be my guest, and I will ask the Trustees of the Faculty to meet you at dinner. Please do not say no, as you will never again have an opportunity of doing so good a piece of missionary work. The profession here needs to be stirred up a bit.

As orator of the occasion, Chadwick in his address on 'Medical Libraries' did what Osler had anticipated, stirred the old 'Faculty' to its depths, and the records of the occasion state that added enthusiasm was aroused 'when the speaker offered to make a contribution to the Faculty Fund if others present would do the same, and within a few minutes $3,500 was collected'. It may be presumed that this was the outcome of a conspiracy prearranged at 1 West Franklin Street.

The third-year clinical teaching for the fifteen survivors of the first entering class was by this time in full swing, and Osler's unusual gifts as an inspirer of youth began for the first time to be appreciated at their real worth. To be sure, in Montreal and Philadelphia these gifts had been apparent, as they had been during the preceding five years in Baltimore when he was restricted to graduate teaching; but from this time on, in control of his own clinic, his extraordinary talents had full play. His success lay far less in his thorough familiarity with his subject than it did in his knowledge of young men and of himself. This enabled him to impart something of what he knew in such fashion as inevitably to spur students to take every advantage of their opportunities—not the least of which was that they might be near him.[1]

[1] In the course of an address on March 22, 1920, given in Osler's memory at the Johns Hopkins University (the *Johns Hopkins Alumni Magazine*, 1921, ix. 296–313), William H. Welch, after discussing the qualities that gave Osler his dominant position in medicine ('at the time of his death he was probably the greatest figure in the medical world; the best known, the most influential, the most beloved'), says further that Osler's reputation, though founded on his scientific work, does not rest solely upon that work, but largely upon the inspiring and stimulating character of his clinical teaching. 'I doubt [he

To be sure, the students at this time were not yet in the wards, but a clinical laboratory had been built,[1] with T. B. Futcher in charge, and Osler had started his introductory 'observation clinics' which were held three mornings each week, in a room under Ward H, convenient to the dispensary. The accessories to these stimulating exercises were negligible—chairs informally grouped around a simple couch, a plain deal table, and Osler. Two or three patients selected by his assistants from the morning's ambulatory clinic were in turn brought in—cases the teacher had not seen—and his chief stress was laid on the methods of examination. 'Don't touch the patient—state first what you see; cultivate your powers of observation.' And there would be an informal running comment, practical, amusing, stimulating; with apt illustrations and allusions that served to fix indelibly on his hearers' minds the points of the lesson he desired to bring out. 'Strong, go to the library and bring me Vol. V of Guy's Hospital Reports, and you'll find an account of this on page—' &c. 'Jones, what have you read in French or German this week? Nothing? Well, report next time to the class from the last *Berliner Klinische Wochenschrift* what Ewald says bearing on this subject—' &c. And meanwhile, to the mystification of one who might be looking over his shoulder, '*James Bovell M.D. James Bovell M.D. M.R.C.P.*' is being scribbled across the blotter or pad beside him as he patiently awaits the response of some student labouring with a question.

Of late years there has been so much discussion, particularly in England, about the so-called unit system, that Osler's part in introducing it has been somewhat obscured. In his address, so frequently quoted, and given years later

says] whether the history of medicine records a man who had greater influence upon the students that came under his teaching. He inspired them with a remarkable devotion and loyal affection. He was their example. His life embodied his precepts, and his students cherished his words. "Cultivate peace of mind, serenity, the philosophy of Marcus Aurelius. Think not too much of to-morrow, but of the work of to-day, the work which is immediately before you."'

[1] 'Clinical Microscopy at the Johns Hopkins Medical School.' *British Medical Journal*, 1899, i. 69–70.

in England,[1] he described what at the time was a novel organization, in the following words:

The medical unit consisted of about seventy beds (the number gradually increased to above one hundred), a large out-patient department, and a clinical laboratory close to the chief wards. In charge was the head, *ex officio* Professor of Medicine in the university; a resident staff of first, second and third assistants (nominated by the professor), a fourth assistant in charge of the laboratory; and, in addition, four house physicians appointed annually. The first assistant, a man of experience, remained for some years, and in the absence of the chief was in complete control of the department. He had rooms in the hospital and was paid £200 a year, half by the hospital, half by the university. All of the assistants were engaged in teaching and were paid. The appointments were for no fixed period, and during the sixteen years of my control there were only five first assistants: Dr. Lafleur, now Professor of Medicine at McGill; Dr. Thayer, Professor of Clinical Medicine at the Johns Hopkins Hospital; Dr. Futcher, Associate Professor of Medicine at the Johns Hopkins Hospital; Dr. McCrae, Professor of Medicine at Jefferson College, Philadelphia; and Dr. Cole, at present Director of the hospital connected with the Rockefeller Institute. In each instance, these men had lived as junior and senior assistants in the hospital for seven, eight, or more years. . . .

I have always felt that the success which followed this experiment —for such it was in hospital work in the United States, at any rate— was due to the type of men we had as senior assistants in the various departments. We chose the best that were to be had; the nomination was in the hands of the chief of the department; they were given responsibility, encouraged to teach and to write, and their professional development was promoted in every way. An excellent plan, greatly favoured by the Director of the hospital, Dr. Hurd, was to allow the senior assistants every couple of years a vacation of from four to six months to go abroad for study. The out-patient section of the medical unit was in charge of a separate staff, usually men who had been senior assistants and had gone into practice in the city. There were three: each took two days a week and had his own staff of three or four assistants, and all were directly engaged in teaching. You may gather from this some idea of the size of a medical unit and of the number of men at work in it, at least twenty-three or twenty-four when I left the hospital. This may be said to be an impossible task for one man to control. Not at all: it is all a question of organization, of subdivision of labour, and of co-operation among workers and the introduction into a department of modern business methods.

[1] 'The Hospital Unit in University Work.' *Lancet*, Lond., 1911, i. 211–13.

But this quotation gives no picture of the man who moved on this background, except that it shows his instinctive tendency to give chief credit to others. One of the senior assistants of this day, W. S. Thayer, has given a foreground view of the man himself, in so far as such an elusive personality can be fastened to paper. In this sketch there is an account of the masterful working system Osler put into his life and maintained to the end, for he knew not idleness :

At 7 he rose ; breakfast before 8. At a few minutes before 9 he entered the hospital door. After a morning greeting to the Superintendent, humming gaily, with arm passed through that of his assistant, he started with brisk, springing step down the corridor towards the wards. The other arm, if not waving gay or humorous greetings to nurses or students as they passed, was thrown around the neck or passed through the arm of another colleague or assistant. One by one they gathered about him, and by the time the ward was reached, the little group had generally grown like a small avalanche.

The visit over, to the private ward. For the many convalescents, or the nervous invalid whose mind needed diversion from self, some lively, droll greeting or absurd remark or preposterous and puzzling invention, and away to the next in an explosion of merriment, often amid the laughing but vain appeals of the patient for an opportunity to retaliate. For those who were gravely ill, few words, but a charming and reassuring manner. Then, running the gauntlet of a group of friends or colleagues or students or assistants, all with problems to discuss, he escaped. How? Heaven only knows!

A cold luncheon, always ready, shortly after 1. Twenty minutes' rest in his room ; then his afternoon hours. At half past four, in the parlour opposite his consulting room, the clans began to gather, graciously received by dear 'Mrs. Chief', as Lady Osler was affectionately known. Soon 'the Chief' entered with a familiar greeting for all. It was an anxious moment for those who had been waiting long for the word that they had been seeking with him. After five or ten minutes he would rise, and perhaps beckon to the lucky man to follow him to his study. More often he slipped quietly from the room and in a minute reappeared at the door in his overcoat, hat in hand. A gay wave of the hand, 'Good-bye', and he was off to his consultations.

Dinner at 7 to which impartially and often, his assistants were invited. In the evening he did no set work, and retired early to his study where, his wife by the fire, he signed letters and cleared up the affairs of the day. Between 10 and 11 o'clock, to bed. Such were his days. Three mornings in the week he took at home for work. He utilized every minute of his time. Much of his summer vacation went to his studies. On railway, in cab, on his way to and from consultations, in tramway, and in the old 'bob-tailed' car that used to carry us to the hospital, book and pencil were ever in his hand, and wherever he was, the happy thought was caught on the wing and noted down. His ability at a glance to grasp and to remember the gist of the article that he read was extraordinary.

His power to hold the mastery of his time was remarkable. He escaped as by magic, but so graciously, so engagingly that, despair though one might, one could hardly be irritated. No one could speak consecutively to Osler against his will. How did he do it? I know not.[1]

As yet there was no fourth-year teaching, and he continued therefore with his exercises for the post-graduates, of whom there was always a goodly number. During this winter semester a series of clinical lectures[2] was delivered for their benefit on the subject of 'Angina Pectoris and Allied States'. This disease has victimized many celebrated people, and Osler related fully the well-known story of John Hunter's attacks which ended in his sudden death at St. George's Hospital following a fit of silent rage. He also cited instances in which the disease has shown hereditary or familial tendencies. Thus:

The best-known instance is that of the Arnold family. William Arnold, collector of customs of Cowes, died suddenly of spasm of the heart in 1801. His son, the celebrated Thomas Arnold of Rugby, whose case I will narrate to you shortly, died in his first attack. Matthew Arnold, his distinguished son, was a victim of the disease for several years, and died suddenly in an attack on Sunday, April 15, 1888, having been spared, as he hopes in his little poem called 'A Wish'—

. . . the whispering, crowded room,
The friends who come, and gape, and go;
The ceremonious air of gloom—
All that makes death a hideous show!

At the time of his death, the accounts which appeared in the *Lancet* and *British Medical Journal* were not clear as to the existence of attacks of angina. The various stages in the progress of his illness

---

[1] W. S. Thayer, 'Osler.' The *Nation*, N. Y., Jan. 24, 1920.

[2] Published serially in the *New York Medical Journal*, 1896, lxiv, Aug. 8th, 22nd, 29th, and Sept. 12th; and subsequently gathered with some additions in a volume, dedicated to W. T. Gairdner of Glasgow.

can be traced very well in his 'Letters', in which you will find an account of numerous attacks from May 1885 until the time of his death. . . .[1]

Always in great demand, such spare time as he had free from school and hospital duties was apt to be booked up long ahead. Early in January he wrote to J. G. Adami: 'I have an engagement for Friday the 24th which I could not possibly postpone as it is an address at one of the Philadelphia colleges,[2] the invitations for which are already out. I will speak to Mr. Gilman, though I am afraid in his present overworked state it is unlikely that he could afford the time.' Naturally enough, his own engagements often became complicated and he, too, was apt to be overworked. On April 14th he wrote to Simon Flexner:

> This is the devil's own luck! The invitation to the dinner & the Programme of the Med. Chir. Faculty came by the same mail, & I see we have the Diabetes discussion on that evening. Welch & I are both down for remarks & I do not see that we can get out of it—much as I should like to. We shall I suppose be able to get away by 9.30.

His active interest in the old Maryland society never flagged, nor did he permit anything to interfere with his regular attendance at its meetings, for this letter refers doubtless to the annual spring session held April 28th to May 1st, when he was elected President for the ensuing year. As stated, the Faculty—though at the price of a heavy mortgage—had moved to their new quarters on Hamilton Terrace, North Eutaw Street, where an old residence had been made over and a bookstack erected in

[1] On the fly-leaf of Osler's own copy of the lectures, published in monograph form, he subsequently inserted the paragraph from Lytton Strachey's 'Eminent Victorians' (1918, p. 211) describing Dr. Arnold's death.

[2] This alludes to a talk before the classes of the Medico-Chirurgical College (*Medical Bulletin*, Phila., 1896, xviii. 81–4) in which he drew an analogy between Addison's disease and Myxoedema and reported a case benefited by the use of suprarenal extract (cf. also *International Medical Magazine*, Feb. 1896). Similarly, he often gave sufficient time to the preparation of many of his undergraduate clinics to justify their subsequent publication. For example, his subject in one of the December clinics was Hemiplegia in Typhoid Fever (*Journal of Nervous and Mental Diseases*, N.Y., May 1896), and on Jan. 13th it was on Mitral Stenosis with Ball Thrombus in the Left Auricle, published a year later (March 1897) in the *Montreal Medical Journal*.

the rear, large enough to shelve, for a few years at least, its rapidly growing collection. Nor did his attendance flag at the Hopkins Society meetings, certain of which, particularly those of the Historical Club, would probably have lapsed had it not been for his untiring support. Historically minded physicians like James G. Mumford of Boston or Robert Fletcher, the editor of the *Index Medicus*, were certain to respond to his call,[1] and Osler's method was to collect for dinner, at the club or at 1 West Franklin Street, the nucleus of an audience, who somehow by tramcar were landed 'across town' on the dot of 8.15. Students and staff meanwhile had been rounded up in his amphitheatre —an easy task, be it said, for meetings which Osler and Welch attended brought students, whether the subject was directly concerned with their immediate studies or not. They knew, moreover, that these meetings would begin at the appointed hour, for the Chief lived up to his dictum —the primary requisite of a physician is punctuality.

On May 1st the Association of Physicians, with Abraham Jacobi as President, held its eleventh annual session. The four events of the meeting of chief historical interest were: the action taken protesting against the antivivisection legislation which shortly before had been introduced in Congress (Senate Bill, § 1552); the great number of articles on diphtheria, its toxin and antitoxin; Theobald Smith's paper differentiating human and bovine strains of the bacillus of tuberculosis; and the paper by Francis Hodder-Williams on the X-ray in Medicine. Röntgen's discovery announced the year before from his laboratory in Wurzburg was, from the outset, obviously adaptable to the diagnosis of many surgical lesions, but Dr. Williams's audience could hardly have realized when listening to his brief account of the fluoroscopic examination of an enlarged heart, of a case of pneumonia, and of two cases of pulmonary consumption, that the X-ray would become a diagnostic aid of such reliability in thoracic diseases that Auenbrugger and Laennec would soon have to make room for Röntgen on their

[1] Thus, on April 13th Fletcher gave a paper on the 'Witches' Pharmacopoeia', as he had done the year before on 'The Medical Lore of the Older English Dramatists'.

pedestal. Though in the discussion of Williams's paper Osler asked about the possible fluoroscopy of gall-stones, not even his imagination could foresee that the X-ray would have an effect on medicine almost as revolutionary as the gifts of just 100 and just 50 years before, namely, Jenner's vaccination and Morton's demonstration of surgical anaesthesia.

He must have gone, possibly in company with H. M. Hurd, immediately to Atlanta, where the Academy of Medicine, of which Hurd was President, met on May 4th. That afternoon the affiliated Association of Medical Colleges, together with the Association of State Board Examiners, listened to 'the introductory remarks of William Osler the presiding officer'—remarks which were said to have been 'given extemporaneously, in a charming and effective manner'—completely lost, be it said, in the abstract of the Proceedings subsequently published. This was preliminary to the annual meeting of the A. M. A., when 'Atlanta with flowing speeches of welcome and a Georgia barbecue greeted and entertained for three days a thousand or more physicians'; and when, as is also recorded, 'unity prevailed on nearly all questions except the perennial one of change of the Secretary'.[1] On the 6th Osler gave the general Address on Medicine, having chosen as his topic 'The Study of the Fevers of the South',[2] a by-product of which had been the discovery of the 'Alabama Student' already referred to. This stirring, timely, forceful address opened as follows:

Humanity has but three great enemies: fever, famine and war; of these by far the greatest, by far the most terrible, is fever. Gad, the seer of David, estimated aright the relative intensity of these afflictions when he made three days' pestilence the equivalent of three months' flight before the enemy, and of three (seven) [3] years of famine. As far back as history will carry us, in ancient Greece, in

---

[1] At this Atlanta meeting, resolutions signed by Osler and others protesting against the passage of Senate Bill § 1552 were introduced and passed.

[2] *Journal of the American Medical Association*, 1896, xxvi. 999–1004.

[3] The word which Osler has bracketed perhaps needs explanation. He took much for granted on the part of his reader, to whose hand, however, Cruden's Concordance may not be as conveniently near as it was to Osler's. There are two accounts of David's 'great strait': in 2 Sam. xxiv. 13, the years of famine are seven; and in 1 Chron. xxi. 12, they are three.

ancient Rome, throughout the Middle Ages, down to our own day, the noisome pestilence, in whatsoever form it assumed, has been dreaded justly as the greatest of evils.

From this he went on to say that one of the most conspicuous contributions of the century had been the differentiation of the continued fevers. He recalled the confusion that existed in the days of Benjamin Rush, who, representing the views of our grandparents, claimed there was but one fever—that all were correlated—that under different conditions yellow fever, malaria, typhus, and so on, could pass into one another. After his usual tribute to the American pupils of Louis, of whom Stillé alone survived, he went on to say that typhoid was—

. . . in the United States *the fever*, just as it was when the old New England physicians recognized its recurrence year after year with the fall of the leaves. Of no disease is the history better known; the measures for its prevention are everywhere recognized; the incidence of its occurrence is an unfailing index of the sanitary intelligence of a community. With good drainage, pure water and pure milk, typhoid fever goes the way of typhus and cholera. The greatest sanitary triumphs of the century have been in reducing to a minimum the mortality from this disease in the great centres of population in Europe. The mortality returns of Washington and of Baltimore, and of many smaller cities demonstrate that we are culpably negligent in allowing this most easily preventible disease to continue its ravages. I estimate that in the latter city there were during the year 1895 not less than 2,500 cases.

And he drew a most graphic picture of the bleedings and cuppings and purgings and blisterings of the early days of the century; but even then physicians were not all addicted to these measures, for he says: 'If I had typhoid fever and had a theosophic option as to a family physician I would choose Nathan Smith, nor would I care whether it was while he laboured in the flesh in the little town of Cornish, N. H., in 1798, or after he had become the distinguished Professor of Medicine in Yale.' He proceeded in no uncertain terms to condemn the antiseptic treatment of typhoid, then very much in vogue, and characterized the paper on the subject, which had recently appeared in the society's journal as a 'heterogeneous jumble unworthy the traditions of the profession or of a subject connected in this country with the names of Bartlett, Gerhard, James Jackson and Flint'. Towards the end of the address there occurs what for him was rather a gloomy prophecy—not about pestilence nor famine, but about the third great enemy of humanity which recent incidents had brought so near:

> For one only of the three great curses the close of the century brings no gleam of hope. It will be in another democracy, in another century, perhaps far distant, that the race will realize the earnest longing of the son of Amos, that 'nation shall not lift up sword against nation, neither shall they learn war any more'. The gradual growth of a deep sense of the brotherhood of man, such an abiding sense as pervades our own profession in its relation to the suffering, which recognizes the one blood of all the nations, may perhaps do it. In some development of socialism, something that will widen patriotism beyond the bounds of nationalism, may rest the desire of the race in this matter; but the evil is rooted and grounded in the abyss of human passion, and war with all its horrors is likely long to burden the earth.

On May 25th came the annual meeting of the Pediatric Society in Montreal, where he read a paper [1] in which he spoke of the lack of order or system in our classification of diseases, particularly of the nervous system, owing to our want of full knowledge concerning them; and he referred to the hopeless attempt made by 'Linnaeus, who found botany a chaos and left it a cosmos', to write a *genera morborum*. Osler usually gave rein to his spirits while in Montreal, and it may be assumed that all old friends were called upon, and that allusions may have been made to his and E. Y. D.'s former escapades. At all events, it is related that he played an outrageous prank on an unoffending and gullible Boston paediatrist and his wife who, with several other members of the society, were being entertained at lunch by his old friend Blackader. Osler, uninvited and unannounced, blew in towards the end of the meal, drew up a chair beside the Boston matron, asked what she had seen in Montreal and whether she had paid a visit to Caughnawauga. Finding the lady devoid of humour he was led on to describe an imaginary suburb of Montreal across the river—built by an American army surgeon,

[1] 'On the Classification of the Tics or Habit Movements.' *Archives of Pediatrics*, N.Y., Jan. 1897, xiv. 1–5.

E. Y. Davis—schoolhouses, parks, theatres, paved streets, a fine hospital for children—quite a wonderful place—but Davis, poor fellow, had a dreadful end—drowned in the rapids—drunk, they say. There doubtless was much more of this, to the great amusement of the table; but the unsuspecting Bostonians never quite forgave him, for, as was subsequently learned, they spent most of the afternoon in an effort to locate Caughnawauga.

On his return to Baltimore he is found pursuing a favourite historical subject, as the following letter of June 2nd shows. It indicates his flair for possible sources of material, for having learned that Dr. Amariah Brigham, the first Superintendent of the Utica State Hospital, had studied in Europe in the days of Louis and had left a journal of the period, he wrote to Dr. G. Alder Blumer (then of Utica) as follows:

I am interested in the Paris medical men between '20 and '40, particularly in Laennec and Louis, and I am looking up at odd intervals the history of the American students who were in Paris at that time, particularly with Louis. I thought perhaps Brigham's notes might contain something of interest. I wish you would ask his nephew. Many thanks for the copy of the Journal. We shall be awfully sorry to lose your cousin. He is a trump, and I think has stability enough to withstand even early success, which is such a cruelty to so many of us.

But such pursuits were restricted to 'odd intervals' indeed, for the American Neurological Association met in Philadelphia the next day; and at this gathering he read a paper on certain of the cerebral complications of Raynaud's disease,[1] in which subject he had long been interested. And so the spring had passed, 'very happy in my professional and college work', as he wrote his old Barrie schoolmate, 'Ned' Milburn; but it may be assumed that when all this gallivanting was over, 1 West Franklin Street without wife and baby proved an empty place, for they, meanwhile, had wisely fled to New England. However, July and August found the family reunited at The Glades Club, where the previous summer had been so agreeably spent.

To W. S. Thayer from W. O. Wednesday [July, 1896].

Dear Thayer, We reached here on Friday—after a very comfortable journey. I hope you have got on with the lectures. Miss H.

[1] *American Journal of the Medical Sciences*, 1896, cxii. 522.

told me that she wanted to get off for the last week of this month & return for the last week of Aug. I told her to arrange it with you. Give her all the dictation you can as she can finish any after her return Sept. 1st. I went to town [Boston] on Monday & saw several old friends at the library & the Tavern Club—Prince, Bowditch, Bullard & Reynolds. I have almost finished the angina lectures—which have extended into seven. I suppose they will be appearing soon. This is a fine spot, plenty of fresh air & the bathing is splendid. The past few days have been rather sweltering. Mr Egerton is flourishing—21 lbs. . . .

So the time was passed between work and play, interspersed with visits to his Boston friends—with Fitz at Beverly, with Bowditch in the 'new Public Library which is a paradise'. 'I am deep in golf', he writes, 'and take headers off the rocks twice daily.' In another letter to Thayer on August 14th he says:

We have been sympathizing with you all in this terrible heat—it has been a baking week here also—so still & moist too & the nights very bad. Fortunately the baby has not felt it at all. You must be used up. Get Smith to come up for a few days & 'mind shop' while you go off to Atlantic City. I too thought of Jacobs—he has age &c, & would I think like the job very much & moreover will have the time. He will be here in a few days & I will pump him as to plans. You & I could arrange the details on Saturday the 6th when I come back. I see you mention sailing on the 5th which would be all right. I could get down on Friday. It would be very nice to go over & see Jack [Hewetson] off. Better get the 3rd year schedule made out for Oct. & Nov. They could have in the two sections as you suggest 2 exercises weekly, independent of the regular class which for these months I could take at 12 instead of 11 on T. T. & S. We shall have to consider the other branches & not take an undue amount of time. Find out if they have anything on M. W. & F. at 11. One section could go then & the other at 11 T. T. & S. Then at 12 T. T. & S. I could talk & quiz for these two months before beginning our regular Dispensary hours. I think the quizzes should be more systematic. You arrange it as you think best. Ultimately you will be responsible for the 3rd year teaching I think. We must put thro. the Asso. Prof. for you & Barker in Sept. The matter came up in June & would have gone thro. all right but the meeting was so small that it was thought wiser to defer. Mrs Osler & Egerton send love to all. I hope Hurd has stood the heat—he should get off for a good rest.

During the last week of August he was in Toronto, possibly to see his brother Britton, who had not been well. At all events, from his brother's house on the 23rd he writes to Thayer again, saying: 'Get the additional things done as reasonably as possible. Our fund will stand it—if not my pocket will.' Needless to say, with his senior assistant abroad at the opening of the school year, he had abundant teaching on his hands, for in addition to what he had mapped out in his letter of August 14th for 'M. W. & F.', as well as 'T. T. & S.', the fourth-year students now came into the wards for the first time as clinical clerks. With them, and for a year or two with the graduates as well, until the undergraduate classes grew so large as to make this combination impossible, he regularly made his formal ward visits three mornings in the week from 9 to 11 for the next nine years. It was here, in the wards and at the bedside, that Osler was at his best. Something of his epigrammatic manner in driving home his views has been put into words by Thayer, as follows:

Observe, record, tabulate, communicate. Use your five senses. The art of the practice of medicine is to be learned only by experience; 'tis not an inheritance; it cannot be revealed. Learn to see, learn to hear, learn to feel, learn to smell, and know that by practice alone can you become expert. Medicine is learned by the bedside and not in the classroom. Let not your conceptions of the manifestations of disease come from words heard in the lecture room or read from the book. See, and then reason and compare and control. But see first. No two eyes see the same thing. No two mirrors give forth the same reflection. Let the word be your slave and not your master. Live in the ward. Do not waste the hours of daylight in listening to that which you may read by night. But when you have seen, read. And when you can, read the original descriptions of the masters who, with crude methods of study, saw so clearly. Record that which you have seen; make a note at the time; do not wait. 'The flighty purpose never is o'ertook, unless the deed go with it.' . . .[1]

'The flighty purpose'—these words were often on his lips, and he needed not with his familiars to finish the quotation. A subject would come up at table—the derivation of a word—the source of a quotation—an historical allusion, or what not—'The flighty purpose', he would say, and he himself or some one else would consult the necessary dictionary or

[1] W. S. Thayer: 'Osler the Teacher.' *Johns Hopkins Hospital Bulletin*, July 1919, xxx. 198–200.

return with a book of reference, so that a meal usually ended with volumes on the table or beside his chair.

Scraps of letters scribbled to Lafleur during these two strenuous months show that among other things he is getting his Angina Pectoris lectures ready for publication. 'We are very busy just now', he says; 'the teaching & wards keep us hard at work. I have recommended Thayer as assoc. Prof. & Barker has also been recommended by Mall. Egerton is a jewel—weighs 24½ lbs & is a lump of good nature.' And, on November 4th, again to Lafleur about an old hospital servant:

Wednesday.

Dear L. You will be very sorry to hear of the death of your old friend Gus. He slipt away on Sunday while sitting peacefully in his chair. He did not seem to have been ailing in any way. It really is a great blessing for the poor old fellow. I could not get to the funeral today as I was detained in Phila, but I sent some flowers, & a nice wreath or cross (I forget wh. Mrs Osler attended to it) from you as I knew you would like it. I hear that there are hosts of applicants for the R. V. If Miss Marion Smith of the Phila Hosp. Training School applies say a good word for her she is a trump.

And a week later to the same: 'Thanks for the 10 the balance of or all of which I will hand over to Mrs Gus for the kids if you do not mind, & I know you wont. Egerton sends love.'

On November 10th and 11th, he with Simon Flexner, Finney, and others from the Hopkins group attended the autumn meeting of the Maryland Faculty held in Hagerstown, Washington County. There Osler as presiding officer made a few sensible remarks to the effect that the Faculty was a State organization, not a Baltimore society; that it was coming rapidly into the possession of a good working library; and that a Nurses' Directory had been established, both of which the practitioners throughout the State should use. He also contributed to the programme by giving a paper on diffuse scleroderma—a rare condition and one which always interested him—whereas Dr. Flexner, who confesses to no recollection of ever having been at any such meeting, nevertheless must, as he admits, 'have performed some sort of antics'[1] because of this

[1] It was a demonstration of the recently discovered serum diagnosis (Widal) of typhoid fever adaptable to State Boards of Health. Much of the

characteristic note written from 1 West Franklin Street, Saturday evening, after their return:

Dear Flexner, You took the *cake* at the *walk* in Hagerstown. The demonstration was A.1. & did much good. Your presentation of the subject was greatly admired. Ellis & others were talking of it on the way down. Leave in my box tomorrow a memo of the Diener's expenses. Yours W. O.

The researches of the senior undergraduate students by this time were beginning to be reported at the Hopkins' meetings. All of them had a problem of one sort or another which usually overlapped the clinic and laboratory. Perhaps the most notable single piece of work was that by Opie and MacCallum upon the Malarial Infection of Birds, reported at the meeting of November 16th,[1] but there were others almost equally so, such as C. R. Bardeen's studies of the effect of burns, and T. R. Brown's discovery of eosinophilia in trichinosis which must have given particular gratification to Osler. The interest and enthusiasm of these bi-monthly meetings, held at the time in a basement under one of the wards—for the hospital as yet boasted no amphitheatre—can hardly be exaggerated. But this new spirit was not being felt at the Hopkins alone. One need only turn the pages of the *Maryland Medical Journal* to realize what Osler during his year as President of the Faculty managed to accomplish for the local profession. That he succeeded in arousing the venerable society from its lethargy, in fusing its divergent interests, in forcing it to take a definite stand on issues relating to public health, in elevating the standards of the profession among the practitioners of city and state, is nothing short of amazing. He even managed to enlist the interest of some prominent laymen in the needs of the old society and, accordingly, had been able at the Hagerstown meeting to announce a gift from the Frick brothers to endow a section of the library in memory of their brother, the late

meeting was given over to typhoid fever, which Osler persisted in bringing to the attention of the profession and the people. Baltimore at this time rejoiced in a 'new' State Board of Health, which had a $5,000-budget! when it needed half a million.

[1] *Johns Hopkins Hospital Bulletin*, Mar. 1897, viii, 51.

Dr. Charles Frick. It was a paltry sum of $1,000, to be sure, but it was a beginning, and Osler determined to make the very most of it as an example to others. Thus, on November 26th he wrote again to his friend Chadwick of Boston:

You cast your bread upon our waters & we are finding it daily. The impetus which your talk gave the old Faculty has done great good. The Fricks have fitted up a very nice room & have given us a good sum to buy new books. We shall have an opening of this new Frick Library on Dec. 10th. Could you be present with us. Chew [Samuel C.] will speak of the late Dr. Frick & one of his old friends Reverdy Johnson will also make a brief address.

Chadwick must have thought he had done enough for the Maryland profession by his address the year before; but, undeterred, Osler finally secured as speakers J. M. Da Costa, then President of the College of Physicians of Philadelphia, and Joseph A. Bryant, who similarly represented the New York Academy of Medicine. The meeting forms a landmark in the history of the institution, and the several committee reports made at the time show what a period of rejuvenation was being entered upon. After the speeches there were many reports—of the Book and Journal Club and the funds it had raised; of the enthusiastic young Librarian who had recently been appointed; of the new Nurses' Directory; of the Committee on General Sanitation organized to promote the cause of hygiene in Maryland by quickening an enlightened public interest in sanitation; of the committee appointed to secure a pure milk supply for Baltimore, and so on. How much of all this was due to Osler, who kept himself completely in the background, can be gathered from this letter from one of the older Baltimore physicians, sent the next day:

To W. O. from James Carey Thomas. 1822 Madison Avenue,
11th December, 1896.

Dear Dr. Osler,—I feel that I must tell you how beautifully you obliterated yourself in the exercises of last evening. Every thing we saw & heard was due to you—your influence & personal effort——& yet nobody was permitted to say so. May I be allowed to take this quiet method of throwing up my hat & shouting, Osler! Osler! long live Osler!!! Yours truly,

J. W. Carey Thomas.

CHAPTER XVII

1897–8

LETTERS, SCIENCE, AND PRACTICE

LITTERAE : SCIENTIA : PRAXIS. This was the legend inscribed under the panel of Linacre, Harvey, and Sydenham, his chief medical heroes, which by now had come from Acland to adorn his library mantel.[1] There was something of each of them in his own composition, and a future panel could well include Osler himself, with the addition of DOCTRINA in its legend. Whatever was interesting or novel in the cases brought to him, he was quick to observe, to investigate, to write about, to teach over. His carefully prepared clinics were often on subjects suggested by cases he had seen in consultation, and though he did not teach from his preparatory notes they often found their way into print. This was true, for example, of a clinical lecture given January 22nd on 'The Ball-valve Gall-stone in the Common Duct'[2]—a subject on which he had evidently been cogitating during the previous summer. It was one of his more important and original contributions—important both to physician and surgeon—and the combination of symptoms of intermittent jaundice with paroxysmal chills and fever, so often at the time mistaken for malaria but usually due to a single gall-stone imprisoned above the orifice of the duct, deserves being known as Osler's syndrome.

In a letter of February 4th to J. G. Adami, mentioning plans to entertain some British scientists expected in the autumn, he exclaims, 'What a year of meetings! We shall be used up with them. Foster writes that he is coming to Toronto—to Montreal too, I hope. They have asked me to give the address in medicine, deuced good of them!

[1] He had ordered a duplicate set, which was presented to the William Pepper Laboratory recently opened at the University Hospital in Philadelphia. Pepper must have written regarding them, for on Jan. 13th Osler replied: 'Drummond has sent me word with reference to the pictures. The Linacre was copied from the picture by Holbein; Sydenham from the one by Sir Peter Lely; Harvey from the painting by Cornelius Jansen [Janssen] in the College of Physicians.'

[2] Published in the *Lancet*, Lond., May 15, 1897, i. 1319–23.

The Fates.

W. S. Atropos — Wm. Lachesis — Howard. A. Clotho

I shall be delighted. The prospects are A.1 and we shall get many of the very best men.' Even thus early in the year it was evident that there was to be a surfeit of medical meetings, national and international. In many of them he participated from the same sense of duty which took him to the local societies of hospital, city, and state. Then too, appeals that he appear at such functions as the commencement exercises of the Training School for Nurses at the old Blockley Hospital, where he gave an address this same month, he found irresistible and if there were groans he concealed them well. He did not compose without effort, as the fragments of writing leading up to the successive drafts of his addresses bear testimony.

He had by this time come to give over his Saturday evenings to his fourth-year group of clinical clerks—a custom he continued throughout his entire Baltimore period. He had a definite routine for these evenings. Two students were invited in turn for dinner at 7 p.m.; the rest of the group came at 8 p.m., and gathered around the dining-room table. An hour was passed in a discussion of the week's work, each student being asked about his patients and his reading. Then over biscuits, cheese, and beer he would give an affectionate discourse on one or two favourite authors—perhaps Sydenham this week, Fuller or Milton the next—illustrated by early editions of their works. This was the Osler his pupils of Baltimore days best remember, and naturally at these informal gatherings he came to know them individually with a degree of intimacy unusual in these later days for one in his position.[1] In these surroundings he was at his best.

A few only of the formal meetings with which the year

[1] Dr. J. F. Mitchell, one of the fourth-year students in this spring of 1897, with a small camera took a photograph of the house staff, for which he had captured three of the chiefs (Halsted, Osler, and Kelly) who were posed in the centre of the picture. Dr. Mitchell subsequently had a separate enlargement made of these three figures, and one day, carrying a print of this, he encountered Osler in the hospital corridor. 'The Chief' scanned the picture a moment and promptly added an appropriate legend, saying: 'The obstetrician holds the distaff; the physician spins the thread; the surgeon cuts it off.' Under another copy he wrote 'Godliness—Sobriety—Respectability'.

was punctuated need be mentioned. Under the auspices of the Maryland 'Faculty' a conference of health officers from various parts of the state was held on February 17th–18th, for which John S. Fulton was in part responsible, though Osler was the prime mover. He had prevailed upon the Governor as well as his neighbour Cardinal Gibbons to attend; whereas the Attorney-General, Mr. Bonaparte, D. C. Gilman, and others had agreed to preside at the different sessions, thereby calling public attention to the meeting and its purposes. For though a bacteriologist, trained in Welch's laboratory, had finally been appointed to the local Health Board, it was still a dormant body and sorely needed the awakening which could only come from an enlightened public opinion. In the address of welcome Osler emphasized the five things on which the public needed guidance: a reorganized Board of Health, remodelled lunacy laws, proper milk inspection, proper control of water supplies, and a hospital for infectious diseases. One full session of the conference was given over to vital statistics, another to diphtheria, and a third on the last evening to typhoid fever, to which he contributed a brief paper [1] reiterating, in new and telling phrases, the difficulties of distinguishing in many cases without proper laboratory methods between typhoid, malaria, meningitis, and even pneumonia. 'Is there a typho-malarial fever? Yes, in the brains of the doctors, but not in the bodies of the patients.' And he went on to say that hereafter the Board of Health should return his blank to every physician who sent in such a diagnosis, asking for something better.

As an outcome of all this, the Maryland Public Health Association, with Dr. Fulton as its Secretary, was organized for the purpose of calling attention to sanitary measures throughout the state and thereby forcing reforms upon a timid and reluctant legislature. Mr. Gilman's subsequent comment upon the conference was that it was the most hopeful sign of progress seen in Maryland in twenty years. Nor was Osler's voice raised in the public-health campaign solely in the city of his adoption. A few days later (Feb. 22nd)

[1] 'The Disguises of Typhoid Fever.' *Maryland Medical Journal*, 1897, xxxvi. 423.

in an address[1] before the Medical Society of the County of New York, he made an appeal for more accurate studies of malaria. 'North of Mason & Dixon's line [he said] physicians are prone to diagnose malaria for other diseases; south of the line they are more prone to diagnose other diseases for malaria; in both regions it is a source of greater errors in vital statistics than any other affection.'

In turn came the annual meeting of the state society, held on April 27th, when he discussed 'The Functions of a State Faculty', in his presidential address. The old society, nearing its centennial anniversary, shared, as he pointed out, the designation 'Faculty'—now used for a group of teachers rather than of practitioners—with but one other similar body, namely the Faculty of Physicians and Surgeons of Glasgow. He emphasized that the society by its act of incorporation had a dual function—that of a licensing body, now given up, and a means whereby the advances in medical knowledge could be disseminated throughout the State of Maryland. The chief weakness of the profession he said lies in its tendency to break 'into cliques and coteries, the interests of which take precedence over others of wider and more public character'; from this a baneful individualism is likely to arise, with every man for himself—'a centrifugalizing influence against which this Faculty is and has been the only enduring protest'. And with expressions reminiscent of those he had used in his Montreal days in regard to the importance of medical meetings, he said:

> No class of men needs friction so much as physicians; no class gets less. The daily round of a busy practitioner tends to develop an egoism of a most intense kind, to which there is no antidote. The few setbacks are forgotten, the mistakes are often buried, and ten years of successful work tend to make a man touchy, dogmatic, intolerant of correction, and abominably self-centred. To this mental attitude the medical society is the best corrective, and a man misses a good part of his education who does not get knocked about a bit by his colleagues in discussions and criticisms. . . .

Then in regard to the educational function of the Faculty's

[1] 'The Diagnosis of Malarial Fever.' *Medical News*, N.Y., Mar. 6, 1897, lxx. 289–92.

library, to which he had already given and continued to give so much time and labour, he said :

> Books are tools, doctors are craftsmen, and so truly as one can measure the development of any particular handicraft by the variety and complexity of its tools, so we have no better means of judging the intelligence of a profession than by its general collection of books. A physician who does not use books and journals, who does not need a library, who does not read one or two of the best weeklies and monthlies, soon sinks to the level of the cross-counter prescriber, and not alone in practice, but in those mercenary feelings and habits which characterize a trade. . . .

During the first week in May, the fourth of the triennial Congresses of the Special Societies was held in Washington, under the presidency of William H. Welch, who gave at the time his notable address on ‘ Adaptation in Pathological Processes ’. One of the general meetings which brought all the societies together was given over to the subject of the Internal Secretions, and W. H. Howell, R. H. Chittenden, J. George Adami, James J. Putnam, Francis P. Kinnicutt, and Osler were the participants.[1] That such a session as this should have been held is interesting historically, in that it marks the beginning of the extraordinary period of professional interest in the ductless glands, an interest which has grown to such proportions—indeed to such disproportions—as to have a dominating influence, under the comprehensive name of ‘ endocrinology ’, on many of the present-day conceptions not only of certain obscure diseases but of human types presumably normal both physically and mentally.

For his part in this symposium Osler reverted once more to the subject of Sporadic Cretinism in America, with which he had formerly dealt in 1893 when he was cognizant of only eleven cases. But he was now able to present

[1] At the Congress, Osler appears to have spent most of his time with the physicians, before whom he read on ‘ The Hepatic Complications of Typhoid Fever ’, emphasizing the relation of gall-stones to typhoid infections, a subject just then exciting great interest. He also gave a paper before the paediatrists on ‘ Adherent Pericardium in Children ’; but as this does not appear in the Transactions he probably had been so swamped by the elaborate study of Cretinism that he failed to finish it for publication.

abstracts of sixty examples of this extraordinary malady, of which he painted this graphic picture :

No type of human transformation is more distressing to look at than an aggravated case of cretinism. It recalls Milton's description of the Shape at the Gates :

> If shape it might be called, that shape had none
> Distinguishable in member, joint or limb,

or those hideous transformations of the fairy prince into some frightful monster. The stunted stature, the semi-bestial aspect, the blubber lips, retroussé nose sunken at the root, the wide-open mouth, the lolling tongue, the small eyes, half closed with swollen lids ; the stolid expressionless face, the squat figure, the muddy, dry skin, combine to make the picture of what has been well termed 'the pariah of nature'. Not the magic wand of Prospero or the brave kiss of the daughter of Hippocrates ever affected such a change as that which we are now enabled to make in these unfortunate victims, doomed heretofore to live in hopeless imbecility, an unspeakable affliction to their parents and to their relatives. . . .

And at the conclusion, before showing his lantern slides he said :

That I am able to show you such marvellous transformations, such undreamt-of transfigurations, is a direct triumph of vivisection, and no friend of animals who looks at the 'counterfeit presentments' I here demonstrate will consider the knowledge dearly bought, though at the sacrifice of hundreds of dogs and rabbits.

He had good reasons for the insertion of this timely statement. For the antivivisection bill under Senator Gallinger's control, which had been before the United States Senate for more than a year, had for a second time been reported favourably out of Committee. Dr. Samuel C. Busey and Surgeon-General Sternberg had expressed the opinion before the business meeting of the Congress that those residing in the District of Columbia were powerless to combat the existing trend of opinion in the Senate, and that pressure would have to be brought to bear by the voting population in other parts of the country.[1] It was

[1] Public opinion had for years been largely fed by Mr. Mitchell, the Editor of *Life*, who for some unaccountable reason made the doctors the chief target of his wit and satire. Some of this was amusing, some of it deserved, and all of it could be endured by a profession which had survived Molière. But it was a different matter when, as champion of the anti-

left with Welch, the President of the Congress, to appoint a committee to act on this proposal, and he did the unusual thing of putting himself on the committee and subsequently of assuming the chief burden of its activities. In view of Osler's testimony two years later the story touches him sufficiently to justify a statement here of the essential facts.

Propaganda on the part of those opposed to medical research had been indulged in more or less continuously since the '60's, and frequent bills opposed to the use of animals for experimentation had been introduced into various state legislatures—always without success. As the result of these agitations, resolutions protesting against any legislative interference with experimental research had from time to time been passed by various of the leading medical and scientific societies. But a more serious attack than any before had been made early in 1896, when what was known as Senate Bill § 1552 was introduced in Congress by Senator Gallinger under the misleading title of 'A Bill for the Further Prevention of Cruelty to Animals in the District of Columbia'. The real significance of the bill, which had been fostered by a group of antivivisectionists of the District, had been unsuccessfully camouflaged by its innocent-sounding title, and because of protests a hearing was called. The hearing, however, was a hurried one; the natural opponents of the measure, like the Surgeon-General, were given scant notice; the bill, slightly modified, was presented out of Committee to the Senate, and might have passed but for the outcry on the part of most of the medical and scientific societies, as well as educational institutions of the country.[1]

We knew nothing [writes Professor Welch] about the first Gallinger bill until it had been reported favourably, and unanimously so, by the Committee on the District of Columbia, and it would un-

---

vivisection controversy, he saw fit in outrageous cartoons to hold up physiologists like Osler's friends Bowditch and H. C. Wood to public abuse and misrepresentation. In an open letter of Oct. 21, 1895, describing these attacks as 'venomous and malicious', Osler repudiated *Life* and withdrew his subscription. To this Mr. Mitchell replied in an unwise editorial over which a curtain may be drawn now that *Life* has atoned for its unfortunate antivivisection attitude of the past.

[1] Cf. Senate Document § 31, 54th Congress, second session, 1896.

doubtedly have passed if we had not bestirred ourselves. It was then that Osler and I spent an entire evening in his house in Washington with Senator Gorman, who promised to have himself placed on the Committee and to keep the bill in Committee. He said we would have to prepare a speech for him, if the bill got before the Senate. It never did. . . . The next session, a somewhat amended bill was introduced and it was then that I gave so much time—the better part of a winter—to organizing the profession in each State in opposition. I was then President of the Congress of Physicians and Surgeons, and acted more or less officially in that capacity. I think this was as critical a time for animal experimentation as had occurred in this country.

The second bill, to which this letter refers, known as Senate Bill § 1063,[1] was little more than the original bill with slight changes in form but not in purpose. Promises of votes sufficient to secure its defeat were obtained through the family physicians or influential constituents of a number of Senators, and President Cleveland, indeed, promised to veto it if it ever reached him. A third and last attempt by Senator Gallinger to get action upon this ill-considered legislation was made two years later, as will be seen.

The Washington Congress was the first in order of a succession of spring meetings, some of which Osler attended, and to others he sent his assistants. Moreover, two important British associations were to meet in Canada in the autumn, as he indicates in this note:

To Edward A. Schäfer from W. O. 1 West Franklin Street, May 14.

The 2nd edition of the Histology which I have received this week was welcomed as an old friend. I have looked it over with great interest, not too without regrets since I now have travelled so far from my first love. Appletons will send you in a week or ten days a little volume of Lectures on Angina Pectoris—a disease which has interested me deeply for several years. I wish that we could

---

[1] Cf. 'Objections to the Antivivisection Bill now Before the Senate'. William H. Welch. *Journal of the American Medical Association*, Feb. 5, 1898. It is related in the Introduction to vol. v of Allbutt's 'System of Medicine' [1898] that the volume had been delayed because one of the chief contributors [Welch] had been unable to prepare his chapter for the reason that he had been spending six months in a campaign against an American antivivisection bill, the more difficult to defeat because the passage of a similar bill in England some years before had been permitted.

visit England this year but I must be in Toronto at the Meeting of the B.A.A.S. and then at Montreal for the B.M.A. I was sorry to hear that you cannot come out, but I suppose it is impossible. You have to be now both father and mother to the children. Mrs. Schäfer and Jack's photos in the little case she gave me, are on the mantel-piece.

I have just had a tempting offer from New York—the Dept of Medicine in the United Schools—University & Bellevue—at £2,000 salary, with of course splendid prospects for consultation work. I have however such exceptional facilities here and we are so comfortable that I have declined. My small boy, now 16 mos. is a very fine specimen.

The nurses' graduation exercises at the Hopkins came on the 3rd of June, and Osler read the address on 'Nurse and Patient',[1] which did not entirely please those members of the nursing profession who took themselves too seriously. Any one knowing Osler's peculiarities on the few occasions when he was sufficiently ill to have a trained nurse forced upon him, can but smile at re-reading these lines:

The trained nurse as a factor in life may be regarded from many points of view—philanthropic, social, personal, professional and domestic. To her virtues we have been exceeding kind—tongues have dropped manna in their description. To her faults—well, let us be blind, since this is neither the place nor the time to expose them. I would rather call your attention to a few problems connected with her of interest to us collectively—and individually too, since who can tell the day of her coming.

Is she an added blessing or an added horror in our beginning civilization? Speaking from the point of view of a sick man, I take my stand firmly on the latter view, for several reasons. No man with any self-respect cares to be taken off guard, in mufti, so to speak. Sickness dims the eye, pales the cheek, roughens the chin, and makes a man a scarecrow, not fit to be seen by his wife, to say nothing of a stranger all in white or blue or gray. Moreover she will take such unwarrantable liberties with a fellow, particularly if she catches him with fever: *then* her special virtues could be depicted by King Lemuel alone. So far as she is concerned you are again in swathing bands, and in her hands you are, as of yore, a helpless lump of human clay. She will stop at nothing, and between baths and spongings and feeding and temperature-taking you are ready to cry with Job the cry of every sick man—'*Cease then*, and let me alone.'

---

[1] Reprinted as No. IX in 'Aequanimitas and other Addresses'.

For generations has not this been his immemorial privilege, a privilege with vested rights as a deep-seated animal instinct—to turn his face towards the wall, to sicken in peace, and, if he so wishes, to die undisturbed? All this the trained nurse has, alas! made impossible.

Certainly there was little dropping of manna or giving out of bouquets in this address, as unlike the perfunctory one usually given on such occasions as could well be, filled as it is with warnings and counsels to those who have come to take their place beside the physician and priest. And he ended by cautioning trained nurses against the benumbing influence of institutional life which, for many, dulls the fine edge of sympathy; and advised 'the practice towards patients of the Golden Rule as announced by Confucius: "What you do not like when done to yourself, do not do to others," so familiar to us in its positive form as the great Christian counsel of perfection, in which alone are embraced both the law and the prophets.'

Two weeks later, on June 15th, came the commencement exercises of the first graduating class from the medical school, fifteen in all, the majority of whom were to remain another year as house officers or as assistants in one or another of the laboratories. A group of these students had organized what was known as 'The Pithotomy Club', a term which indicates the making of a hole in a keg, and there had been festive occasions with song and refreshments in which students and teachers had participated, and in which the foibles of the teachers in particular were not spared in burlesque. Those were indeed informal days at the Hopkins.

With his first assistant away—for Thayer had gone to Moscow to attend the XIIth International Medical Congress that summer—and with some addresses to write for meetings to come in the autumn, he appears to have stayed on in Baltimore for a part of July, while Mrs. Osler, with Revere and the boy's coloured 'Mammy', visited her friends in Wilkesbarre. He subsequently joined them at his brother's house in Toronto; but it was a torrid summer, the boy was teething, and they proceeded to Montreal, whence Sir William van Horn sent them on comfortably in his private car to St. Andrews, New Brunswick, where they had made arrangements for a cottage.

During this month of July, with the aid of a medical dictionary, a copy of Osler's Text-book was being read word for word by a layman passing his summer in the Catskill Highlands—an event of far greater importance to medicine and of greater biographical importance than the mere happenings of Osler's own summer vacation in New Brunswick. This gentleman happened to be the member of John D. Rockefeller's philanthropic staff who was successful in directing his interests towards medical research, and as Osler's volume was an essential link in this process, the story deserves telling here in his own words, though five years elapsed before Osler knew of the incident.

In the early summer of 1897 my interest in medicine was awakened by a . . . Minneapolis boy who in his loneliness in New York used often to spend his week-ends with us in Montclair. His deceased father had been a homeopathic physician but he himself was studying in the regular school. I determined as a result of my talks with this enthusiastic young student to make myself more intelligent on the whole subject of medicine, and at his suggestion I bought a copy of Dr. Osler's 'Principles and Practice of Medicine'. . . . I read the whole book without skipping any of it. I speak of this not to commemorate my industry or intelligence but to testify to Osler's charm, for it is one of the very few scientific books that are possessed of high literary quality. There was a fascination about the style itself that led me on, and having once started I found a hook in my nose that pulled me from page to page, and chapter to chapter, until the whole of about a thousand large and closely printed pages brought me to the end.

But there were other things besides its style that attracted and intensified my interest. . . . To the layman student, like me, demanding cures, and specifics, he had no word of comfort whatever. In fact, I saw clearly from the work of this thoroughly enlightened, able and honest man, perhaps the foremost practitioner in the world, that medicine had—with the few exceptions above mentioned—no cures, and that about all that medicine up to 1897 could do was to suggest some measure of relief, how to nurse the sick, and to alleviate in some degree the suffering. Beyond this, medicine as a cure had not progressed. I found further that a large number of the most common diseases, especially of the young and middle-aged, were infectious or contagious, caused by infinitesimal germs that are breathed in with the atmosphere, or are imparted by contact or are taken in with the food or drink or communicated by the incision of insects in the skin.

I learned that of these germs, only a very few had been identified and isolated. I made a list—and it was a very long one at that time, much longer than it is now—of the germs which we might reasonably hope to discover but which as yet had never been, with certainty, identified; and I made a longer list of the infectious or contagious diseases for which there had been as yet no cure at all discovered.

When I laid down this book I had begun to realize how woefully neglected in all civilized countries and perhaps most of all in this country, had been the scientific study of medicine. . . . It became clear to me that medicine could hardly hope to become a science until it should be endowed, and qualified men could give themselves to uninterrupted study and investigation, on ample salary, entirely independent of practice. . . . Here was an opportunity for Mr. Rockefeller to become a pioneer. This idea took possession of me. The more I thought of it the more interested I became. I knew nothing of the cost of research; I did not realize its enormous difficulty; the only thing I saw was the overwhelming and universal need and the infinite promise, world-wide, universal, eternal. Filled with these thoughts and enthusiasms, I returned from my vacation on July 24th. I brought my Osler into the office at No. 26 Broadway, and there I dictated for Mr. Rockefeller's eye a memorandum in which I aimed to show to him the actual condition of medicine in the United States and the world as disclosed by Dr. Osler's book. I enumerated the infectious diseases and pointed out how few of the germs had yet been discovered and how great the field of discovery; how few specifics had yet been found and how appalling was the unremedied suffering. I pointed to the Koch Institute in Paris. I pointed out the fact, first stated by Huxley I think, that the results in dollars or francs of Pasteur's discoveries about anthrax and on the diseases of fermentation and of the silkworm had saved for the French nation a sum far in excess of the entire cost of the Franco-German War. I remember insisting in this or some subsequent memoranda that even if the proposed institute should fail to discover anything, the mere fact that he, Mr. Rockefeller, had established such an institute of research, if he were to consent to do so, would result in other institutes of a similar kind, or at least other funds for research being established, until research in this country would be conducted on a great scale; and that out of the multitudes of workers we might be sure in the end of abundant rewards, even though those rewards did not come directly from the institute which he might found.

These considerations took root in the mind of Mr. Rockefeller and, later, of his son. Eminent physicians were consulted as to the feasibility of the project, a competent agent was employed to secure the counsel of specialists on research, and out of wide consultation the Rockefeller Institute of Medical Research came into being. It had its origin in Dr. Osler's perfectly frank disclosure of the very narrow limitations of ascertained truth in medicine as it existed in 1897.[1]

All unconscious of what was taking place at No. 26 Broadway, Osler from St. Andrews was sending scraps of letters to various people to the effect that he had invited Richet to stay with him; that he had arranged for Bowditch and the Fosters; that his nephew would not be back, so another small room would be free; that he would reach Toronto 'Tuesday eve' which presumably was August the 17th. All this was in preparation for the British Association for the Advancement of Science, which after a thirteen-year interval met for a second time in Canada this hot summer. Mrs. Osler, possibly mindful of a B.M.A. meeting in Nottingham a few years before, preferred to go with the baby to her mother in Canton, while her gregarious husband, indifferent to crowds and heat, entertained a houseful of guests in his brother Britton's abode in Toronto. The meeting (August 18th–21st) was memorable for one thing at least, and this was registered in terms of the thermometer so high that frock-coated Englishmen with top hats were reduced to mopping their brows and appearing in the streets in their shirt-sleeves. There were many notable guests and many old friends; but of all, Lister, just elevated to the peerage, President of the Royal Society, President also of the Association, was the outstanding figure, and Osler must have been gratified to have him pay special attention to an exhibit in Ramsay Wright's lecture-room by one of the newly fledged Hopkins graduates, W. G. MacCallum, of a discovery he had made while studying the malarial parasite of crows.

There followed a week's intermission before the Montreal meeting, which gave the foreign guests an opportunity to enjoy the beauties of Upper Canada, though probably none of them made a pilgrimage to Weston or Bond Head, for by now the forests had retreated well north of the Muskoka Lakes, where Lister apparently was taken. Osler

[1] From unpublished archives which deal with the early history of the Rockefeller Institute, through the kindness of Mr. F. T. Gates.

meanwhile had rejoined his family, and from Canton on August 28th wrote to his absent assistant:

Dear Thayer, I hope you have had a jolly & profitable time. We saw in the cable dispatches that you had been presented to the Czar at Peterhof. I write to catch you in London. Draw on me the National Union Bank of Baltimore for the $200. I have arranged it. You will need it I am sure. Everything seems smooth at the J. H. H. Camac is engaged & leaves in Oct. This will put McCrae in his place—lucky we have so good a man. MacCallum has a great find in the crows blood—conjugation of organisms—the flagella definitely penetrating certain bodies which undergo changes &c. It seems quite straight & will of course be most important. His paper was very well received. Lister moved the vote of thanks & spoke most appreciatively of the work. We have been at St. Andrews, delightful spot. I go to Montreal for the meeting & then on the 4th to Baltimore. Mrs Osler & Ike are very well & send love. . . .

Apparently he left the same evening for Montreal, for on the following day, Saturday, he sent word to Adami regarding the houseful of friends being gathered at the home of his former colleague, Gardner:

I have not made any arrangement for Welch. Gardner offered me four rooms which I have filled with J. C. Wilson, F. C. Shattuck, Fitz and Musser. I shall also be there. G. may be able to give another room. He is asking Chadwick and one or two others I believe. G. will be here next week, and I can arrange it if you have not seen him meanwhile.

It was the first time in its sixty-four years of existence that the British Medical Association had ventured to hold one of its meetings overseas, but, taken in combination with the meeting in Toronto of the science association of which Lister was President, a large attendance from Great Britain was guaranteed. T. G. Roddick, Professor of Surgery at McGill, one of the dinner-club members of Osler's Montreal days, was President of the 'B.M.A.', but Lister of course figured largely in the proceedings, and the old Medico-Chirurgical Society gave a special dinner in his honour. Also, from beginning to end, another old friend, the Chancellor of the University, Lord Strathcona and Mount Royal—he who had been Sir Donald Smith a few days before—lent his presence to the more important general sessions. At one of these, on Wednesday, September 1st, came Osler's address, a feature of the week's ceremonies, in which, speaking more as a Canadian than an American, he dwelt on 'certain of the factors which have moulded the profession in English-speaking lands beyond the narrow seas—of British Medicine in Greater Britain'.[1]

Evolution [he said] advances by such slow and imperceptible degrees that to those who are part of it the finger of time scarcely seems to move. Even the great epochs are seldom apparent to the participators. During the last century neither the colonists nor the mother country appreciated the thrilling interest of the long-fought duel for the possession of this continent. The acts and scenes of the drama, to them detached, isolated and independent, now glide like dissolving views into each other, and in the vitascope of history we can see the true sequence of events. That we can meet here to-day, Britons on British soil, in a French province, is one of the far-off results of that struggle. This was but a prelude to the other great event of the eighteenth century: the revolt of the colonies and the founding of a second great English-speaking nation—in the words of Bishop Berkeley's prophecy, 'Time's noblest off-spring'. Surely a unique spectacle, that a century later descendants of the actors of these two great dramas should meet in an English city in New France! Here the American may forget Yorktown in Louisbourg, the Englishman Bunker Hill in Quebec, and the Frenchman both Louisbourg and Quebec in Châteauguay; while we Canadians—English and French—in a forgiving spirit, overlooking your unseemly quarrels, are only too happy to welcome you to our country—this land on which and for which you have so often fought.

When and where the writing was done, far less the collateral reading,[2] is not apparent, but in all probability it followed the receipt of Acland's panel, for after drawing a comparison between Hellas and her colonies and England and hers, the address was largely woven about Linacre, the type of literary physician to whom was largely due the revival of Greek learning in England in the sixteenth century; Harvey, practitioner and hospital physician, as well as experimental scientist; and Sydenham, the model of the practical physician of modern times.

[1] Reprinted as No. X in 'Aequanimitas and other Addresses', 1904.

[2] He had been reading things as unrelated as 'The Life of Thomas Wakley', Hooker's 'Ecclesiastical Polity', Hawthorne's 'Scarlet Letter', Parkman's 'Jesuits in North America', 'The History of Aryan Medical Science', 'In the Days of the Canada Company', and the 'Breakfast Table' series.

A Physician [he went on to say] may possess the science of Harvey and the art of Sydenham, and yet there may be lacking in him these finer qualities of heart and head which count for so much in life. Pasture is not everything, and that indefinable though well-understood something which we know as breeding is not always an accompaniment of great professional skill. Medicine is seen at its best in men whose faculties have had the highest and most harmonious culture. The Lathams, the Watsons, the Pagets, the Jenners, and the Gairdners have influenced the profession less by their special work than by exemplifying those graces of life and refinements of heart which make up character. And the men of this stamp in Greater Britain have left the most enduring mark,—Beaumont, Bovell and Hodder in Toronto; Holmes, Campbell and Howard in this city; the Warrens, the Jacksons, the Bigelows, the Bowditches and the Shattucks in Boston; Bard, Hosack, Francis, Clark and Flint of New York; Morgan, Shippen, Redman, Rush, Coxe, the elder Wood, the elder Pepper, and the elder Mitchell of Philadelphia—Brahmins all, in the language of the greatest Brahmin among them, Oliver Wendell Holmes—these and men like unto them have been the leaven which has raised our profession above the dead level of a business.

Nor did he forget to mention Father Johnson in connexion with a lament that medicine had become severed from the old-fashioned natural history. And there was much more of equal and greater interest, as he traced with a sure historical perspective the development, and portrayed the conditions of the profession in America and the British colonies. September 4th, according to his programme, found him back in Baltimore, and though he had pledged himself for another formal address which must be written, nevertheless he appeared ten days later in Ocean City for the autumn meeting of the Maryland 'Faculty', where he read a paper on haemorrhage in typhoid fever. A day later he left for Boston, as told in the following note written from the Maryland Club on the 16th to Palmer Howard's younger son, who was just entering McGill:

Dear Campbell, Just a line to wish you good luck and God-speed in your Medical work. The hopes of all your father's dear friends are set on you. I know you will work steadily and surely. Let me know of any of your troubles and worries. I should like to stand to you in the same relation your father did to me. I can never repay what he did in the way of example and encouragement. Aunt Grace is not yet back. I am going to Boston tonight to see her.

As a result of this visit, having been called to see a patient in Nahant, he was exposed while driving across the Nahant Neck and came down with one of his periodical bronchial attacks which, occasionally verging on pneumonia, subsequently came to cause his friends so much anxiety and of which ere long he began to make some personal observations, jotted down in his account-book.

There were two topics, it may be noted, on which he particularly dwelt year after year in his fourth-year instruction—pneumonia and typhoid—for he felt that if these two diseases, one primarily thoracic and the other primarily abdominal, were thoroughly understood by the students, it would give them a satisfactory foundation on which to build their later experience. Accordingly, during the autumn and winter semesters every case entering the hospital was listed under the patient's name on the ample blackboard in his clinical amphitheatre, and the subsequent complications and ultimate issue of the disease were added, so that the students came to know these cases almost as intimately as if they had been private patients of their own. The exercises in connexion with these topics, as the course progressed, led Osler frequently into print: as, for example, in his paper 'On Certain Features in the Prognosis of Pneumonia', published early in this year, where he analysed the mortality of the first 124 cases of pneumonia which had been admitted to or had developed in the hospital. He said: 'No other disease kills from one-fourth to one-third of all persons attacked'; and 'so fatal is it, that to die of pneumonia in this country is said to be the natural end of elderly people'.

1 West Franklin Street saw a succession of guests during the early weeks of the autumn term, members of the B. M. A. or B. A. A. S. who had drifted down after the Toronto and Montreal meetings. 'I do wish you would come on here and stay a couple of weeks', he would write. 'You can breakfast at 10, play with Ikey till 12, spend a couple of hours in the laboratory with Futcher & amuse yourself the rest of the day.' The burden, of course, fell on the willing shoulders of the mistress of the house, who, fortunately, amused by the circus which revolved around

them, played her rôle with an imperturbability matching his own. Somehow, despite school duties, a speech at the opening of the new hospital of the University of Maryland, and other calls, he managed to compose another important address, delivered on October 19th at New York, on 'Internal Medicine as a Vocation'.[1] In this he set out to emphasize the fact that the student of internal medicine cannot be a specialist; and he proceeded to explain what elements in his estimation went to make the great physician—men of the type of Austin Flint, of James Jackson, and Jacob Bigelow. He warned the New Yorker against the besetting sin of '*Chauvinism*, that intolerant attitude of mind which brooks no regard for anything outside his own circle and his own school'. And he recommended the breadth of view which only comes from travel, though not heedless of the truth of Shakespeare's sharp taunt:

> How much the fool that hath been sent to Rome
> Exceeds the fool that hath been kept at home.

The address might almost be transcribed as an autobiographical sketch, so closely does it reflect his own *modus vivendi*. Visualizing a young Lydgate, who does not get entangled in the meshes of specialism and whose object is to become a pure physician, he took him through what Sir Andrew Clark had spoken of as the three stages—the dry-bread period, the bread-and-butter period, and the period of cakes-and-ale. All things come to him who has learned to labour and wait, but 'let him not lose the substance of ultimate success in grasping at the shadow of present opportunity'.

. . . How shall he live meanwhile? On crumbs—on pickings obtained from men in the cakes-and-ale stage (who always can put paying work into the hands of young men), and on fees from classes, journal work, private instruction, and from work in the schools. Any sort of medical practice should be taken, but with caution—too much of it early may prove a good man's ruin. He cannot expect to do more than just eke out a living. He must put his emotions on ice: there must be no 'Amaryllis in the shade', and he must beware the tangles of 'Neaera's hair'. . . [And:]

. . . at the end of twenty years, when about forty-five, our

[1] Reprinted as No. VIII in 'Aequanimitas and other Addresses', 1904.

Lydgate should have a first-class reputation in the profession, and a large circle of friends and students. He will probably have precious little capital in the bank, but a very large accumulation of interest-bearing funds in his brain-pan. He has gathered a stock of special knowledge which his friends in the profession appreciate, and they begin to seek his counsel in doubtful cases and gradually learn to lean upon him in times of trial. He may awake some day, perhaps, quite suddenly, to find that twenty years of quiet work, done for the love of it, has a very solid value.

He went on to consider the cakes-and-ale period, and divided the consultants as a class into intra- and extra-professional. The latter, caught in the coils of the octopus, were deserving of sincerest sympathy :

One thing [he says] may save him. It was the wish of Walter Savage Landor always to walk with Epicurus on the right hand and Epictetus on the left, and I would urge the clinical physician as he travels farther from the East, to look well to his companions—to see that they are not of his own age and generation. He must walk with the 'boys', else he is lost, irrevocably lost ; not all at once but by easy grades, and everyone perceives his ruin before he, 'good, easy man', is aware of it. I would not have him a basil plant, to feed on the brains of the bright young fellows who follow the great wheel uphill, but to keep his mind receptive, plastic, and impressionable he must travel with the men who are doing the work of the world, the men between the ages of twenty-five and forty.

And finally, after warning against 'the temptation to toy with the Delilah of the press', who, sooner or later 'sure to play the harlot, has left many a man shorn of his strength', he ends with this paragraph :

In a play of Oscar Wilde's, one of the characters remarks : 'There are only two great tragedies in life : not getting what you want—and getting it !' and I have known consultants whose treadmill life illustrated the bitterness of this *mot*, and whose great success at sixty did not bring the comfort they had anticipated at forty. The mournful echo of the words of the preacher rings in their ears, words which I not long ago heard quoted with deep feeling by a distinguished physician : 'Better is a handful with quietness, than both hands full with travail and vexation of spirit.'

These quotations grow too many and long. 'Twere better for medical students young and old to ponder over the original address—even to its single foot-note to Lydgate, which says : 'This well-drawn character in George Eliot's

" Middlemarch " may be studied with advantage by the physician ; one of the most important lessons to be gathered from it is—marry the right woman.'[1] Most happily married himself and knowing how often the tragedy of Lydgate was repeated in the profession, Osler used to reiterate the warning to his young friends to keep their affections on ice. His advice was not always taken. There was found among his papers this draft in pencil of an unfinished letter to a young graduate, which tells its own story :

Dear ——, Do not worry, you could not offend me, nor did you fool me altogether. Although I did not refer to it, I had a feeling that you had made up your mind. Long experience has taught me that, in these cases, advice is sought to confirm a position already taken. In the affairs of the heart, in which I have had a long and curious experience, I do not remember an instance in which my adverse counsel was taken. From the West, one day, a family group of anxious Hebrews came to consult me on the advisability of the son—an early phthisiker—marrying. There could be no two opinions ; the old people on both sides were greatly pleased, and the young ones, though sad, seemed contented and agreed to wait until he was quite well. As they streamed out, the patient said : ' Doctor, a word with you please, alone. I think it only fair to say that, knowing very well what your advice would be, we got married before we left Kansas City.'

I was quite touched by your letter. Of course, I know you love her, or think you do, which at this stage of the game is the same thing. Only remember that the blind bow-boy plays the devil

---

[1] Among Osler's notes for an intended Introduction to the *Litteraria* section of his library catalogue there is a long one which reads in part as follows : ' Ask the opinion of a dozen medical men upon the novel in which the doctor is best described, and the majority will say *Middlemarch*. Lydgate is at once an example and a warning. . . . An unmitigated calamity, his marriage ruined his intellectual life in a soul-wasting struggle with worldly annoyances. . . . George Eliot was happy in her relations with the profession, and we owe her a deep debt for this Early Victorian sketch of it in a provincial town. It is often said that my Brother Regius of Cambridge, Sir Clifford Allbutt, was the original Lydgate. Nothing in their careers is in common, save the training and the high aspirations. There is a basis for the statement. When Dr. Bastian lived at Hanwell, one Sunday afternoon he had just returned from a visit to George Eliot, and the conversation turned on *Middlemarch* which had recently appeared. He said that the matter had been discussed in her house that afternoon, and she confessed that Dr. Allbutt's early career at Leeds had given her suggestions.'

with us sometimes. I tried to warn you against what I felt was an indiscreet marriage. You have a career ahead of you which the right woman will help, the wrong woman wreck. A level-headed fellow can do anything he wishes with a wife if love blossom into trust, gentleness and consideration. A doctor needs a woman who will look after his house and rear his children, a Martha whose first care will be for the home. Make her feel that she is your partner arranging a side of the business in which she should have her sway and her way. Keep the two separate. Consult her and take her advice about the house and the children, but keep to yourself, as far as possible, the outside affairs relating to the practice. . . .

A meeting of the newly formed Maryland Public Health Association, organized early in the year and of which Welch had been made President, was held in the hall of the Faculty, November 18th–19th, when abattoirs, water filtration, school sanitation, and such subjects, were discussed. The deliberations of one whole evening were given over to the old question of Baltimore sewerage, and in this relation Osler again spoke vividly of the existing conditions, and their connexion with typhoid mortality:

. . . The penalties of cruel neglect have been paid for 1896; the dole of victims for 1897 is nearly complete, the sacrifices will number again above 200. We cannot save the predestined ones of 1898, but what of the succeeding years? From which families shall the victims be selected? Who can say? This we can predict—they will be of the fairest of our sons and of our daughters; they will not be of the very young, or of the very old, but the youth in his bloom, the man in the early years of his vigour, the girl just wakening into full life, the young woman just joying in the happiness of her home. These will be offered to our Minotaur, these will be made to pass through the fire of the accursed Moloch. This, to our shame, we do with full knowledge, with an easy complacency that only long years of sinning can give. . . .

By means of its published report, widely distributed throughout the State, this meeting served to stimulate even the smaller hamlets to some conception of their public health obligations. And though, as H. B. Jacobs has said,[1] such writing as Osler's was not only convincing but was intensely moving, and played no small part in securing, in

[1] 'Osler as a Citizen and his Relation to the Tuberculosis Crusade in Maryland'. *Johns Hopkins Hospital Bulletin*, July 1919.

the end, proper sewage disposal for Baltimore, it is not unlikely that the imagination of the Marylander accustomed to frequent, on occasion, what is known as a 'raw bar' was still more moved by the paper of W. K. Brooks the zoologist, who hinted that every drop of water entering the Chesapeake Bay had a good chance of having its bacilli filtered through the gills of an oyster.

He took upon himself at this time the onerous task of collecting funds for the purposes mentioned in the subjoined note sent to the doctors throughout the State. There is nothing about it, however, which would suggest the kindness of heart that was his underlying impulse, for one purpose was to supply a scholarly physician in Baltimore, who was in needy circumstances, with a literary task he was well fitted to accomplish. The notice read: 'The Medical & Chirurgical Faculty at the celebration of its one-hundredth anniversary will issue a volume containing the annals of the profession of Maryland, and an account of the Proceedings of the Centennial Meeting. The price of the volume will be $2.00, and all names should be sent to Dr. William Osler, 1 West Franklin street, Baltimore.' And so, with the usual shower of brief Christmas notes, such as 'Dear Flexner, that is a bully piece of work! I am obliged for it in such a handsome dress. Do not work too hard this winter. Yours, W. O.', which rained from 1 West Franklin Street, the year passed, and with it Revere's second birthday.

1898

Consultations were beginning to call him afield, and his triennial Text-book revision was impending, as he indicates in this note to Lafleur on January 27th:

Dear Laffie, How are you? Well & strong again I hope. I heard of your return through Mrs Bullitt. If Pepper writes you about some articles for the Am. Text Bk of Med. 2nd Edition—do undertake them. We are all well—rather sad at Weir Mitchell's severe loss. His daughter aet. 23 died on Thursday of Diphtheria & Mrs. M is still seriously ill. I have been tramping the country this month—Florida, Richmond & Rochester in rapid succession. Send me memos as to alterations in my text book. Mrs Osler sends love & Tommy would if he could.

'Tramping the country' though he was, his institutional responsibilities were ever in his mind. So, on February 9th one finds that one of the first donations ever made to the Johns Hopkins Hospital, as mentioned in the IXth Report of the Superintendent, is a fund for the study of tuberculosis, 'through the liberality of benevolent individuals who desire that their names be not mentioned, . . . that tuberculosis be studied in all its aspects, as to causes, means of communication, prophylaxis and treatment.'[1] This, apparently, is the donation he subsequently referred to as having been given by 'two ladies—God bless them', and it is quite probable that he was led to contribute to it himself, because just at this time the ill health of a number of the students made it clear that their living conditions, no less than those of the consumptives who came to the dispensary, needed to be thoroughly looked into.[2]

The many incidents of this busy winter must be briefly passed over. Fanned by the yellow press and the war-cry of 'Remember the *Maine*', the smouldering embers of war threatened frequently to burst into flame, and Osler thought about it what other intelligent people did. Meanwhile, a new building was going up in the medical school lot, to house physiology and pharmacology. A leper by mistake got admitted to the hospital; a nurse was discharged who refused to attend to her; and Osler made the patient the subject of a clinic.[3] An announcement went forth that the

[1] In later Reports this announcement was changed to the following: 'Through Dr. William Osler, from himself and other interested friends, as a fund for the study of tuberculosis.'

[2] Welch and Osler were appointed a committee to supervise these studies, and their first report, which recorded that Charles D. Parfitt was appointed to take charge of the work, appeared in the Superintendent's Report published a year later. Dr. Parfitt himself shortly became victimized by the disease.

[3] 'Leprosy in the United States, with the Report of a Case.' *Johns Hopkins Hospital Bulletin*, Mar. 1898. It is recalled by one of the students of the day, now Professor C. R. Bardeen, that this patient had been studied for some days in the dermatological clinic, where one physician by detailed differential methods had proved before the class that the case was one of cutaneous syphilis, and another physician on the following day had proved with equal conclusiveness that it was tuberculosis. At this juncture Osler happened to walk through the dispensary one morning with his satellites, caught sight of the woman sitting on a bench, and exclaimed: 'Look at this! This is the first case of leprosy I've seen since I was in Tracadie.'

"And on his shoulders, not a lamb, a Kid"!
3. 6. 98.

Frick Committee of the Faculty had come into possession of $600 to be spent on books, and the committee would be glad to receive suggestions from physicians of their needs, which 'may be sent to Dr. William Osler, 1 West Franklin Street'. The Book and Journal Club was thriving, and had managed since its inception to put $1,200 worth of books on the shelves of the Faculty's library. Meanwhile, his Wednesday clinics on the winter crop of pneumonia had begun. Some got into print and serve to give an idea of the intimate character of these exercises. On March 1st he wrote to Ogden, making idle promises about playing golf:

Dear Ogden, D.V. I leave for England immediately after my exams—early in June. Sorry not to be able to go to Denver [the annual A. M. A. meeting for 1898] but I need a good rest & hope to get off for three months if I can induce Mrs. O to take Ike. I wish you could take ten days or two weeks with us this spring—say May. You would enjoy a good rest & it would be a great pleasure to have you. I will promise to play golf with you three or four times a week. The boy thrives. I have been horribly driven—literally from Dan to Beersheba. I never have been so much away.

Other letters of the time indicate that, however 'horribly driven', he was dipping into the Text-book revision preparatory to the third edition; also that Ogden paid his visit earlier than May, and his kodak of Revere on his father's back shows that the boy was thriving. During the spring recess, accompanied by his nephew and Barker, he took a brief holiday in the South, coming back 'much refreshed', as told in one of Mrs. Osler's letters written behind the scenes on April 19th; and the letter states further that she has 'just written thirty dinner invitations for the 26th, which verifies what you say about my constantly being at my desk'.

The Maryland Faculty held its one-hundredth annual meeting with a four-day programme, beginning on April 26th, which accounts for the 'thirty dinner invitations'.[1] As Chairman of the Executive Committee Osler announced

[1] The President for the year was Dr. Charles M. Ellis of Elkton, a man of unusual attainments, the *beau idéal* of a country practitioner. W. T. Councilman came from Boston and gave the principal address of the occasion, on cerebrospinal meningitis, which had appeared in epidemic form in Eastern Massachusetts.

at the business session that, in response to the circular issued the previous spring, $4,300 had been subscribed towards the $7,000 debt on the building. 'Our present home', he declared, 'is an advance on our old one, but it does not represent suitable quarters for the profession of a city of 500,000 inhabitants. We need a new building, and an endowment fund for the library; and what we need, Mr. President, we can get with concerted action on the part of the profession and our friends.' Osler was determined this mortgage should be lifted, but the attention of his hearers was doubtless distracted by other matters. For on the day before the meeting convened, Congress had declared the existence of a state of war with Spain, and there was talk of an invasion of Cuba, where more to be feared than Spanish guns were typhoid and malaria, smallpox and dysentery. Worse even than these was yellow fever, and the Surgeon-General, who read a paper at this centennial meeting, had promptly issued a call for immunes among the profession to accompany the troops as contract surgeons.[1] They were not difficult to find, for yellow fever had been rampant in the Southern States the preceding year.

The 'American Physicians' held their thirteenth annual meeting in Washington the next week,[2] with F. C. Shattuck as their President. On this occasion Sternberg gave another paper on the subject of yellow fever, quoting with disapproval Sanarelli's experiments and discrediting his claim that the *Bacillus Sanarelli* was the causal agent of the disease, for it proved to be identical with his own previously described 'Bacillus X', on which Walter Reed and James

[1] Surgeon-General Sternberg himself had had yellow fever, was considered an authority on the subject, and had written much on the bacteriology of the disease. A veil had best be drawn, however, over the medical history of the expedition to Cuba. Nor need the British War Office be much more proud of what happened that same year in the Soudan under Kitchener, where medical officers were hardly thought necessary.

[2] The day before this meeting, on May 2nd, with Osler's backing, the late George M. Gould, then Editor of the newly established *Philadelphia Medical Journal*, called a meeting in Philadelphia which resulted in the organization of the Association of Medical Librarians, whose purpose was the fostering of medical libraries and the maintenance of an exchange of medical literature. Of this society Gould was made the first President, and subsequently under Osler's influence the organization was held together in ways that will be seen.

Carroll had been working. V. C. Vaughan in the discussion had mentioned as 'ridiculous' Sanarelli's experimental inoculations on man, and Osler is reported to have followed with an emphatic denunciation of these experiments. Even granting, he said, that every dose of medicine we give is an experiment, to deliberately utilize a human being for the purpose without the sanction of the individual 'is not ridiculous, it is criminal'. It was a condemnation, the publicity of which stood Osler in good stead two years later.

Thus were the pieces fitting together. The invasion of Cuba; yellow fever; Reed and Carroll; a God-sent Governor-General who had been a doctor; experiments on man—for U.S. soldiers *did* give their sanction; the discovery of the transmitting agent; Havana freed from the disease and yellow fever driven into its last ditch—all of which might not have happened—so soon, at least—if the battleship *Maine* had not been blown up in Havana harbour on January 24 of this year.

Some time during the month it became noised about that Osler had been elected a Fellow of the Royal Society of London,[1] of which Lister was then President. This honour had previously been accorded to few Canadians, though before the revolt of the colonies farther south, there had been several, like Benjamin Franklin, entitled to write 'F.R.S.' after their name. His mother wrote on May 19th:

My dear Willie,—A line to congratulate you on the step up the Ladder of Fame. I do not think it will exalt your pride or vainglory but it is certainly most gratifying to us all and must be especially so to you and Grace. Nellie was going to send a Tel. but I did not like her going over late in the evening and said I would write but could not manage it somehow yesterday. . . . W. F. generally sends all sorts of scraps to his mother about your precious little lad and I get them through Jennette, most amusing some of them are. I am longing to see you all, and counting off the days as they pass till the 5th or 6th of June. Do come as soon after that as you can, but you must be very much rushed here and there—and sorely need a sea voyage to rest you. I know you have to go to England and nothing will be better for you—there were disappointments when you did not come on from Buffalo and I know that as usual you will

[1] He was recommended for election by the Council, May 5, 1898; formally elected June 6, 1898; 'admitted' June 8, 1899.

not get much rest in Toronto. . . . My heart goes out towards you all ; dear Grace I'm sure feels low about this horrid war. . . .

Too much was made of this Fellowship, by press and public, for his peace of mind, and though he submitted to a complimentary dinner on May 24th he escaped the next day to New York for a meeting of the Neurological Association, held at the Academy of Medicine. He was on the programme and read a paper, though it may be assumed that he spent a good deal of his time browsing among the old books in the rich collection of the Academy, enviously comparing it with the library of the 'Faculty'. He stayed at the University Club, for he abhorred hotels and hotel lobbies where he was apt to be waylaid by reporters and by bores, whom he never suffered gladly. 'This is Dr. Osler, I believe?' To which he would be likely to reply: 'No—sorry—often mistaken for him. My name is Davis—E. Y. Davis of Caughnawauga.'

To F. J. Shepherd from W. O. 1 West Franklin St. [June 8]

Dear F. J. Sorry to hear you were knocked out. I wish you had come on here for repairs. The F R S was a great surprise. I suppose Foster set it up. I had no idea that my name had been proposed. We have changed our plans. We had berths for the 13th but [Revere's coloured] 'Mammy' struck & would not go, fearing the dangers of the sea. Then Mrs O's heart failed & she decided to go to Bar Harbour for the summer & has given me six weeks leave for a trip to England. I sail on the 9th of July. Wish we were going together I shall see you in London 40 Clarges St. will be my address. . . . Mrs O & Ike left for Toronto on Monday I go on the 18th. I am over head & ears in my 3rd Edition—infernal nuisance

Early in the preceding month the Maryland Public Health Association, which in its short year of existence had accomplished such unlooked-for results under Welch's presidency, held its second meeting at the 'Faculty' hall. The affairs of the organization were coming to take more and more of Welch's time. He had acted as Dean of the Medical School since its opening, and after presenting to Mr. Gilman on June 14th at the commencement exercises the second group of candidates for graduation, 26 in all, he resigned his deanship in favour of Osler—another 'infernal nuisance', which, however, he assumed with his customary imperturbability, though it is not certain that he was a very energetic Dean. He took the responsibility lightly; there was, indeed, little at any time about the school machinery to require more than occasional oiling, and he was good at this. With the close of the school session, the usual post-graduate courses began, and though these were largely taken over by the junior members of the hospital staff, who thereby eked out their meagre university salaries, Osler always participated. Thus on June 18th he gave them a clinical lecture, using cerebrospinal fever as his text; for the epidemic had in mild form reached Baltimore, and there were seven cases in his wards. He probably, too, as was his custom, gave the graduate students a reception, though with Mrs. Osler away, and floors, tables, and chairs doubtless strewn with the manuscript of his Text-book revision, this year's reception could hardly have been held at 1 West Franklin Street. Before leaving Baltimore some two weeks later, he scribbled this note to W. S. Thayer:

> Miss H. will tell the postman to leave all my mail at the Hospital until after Aug. 1st. Will you open the letters (unless marked personal) and answer those to patients—nabbing any you can. The Trustees, under a misapprehension (W. tells me) did not pass your salary increase. It is all right W. says & can be arranged without question. So if you hear of it do not be worried in the slightest. Hope you will have a good summer. My address is 15 Queens Park till July 1st. I sail 9th on Etruria.

So to 15 Queens Park, his brother 'B. B.'s' house in Toronto, he repaired, 'bringing with him plenty of work', as stated in one of his mother's letters; and from there in anticipation of the coming Edinburgh meeting of the British Medical Association he wrote to J. G. Adami on July 1st:

> Friday.
>
> Dear Adami, Yours of the 28th reached me here, where I have been for a week with Mrs. Osler and Egerton Y (Jr.). I am delighted to hear of the cirrhosis work. Do send the material &c. with Stewart. I shall be only too glad to read the paper for you and show the specimens. Have you notified the secretary of the Med. Section? The discussion on cirrhosis is in it—I think. It will be quite startling —but what a comfort to the thirsty Scotsmen! Thanks for the congratulations upon the F. R. S. It was very unexpected, and very

much appreciated. I have been in the depths—a revision of my text-book. I have knocked it to pieces. Sins of omission begin to haunt me—as the sections are printed off. I had a note about your interesting lipoma—and forgot it! I shall look out for the paper and specimens by Stewart. Love to 'little Mary Cantlie.'

In a letter of the next day to President Gilman, stating that he is leaving for Bar Harbour on Monday and sailing on Saturday 'to be absent only five weeks', he adds something, in effect that he sees no reason why Mr. Gilman should be called upon in any way to help a certain Miss J. to finish her biological studies because he has promised to do this himself. In such ways Osler managed to keep his pocket-book empty —'to sanctify' his professional fees. The education of the Locke children; Miss J.'s biological studies; the continued support of certain boyhood friends who were having hard sledding; numberless things of this sort hardly to be specified. He was not a good business-man, if that means the accumulation of capital. A Canadian physician recalls that during his student days he was once caught penniless in Washington, and recognizing Osler, with whom he was unacquainted, asked with embarrassment if he could borrow $25 to get home. Osler said: 'That's not enough; here's fifty.' He was the bane of the Baltimore charity organizations. In an attempt to stop house-to-house begging they had issued tickets which householders could give to beggars, referring them to a central agency where they would be given a night's lodging and a breakfast in return for wood-chopping. Osler nevertheless had an agreement with black Morris that no one asking aid should be turned away without money, and there was a box at the door with ready coins for the purpose. Better a thousand mistakes than one chance missed really to help some poor devil in actual want. 'There was no discrimination', he once said, 'in the charity of the Good Samaritan, who stopped not to ask the stripped and wounded man by the wayside whether it was by his own fault the ill had come; nor of his religion, nor had he the wherewithal to pay his board.' In other ways too he was irregular. He had circularized the profession, as will be recalled, late in December of the previous year, asking for two-dollar subscriptions to enable the Maryland 'Faculty' to publish a centennial volume which Dr. E. F. Cordell was to edit. The subscriptions were few. It grew to be a large volume. The cost of the printing was heavy, and in the end Osler made up the entire deficit of two or three thousand dollars, though there is no written record of this. Moreover, his name headed the list of contributors to the University of Maryland Endowment Fund being raised at this time, though only the friends and alumni of the old school had been asked by Dr. Cordell 'to rally to its support'. Such a chance he never missed—and usually gave doubly in that he gave first.

The Text-book he had indeed 'knocked to pieces'.[1] In the preface, evidently written in New York at the Waldorf Hotel the evening before sailing, he says that a text-book six years old needs a very thorough revision, and that the present one had been wholly recast though without being materially increased in size. He enumerated the sections which had been rewritten or were new; mentioned those who had given help, especially Flexner, Thomas, and Barker, in addition to those of his own staff; and at the end spoke of his obligations to Livingood, a victim of the *Burgogne* disaster, who had been on his way for a year's study abroad and 'by whose untimely death the Johns Hopkins Medical School has suffered a grievous loss'. From this he turned to send word to Flexner:

> What an awful calamity this is! Poor Livingood! I cannot realize it. Write a nice obituary notice of the poor fellow for the Philadelphia Jour. next week. You know the details. Gould will be very glad to have it. I left Mrs. Osler and Tommy at Bar Harbour. What have you done about Cordell?

The revision had been a great labour. He wrote to Mrs. Osler from the steamer on July 9th: 'It's a great relief to have the book off my hands—I slept so happily—it has

[1] The unprecedented success of the volume is shown by a note from his publishers stating that 'the whole number of the second edition printed was 17,500; total of the two editions 41,000'. Naturally it was the source of imitations, but by his revisions Osler kept well ahead of them. His friend James M. Anders of Philadelphia had issued, through a rival publishing-house in 1897, a 'Text-book of the Practice of Medicine' arranged on similar lines. Some wag wrote a review of it, under the title *Osler mit etwas Anders*.

been a little too much on my mind. Roddick and Stewart are here and one of the Brocks so we shall have a pleasant time. My cabin looks very well. My companion has not turned up—a Mr. White I think. I enclose a list of the passengers. Look out for a cable from Liverpool.' Later, from 12a Curzon Street in London, where he was giving the younger Francis cousins a good time, he sent home under the postmark of July 22nd this quasi-journal:

Two LL.D's, a D.C.L. and the F.R.S. make 1898 a pretty full year in the life of your old man—But keep humble—lest we forget! I got the notice this a m of the Edinboro' Degree, which is to be conferred on the Saturday after the meeting. Roddick is to have it also, I am glad to say. I took Gwen in a Hansom to get my ticket—i.e. pay for it. Then we spent an hour in the National Gallery—and at 12 met May and a very sweet faced woman, Mrs. Clayton, at the Academy. Pictures are very good this year. Two of Harry Tuke's are A.1. May took us to the Empress Club in Dover Street—where she is a member—to luncheon, and at three we took hansoms for Lords where the great match of the season—Gentlemen vs Players—is on. We saw some first class cricket—but not W. Grace who had been put out a few minutes before we came. Went to Mrs. Clayton's to tea—near Regents Park. I left the girls at Peter Robinsons and came home. We have tickets for the Little Minister—at the Haymarket—this eve. You see we are doing the town. Gwen is enchanted. This is a very nice place, attendance perfect. Mrs. Russell is a very nice woman. I have asked Margery to come in for Thursday and Friday.

Wednesday a m. Waiting for the girls for bkfast. The play was charming. Winifred Emery so sweet and a much better actress than when we saw her a few years ago. Splendid weather—not too hot. 5.30 Have just left the girls at the American Shoe Store in Regent St. while I came in to order tea. George Francis came to lunch. Looks so well. Hal and I took the girls to the Tavern—we went down the river by boat. It was great fun. Gwen was enchanted. Tonight we dine at the Criterion and go to the 'Liars'—Wyndham—It is just too bad that you are not here.

Thursday, 2.30. Such fun at the Liars. Wyndham is splendid and Miss Moore very good—a little off from what you remember. This morning I went to Clovell's and to the shirt-maker. Then to Euston to meet Margery Howard who is to be with us until Friday eve (she sends her love). Got a leather portmanteau and a hat-box at the Stores. We have just had luncheon and are off to Earls Court to see the Naval Show. Such weather! no rain and bright sunshine and crisp east wind—Bostonian—fresh air. I am just disgusted that you are not here. Your letter has just come—so glad to have good news. I will cable on Saturday, I am delighted that you like everything. Do take drives and spend all the money you wish.

Friday a m. We went to Earls Court in the afternoon—saw the sham naval battle—wonderful performance Margery enjoyed it so much. The girls went to tea at 5 with Pa at the Jr Constitutional Club. M. came home with me. At 7.15 we all dined with Hal at a very swell restaurant and then went to Daly's to see the Greek Slave. Marie Tempest was so good. We enjoyed ourselves greatly. With the exception of Ewart I have not seen a Doctor. My clothes are progressing. I am going this a m about your cloak, and the reefer for Tommy. I shall be very careful about the former. We go tonight to the—I forget—at Ealing to dine, and this afternoon to the Imp. Institute. It seems very long since I left you, but Aug. 6th will soon be here. . . . Yours

EGERTON.

If for the sake of his nieces he had eluded doctors and formal dinners in London, it was to be otherwise in the North, for after receiving his LL.D. at Aberdeen on July 21st, and reaching Edinburgh for the British Medical Association meeting, his note-book records: '25th, dinner Stewart 7.30; 26th, Gibson 7.15; 27th, Chiene—Turner 7.45; 28th, Fraser; 29th, Thompson—Greenfield 7.15.' Thomas Grainger Stewart, who held the Chair of Medicine at Edinburgh (a position offered to Osler a few years later, it may be added) was the President-Elect of the B. M. A., to succeed Roddick of Montreal; and at the annual dinner of the association, where was dispensed Scottish hospitality at its best—to haggis and pipers—a good deal of banter seems to have passed when Osler proposed Stewart's health.

From the opening service at St. Giles's Cathedral, to the university ceremonial of the last afternoon given in the beautiful McEwan Hall, there was probably little he missed in the way of excursions, receptions, and scientific sessions. Certainly he was at St. Giles's, for the Rev. Alexander White, D.D., Moderator of the Free Church of Scotland, taking as his text 'The greatest of these is Charity', gave a discourse on none other than the man Osler knew by heart, and of whom the minister said: 'The properly prepared and absolutely ingenuous reader of the "Religio Medici" must be a second Sir Thomas Browne himself. If ever any man were a true Catholic Christian it was surely he.'

Certainly, also, he was at McEwan Hall, for there before an audience of 3,000, he, with H. P. Bowditch of Boston, Jonathan Hutchinson, Lauder Brunton, Broadbent, Kocher, Mikulicz, Roddick, and others (including two Dutchmen whom he was to visit the next summer) made up the nineteen to whom the LL.D. had been accorded by the Senatus Academicus of the University. He appears to have taken no part in the scientific sessions except to make the promised presentation of Adami's paper,[1] to whom he scribbled a note saying: 'Your paper went off very well—good audience. No discussion. I think it rather paralysed them.'

He must have returned to London, and soon after went on one of the quests in which he so delighted—this time in search of field-records of Thomas Sydenham, for he had exhausted the British Museum sources in the summer of 1894 and on this visit as well. His pocket note-book is filled with notes relating to Sydenham and his contemporary John Locke, to the Countess of Shaftesbury, and so on. Among his papers, too, has been found a fragmentary sketch, partly in pen, partly pencil, which begins thus:

I took the 11.45 from Paddington, and reached Maiden Newton, Dorset, in about three hours. I wished to see the birthplace of the great Sydenham and also to verify the entries in the parish register. Wynford Church is only a chapel of ease connected with Little Toller and as all conveyances of the villages were engaged at a picnic I walked to the latter place about 1½ miles distant. . . . The Hospitalers of St. John chose a pleasant site for the monastery of Toller Fratrum. In one of the extensive valleys of Frome on the brow of a small hill which rises abruptly from the banks of a small stream, a farm-house and barn embody all that remains of the once spacious establishment. The church is new and uninteresting save for a remarkable font and the old Register from which I have given you extracts.

Far from the madding crowd at Wynford Eagle, a hamlet or chapelry belonging to Little Toller, in the garden of England, as Dorset has been called, Thomas Sydenham was born. The place belonged to the great honour or barony of Aquila or Eagle in Sussex, which name it received from a Norman family named Aquila. The estate passed from the Zouch's to Thomas Sydenham, the physician, through an ancestor in the reign of Henry VIII. The Sydenhams were an ancient family divided into many branches. They were

[1] 'On the Bacteriology of Progressive Portal Cirrhosis.'

originally seated at Sydenham near Bridgewater and Kilsford (Somerset) in the reigns of King John and Henry III. Hence issued the various Sydenham families of Somerset and the Wynford Eagle Sydenhams of Dorset.

And from here at some other time, possibly on the steamer, he has gone on in pencil, very illegibly it may be said, to describe the manor house at Wynford Eagle, where 'without a suspicion of the three centuries of world change' Sydenham might return with no sense of that estrangement which is given by the alteration of places familiar to our childhood. He may have been thinking of Bond Head and his own boyhood as he wrote these lines:

Of the childhood and youth of Sydenham we know nothing, or to speak more correctly we have no records. In reality we know everything; childhood and youth are among the immutable things. On the occasion of my visit I saw the little Sydenham running into a lane near Toller Fratrum; a group of children rushing helter-skelter down the hill were followed at a distance by a bright-faced little lad who at the sight of a stranger looked and screamed to his mother. At the gate by the church at Wynford Eagle a chubby boy of five was shouting to the shepherd dogs as they turned the flock from the road into the field. Into the same field the little Sydenham had doubtless often helped to drive the flock and I saw him in my mind's eye in the boy who with mimic stride went down the road with the shepherd. And again as I sat on a stile, a lad of twelve came through the hedge with a rabbit in his hand and a snare. Joyous, happy days, full of those joys of country life which for children are so much heightened in a large family of boys and girls.

Pressed in the book is a flower, 'from the vine over the door of the birthplace of Sydenham July 26, 1899'; so the reader may expect to find him back in the garden of England in another twelve months. He sailed on the *Campania*, reaching New York on August 8th, when he first learned the sad news of Pepper's sudden death, and of the interment on the 6th in Philadelphia. Too late to pay by his presence the tribute he would like to have rendered, he went on immediately, as planned, to join his family at Bar Harbour, where he was laid low by one of his periodical infections.

To W. S. Thayer from W. O. Wednesday [Aug. 12]

I should have written at once but I am deep in a horrid cold which I caught in an upper berth on the N. Y. N. H. & H. R. R. I am delighted with everything here—the links are A.1. tho I have only been out once. Campbell & Muriel Howard are here. Mrs. Osler asked them as a surprise for me. What about the Smith house, Would it not be better than the Carrolls'. I suppose it would not be furnished. Perhaps Van Ness may be going to live there. I am so glad that Flexner has decided to stay. Welch could not well have spared him. It would be hardly worth while to go to Santiago now—the troops would all be away in a few weeks. I believe we would see quite as much in some of the northern hospitals to which the troops are being sent. But you need fresh air & rest—not any more Hospital work.

I see they have me secured for Pepper's chair—even my photo in the Ledger. Poor Pepper!—they will never have his equal again in Phila. They did not half appreciate him or what he did for them. The U. P. would have been still on 9th Street, a three year school & the other depts undeveloped had it not been for his amazing energy & push. There is likely to be heart-burning over the appointment. Mitchell insists that I shall not say nay until after the Faculty have met but I should only be worried to death by practice in Phila. I see your sister every day. She is doing a miniature of Tommy. Your father is away. Very glad to hear that Barker is off & free—He must now buckle down at one or two good bits of original work.

And so Philadelphia, not large enough to hold at one time both these men, was to have neither of them. Always deeply moved by the death of one of his friends, Osler immediately sent a long obituary notice of Pepper to the *British Medical Journal*, and also set to work to prepare a more formal memorial sketch.[1] This he had intended to read at the opening session of the medical school, but was prevented from doing so by an attack of his periodical bronchitis, more serious than usual, and contracted under circumstances to be related. By the middle of August he had written: 'I am lowering my record at golf which is the only matter of interest to me just now.' But the remainder of his summer was to be badly broken up and spent for the most part in trains. He had been summoned to Buffalo, and from there had gone on to see a patient somewhere in Iowa. Soon after his return, he was called over one day late in August to Winter Harbour to see Captain Arthur Lee, and while there received an urgent message begging

[1] Reprinted in 'An Alabama Student and other Biographical Essays' Oxford, 1908. The gist of this more finished sketch he sent later in the autumn to the Mahogany Tree Club of Philadelphia, for a memorial meeting.

him to come to Minneapolis because of the serious illness of Walter S. Davis, one of the recent Hopkins graduates. Davis, one of the most promising members of his class, illustrates that curious tendency of physicians to become victims of the malady in which they have specialized. He had been doing some research work on pigments in Abel's laboratory, and during the year had begun to show such a degree of pigmentation of his own skin that it was evident that he had Addison's disease, though up to that time there had been no serious symptoms. From Minneapolis Osler returned to Canton to join Mrs. Osler at her mother's, and immediately had to leave for Toronto to see his brother Edmund's son, who was critically ill. During this entire week, moreover, the country was prostrated by an unseasonable and excessive heat wave. All this he tells in the following letter from Canton to W. S. Thayer:

I found Davis very much better. He returned from the yacht (Abel's) feeling badly having had attacks of giddiness & nausea—once or twice vomiting as well. On Tuesday & Wednesday he had three or four fainting spells, one very prolonged & with a good deal of collapse. They then telegraphed me. I was away in Winter Harbour & did not get back until the eve. I left on Thursday & got to Minneapolis Monday a m. He was very much better—quite bright & it was simply impossible to realize, as we sat & talked to the poor fellow, that his condition was serious. . . . I have told him that we would arrange leave for six mos. which will relieve his mind very much. . . . Unfortunately I have to leave for Toronto tomorrow morning, a nephew is seriously ill. I shall not return here but go down to Balt direct—reaching there on the 15th. What a deuce of a summer you must have had! I saw many in St. P & M who asked after you. It is delightful to see the condition of the school. Their laboratory equipment is A.1. Mrs. Osler came this a.m. I got in at 6 p.m. She says you have sent on letters but I shall have to defer the reading until the train.

On the next Saturday, from his brother Edmund's home, Craigleigh, Toronto, he again wrote to Thayer:

I found my nephew with (I hope) a sharp attack of peripheral neuritis. The suddenness of onset looked alarming, as tho it might be an anterior poliomyelitis, but the distribution & the condition now are reassuring. I shall stay, to see that all goes well, until Wednesday [14th]. Back Thursday a m [i.e. September 15th] early.

All this need hardly be mentioned except that it indicates

how a physician of his standing may be called upon to pass his vacation if he is within reach, and has a heart. Three strenuous days—September 16–18—were spent in Baltimore over professional consultations, for patients and their physicians were waiting to waylay him on his very doorstep. On the 19th came an appeal from James G. Mumford, a young Boston surgeon of literary tastes to whom he was greatly attached, that he see a critical case with him in consultation in Nahant. He acceded, and after a glimpse of his wife and boy, who were still at Canton, he proceeded to Toronto for another look at his nephew. The 'appointments' noted in his account-book for the year ended abruptly on September 24th, and were not resumed till the end of October. The reason is as follows:

On his way from Toronto in the middle of the night he was called out of his berth by the porter, to see a woman, the wife of a Baptist minister in Baltimore, who had recognized him. She, poor thing, was in labour. Osler, in little more than his pyjamas, with the porter's aid got her into an empty compartment in another car, gave her some chlorodyne which he happened to have, telegraphed ahead to her husband and her doctor, and stuck to the distasteful job himself till, reaching Baltimore, he brought the woman to her doorstep in the very nick of time, for 'plump' the baby was born in the vestibule. He must have dictated a few letters that morning, as the following indicates:

To J. G. Adami from W. O. Sept. 23, 1898.

Dear Adami, Your former letter reached me just as I was leaving for Minneapolis, and I have since then been off to Toronto and back to Boston, and have only just returned. I was very much interested in it, and will give it to Flexner to read when he returns. The other paper of which you speak in the letter received to-day I will look for with interest. Thanks for the reprints. I was reading on the cars this morning the hepatitis paper. The subject is one in which I am greatly interested. You will see in the Text-book that I have rewritten the sections on diseases of the liver, and I hope have made them a little more practical.

And perhaps he saw a few patients, but later in the day he took to his bed with fever and a bad cough. He was evidently very ill, so much so that either Futcher or McCrae for several days hardly left his bedside, and Mrs. Osler, 'smelling a rat', hurried home. As a patient he behaved very badly, would not have his windows open, would not have a nurse, twisted his coverlets up, and, disliking to be fussed over, refused to have his bed made—behaving, in short, much as he said in his 'Nurse and Patient' address a man would behave, 'wishing to turn his face to the wall and sicken in peace'.[1] The crisis came on the eighth day, to the great relief of all, and though much used up he wrote from his bed a note to Thayer, who had been away for his holidays, giving some details of his illness and adding:

The Trustees passed on your salary all right—there had been a misunderstanding. Jacobs is taking the 3rd year McCrae the noon class & Futcher the 4th & clinic. Brown has decided not to come to us [to take Davis's place]. This leaves us stranded for the Clin. Labor. I do not see what we are to do. Some one may turn up. The weather has been infernal—87–88 & saturated with moisture. I shall go off for two weeks after a while—probably not before your return. Do not hurry—All is going well.

This illness had interfered with many plans—among them the giving of two promised addresses. One was the memoir of Pepper; the other was to have been delivered on October 4th before the Medical School branch of the Y.M.C.A. at the opening of the school. A rough draft of this has been preserved, on which is pencilled this note: 'Written chiefly on the train from Minneapolis to Boston, copied Sept. 24th and 25th.' Evidently, therefore, he had it on his mind during the first days of his illness. In a later hand he had written: 'Just as well perhaps that I could not go.' He began the address by saying:

In such a gathering I have a feeling of embarrassment such as that which overtook the son of Kish in the memorable incident after the

[1] Apparently it was during this illness—for he always wrote a good deal propped up in bed—that he had gone over the notes of his pneumonia cases of the past winter's session in preparation for a 'leading article' solicited by one of his friends, Burnside Foster, who was about to launch a new medical journal. The article ('On the Study of Pneumonia', *St. Paul Medical Journal*, St. Paul, Minn., Jan. 1899, i. 5–9) is largely devoted to the analysis of the series of cases made by a fourth-year student, Mr. L. W. Ladd. It contains a paragraph which explains why he laid such stress on the disease before his students; and ends with his favourite lines from Cowper which so clearly distinguish between knowledge and wisdom.

finding of his father's asses. It has been my practice for years not to talk on religious questions, holding with Mr. Rogers who when asked of what religion he was, replied, 'The religion of all sensible men.' 'And pray Mr. Rogers, what is that?' 'Why all sensible men keep that to themselves.' In many ways a very poor answer since it comes within the scathing denunciation of —— . . .

And he goes on to divide people into Theresians, Laodiceans, Rimmonites, and Gallionians, for into one or the other of these 'categories we are all ranged, not all of us knowing in which'. Of all this there is much more; traces of what he wrote are to be found in his Ingersoll Lecture six years later. By October 7th he must have been well enough to be up and about, for in a letter to J. G. Adami he says:

I was on the point of writing to you this morning, asking if you had heard anything from Allbutt, when I received a letter from Chicago.[1] He has fixed the 17th as the date of his visit here. I am sorry to say I shall be away, as I am going to the mountains for a couple of weeks to recuperate. We hope, however, that the Allbutts will use our house. My nephew and Welch will look after them, and they can be very comfortable and feel quite at home. I am feeling all right again, though rather used up by the attack.

And not long after, on a Sunday there was posted from Trucksville, Pennsylvania, the following undated note:

Dear Thayer & Barker, Greetings! You would not know me—hardly—after three days in this earthly paradise I have gained 5½ lbs. & a few cc additional. To-day I have been out for several hours walking over this beautiful farm, inspecting stock & mangels & instructing the farmer on new points about clover as a fertilizer. They have first class links here—greens in fine condition & my nurse suggests that I telegraph for permission to do a little putting. I take whiskey twice & milk thrice daily & I have gathered yarrow enough for a good tonic and appetizer. I am reading Dr. Locke's life & works and altogether leading a dietetic philosophical & bucolic life. Mrs Osler & Tommy send kind regards mingled with love.

Later in the month, a letter to Ogden postmarked October 25th gives a *résumé* of the summer happenings:

I had a bit of a knockout—ten days in bed with bronchitis & a patch of flatness at the left base but no rusty sputa or tubular breathing. Fever for 7 days & cough for ten—sudden stoppage of both & rapid convalescence. I am at Hillside near Wilkesbarre with

---

[1] Clifford Allbutt had been in San Francisco giving the Lane Lectures.

the Conynghams, a delightful country place in the mountains. I have gained 10 lbs. & am feeling very fit. I go back at the end of this week. . . . Mrs O & the boy are with me. The latter is getting quite companionable. Do come on for another visit before long. Mrs. O. thinks no one who stays with us is quite so nice. I had a delightful time abroad. May Bath & Gwen Francis who is staying with her came up from Swansea & stayed 10 days with me in London. We had a royal time. Edinboro was a great treat. Two Scotch LL.D's warrant the addition of a Mac to my name. The F.R.S. was a great surprise & a very pleasant one. The number of M.D.'s of late years has been diminishing. All the boys are well. Thayer has gone from the Hospital—is to practise in cons. Still helps with the teaching. Futcher succeeds him.

He was back in harness by November, to the jubilation of all at the hospital—staff, students, patients, and servants. One who particularly rejoiced at the reappearance of this man, ' with a drooping moustache, an olive complexion, and unusual ways—a man unlike any other ', was Miss Elizabeth Thies, the Librarian, whom he insisted on calling by a variety of names, notably ' Miss Thesis '. ' I do not think ', she writes, ' that Dr. Osler ever missed coming into the library when he came to the hospital. He had a warning whistle which I grew to know as did the little children in the ward. When they heard his whistle, they would look to the door, never too sick to sit up and take notice and feel happier for having seen the man we all learned to love and worship. Many a scrap of a note he left on my table '—and she sends many of them, of which these are samples :

8.55½ It seems a very shocking hour for you to arrive or not to arrive. I want the Revue de Chirurgie of last year. Badly. Wm Osler.

[Again] Would the kind Fraülein look in the Am. Jr. of the Med. Scien. for years 1887–1893 for references to Endocarditis? Wm Osler. PS. Will be in at 11^{05}:3 secs.

[Again] *Um Gottes Willen* pasten sie nicht these labels over the titles in the contents. Wm Osler.

As the last letter to Ogden indicates, Thayer had left the hospital to enter consultation practice. He and H. B. Jacobs had rented No. 3 West Franklin Street adjoining the Oslers' —the one-time fashionable abode of a branch of the Carroll family, still full of their beautiful old furniture and bric-àbrac. Here for the remainder of Osler's Baltimore period a succession of 'latch-keyers', who were as much at home in No. 1 as No. 3, had their abode, until one by one they were picked off by marriage. No. 3 had the only telephone, an abomination always to 'the Chief', though occasionally he was dragged reluctantly to it through the hole cut in the fence to facilitate the circulation of the denizens of the two dwellings; and guests flowed freely from one house to the other.

Dr. Thayer recalls a typical incident of the first day they had set up housekeeping. Osler had said to him that morning: 'What's the name of that old codger from Boston with a white beard down to his middle I met at the Maryland Club last night? He wanted to know your address.' Thayer did not identify 'the old codger', but on returning home found that a large box of provender—cigars, interesting bottles, cheeses, and the like—had been sent from the club, and though nothing was acknowledged he knew that the Bostonian with the white beard was an autumnal Santa Claus—and Osler did not brook being thanked for his kindnesses.

In January of this year there had appeared the first number of a new 'weekly'—the *Philadelphia Medical Journal*—which had been launched with the financial backing of Musser, Keen, Osler, and many others, and of which George M. Gould was the editor. To this journal, which had an all-too-short though successful career, the following letter of December 31st refers:

Dear Musser, The Devil! I suspected that the trustees would be after Gould. The P. M. J. has been an eye opener to them. As a matter of public (i.e. professional) policy I should say let him go. The J. A. M. A. needs him now more than we do & he could put the Journal on a first class basis which would be a good thing for the rank & file. Phila is surely not so reduced that a good successor to G. could not be found. Da Costa would be the man of my choice. He has both brains and energy & could hold the younger men who have to do the work. With our sub. list & start, there should be no risk of failure—not the slightest. The essential point is to have a strong editor who commands the respect of his juniors & who can get work out of them.

I have been laid up for three days with the grippe—not a bad attack fever for only one day. Kelly was in last night—he had just returned from Phila very much disgusted with the outlook at U. P. He says that there is a strong feeling against White among the younger men, who feel that with him in charge alone, the able men among them would have very little chance. I did not know the feeling was so strong. In medicine the fusion of the two departments would be a good thing. Save only that it cuts you out of a full chair. Tyson who is a clear minded soul feels thus, & spoke of it while here a few weeks ago. Happy New Year.

CHAPTER XVIII

1899

AFTER TWENTY-FIVE YEARS

'I AM so distressed to hear of Kanthack's death—it is a grievous loss to all of us. Poor fellow! and he had so much to live for and so much to do.' So Osler wrote early in the year in a note to Adami regarding the untimely death of the man who had filled the Chair of Pathology in Cambridge for only a short few months. And in another note sent later the same day he urged Adami to write an obituary notice for Gould's journal, saying: 'If you send it by Saturday eve it will be in time.' Thus he would have others heed 'the flighty purpose'. It is tempting to dwell on this habit of impulsive note-writing: for whenever occasion offered, a card always convenient to his hand was scribbled and posted. Even when he received reprints of other people's papers—instead of the usual perfunctory acknowledgement, if any at all, he would invariably send some sort of personal message. So, in a note of this time to H. P. Bowditch:

Dear H. P. Greetings to you and yours! I have just been reading your 'Reform in Medical Education' with every bit of which I fully agree. To one relief of the early congestion you did not refer—viz. the exclusion of Chemistry (Gen. & Lab.) from the strictly Medical curriculum. We found here that it is a great boon—the students have a three months course only in Physiological Chemistry. There are schools in the country (U. P. for ex.) in which the Chemistry takes up more time in the first two years than any other subjects. I have abandoned didactic lectures altogether—but I talk a great deal (with my feet dangling from a table which I find is a great help). Your lecture will do good. Love to all at home.

Even his briefer messages were apt to have some twist out of the ordinary, like the following on the back of a calling-card left for one of the nurses who had come down from Hamilton, Ontario, to enter the training school:

Will you please if you can get off (without disturbing the equanimity of the Vestalia, and without distress to any of your youthful companions) come to tea at 4.30.

And at this time a succession of notes was being sent to Dr. and Mrs. John A. Mullin or to their son, in Hamilton, Ontario. His acquaintance with the old doctor dated back to the days when as a medical student he had gone from Montreal to Hamilton to see a case of trichinosis with Archibald Malloch, Sr., who was Mullin's friend and contemporary. During his recent Christmas visit to Toronto he must have stopped off to see Dr. Mullin, who was ill, and on his return wrote encouragingly asking for news. Every few days a cheerful message of some sort went to the old doctor :

Dear Mullin, How goes the battle? With Israel I hope. I left you in bed & rather wretched after a sharp attack of pain. I hope you are up again and doing what you can in the way of work without tiring yourself. Let me hear soon how you are.

Dear Mullin, I was very glad to have your letter to-day—to hear the more cheerful news of your breadbasket. Do take it easy & make the young Doctor do most of the work. I should have answered Mrs. Mullins letter which I was very glad to have, but I have been very much driven for the past ten days.

An epidemic of influenza prevailed at the time, nor did Osler escape, as is evident from his mother's letters, which express concern about her 'Benjamin', and which admit that she herself, because of the infirmities of ninety-four years, 'often feels the grasshopper a burden'. But when housed by temporary illness his wheels nevertheless continued to revolve. On January 9th he wrote to H. M. Hurd, who for years had shouldered the responsibilities of editing the hospital publications :

We should have a meeting at an early date about the Bulletin. I have asked Mall to have a chat with you about it. I think there should be an Editorial Committee composed of you and Mall and Abel and Howell and a couple of the younger men, with Smith as Secretary to do the proof-reading and to relieve you of all the worry of it. There should be not the slightest difficulty in arranging for the Medical School fund to stand some of the expense, as it has practically been the organ of the Medical School since the School started. I hope to take up work tomorrow. I feel quite myself to-day.

He was sufficiently himself to put together another of his stirring addresses on 'The Problem of Typhoid Fever in the United States'—an arraignment of the national shortcomings in matters of public hygiene and sanitation—given in Albany on February 1st before the Medical Society of the State of New York. To-day, in spite of our many schools of hygiene, our special laboratories and princely funds devoted to the purpose, there is no voice or pen comparable to his—able in like fashion to rouse the profession and the people to their duties. He said that the very staleness of his subject was a warrant for repetition, that its triteness made earnest reiteration necessary, for the country had had a very bitter lesson in the war—a sad conclusion to a brilliant victory. He reviewed the history of typhoid in the country; told of the labours of Louis's pupils and their writings on the subject; and outlined the progress of our knowledge leading up to the triumphs of sanitation. 'That imperfect drainage and a polluted water supply means a high mortality rate from typhoid fever is the very alphabet of sanitary science.'

Let us turn [he said] from this picture with its glowing colour to a more sombre canvas. Last autumn this nation, in the moment of victory, had a rude awakening, a sudden conviction, a hard lesson. A voice like that heard in Ramah went up throughout the land—'lamentation and weeping and great mourning'. From Montauk Point to San Francisco, from Minneapolis to Tampa, Rachels were weeping for their lads, cut off by a cruel disease. The most bloodless campaign in history was followed by a relatively greater mortality from disease than in any recent war, and chiefly from this very disease over which I have been chanting the paeans of the triumph of our profession. To us these autumnal dirges rang no new tune; we had heard the same in the palace of the rich, in the crowded tenement, in the hospital ward, in peaceful New England valleys, in the settler's shanty of the far West, in the lumberman's shack, in the mining camp. Year by year we had listened to the Rachels of this land weeping for their fair sons and fairer daughters, not killed by any pestilence that walked in darkness, but by a preventable sickness that destroyed in the noon-day—the noon-day of the intelligence of a civilized people. People asked each other, what did it all mean? Nothing more than a slight extension of the judgement upon criminal neglect of sanitary laws. . . . This is a nation of contradictions and paradoxes. A clean people, by whom personal hygiene is carefully cultivated, displays in matters of public sanitation a carelessness which is criminal. A sensible people, among whom education is more widely diffused than in any other country in the world, supinely acquiesces in conditions shameful beyond expression. I do not propose to weary you with statistics, of which our Journals and Reports are full, but I will refer to a few facts drawn at random from three cities and three States, illustrating this shocking neglect.

And he went on to expose Philadelphia, Baltimore, and the national capital as examples of how in sanitary measures we were a generation behind Europe:

The solution of the problem is easy. What has been done in many parts of Europe can be done here; the practical conviction of the people is all that is necessary. Upon them is the responsibility. Let us meanwhile neither scold nor despair. The good-natured citizens who make up our clientèle, pay our bills and vote the straight party ticket, have but little appreciation of a scientific question, and are led as easily (more easily) by a Perkins or a Munyon than by a Lister or a Koch. Under the circumstances it is marvellous so much has been achieved in fifty years. 'The larger sympathy of man with man', which we physicians are called upon to exercise daily in our calling, demands that we continue our efforts—efforts often fruitless in results, but very helpful to ourselves—to educate this foolish public. What is needed seems so easy of accomplishment—the gain would be enormous! We ask so little—the corresponding benefits are so great! We only demand that the people of this country shall do what Elisha asked of Naaman the Syrian—that they shall wash and be clean—that they shall scour the soil on which they live, and cleanse the water which they drink.

On the same day, in an extemporaneous address [1] to the Albany medical students, he emphasized three things: the good fortune which was theirs in entering medicine just at that time; the doing of the day's work without too much thought of the morrow, which gave a chance for his favourite quotation from Carlyle; and lastly, the need of cultivating equally the head and heart:

There is [he is quoted as saying] a strong feeling abroad among people—you see it in the newspapers—that we doctors are given over nowadays to science; that we care much more for the disease and its scientific aspects than for the individual. I don't believe it, but at any rate, whether that tendency exists or not, I would urge upon you in your own practice to care particularly for John and Elizabeth, as George Eliot says,—but I will not add, especially for Elizabeth—but to care more particularly for the individual patient than for the special features of the disease. . . . Dealing, as we do,

---

[1] Cf. *Albany Medical Annals*, 1899, xx. 307.

with poor suffering humanity, we see the man unmasked, exposed to all the frailties and weaknesses, and you have to keep your heart soft and tender lest you have too great a contempt for your fellow creatures. The best way is to keep a looking-glass in your own heart, and the more carefully you scan your own frailties the more tender you are for those of your fellow creatures.

Science, however, was by no means forgotten, for the staff at the Hopkins one and all were busily engaged in forwarding knowledge as best they could. This spirit even pervaded the undergraduates, and such a discovery as had been made by T. R. Brown two years before regarding the eosinophilia of trichinosis well atoned for the hours over the microscope counting blood-cells to which the Hopkins students of the day were subjected. Brown at this time having just reported his fourth case, Osler was led to review his own personal experiences with the disease,[1] and to his former assistant, C. N. B. Camac, wrote as follows:

2.9.99.

. . . So glad of the gall-bladder article. It will do too for our third Typhoid studies at which I am at last at work. I have been much driven this winter—so much on hand and so many calls. By the way look out for the mild cases of trichinosis at Bellevue—The eosinophilia is most remarkable. Thayer has just found a 6th case in a nurse in town. It is really a very good blood find. You remember one of the cases when you were here. The Associate Professor [Thayer] is doing so well—a good many calls out of town. We still miss you & your good system—The new school I hope will make progress Schurman was here a few weeks ago—full of hopes & plans. Mrs. O & Ike are well—I hope to see you at an early date.

'So much on hand and so many calls.' From January to May of this year consultations were incessant—his afternoon hours filled, and many demands from out of town. Yet his other activities did not suffer, and each month saw one or two papers published, not a few of them being sent off to rejoice the editors of struggling medical journals of little more than local reputation, to many of which he permitted his name to be attached as collaborator. By this time, also, announcements had begun to appear regarding the coming anniversary of the Maryland Faculty, for

[1] 'The Clinical Features of Sporadic Trichinosis.' *American Journal of the Medical Sciences*, Mar. 1899.

which a liberal sum of money must needs be subscribed—'contributions to be sent as soon as possible to Dr. William Osler at 1 West Franklin Street'; and he took advantage of every opportunity to appeal for funds, as he did on January 25th at a meeting of the Book and Journal Club, at which time he described his visit of the summer before to Sydenham's birthplace.

February was the month of a memorable blizzard, and on the 18th he wrote to Dr. Lawrason Brown, one of the students who during his third year had contracted tuberculosis and had gone to join Trudeau:

PS. Adirondack drifts at—1 West Franklin Street,
2.18.99.

Dear Brown, Greetings! & best wishes for your pulmonic health! A nephew, Rev. H. C. G——, of Toronto, has just developed Tub. laryngitis 8 weeks duration. No trouble *evident* in lungs—condition good—no fever but bacilli found. I wish him to go to the Adir. at once. I have written Trudeau asking about the Sanitarium's private rooms but I tho't it would save time to ask you to let me know of some good boarding houses—with prices, &c. Love to Oliver—I hope you are both on the primrose path!

A light-hearted letter, but, with another sent at the same time to his nephew, telling him to cheer up his mother, for 'to know one's enemy is half the battle', it shows that he was serious enough and overlooked nothing in his behalf.

Early in the year he had accepted the invitation from the West London Medico-Chirurgical Society to give the Cavendish Lecture, and plans for another summer abroad were already being made, as indicated in a note of March 24th to one of the Francis 'nieces' from 'her loving old doctor', which says: 'We shall spend July & August somewhere by the sea quietly & if you are in England it will be very jolly to have you with us, with sister too—the bad thing. Revere is fun now, & so full of mischief.' But lest one lose track of Osler in his daily rounds in the hospital wards during the recital of all these extracurricular matters, a bedside incident of the period recalled by Dr. Joseph Walsh may be related:

In the spring of 1899 [he writes] shortly after my return from two years' medical study in Europe I first met Osler in the Johns Hopkins

Hospital, and he invited me to his house. . . . One of the cases he showed me on his ward rounds next morning I have frequently quoted since, on account of its encouragement to people afflicted with less serious ills. She was an old woman of seventy-five, in the hospital for acute rheumatism, who also showed a wind tumour of Steno's duct the size of a walnut, which she could inflate and deflate at pleasure. Osler said it was the second one he had seen. Both of these conditions, however, were incidental to her general history.

'Mother,' said Osler, 'I would like you to tell Dr. Walsh something about your past life. When were you first in a hospital?' 'At twenty-seven.' 'What was the matter?' 'I had sarcoma of the right knee.' 'What did they do for it?' 'They cut off the right leg at the hip.' 'Did you get entirely well?' 'Yes, entirely well.' 'When were you in again?' 'At forty-two.' 'What was the matter?' 'I had cancer of the left breast.' 'What did they do for it?' 'They cut off the left breast and left arm.' 'Did you get entirely well?' 'Yes, entirely well.' 'What are you in the hospital for, now?' 'For rheumatism; and Doctor,' she said, with tears in her voice, and catching his hand, 'I hope you will make me well in a hurry, because I have to go home to take care of my grandchildren.'

Osler, in short, never forgot the patient in his interest in the malady, and this incident which has stamped itself on Dr. Walsh's memory could be reduplicated a hundred times by the students. There was a tradition among the clinical clerks that 'if you want to see the Chief at his best watch him as he passes the bedside of some poor old soul with a chronic and hopeless malady—they always get his best'.

It is evident from the following note that some one had offered a hospital ship to go to the tropics, but more important at this juncture is the allusion to a missionary tour nearer home:

To D. C. Gilman from W. O. 3.29.99.

It does seem a thousand pities not to do something with such an offer & such a ship—but what? She would be invaluable as a floating Hospital in Manila. In Cuba the Government will doubtless feel that private charity of this kind reflects somewhat on the War Dept. A three months' study of the malaria problem in the West Indies would be worth undertaking. We could supply the men for such work. I am off with Tiffany on a missionary tour to Garrett & Alleghany counties & will not return until Friday noon. I should be glad to meet you & Mr Baker at any hour after then.

The 'missionary tour' was for the purpose of arousing

in these counties an interest in the coming centennial of the State Faculty. During the year he and a few others with renewed ardour endeavoured to elevate the ponderous and inactive old society by its very boot-straps; and by trips to the counties, such as he mentions taking with McLane Tiffany, who also was a member of the Executive Committee, they succeeded in enrolling one hundred new members. He even appears to have entertained the hope that an endowment might be raised for a new building, and wrote to James R. Chadwick, urging him to come and make another speech. 'You stirred up the brethren here & they have not forgotten it.' It was a vain hope. It was difficult indeed even to raise funds sufficient to cover the expenses of the meeting, which was planned on a generous scale fitting such an anniversary. The responsibility of the affairs and general policy of the society rested largely upon the shoulders of the small Executive Committee of the Faculty, of which for some years he had been Chairman. But in addition, he was this year on the Board of Trustees, on the Library Committee, and President of the Book & Journal Club, through whose agency most of the book-purchasing funds were raised.

For months there had been advertisements in the journals to the effect that persons knowing of old portraits or relics of interest in connexion with the Faculty or the profession of Maryland were requested to notify Dr. William Osler; and that every physician of the State, of whatever society, creed, or school, was urged to attend a meeting which had such historical significance. Osler, of course, did not do all this alone, but those who participated recall that he was the chief moving spirit. There is little in the printed records [1] about him except that he gave on the opening night a dinner at the Maryland Club to the Trustees, officers, and chief guests, a large reception at his house on another evening, and a clinic on cerebro-spinal meningitis one morning—but then, others did similar things, too.

The centennial exercises were more like those of the

[1] There is a long account of this successful meeting in E. F. Cordell's large centennial tome—'The Medical Annals of Maryland'—finally issued in 1903.

great congresses, so successfully staged in later years, but which were then less common—with clinics at all the hospitals, with demonstrations, lectures, and exhibits at set hours day by day, in the hope of arousing the interest of the profession at large in their State society. An immense amount of labour had been expended on the exhibits, which for lack of space in the small Faculty home were put up in McCoy Hall, one of the Hopkins University buildings—the published works of the Maryland profession, works relating to the chief epochs of medical history, largely borrowed from the Surgeon-General's Library, portraits of distinguished Maryland physicians, and so on—for all of which Osler and Welch were chiefly responsible. And a memorable occurrence at one of the evening meetings, which had a thin programme because of the non-appearance of two out-of-town speakers, was when Welch stepped into the gap and gave extemporaneously a *résumé* of medical history as illustrated by the exhibits in the hall. How the local profession felt about the man in the background of all this, can be surmised by the fact that at the fully attended annual dinner held on the last evening, the President-elect, Dr. Clotworthy Birnie, a country doctor, referred at the close of his speech to the new county members who had been drawn into the society, and to the good-will existing between them and the Baltimore profession, saying: 'The tact that was necessary to bring this condition about, and the industry to apply it, is due in great measure to one man.' When he had taken his seat there were insistent calls for 'Osler!' who arose, and said:

> It may not be known to the members of this Faculty that part of the reason why I love my fellow practitioners in the country rather more than my fellow practitioners in town is that I narrowly escaped being a country doctor. I was brought up in the office of a country doctor, and he has told me that the saddest hours of his life were those he spent while I was his office student. I never did appreciate drugs, and didn't even understand the importance of keeping each one in its proper place, but generally managed to put the morphia bottle where the quinine ought to be, so my preceptor had difficulty in the dusk to find them, and on one occasion he nearly poisoned his best patient.

All of which probably refers to his days in Dundas assisting

Dr. A. H. Walker, and the 'speck in cornea 50¢' entry. But he went on in more serious vein to tell of the growth of the library, the needs of the institution, the necessity of an endowment, and the importance of a new building in some degree commensurate with the age of the society and its importance to the city and state. There was no reason, he said, why, with united effort, they could not have a first-class, well-equipped home; there was no reason why it could not be obtained within a short period. 'I would urge the members of the Faculty', he said in closing, 'to take this to heart, and I intend to ask at the business meeting tomorrow evening that a committee be appointed to take this matter in hand and work it systematically during the next year.'

Following the centennial came a visit from Trudeau, who talked to Osler's class on some questions relating to tuberculosis; and together, while Mrs. Osler took Revere for a visit to his grandmother in Toronto, they went over to Washington for the annual meeting, held May 2nd to 4th, of the Association of Physicians. There, as usual, he took an active part in the discussions and was down on the programme for a paper on a peculiar form of bronzing of the skin (Haemochromatosis), and presented a patient with this rare malady, which was beginning to excite attention.[1] In this paper due credit was given to his recent house officer, Dr. Eugene Opie, for the special studies he had made on the subject. In these matters he was most punctilious. There is a story told of a visit William Pepper made to the Hopkins to see the clinical laboratory at the time he was planning to erect a similar laboratory in memory of his father at the University of Pennsylvania, and in the course of their conversation, according to a bystander, Pepper said: 'Osler, if discoveries are made in such a laboratory as this, does the Director get the credit?' The answer came immediately: 'Why Pepper, no; the worker of course! Suppose we go to lunch.'

He must have busied himself during May with the assembling, at least, of the material for his Cavendish

[1] He was evidently hard pressed and used the same material for his paper before the British Medical Association meeting later on.

Lecture,[1] which contained an elaborate *résumé* of the experiences with all forms of meningitis in his clinic. The paper, however, was devoted largely to the epidemic form of the disease which had so widely prevailed in the United States with a very high mortality—as high as 68·5 per cent. in some localities. Such diagnostic procedures as lumbar puncture were at this time only just being introduced, and a serum treatment of the disease was hardly dreamed of—indeed, the man who was to elaborate it was at this time serving on a commission in the Philippines.

Their passages had been taken for May 31st, and he wound up his curtailed school year with notes like the following to John H. Musser: 'Janeway has appointed you and Fitz and me a Committee to get up a memorial to Dr. W. W. Johnston on the occasion of his retiring from the treasurership of the Association. I am sending out a little circular, and my secretary will collect the money.' Probably the memorial to his friend Johnston had been his own suggestion, and E. G. Janeway[2] of New York, who was President of the Association of Physicians, had, as is usual under such circumstances, put the suggester on the committee. And there were other brief notes, such as: 'Dear Mr. Coy, please call a meeting of the Medical Faculty for Friday May 26 at 4.30. Sincerely yours', &c. Beyond such missives there is little trace of Osler's short service as Dean of the Medical School; and after holding the position for this single year he was succeeded by W. H. Howell, the Professor of Physiology, when the office of the Dean became installed in a small room in the new building for Howell's department. Indeed, the medical school had a way of running itself, with the aid of one person, this selfsame Mr. George J. Coy to whom this request had been passed.

From London, June 8th, he wrote to Ogden of a delightful voyage, and added: 'Very interesting meeting of the

[1] 'On the Etiology and Diagnosis of Cerebrospinal Fever.' *The West London Medical Journal*, 1899. Reprinted by W. O.

[2] It was Janeway who, a short time before, had, as the British papers put it, saved 'to the cause of letters and mankind the life of Rudyard Kipling'.

Royal Society this afternoon. I was admitted and had to sign the book and be cordially shaken by the hand by Lord Lister.'[1] And a few days later to W. S. Thayer from 36 Half Moon Street:

We had a jolly trip over—fine skies & smooth seas. I really enjoyed it. We did not get in until Wednesday night. I finished my address on the S. S. & it is now in type. It will come out in Lancet & B. M. J. of the week after next. I have been loafing since coming here & have seen very few Doctors except at the Royal Society where I heard Haffkine talk in very good form on India & the plague inoculations. Glorious weather—hot for the Londoners. We had a jolly day with Schäfer in the country yesterday. He hopes to get the Edinboro appointment in Physiology. Revere had the time of his life on the S. S. Love to the boys.

Revere had 'the time of his life' whenever he was with his father, and no child ever found a father a better playmate. Some weeks later, from Swanage on the Dorset coast, the boy of four summers dictated for H. B. Jacobs this laboured note:

Dear Dr. Jacobs, I am having a good time. We have been in London very hard. I like London. I got lots of toys at London—some blocks too. We are at the seaside now. 1, 2, 3, 4, 5. We have a nice little house and a bathing tent and a pony. E. R. Osler.

They were indeed in London 'very hard'. The Cavendish Lecture was delivered in the Town Hall, Kensington, on June 16th; at the conclusion of which, after being subjected to the more than usually flattering votes of thanks, in which he was likened to a modern Hippocrates and his great diversity of talent was pointed out, he briefly thanked the society for their reception and added that whatever he had been able to do in his life had been accomplished by hard and persevering work. With this carefully prepared and technical lecture off his hands there began a round of book shops and libraries, interspersed with dinners and entertainments from which there was no escape, since his old friends, E. A. Schäfer, Sir Andrew Clark, Lauder Brunton, Stephen Mackenzie, Jonathan Hutchinson and others clamoured for him in turn. The

[1] On June 10th Osler was given a LL.D. (*in absentia*) at the commencement exercises of the University of Toronto.

only cloud to the summer's happiness was the news of the death on July 7th of his old schoolmate, James E. Graham, Professor of Medicine at Toronto, who in recent years had selected for him from among the promising Toronto graduates a number of the men who had become his assistants in Baltimore.

> Dr. Graham was one of my oldest friends in the profession [he wrote]. During the session of 1868–9 he was a senior student in the Toronto School when I was a freshman, and every Saturday morning throughout the session we met at Dr. Bovell's to work with the microscope. To both of us the memory of those happy days was ever dear. It was a great privilege after the dry programme of the week, to be brought into contact with a genuine enthusiast who loved to work at as well as to think about the problems of disease. On these occasions the only annoyance to Dr. Bovell was the 'damned guinea', in Hunter's phrase, and how often have we laughed at the involuntary anathema which would escape the lips of the good pious man when the maid announced a patient! . . .[1]

They had gone out to Haslemere to pay a visit to Jonathan Hutchinson, and to see the educational village museum and the Memorial Holiday Home for London Children which that high-minded old man had established. It was Hutchinson who suggested Swanage to them as a suitable place for their summer outing, possibly because it was near Wynford Eagle. However this may be, it proved a great success, as the following extract of a letter from Mrs. Osler to Dr. Jacobs testifies:

> . . . I wish you could see the dear little house and garden we have taken for six weeks. Swanage is below Poole and Bournemouth, a quiet little place on a pretty bay with cliffs at either end—no mosquitoes—no flies—no invitations—no southwest wind—no one to bother us. We have two servants with the house and all the tradespeople call at the door, so housekeeping is no trouble. I am enchanted with the garden. One end of the house is covered with a rose vine and I am having a perfect treat. We are about one minute from the beach where we have a bathing tent. Dr. Osler is very happy. He has golf in the morning—then a swim, and loafs all the afternoon. We hope to have Dr. McCrae here for a few days and perhaps Dr. Halsted for a night. We were ready to leave London—we had lunched and dined until we were nearly dead.

[1] *British Medical Journal*, July 29, 1899, ii. 317.

Revere is so happy, it is a joy to see him. We will stay until August 25th, then have a week in London before sailing on Sept. 2nd. . . .

To H. B. Jacobs from W. O. The Gwyle, Swanage, Dorset. 20th.

Many thanks for the chart. I am going to discuss endocarditis at the B. M. A. I would try to get M. S.'s early record if possible. You should report the case—the embolic features are remarkable. Poor lassie! It was a sad business. I hope Mr. D. has paid you. I had not sent him any bill & I forget whether I put it on the July list for Miss Humpton. We are enjoying this place greatly—fine bathing, good driving, beautiful country, superb downs (R. calls them 'ups') & a most comfortable little house with good servants. Mrs. Osler says it is a god-send. I sent a reprint of the Cavendish Lecture to 3 W. Fr. I hope T. has forwarded it. Revere looks well, badly sunburnt on his bare legs. We have had one day's rain in six weeks. The country is very dry—an occasional fog here keeps the coast-line green. Kindest regards to your mother.

That Thomas McCrae, then an assistant-resident on Osler's staff, paid his expected visit is evident from a pocket note-book of the period in which this has been scribbled:

A game of Sixes on Poundburg Ring. Players: Tom Lovell, Ed Rowe, Dave Hayes, E. Y. D., T. McC. and a wall-eyed sheep dog. On the north side of the celebrated Poundburg Ring, on the turf-walk of the rampart at 3 p.m. July 26th lay three boys, two men and a venerable dog. The positions were as in annexed diagram. Tom, a tow-headed lad of 16, bossed the party and had the cards—a small dirty, dog-eared but complete pack. The game he said was sixes,

Tom Ed.
Dog Dave
T. McC. E. Y. D.

which I did not know, so I put up 3*d.* in middle to be played for by the boys, and that we could catch the trick of the game. Tom dealt one first, then two, then three, not always in order and it was evident that so long as each boy got six it did not matter how the cards came. Ed led off with the ten of hearts which he called spades, in ignorance I thought as he was young and looked a green hand; Dave covered it, trumped it he said, with a four or six of spades, and Tom took the trick proudly with a face-card—the knave of hearts.

It was an episode which Osler might have used to adorn a tale and point a moral, but what was in 'E. Y. D.'s' mind does not appear, though it shows an interest in children and a capacity for amusement. There are other notes, which indicate that he had been reading Jessop's 'Life of John Donne', T. Longueville's 'Sir Kenelm Digby', the 'arch-amateur of all history'; and the 'Letters and Unpublished Writings of Walter Savage Landor', by Stephen Wheeler. Then under the date of August 12th occurs the long description of a visit to the house of Benjamin Jesty, the pre-Jennerian vaccinator—a note subsequently turned over to McCrae to incorporate in his interesting account of Jesty, read in the autumn before the Hopkins Historical Club:

Downshay (pronounced Dunsai). The farm occupies a delightful situation in a valley between the Purbeck Hills and Nine Barrow Downs, four miles from Corfe Castle. Leaving the Kingston Road the house is reached by a rough and rutted road through the fields, with many steep descents. It is not seen at first, indeed we did not look for it as our whole attention was centred on the superb outlook; to the left in the setting sun the ruins of Corfe Castle, guarding the gateway to the Isle of Purbeck—to the right the town of Swanage with its fine blue bay, and far off on the horizon the white cliffs of the Isle of Wight (the Needles), while across the valley rose the fine sweep of the Nine Barrow Downs. Encircled by trees and in a depression we did not see the house until we reached the barnyard where we were cordially greeted by a jolly-looking dairyman who had just driven out one herd and was preparing to finish the evening milking. . . .

They made other expeditions—to see the Roman remains at Dorchester, where they spent the night, and there is an amusing story of an old man in the tap-room who was furious because the chimes kept ringing in the church near by, and whom W. O., to pass the evening, egged on to expostulate about chimes in general. From there they went to Wynford Eagle, and it was on this visit that he picked the 'rose from the vine over the door of Sydenham's birthplace'. And then to the little hamlet of Rampisham in Dorset where Glisson is supposed to have been born, and where they tried in vain to find the entry of his birth in the parish church records of the sixteenth century.

Meanwhile, during the first week in August they had attended the B. M. A. meeting at Portsmouth, and here, in addition to giving his formal paper, he participated in the discussions which had been prearranged for two of the more important sessions of the medical section. The subject at one of them—a subject just beginning to be thoroughly ventilated—was the Prevention and Remedial Treatment of Tuberculosis, in which Clifford Allbutt, Sir William Broadbent, R. Douglas Powell, Osler, James Tyson of Philadelphia, who had just been appointed to succeed Pepper, and others, all took part. Another session was devoted to the Medical Tests for Admission to the Public Services, and in the course of his remarks Osler referred to 'the beneficial effects of general military training on the young men of the nation, as exemplified in Germany, a benefit seen not less on their bodies than on their minds, which while plastic learned the all-important lesson of life—discipline'. Little did he realize that these plastic young minds and bodies were being so disciplined that they might react to a call to arms when 'the day' should arrive. And during this very summer, it may be added, the delirium of the Dreyfus case was stirring France to its depths, and the ill-fated Czar was making proposals for a peace conference at The Hague.

Swanage proved, as the August letters testify, to have been a 'haven of rest'; and though with 'only one shower in seven weeks the cattle were suffering and the sheep being fed on the ill-grown carrots', it had been perfect for the three who, before the summer was over, were all 'as dark as Rebecca, Mammy's substitute'. Leaving his golf-clubs behind, which 'looked like another summer in Dorset', towards the end of August Osler went for a week-end to visit the Allbutts and Nuttall in Cambridge, while Mrs. Osler took Revere, who 'had not cried three times this summer', to London preparatory to their sailing on September 2nd. There, while W. O. was grubbing in the British Museum, a Scotch nurse was engaged who was 'to come out in October and take the place of the boy's Mammy' whom he had now outgrown. The last entry in the pocket notebook of the summer reads as follows:

Brown, Sir Thomas, bought the 1st authorized edition of the Religio Medici 1643, from Quaritch, August 1899. £7. 7.

Aug. 29th. Saw to-day the two unauthorized editions:—(a) British Museum. Same publisher as authorized, Andrew Crooke, 1642. Same figure on title page, but between the extended arm and the rock are the words 'Religio Medici', and at one corner, Will: Marshall. scu:. There are 159 pages. K. Digby's Observations follow. (b) at Coll. Phy. Bound alone without Digby's observations. Title page same as B. M. copy, 190 pp. (on a slip W. A. G. [Greenhill] says 'This is a copy of the unauthorized edition and is probably very scarce').

As likely as not, it was the purchase of this early edition of the 'Religio' that led him into the bibliophilic pursuit of gathering a complete set of all the editions.[1] He probably had seen while in Portsmouth a good deal of J. Frank Payne, an ardent book-collector, who happened to be President of one of the B. M. A. sections, and, as may be recalled, an effort was being made at this time to collect funds for the erection of a monument to Sir Thomas Browne to be placed in the shadow of St. Peter Mancroft.

From Canton, Mass., on September 12th he wrote to his friend Shepherd in regard to an address promised for the opening of the McGill session; and three days later from 1 West Franklin Street this to Simon Flexner:

Welcome home! with, I hope, an undefiled liver and a smooth colic mucosa. We were on the look-out for you in London, but I suppose you hurried back via Frisco. I am most anxious to see you and hear of your doings. What a delightful experience! We had a peaceful summer on the south coast. I saw Nuttall who has taken Cambridge by storm. I have just returned. Let me know if I can be of any use to you in the way of introductions.

The Spanish War, the responsibility of the Philippine Islands, Leonard Wood's great success as Governor-General in rehabilitating Havana and the Province of Santiago, had aroused Americans to some conception of the importance of 'the white man's burden'. A very important part of the load in Cuba, the Philippines, and soon in the Canal Zone, had to fall upon the medical profession, and early in the year a commission headed by Barker and Flexner had been sent to the Philippines to investigate and to make a report upon the diseases of the archipelago.[2] To be sure, this was only preliminary to what had to be done there,

[1] Cf. Geoffrey Keynes, 'Bibliography of Sir Thomas Browne', Camb. Univ. Press, 1924: dedicated to Sir William Osler.

[2] Barker, with J. M. Flint, one of the undergraduate members of the commission, had returned home by way of India in order to study the plague which was then rampant there.

and ere long Leonard Wood, though not in his medical capacity, volunteered to go to the Islands and persuade, in one way or another, the head-hunting Moros to engage in more peaceful pursuits.

As part of all this, great interest was being aroused in the comparatively new specialty of tropical medicine. A school had been established in Liverpool. A course to be devoted especially to the study of tropical diseases was announced by Osler, to be given at the Hopkins in the autumn. Guitéras, himself a Cuban, had resigned from his position as Pathologist at the University of Pennsylvania so that he might go to Havana and work with the American Commission which was investigating yellow fever. To his post Flexner was to succeed, and hence Osler had asked if he might be of use in the way of introductions.

To John H. Musser from W. O. 1 West Franklin Street, Sunday

Dear J. H. I was on the point of writing to you last eve, when someone came in. We returned last Sunday & I took Mrs O & Ike to Mrs Revere's & came here on Friday. The summer was a great success. We took a house on the Dorset coast & had two months of peace sunshine sands & sea. The first month in London was very pleasant. . . . I have been book hunting & grubbing in the British Museum & Record Office. I go to Montreal on Wednesday to give the opening address at the college. I have not a copy of the B. M. J. article. So glad to hear that the prospects are good at the University. I forgot to congratulate you on your appt. I did not hear definitely until I saw Tyson at Portsmouth & after that forgot. I am sure you will be able to arrange the work very comfortably. Do come down soon.

On September 21st he gave before the assembled faculty and students of McGill the address, 'After Twenty-five Years'[1]—from which the paragraphs reminiscent of his days in Montreal have already been quoted in an earlier chapter. For the benefit of the faculty he discussed the many and different ways in which successful teaching may be carried out, one of them, when classes are small, being the elbow-to-elbow method under trial at Baltimore:

Undoubtedly [he said] the student tries to learn too much, and we teachers try to teach him too much—neither, perhaps, with great success. The existing evils result from neglect on the part of the

[1] *Montreal Medical Journal*, Nov. 1899, xxviii. 823–33.

teacher, student and examiner of the great fundamental principle laid down by Plato—that education is a life-long process, in which the student can only make a beginning during his college course. The system under which we work asks too much of the student in limited time. To cover the vast field of medicine in four years is an impossible task. We can only instil principles, put the student in the right path, give him methods, teach him how to study, and early to discern between essentials and non-essentials. Perfect happiness for student and teacher will come with the abolition of examinations, which are stumbling-blocks and rocks of offence in the pathway of the true student. And it is not so Utopian as may appear at first blush. Ask any demonstrator of anatomy ten days before the examinations, and he should be able to give you a list of the men fit to pass. Extend the personal intimate knowledge such as is possessed by a competent demonstrator of anatomy into all the other departments, and the degree could be safely conferred upon certificates of competency, which would really mean a more thorough knowledge of a man's fitness than can possibly be got by our present system of examination.

From this he went on to consider the congested state of the curriculum, suggesting measures of relief that he 'would recommend particularly to the younger men, in whose hands alone such radical changes can be carried out. A man', he characteristically added, 'who has been teaching for twenty-five years is rarely in a position to appreciate the necessity of a change, particularly if it touches his own special branch'. Then, addressing himself more directly to the students before him, he advised them to start with no higher ambition than to join 'the noble band of general practitioners', who 'form the very sinews of the profession—generous-hearted men, with well balanced cool heads, not scientific always, but learned in the wisdom not of the laboratories but of the sick-room'. And after referring to the cultivation of interests other than purely professional ones, he urges outside reading, and says, perhaps with his summer's purchase in mind, that 'the "Religio Medici", one of the great English classics, should be in the hands—in the hearts, too—of every medical student'.

As I am on the confessional to-day, I may tell you that no book has had so enduring an influence on my life. I was introduced to it by my first teacher, the Rev. W. A. Johnson, Warden and Founder of the Trinity College School, and I can recall the delight with which I first read its quaint and charming pages. It was one of the strong influences which turned my thoughts towards medicine as a profession, and my most treasured copy—the second book I ever bought—has been a constant companion for thirty-one years—*comes viae vitaeque*. Trite but true, is the comment of Seneca—'If you are fond of books you will escape the ennui of life, you will neither sigh for evening disgusted with the occupations of the day—nor will you live dissatisfied with yourself or unprofitable to others.' And, finally, gentlemen, remember that you are here not to be made chemists or physiologists or anatomists, but to learn how to recognize and treat disease, how to become practical physicians.

'After twenty-five years.' It was a more mature Osler, who spoke with experience and authority, but the ideas in the address were not very different—perhaps they never are in such addresses—from those in his first valedictory lecture of 1875, even to the inclusion of Sir Thomas Browne. It seemed, however, less necessary than before to warn against the temptation of drink, for 'nowadays', he said, 'even the pleasures of a medical student have become respectable, and I have no doubt that the "footing supper", which in old Coté Street days was a Bacchanalian orgy, has become a love-feast in which the Principal and even the Dean might participate'. Hundreds of introductory talks for students, consisting, as a rule, of perfunctory admonitions, are being given every autumn to the groups of young men in all countries, who are entering medicine. But this was an address of a different order: picturesque, appealing, and written with apparent ease, which merely means that he had learned to conceal the effort which all good writing requires, even in the gifted. The notable thing is that he was willing to take so much trouble for such an occasion.

Of his other doings in Montreal there is no trace, but it may be assumed that no old friend was forgotten; that the Howard children were very much excited; and that 'Damphino Cook', looking very proud, was circulating to the new-comers, stories, on the side, of the good old days—'me and the Dean'. There must, too, have been talk of the South African War, for a small Canadian contingent had already been dispatched and Strathcona's Horse was being organized. How this distant war of none-too-happy origin touched Osler does not yet appear, though one of his house staff at this time, 'Jack' McCrae, newly appointed, was straining at the leash. 'If I can get an appointment in England by going, I will go', he wrote. 'My position here I do not count as an old boot in comparison.' The autumn semester at the Hopkins began on October 1st, and a few days later [1] he sent this note to Musser:

1 West Franklin Street,
10. 5.

Dear J. H. So glad to hear of the new Edition. I will show it at once to the class. What a nuisance that the publishers are always ten days late! Those new cuts are beauties. I began work this week—larger classes alas! but we have doubled the size of the 3rd year dispensary class room. They are after Futcher for Graham's place but I cannot let him off until a year from this date. We are all delighted at Clark's success.[2] You must have had the Provost's ear. I wrote warmly to Da Costa & to Tyson. The former sent a most encouraging reply. It was a brave move on the part of the faculty as C of course is not widely known thro the state. He is a trump—we never had a better fellow about the Hospital. Barker is back—full of interesting information about the Plague in India. Do come & see us soon. Yours ever, W. O.

Preparations at this time were under way for the next international congress, to be held in Paris in connexion with the World's Exhibition, and as Osler had been called upon to organize an American Committee, a vast deal of correspondence followed with the several 'Presidents of the American Medical Association and the Congress of American Physicians and Surgeons, and of the national societies forming part of the Congress, and the Surgeon-Generals of the Army, Navy and Marine Hospital Service', who were chosen to constitute the Committee. Meanwhile the hospital wards were filled with the autumnal crop of typhoids, and his pen was again busied with this more interesting subject. As usual, he combined the duty of his antityphoid propaganda with the pleasure of collateral

[1] On that same day, October 5th, the Association of Medical Librarians held their annual meeting, a constitution was adopted, and 34 medical librarians had become enrolled.

[2] John G. Clark's appointment to the Chair of Gynaecology at the University of Pennsylvania.

reading and writing. Having promised to attend two society meetings, one in New York and the other in Rhode Island, he prepared for the first a succinct statement concerning 'The Diagnosis of Typhoid Fever', and alongside of this, for the second, he was engaged in a task far more to his liking—the putting together of his sketch of Elisha Bartlett:

To Dr. F. C. Shattuck from W. O. Monday eve

I have been enjoying a quiet evening with old Elisha Bartlett, W. W. Gerhard, G. C. Shattuck Jr. & James Jackson Jr.—delightful company after the Medico-Chirurgical Bulletin and trash of that kind! Your father's papers I found in the Med. Examiner for 1840 and Valleix gives a very full summary in Archives Générales for Oct–Nov 1839. The contribution is admirable. I had never seen it before. Stillé too has a paper which he read at the Société d'Observation some months before your father's. It has never been printed. I must get a copy from the old man for I should some day like to collect the essays of W. W. Gerhard, your father and Stillé & publish them together. I see dear old Sam Wilks is still under the delusion that Jenner in 1849–50 first clearly separated typhus and typhoid! Yours [etc.]. P.S. Do come down this winter & spend a quiet week. Soft old bed, breakfast in it at 9.30. Scotch (hot) at 10 p.m.

This was his form of taking literary recreation, just as in preparing his paper on the continuous fevers of the South he had turned to an account of John Y. Bassett. Unlike the 'Alabama Student', however, Bartlett needed not to be rescued from oblivion, for he already occupied an important niche in medical history, and his name as one of Louis's American pupils was often on the tip of Osler's tongue and at the nib of his pen.

In the first of these papers[1] he somewhat severely arraigned certain members of the New York profession (one of whom, it may be added, in somewhat sarcastic vein subsequently replied) on their evident failure in many cases to differentiate properly between malaria and typhoid:

One has [he said] to sympathize a bit with him—clinical fetishes are given up with difficulty and regret: To many good, easy men

[1] Contributed to a general discussion on typhoid at a meeting of the New York State Medical Association, held on October 25th. *N. Y. Medical Journal*, 1899, lxx. 673.

it came as a shock, to find that malaria was really a well-defined, easily recognizable disease. Naturally, it was hard to abandon a word like *malaria*, which carried with it as much clinical comfort as did that blessed word *Mesopotamia* spiritual unction to the old lady. My sympathies have been deeply aroused by the distress which has been felt in many quarters of this city where you have been, until recently, with some notable exceptions, heretics of the worst kind. Nowhere, perhaps, has malaria ever covered such a multitude of diverse maladies. . . .

He proceeded to give clinical rules of diagnosis which should guide practitioners above Mason & Dixon's Line, emphasizing that in these regions an intermittent fever which resists quinine is not of malarial origin, nor is a continued fever due to malarial infection, even though for variability of symptoms the aestivo-autumnal infection takes precedence even of typhoid fever. And he drew an amusing comparison between the temperature charts of the two diseases —typhoid which has a 'Pennsylvania-Railway-like' directness, in marked distinction to the zigzag 'Baltimore-and-Ohio-Railway' chart of aestivo-autumnal fever. He begged the hard-worked practitioners of the smaller towns and country districts, who found it difficult to apply the modern scientific methods of diagnosis, to use their common sense and learn to suspect typhoid and not malaria in every case of fever of six or seven days' duration. And in the course of the paper he spoke of the country's recent experience with typhoid at the Chickamauga Camp, which was 'a wholesale demonstration of the ignorance among the profession of the essential elementary facts concerning the two diseases'. Had he known of the fact he would probably have added that steps were being taken elsewhere to prevent a repetition of the experience of the American army camps; for the Professor of Pathology at Netley, Almroth E. Wright, whom Osler must have seen at the Portsmouth meeting of the B. M. A. the summer before, was, at this very time, making his first tentative inoculations of the British troops being mobilized for the South African War, among whom severe outbreaks of typhoid had already occurred.

The autumn meeting of the Maryland 'Faculty' was

held on November 14th in Westminster, Maryland, with Osler as usual in attendance, and though the starred feature of the programme was undoubtedly the report, by Barker and Flexner, upon the medical conditions in the Philippines, Osler's short paper on 'The Home Treatment of Consumption' should not be overlooked, for it is of historical importance.[1] He estimated that there were some eight or ten thousand cases in Baltimore alone, of whom only a possible 5 per cent. could receive treatment in sanatoria; and he made a strong plea for greater attention to the living conditions of consumptives, instancing the case of the brave young woman who at this time (he had just been to Cumberland to see her) was, on his advice, living out of doors *at her own home*—a novel idea in the 90's. He never forgot her and she still lives to bless him.

The campaign against the 'white plague' was still confined to a few members of the profession, and had not yet reached the public. But the ball he had set rolling the year before in Baltimore was already gaining momentum. An active crusade to enlighten the public seemed to be the only way to conquer tuberculosis, and traces of the movement had already been apparent—an International Tuberculosis Congress at Berlin—the session at the B. M. A. the summer before—the subject brought up at a State medical meeting—finally brought home to a single institution which was among the first to gain recruits under the banner of the white cross on a red field. Out of all this, as will be seen, the Social Service movement took its origin.

As a result of his McGill address two months before, there had been a shower of letters from his old students—to each of whom a personal hand-written acknowledgement went in return: thus to Dr. J. H. Darey, whom in 1886 he had sent out to Iowa for his health:

11. 17. 99.

I was very glad to hear from you. My address has called out letters from several of my old Montreal boys. What a hard road you have had to travel! I feel sure you will settle down to peace & mental quiet as the years pass. A steady uniform life, 1/2 speed, as little stress & strain as possible should obviate the tendency to these

[1] *Maryland Medical Journal*, 1900, xliii. 8–12.

recurrent attacks. You probably do not heed your domestic counsellor enough. I was delighted to see the progress at McGill—the outlook is good for a great medical centre. I am pegging away here, very interested in the teaching of which I have a great deal. I send you a bundle of reprints some of which may amuse you.

The address, 'Elisha Bartlett: A Rhode Island Philosopher', a by-product, as has been seen, of his historical studies regarding typhoid fever, was given in Providence on December 7th, before the Rhode Island Medical Society. He was forever arousing in people in different localities an interest in their local medical worthies. It was, for example, customary for him to ask any one hailing from Cincinnati when they were going to put up a monument to Daniel Drake, for he had made a vow never to visit there until one was erected. It was usual for them to admit that they did not know who he was.[1] So, on this occasion, in his introductory paragraph he mildly rebuked his audience for their neglect of Bartlett:

> Rhode Island can boast of but one great philosopher—one to whose flights in the empyrean neither Roger Williams nor any of her sons could soar—the immortal Berkeley, who was a transient guest in this State, waiting quietly and happily for the realization of his Utopian schemes. Still, he lived long enough in Rhode Island to make his name a part of her history; long enough in America to make her the inspiration of the celebrated lines on the course of empire. Elisha Bartlett, teacher, philosopher, author, of whom I am about to speak, whom you may claim as the most distinguished physician of this State, has left no deep impression on your local history or institutions. Here he was born and educated, and to this, his home, he returned to die; but his busy life was spent in other fields, where to-day his memory is cherished more warmly than in the land of his birth. . . .

He had secured from Bartlett's nephew the letters and family papers that enabled him to put together a biographical sketch, in which he particularly stressed his student years abroad. And most sympathetically he treated

[1] Osler's interest in Drake must have gone back to 1894, for there are two or three letters in October of that year indicating that he was in correspondence with certain members of Drake's family and had secured some letters and documents regarding him. They are inserted in the copy of Drake's 'Pioneer Life in Kentucky' in his library.

of his career as a medical writer, of his brief experience as editor of a medical journal, and of his life as a peripatetic professor:

For many years there was in this country a group of peripatetic teachers who, like the Sophists of Greece, went from town to town, staying a year or two in each, or they divided their time between a winter session in a large city school and a summer term in a small country one. Among them Daniel Drake takes the precedence, as he made eleven moves in the course of his stirring and eventful life. Bartlett comes an easy second, having taught in nine schools. Dunglison, T. R. Beck, Willard Parker, Alonzo Clark, the elder Gross, Austin Flint, Frank H. Hamilton, and many others whom I could name, belonged to this group of wandering professors. The medical education of the day was almost exclusively theoretical; the teachers lectured for a short four months' session, there was a little dissection, a few major operations were witnessed, the fees were paid, examinations were held—and all was over.

Teacher, philosopher, author, orator, and poet—on all of these aspects of Bartlett's remarkable career he touched; and appended to the essay, when published,[1] he reprinted one of Bartlett's latest writings, the sketch of Hippocrates, containing that imaginary scene of Pericles upon his death-bed with the young physician from Cos in attendance, which Osler regarded as a masterpiece worthy of Walter Savage Landor—exceeded by few word-pictures in the English language.

[1] In 'An Alabama Student and other Biographical Essays.' Lond., Henry Frowde, 1908.

CHAPTER XIX

1900

THE EDINBURGH CALL; AND THE BEGINNINGS OF SOCIAL SERVICE

To Humphry Rolleston from W. O. 1 West Franklin Street,
Jan. 1, 1900.

Greetings and best wishes for the New Year! I have just read the review of the concluding volume of Allbutt's System, and it occurred to me that the contributors should express in some way their appreciation of the Editor's labours. What do you think? I should be very glad to join in anything. . . .

Friendly thoughts and reactions of the sort relating to Clifford Allbutt were by no means restricted to the first day of the year. He was at it again two days later in a letter to D. C. Gilman urging that Dr. E. F. Cordell, who by this time had about completed his expensive and voluminous 'Medical Annals of Maryland', be appointed to the vacant position of Custodian of the Toner Collection of the Congressional Library. But there were other more important matters to engage him, one of them the health of the medical students, now becoming a matter of great concern to the faculty, and he wrote to Mr. George Coy to go over the lists and to 'find out how many have been ill with typhoid or any other protracted illness'. There was abundant reason for apprehension, with the students increasing each year in number, and scattered in cheap boarding-houses whose landladies looked upon an occasional consumptive as nothing out of the ordinary. Tuberculosis and typhoid, indeed, provided the bread and butter of the doctor in those days—even of the consultant, as numbers of Osler's laconic notes, like this to Edward R. Baldwin of Saranac Lake, imply:

1. 12. 00.

Dear Dr. Mr. Nyce has the white plague—I hope he may do well. Thanks for your kindness to Gwyn. Yours,

Wm Osler.

All very well for Mr. Nyce, who probably recovered, as did Osler's nephew and one or two of the Hopkins students already under the supervision of Trudeau in the Adirondacks ; but it was a different matter for the Baltimore poor, who crowded the dispensary, and whose home conditions, as will be related, had for the past year or more been made a subject of investigation.

As the guest of the Students' Societies of the Medical Department of the University of Pennsylvania, he gave on January 16th one more of his biographical essays, choosing for his subject another physician-philosopher, though, unlike Bartlett, whose philosophy was secondary, John Locke was 'in all the colleges' and his medical career largely forgotten. As Osler had written to Musser in the preceding autumn after his return from abroad, he had again been 'hunting and grubbing in the British Museum and Record Office', much as on previous visits to London. From Sydenham, with whom he began, he had been led by the nose to Sydenham's contemporaries, and the great mass of manuscript relating to the medical career of the philosopher Locke had evidently come to his attention and been thoroughly gone over.

His chief source of information regarding the intimacy between these well-paired friends, Sydenham and Locke, was the Shaftesbury papers, which had come to light since John Brown's essay had been written—an essay he had reviewed thirteen years before in his 'Notes and Comments'. In this present address he dwelt at length on Locke's account of Lady Northumberland's tic douloureux, but more especially on Lord Shaftesbury's malady—for the Lord Chancellor had a suppurating hydatid cyst of the liver, which, according to Pepys, Locke himself had operated upon ; the cyst was for years drained by a silver tube popularly known as 'Shaftesbury's spigot', of which the satirists and wits of the day made much sport. Having considered Locke's other medical writings, journals, records, and commonplace-books, he ended as follows with the philosopher's rule of life which was much like his own :

For each one of us there is still a 'touch divine' in the life and writings of John Locke. A singularly attractive personality, with a sweet reasonableness of temper and a charming freedom from flaws and defects of character, he is an author whom we like at the first acquaintance, and soon love as a friend. Perhaps the greatest, certainly, as Professor Fowler says, the most characteristic English philosopher, we may claim Dr. Locke as a bright ornament of our profession, not so much for what he did in it, as for the methods which he inculcated and the influence which he exercised upon the English Hippocrates. He has a higher claim as a really great benefactor of humanity, one of the few who 'reflected the human spirit always on the nobler side'. One of Locke's earliest writings was a translation for Lady Shaftesbury of Pierre Nicole's 'Essays', in one of which, on 'The Way of Preserving Peace with Men', Locke seems to have found a rule of life which I commend to you: 'Live the best life you can, but live it so as not to give needless offence to others; do all you can to avoid the vices, follies, and weaknesses of your neighbours, but take no needless offence at their divergence from your ideal.'[1]

His interest in Locke was long-enduring, and when five years later he, too, came to be a 'Student' [i. e. Fellow] of Christ Church and was given rooms there, he always claimed that they were the ones Locke—until the time of his expulsion by the peremptory order of the King—had occupied before him.

On February 5th he wrote to Rolleston again about the proposed tribute to Allbutt, adding:

I wish that I could go to South Africa. We are of course most deeply interested in the war. I am an optimist of the first water, and see no reason for hysterics. What a bagatelle it is after all for the Empire! What are 200,000 men in the field! And as for the reverses—well 'sweet are the uses etc.' It is sad for the poor chaps who fall, but the stake is worth the sacrifice. England spent more blood and money to make North America English than will be needed to do the same for South Africa. All the decent people here are with us and the war has done more to promote an Imperial Spirit than anything that has ever happened in the recent history of the colonies. . . .

As he himself had stated, Osler was British to the core, and though a Christ Church studentship and the occupancy of John Locke's rooms could not at that time have existed even in his dreams, there came shortly after this a call from farther north which must have been exceedingly upsetting even to his well-practised equanimity. A hint of what was

[1] 'John Locke as a Physician.' Cf. 'An Alabama Student and other Biographical Essays'. Lond., Henry Frowde, 1908.

brewing was given in the postscript to a letter from Edward A. Schäfer, written on January 23rd, which says: 'I suppose you would not consent to transfer yourself to Edinburgh in the event of a vacancy in the Chair of Medicine which is extremely likely to occur before long.' He could hardly have taken this very seriously, though Schäfer's implication that his old friend Grainger Stewart was near his end must have sorely grieved him. Stewart's death, indeed, occurred on the 3rd of February, and Osler had knowledge of it when three days later, in reply to Schäfer's query, he said in effect that he would be loth to leave Baltimore, where he was happy and had a really good clinic. He admitted, nevertheless, that both he and Mrs. Osler would prefer to have Revere educated in the old country and had been planning to retire to England in eight or ten years.

On the very day this letter was posted in Baltimore Professor W. S. Greenfield was writing from Edinburgh, using all the arguments he could summon: that Stewart had hoped he would become his successor; that he would be certain to get the post if he would only announce his candidacy; that no time was to be lost, and 'a wire would be desirable'. It was a tempting proposal—the blue-ribbon position in British Medicine—the famous Chair which had been occupied by the Gregorys, Cullen, Allison, and Laycock. That his immediate reaction was favourable is indicated in this note to his sister Mrs. Gwyn—the 'Chattie' of other letters:

1 West Franklin Street, [no date]

Dear Lisbeth, So sorry not to have written before but I have been in the traces as usual and hard at it between 8[30] & 10 p m with the daily routine. I have never been so busy or so much pressed particularly with arrears of literary work. Ike is thriving finely—still angelic, living a delightful life with Mowgli & Baloo & Bagheera & his jungle friends. The Scotch girl is a great success & he is devoted to her. My friends in Edinburgh are very anxious that I should be a candidate for the chair of medicine there vacant by the death of Sir Grainger Stewart—'Tis a great temptation & if it is offered to me I may accept. . . .

But when he was confronted by the necessity of formulating an answer to Professor Greenfield's letter that was at all satisfactory, his pen actually balked, as is evidenced by his first draft of the reply which was posted February 14th. It is so interlined and scratched as to be nearly illegible, but it says: 'I really am very comfortable here and have work very much to my desire, but I tell you frankly I would rather hold a Chair in Edinburgh than in any School in the English speaking world.' To judge from the halting way his sentences were formed, the composition of this letter must have tried his very soul. There is only one thing missing to indicate his mood—the name of James Bovell scribbled somewhere on the margin of the sheet. He must have written to Schäfer also, expressing how repellent it would be to him to appear to be seeking the position by announcing his candidacy and to engage in the contest by soliciting testimonials—a procedure which characterizes professorial appointments in British universities. But however distasteful, he knew well enough that the appointment was made by a lay board, who had to be instructed, and that an invitation was out of the question. Moreover, some of his greatly admired friends—all of them Edinburgh men, were already in the field.[1]

From E. A. Schäfer to W. O. University Club, Edinburgh, Feb. 20, 1900.

My dear Osler,—Nothing for a long time has given me so much pleasure as hearing that you would be willing to come. The gift is in the hands of the Curators of Patronage who are seven in number: four appointed by the Town Council and three by the University Court: permanent appointments. I am working all I can to get them to *invite* you but everyone says it is useless as they have never done such a thing before—however I am making out a strong case and hope to be able to move them. [Sir William] Turner is the most influential man in this University and I believe I have enlisted him for you. The possibility of your coming here is being freely discussed and in spite of local interests I do not doubt that you will carry all before you from all that I can hear. In the meantime I have written to Clifford Allbutt, Sanderson, Foster, Lord Lister, Brunton, Pye-Smith, and am writing to others so that they may not pledge themselves to support anyone else.

In the event of my being unable to induce the Curators to *invite*,

[1] One of them, at least, withdrew in favour of Osler on learning that he might be induced to stand.

and considering who they are it is unlikely they will do so (that I must admit), you must send in a formal application after the post is advertised, with a statement of your career and a list of published works. You do not of course want testimonials except as a matter of form, but I would get all those people I have mentioned to write to the Curators and press your claim, and any others you might think of. I will write further and let you know how the matter progresses.

Yours ever,

E. A. Schäfer.

Many other letters passed, those from Edinburgh stating that there was no mechanism by which a man could be invited; that, although the Curators felt bound to proceed in the usual fashion and to advertise the vacancy, the date for the closing of applications had been advanced for his benefit till April 14th; that *Nature*, the '*British Medical*', and the *Lancet* would all insist on his paramount claims, but that he must go through the usual form of making application and submitting testimonials. The rival candidates were Byrom Bramwell, John Wyllie, G. A. Gibson, and Alexander James; all Edinburgh men of unquestioned distinction, most of them teachers of experience in the extra-mural school. Against these men and their expressed wishes and deserts Osler was loth to submit his name as a contestant:

To E. A. Schäfer from W. O. 3. 4. 00.

It is so kind of you to take all this trouble. If offered the Chair I will take it; but I cannot go into a canvass which would be most repulsive to me, particularly as both Bramwell and Gibson are warm personal friends. If on the ground, or in the country, it might be different, but I feel very sensitive in applying for a position without an intimation that I am wanted, except from you and Greenfield—old friends. I do not like to be over scrupulous but I think it best to write you just as I feel in the matter. . . .

More letters followed, those from London and Edinburgh containing assurances of an enthusiastic welcome from the profession: the position was the best Great Britain could offer; it would be a worthy crown to his career; his terms would surely all be accepted; and he was requested to cable his decision. It was made clear, however, that by no possibility could an invitation of a formal kind be given; an application at least must be sent in; others if necessary could supply the information about his career demanded by the Curators of Patronage. One of them, Lord Robertson, in answer to a letter from Sir Michael Foster, urging Osler's election without the customary formalities, very properly replied :

While I fully believe that to those who know Professor Osler it may seem absurd and superfluous that he should produce testimonials, yet your own experience will probably suggest that he must remember that the electors are outside the circle in which even the highest scientific reputations are known, and accordingly it would be wise that this tribute be paid to our ignorance.

To E. A. Schäfer from W. O. March 13, '00.

After the receipt of your letter by this week's mail I felt that there was nothing left but to comply. I cannot tell you how deeply I appreciate all the trouble you have taken in the matter. I have sent in the application, and will send in a list of my published works and papers by the S. S. of the 17th, if I can get it printed in time. I think copies of my collected Reprints are in the Library of the R. C. of Physicians in Edinburgh, if not the 1st, at any rate the 2nd and 3rd series of 1897. I have sent copies of some of my general addresses to each of the Curators. Lord Strathcona and Lord Mount Stephen would no doubt know some of the Curators, and I shall write and ask them for letters. I have to hurry with this to catch the steamer. I have been 'on the road' and very much driven. Love to the children, [etc]. PS. We too have been rejoicing in the news from South Africa.

Undoubtedly the real explanation of his decision lies in the sentence which says he has been very much driven, and there may have been a subconscious thought of escape from his accumulating professional burdens. The moment may have come when a coin was tossed, as it had been in Leipzig in the summer of 1884, and the next morning, March 14th, a cable went to Schäfer, saying: 'ALL RIGHT APPLICATION SENT OSLER.' He had submitted, and an announcement of the fact appeared in the *British Medical Journal* for March 17th, to the jubilation of his many British friends. But on this same day, at 1 West Franklin Street, Osler was laid low, thereby escaping the perfect hullabaloo in Baltimore which his decision produced, for it had been cabled back from England and was headlined in the press. In his account-book of the year, against the dates March 17–25, there occurs the single entry—'Influenza—in bed'. His illness, the doubt it raised as to whether with his susceptibility to pneumonic attacks he could endure the rigours of many Edinburgh winters, the pressure from all sides to hold him in Baltimore—all these led to a second cable on March 26th to Schäfer: 'APPLICATION WITHDRAWN LOCAL PRESSURE TOO STRONG SO SORRY OSLER.'

To E. A. Schäfer from W. O. Mar. 27th.

I felt very badly to cable yesterday as I did, but I was quite unprepared for the outburst which followed the announcement to my colleagues that I was a candidate for the Chair. I had no idea that they would make it such a personal matter, and my special associates and assistants in the Medical Department were so stirred about it that my feelings were terribly harrowed. I suppose I should have counted on a strong local opposition but I had no idea that I should have to yield. After all, these men have stood by me for ten years in getting the School organized and the Hospital in working order. I am mortified to think that I should have caused you so much trouble. It is in many ways a great disappointment to me as I feel that I could have been very happy in Edinburgh. Mrs. Osler, too, is quite disturbed. She was very willing to go. All my friends in Canada have been very excited about it. . . .

The following letter from President Gilman expresses as well as any the relief produced by his decision:

614 Park Avenue, Baltimore,
March 24, 1900.

My dear Dr. Osler,—I have just heard through Dr. Welch that you have declined the extraordinarily attractive overture from Edinburgh. You may be sure that every one of your associates, Trustees, Professors, & Students, would have grieved deeply if your decision had been different. In the short period of your residence in Baltimore, you have won such a position, as no one else has held, and such as no one can fill, if you ever give it up. In the hospital, and in the medical school you have the utmost influence, while your love of letters and your skill as a writer would give you the same influence among our literary co-workers if they could only see and hear you more frequently. Now I hope that nothing more attractive than a call to Edinburgh will ever reach you, and that through a long life you will continue to add to the distinction of the Johns Hopkins foundations. Ever your sincere and grateful friend

D. C. GILMAN.

Subsequent appeals from abroad that he would reconsider; that they thought none the worse of him for having won the hearts of the Baltimoreans; that it was a call of duty; and that something tantamount to an invitation he could not refuse would be issued, left him unmoved once he had definitely altered his decision; and though grieved to have been the cause of so much trouble, he, outwardly at all events, promptly dismissed the episode from his mind and rarely if ever referred to it again.[1]

While all this was going on during February and March, to the distraction of all concerned, there were other matters, too, deserving of mention—the relief of Kimberley, for example, and of typhoid-ridden Ladysmith—so that after months of depression things were looking better in South Africa—at least for those who were not Dutch. Then, too, what was important, Revere had acquired a new pet, also certain E. Y. D.-ish habits, of which his grandmother speaks in a letter to her Dear Chattie:

> In Willie's last week's letter he tells me that someone has presented Revere with a young alligator for a plaything—worse than a pet toad or rat I should think. W. F. says that he has generally to turn down the clothes of his bed to look for slipper, comb or brush, but now will have to be doubly careful or may find a still more unpleasant bedfellow.

Moreover, during these months, the antivivisection controversy, which had received an apparent quietus in 1898 in consequence of Welch's activities, had again come to a head. It was the third and last attempt of the opponents

[1] There is a volume in the Osler library, of collected papers entitled 'Testimonials, Edinburgh University, Chair of Medicine, 1846.' Osler's abhorrence of the testimonial custom is expressed in the following note which he had written in the back of this volume fifteen years later:

'xii.26.15. Given to me by Dr. Harvey Littlejohn of Edinboro from his father's library. I am glad to have this tragic volume illustrating the most venomous system of election to professorships, still perpetuated in the Scotch universities, as the candidates seek testimonials far and near. One rarely sees so extensive a list as that of Goodsir. The list of voters and the result of the ballot at the end of Goodsir's testimonials show that the election was entirely in the hands of the Town Council, a committee of which still shares in the election—the proportion I do not know. When in (?) I had consented to be a candidate for the Chair of Medicine at Edinboro, Turner and Schäfer guaranteed me the majority of the votes of the Town Council. In the depression associated with an attack of influenza, I cabled withdrawing my name. I wonder what would have become of me at Edinboro—whiskey or John Knox? I think I could have got on with the men as I have always liked the Scotch. W. O.'

of research to pass a regulatory law through the national legislature; and towards this end Senator Gallinger had introduced before the 56th Congress an amended or substitute measure under a slightly modified name and now called 'Senate Bill § 34'. When this became known to the scientists, a public hearing [1] was demanded, and on February 21st the advocates and opponents of the bill appeared before the Senate Committee of the District, with Senator Gallinger in the chair. W. W. Keen, H. P. Bowditch, Bishop Lawrence, General Sternberg, Mary Putnam Jacobi, and others including Welch and Osler, all spoke in opposition to the bill. The major task, that of drawing up an elaborate argument, had been assigned to Welch, and his statement ended with this paragraph:

Surprise has been expressed that scientific men and the great body of the medical profession in all parts of this country should concern themselves so actively with contemplated legislation which in its immediate effects relates to a very limited area and affects directly the work of probably not more than a dozen men, if indeed of that number. Our solicitude to prevent the passage of this act is not greater than that of antivivisectionists throughout the country to secure it. Our opponents have hitherto signally failed in their repeated efforts to obtain the enactment of similar laws in the various states. They now seek Congressional sanction in the hope that it will promote their 'Cause' throughout the country. We know, and scientific and medical men alone can fully know, the dangers to science and humanity which lurk in what may seem to some of you this unimportant bit of legislation. The medical and biologic sciences have advanced in these later years with strides unapproached and in directions undreamed of but a quarter of a century ago. New vistas of knowledge and power have been disclosed, the full fruits of which will be gathered by coming generations. The main cause of this unparalleled progress in physiology, pathology, medicine and surgery has been the fruitful application of the experimental method of research, just the same method which has been the great lever of all scientific advance in modern times. Strange as it may seem at the turning-point of the century, we are here, not as we should be, to ask you to foster and encourage scientific progress, but to beg you simply not to put legislative checks in its way. Our own contribution to this progress may now be small, but America is destined to take

[1] Senate Document No. 337, Government Printing Office, Washington, 1900, 222 pp.

a place in this forward movement commensurate with her size and importance. We to-day should be recreant to a great trust, did we not do all in our power to protect our successors from the imposition of these trammels on freedom of research. Our appeal to you is not only in the name of science, but in the truest and widest sense in the name of humanity.[1]

Throughout the hearing there was left no doubt in any one's mind of the Chairman's position regarding the measure. He had obviously been thoroughly coached upon the usual antivivisection mis-statements, and under the mask of senatorial politeness there was a good deal of sarcasm, short of heckling, which must finally have upset Osler's customary imperturbability. His own testimony was very brief and was confined to the single issue of human experimentation—a matter on which, as may be recalled, he had expressed himself vigorously before the Association of Physicians in 1898, when, in discussing Sternberg's paper on yellow fever, he had denounced Sanarelli's experiments. One episode had a humorous touch. Senator Gallinger persisted in cross-questioning him[2] about the possibility that some one, sometime, might possibly have permitted unnecessary suffering in the performance of his experiments ; and Osler, holding up an antivivisection pamphlet, replied with considerable warmth that there was no profession about which a similar set of disgraceful statements might not be made and sown broadcast—' no profession, from politics —up ! '

Senator Gallinger : I hope that nothing very violently personal may be indulged in. I will say that when I used the name of Mantegazzi, I meant Sanarelli. If I understand it, Mantegazzi made experiments upon animals, but Sanarelli experimented with yellow fever upon human beings. Of course we are glad to hear the remarks of the gentleman with regard to vivisection. I will not call attention to some matters that I had noted in that connection, because Dr. Osler has denounced them vigorously. I will ask him this however : Supposing, Dr. Osler, that I should offer a bill preventing human vivisection, would you oppose it ?

Dr. Osler : Yes, sir ; as a piece of unnecessary legislation.

---

[1] ' Argument against Senate Bill § 34, Fifty-sixth Congress, First Session, generally known as the " Antivivisection Bill ".'

[2] The stenographic report of the tilt may be found in the same ' Senate Document No. 337, pp. 64–5.

A short three months later (May 1900) on the recommendation of General Sternberg, a board composed of Reed, Carroll, Agramonte, and Lazear was sent to Quemados, Cuba, to pursue investigations relating to yellow fever which had broken out among the troops stationed in Havana. By a series of painstaking experiments conducted on human beings who had the moral courage to volunteer for the purpose, they first disproved conclusively that the disease was contagious in the ordinary conception of the term, and subsequently demonstrated, before the end of the year, that the female of a certain species of mosquito (*Stegomyia fasciata*) was alone responsible for its transmission. Had the discovery not been made, had one of the soldier-volunteers who contracted the disease (rather than the lamented Lazear, one of the Commission) died as a result of the experimental inoculations, one can imagine what a howl would have been raised on the floor of the Senate in Washington. Had there not been an intelligent and courageous Military Governor in Havana willing to take the responsibility for the carrying out of these experiments without getting the permission of Congress—well, the Panama Canal project would have been an impossibility.

During the Easter recess, April 4–10, a much needed outing to recuperate from his influenza, no less than from the Edinburgh distraction settled only a few days before, was taken with H. B. Jacobs and T. B. Futcher—Thayer's successor as Resident Physician. They departed together for Old Point Comfort, and put up at the old Chamberlin Hotel,[1] whence they made various amusing trips by boat to Mobjack Bay, Virginia, and also to the Dismal Swamp, which accounts for a telegram to Mrs. Osler stating: 'SAW DREDS MOTHER YESTERDAY.'

W. O. [writes Futcher] had always been fascinated by Tom Moore's poem, 'The Lake of the Dismal Swamp', and had always wanted to visit the lake. Accordingly, he planned a trip for Easter Monday. We (the Chief and I only) left by boat early for Portsmouth, Virginia, where we hired a conveyance and drove about five miles across

[1] It was at this time that he saw in consultation with the Post Doctor, a patient, Miss Mabel Tremaine (Mrs. Robert Brewster), which began a friendship providing many letters for this biography.

country to the Albemarle Canal. After purchasing some cheese, crackers and fruit at a little country store, we hired the gasoline launch of the contractor (the canal was then under construction) for the day. We went along the canal for about two hours and arrived at the 'feeder' which is the only outlet of the lake. This is a deep ditch about fifteen to twenty feet wide and two or three miles long. The banks are eight to ten feet high and made up of a rich vegetable humus aeons old. Just before the lake is reached, there is a small lock which raised us up to the level of the water in the lake. Passing along this stream for a few hundred yards, we finally reached the lake, which has no visible banks, the waters of the lake seeming to merge with the trees of the swamp surrounding it. The weird cypress trees, with their numerous roots rising out of the water and merging to form the trunk several feet above the water's level, extending far out into the lake, produce the illusion that the lake has no shores. We motored about the lake in the launch for about an hour and then started on our return trip. On our way back, and while we were eating our frugal lunch, the Chief wrote a most imaginative account of our experiences for Revere on the blank pages in the back of Burton's 'Anatomy of Melancholy' which he had brought along with him. In this he described how we passed between the roots of the cypress trees; how brilliant-hued moccasin snakes had dropped into our boat from the limbs of the trees as we passed under them; how we had met a man with a 'vertical eye'; and also of the negroes who had not yet heard of 'Emancipation'. We tried to persuade W. O. to publish this amusing tale in *St. Nicholas*, but he never did.[1]

There was another episode of the Chamberlin Hotel, one which Futcher does not mention; it concerned a celebrated actress of the day named 'Cissie', who having fallen off the pier one night, conveniently near a passing rowboat, was immediately fished out, and brought to the hotel in hysterics. 'The Chief', when subpoenaed by the manager, said: 'How fortunate! We have Dr. Futcher here; he is our specialist in drowning, at the Hopkins. I will send him.' And from this there grew up a story, more or less credited, probably attributable to 'M'Connachie', of how Futcher had plunged into the bay and had swum

[1] The original account, written on the fly-leaves of A. R. Shilleto's 1893 edition of Burton, had long been lost, but the volume has turned up among those Osler placed in the collection of Burton's works at Christ Church, with no expectation that its added contents would ever be deciphered, if indeed they had not been forgotten. This book has kindly been restored to the Osler library.

an incredible distance to shore, bravely bearing the said 'Cissie' on his shoulder.

On May 4th and 5th pleasant tributes were paid to two outstanding figures in the profession—one in Baltimore to Welch on the twenty-fifth anniversary of his doctorate; the other in New York to Abraham Jacobi to celebrate his seventieth birthday.[1] That in honour of Welch was largely a family affair, with a dinner given at the Maryland Club and the presentation by Councilman of a *Festschrift* volume to which Welch's Hopkins students and co-workers had contributed. The Jacobi festival, held the next evening in New York, was more national in scope, to honour the man who in 1858, seven years after his escape from Germany as a young political refugee, had succeeded in making such a name for himself as a children's specialist that the first professorship in paediatrics in the country was established in order that he might fill the position. Osler's amusing remarks at the Welch dinner were not recorded, but his comparatively serious ones made in New York have been.[2] On both occasions E. Y. D. got the better of him. After a fitting introductory tribute to the guest of honour, he is quoted as saying:

There is no single question before this nation to-day of greater importance than how to return to natural methods in the nurture of infants. The neglect is an old story in Anglo-Saxondom. St. Augustine, so Bede tells us, wrote to Pope Gregory complaining that the question of infant feeding was worrying him not a little! I understand that a systematic effort is being made to supply every child born in this land its rightful sustenance for one year at least. Under the auspices of the Pediatric Society and the Woman's Christian Temperance Union, a *Woman's Infants' Suckling Union* is to be established, which will strive to make it a criminal offence against

---

[1] For an account of the Welch *Festschrift* volume and its presentation, see *Maryland Medical Journal*, 1900, xliii. 314–19.

The Jacobi *Festschrift* contained contributions from over fifty distinguished writers. Among them was Osler's paper on the subject of 'The Visceral Lesions of the Erythema Group', a sequel to the 1895 paper on a similar dermatological subject, one which interested him greatly, chaotic though it was—and is. He confessed that 'what is needed is a dermatological Linnaeus to bring order out of the chaos at present existing in the group of erythemas'.

[2] *Maryland Medical Journal*, 1900, xliii. 320–2.

the state to bottle-feed any baby, and which will provide in large and well-equipped sucklingries ample sustenance when a mother from any cause is unable to do her duty. Dr. Rotch tells me that the action on the part of the Pediatric Society has been influenced by an exhaustive collective investigation which has been made on the future of bottle-fed babies, in which it is clearly shown that intellectual obliquity, moral perversion and special crankiness of all kinds result directly from the early warp given to the mind of the child by the gross and unworthy deception to which it is subjected—a deception which extends through many months of the most plastic period of its life. According to these researches, you can tell a bottle-fed man at a glance, or rather at a touch. *Feel the tip of his nose.* In all sucklings the physical effects of breast pressure on the nose are not alone evidenced in the manner set forth so graphically by Mr. Shandy, but in addition the two cartilages are kept separate and do not join; whereas in bottle-fed babies where there is no pressure on the tip of the nose the cartilages rapidly unite and, in the adult, present to the finger a single sharp outline, entirely different from the split bifid condition in the breast-fed child. The collective investigations demonstrate that all silver democrats, many populists, and the cranks of all descriptions have been bottle-fed, and show the characteristic nose-tip. Utopian as this scheme may appear, and directly suggested, of course, by Plato, who can question the enormous benefit which would follow the substitution of sucklingries for Walker-Gordon laboratories and other devices!

And in phrases prophetic of his 'Fixed Period' address, he went on in more serious vein to say:

Mr. Chairman, this magnificent demonstration is a tribute not less to Dr. Jacobi's personal worth than to the uniform and consistent character of his professional career. The things which *should* do not always accompany old age. The honour, love, obedience, troops of friends are not for all of us as the shadows lengthen. Too many, unfortunately, find themselves at seventy nursing a dwindling faculty of joy amid an alien generation. Fed on other intellectual food, trained by other rules than those in vogue, they are too often, as Matthew Arnold describes Empedocles, 'in ceaseless opposition'. Against this interstitial decay which insidiously, with no pace perceived, steals over us, there is but one antiseptic, one protection—the cultivation and retention of a sense of professional responsibility. Happiness at three-score years and ten is for the man who has learned to adjust his mental processes to the changing conditions of the times. In all of us senility begins at forty—forty sharp—sometimes earlier. To obviate the inevitable tendency—a tendency which ends in intellectual staleness as surely as in bodily weakness—a man must not live in his own generation; he must keep fresh by contact with fresh young minds, and ever retain a keen receptiveness to the ideas of those who follow him. Our dear friend has been able to do this because he was one

> whose even-balanced soul
> Business could not make dull nor passion wild,
> Who saw life steadily and saw it whole.

During May and June he was pushed to the limit with consultations, the number of which he found difficult to restrict, for he was coming to be the doctors' doctor, and appeals for advice from his professional fellows when they or some member of their families were ill were impossible to refuse; and calls to see people of national prominence could hardly be ignored. Epistolary scraps of early June, such as this to H. V. Ogden, tell of his summer plans:

Dear O. We are off on the 16th. I am horridly full of work, & arrears of all sorts stare me in the face. Mrs Osler & Ike have gone to Boston. We shall stay quietly by the sea after two weeks in London. We have the same little cottage at Swanage. Love to your mother. Yours, Wm Osler. The Edinboro chair was a great tempt. but I am 50+ & the fear of changes perplexes now as it did not 10 years ago. They cabled the day before the election saying I could have it if I signified my acceptance. They made a great mistake in overlooking Bramwell.

In his commonplace-book are jottings which indicate that on the steamer he immersed himself in Bunyan, whose 'Life' by John Brown he was reading:

Bunyan was 47 when he wrote the Pilgrim's Progress. 'Afar off the Publican stands.' Said to have been the last work written in England without any thought of a reviewer—without too any thought of a reader.

> I only thought to make
> I knew not what; nor did I undertake
> Thereby to please my neighbour; no not I,
> I did it mine own self to gratifie.

In the Jerusalem Sinner Saved he says 'Physicians get neither name nor fame by pricking of wheals or picking out thistles or by laying of plasters to the scratch of a pin; every old woman can do this. But if they would have a name and a fame, if they will have it quickly they must, as I said, do some great and desperate cures. Let them fetch one to life that was dead; let them recover one to his wits that was mad; let them make one that was born blind to see, or let them give ripe wits to a fool; these are notable cures and he that can do thus—if he doth thus first he shall have the name and fame he deserves ; he may lie a-bed till noon.'

Taking rooms at 40 Clarges Street, a few weeks were passed in London engaged in the now familiar round of activities, including the book shops and auction sales, many of his purchases being destined to fill gaps in the library of the Maryland Faculty. Meanwhile he managed to put the final touches to a promised address.

The name of Jonathan Hutchinson was made familiar to Osler's students, for when anything anomalous or peculiar turned up, 'anything upon which the text-books are silent and the Systems and encyclopaedias are dumb,' he always advised them to turn to the volumes of Mr. Hutchinson's 'Archives of Surgery'. Though of an older generation, though a surgeon, and though something of a nonconformist in medicine, at least in the view of the conservative Londoner, Hutchinson was a man after Osler's own heart in his humanity and in his all-roundness. On July 4th there was a gathering of some thousand medical men at the opening of the 'Medical Graduates' College and Polyclinic', an institution which owed its existence largely to Mr. Hutchinson, who for years before its establishment had given over each Wednesday afternoon to a widely attended consultation clinic held at his house for graduate students from any part of the world who happened to be in London. Osler had been induced to give an oration appropriate to the occasion, and chose as his title 'The Importance of Post-graduate Study'.[1] In this address, which contains much that is autobiographical, he expresses doubt as to whether the medical world is as cosmopolitan as it was in the 17th and 18th centuries ; he extols the advantage of graduate studies abroad ; and in speaking of post-graduate teaching he says :

Post-graduate instruction is needed in all classes among us. The school for the young practitioner is a general practice in which the number and variety of cases will enable him at once to put his methods into daily use. A serious defect may warp his course from the outset. Our students study too much under the one set of teachers. In English and American schools they do not move about enough. At a tender age, four or five years give a man a sense of

---

[1] *Lancet*, Lond., July 14, 1900, ii. 73–5.

local attachment to place and teachers which is very natural, very nice, but not always the best thing for him. He goes out with a strong bias already in his mind and is ready to cry 'I am of Guy's', 'I am of Bart's', or 'I am an Edinburgh man'. To escape from these local trammels which may badly handicap a man by giving him an arrogant sense of superiority often most manifest when there is least warrant, is very difficult. I knew three brothers, Edinburgh men, good fellows at heart and good practitioners, but for them the science and art of medicine never extended beyond what their old teachers had taught. A Guy's man they could just endure, for the sake, as one of them said, of Bright and Cooper and Addison, but for men of other schools they entertained a supreme and really ludicrous contempt. . . .

'There are', he said, 'two great types of practitioners—the routinist and the rationalist'; and 'into the clutches of the demon routine the majority of us ultimately come'.

After all, no men among us need refreshment and renovation more frequently than those who occupy positions in our schools of learning; upon none does intellectual staleness more surely steal 'with velvet step, unheeded, softly', but not the less relentlessly. Dogmatic to a greater or less degree all successful teaching must be, but year by year unless watchful this very dogmatism may react upon the teacher who finds it so much easier to say to-day what he said last year. After a decade, he may find it less trouble to draw on home supplies than to go into the open market for wares, perhaps not a whit better, but just a wee bit fresher. After twenty years, the new, even when true, startles, too often repels; after thirty, well, he may be out of the race, still on the track perhaps, even running hard, but quite unconscious that the colts have long passed the winning post. . . .

From this he went on to his favourite theme that 'men above forty are rarely pioneers, rarely the creators in science or in literature'; and he cited Harvey's statement that he did not think any man above forty had accepted the new truths regarding the circulation of the blood. He recommended post-graduate study as an antidote against premature senility, mentioning 'the three signs by which, in man or institution, one may recognize old fogeyism'. And after telling how graduate students during the last three centuries had frequented in turn the fountains of learning in Italy, Holland, Great Britain, France, and Austria, he hinted that the lines of intellectual progress were veering strongly to the west. 'I predict', he said, 'that in the twentieth century the young English physicians will find their keenest inspiration in the land of the setting sun.'

On the following day, it may have been while *en route* to Norwich, judging from the next letter, he must have finished the 482 pages of Brown's 'Bunyan', for in his note-book appears 'vii. 5. '00. Good story of Thackeray and his "Vanity Fair" p. 479'. And it *is* a good story. But the point to be made here in connexion with Osler is that he was one of the rare people able to write '*perlegi*' at the end of his books. The following note to J. William White may have been written before his departure that same morning of July 5th; and it is characteristic that he dated the annotation just given, and not his letter.

40 Clarges St. [undated].

Dear White, I had an opportunity on Tuesday evening to talk with MacCormac & the Secretary of the Com. about the Hon. Fellowship affair. As there were to be only four they felt that two could not be selected from one city & Keen was your senior. Evidently the question was very fully discussed & they knew all about you. I am very sorry. I hope we may see you. We are off to Norwich for a few days & then go on the river for two weeks before taking to the seaside—Dorset again for a steady rest. Kind regards to your *very* VERY VERY much better half. Yours, W. O.

With his Sir Thomas Browne collection growing apace, another pilgrimage to Norwich was natural enough, and he at this time arranged with Sir Peter Eade to have constructed a dignified receptacle properly inscribed, to hold the skull of Sir Thomas, which though not exactly 'made into a drinking-bowl', had nevertheless since 1847 been knocking about the Infirmary Museum uncared for.[1] They subse-

[1] This casket, according to an editorial in the *British Medical Journal* of February 15, 1902, had been presented by Mr. Williams to the museum in the name of Professor Osler, who had directed that an appropriate pedestal should be made on which the casket should permanently stand. The casket, manufactured by the Goldsmiths' & Silversmiths' Company of London, was described as 'an exceedingly choice work of art', and the four plates, one on each side, bore the following inscriptions:

1. 'I believe that our estranged and divided ashes shall unite again; that our separated dust, after so many pilgrimages and transformations into the parts of minerals, plants, animals, elements, shall at the voice of God return into their primitive shapes and join again to make up their primary and predestinate forms.'

quently went to a charming place on the Thames, namely, Wargrave, at the 'George and Dragon', where the Francis 'nieces' and others joined them, and where Revere had his first taste and fill of boating. It was a scorching summer and they were glad by July 18th to get away to the region of Hardy's novels and to their cottage on the beautiful Dorset coast:

To Henry M. Hurd from W. O. Swanage, July 20.

I have at last got to the sea and the downs! After two weeks in London we went to the or on (as they say) the river which was most enjoyable. We escaped a good deal of the dining &c. in London. I have been very busy in the book shops completing my set of Sir Thomas & found some treasures of Burton and others. We went to Norwich for a short visit to Sir Peter Eade and I picked up some interesting photos &c. of places connected with Browne. We have seen a good deal of Flexner. We went down to Liverpool to see the two young fellows off—they will have told you about the good time we had. Then we went to Cambridge together & had a most enjoyable visit. Nuttall is very happy and will I think be a permanent resident. Everyone likes him so much and he is stirring up a great deal of enthusiasm. You will have heard I suppose that Halsted is to be one of the four Americans (Keen, Weir and Warren the others) to receive the honorary F.R.C.S. at the centenary next week. I am going as MacCormac has kindly sent us invitations to all the functions. Jacobs, McCrae and Cushing have been playing about with us in London. McC. passed his M.R.C.S. and L.R.C.P. last week. He is with me here for a week while Mrs Osler is in Paris with some friends. . . . We had a pleasant evening at the Post-graduate College. I hope you & the family are enjoying the Blue Ridge.

A few days later he returned to London to attend the celebration (July 25–27) to which this letter refers—the centenary of the Royal College of Surgeons; and in a long account [1] sent home for local consumption, after giving

2. 'At my death I mean to take a total adieu of the world, not caring for a monument, history or epitaph, not so much as the bare memory of my name to be found anywhere but in the Universal Register of God.'

3. 'In these moral acceptions the way to be immortal is to dye daily. Nor can I think I have the true theory of death when I contemplate a skull, or behold a skeleton, with those vulgar imaginations it casts upon us.'

4. This casket was presented to the Norfolk and Norwich Hospital by William Osler, M.D., F.R.S., Professor of Medicine, Johns Hopkins University, 1901.

[1] *Maryland Medical Journal*, 1900, xlii. 520–2.

the history of the college, and after a description of the exercises at the Hunterian Museum, he went on to tell of the conferring of the honorary fellowships on the thirty-four eminent surgeons from many countries, resplendent in their varied academic robes—'a most delightful ceremony in spite of the heat'. And further:

> At eight o'clock a dinner was given by the college in the hall of Lincoln's Inn, one of the law societies. It was the best-ordered large dinner I have ever attended. We sat down about 8.15, and rose about 11.15. A more distinguished company has perhaps never been gathered to do honour to the profession. To the right of Sir William MacCormac sat the Prince of Wales, the Marquis of Salisbury, the Duke of Northumberland, Lord Strathcona, Lord Kelvin and a group of Honorary Fellows. To his left sat the Duke of Cambridge, Earl Rosebery, the Lord Chancellor, Lord Lister, the Lord Mayor, and other Honorary Fellows. The members of the council occupied seats at the ends of the eight long tables. Among many excellent features of a most exceptional dinner may be mentioned the shortness of the speeches and the softness of the music. The Prince of Wales spoke with great clearness and directness, and was well heard by everyone. He acknowledged most gratefully and gracefully the debt he owed to the President on the occasion of the serious accident to his knee. The only other speech of note was by Lord Rosebery, who, witnessing the harmony existing in the medical profession throughout the world, expressed the hope that perhaps through science might be realized that peace on earth to effect which all other means had failed. There were several remarkable bits of plate on the table—one the silver grace cup presented to the Barbers' Company by King Henry VIII in 1540 in commemoration of the union of the barbers with the surgeons. Pepys mentions this in his Diary: 'among other observables at Chirurgeons' Hall, we drunk the King's health out of a gilt cup given by King Henry VIII to the Company, with bells hanging at it, which every man is to ring by shaking after he has drunk up the whole cup.'

He gave in similar fashion a recital of other incidents of the three-day festival, failing to mention that at the *conversazione* given in the College on the Wednesday evening, a couple—one a dark-complexioned man with a drooping moustache and mischief in his eye, the other the daughter of Professor Keen of Philadelphia—were loudly announced to the receiving dignitaries as Dr. and Mrs. Egerton Yorrick Davis.

At Swanage again, there was always an early morning dip,

much play afterwards, and many excursions and picnic-luncheons on the downs or within the ruined walls of Corfe Castle. There was a succession of young visitors to enjoy all this with them, but he and McCrae meanwhile managed to find time to put together the material for a small monograph (dedicated to the memory of James Elliot Graham) on a clinical topic they had been studying together.[1] During the month, too, as his commonplace-book indicates, he had been devouring Donne's 'Biathanatos', from which he had taken a long list of excerpts that must have coloured his thoughts, as many of them subsequently did his addresses. Thus:

p. 22. 4 sets of readers: 'Sponges which attract all without distinguishing; Houre-glasses which receive and pour out as fast; Bagges which only retain the dregges of the spices and let the wine escape; and Sives which retain the best only.'

p. 45. Wayside fruit. Some need the counsel of Chrysostom. 'Depart from the highway and transplant thyself in some enclosed ground, for it is hard for a tree which stands by the wayside to keep her fruit till it be ripe.'

p. 73. Sexagenarii were by the laws of wise states precipitated from a bridge. In Rome men of that age were not admitted to the suffrage, and they were called Depontani because the way to the Senate was *per pontem* and they from age were not permitted to come hither.

As the following letter indicates, he was compelled to miss the XIIIth International Medical Congress, which met in Paris during the week of August 2nd and for which as Chairman of the American Committee he had taken so much trouble. A huge assemblage it was, of 6,000 medical men, with Virchow and Lister the two outstanding figures. To countless young Americans, Osler's absence marred the congress, for it was too large a gathering, and with him as with no other they would gladly have escaped; for he

[1] A series of papers reviewing 150 cases of cancer of the stomach had already appeared under their joint names. The first, in the *Philadelphia Medical Journal* for Feb. 3rd, was the report of seven cases which had come to autopsy and in which the disease had been suspected during life; interesting to-day chiefly in showing that the X-ray had not as yet come to be used in detecting lesions of the alimentary canal, and that surgical explorations were still infrequent. For the second and third papers, see the *New York Medical Journal* for April 21 and May 19.

would have known best where to go in order to see old medical Paris.

To Henry Barton Jacobs from W. O. The Gwyle, Swanage, [no date]

Dear Von J. I had a cable yesterday that my brother was worse, & I feel that I must go out. It does not seem right to leave him at this crisis. I shall sail by the Teutonic with my brother E. B. and family, & I hope to be able to get back by the 25th, so as to have a couple of weeks here. I am desolated to miss the Congress. Greet the men from me & say how sad I am to miss seeing them—tell the Keens particularly. Mrs Osler and Ike are well. You must come here—an ideal spot for air & sea & sand. Yours W. O.

It made a sorry break in the summer. In his note-book he has written: 'On Teutonic read Froude, Life of Bunyan.' And he probably amused himself aboard ship with his essay on 'The American Voice'—an article never completed though he always carried it with him when crossing, for it is then that changes in intonation strike one most forcibly. Thus he has jotted down: 'Voice. Lucian says that at Athens he got rid of his "barbarous Syrian speech and perfected himself in a pure Attic diction". See Classics for English Readers. Lucian p. 7.'

From his brother Featherston's house in Toronto he wrote to W. S. Thayer:

125 College Street, Saturday.

I came out unexpectedly after a somewhat urgent Cable as to my brother's condition. He had had a very bad attack about 10 days ago but he is now better. I shall probably take the Teutonic Wednesday from N. Y. unless there should be any more serious symptoms in which case I shall remain & let Mrs Osler & Ike return alone. The weather here was + + 97° yesterday. I hope you are standing the wear & tear without losing that eusarkoid aspect which has so long distinguished you.

As foretold, he was again at sea on the Wednesday, this time with Froude's 'Life of Erasmus' as his companion; and from it many excerpts were taken down, such as these:

Advice to students, p. 65 excellent. Read the best of books—the important thing is not how much you know, but the quality of what you know—never work at night; it chills the brain and hurts the health. Remember above all things that nothing passes away so rapidly as youth.

E. P. 79. Do not repent of having married a widow, if you buy a horse you buy one broken in already. Sir Thomas More said that if he was to marry a hundred wives he would never take a maid.

He was back in Baltimore by the end of September,[1] and with the opening of the autumn term there was organized at his suggestion a new society, which was to hold monthly meetings at the Hopkins. It was called 'The Laennec—a Society for the Study of Tuberculosis', the purpose of which, in his own words, was 'to promote the study of the disease among physicians and surgeons of the hospital, the senior students of the medical school, and any physicians who might wish to attend the meetings'. Believing in the inspiration of great names, the society had been called after the greatest student of the disease, and it was planned in the course of the meetings to review the historical epochs of tuberculosis; to study the conditions existing not only in Baltimore but in the country at large; and to make reports upon the work of the hospital in connexion with the disease during its first decade. It was but one further step of the many that Osler took in the campaign against the white plague, and were all of them to be mentioned a volume devoted to this subject alone would be required. This new society held its first meeting on October 30th, with Osler presiding, and in the course of his introductory remarks he said:[2] 'Two years ago I was much impressed with the number of cases applying at our out-patient department, and some kind friends placed at my disposal a sum of money which was to be used to promote the study of tuberculosis and to diffuse among the poor a proper knowledge of how to guard against the dangers of the disease.' With no mention that a portion of this sum had come from two ladies whose sister had died of tuberculosis, and the rest from his own pocket, he went on to tell how the fund had been disposed. It will be remembered that a laboratory had

[1] It was on Sept. 25th that Jesse Lazear, one of his students on the Commission and a quondam assistant, died at Quemados, Cuba, of yellow fever acquired from an infected mosquito which he had allowed to bite him.

[2] These were published in a special number of the *Philadelphia Medical Journal*, devoted to tuberculosis, Dec. 1, 1900. This was merely a part of his propaganda, for he had persuaded the Editor, Dr. George M. Gould, to devote the entire issue to tuberculosis.

been equipped, of which C. D. Parfitt had been in charge until he himself unhappily became a victim of the disease. Then, also, two of the third-year students—Miss Blanche Epler during the 1898–9 semester, and Miss Adelaide Dutcher the next year—had followed the consumptive out-patients to their homes to investigate the conditions under which they lived and to see that proper hygienic directions given in the hospital were actually carried out.[1] So at this first meeting of 'The Laennec', Miss Dutcher gave a report on the social and domestic conditions of 190 cases of pulmonary tuberculosis which had thus been followed up,[2]

[1] 'It was in my third year in the medical school [writes Dr. Dutcher] that I did the house visitation to tuberculous patients of the Johns Hopkins Dispensary, from October '99 to October 1900. In the fall of 1899 Dr. Osler called for a volunteer from the fourth-year class, but without response. This led me to offer my services and he at once assigned me to the work. We never had any written communication. Dr. Osler's verbal instructions to me were simple and direct. I cannot pretend to repeat his words literally, but the impression lingering in my mind is as follows: He was of the opinion that much could be done to prevent the spread of tuberculosis in Baltimore if the consumptive and his family knew more of the nature of the disease. He asked me to make a friendly visit, warning me against antagonizing the patient which naturally would prevent coöperation. My duty should be to learn all I could about the patient, his family, and his environment; to advise him of the nature of his disease, its mode of contagion, and method of prevention; to teach him first of all to destroy his sputum because it contained the seed which caused the disease and was the only way of transmitting the disease to others; to give him a moral reason for cleanliness to help him out when natural instincts were lacking; to give the reason why sunlight and fresh air were of preventive and curative value; and to make any suggestions that would be of help in each home that I went to. I reported to Dr. Osler once a month at his home throughout the year. In October 1900, Dr. Osler told me that he and Dr. Welch were about to organize a society for the study of tuberculosis, and asked me to prepare a written report of my year's work to read before the first meeting.'

[2] Though the name of 'social service' was not yet coined, the movement, in America at least, appears to have had its beginnings in these studies and reports made by Miss Epler and Miss Dutcher. Osler's connexion with the movement, which through Dr. Richard C. Cabot's work has become one of the recognized extra-mural obligations of all large hospitals, seems to have been entirely lost sight of. Indeed, he left no stone unturned whereby others might get the credit of the idea, and his original contribution to it remains obscured. Subsequently one of the members of the Hopkins class of 1899, Charles P. Emerson, who succeeded Futcher as director of Osler's clinical laboratory, organized a group of students who had a missionary spirit, and they, in association with the Charity Organization Society, made a study of the

and Welch in a talk on the bibliography of tuberculosis made suggestions for the establishment of a special library. But Osler's remarks, after all, were the keynote of the meeting, and in the course of them he said:

If we add the deaths due to tuberculosis of other organs, we are well within the mark in saying that one-tenth of the deaths in this city are due to this disease. It is estimated that above a million of persons are suffering with consumption alone, in this country, of whom at least 150,000 die annually. The white plague, as Holmes called it, is the great scourge of the race, killing 5,000,000 yearly. Let me read you an abstract from De Quincey, which, while expressing an old, erroneous idea, gives in his strong and characteristic language the terrible, the appalling nature of this annual slaughter: 'Are you aware, reader, what it is that constitutes the scourge (physically speaking) of Great Britain and Ireland? All readers, who direct any part of their attention to medical subjects, must know that it is pulmonary consumption. If you walk through a forest at certain seasons, you will see what is called a *blaze* of white paint upon a certain *élite* of the trees marked out by the forester as ripe for the axe. Such a blaze, if the shadowy world could reveal its futurities, would be seen everywhere distributing its secret badges of cognizance amongst our youthful men and women. . . . Then comes the startling question—that pierces the breaking hearts of so many thousand afflicted relatives—Is there no remedy? Is there no palliation of the evil?' Let us be thankful that we can answer to-day—There is!

During the autumn months, judging from his appointment books, he was much away on consultations, many of

social and hygienic conditions existing in the homes of the dispensary patients. Another student, Joseph H. Pratt, who after graduating in 1898 removed to Boston, subsequently organized at the Massachusetts General Hospital in July of 1905 a 'tuberculosis class' in connexion with which a 'friendly visitor' was provided. Dr. Pratt appreciates that this was done more or less unconsciously under Osler's influence, and states that Osler was among the first publicly to support him in the development of the class method of handling these cases. In October of 1905 Dr. Richard Cabot at the same hospital was the first to employ a full-time, paid 'social service' worker, and by his effective writings did much to advance and popularize a conception of this new kind of hospital service.

Dr. Blanche Epler, the first of these 'follow-up workers', subsequently at her home in Kalamazoo, Michigan, was one of the pioneers in developing the principle involved, and through the agency of the County Federation of Women's Clubs was instrumental in so developing the local public health activities that they came to receive recognition throughout the country.

them family affairs in Toronto. His mother wrote: 'We were all up to breakfast with Willie this morning. He saw all his relatives and administered advice to one and another. We shall look anxiously for his report this afternoon [on 'B. B's' condition] and can but hope it will still be favourable.' But as a relief to these professional duties and anxieties one may imagine him again in Baltimore on the late afternoon of Guy Fawkes Day, notice having been served in strange handwriting both on Revere and on the little girl some one had named Doris—a notice reading:

'Remember, remember the fifth of November,
Gunpowder, treason and plot;—'

and with all the lights out there would be rustling of hidden conspirators behind curtains, and weird noises to make one's flesh creep would issue from the region of the furnace—all very hair-raising. Or one, in imagination, may hear a familiar tuneless chant 'Oh, for Thy many mercies, *Gott—sei—dank!*', issue from his room, called forth by the receipt of the book packages containing his purchases of the summer; for they were beginning to come in, as the next two letters show:

To John H. Musser. Nov. 7, 1900.

Thanks for your fourth edition, which looks tip-top. I have not had time yet to more than just look into one or two sections. I do not see how you have found time to keep it up so thoroughly. I send you to-day a nice old copy of Sir Thomas Browne's 'Vulgar Errors' and 'Urn Burial', which I picked up for you in London, and which just arrived in a case the day before yesterday. I was fortunate in getting some great treasures this summer, and have picked up two or three very nice things for the College of Physicians' Library, which I will send over as soon as a Linacre's Latin Grammar, which I left to be bound, arrives. . . .

To H. V. Ogden. Nov. 21, 1900.

So glad to hear from you, and to know that the Sir Thomas pleased you. Greenhill's edition represents an immense amount of work on his part. You must come on this winter and spend a couple of weeks with us. You can have your breakfast in bed, and you will be perfectly enchanted with my corner in the library now, where I have gradually collected some great treasures. I have almost completed the Sir Thomas editions. Do try and arrange it. I am sure it would do you a great deal of good. . . . The small boy is thriving, and whenever I mention you Mrs. Osler says: 'When can we get Dr. Ogden to come?' You are one of her special favourites. I am sending you a paper on Elisha Bartlett, and a talk I gave in London; and this week there will be the Locke paper which will, I think, interest you. Send me word pretty soon that you will be able to join us. . . .

On that same day, the 21st, there was a dinner for J. Collins Warren, who had come from Boston to give 'Some Reminiscences of an old New England Surgeon' before the Book and Journal Club of the Maryland 'Faculty'—a club which had to be kept going; and, to retrace his steps, the week before Osler himself for some occasion had been the guest of the University of Pennsylvania; and on the 12th had talked before the Johns Hopkins Historical Club on 'The Sympathetic Powder of Sir Kenelm Digby'. Nor was this enough to round off November, for the 28th found him in Troy, New York, where a local hospital was having its semi-centenary, and where he gave an address 'On the Influence of a Hospital upon the Medical Profession of a Community'.[1] This address began with a happy quotation from Sir Thomas More, regarding the 'well appointed hospitalles' in Utopia, which were so well appointed and attended 'that, though no man be sent thether against his will, yet not withstandinge there is no sicke persone in all the citie, that had not rather lye there, than at home in his owne house'. So he went on with well-chosen words, fit for the ears of trustees as well as staff, regarding the functions of a hospital, which in an educated community has a value that cannot be over-estimated:

It is a great pity [he said] that in the administration of this Christ-like gift we have, in this country, linked sectarian names with anything so sacred. While I know that in Episcopal, Methodist-Episcopal, Baptist, Presbyterian and other denominational hospitals, much indiscriminate charity is practised, naturally preference must be given in them to sufferers who are 'of the household of faith' which the institution professes. In nothing should the citizens of a town take greater pride than in a well established, comfortable Hôtel Dieu—God's Hostelry—in which His poor are healed. And it should be to them a personal care. There is to-day far too much of the second-hand charity of the ten- or fifty-dollar subscription. Let

[1] *Albany Medical Annals*, 1901, xxii. 1–11.

me paraphrase the well known words in which Milton describes the man who consigns his religion to the care of his parson. It is equally applicable to the man who consigns his charity to the Secretary of a Hospital Board: 'A wealthy man, addicted to his pleasure and to his profits, finds "charity" to be a traffic so entangled, and of so many peddling accounts, that of all mysteries he cannot skill to keep a stock going upon that trade. What should he do? Fain he would have the name to be "charitable", fain would he bear up with his neighbours in that. What does he, therefore, but resolve to give over toiling, and to find himself out some factor to whose care and credit he may commit the whole managing of his "charitable" affairs, some man of note and estimation that must be. To this he adheres, resigns the whole warehouse of his charity, with all the locks and keys, into his custody.' 'The simple dispensation of money to be converted into virtue by the piety of other men' is as the crumbs which fell from the rich man's table, ample for Lazarus, and most acceptable, but of no avail to save Dives. . . .

He touched further on his favourite theme that no hospital could fulfil its mission that was not a centre for the instruction of students or doctors; and he told how a staff should be organized; what their relations should be to the board of government; that they should make the best of existing conditions, for 'some of the greatest clinicians have had wretched facilities in very small wards: the little farm well tilled is most profitable'. He went on to pay a fine tribute to his colleague Welch and the thorough organization of his Department of Pathology, adding that the pathologist should be a well-paid officer of an institution (all this indirectly to help a former member of his staff, Dr. George Blumer, then in charge of the Bender Hygienic Laboratory). Finally in autobiographical vein he continued:

On one other point I may speak plainly as one of the few salaried attending physicians to a hospital in this country. Look over the organizations of our great corporations—the Railways, the Warehouses, the Insurance Offices, the Universities and Colleges—and you will everywhere find the work to be done upon the good old principle—'the labourer is worthy of his hire'. But when we turn to hospitals we see an enormous staff of men, who ungrudgingly year by year devote their time and energies to the service of these institutions 'without money and without price'; men, too, who have risen to the very highest distinction and whose hours are bank notes, and who often devote to the poor, time which should be given to refreshment and recreation. Think of the long years of gratuitous service the late Austin Flint of Buffalo, in Louisville, in New Orleans and in New York gave to the hospitals of those cities; Da Costa, of whom we have been bereft so lately, a hospital physician, assiduous and devoted for long years, whom death found 'on duty'; Weir Mitchell, still in harness at the Infirmary for Nervous Diseases, still glad to give freely of the treasures of his ripe and unique experience to whosoever needs them. Tomorrow morning in some hundreds of institutions, from the General Hospital, Winnipeg, in the north, to the Charity Hospital of New Orleans in the south; from the General Hospital in Halifax, to the Cooper College Hospital in San Francisco, the public has a band of servants doing some of the best work in the world, not on business principles. I do not ask that doctors should always be paid for their services; there are many hospitals in which it would be impossible, and there are wealthy corporations, which should not ask, particularly of young men, long and arduous duties without remuneration. Hospitals might fitly recognize this enormous debt by more frequently placing a physician on the Committee of Management, or on the Board of Trustees. Fortunately the medical profession can never be wholly given over to commercialism, and perhaps this work of which we do so much, and for which we get so little—often not even thanks—is the best leaven against its corroding influence. While doctors continue to practise medicine with their hearts as well as with their heads, so long will there be a heavy balance in their favour in the Bank of Heaven—not a balance against which we can draw for bread and butter, or taxes, or house-rent, but without which we should feel poor indeed.

One thing more must be mentioned in this crowded year, for it saw buried in Volume III of the *Johns Hopkins Hospital Reports* a series of seventeen papers, four of them from his own pen, comprising the third fasciculus on the subject of typhoid fever—there having been 829 cases of the disease in his wards during the ten years since the opening of the hospital.[1] The year had been a trying one. The world was ridden with pestilence, war, and famine. The conflict in South Africa was still dragging on, with De Wet, Botha, dysentery, and typhoid companions-in-arms against the British. The tragedy of the legations at Peking during the Boxer Rebellion had horrified the western nations.

[1] Some time during that year he must also have prepared for the supplementary volume of Keating's 'Cyclopaedia of the Diseases of Children', Phila., J. B. Lippincott Co., 1901, two chapters—one on 'Sporadic Cretinism', and the other on 'Cerebrospinal Fever' in which the then comparatively novel procedure of lumbar puncture was fully discussed.

Plague, cholera, and famine were stalking through India. The people had grown indifferent to vaccination and many outbreaks of smallpox had occurred. Yellow fever was still having its own way in Cuba. Even in San Francisco plague had broken out in the unsavoury quarter of its Chinatown. Mr. Mitchell of *Life*, and other antivivisectionists, were meanwhile abusing those of the profession who alone might be able to check the horror of pestilence.

A gloomy picture! But let the last hours of the year and century be brightened by two letters concerning men who were quietly working to make the world more habitable.

From S. Weir Mitchell to W. O. Sunday, Dec. 31, 1900.

Many thanks my dear Osler for the scholarly address. There is here what is said to be an original portrait of Locke. I shall be in Baltimore in Jan. for a day and a night, to talk to the Sheppard Hosp. Board. A fine chance. Can you take me in for a night? It will be not earlier than the 8th Jan. Your Browne books were fine and the predictions new to me. I bought yesterday a charming pencil original of Charles Lamb, by Geo. Dance. I wish you and yours a happy century, and all good gifts of God's sending or man's giving. What a fine fellow is Flexner. I have got him on to snake poisons, and have planted him full of suggestive ideas, for now I am at the time when I can sow and let others reap. Yours always and all ways.

From Dr. Walter Reed to Mrs. Reed. Columbia Barracks,
Quemados, Cuba.
11.50 p.m., Dec. 31, 1900.

. . . Only ten minutes of the old century remain. Here have I been sitting, reading that most wonderful book, 'La Roche on Yellow Fever', written in 1853. Forty-seven years later it has been permitted to me and my assistants to lift the impenetrable veil that has surrounded the causation of this most dreadful pest of humanity and to put it on a rational and scientific basis. I thank God that this has been accomplished during the latter days of the old century. May its cure be wrought in the early days of the new! The prayer that has been mine for twenty years, that I might be permitted in some way or at some time to do something to alleviate human suffering has been granted! A thousand Happy New Years! . . . Hark, there go the twenty-four buglers in concert, all sounding 'Taps' for the old year.

CHAPTER XX

1901

THE NATURAL METHOD OF TEACHING

Osler had other ways of ' sanctifying a fee ' than by the purchase of rare books to add to his library, and the year may well begin with a note which shows what a Baltimorean, professor in another school and long-time treasurer of the old Medical and Chirurgical Faculty, thought of him. The note indicates that a renewed effort was being made to lift the debt which was still burdening the society :

From Thomas A. Ashby to W. O. Jan. 2, 1901.

I think to have a big generous heart and then to have the means of making it happy through generous acts and deeds is the nearest approach to Heaven we can get in this life. I never saw a man who enjoyed giving as much as you do, and I presume this is one reason why you are always happy. If I should outlive you I will make the old Faculty erect a monument to your memory if I have to give all the money myself. I rejoice with you in the good work you are doing and am sure we will have the debt wiped out by the April meeting. The small donations will come in later. . . .

A New Year's Day letter to Lafleur, in which he says, ' Send me any memoranda of corrections or suggestions you may have for a new edition of my vade-mecum ', recalls that the burdensome triennial text-book revision was due, but this had to be crowded in among other things. Among physicians he was one of the first to appreciate the necessity of immediate operation for intestinal perforation in typhoid, and to urge that surgeon and physician together visit all typhoid patients showing symptoms, even suggestive ones, of this desperate and usually fatal complication. A younger generation will happily never know what this was all about and what Osler's backing meant to the surgeons of that time. On January 9th he read a paper on the subject before the Philadelphia County Medical Society ; and to-day, when the students look upon a stray case of typhoid as a curiosity, it is merely of historical interest that he should have felt impelled, little more than two decades ago, to write:

Our senior students should receive a practical, first-hand day-by-day acquaintance with typhoid fever. Heaven knows there are cases enough and to spare in every city in the Union to provide instruction of this sort. But is it given? I do not mean lectures on typhoid fever, or recitations on typhoid fever. I mean seeing typhoid-fever patients day by day, practically having charge of them and watching their progress from week to week. This can be done, and this should be done in the case of an all-important disease of this character. The worst indictment ever brought against the medical schools of this country is contained in the recently issued report by Reed, Vaughan and Shakespeare on the prevalence of typhoid fever during the Spanish-American War. Shades of W. W. Gerhard and of Austin Flint! The young doctors, to whom were entrusted scores of valuable lives, had practically not got beyond the nosology of Rush. Of the total number of 20,738 cases of typhoid fever, only about 50 % were diagnosed [correctly] by the regimental or hospital surgeons.[1]

Three days later he was in Boston to participate in the dedication of a new building for the Boston Medical Library, which explains a characteristically brief note sent the month before to James R. Chadwick—a note which merely said: 'No indeed! I shall not disappoint you—only too glad of the opportunity! It is very good of you to ask me.' Since 1875—since the days, in fact, when Osler first went down from Montreal to visit Boston—Chadwick had served in the capacity of a voluntary but indefatigable Librarian for the Boston Medical Library Association, a society which holds a relation to the local profession similar to that held by the College of Physicians of Philadelphia, the Academy of Medicine in New York, and the Maryland Medical and Chirurgical Faculty. But whereas the century-old Maryland Faculty, as T. A. Ashby's letter has shown, was vainly soliciting funds in Baltimore, even to get out of debt, the Boston society in this its twenty-sixth year had raised a sufficient sum to erect a palatial building worthy of the man after whom its chief hall was appropriately named: for Oliver Wendell

[1] 'On Perforation and Perforative Peritonitis in Typhoid Fever.' *Philadelphia Medical Journal*, Jan. 19, 1901.

Holmes, after serving thirteen years as its first President, had then made the library the repository of his books.

At this dedication Osler, John S. Billings, Weir Mitchell, and H. C. Wood had been invited to speak. Certainly none of them could have sent a more brief, prompt, or satisfactory note of acceptance than that quoted above. And in the course of his address,[1] which he entitled 'Books and Men', evidently with the new edition of his 'vade-mecum' in mind, he told how difficult it was for him to speak of the value of libraries in terms which would not seem exaggerated; how they had been his delight for thirty years, as well as having been of incalculable benefit, and he used the striking simile, 'to study the phenomena of disease without books is to sail an uncharted sea, while to study books without patients is not to go to sea at all'.

He went on to speak of the use of a great medical library for the teacher, for the general practitioner, and finally for another group to which he belonged:

> There is [he said] a third class of men in the profession to whom books are dearer than to teachers or practitioners—a small, a silent band, but in reality the leaven of the whole lump. The profane call them bibliomaniacs, and in truth they are at times irresponsible and do not always know the difference between *meum* and *tuum*. In the presence of Dr. Billings and of Dr. Chadwick I dare not further characterize them. Loving books partly for their contents, partly for the sake of the authors, they not alone keep alive the sentiment of historical continuity in the profession, but they are the men who make possible such gatherings as the one we are enjoying this evening. We need more men of their class, particularly in this country, where everyone carries in his pocket the tape-measure of utility. . . .

During this same month there were frequent visits to Canada because of his brother's illness, and at home there was equal cause for anxiety over the ill health of his colleague Rowland. Meanwhile there were other things to occupy him, among them a series of evening lectures to be given to the post-graduates, one of which on Sir Thomas Browne he promised to give himself. With all this he nevertheless

[1] Reprinted in 'Aequanimitas and other Addresses'. For a full account of the proceedings, see *Boston Medical and Surgical Journal*, Jan. 17, 1901.

managed to write one[1] of a series of articles on 'The Past Century: its Progress in Great Subjects', which were published during the month. It was a difficult task, most successfully handled—a presentation, suited for popular consumption, of the advances made by Medicine in its most remarkable century. Of particular interest, possibly, to the profession, was the section in which the revolution that had taken place in the treatment of disease was discussed under the caption of 'The New School of Medicine' —one 'with firm faith in a few good, well-tried drugs, little or none in the great mass of medicines now in use'—a new school which cares nothing for homoeopathy, and less for so-called allopathy, but 'seeks to study rationally and scientifically the action of drugs old and new'. One paragraph may be quoted:

> A third noteworthy feature in modern treatment has been a return to psychical methods of cure, in which *faith in something is suggested* to the patient. After all, faith is the great lever of life. Without it man can do nothing; with it, even with a fragment, as a grain of mustard-seed, all things are possible to him. Faith in us, faith in our drugs and methods, is the great stock-in-trade of the profession. In one pan of the balance, put the pharmacopoeias of the world, all the editions from Dioscorides to the last issue of the United States Dispensatory; heap them on the scales as did Euripides his books in the celebrated contest in the 'Frogs'; in the other put the simple faith with which from the days of the Pharaohs until now the children of men have swallowed the mixtures these works describe, and the bulky tomes will kick the beam. It is the *aurum potabile*, the touchstone of success in medicine. As Galen says, confidence and hope do more than physic—'he cures most in whom most are confident'. That strange compound of charlatan and philosopher, Paracelsus, encouraged his patients 'to have a good faith, a strong imagination, and they shall find the effects' (Burton). While we doctors often overlook or are ignorant of our own faith-cures, we are just a wee bit too sensitive about those performed outside our ranks. We have never had, and cannot expect to have, a monopoly in this panacea, which is open to all, free as the sun, and which may make of everyone in certain cases, as was the Lacedemonian of Homer's day, 'a good physician out of Nature's grace'. Faith in the gods or in the saints cures one, faith in little pills another, hypnotic suggestion a third, faith in a plain common doctor a fourth.

[1] 'The Progress of Medicine in the Nineteenth Century.' The *New York Sun*, Jan. 27, 1901. Reprinted in 'Aequanimitas and other Addresses'.

In all ages the prayer of faith has healed the sick, and the mental attitude of the suppliant seems to be of more consequence than the powers to which the prayer is addressed. The cures in the temples of Æsculapius, the miracles of the saints, the remarkable cures of those noble men the Jesuit missionaries in this country, the modern miracles at Lourdes and at Ste. Anne de Beaupré in Quebec, and the wonder-workings of the so-called Christian Scientists, are often genuine, and must be considered in discussing the foundations of therapeutics. We physicians use the same power every day. If a poor lass, paralysed apparently, helpless, bed-ridden for years, comes to me, having worn out in mind, body and estate a devoted family; if she in a few weeks or less by faith in me, and faith alone, takes up her bed and walks, the saints of old could not have done more, St. Anne and many others can scarcely to-day do less. We enjoy, I say, no monopoly in the faith-business. The faith with which we work, the faith, indeed, which is available to-day in every-day life, has its limitations. It will not raise the dead; it will not put in a new eye in place of a bad one (as it did to an Iroquois Indian boy for one of the Jesuit fathers), nor will it cure cancer or pneumonia, or knit a bone; but in spite of these nineteenth-century restrictions, such as we find it, faith is a most precious commodity, without which we should be very badly off.

Osler's was the last and best of this excellent series of articles; but more than this, what concerns us here is the fact that his honorarium went to the Faculty's fund, for his name headed the list with the first and largest contribution, which accounts for the enthusiastic letter from Dr. Ashby with which the year began.

Britton Bath Osler, great orator and lawyer, whose name as Crown counsel was a household word in Canada, died on February 5th—the first loss in the circle which, as the Canadian papers said, 'had produced more distinguished men than any other contemporary family in the Commonwealth'—a man who 'possessed in large measure that indescribable gift which goes by the name of personal magnetism'. In a letter to his old Montreal friend Shepherd, Osler in his characteristic, off-hand way, while expressing sympathy for a loss his friend had sustained, conceals the anxiety he himself had been under for so many weeks:

ii.11.01.

Dear Shepherd, I am so sorry to hear of the death of your mother. I knew she was in feeble health but I had not heard of anything serious. It will make a sad break in your circle. Give my kindest regards to your sisters. I have just returned from Toronto. B. B. went off with coronary artery disease. He has had slow pulse with syncopal attacks for a year. 'Twas a mercy that he died suddenly as he dreaded a long illness. So sorry that you cannot come down for the Surgical association. Love to Cecil.

The year 1901 was a critical one for the Hopkins. Some liberal citizens had offered the 'Homewood' property as a new university site on condition that an endowment of a million dollars be raised, but there seemed little prospect of this, for in those days, especially in Baltimore, this appeared an enormous sum. Mr. Gilman's resignation, moreover, had been handed in, and the university was seeking a new president. Among others, the names of both Welch and Osler had been mentioned, but they had other aims in life. Osler's chief aim was to keep in touch with undergraduate students, though little may have been said of them during the recital of these past few years. 'Could you look in here now', wrote Mrs. Osler on the evening of February 23rd, 'you would find Dr. Osler at the head of the dining-room table with 12 clerks of the 4th year listening to his Saturday evening talk; and beer, books and tobacco before them. They all seem to enjoy these evenings.' And yet she wrote the same evening a letter to Ogden urging him to come 'prepared to spend a month and have a nice loaf', adding that 'Dr. Osler has felt his brother's death very much—the first break among the six brothers and altogether very sad.'

With these Saturday evenings at home given over to the successive groups of clinical clerks nothing was allowed to interfere; but he was no less punctilious in attending the local medical meetings, not only at the Hopkins, but those under the auspices of the Maryland Clinical Society which met at the Faculty hall. His mere presence was enough to stimulate an interest in these gatherings, for even if his name did not appear on the programme he was almost certain to participate entertainingly in the discussions. Of his own more formal contributions to one or the other of these societies it need only be said that they were frequent and timely, and that several of them early in this particular year found their way into the pages of a new journal, *American Medicine*, which was in need of professional backing.[1] Meanwhile other things were on his conscience if not actively on his hands, which seemed full enough; one of them, the chairmanship of the American Committee to prepare for the great Tuberculosis Congress to be held in London that coming summer; another the text-book revision.

At this juncture he was laid low with one of his periodic attacks of bronchitis, and took advantage of his several days in bed to devour Gomperz's 'Greek Thinkers', the first volume of which Scribner had just issued. It was on such occasions that he managed to do some consecutive reading, time for which ordinarily was snatched on the wing—when dressing, breakfasting, or retiring. His nephew, who had lived at 1 West Franklin Street or next door with the 'latch-keyers' during his medical course, has written this intimate note of W. O.'s bath and 'the phenomenon', which tells incidentally how time for reading may be found:

He took a warm bath every evening about 10.30. My room was next the bathroom at 1 West Franklin Street and I would get the bath ready when he called out to me on coming upstairs. Or if I were downstairs, I always went up with him for the ceremony. This consisted in my reading to him for ten minutes or so while he was brushing his teeth, taking his bath and drying himself. In the course of six years (the seventh I slept at No. 3) we went systematically through several books: Chapman's Homer ('Iliad' and 'Odyssey'), Morley's 'Jerome Cardan', Izaak Walton's 'Lives', Hilton's 'Rest and Pain' etc., and—during my anatomy days—Holden's 'Landmarks' (apropos of surface markings, I expect you have gone swimming with him and seen the hole in one of his shins from periosteitis following a football injury when he was a boy), using him as a subject. Sometimes we talked about things in general, or what I was learning at the time.

In his bath he seldom failed to test what he called the phenomenon—lying flat in the bath with your toes covered with the water, flex your thigh so as to raise the extended leg *sharply* out of the water. You are conscious of no effort until the heel has cleared the water

---

[1] Its first number appeared in April, under the editorship of George M. Gould, who for sufficient reasons had withdrawn from a similar post on the *Philadelphia Medical Journal*.

by a few inches, when *suddenly* the motion stops. It is then almost impossible to prevent a slight recoil, and it is only with the greatest effort, and after an appreciable interval of immobility, that you can begin again to raise the leg any higher. In this third stage the amount of effort rapidly diminishes to that normally required for elevating the leg through the same angle when you are lying on a dry floor. I used to have to test it for him passively by raising his heel with my hand, and to acknowledge that my effort went through the same three stages.

I would hear the *swish* and expect the usual interruption: 'How d'ye account for it?' or 'Really, Bill, it's extraordinary', etc., etc. No explanation ever satisfied him, and indeed towards the end I gave up arguing it with him and agreed that it was inexplicable. 'Buoyancy? Momentum? Action and reaction? You old tom-cat fool! Buoyancy ought to cease the *instant* the leg leaves the water and the momentum ought to diminish *gradually*. They really don't know much physics nowadays. Archimedes could have solved it for me in a jiffy!'

During April and May came the usual succession of meetings, of Osler's part in which some trace has been left in print or in his correspondence. On April 23rd came the annual gathering of the 'Faculty', with a dinner for Walter Reed, who delivered the oration, taking the recent researches on yellow fever as his text. Then on the 30th, at a meeting of the 'American Physicians' in Washington with Welch presiding, Osler spoke on the subject of the spinal form of arthritis deformans, and there was also a paper by Trudeau on the early recognition of tuberculosis, in the course of which he made what was an extraordinary statement for the time, namely that 75 per cent. of cases of pulmonary consumption might be expected to recover if recognized in time and placed in favourable surroundings. Two outstanding features of the meeting were the accounts given by Reed and Carroll of their Cuban experiences, and by Barker, Flexner, and Novy of the plague situation in San Francisco which they had recently been investigating; and subsequently an event not on the printed programme took place. For a group of five men—Welch, Prudden, Holt, Herter, and Biggs—all members of the association, met in the Arlington Hotel on the invitation of John D. Rockefeller to consider the question of the establishment of an institution to promote research in medicine,[1] a project not then a matter of public knowledge. Osler, whose Text-book had been indirectly responsible for this gathering, had meanwhile returned with Trudeau to Baltimore for a meeting of the Laennec Society, before which body Trudeau gave an account of his work in Saranac. It was in the course of this address that he related the following incident:

About this time [1893], while ill in New York, my house burned to the ground, the fire having originated during the night from the explosion of the kerosene lamp of the thermostat in my little laboratory, and everything in the house and laboratory proved a total loss. Two days after the fire I received from Dr. Osler a brief note, which shows that his great reputation should not be limited to his attainments as a physician, but that he may lay claim also to some reputation as a prophet. The entire substance of the note was as follows:

'Dear Trudeau: I am sorry to hear of your misfortune, but, take my word for it, there is nothing like a fire to make a man do the Phoenix trick.'

Dr. Osler's prophecy very soon began to be realized. A friend and patient of mine, . . . told me that as soon as I was well enough he hoped I would return to Saranac Lake and build a suitable laboratory, one that would not burn down; that he wanted me to build the best I could plan for the purpose, and that he would pay for it. . . .

On the heels of one meeting came another: the American Surgical Association met in Baltimore the first week in May; on the 13th James G. Mumford came to address the Historical Club. Two days later there was a meeting in Chicago; on the 20th another in Philadelphia; and on the 25th the Association of Medical Librarians met in Baltimore. This society, as may be recalled, had been launched with Dr. Gould three years before, for the purpose of heartening the group of people, most of them young women, who were engaging themselves as medical librarians. This was the first meeting of the society to be held in Baltimore, where subsequently, with Osler as President and with Miss Marcia C. Noyes as manager of its book exchanges, its head-quarters were established;

1 The Rockefeller Institute was incorporated a month later, on June 14th, when a pledge of $200,000 was made to the Board (to which the names of Theobald Smith and Flexner had been added), to be drawn upon at their discretion during a period of ten years for preliminary work.

and it hardly needs saying that Osler made it possible for the underpaid librarians of both the 'Faculty' and of the Hopkins Library regularly to attend the meetings of the association elsewhere, for in time it came to hold its sessions in conjunction with the annual A. M. A. gatherings.

But 'Association' is a large word for the small group of seven earnest people and a few invited guests who that afternoon heard Osler give an account of his two visits made the previous summer to the Hunterian Library at Glasgow [1]—visits which had left him 'bewildered with the impression of the extent and value of the collection', the uniqueness of which the Glasgow University authorities scarcely appreciated. And though small, it was a happy group that later on dined with the Oslers and spent an evening at 1 West Franklin Street, which served as a tonic sufficient to tide them over another twelve months in their difficult and unremunerative positions.

How he ever found time for his writing is hard to see. Only two days before this meeting of the librarians, on the occasion of his visit to Chicago, he had given, before the Society of Internal Medicine, an important address [2] in which he attempted to tell, as he says, 'a plain tale of the method of teaching at the Johns Hopkins Hospital'. There was nothing extraordinary about it, except that in the third and fourth years the hospital was made the equivalent of the laboratories of the first and second; and that the student learned the practical art of medicine at the bedside. He spoke of the novel conditions which confronted the Hopkins teachers at the outset; gave a skeleton of the staff organization; told in detail how the clinical instruction was begun; how he believed in the old maxim that 'the whole art of medicine lies in observation'—and he dwelt particularly on his favourite third-year observation class, where the students saw 'close at hand the unwashed

[1] *Bulletin of Association of Medical Librarians*, Balt., 1902, i. 20–3.

[2] 'The Natural Method of Teaching the Subject of Medicine.' *Journal of the American Medical Association*, June 15, 1901, xxxvi. 1673. The article was illustrated by several snapshot pictures of the classes, taken by one of the students. There were many others stolen of him in characteristic attitudes at the bedside, four of which are here reproduced.

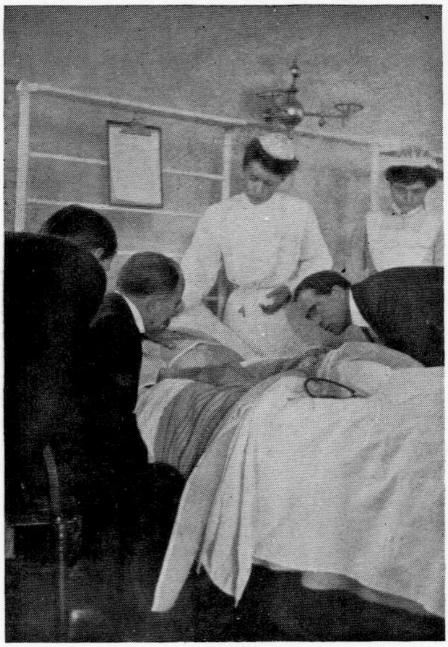

Inspection

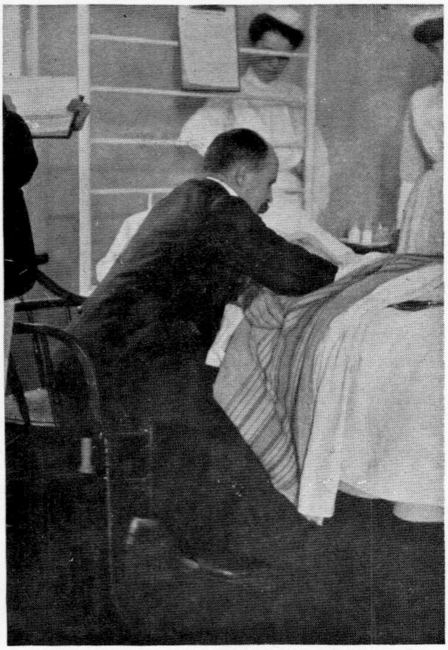

Palpation

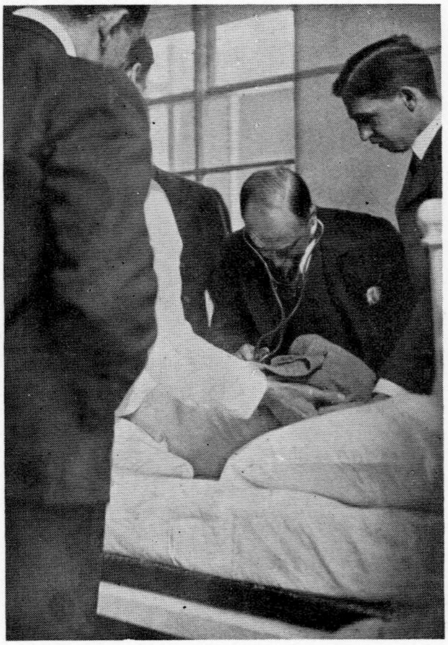

Auscultation

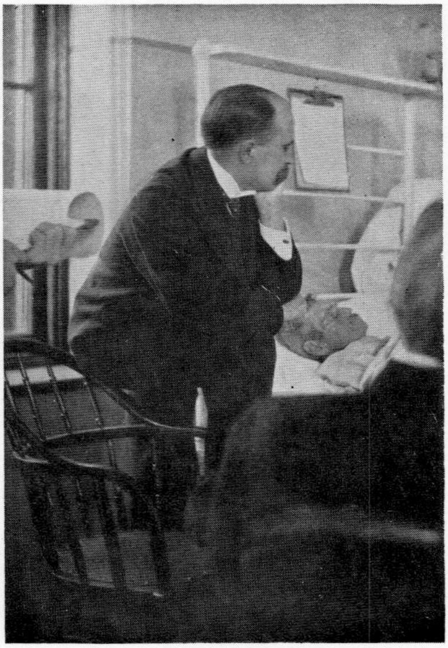

Contemplation

SNAPSHOTS OF OSLER AT THE BEDSIDE

From snapshots taken by T.W. Clarke

maladies' from the dispensary. He described the class in physical diagnosis and clinical microscopy, the general medical clinic, the work of the clinical clerks, his general clinic in the amphitheatre on Wednesday noon when the 'typhoid committee' and the 'pneumonia committee' made their reports. 'Great emphasis', he said, 'is laid on the teaching of pneumonia, the great acute disease, the present "captain of the men of death", to use a phrase of John Bunyan.'

It was all very simple. There was nothing new about it. This he fully emphasized, quoting in evidence what Professor Gomperz in his 'Greek Thinkers' had said of the rational science of Hippocrates and his contemporaries. And he ended with this reference to his old teacher:

Years ago my preceptor, Dr. Bovell, placed in my hands Latham's 'Clinical Medicine', and he marked a passage which contains the Alpha and Omega of clinical teaching, and with it I will conclude: 'In entering this place,' speaking of the wards of St. Bartholomew's Hospital, 'even this vast hospital where there is many a significant and many a wonderful thing, you shall take me along with you, and I will be your guide. But it is by your own eyes, and your ears and your own minds and (I may add) your own heart that you must observe and learn and profit. I can only point to the objects and say little else than "see here and see there".'

Yes, it was all very simple—the method—but there was something far more important than method—the personality of the teacher, needed to make this or any other system a success. One can easily conjecture the existence of this essential element by reading between the lines of the address; but given some years later in the words of one of those students, it is more vivid:

To us who were his students in the early days of the Johns Hopkins Medical School, his memory is so vivid, so fresh, that it seems as if yesterday when he worked and played in our midst, and we have but to close our eyes to see him in fancy, almost as clearly as we saw him in fact in the late '90's, the great teacher and the great student in his manifold relations to his students. Now we can see him riding to the hospital in the Monument Street car, and to the group about him prophesying with keen yet ever kindly vision the ills—physical, mental and spiritual of the derelicts *en route* to the dispensary; here in the wards demonstrating the complex psychology of Giles de la Tourette's disease, as exemplified by a poor bit of sodden humanity whose coprolalia but exemplified—in a way a bit embarrassing at times, it is true,—the symptom-complex he was discussing; or in an alcove off the ward playing with little Theophilia as she was emerging from the night of cretinism into the day of normal happy childhood under his skilful guidance; now in the classroom of the dispensary . . . solving a case of great complexity . . . now in the clinical laboratory studying a blood specimen, and suggesting to the student some line of original investigation which might, perhaps, light into flame the dormant investigator and research worker; now in the autopsy room studying in death the puzzles that he had helped to unravel during life; now walking through the wards and corridors of the hospital with a smile or an epigram for every doctor and nurse who passed; a kindly word, and his ever-stimulating psychotherapy—encouragement, optimism, hope—to every patient he saw; in his myriad activities always making each student feel that he also was but a student of health and disease, of men and morals, and yet such a student as to fire our minds, our souls and our bodies to renewed efforts so that we might, in some measure at least, prove worthy of this fraternity. To us who were privileged to be his students—his fellow students in those days—he was, and still is, always our inspiration and always our model.[1]

By the end of May, leaving him knee-deep in proofs, Mrs. Osler had departed, taking Revere for a visit in Canton, thereby exchanging for her exciting life a very quiet one. And she wrote to one of the 'latch-keyers' that she was homesick and blue at the thought of 1 West Franklin Street full of people—but that she would struggle along till the 15th. This was the date set for their sailing on the *St. Paul*, and, sure enough, by then the Text-book revision was completed and the pages forwarded to the publishers, though the preface does not appear to have been written till after they had reached London. Inserted in his own library copy of this 4th edition, is a slip on which Osler has written:

This very clever examination paper on my Text-book was written by Dr. Scott, afterwards demonstrator of histology in the University of Oxford, and appeared in the St. Thomas' Hospital Gazette, 1902. Additions were made to the original by one or two of my assistants in Baltimore. About a month after the examination appeared,

---

[1] 'Osler and the Student.' T. R. Brown, *Johns Hopkins Hospital Bulletin*, July 1919, xxx. 200.

a complete set of answers was sent to me by my friend J. William White, the well-known Philadelphia surgeon.

It was a most amusing skit—this paper—and tickled Osler greatly. It was signed 'D. M. S.' and really was composed by three St. Thomas's men: L. S. Dudgeon, A. Mavrogordato, and S. G. Scott. The skit, with its 19 questions (expanded later to 24) began in this wise:

An Examination Paper on Osler (*4th Edition*)

There seems to be a certain monotony about medical examinations, so we suggest the following, by way of variety:

1.—Who was Mephibosheth? What parental superstition dates from his time?

2.—What is 'one of the saddest chapters in the history of human deception'?

3.—Give Osler's quotations from the following authors: John Bunyan, Byron, John Cheyne, George Cheyne, Montaigne. Explain the context where necessary.

The first trace of Osler's footsteps in London this summer of 1901 occurs as a note on the fly-leaf of Scott's 'Letters on Demonology and Witchcraft', addressed to J. G. Lockhart, 1830. 'This is the first Edition', he wrote. 'I bought it at Sotheby's June 30 1901 for £1. 8. 6. W. O.' And from the Savile Club he sent word to George Nuttall that they had changed their plans about Cambridge, since they were off to Holland on Monday, and would hope to see him later at the Tuberculosis Congress.

It was again a scorching summer and some one had suggested that it might be cooler in Holland, where there were so many windmills. Heat, however, bothered Osler very little, due, as he was wont to say, to the chill of thirty Canadian winters lingering in his veins. The trip, long planned, was to be taken with George Dock, his former Philadelphia assistant, but at the last moment, braving the thermometer, Mrs. Osler accompanied them with the understanding that she was in no way to interfere with their programme. This was largely a medico-biblio-historical one, which was to begin with 'The Anatomy Lesson' at The Hague. They had written ahead to some physicians in various places they intended to visit, and started out, Osler with a Life of Boerhaave and Foster's

'Lane Lectures', just published, under his arm. These he would be found perusing in some corner of the Mauritshuis, for example, while the others were led on beyond the one or two pictures to which they had definitely agreed to confine themselves.

A most amusing though trying day, with the temperature about 100° F., was spent in Leyden with Professor Rosenstein, then an old man, a Teuton who for many years had occupied Boerhaave's Chair as Professor of Medicine. But alas! he had never been to Oud-Poelgeest, nor did he know where was his immortal predecessor's tomb—indeed, insisted there was none. The good old man learned a great deal of medical history on this particularly red-hot day, and finally got his guests home, where in their shirt-sleeves, seated on a horse-hair sofa, they were refreshed by some warm lemonade. Nor was this all—for a sweltering evening with much feasting and toasting was passed with the professor's family at a waterside resort—but it must suffice. A second day was passed in Leyden, looking in vain through the university register for the signature of a quondam matriculant named Thomas Browne of *circa* 1633; but they had better luck elsewhere, for later in the day they stumbled upon a sale at which the belongings of the last female descendant of Boerhaave were being disposed of, and Osler purchased items from the collection, including a large brass quadrant which had once been Boerhaave's. He also appears to have made this entry in his pocket note-book late one evening, possibly on the way back to The Hague:[1]

July 11th 1901.

Dr. George Dock and I dined with Professor Rosenstein and about 8 o'clock strolled out along the Trekvaart for about half a mile, then turned into a narrow country lane, which with many windings

[1] Osler evidently was pursuing the 'flighty purpose', viz. to jot down his impressions for use in a subsequent paper. The plan was never fulfilled. He did speak on Boerhaave the next autumn before the Historical Club, but his remarks were never published. Sixteen years passed before he touched this material again, and then before the Historical Section of the Royal Society of Medicine (1918) he gave a paper on 'Boerhaave's Position in Science', the manuscript of which is preserved, though it was never printed. In this article he particularly defends Boerhaave's position as an experimental chemist; 'Not even the erudite Haeser refers to it, nor indeed does Meyer,

led to Oud-Poelgeest (Old Pond Marsh), the country home of Boerhaave. High stone pillars and massive iron gates of unusual height open on a drive which leads to the house through an avenue of magnificent beeches. . . . The trees come very close to the house, which is a spacious square building of old brick, flanked by wings which are set forward a little from the main building. Coming out from the dense avenue it looked as sombre as the 'House of Usher', but the weird and solemn stillness was soon broken by the furious barking of two great dogs, which were kenneled and chained opposite either corner. A hedge of box, in the letters Oud-Poelgeest, threw a fragrance on the damp evening air. It was a great deprivation not to be able to enter the house. On either side there was a dense shrubbery, in the midst of which to the left stood the magnificent ruins of what is known as Boerhaave's tree, an American tulip tree which he had planted some two hundred years ago. The main trunk had split some years ago and had been girded with irons; one or two of the large branches remained, and there were vigorous shoots which bore beautiful blossoms. One could not but feel that the tree was emblematic in a way of the great school of Leyden, which had as it were lived its life, but which now shows new and vigorous shoots. A tablet was placed upon the tree in 1817 with an inscription referring to Boerhaave and his reputation.

On passing to the back of the house what was our surprise to find that it rose directly out of the basin or expanded termination of one of the canals leading directly to Leyden, and Professor Rosenstein pointed out at one angle the doorway through which tradition says Boerhaave took his barge to go to town. Here, too, Peter the Great anchored his boat when he paid a visit to the great Professor. From the bridge over the canal one got a fine view of the old house, the foundations of which rose directly from the water. The dampness of the place may have accounted for the attacks of serious arthritis from which Boerhaave suffered. Perhaps in his time the place was more open and the trees had not grown so close to the house; but here, after the toils and cares of the day he retired for recreation and repose. . . .

A few days were passed in Amsterdam—the mornings by Osler in his shirtsleeves up a ladder selecting from the shelves of Muller's *magasin de livres* a stock of books for the 'Faculty' library and incidentally some few for his own. On a table conveniently near for consultation stood the volumes of the Index Catalogue of the Surgeon-

while Garrison, so accurate and liberal, is positively unjust and is supported by my Cambridge brother [Allbutt] whose astonishing statement is quoted— "he made no experiments in Medicine".'

General's Library, and Foster's new 'History of Physiology' lay open exposing the page with a chronological list of rare historical works;—a pitcher of drinking-water completes the picture. Meanwhile Mrs. Osler writes to one of the 'latch-keyers' in Baltimore that her two men are very happy hunting old books; and incidentally a fifty-second birthday is recorded:

. . . They found nothing in the Hague or Rotterdam, but have had splendid luck here and got some Boerhaave things in Leyden. We are going north to-morrow to Groningen; then to Utrecht and Antwerp—on to Ghent and some epileptic-hospital place; and cross from Ostend on the 21st. . . . Revere is so happy in Scotland. He joked up to the last moment about leaving us, but when we put him on the train he said: 'Oh, I do care—I feel queer in my heart under my arm.' . . . Dr. Osler has been really sightseeing on this trip and is very amusing. He looks at one picture in the collection and then flies to a book shop. I got him a lovely Keats for his birthday. I think I told you he would not bid against Quaritch at this sale so we had to take it at his price, but no matter, he is so happy over it. He has a consultation in the country next week and the fee will cover many indiscretions.

From Amsterdam they crossed the Zuyder Zee to visit the new clinics in course of erection at Groningen, and there a lifelong friendship was started with K. F. Wenckebach, the newly appointed young professor, who vividly recalls one incident of the visit, for after they had gone over the buildings Osler announced that he would like to see 'the Bible'. 'What Bible?' 'The Bible', replied Osler, 'that belonged to Martin Luther and afterwards came into the hands of Erasmus who made annotations in it; it must be in the University Library.' 'And lo', Professor Wenckebach adds, 'there the Holy thing was'—much to his amazement, for he knew nothing about it. They subsequently went on to Friesland, and that enchanting spot Leeuwarden; and from there the story may be taken up from another letter, written by the third member of the party:

. . . I believe I wrote you from Amsterdam. We really had a delightful trip, though Drs. Dock and Osler became utterly disgusted at every place where old books were not forthcoming and promptly wanted to leave. We went far north into Friesland and came to a most fascinating place, Leeuwarden, where we had the good luck to hit on a kermess and saw the natives in their charming prosperity and beauty. There also we found the factory for 'antique' silver—and know why it is so plentiful. The spoons cost almost nothing there. Utrecht was a great disappointment. The Professor wrote Dr. Osler a note and called him 'dear Professor Hopkins' which afforded us much amusement. In Antwerp it was so boiling hot we could not breathe and made up our minds to skip Bruges and Ghent and rush on to Ostend. There we stayed three days in a most charming hotel and had sea baths and generally refreshed ourselves. . . .

So they did, and some one else tells that the 'Life of Boerhaave' was forgotten, and a peculiar amphibious dark-skinned person who had learned his water-tricks in the ponds of Upper Canada proceeded to walk around the floor of the ocean on his hands, waving aloft a pair of legs to the amazement of the natives and to the anticipated embarrassment of his wife in the water alongside. From this digression we may return to Mrs. Osler's letter:

[From Ostend] we went back to Clarges Street. I stayed two days at the Congress. It was very impressive—the Duke of Cambridge opened it. I nearly had a fit. I did not know Dr. Osler was to speak and I was overcome with astonishment. Entre nous—he and Lord Lister had more applause and a better greeting than any of the others. The thermometer was about 98° and I was so excited I really could hardly sit still. I was alone and had no one to poke. The meetings were most successful and the social functions wonderful. I asked Mother to send you on a menu from Sir James Blyth's dinner. . . . The Duke of Cambridge asked Dr. Osler to sit down and chat with him, and said: 'Oh, you Americans are so joky, I do like you.' Wasn't it delightful. We went to a most lovely tea at Apsley House—there the Duchess of Wellington made us feel that we were really the only people in the world she wanted to see. It gave me a good lesson. I left the men having this very festive time, and came to Edinburgh by sleeping-carriage—then on to Falkirk.

She had gone to Scotland to get Revere, who by this time was probably feeling less 'queer in his heart under his arm', leaving behind her in London Drs. Dock, Musser, and Osler 'tuberculously daft', as she expresses it in another letter. But this British Congress on Tuberculosis, the second of these special congresses to be held on an international basis, which opened on Monday, July 22nd, with some 2,500 persons in attendance, cannot be so lightly dismissed. It was indeed a most successful affair, and royalty by lending its patronage had lined itself up in the campaign against the disease which had spared no families, those of prince or pauper. A short six months to the day had elapsed since the cousin of the Duke of Cambridge—who eighty-three years before had unexpectedly stepped between him and the throne—had ended her long career. Otherwise she, rather than her son, would have been the person to command the aged Duke, who had served in the Crimea when Osler was wearing a smock-frock in Bond Head, Upper Canada, to be temporary G.O.C. in this new and peculiar campaign which was to be fought by a species of propaganda.

The exciting occasion—when there was no one for Mrs. Osler to poke—was the opening ceremony at St. James's Hall when, in the presence of Ambassadors innumerable, Mr. Choate among them, of Strathcona the High Commissioner of Canada, of Bishops, Lord Mayors, Earls, Marquises, and other dignitaries too many to mention, the Earl of Derby called upon the representative delegates of each of the foreign countries—Osler first, as representing America—and in turn presented them to the Duke. Osler spoke briefly, and the reader knows how it was that he came to apply Bunyan's phrase in speaking of consumption as 'captain of the men of death'; the captain, he said, had nevertheless been reduced to a lieutenant and would soon be reduced to the ranks, though it was almost too much to expect that he would actually be drummed completely out of the regiment. All of which may have been what H.R.H. the Duke termed 'joky'. In alphabetical order, the Belgian, Danish, French, German, and other delegates were then presented, each of them responding in turn with appropriate and brief remarks—less 'joky', be it said, than were Osler's. A deputation, Osler among them, was subsequently received by the King at Marlborough House; and there were great receptions, one at the Mansion House, and elaborate dinners to be attended.

During the serious sessions of the congress which followed, the outstanding, and, be it said, somewhat disconcerting, episode occurred on the second day, when, introduced by Lord Lister, 'Geh. Med. Rath. Professor Dr. Robert Koch, Direktor des Instituts für Infektionskrankheiten in Berlin', discoverer of the tubercle bacillus, gave a notable address,[1] a certain portion of which provoked most unexpected commotion. Koch gave an exceedingly interesting analysis of the ways in which different infectious diseases must be combated, and laid down a most sensible programme for the fight against tuberculosis. Much of the value of this was lost, however, because of the one section of his paper in which he dwelt on the difference between human and bovine tuberculosis. For what riveted the attention of his audience to the exclusion of all else was his statement that human tuberculosis was practically non-transmissible to animals; that the reverse was probably also true; and consequently that the attempt by legislative action, particularly rigorous in England, to stamp out the disease in cattle as a source of human infection, had been misdirected. This led to a storm of protest and disagreement among sanitarians, which lies outside this story. Suffice it to say that Koch again, as with his tuberculin, had been a little premature in his conclusions; and in the discussion that immediately followed the address, Lister with extreme clearness of thought promptly put his finger on the weak point in the deductions Koch had drawn from his experiments.[2]

[1] 'The Fight Against Tuberculosis.' *British Medical Journal*, July 27, 1901, ii. 189–93.

[2] In these experiments Koch had shown that it was impossible to infect cattle, swine, or other animals with the bacillus taken from cases of pulmonary consumption in man, whereas they were readily susceptible to transmission of infected material from animal to animal. The reverse experiment, of course, could not be tried without personal 'sanction' of a group of human volunteers. However, involuntarily, experiments are continually being conducted, particularly in the case of children who are fed on butter and milk containing living bacilli from infected animals. Koch did not believe tuberculosis could be contracted by humans in this way. Others who disagreed with him were apparently correct, but his, just then, was the greater voice. The aftermath of all this can be followed in the correspondence, editorials, &c., in the *British Medical Journal* of July 27, 1901, and succeeding issues. It may be said that a Royal Commission on Tuberculosis was soon appointed which sat for ten years, with a net expenditure of £75,557, and published an elaborate report in 1911, to the effect that man *is* infectible by the bovine bacillus, Professor Koch notwithstanding.

There was one man greatly missed at the congress, and in the midst of the three days' busy sessions Osler found time to say so in a letter of July 23rd to Dr. Lawrason Brown at Saranac:

40 Clarges Street.

Dear Brown, You will not find it easy I fear to get an assistant unless he is a healed 'lunger'. I do not know of the right man at the moment but I will bear it in mind. We are having a delightful meeting, only we miss Trudeau sadly. So many inquire for him & speak of his work. So glad you are going to take charge of the Sanitarium. The outlook for you should be first-class. Love to Dr Trudeau.

A meeting of the British Medical Association at Cheltenham followed upon the heels of the Tuberculosis Congress, and though Osler was in attendance and participated in the programme, the occasion need not detain us except to point out that, as told by G. A. Gibson,[1] he seems to have devoted himself largely to his old friend Sir William Gairdner, whom he was to see for the last time. This meeting over, he rejoined Mrs. Osler and Revere at North Berwick, where they had meanwhile gone and where rooms had been taken for the remainder of the summer near his friends the Schäfers, who resided there. A few days later he wrote to John H. Musser, saying:

We were very much disappointed that you did not turn up on Tuesday. I only found out the Sabbatarian character of the North British RR in the afternoon. It was very nice to see you in London. I only wish that you had come earlier as there were many things that we might have done together. It has been delightful I feel sure for John to have trotted about with you. Mrs. Osler sends love & thanks for the books. . . . This is a delightful place & I shall enjoy the golf greatly. I hope you will have a good trip. Kind regards to Janeway. It was nice to have him here as one of our representatives. Do not forget to tell the Provost what a strong impression Ravenel made. He appeared before the Local Gov. Board on the tuberculosis question.

In North Berwick he feigned to devote himself to the links, but there are recollections of a succession of visitors; of expeditions to Bass Rock, which William Harvey visited with amazement in 1633, as described in his treatise on

[1] 'Life of Sir William Tennant Gairdner'. Glasgow, 1912.

'The Generation of Living Creatures'; of Tantallon Castle and Berwick Law, from which one can see on a fine day Arthur's Seat and the smoke of Edinburgh, some twenty-five miles up the Firth of Forth. Nor was Edinburgh so far away but that expeditions were made there too, as verified by the note, 'I bought these volumes in Edinburgh Aug. 1901', written in such a peculiar set as William Hayley's 'Essay on Old Maids' in three volumes. And likely enough there were purchases for the Faculty, to whose Librarian, Miss Marcia Noyes, he sent a belated note:

Dear Miss Noyes, I was very distressed (truly) to leave without saying good-bye but I had such hard work to get away—that confounded text-book kept me right to the very last moment. I hope by this time you are away on your holiday. I will send by Sept 1st the circular letter which I wish to have sent to all those interested in Libraries asking them to subscribe. I have some treasures for the Library. Muller & Co of Amsterdam had a loft full of fine old books which I looked over. They will send out a box about Sept. 15th. Let me know if there is anything special wanted from Germany as it could come in Muller's box. We had a delightful trip in Holland. We came here ten days ago. I have forgotten all about medicine & Doctors & my sole ambition in life now is to reduce my score at golf. I hope your sister keeps well.

Nor had he forgotten the McGill Library, for a few days later a similar letter went to its supervisor, Miss Margaret Charlton, announcing some rare books he was sending, and later on he wrote to the son of his old preceptor, who had graduated from McGill the previous spring, and with whose plans he was naturally concerned, saying:

Incheuen, North Berwick,
Aug. 21st 1901.

Dear Campbell, I am delighted to think that you will be in the M. G. H. on Sept 1st. How long is your service, 1 or 1 1/2 years? I think if you wish it I could arrange to take you on my service next year (after finishing the M. G. H.). You could come in as one of the four senior Residents and the work would be mainly bacteriological but you would see all the work and have to help in teaching. If you think of it as likely, pay special attention to bacteriology this winter with [John] McCrae your Resident Pathologist—in fact it would be well to get him to coach you. Of course if you think two years of Hospital work too much, with what you wish to spend abroad, it might be possible to arrange for some special work, but you would not have the advantage of living in the Hospital. Aunt Grace and Revere send love. We sail Sept. 14th.

And this allusion to Palmer Howard and to days gone by makes it appropriate to recall the Rev. W. A. Johnson, and his son 'Jimmie', who had helped grind the cow's molar; and who, having long since left medicine to enter the Church, now had a parish near London:

To James Bovell Johnson from W. O. U.S.M.S. *St. Louis*, 18th.

Dear Jim, We had to change our plans & did not leave North Berwick until nearly a week later than we had anticipated. I am so sorry to hear that you have had financial troubles, & am sure your suspicions must be unfounded. . . . X. has done well but I am afraid he has not saved much money. You know how hard it is to put by anything in our profession unless you are keen after the 'baubees' and successful in investments. I worked 20 years before I had saved a shilling. I doubt if I shall be over next year as I have a lot of heavy literary work on hand. Let me know if I could help you in any way. . . .

On the steamer he was probably kept busy between Revere and 'The American Voice', but he found time to write—or to promise, for he procrastinated about this—a review of Sir Michael Foster's 'Lane Lectures', which, as noted, had trotted about with him during the summer. On landing, they paid a brief visit to the Conynghams in Wilkesbarre, and to judge from a series of letters to Mr. George Coy, the idea must have struck him of the desirability of publishing in the School Catalogue a list of the former graduates with the positions they had come to occupy, as well as a list of the papers written by members of the staff. At least, from this time on, such a list became a feature of the Medical School Catalogue. These letters show also that the health of the students, many of whom were living in unsanitary boarding-houses, was a source of unending anxiety, which fell even more heavily on him than on the Dean, for the Professor of Medicine had to care for them and take the blame. In a later paper [1] he mentions the case of one of the third-year students, a Baltimore boy, who, used up by his June examinations, had

[1] 'Typhoid Fever and Tuberculosis.' *American Medicine*, Dec. 26, 1903.

been admitted to the hospital with fever, and for a time typhoid instead of tuberculosis was suspected, for which both he and Thayer were severely censured by the family. The death of Davis while a house officer had been the occasion of immeasurable distress, and first and last there had been a good deal of illness. In the class of 1899 alone four of the students had developed consumption, and at this particular time John Bruce MacCallum, possibly the most brilliant student ever graduated from the school, had begun to show while at work in Mall's laboratory unmistakable signs of the disease, which ended in four short years a career of unusual promise.

Thayer had married during the summer, and T. B. Futcher with another had come as neighbours to share his place in the 3 West Franklin Street house with H. B. Jacobs. Then, too, the circle had been further increased by the arrival for Revere of a black puppy, designed to be a long-haired spaniel and selected with due regard for his pedigree by Dr. Malloch of Hamilton. Revere at that time was having a severe attack of mythology and could think of little else. The puppy consequently was promptly named 'Hector', which must have considerably modified his destiny, for he turned out to be more of a Trojan and less of a spaniel than was expected (W. O.'s diagnosis was a Hamiltonian terrier). At about this time, also, the foreign book packages began to come in, and, to judge from the following letters, were being distributed, George Cheyne's 'Essay of Health and Long Life' accompanying the first letter:

To George C. Shattuck from W. O. 1 West Franklin Street.

I am sure you will enjoy reading the old man's book on Health. There are some very delightful things in it. I am glad to see that you sign yourself only George C. Perhaps we might compromise on that, but I dare say as you grow older & get well into the profession & appreciate the virtues of the original George Cheyne & of your great-grandfather & grandfather you will then insensibly be compelled to use the Cheyne for the Cheever. With kind regards for all at home, &c.

To F. J. Shepherd from W. O. x.18.01.

Very glad to have your letter this evening. We got back three weeks ago. Mrs. O & Revere have just returned from Canada.

I could not go with them as there were a score of things to do before the session opened & we were arranging a new scheme for our 4th year work by which the men would have more time in Medicine & Surgery and bunching the specialties to practical demonstrations & work in the Dispensaries. . . . I have been book hunting all summer and secured some treasures in Holland, chiefly from Muller of Amsterdam who keeps a good stock. I sent out one or two books for the Library & I got in London a good copy of Harvey's De generatione Animalium, Eng Edition, which I left to have bound & forwarded. All goes well here, except that I am bothered to death with practice—hard to keep it within decent limits so as to have time for teaching & private work. What is the Date of the C M A? If it is after the middle of Sept I can be with you & would be only too glad to give the Address in Medicine or anything else you wish. So glad that you are the President this year. Love to Cecil and Dorothy. I hope you will be down this winter, & bring Cecil. I saw Stephen Mackenzie several times—he is better but looks far from well. I have been reading with interest Macallum's Addresses —they bring back old days & ways. What a shame that we never had his portrait painted. Is it too late? Wright's too? Yours ever

Wm Osler.

From October 21st to 23rd there was a gathering at New Haven to celebrate the bicentenary of Yale—an occasion which brought together delegates from countless universities at home and abroad, as is the way with such festivals. The exercises culminated in a ceremony remarkable in many respects, but particularly in that it gave opportunity to bring out the extraordinary qualities of two very unusual personages—Hadley, then President of Yale; and the man whom fate a short time before had made President of the Nation. Some threescore men of letters, of science, and statesmanship from various parts of the world were presented for degrees—John Hay, Marquis Ito and so on; from the Johns Hopkins were Remsen, Gildersleeve, and Osler; and, youngest of all, the Professor of Jurisprudence and Politics at Princeton University, by the name of Woodrow Wilson, to mention but a few of them. To each of these sixty as they were presented in turn, without reference to any notes, Mr. Hadley addressed himself appropriately and briefly in conferring the honorary degrees—the last of them on a man to whom, as a private citizen a few short months before, the invitation had been sent.

Turning to Theodore Roosevelt, he said: 'But one name now remains', whereupon an extraordinarily moving scene was enacted—which perhaps, after all, lies outside this narrative.

To Francis R. Packard from W. O. Nov. 2, 1901.

Pardon the delay in replying to your letter, but I have been on the road. Yes, I will come over with pleasure on the 13th, and will gladly dine with you at the club and stop the night. I am so glad to hear that you have started a historical club. It will be most useful. I am arranging a programme for our Book & Journal Club for this winter. Could you give us something at one of the meetings? It is a club of the Medical & Chirurgical Faculty, with about sixty or seventy members, and we have four meetings a year, at which we generally have somebody from outside to give us a little talk on any matters of bibliographical or historical interest. If you can come would December 18th [1] be convenient?

November 9th records a dinner at 1 West Franklin Street in honour of the King's birthday. The 19th finds him in Elkton, the home of his country-doctor friend Ellis, in attendance at the autumn meeting of the Faculty. The month also saw published a number of brief clinical papers,[2]

[1] Packard did come, and spoke on the Resurrectionists [i.e. body-snatchers] of London and Edinburgh; while on the same programme Osler was down for a paper (unpublished) entitled 'Pickings from London Book Shops'. He presented a number of the 'pickings' to the Faculty Library.

[2] Two of them are especially noteworthy. One was his first paper (three others followed) on 'Multiple Hereditary Telangiectases [&c.]' (*Johns Hopkins Hospital Bulletin*, 1901, xii. 333–7).

The other bears the paradoxical title of 'The Advantages of a Trace of Albumin and a Few Tube Casts in the Urine of Certain Men over Fifty Years of Age' (*New York Medical Journal*, Nov. 23, 1901), in which he belittled the chance laboratory-finding of a trace of albumin and a few tube casts. He pictured the successful business man, who having overstoked his engine has a rude shock when some life-insurance company declines the extra sum he wishes to place on his life. He proceeded to give a few striking illustrations, one of them, Osler subsequently admitted, being the case of Sir Charles Tupper—then 'still alive and an octogenarian of exceptional vigour'. And he went on to tell of the man who in the Cathedral of Antwerp, the past summer, had touched him on the shoulder and whispered in his ear, 'Not dead yet', and on turning he had seen an old patient who ten years before had been rejected because of Bright's disease. Sir Charles Tupper, who, before Strathcona, had been Canadian High Commissioner, lived to be ninety-three; and in an obituary notice which Osler wrote of him (*British*

and the appearance of a large volume on typhoid fever of which he was the editor.[1] So the time was amply filled both at home and 'on the road'. In December he is found at a meeting in Ann Arbor, where he addressed the students; and, later on, the Christmas recess was passed with Mrs. Osler's relatives. Some time before, he had sent this undated note to his friend Chadwick in Boston:

> You are a Saint. That dictionary[2] will be of such help—I have long wanted just such a volume. *Le Peter* is most flatulent & will please some of the boys. Thank you so much for both of them. The 27th or 28th would suit me for a talk—Thomas Linacre, the first of the Great Medical Humanists. If this is too long just Thomas Linacre. Yours sincerely. [P.S.] I will bring the volumes as a text.

Thus the Boston Medical Library, and a sort of book and journal club which had been started there by Chadwick, profited by this Christmas visit; and though he chose Linacre as his topic, several years were to pass before this material was whipped into its final form as a finished essay.

Medical Journal, Nov. 6, 1915) he returns to the subject, saying: 'The advantage of the discovery [made in 1880 in Sir Charles's case] was never better illustrated, as he ever after lived a careful life.'

[1] Under the supervision of Dr. Alfred Stengel, a successor to Osler's former position in Philadelphia, a translation from the German, of Nothnagel's great 'Encyclopaedia of Practical Medicine' had been made during the year. The volume on Typhoid and Typhus Fevers was edited by Osler with the help of Dr. Rufus I. Cole, then one of his assistant resident physicians, and judging from Osler's preface many of the chapters in the volume of over 600 pages had been thoroughly revised or practically rewritten.

[2] Cappelli's excellent 'Dizionario di Abbreviature latine', Milan, 1899.

CHAPTER XXI

1902

BOOKS AND THE MAN

During the year the subject of tuberculosis continued to be very much to the fore, and the community at large had begun to be sufficiently aroused to appreciate the significance of an anti-spitting ordinance, if nothing more. Nor was the public allowed any rest at this stage of its education. On January 13th Osler wrote to the Dean: 'I think a very good subject for an evening lecture would be Municipal Sanatoria in Tuberculosis; Dr. Warren Buckler has the whole matter in hand.' The time had come, indeed, when an assault on the State legislature was justified, and with this both Welch and Osler in their different spheres had much to do.

The local Board of Health, of which Welch continued to be President, and which had a most active Secretary in the person of Dr. John S. Fulton, had recommended through the Governor to the legislature the appointment of a Tuberculosis Commission which, though unsalaried and removed from politics, was, however, to be granted certain powers. In order to secure some popular backing for this recommendation, it was decided that a public meeting should be held under the combined auspices of the Laennec Society, the Medical and Chirurgical Faculty, and the Maryland Public Health Association. This last-mentioned body, of whose origin mention has been made, had in the short four years of its existence come to play an increasingly important rôle in turning public attention towards matters of public health.

In these matters, particularly as regards tuberculosis, Massachusetts was far ahead of the other States, and Dr. Vincent Y. Bowditch had been asked to come from Boston to give the main address of the evening. McCoy Hall was packed to the doors. Dr. Fulton, in explaining the status of the tuberculosis question so far as it concerned the welfare of Baltimore and the State, vividly laid bare the 'ignorance, vice and greed which propagate the disease'. Bowditch followed with his address, which began with a quotation from Osler's 'Practice', and ended with a plea for a state sanatorium for Maryland. The Mayor of Baltimore made a few feeble remarks. And then Osler was called on. The situation may be contrasted with that of the summer before, when royalty had aligned itself with the crusade and he spoke in the presence of the old Duke of Cambridge on the same subject. The rather-more-than-usually apathetic Mayor found Osler distinctly less 'joky' than had the Duke—indeed, to the amazement of Baltimore, Osler publicly shook his finger in the Mayor's face—but apparently it turned the trick. He was quoted, in a mild version, as having spoken impromptu, as follows: [1]

Mr. Chairman and my long-suffering, patient, inert fellow-citizens: You have heard two aspects of the tuberculosis question—first, the interesting statement, with reference to the existing prevalence of the disease, from Dr. Fulton; and second, the modern means whereby the disease in a very considerable number of cases may be arrested. Now, what is our condition in this city, and what are we doing for the 10,000 consumptives who are living to-day in our midst? We are doing, Mr. Mayor and fellow-citizens, not one solitary thing that a modern civilized community should do. Through the kindness of a couple of ladies—God bless them!—I have been enabled in the past three or four years to have two medical students of the Johns Hopkins University visit every case of pulmonary consumption that has applied for admission to the dispensary of our hospital, and I tell you now that the story those students brought back is a disgrace to us as a city of 500,000 inhabitants. It is a story of dire desolation, want, and helplessness, and of hopeless imbecility in everything that should be in our civic relation to the care of this disease. No instruction on the part of the State or city, none whatever. These people have had no instruction except what these two young women have given them. . . .

This is the whole matter in a nutshell, Mr. Mayor and fellow-citizens. Now, what are you going to do about it? Nothing. It is not the fault of the Mayor and City Council, but of the citizens, and unless you get them awake nothing can be done. If you can once get the people awake it doesn't make any difference if the Mayor and City Council are asleep. It is you, fellow-citizens, that must wake up, and if you would get wide awake, and remain awake a short time, I would like to tell you what to do.

Mr. Mayor, you may close your ears, because I know you are

---

[1] *Maryland Medical Journal*, 1902, xlv. 133–5.

a good hard-working fellow, and don't get your deserts. But . . . we want a new charter in this old town. We are sick to death of mayors, and first branches and second branches. In heaven's name, what have they done for us in the past? I can tell you what they have done for us in the thirteen years I have been here. To my positive knowledge they have paved two or three streets east and west, and two or three streets north and south, and by the Lord Harry! I could not point to a single other thing they have done. They haven't given us a municipal hospital, they haven't given us a sewerage system, and we are still begging for lots of other things. I would say to Mr. Carter: We want something new, and something good, and just you frame a charter without any of the ancient tomfoolery, old-time Mayor and City Council. Give us a couple or three good men and true who will run this city as a business corporation. It would not take us a year then, Mr. Mayor, not a year, to get a start on a sewerage system and an infectious-disease hospital, and everything else that the public welfare demands. We would have a sanatorium-system complete within a few years; and, what is more, your taxes would be reduced. . . .

Dr. Bowditch, the guest of the evening, recalls that this unlooked-for tirade made his very hair stand on end, and he fully expected that a southern duel would be precipitated, but to his surprise, later in the evening, he saw the Mayor with his arm over Osler's shoulder, talking to him in a most affectionate manner. 'Osler was nothing if not frank', he adds; 'and the curious thing about it is that no one ever seemed to take offence.' It did not occur very often that Osler thus let himself out, but this sort of direct outspokenness was under the circumstances absolutely necessary to get action on the part of the people. There was one touch in his fiery speech to which attention may be drawn—his inevitable reaction of sympathy for the man whose civic apathy he was exposing—for, after all, he probably *was* 'a good hard-working fellow' who didn't get his deserts.

Some one has expressed concern lest the Osler in these pages convey the impression of a 'plaster saint' because of the inherent kindness of heart which made him so greatly beloved, and because he would never permit any one in his presence to speak ill of another; whereas in truth 'what adverse opinions he had to give were handed to the man himself, full in the face'—as happened here and in the episode of the A. M. A. meeting in May 1895.

The sequel may be briefly told. At the next meeting of the Maryland General Assembly a Tuberculosis Commission was created without opposition. Meanwhile a group of young society women called the 'Quarter Club' set out to raise, by small sums, for which twenty-five-cent coupons were given, a fund for the care of early cases of tuberculosis. From this came the employment of a full-time tuberculosis nurse; and, in due sequence, the Maryland Association for the Prevention and Cure of Tuberculosis; a special department at the Johns Hopkins with a bequest from Mr. Phipps; the Baltimore tuberculosis exhibit; the national association; and much else besides. In these and other ways they were, as Osler expressed it in a contemporary letter, 'enjoying a quiet winter', which, however, was soon to be interrupted by a university function that meant for them a houseful of guests—no uncommon thing, to be sure.

Meanwhile Revere and his little friend Doris had formed a secret society of two, and there were mysterious goings-on, only vague hints of which were permitted to leak out even to their especial playmate, who to the outside world was a learned professor of medicine. And one may imagine the bursts of joy and the swift and dire revenge when they discovered that he was the perpetrator of the note, in a disguised hand, sent to the female member of the society, which read:

Office of the Chief of Police,
Ma'am Baltimore, Feb. 21st.

Your Club is illegal and must be disbanded. Report to me, with E R Ike O'Slur at 12 tomorrow or a policeman will come for you both. JOHN McADOO, Chief of Police.

This threat of criminal proceedings did not interfere with the ceremonies attending the twenty-fifth anniversary of the founding of the university, which was celebrated on this and the following day, Saturday, February 22nd. The occasion marked the retirement of D. C. Gilman as President, for, having reached the age of seventy, he wished to devote his remaining years to the affairs of the Carnegie Institution.

The birthdays of the Johns Hopkins fall at a time of year when weather conditions are unpropitious for the parading of streets in academic costume, and though worse than usual on this particular occasion, the weather could not dampen the interest of the group of representatives who had come from all the principal institutions of learning in the United States and Canada. Mr. Gilman's valedictory; the congratulatory address to the retiring President delivered by Woodrow Wilson, representing the alumni; the address by Principal Peterson of McGill, who could not refrain from complaining that the university was keeping Dr. William Osler from his Alma Mater, which wanted and needed him; the inaugural of Ira Remsen, the new President—these and the many other addresses need not detain us. Nor need the list of distinguished men whom Mr. Gilman then presented to his successor as recommended for various honorary degrees, among them Professor Wilson of Princeton University, 'whose vision is so broad that it includes both North and South; a master of the principles which underlie a free government'.

The ceremonies ended on Saturday night with a large alumni dinner at which there were so many to be called upon that when it came to the turn of President Alderman of the University of Virginia to speak, he glanced at the clock and said: 'Last week when this banquet began', &c. It was two minutes past 12, and though there were other speakers to follow, it is time to end this account of an important episode in the history of the Hopkins, when its leadership first changed hands.

Not many months before this event took place, announcements had gone forth in the daily press that the Harvard Medical School had been the recipient of princely sums of money from J. Pierpont Morgan and John D. Rockefeller, the latter stipulating that a sum comparable to his own gift be raised by the community. How it happened that Mr. Rockefeller came to be first a benefactor to Harvard and subsequently to medicine in a far larger field, is made clear in an exchange of letters of this time. The first of them was written under the date of March 4th by Mr. F. T. Gates, who introduced himself as 'Mr. Rockefeller's representative in many of his business enterprises and philanthropies, beginning with the establishment of the University of Chicago'. The letter went on to give Osler for the first time much of the information previously set down at length regarding Mr. Gates's occupation during the summer of 1897 and the resulting establishment of the Rockefeller Institute. It also went on to say:

In the course of our study of the subject, we became acquainted with the very excellent work being done at Harvard, and while it was not thought best to connect the Institute with the Harvard Medical School, we were profoundly impressed with the very superior work done at that institution. Accordingly, after the establishment of the Institute in the tentative way above described, Mr. Rockefeller contributed a million dollars to the Harvard School. Both of these gifts grew directly out of your book. The first, while not as yet large in money, has in it possibilities by no means circumscribed by the present gift. It has occurred to me that possibly you might be gratified to know of an incidental and perhaps to you quite unexpected good which your valuable work has wrought.

To Mr. F. T. Gates from W. O. March 5, 1902.

Dear Sir,—Your letter is, of course, very gratifying. I have been greatly interested in the Rockefeller Institute, and feel sure that good results will come of it. We are still far behind Germany in this question of the scientific investigations of disease. Even our best laboratories connected with the universities are imperfectly equipped, the men in charge have too much teaching to do, there are not enough assistants, and there is an increasing difficulty in getting the best sort of men to devote themselves to scientific work. One serious difficulty is the limited number of positions with which living salaries are attached. For example, only last week a doctor connected with the leading school in St. Louis came to me wishing a pathologist and bacteriologist. They offered a salary of $2,000! and that is more than is paid by any of the other schools in the city. Did you see the brief summary which I gave of the progress of bacteriological science in the *New York Sun* last year in the general reviews of the subject of science? If you did not, I can have a copy sent to you.

One can hardly believe from the character of Osler's reply that he could have fully grasped all that Mr. Gates had in mind, for the comparatively small sum which, at the outset, had been placed in the hands of the seven Directors of the Institute was a mere feeler. That Mr. Gates had chanced upon his 'Practice of Medicine' rather than upon one of the many text-books in which, with therapeutic enthusiasm, drugs were prescribed for every disease and every symptom, was 'of course very gratifying', but nothing more. The letter was tossed to Mrs. Osler, who fortunately preserved it and called it to his mind two years later, when it stood the university in great stead.

There was another happening in this month of March which was followed by the bestowal of large funds for educational as well as other purposes, and which in an unexpected way was to touch Osler in his later years. The long-drawn-out war in South Africa, though victory for the British was practically assured, was not yet over when on March 26th Cecil Rhodes died. He, too, though a very different person, was the youngest of several sons in a clergyman's family; had expected to enter the Church; and in the world of affairs had reached the top, as had Osler at the same age in the world of medicine. With vision and idealism, Rhodes had left the bulk of his large fortune to found scholarships at Oxford to be held by picked men from each of the United States, from the British Dominions, and from Germany, with the object of fostering an understanding between the three great powers which would render future wars impossible. With these Oxford Rhodes Scholars Osler will have much to do; though the object, alas, for which Rhodes wished these representative young men to be brought together was not attained. Nor, seventeen years later, was the world ready to accept a still more ambitious programme to ensure future peace, introduced by the young Princeton professor who had just played so prominent a part in the Hopkins celebration a month before.

Meanwhile, his collection of books was growing, and one acquisition he mentions in a note of early March to C. N. B. Camac: [undated].

So sorry to have missed you—will try to give you warning next time. When are you coming down? There are many things I wish to talk about with you & some of my new old treasures would delight you. Hunter McGuire left me a set of Jenner's Vaccination Monographs—all autograph copies to his friend [Henry] Shrapnell. It is really a great treasure. . . . Mrs. O & Ike are well. So glad to hear you are getting consultations. Get out 2 or 3 good papers each year —they help.

It was a characteristic ending, and a form of advice in which he set abundant example, as his own bibliography continues to testify. The letter merely shows that he had dropped in on one of his old house officers while on a fleeting visit to New York. This was his invariable habit when chance took him to their places of residence, and some incident of such an occasion rarely failed to stick in the memory of the person thus favoured. Thus Dr. Camac relates that having once received a telegram that W. O. would be in town and asking could they dine together, a few young men were invited to meet him. After dinner the talk ran to books, and on Camac's producing a copy of Brillat-Savarin's 'Physiologie du Goût', one of the party mistaking the French word *goût* for the English word, became somewhat involved, whereupon Osler, to save him embarrassment and to put him right in a gentle way, quoted the well-known epigram:

> The French have taste in all they do,
> Which we are quite without;
> For Nature, which to them gave *goût*,
> To us gave only gout.

A trifling incident, to be sure, but a good example of the same kindly way in which Osler would lead one of his class-room pupils aright without permitting the young man to blush before his fellows.

On April 2nd the Philadelphia College of Physicians held a memorial meeting for Alfred Stillé, who had died at eighty-seven, the last survivor of the group of Louis's pupils. Osler gave the chief address,[1] and largely in the words of his old friend recounted anew the story of the differentiation of the two fevers, typhoid and typhus, which had been worked out in the old Blockley Hospital during the epidemic of 1836 by Gerhard and Pennock and their junior co-worker, Stillé. The address ended with the line, borrowed from Stillé, that 'only two things are essential, to live uprightly and to be wisely industrious', a line which might be made the text of this present biography.

But with all these absences—and there were many others which might be mentioned—his local, routine activities must not be overlooked. 'No, I cannot possibly take more than

[1] Reprinted in 'An Alabama Student and other Biographical Essays', 1908.

twenty-five men', he writes to the Dean on April 22nd. 'All through May we have the undergraduates as well, which makes too great a crowd altogether in the wards. I was very sorry that I could not get over to Gaule's lecture, but there was a meeting of the Executive Committee of the State Faculty at that time, and as I am Chairman I was obliged to be present.' Indeed the annual gathering of the Faculty was being held at the time, and to the programme he contributed a timely lecture on 'The Diagnosis of Smallpox'—a subject with which he was all too familiar. There had been many increasingly severe outbreaks of the disease, not only in Maryland but in other parts of the country, due to the neglect of vaccination, which had got a bad name because of an impure lymph which had been put on the market.

Though the usual distracting succession of spring meetings soon followed, he was at work meanwhile on an unexpected revision of the Text-book. To this he refers in the following letter to Joseph H. Pratt, one of the Hopkins students, who since his graduation in 1898 had been in the pathological department of Harvard, and was now abroad:

May 9, 1902.

Dear Pratt,—It was very nice to get your letter of the 25th, and to find that you are in good hands. I am sure you will find Krehl a most satisfactory man. Please give him my regards. I will have a copy of my Text-book sent to him, and a volume of our Studies in Typhoid Fever. I will send you this week the list of books for the tuberculosis library. I haven't had them copied, so please take good care of this list, which is in Dr. Welch's handwriting. I will enclose a memorandum with reference to certain ones which we have. Keep a close eye on some corrections for the Text-book like a good fellow. Use your pencil freely. Suggestions for rearrangement will be in order. . . . Take good care of yourself and do not work too hard; and sample a fair amount of beer in the course of a week.

Though only a year had elapsed since the last revision, a new edition was necessitated by the fact that, owing to an oversight, copyright had not been taken out in Great Britain. An unauthorized edition had promptly been issued at a much reduced price, which had greatly interfered with the legitimate sale of the book in Great Britain and Canada. As Osler said in a later letter of explanation,[1] 'the

[1] *Lancet*, Lond., April 11, 1903, i. 1058.

circumstances justified what Rabelais calls "the pretty perquisite of a superfoetation".'

He was laid up with one of his periodical attacks the latter part of the month, and from his bed sent letters which say that not for years had he enjoyed a book so much as Kussmaul's 'Jugenderinnerungen'—'nothing so good that I know of in the way of medical autobiography'. In his engagement book, opposite the dates May 18–23, where entries for his afternoon consultations would occur, there is written, 'Influenza: frontal sinus'; and opposite May 24–31, 'Atlantic City'. This was the occasion when he impishly signed the name of Egerton Y. Davis under that of Mrs. Osler on the Hotel Chelsea register. Among letters written on his return is this cryptic note to H. V. Ogden, who had evidently heard rumours of his ill health:

vi.1.02.

Dear O. I am all right. I had a Schnupfen which rose into my sinuses & used me up for a week. They telephoned me one night to come & see L P[1] but as it was 1 a m and I had had a hot bath I declined & sent Thayer. I had seen the old boy the day before & there was nothing to do. Mrs O is well & Morris is back from the hospital so the family is again 'gesund'. Thanks for the memo—about Ex Ophth G. We go to Murray Bay. We had our passage for the 25th, but as we would have to return early—I give the address in Med.—Can Med in Montreal—we decided to give it up. I wish to get over early next year and have a 6 weeks period of study in Paris.—Come. Love to all of you. Am rejoicing in a sumptuous copy of Fuller's Worthies, 1662, from B. Q. Yours,

W. O.

There had been a good deal of discussion in the pages of the journals at this time about the teaching of medical history—no new thing, be it said, for in Vienna, Berlin, and in most of the Italian medical schools there had actually been professorships of the subject. Osler, though he did not believe, with the existing crowded state of the curriculum, that a full course could be offered, was aroused by an editorial in the *British Medical Journal* to send a description

[1] 'L P' was Lord Pauncefote, the first British Ambassador, who during his long period of service in Washington had with John Hay been quietly clearing away the many disputed problems, long sources of misunderstanding between the two countries.

of what was being done in Baltimore in this direction.[1] In this he spoke of John S. Billings's lectures ; of the work of the Historical Club ; of the effort even in the everyday ward-work to make the student get the habit of going to original sources ; of his Saturday evenings with the students when, over a little ' beer and baccy ', he was apt to give a short talk on one of the ' masters of medicine ' ; and he ended with this quotation from Fuller, the sumptuous copy of whose ' Worthies ' had so recently come from Bernard Quaritch :

> History maketh a young man to be old, without either wrinkles or grey hairs ; privileging him with the experience of age, without either the infirmities or inconveniences thereof. Yea, it not onely maketh things past present, but inableth one to make a rationall conjecture of things to come. For this world affordeth no new accidents, but in the same sense wherein we call it *a new Moon*, which is the old one in another shape, and yet no other than what had been formerly. Old actions return again, furbished over with some new and different circumstances.

Not only in medical history was he beginning to be thoroughly steeped, but his infection with the bibliomania was becoming chronic. Among his posthumous papers were a number of stray leaves, representing the rough draft of an article, some of which may have been written at this time of comparative idleness at the seashore when Thomas Fuller was in his mind, and E. Y. D. in his reactions :

BURROWINGS OF A BOOKWORM

by

Egerton Yorrick Davis, Jr.

1. *Apologia.* In the final stage of the malady, sung of so sweetly by John Ferriar, and described so minutely by Dibdin, the bibliomaniac haunts the auction rooms and notes with envious eyes the precious volumes as they are handed about for inspection, or chortles with joy as he hears the bids rise higher and higher for some precious treasure already in his possession. Of this final enthraldom the chief symptom, not mentioned indeed by Dibdin, is the daily perusal of the catalogues of auction sales. . . . Like the secret drinker with a full bottle by his side and the kettle on the trivet the victim in this last stage indulges his passion alone and is never so happy as [when] with a Sotheby catalogue and the help of Livington or Karslake, he prepares

[1] ' A Note on the Teaching of the History of Medicine.' *British Medical Journal*, 1902, July 12, ii. 93.

to send his bids to the auction firm. Though the spirit of the gambler is upon him there is method in his mania, for he makes his calculations with shrewdness and knows the prices which his favourite books have brought. He is never disappointed, for he has a strong conviction that the world is one big auction room in which the gods sell everything to the man who can work or to the man who can wait. If he loses to-day tomorrow may bring luck, and this element of uncertainty gives zest to the dispute. Into this final stage I confess to have lapsed, gradually and insensibly, and without the loss of my self-respect. Nor is he an indiscriminate buyer, seeking incunabula and *editions de luxe* with equal avidity, but one guiding principle, *deep interest in an author* limits the range of his desires and keeps his library within the compass of his house and purse. The great difficulty is to keep the passion within bounds, so fascinating and so numerous is the company into which it brings him ! Any one of the elect may absorb his energies for months. Charles Lamb says that he lived on Landor's little poem *Rose Aylmer* for a week. After first finding Fuller I lived on him for six months ; and when hungry or thirsty after the mental labours of the day, I find refreshment in the *Worthies* or in any page of the *Holy and Profane State*. Before this happy stage is reached you must know the man—not that biography should precede, rather indeed it should follow, the systematic study of a man's work, but to get on terms of refreshing intimacy you must love the man as a friend and know the phases of his mind as expressed in his writings. To be supremely happy, to the instinct of the collector must be added the mental attitude of the student. Either alone lacks completeness ; the one supplements the other. I can read with pleasure a classic such as Rasselas though issued in ' penny dreadful ' form by Mr. Stead, [but] feel nearer to the immortal Samuel when I hold the original in my hand. It is all a matter of sentiment—so it is, but the very marrow of my bones is full of sentiment, and as I feel towards my blood relations—or some of them !—and to my intimate friends in the flesh, so I feel to these friends in the spirit with whom I am in communion through the medium of the printed word. . . .

The Association of Medical Librarians, with sixteen members present and Osler in the chair, met in Saratoga on June 10th, the day before the sessions of the American Medical Association opened. Osler had ' packed ' the meeting by bringing in a few of his assistants, and they were well repaid, for he read a delightful address on ' Some Aspects of American Medical Bibliography '—an address [1] prepared with no less care for this small group of people than it would have been for a larger audience. A single

[1] Reprinted as No. XV in ' Aequanimitas and other Addresses '.

example of what he called his ' splintery ' and rambling remarks regarding ' that aspect of medical bibliography which relates to writings which have a value to us from our interest in the authors ', may be given :

There are many single volumes for which you will be on the lookout. Caldwell's ' Autobiography ' is a storehouse of facts (and fancies !) relating to the University of Pennsylvania, to Rush and to the early days of the Transylvania University and the Cincinnati schools. Pickled, as it is, in vinegar, the work is sure to survive.

Have carefully re-bound James Jackson's Memoir of his son (1835), and put it in the way of the young men among your readers. Few biographies will do them more good.

For the curious, pick up the literature on the Chapman-Pattison quarrel, and anything, in fact, relating to that vivacious and pugnacious Scot, Granville Sharpe Pattison.

There are a few full-blown medical biographies of special interest to us : The life and writings of that remarkable philosopher and physician, Wells, of Charleston. The life of John C. Warren (1860) is full of interest, and in the ' Essays ' of David Hosack you will get the inner history of the profession in New York in the early years of the last century. In many ways Daniel Drake is the most unique figure in the history of American medicine. Get his ' Life ' by Mansfield, and his ' Pioneer Life in Kentucky '. He literally made Cincinnati, having ' boomed ' it in the early days in his celebrated ' Picture of Cincinnati ', 1815. He founded nearly everything that is old and good in that city. His monumental work on ' The Diseases of the Mississippi Valley ' is in every library ; pick out from the catalogues every scrap of his writings.

And he concluded with this paragraph :

What should attract us all is a study of the growth of the American mind in medicine since the starting of the colonies. As in a mirror this story is reflected in the literature of which you are the guardians and collectors—in letters, in manuscripts, in pamphlets, in books and journals. In the eight generations which have passed, the men who have striven and struggled—men whose lives are best described in the words of St. Paul, in journeyings often, in perils of water, in perils of the city, in perils of the sea, in weariness and painfulness, in watchings often, in hunger and thirst and fastings—these men, of some of whom I have told you somewhat, have made us what we are. With the irrevocable past into which they have gone lies our future, since our condition is the resultant of forces which, in these generations, have moulded the profession of a new and mighty empire. From the vantage ground of a young century we can trace in the literature how three great streams of influence—English,

French and German—have blended into the broad current of American medicine on which we are afloat. Adaptiveness, lucidity and thoroughness may be said to be the characteristics of these Anglican, Gallic and Teuton influences, and it is no small part of your duty to see that these influences the combination of which gives to medicine on this continent its distinctive eclectic quality, are maintained and extended.

Immediately after the A. M. A. meeting there was a large subscription dinner given on June 13th at Delmonico's in New York in honour of Surgeon-General Sternberg, whose retirement had just taken place. There had been some idle claims put forth, by partisans rather than principals, as to who deserved chief credit for the yellow fever discoveries in Cuba, the only thing about the Spanish War and its aftermath from which any special credit was to be drawn. Well-deserved tributes for his pioneer work on this subject were paid to Sternberg by the speakers at the dinner, among whom were E. G. Janeway, Welch, Gorgas, Osler, and others. And it was Gorgas, ere long to be Sternberg's successor, who put his finger on the point at issue, in his statement that had the work of the commission been less fortunate in its outcome General Sternberg would have received the entire blame, and consequently the success should be his also.

As stated in his cryptic letter of June 1st to Ogden, the Oslers had decided not to go to England for the summer, but to Murray Bay on the St. Lawrence. They had been influenced by several things. His mother, who was ninety-six, seemed less vigorous than usual; moreover he had two addresses to prepare, one for the Canadian Medical Association, which was to meet in Montreal under F. J. Shepherd's presidency, the other to be given later on in St. Louis. 'We have taken a house,' he wrote, 'and I doubt if I shall be bothered much with patients. It will give me a good fourteen weeks' rest.' On the eve of his departure he wrote:

To Henry M. Hurd from W. O. 1 West Franklin Street,
June 21, 1902.

Dear Hurd,—So sorry to go off before your return. I hope you had a good meeting in Montreal. I am terribly distressed to hear of the death there of poor Wyatt Johnston. He was a nice, good fellow and a very dear friend of mine. I am going to Toronto to the Celebration at Trinity, and then on to Murray Bay, where I hope to remain peacefully and quietly for the summer.

One point about the new buildings rather distressed me. I wrote to Mr. Archer about it, but have had no reply. I understand from a conversation with Emerson that they will cut off four of the rooms of the Clinical Laboratory, which is a very serious loss, considering how cramped we are there at present, and as the classes increase it will be a very serious matter. Would it not be possible to arrange that on the upper floor, at any rate, the same space as at present could be utilized? The rooms for preparations and for special workers of course ought to be close at hand. Emerson is really getting out some first-class work from his department, and we should encourage him as much as possible. It is the sort of work that has not been done here before and I think will tell.

I am having one of my young protégés, a very bright fellow, a senior student at Toronto University, come down for the months of July and August to work in the wards and dispensary. His name is Locke, and he is the son of a very old and dear chum of mine. I told McCrae to look after him, and have asked him to call upon you. Another point—do you not think it would be well to put Cordell's picture in the front of that volume? Ask Ashby and Preston what they think about it. He has done so much work that there ought to be some recognition. I hope in October to get up a little fund for him and hold a reception. I have arranged with Thayer about the private ward, and he and Futcher will be on hand to help McCrae with anything special in the public wards.

'He has done so much work that there ought to be some recognition'—this is a characteristic phrase in Osler's letters, and he was for ever getting up funds for deserving people. Dr. Weir Mitchell was once heard to say that the first thing to be done by a biographer in estimating character is to examine the stubs of his victim's cheque-books. Osler's expenditures, however, can be easily traced between the lines of his brief letters. Just at this time he is paying the expenses, as mentioned in this letter, of the son of his old-time chum, Charles Locke; there is a distant cousin of a younger generation, whom he had never seen, with consumption, and for whom a twelve-months' sojourn in Saranac has been made possible; a monthly cheque goes to his nieces; the assistants that he takes with him to Saratoga, as well as the librarians, have their expenses paid; and Morris, meanwhile, gives out something to every one who knocks, or plays a hurdy-gurdy, at the door.[1] One need not examine the stubs of Osler's cheque-books.

The 'celebration at Trinity' which preceded the Murray Bay sojourn was the occasion of his receiving a D.C.L. at the hands of his first Alma Mater. Since 1874 there had been sporadic efforts to amalgamate Trinity College with the University of Toronto. Not without some heart-burning this union was about to be accomplished, for the old mischievous cry of a 'Godless college' which would have been raised in Father Johnson's time was ere this represented by a very feeble voice. It was the last convocation held separately by Trinity, and degrees were bestowed on a number of distinguished Canadians. One of them, in all probability, as he sat on the platform in his old college with thoughts far away, was engaged in writing 'James Bovell' on his programme.

On the Saguenay boat from Quebec they encountered, in addition to a pair of rabbits and a pet billy-goat, seven children, whose mother proved to be the widow of his old Montreal fellow-student, Harry Wright. Then and there began an intimacy which meant the quasi-adoption of these children, like those of Palmer Howard, as members of his family. With them, and with the children of the Tafts, the Blakes, the Wrongs, and other neighbours at Pointe-à-Pic, P.Q., there were many games played and dams constructed and picnics held during the summer, which with golf and fishing and reading betweentimes was most happily passed. He was much sought after, not only by the children but by their elders. As Chief Justice Taft recalls:

> We had cottages which were not very far apart, and I used to see a great deal of him on picnics as well as informal gatherings in that very delightful community. Revere was just about the age of my son Charlie and all the children were in and out of the Osler house. He had a love of humour and a disposition to joke others in a playful way. The wonder that came over me was at the universal knowledge of the man. He was not only most learned, but applied that learning with a keen common-sense and a sense of proportion that must have

[1] Morris's petty-cash account was good reading: 'Parcel 50 cents, music 5 cents, beggar 10 cents, Dr. Osler 15 cents,'—the last in response to the frequent appeal, as the tram was heard rattling down the hill, 'Here's the car! Morris, quick, some change!'

been the basis of the influence he wielded not only in his profession but in the community at large.

This hint of 'picnics and informal gatherings' is not betrayed in the many notes which issued from Pointe-à-Pic during the summer to his librarian-friends at McGill and Toronto, asking for some journal or other, or for information: 'Do you know if the complete typhoid figures of the S. A. war are at hand, i. e. the total cases and the total deaths up to say May 1st. Look, like an angel, in the Lancet index, for the last half year and the B. M. J. and let me know.' And to Miss Thies, who was being kind to his young protégé in Baltimore:

21st.

Dear Miss Thesis, How many have subscribed to the volume which Dr. Cordell is preparing? Did you and Miss Noyes send out postal cards to all the members of the Faculty who had not yet subscribed? I hope you are not over-worked. You must get a good holiday when your 'chiefess' comes back. Mr. Locke writes that you are all very kind to him—many thanks.

Nor did he entirely escape from patients. One of his little companions of the dam-making coterie must have an operation for blood-poisoning, and he insisted on coming every day to dress the wound himself. Then a bishop was taken ill, so a microscope must be procured from Montreal, and there followed a shower of postcards like this to W. S. Thayer:

Pointe-à-Pic, vii. 27. 02.

I am sending cover slips—bad ones too—of case—fever 9 w. duration—B. of Can. Diagnosis of malaria aestivo-autum. in N. Y. Parasites in blood. Slides sent to Martin in Montreal, report negative Report from relative of patient in Chicago positive—Martin sent microscope to-day & I have gone over 4 specimens without finding ring-bodies pigment or crescents. No spleen—this [diagram] T. 100–103. Old Corrigan's disease; no signs sub. or obj. of fresh endocarditis save the fever. Please go over the slides with the greatest care & telegraph me. Put down his name on your visiting list for consultation &c. Love to S. S. so glad to hear she is better W. O.

Meanwhile Mrs. Osler writes to the 'latch-keyers' at 3 West Franklin Street that they are very comfortable, with plenty of room (for guests) and a lovely view; that W. O.

is enjoying every moment, with 'good golf and nice men to play with', there being many old friends from Montreal and other parts of Canada. His much-worn commonplace-book records that during July he read F. S. Stevenson's 'Life of Robert Grosseteste', from which many quotations are taken. And from ecclesiastical reforms in the thirteenth century he slid the next month into John Richard Green's 'Letters', edited by Leslie Stephen, from which also he makes many excerpts, one of which, the following, crops out in an address he was preparing: 'It is the single advantage of being a sceptic that one is never very surprised or angry to find that one's opponents are in the right.' He had been persuaded by Dr. Shepherd to give the annual oration before the Canadian Medical Association; and that he was having a little trouble with the title of the address is apparent from this note to H. A. Lafleur:

Sept. 4/02.

Dear Laffie, 'La Cocarde Tricolore' 1831 by Cogniard, the play in which Chauvin flourished is not in the McGill library—is it likely to be in any other collection in Montreal? I should like to read what he says about the old Soldier. Ask one of your literary friends please. I have been struggling with the subject of nationalism & provincialism in Medicine—too wide a swath I fear for my scythe.

There is a stage in the preparation of an address when even such as Osler has misgivings, but he need have had no fear for the sweep of his scythe, for in many respects it was one of his best pieces of writing and, contrasted with some others of his addresses, written hurriedly and piecemeal, it showed the effects of his comparatively quiet and uninterrupted summer. He had taken as his subject, 'Chauvinism in Medicine',[1] and gave as his definition of the word, 'a narrow illiberal spirit in matters national, provincial, collegiate or personal'. He spoke first of the FOUR GREAT FEATURES OF THE GUILD, *its noble ancestry, its remarkable solidarity, its progressive character*, and, as distinguished from all others, *its singular beneficence*. He then took up NATIONALISM IN MEDICINE—'the great curse of humanity'. 'There is room,' he said, 'plenty of room, for proper pride of land and birth.

[1] Reprinted as No. XIV in 'Aequanimitas and other Addresses'.

What I inveigh against is a cursed spirit of intolerance, conceived in distrust and bred in ignorance, that makes the mental attitude perennially antagonistic to everything foreign, that subordinates everywhere the race to the nation, forgetting the higher claims to human brotherhood.' There followed the last section, on PROVINCIALISM IN MEDICINE— ' a very unpleasant sub-variety of nationalism '. ' After all these years,' he said, ' that a young man, a graduate of Toronto and a registered practitioner in Ontario, cannot practise in the Province of Quebec, his own country, without submitting to vexatious penalties of mind and pocket, or that a graduate from Montreal and a registered practitioner of this province cannot go to Manitoba, his own country again, and take up his life's work without additional payments and penalties is, I maintain, an outrage ; it is provincialism run riot. That this pestiferous condition should exist through the various provinces of this Dominion and so many States of the Union, illustrates what I have said of the tyranny of democracy and how great enslavers of liberty its chief proclaimers may be.' From this he went on to PAROCHIALISM IN MEDICINE ; in other words, to the personal aspects of Chauvinism which applies to all individuals :

There are [he said] shades and varieties which are by no means offensive. Many excellent features in a man's character may partake of its nature. What, for example, is more proper than the pride which we feel in our teachers, in the university from which we have graduated, in the hospital at which we have been trained? He is a ' poor sort ' who is free from such feelings which only manifest a proper loyalty. But it easily degenerates into a base intolerance which looks with disdain on men of other schools and other ways. The pride, too, may be in inverse proportion to the justness of the claims. There is plenty of room for honest and friendly rivalry between schools and hospitals, only a blind Chauvinism puts a man into a hostile and intolerant attitude of mind at the mention of a name. Alumni and friends should remember that indiscriminate praise of institutions or men is apt to rouse the frame of mind illustrated by the ignorant Athenian who, so weary of hearing Aristides always called the Just, very gladly took up the oyster shell for his ostracism, and even asked Aristides himself, whom he did not know, to mark it. . . .

He spoke of collegiate Chauvinism, so often ' manifest in the narrow spirit displayed in filling appointments '; of its unpleasant manifestations due to the competition existing in scientific circles which leads to a narrowness of judgement instead of a generous appreciation of the work of others; and he warned against the jealous spirit of the 'lock and key' laboratory. But, he continued:

Chauvinism in the unit, in the general practitioner, is of much more interest and importance. It is amusing to read and hear of the passing of the family physician. There never was a time in our history in which he was so much in evidence, in which he was so prosperous, in which his prospects were so good or his power in the community more potent. The public has even begun to get sentimental over him! He still does the work; the consultants and the specialists do the talking and the writing—and take the fees! By the work, I mean that great mass of routine practice which brings the doctor into every household in the land and makes him, not alone the adviser, but the valued friend. He is the standard by which we are measured. What he is we are; and the estimate of the profession in the eyes of the public is their estimate of him. A well trained sensible family doctor is one of the most valuable assets in a community, worth to-day, as in Homer's time, many another man. To make him efficient is our highest ambition as teachers, to save him from evil should be our constant care as a guild. . . . Few men live lives of more devoted self-sacrifice than the family physician but he may become so completely absorbed in work that leisure is unknown. . . . There is danger in this treadmill life lest he lose more than health and time and rest—his intellectual independence. More than most men he feels the tragedy of isolation—that inner isolation so well expressed in Matthew Arnold's line—'We mortal millions live *alone*.' Even in populous districts the practice of medicine is a lonely road which winds up-hill all the way and a man may easily go astray and never reach the Delectable Mountains unless he early finds those shepherd guides of which Bunyan tells, *Knowledge*, *Experience*, *Watchful* and *Sincere*. The circumstances of life mould him into a masterful, self-confident, self-centred man, whose worst faults often partake of his best qualities. The peril is that should he cease to think for himself he becomes a mere automaton, doing a penny-in-the-slot business which places him on a level with the chemist's clerk who can hand out specifics for every ill, from the 'pip' to the pox. The salt of life for him is a judicious scepticism, not the coarse crude form, but the sober sense of honest doubt expressed in the maxim of the sly old Sicilian Epicharmus, 'Be sober and distrustful; these are the sinews of the understanding.'

The address, which ended with the following paragraph,

would almost stand as a fit biography of William Osler, could one read sufficiently widely and far between the lines:

I began by speaking of the art of detachment as that rare and precious quality demanded of one who wished to take a philosophic view of the profession as a whole. In another way and in another sense this art may be still more precious. There is possible to each one of us a higher type of intellectual detachment, a sort of separation from the vegetative life of the work-a-day world—always too much with us—which may enable a man to gain a true knowledge of himself and of his relations to his fellows. Once attained, self-deception is impossible, and he may see himself even as he is seen—not always as he would like to be seen—and his own deeds and the deeds of others stand out in their true light. In such an atmosphere pity for himself is so commingled with sympathy and love for others that there is no place left for criticism or for a harsh judgement of his brother. 'But these are Thoughts of things which Thoughts but tenderly touch,' as that most liberal of men and most distinguished of general practitioners, Sir Thomas Browne, so beautifully remarks; and it may be sufficient to remind this audience, made up of practical men, *that the word of action is stronger than the word of speech*.

Needless to say, there were more people to see and visits to make in Montreal than he could encompass, and notes had to be sent late at night from Dr. Shepherd's, where he was staying—'So sorry to miss you to-day, but I was hard pushed & had some 10 calls to make & the new M. G. H. plans to look over', &c. At the end of the three-days' visit he disappeared, leaving Mrs. Osler to get his nephew settled as a house officer in the Royal Victoria Hospital; and from Toronto a few days later she wrote, saying: 'I sunned myself in my husband's glory in Montreal, and as he departed at dawn Thursday not waiting to hear what was said of his address I was inflated with pride and left very humble-minded and impressed with my utter inability to cope with my position as spouse to such an admired object.'

The 'admired object' had escaped to Saranac Lake to see a distant cousin who had been there for a few months, and to whom reference has been made. Two days were spent with Trudeau; and Lawrason Brown, who was then in the Sanitarium, recalls an incident of the visit; for, on Osler's being shown the clinical records he tapped them and said: 'A man who speaks of his experience and has it recorded in this way knows whereof he is talking.' Up to that time Trudeau, trusting to his unusual memory, had never kept records of his private patients, but this episode started him doing so.

To John H. Musser from W. O. 1 West Franklin Street [undated]

Dear J. H. Glad to see you are back! Thanks for the description of the Rylands Library. I am most anxious to see it. I have heard from one or two men in Manchester since the meeting—all seem to have been delighted with you. We had a charming summer. Mrs O & Ike enjoyed it so much. The place is ideal in many ways. I have my neck in the yoke again. Am very busy with an address on Beaumont. The family put his papers in my hands some years ago. I hope to see you before long. I shall be in Phila the week after next. Glad to have a note from Hare about the Wood-Keen dinner. Yours, W. O. Love to all at home.

Evidently he was no sooner off with the C. M. A. address than he was on with the preparation of another, concerning which among other things he soon dictated a letter to George Dock in Ann Arbor:

Sept. 24, 1902.

I think that the figures given in the *Physician and Surgeon*, published at the time of the Memorial Exercises at Mackinac are sufficient. The old officers' quarters are given and one or two of the old block-houses. I wish I could go out by way of Michigan, but I shall go through Pittsburgh and Columbus. I saw the letters of Shrapnell, particularly about that interesting shipwreck. He was a gentleman at any rate to bind all the [Jenner] pamphlets together. It seems a pity to break them up, but I think they are worth while binding separately in good style, and I shall probably deposit them in one of the libraries.[1] I got back on Sunday. We had a very good meeting in Montreal. You will see my Chauvinistic address in *American Medicine* and the *Phila Medical Journal* this week. I believe I have been curiously led astray by two distinguished professors as to the origin of the word chauvinism. I give it quite different from that given by Brewer who is likely to be right.

Enough has been said already in these pages of Osler's interest in the story of Beaumont and Alexis St. Martin—an interest which goes back to his Montreal days, when he was frustrated in his efforts to secure St. Martin's stomach for the Surgeon-General's Museum. That he should have gone

[1] W. O. had loaned the papers to Dock, who made their study the basis of an address. *New York Medical Journal*, Nov. 29, 1902, *et seq.*

so far afield as to St. Louis to give an address on 'Beaumont, a pioneer American physiologist',[1] is accounted for by the fact that St. Louis had been Beaumont's place of residence after his resignation from the army, and, besides, Osler's friends, Baumgarten and Fischel, intimates in the Association of American Physicians, were both members of the local medical society before which on October 4th the address was given. He introduced the story as follows: [2]

Come with me for a few moments on a lovely June day in 1822, to what were then far-off northern wilds, to the Island of Michilimackinac, where the waters of Lake Michigan and Lake Huron unite and where stands Fort Mackinac, rich in the memories of Indian and voyageur, one of the four important posts on the upper lakes in the days when the rose and the fleur-de-lys strove for the mastery of the western world. Here the noble Marquette laboured for his Lord, and here beneath the chapel of St. Ignace they laid his bones to rest. Here the intrepid La Salle, the brave Tonty and the resolute Du Luht had halted in their wild wanderings. Its palisades and block-houses had echoed the war-whoops of Ojibways and Ottawas, of Hurons and Iroquois, and the old fort had been the scene of bloody massacres and hard-fought fights, but at the conclusion of the War of 1812, after two centuries of struggle, peace settled at last on the island. The fort was occupied by United States troops, who kept the Indians in check and did general police duty on the frontier, and the place had become a rendezvous for Indians and voyageurs in the employ of the American Fur Company. On this bright spring morning the village presented an animated scene. The annual return tide to the trading-post was in full course, and the beach was thronged with canoes and bateaux laden with the pelts of the winter's hunt. Voyageurs and Indians, men, women and children, with here and there a few soldiers, made up a motley crowd. Suddenly from the company's store there is a loud report of a gun, and amid the confusion and excitement the rumour spreads of an accident, and there is a hurrying of messengers to the barracks for a doctor. In a few minutes an alert-looking young man in the uniform of a U. S. Army surgeon made his way through the crowd and was at the side of a young French Canadian who had been wounded by the discharge of a gun, and with a composure bred of an exceptional experience of such injuries, prepared to make the examination. Though youthful in appearance, Surgeon Beaumont

[1] *Journal of American Medical Assoc.*, 1902, xxxix. 1223. Reprinted as 'A Backwood Physiologist' in the 'Alabama Student [&c.]', 1908.

[2] He had used the same account eight years before at the close of his address on 'The Army Surgeon'.

had seen much service, and at the capture of York and at the investment of Plattsburgh he had shown a coolness and bravery under fire which had won high praise from his superior officers. The man and the opportunity had met—the outcome is my story of this evening. . . .

He went on to tell of Beaumont's relations to the young French Canadian, whom he took into his own house and nursed to health, and of his trials in regard to the experiments on digestion which were subsequently undertaken with the wayward and stubborn fellow, 'that old fistulous Alexis' who for so many years survived the man who made him famous. Even as it was, with far less accomplished than Beaumont could have wished, many of the phenomena occurring during the process of ordinary digestion, including the nature and mode of action of the gastric juice, whose acid component was shown to be hydrochloric acid by Benjamin Silliman at Yale, were studied for the first time and made clear.

Osler's appearance in St. Louis to give this address had the usual stimulating effect on the local profession, for due solely to this visit a society for the study of medical history was inaugurated.[1] But for such studies books are tools, and it is quite consistent to find him, two weeks later, presiding at a dinner in Philadelphia given for the Executive Committee of the Association of Medical Librarians and several others interested in the history of medicine. At this time it was proposed that the former bulletin of the association be merged with the *Medical Library and Historical Journal*, the first issue of which, under the editorship of Albert Tracy Huntington, appeared in the following January. During its all-too-short five years of life this excellent journal continued, as the official organ of the association, to print its transactions and book-exchange lists. With the death of Huntington the journal came to its end, and after Osler's

[1] One of its most active members, the late Dr. Jesse S. Myer, ten years later published a complete and copiously illustrated biography of Beaumont for which Osler wrote an introduction. Therein is given the full story of the man who in Osler's words 'recognized, grasped, and improved the opportunity which fell in his path, with a zeal and an unselfishness not excelled in the annals of medical science'. ('Life and Letters of William Beaumont.' St. Louis, 1912.)

departure from America, though the association lost his guiding hand, it resumed the publication of an independent bulletin, restored its exchange bureau to the head-quarters in Baltimore, and has since continued as an active and most useful organization.[1]

Shortly before this, on October 7th to be exact, he had been elected to membership in the Grolier Club of New York, but the fact of his being, if anything, more interested in the building up of libraries in general rather than in the making of a personal collection, has been made sufficiently clear.

To John H. Musser from W. O. Oct. 22, 1902.

I like your scheme very much for the library. It would really be unique in a way. The next time you come down I would like you to see the list of books we have been gradually collecting at the Medical & Chirurgical Library relating to biography and history. I have just received a superb copy of the first edition of Locke's Essay, which I have been after for a good many years. Some years ago I made a list of the most important literary works by physicians. I will try to find it and let you have a copy.

From these things about ' books and the man ', Osler may be picked up again in the hospital wards, for after all it was at the bedside with his students about him that he was at his very best. So picturesque, indeed, were many of his spontaneous bedside epigrams that they have been preserved in many a student's note-book : [2]

There are incurable diseases in medicine, incorrigible vices in the ministry, insoluble cases in law.

Probability is the rule of life—especially under the skin. Never make a positive diagnosis.

Raynaud's disease and chilblains are Tweedledum and Tweedledee.

---

[1] A new journal started, or an old journal revivified, was almost sure to have Osler's name as a collaborator or a contributor, or often as both. Thus the first volume of a new series of the *International Clinics* under the editorship of A. O. J. Kelly begins with a paper from his pen, in which the fourteen cases of a particular form of aneurysm observed in his clinic were fully discussed.

[2] Two of the students, indeed, thinking to turn an honest penny, gathered a sufficient number of what they called ' Oslerisms ' to make a small volume, for which they found a ready publisher who issued an announcement of the book, but Osler promptly ' sat ' upon it.

Who serves the gods dies young—Venus, Bacchus, and Vulcan send in no bills in the seventh decade.

Common-sense nerve fibres are seldom medullated before forty—they are never seen even with the microscope before twenty.

The mental kidney more often than the abdominal is the one that floats.

Although one swallow does not make a summer, one tophus makes gout and one crescent malaria.

Believe nothing that you see in the newspapers—they have done more to create dissatisfaction than all other agencies. If you see anything in them that you know is true, begin to doubt it at once.

Up to this time the Hopkins, as is the way with new and privately endowed foundations, had been obliged to shift for itself, and gifts were hardly to be expected from outside sources until a generation had passed. It consequently must have been heartening in the face of the unexpected poverty of the institution, to have the ice broken through the establishment of a lectureship by a New Yorker, Dr. Christian A. Herter, who had been one of the early group of workers in Welch's laboratory.[1] Hence the following letter:

1 West Franklin Street, xi.3.02.

Dear Herter, The splendid gift which you & Mrs Herter have so generously given has stirred us to a high pitch of enthusiasm. It would have rejoiced you both to have seen Welch's delight as he read your letter. It really means a great deal to the School, and it is so nice to think that our first outside gift came from friends whom we love & appreciate as much as we do you & Mrs. Herter. The minute of the Faculty which you have received by this time does not half express the warmth of our feeling—certainly not of those of us who are your friends. . . .

Only a few things relating to his professional activity during the remainder of the autumn need detain us. At a meeting of the Hopkins Medical Society, on November 17th, he showed an example of the condition—'cyanosis with polycythaemia'—in which he had come to take especial interest and which has since become coupled with his name as 'Osler's disease', for though Vaquez had first described a case of polycythaemia rubra, it was Osler who recognized

[1] The first lecturer on the foundation was Welch's old friend Paul Ehrlich of Frankfort, and there followed Hans Meyer of Vienna, E. A. Schäfer, Almroth Wright, and others.

it as a definite clinical entity.[1] On November 20th he was in New York again, and the next day wrote to C. N. B. Camac :

Find out how much Doring would ask to paint a good portrait of Welch. I was in New York yesterday, only for two hours, a hurried consultation. Sorry I could not see you. I had to come back at once, as poor Ochsner, one of my internes, is desperately ill with typhoid.

Tuberculosis was bad enough—but typhoid—how he hated it ! Until it disappeared there were to be plenty of sacrifices on the part of those endeavouring to check its ravages.[2] Those were days when the wards were full of it, nurses, house staff, and students all being more or less exposed to chance infection despite the utmost care ; and when, after three more anxious days, this promising pupil died, it is evident from the following note jotted down in his commonplace book after returning home that night, how deeply Osler was moved :

Death (Poor Ochsner) The oppressive stillness of the chamber in which he lay dying was made more oppressive by the soft but hurried and just audible respiration. I sat by the bed holding the poor chap's hand & beside me were my two assistants & at the foot of the bed an angel in white, one of the two who had shared the fight with us. For three weeks we had worked in hope but in vain. We silently waited the end with sad hearts & brimming eyes. The young life so full of promise & only just equipped for the race, was dear to us by the association in work of four years, and the thought that those to whom the dear man was vital, were far away—intensified the tragedy of the moment. A strange half frightened look lightened the apathy of his countenance. Far from his home—far from the loved one who had watched with pride his career—and—.

This was all. It is curiously reminiscent of the reaction he

[1] Sir A. E. Garrod (*Proceedings of the Royal Society*, B, vol. xcii, 1921) has attached Osler's name to another disorder. 'An hereditary malady [he says], characterized by multiple telangiectases associated with haemorrhages may rightly be styled Osler's disease.'

[2] By this time, one epidemic disease at least had been conquered, for yellow fever had disappeared from Cuba, never to return, unless people forget and grow careless as they have done with vaccination. On the 22nd of this Nov. 1902, Walter Reed died of appendicitis, and shortly after, the U. S. Senate after much debate provided the meagre pension of $200 a month for his widow ; whereas in one year of yellow fever it was estimated that the epidemic had cost the State of Louisiana alone $15,000,000 and 4,056 lives.

felt after leaving the deathbed of Miss Fisher, the Blockley nurse, when he was similarly impelled to write a few unfinished lines—far different from the message of sympathy subsequently sent to this boy's parents when he was under control. But he cannot be left long in this mood. And that 'symptom of the bibliomania not mentioned by Dibdin' provides a diversion, for at this very time there appeared among other catalogues one from George P. Johnston of Edinburgh, listing 'a series of medical theses by students from America at Edinburgh University', for which he promptly cabled—Johnston replying to ask if he meant *all* of them, which indeed he did. Books could be a great solace.

On December 4th, before the New York Academy of Medicine, he gave an address [1] for which he took as his motto a quotation from Abernethy: 'The Hospital is the only proper college in which to rear a true disciple of Æsculapius.' It was a most timely and important topic, and of particular significance coming from one who expressed the desire that his epitaph should read: 'Here lies the man who admitted students to the wards.' Though he did not say so, his remarks were really aimed at the conditions then existing in most of the New York hospitals, into whose amphitheatres students were admitted by side entrances, but from whose wards they were barred, 'as hurtful to the best interests of the patients'—a fanciful objection, as he clearly pointed out, provided one uses ordinary discretion and is actuated by kindly feelings. It is hardly necessary to-day, when much that Osler pleaded for in these respects has come to pass, to do more than point out how great was his influence in bringing about the transformation, and he made this prophecy, that 'within the next quarter of a century the larger universities of this country will have their own hospitals in which the problems of nature known as disease will be studied as thoroughly as are those of Geology or Sanscrit.'

In what may be called the natural method of teaching [he said], the student begins with the patient, continues with the patient, and ends his studies with the patient, using books and lectures as

[1] 'On the Need of a Radical Reform in our Method of Teaching Senior Students.' *Medical News*, N.Y., Jan. 10, 1903.

tools, as means to an end. The student starts, in fact, as a practitioner, as an observer of disordered machines, with the structure and orderly functions of which he is perfectly familiar. Teach him how to observe, give him plenty of facts to observe and the lessons will come out of the facts themselves. For the junior student in medicine and surgery it is a safe rule to have no teaching without a patient for a text, and the best teaching is that taught by the patient himself. The whole art of medicine is in observation, as the old motto goes, but to educate the eye to see, the ear to hear and the finger to feel takes time, and to make a beginning, to start a man on the right path, is all that we can do. We expect too much of the student and we try to teach him too much. Give him good methods and a proper point of view, and all other things will be added, as his experience grows.

Little realizing what complications were in store for him, Osler had accepted, during that month, with some misgivings and reluctance, an invitation to give one of the series of 'Lectures on Immortality' at Harvard University. President Eliot had long wished that a physician might participate in this, the Ingersoll Foundation, and two years before had approached William H. Welch on the subject, when an exchange of letters to this effect took place: from Dr. Welch—that so far as he could see Science had nothing to say upon the subject of immortality; from Mr. Eliot—that was just what he wanted him to say; from Dr. Welch—that it would not be possible to fill an hour in saying so.

Whether or not Mr. Eliot had forgotten this correspondence does not appear, but the next summer at Seal Harbour he approached Dr. Welch again with no better result. Mr. Eliot then threatened to persist until Dr. Welch gave in, unless he would get some one else to give the lecture in his place, whereupon Welch suggested Osler. Osler was written to, and 'refused energetically', as Mr. Eliot recalls. A conspiracy was then entered upon, it is said, and Mr. Eliot was to write to Osler again and was to advise Dr. Welch, at the same time, that he had done so. Accordingly, a day or two after this second invitation was sent from Harvard, Dr. Welch dropped in at 1 West Franklin Street and the following conversation took place:

W. O.: 'Welch, what do you think? They have asked me to give the Ingersoll Lecture.'

W. H. W.: 'How splendid; you're going to accept of course.'

W. O.: 'Splendid? I wouldn't think of talking before a Boston audience on such an impossible subject as Immortality. I have already refused once.'

W. H. W.: 'Why, you're a perfect coward. You must do it of course; no one could do it better. No one ever refuses an invitation to give an Ingersoll Lecture.'

W. O.: 'Do you really mean it?'—and the long and short of it was, the following equivocal letter was dispatched, and ultimately he was persuaded to accept:

Dec. 19, 1902.

Dear President Eliot,—I regret exceedingly that I have again to decline your kind invitation to deliver the Ingersoll Lecture. The temptation to accept was very strong, particularly as I have been collecting data for some years on 'this business of death', as Milton terms it, but the winter's work is now so exacting that I could not possibly find the necessary time for preparation. If you could give me a year's notice on some other occasion, so that I could have my free summer for the work, I should be only too glad to deliver the lecture.

It had been an eventful year. Mendel's law, after forty years of oblivion, had been rediscovered. The passing of Virchow in his eighty-first year was the last connecting link between the old régime in pathology and a new one of which Paul Ehrlich, to be the first Herter Lecturer, was the chief exponent. Such benefactions as the Carnegie Institution and the Rockefeller Institute were calling attention to the needs of the profession and the means which should be taken to control disease. Sanatoria for consumptives were springing up in all communities, and Mr. Phipps's donations had helped greatly to focus attention upon the antituberculosis crusade in which the public was becoming interested. But on the whole, people were indifferent to the possibilities which had so inspired Mr. Gates, and their elected representatives, in consequence, were utterly deaf.

There had been two striking object-lessons, one in Cleveland, where a bigoted though influential mayor had opposed vaccination and insisted that disinfection with formaldehyde could stem a serious outbreak of smallpox which had occurred there; another in San Francisco, where for political reasons all mention of the existence of plague had been suppressed to such a degree as to jeopardize the safety of the entire country. Then, too, during the year the widespread extent of infection from uncinariasis or 'hookworm' throughout the South began to be appreciated as the chief cause of the filth and squalor among the 'poor-whites' in the Southern States. But, if legislatures were indifferent, the greater was the need for private enterprise, and the field was prepared for the opportunity soon to be grasped by the International Health Board of the Rockefeller Foundation. In all of these things, as has been seen, Osler indirectly had no little part.

CHAPTER XXII

1903

THE MASTER-WORD IN MEDICINE

TWENTY years ago Baltimore was still sufficiently old-fashioned for people on New Year's afternoon to keep open house, with an abundance of apple toddy, cake, and Maryland beaten biscuit, or even a 'julep' for those who relished some mint in their nostrils. Falling this year on a Thursday, there were quiet days left over for the week-end and one may imagine Osler taking full advantage of them. He was writing an address to be given in a few days at New Haven, but the week's instalment of journals had come in, and one of them at least—probably all, for they were soon to be handed on to the Faculty reading-room—he goes over from cover to cover. Few things missed his eye—even in the book reviews; and the number of postcards or notes which were left to be mailed when 10 o'clock came is unrecorded, but there were often a dozen or more. On this second day of January his reading of the London *Lancet* alone led to two of them at all events. The first went to the editor, as follows:

In the *Lancet* of Dec. 20, 1902, p. 1072, the reviewer of a new edition of the 'Religio Medici' states that he cannot call to mind any editor who has pointed out the similarity between Bishop Ken's 'Evening Hymn' and the dormitive which Sir Thomas says he took 'to bedward'. In Gardiner's edition (1845) there is the following note: 'Compare this with the beautiful and well known "Evening Hymn" of Bishop Ken, and these again with several of the Hymni Ecclesiae, especially that beginning "Salvator Mundi, Domine", with which Ken and Browne, both Wykehamists, must have been familiar.' [1]

Having newly familiarized himself with the medical history of Connecticut in view of his coming address, another communication had arrested his attention, and in the *Archives of Pediatrics* for May will be found an article by Dr. Hezekiah Beardsley of New Haven, Conn., entitled

[1] 'Sir Thomas Browne's Evening Hymn.' *Lancet*, Lond., Jan. 17, 1903.

'Congenital Hypertrophic Stenosis of the Pylorus', with this 'foot-note by Professor Osler':

Cautley and Dent in a recent paper (*Lancet*, December 20, 1902) state that the first record of this disease which is now exciting a good deal of interest, dates back to 1841. The report here given by Dr. Beardsley of a very clearly and accurately described case ['schirrosity of the pylorus'] is, I think, worth republishing. It appears in the earliest volume of medical transactions issued in this country, entitled 'Cases and Observations by the Medical Society of New Haven County in the State of Conn.' New Haven, J. Meigs, 1788.

Thus the record of a century-old observation, together with its author, was rescued from oblivion. Still another note, probably traceable to the same evening, was sent to the editor of the *Medical News*,[1] and how many more cards went to the contributors of the various articles in these and other journals, as he cleared his desk of them, can only be conjectured.

The occasion of his New Haven address, given January 6th, was the centennial celebration of the local medical society, and Osler made what he termed 'remarks' 'On the Educational Value of the Medical Society'. Though perhaps somewhat less effective than other things he had written, it nevertheless was included the next year in his collected addresses,[2] by which time he had chosen as the two prefatory mottoes the verse from the Epistle to the Hebrews, chapter x: 'Let us hold fast the profession of our faith,' &c., and the following from Jowett's Introductions (Dialogues of Plato), which indicates sufficiently well the thread of his discourse:

The want of energy is one of the main reasons why so few persons continue to improve in later years. They have not the will, and do not know the way. They 'never try an experiment' or look up a point of interest for themselves; they make no sacrifices for the sake of knowledge; their minds, like their bodies, at a certain age become fixed. Genius has been defined as 'the power of taking pains'; but hardly anyone keeps up his interest in knowledge throughout a whole life. The troubles of a family, the business of making money, the demands of a profession destroy the elasticity of the mind. The waxen tablet of the memory, which was once

[1] 'The Significance of Cutaneous Angiomata.' *Medical News*, N.Y., Jan. 10, 1903.

[2] 'Aequanimitas and other Addresses', No. XVII.

capable of receiving 'true thoughts and clear impressions', becomes hard and crowded; there is no room for the accumulations of a long life (Theæt., 194 ff.). The student, as years advance, rather makes an exchange of knowledge than adds to his store.

The address was an appeal to the practising members of his profession (among whom the 'forty-visit-a-day man' is most to be pitied) to remember that education is a life-long business; that experience is fallacious and judgement difficult; and that attendance on a medical society, particularly one which maintains a library, may prove the salvation of the man who from success in practice 'needs to pray the prayer of the Litany against the evils of prosperity' lest he tend towards slovenliness in his methods of work. Even his foot-notes deserve quoting. One of them reads:

In every age there have been Elijahs ready to give up in despair at the progress of commercialism in the profession. Garth says in 1699 (*Dispensary*)—

> Now sickening Physick hangs her pensive head
> And what was once a Science, now 's a Trade.

Of medicine, many are of the opinion expressed by one of Akenside's disputants at Tom's Coffee House, that the ancients had endeavoured to make it a science and failed, and the moderns to make it a trade and have succeeded. To-day the cry is louder than ever, and in truth there are grounds for alarm; but on the other hand, we can say to these Elijahs that there are many more than 7,000 left who have not bowed the knee to this Baal, but who practise *caute, caste et probe*.

And the reader is struck, even if his listeners may not have been, with the diversity of the author's reading, for he begins with an appropriate line from 'The Autocrat', ends with another from Kipling; and in the body of the address, in addition to the Bible, Bishop Butler, Locke, Browning, Thomas Fuller, and George Eliot in the person of Mrs. Poyser, all make themselves felt. Osler's mind was insatiable. At this very time, as the following letter shows, he was on another hunt, which will account for his presence in York the following summer:

From Dr. George A. Auden to W. O. York, Jan. 11, 1903.

Dear Prof. Osler,—I shall be delighted to hunt up any facts about old James Atkinson of York. His Medical Bibliography is, I am sorry to say, but little known. He was born in 1759, his father being a friend of Laurence Sterne who was Vicar of Sutton, ten miles from here. I have often thought that the Medical Bibliography reminds one a good deal of Tristram Shandy's humour. . . . Another medical celebrity of York has been immortalized as Dr. Slop in Tristram Shandy. This was Dr. Burton who is buried in Holy Trinity, Micklegate. I have in my charge as Secretary of the York Med. Society the midwifery instruments described as the cause of the deformity of Shandy's nose! We have in York a very good collection of mediaeval medical works, some very valuable ones. One I am in hopes of transcribing—a vellum MS. of 1403 by William of Killingholme, I believe unique. If anything should at any time bring you to England and you could spare a few days for York, I should be delighted to offer you my hospitality. . . .

Mrs. Osler had gone to Boston shortly after Christmas because of the illness of a relative, and had returned with a troublesome cough supposedly due to a cold caught on the train; and though exposed to whooping-cough while at her sister's, it could not have been apparent as yet, either to her 'latch-keyer' attendant or to her husband, that she was in for a long-drawn-out illness:

To Mrs. W. S. Thayer from W. O. 1 West Franklin Street, 1. 18. 03.

Dear Sister Susan, So sorry that I shall have to withdraw the very kind invitation to tea which came from you this morning *thro. William Sydney* but—when he came Mrs O seemed so much 'given over' to the effects of Dr Futcher's medicine that it looked hopeless for the day, now she has revived & talks of getting up—under which circumstances, I mean the getting up, it seems more properer & polite that I (as she would be alone otherwise, & *most* unhappy) that I, I say, should stay at home & consequently cannot come. You will understand. Sincerely yours, Wm Osler. PS. 'Tis not the invitation that I withdraw, of course, but the acceptance. [On the envelope, evidently intended for W. S. T., is written: 'Could you send me Huchard—Traité des Maladies du Cœur.']

The following two letters tell their own story:

To John H. Musser from W. O. 1. 19. 03.

Dear J. H. Many thanks for the Bowditch. He was a noble old citizen & the life is well told. I wish there had been a little more about his Paris days. There has been a proposal made to launch a National Medical Historical Society. What do you think of such a move? It seems a pity to start a new society, when there are so many & when we all have such hard work to keep up our interest in existing organizations. Whether it should be started—& if so should it be a section of the Am. Med. Ass. or an independent body—& of unlimited membership or of limited? At your leisure drop me a line. The question has not been discussed openly as yet.

To Charles W. Eliot from W. O. Jan. 19, 1903.

Dear President Eliot,—I feel much honoured by your kind and tempting offer. It would be delightful to spend a winter in Cambridge, quietly thinking and studying, and doing such teaching as you suggest, but I do not see how it could be managed. I have talked the matter over carefully with Mrs. Osler and I am sorry to feel compelled to decline. With kind regards and many thanks, Sincerely yours.

He had expected to attend a dinner of the College of Physicians of Philadelphia, of which Weir Mitchell was again President, on the evening of January 24th[1] at the Hotel Walton, but it must have become all too evident by that time that 1 West Franklin Street was in for a siege of whooping-cough, for he wrote to his niece: 'Aunt Grace is better to-day—but she has c*o*fed & c*o*fed & c*o*fed. Can't you hear her whoop thro this writing, it just gave me a shudder as I heard it. Poor Ike is sure to catch it.' Revere did 'catch it'—badly—and ere long he began to tune up in most brazen fashion. This explains the following, sent on a card from the University Club of New York, postmarked February 3, 1903:

To Egerton Y. Davis Osler Jr., of 1 West Franklin St., Baltimore.

Dear Bandmaster I hear that you are looking for three good players for your band. I play the big drum, my son Josh plays the bugle and my little son Reckcrack plays either the bones or the kettledrum. We charge a dollar a day (each) with meals included.

---

[1] On the morning of the 24th a notice had appeared in the daily papers stating that Mr. Carnegie had included among his various donations to libraries—and one may suppose at Dr. Mitchell's suggestion—the Library of the College of Physicians at Philadelphia. His gift of $50,000 was conditioned, as usual, on the raising of a similar sum by the college itself, and those who attended the banquet will recall that when the formal announcement of this munificent gift was made by one of the after-dinner speakers, he held up and waved a telegram received that morning from Baltimore, stating that the first contribution had already been received. The telegram read: 'Congratulations on the bequest. Put Mrs. Osler and me down for five hundred.'

We like scrambled eggs for breakfast, mushrooms for dinner and buttered toast for tea. We play all day for the dollar, and we sleep in our clothes in the band wagon. We prefer the horse to be white. Yours truly, EZEKIEL TOMTOM.

He had busied himself, meanwhile, with the programme of the Historical Club for the year, and papers had been promised by Roswell Park, Walter R. Steiner, E. F. Cordell, and James Mumford, who gave the first of them, and, despite the whooping-cough, stayed at 1 West Franklin Street. On February 18th Osler was in Richmond, where he gave a clinical lecture before the College of Medicine, on Leukaemia,[1] and on the 24th he sent one of his many letters to Chadwick of the Boston Medical Library:

No, I have not Aikin's Biographical Memoirs, & should like them very much. I know about the old bird & have his Memoir by his daughter Lucy. I am sending you Thacher's Military Journal. It is the first edition and I had it bound this year at Rivière's. It is really a very first-class work & a great credit to the old man. By the way, Thacher's Diploma from the M. M. S. is in the hands of his grandson, Boutelle, of Hampton, Va, who might perhaps leave it to the library. I have a great many letters about the proposed Historical Society. Nearly all of the young men are in favour of it, but I have great hesitation about going into it, as I am so confoundedly driven with so many things.

A week later he sent word to a niece: 'We are having a miserable time thank you. Poor Ike whoops about 24 times in the 24 hours. Aunt Grace has been much better lately and is almost over the whoops. Revere keeps very jolly & joky. Isn't Bea's birthday on the 13th? Get a nice cake and candles &c at Webb's & order flowers at Dunlops.' He does not add that though Revere kept 'jolly & joky', his father with his fingers in his ears would sometimes rush from the house, for he could not endure to hear the boy in one of his bad paroxysms. This went on interminably, as is the way with whooping-cough, but it was even worse than usual, for Revere would 'whoop and put', and went everywhere—to the park or his playhouse—accompanied by a tin basin and a bath-towel. Finally his father got a red and a blue pencil for him to keep score—

1 This has got into his bibliography, though it was merely taken down and published from a student's notes.

a blue mark for a 'whoop' and a red one for a 'whoop and put'. Still, there were some cheering things, especially those derived from book catalogues, and it was at about this time that the Edinburgh theses for which he had cabled the previous December must have arrived, to his great delight. In the sale-list which remains in his library he subsequently wrote as follows of this purchase:

This Edinboro' Catalogue here appended came from G. P. Johnston one Sunday morning while I was still in Baltimore. I cabled at once for all the American Theses, and secured them (J. cabled me 'Do you mean all of them?'). The following summer when in Edinboro I called at Johnston's and he showed me a group of cables which he had received. Mine came early Monday morning before the shop was opened. Then in quick succession came cables from the Surgeon-General's Library, Washington, the College of Physicians, Phila., the Academy of Medicine, New York, and from Dr Wm Pepper, Phila. It is a very remarkable collection and came chiefly from the libraries of the Professors Hope to whom they were presentation copies. There are the theses of some of the most distinguished of American physicians, Bard, Archer, Almon of Nova Scotia (the father of Senator A. and the grandfather of my friend Tom A.), Shippen, Morgan, Kuhn, Logan of Phila, Benj. Rush, Physick, Arthur Lee and others. I gave the collection to the Frick Library of the Medical & Chirurgical Faculty of Maryland.[1]

One of the first acts of the Carnegie Institution, of which D. C. Gilman had become President, was to set aside funds to make possible the resumption of the *Index Medicus* under the editorship of Robert Fletcher. This action was probably taken at the solicitation of Weir Mitchell and John S. Billings, both of whom were members of the Board, for its general policy has been from the outset to leave medical and public health interests to the Rockefeller foundations and to support research in other fields. Osler and Welch promptly arranged for a dinner at the Maryland Club to celebrate the occasion, and many notes like the following to Dr. H. C. Yarrow issued from 1 West Franklin Street:

iv. 8. 03.

Dear Yarrow, Are there any special friends of Dr. Fletcher—other than H. C. Y.—who should be asked to our little gathering on the 18th to commemorate the Index Medicus redivivus?

---

[1] The 123 Theses were presented at a meeting of the Book and Journal Club, Thursday, March 26th.

Most of the letters of this time which have been recovered are brief lines relating to matters of this sort: a reception at the Faculty hall for Dr. Cordell as a mark of appreciation for his centennial volume,[1] which by now had appeared, a somewhat overgrown and expensive child for the committee of five who had fostered it; arranging for another public meeting in McCoy Hall under the auspices of the Tuberculosis Commission; arranging for a luncheon in New York for Professor Ewald of Berlin; for the Laennec Society meeting; the post-graduate lectures; and much else besides. Not content with the dinner for Robert Fletcher, he had set on foot a movement for a portrait, and from the University Club in New York on the day of the Ewald luncheon, he wrote to J. R. Chadwick:

6th [May 1903]

Many thanks for the Cardan. I had not the volume. It is most interesting. The horoscope of Andreas Vesalius is excellent—I found it accidentally. I have just had four of the original editions of C. from Muller & Co with several treasures. About the Fletcher portrait—will you stir up the Boston men. I will attack some of the N. Y. fellows tomorrow & next week we can canvass the men in Washington. Shall you be at the Meeting? I shall be at the New Willard. Join me often in the Café!!

The meeting to which he refers was the eighteenth session of the 'American Physicians' held in Washington on May 12th to 14th, under the presidency of his old Montreal colleague, 'silent' James Stewart.[2] Osler had written to

1 'The Medical Annals of Maryland, 1799–1879.' Baltimore, 1903. (Privately printed.)

2 It was the year of the VIth triennial Congress of American Physicians and Surgeons, over whose general sessions W. W. Keen presided. At the combined sessions symposia were held; Fitz, Opie, Flexner, R. H. Chittenden, and Mikulicz of Breslau were the chief speakers on the subject of the pancreas, an organ which occupies the region that Osler, before his students, was accustomed to refer to as 'the area of abdominal romance, where the head of the pancreas lies folded in the arms of the duodenum'. On the subject of the gall-bladder there were papers by Ewald of Berlin, Klebs of Halberstadt, Musser, Christian Herter, W. J. Mayo, and Moynihan of Leeds—later Sir Berkeley, whom Osler always playfully addressed as 'Carnifex Maximus'. There were other papers no less notable. Thus at another session, Theobald Smith and Trudeau made clear that Koch had been rash in his statements made at the London Congress in 1901, for Smith had succeeded in isolating the bovine bacillus from the mesenteric glands of a child, and Trudeau had

Lafleur urging his attendance, stating that the prospects were good for an exceptional meeting—and such it proved to be. One of the afternoon sessions was given over entirely to a symposium on Disorders of the Spleen, and Osler read one of the more important papers,[1] which led to a lively discussion. That a dinner of the association followed, which proved unexpectedly expensive for some of the participants, is evidenced by the following, scribbled without date, and again from the University Club of New York, to his friend Chadwick :

Many thanks for the books. The large paper copy of the Religio I had never seen—tis a fine addition to my collection. I will send you the small paper copy in exchange. I have a duplicate *2nd Edition.* I did not know of Jackson's 2nd letter—though I had read somewhere of his 'Death of Washington'. We have just finished the meeting of the Association of Medical Librarians.[2] The work is progressing well. I bagged $250 for the Fletcher portrait at our Assoc. of Am. Phy. dinner. Garrison writes discouraged from Washington. I shall stir up some men 'at large'. Will you attack the Boston men.

But he was not permitted invariably to be the host and the suggestor of tributes to others. Occasionally he was subjected himself, and nothing could have been more spontaneous or delightful than the dinner given at the Maryland Club on the evening of May 15th when a group of the 'old timers' at the Hopkins gathered together to make fun of him and each other ; and on the menu they were recommended among other things to 'cultivate the virtue of taciturnity' ; to 'remember the words of Publius : "I have often regretted my speech, not my silence"' ; and to 'read the advice to a young physician by Egerton Y. Davis'.

produced a relative immunity with an avian bacillus. Both of these studies indicated the essential identity of the various bacillary groups of tuberculosis.

[1] The title was 'Chronic Cyanosis with Polycythaemia and Enlarged Spleen : a New Clinical Entity' (*American Journal of the Medical Sciences*, Phila., Aug. 1903, p. 187). It was a further consideration of the so-called 'Osler-Vaquez disease' with the report of additional cases.

[2] The meeting, with fifteen in attendance, was held on the morning of May 16th in Brooklyn in the Library of the Medical Society of the County of Kings, and in the afternoon in the New York Academy of Medicine. Osler was again elected President and, indeed, was the main source of inspiration of the Society. The Transactions appear in the *Medical Library and Historical Journal*, 1903, i. 206–21.

Late in the evening a procession filed from the club and marched to 1 West Franklin Street, trundling barrow-loads of books to deposit in his library. For the real purpose of this gathering was a gift—that monument of George M. Smith the publisher, the sixty-three volumes of the 'Dictionary of National Biography', completed shortly before, 'after eighteen years of unremitting labour'.

They sailed on May 29th on the *Cedric*, and the following letters tell something of their summer; of a gift from Henry Phipps; of a fictitious portrait of Harvey; of the aftermath of Mrs. Osler's whooping-cough; of Paris, Guernsey, Harrogate, York, Norwich, Beauly, and London:

To H. M. Hurd from W. O. Paris [undated]

Dear Hurd, That was a kindly act of Mr. Phipps—and shows a discerning mind. I have told Brown Shipley & Co. to pay the money to the Johns Hopkins Hospital and we can determine later what is best to be done. Either to invest & spend the interest in the tuberculosis work or to spend the whole amount in rearranging the Dispensary (which needs it badly) and adding special rooms for the tuberculosis patients. Making a modest out-patient dept. of this sort might appeal to Mr. Phipps & he might double his subscription. In any case it is an encouraging sign and we can use the money to great advantage. I am here with Emerson & Jacobs. E. has had a most profitable visit. [Pierre] Marie has been most kind and he has the run of the Bicêtre. We go about July 1st to Brittany or the Channel Islands. Love to all at the Hospital, [etc].

The allusion to the 'kindly act of Mr. Phipps' deserves explanation. One of Henry Phipps's children had been a patient of Osler's and he had been to see them from time to time in New York. Quite possibly on one of these occasions something may have been said commendatory of Mr. Phipps's project to establish an institute in Philadelphia for the special study of tuberculosis, the first institution of its kind, newly established under the directorship of Dr. Lawrence F. Flick.[1] Osler in all likelihood must have told him

[1] The Henry Phipps Institute for the Study, Treatment, and Prevention of Tuberculosis—'the embodiment of a new idea, namely the concentrated effort upon a single disease for its extermination'—had been founded on Feb. 1, 1903, and was in operation in temporary quarters at 238 Pine Street, Philadelphia. After a period of excellent work it was subsequently taken over by the regents of the University of Pennsylvania.

of the great importance of the work, and may have mentioned the conditions which the students in Baltimore had disclosed in visiting the homes of the consumptives who had reported at the dispensary. In any event, Mr. Phipps had come to feel that he would like to do something for Baltimore as well as Philadelphia. Having acquainted Dr. Flick of this intent, one evening early in June, when at dinner in Philadelphia with the staff of the Institute, he excused himself, left the table for a moment, and returned with a small sheet of club stationery partly torn in two, on which he had scribbled, 'Pay $10,000 to Dr. Osler. [signed] Henry Phipps.' 'Would you mind taking this to Dr. Osler?' he said, 'and tell him that if he uses it well I will send him more.' This slip, promptly taken to Baltimore by Dr. Flick, was forwarded to London by Dr. Welch, where it was thought to be a hoax, and Brown, Shipley & Company forwarded it in turn to Paris, where its genuineness and purpose was recognized. In reply to Osler's letter of acknowledgement Mr. Phipps wrote: 'I hear you are married. We have taken Beauly Castle and hope you will pay us a visit.'

To W. S. Thayer. Hotel de Castiglione, Paris [no date]

Dear Thayer, We had a delightful crossing, pleasant people & smooth seas. After a week of rain and bustle in London I came on here and am with the Baron von Jacob [H. B. Jacobs] & Emerson. Enjoying Paris very much. E. J. & I start out every morning about 9 for one of the Spitals. We have been 3 times at Bicêtre with Marie who is charming and yesterday we saw his collection of odd & anomalous cases—an extraordinary show. I have been 3 times at the St Louis & have been going thro the museum carefully. The trophic & other lesions are remarkable. Dieulafoy we missed & Debove, but we have heard three delightful lectures by Brissaud on the forms of oedema & the vasomotor disorders. Norton turned up yesterday—just on from Wien. He seems well & happy. Whitman I have seen twice; dined with him on Friday. . . . I shall stay here for another two weeks.

Was not Mr. Phipps gift a surprise. We should either convert it & spend the $400 a year in some special way associated with Tuberculosis or what I think would be better still devote it to help reorganize our Out-patient Dept. & make one special part for Tuberculosis. We could leave the waiting room as it is & pull down & rearrange all the rooms to the left & possibly to the right. This should not cost more than 20,000 dollars & the Trustees should go

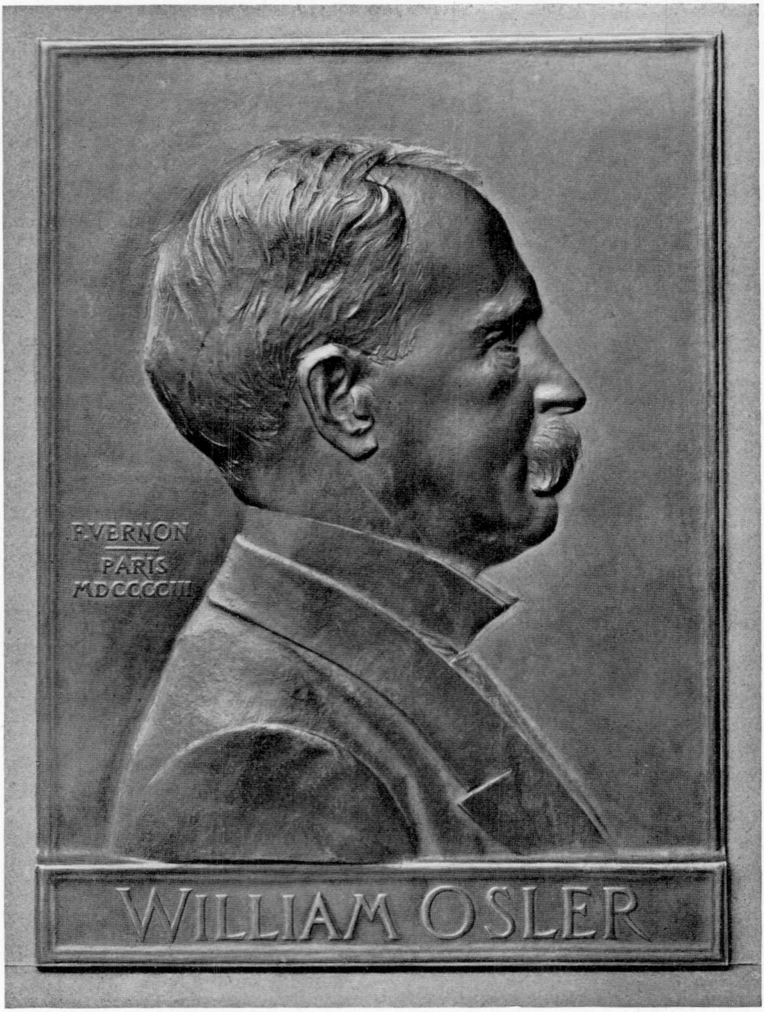

THE VERNON PLAQUE

Paris, 1903

shares. . . . Drop a line before long. Do arrange with Smith & Futcher about the summer dispensary work so as to be sure there are a couple of men on hand each day. Ever yours, W. O. Send word of any special French books we should have I have a box coming out from Welter.

Subsequent letters tell of prowling along the Quais in and out of old book shops ; of visits with Raymond, Charcot's successor at the Salpêtrière ; of a supposed picture of William Harvey by Janssen they had discovered ; and it was during this sojourn in Paris that H. B. Jacobs had the medallion by Vernon made of him, to which the following letter of recent date from Pierre Marie refers :

Je me félicite d'avoir été tout au moins l'occasion de l'éxécution de sa médaille par Vernon (notre grand médailliste — mort, lui aussi). Sir William était venu dîner à la maison avec un de ses compatriotes, et après le dîner j'avais pensé que tous deux prendraient peut-être quelque intérêt à regarder les médailles des médecins et chirurgiens connus de Paris ; c'était alors la coutume que les amis et les élèves fissent cadeau à leurs maîtres de leur médaille, par souscription, et j'en avais un grand nombre. Sir William et son ami avaient beaucoup admiré les médailles faites par Vernon. En nous quittant l'ami me prit à part et me demanda de le mettre à même de faire faire par Vernon, en quelques jours, la médaille de Sir William—elle fut très réussie et j'en fus très heureux.

To H. B. Jacobs. Glen View, St. Martins, Guernsey, July 8th.

Surely the dealers are children of Ananias & of the sons of Belial. Col. Bramston writes a very nice letter. He knows of no such picture [of Harvey], never had one & had he had one he never could have parted with a family relic of such value !

We are most comfortable here—the weather is superb & the bathing first class. The roads are excellent & we have already had several delightful five o'clock tea picnics in different parts. The sea & the rocks on the south shore, near us, are very fine, & as in the Isle of Wight, chines run up from the Coast. Mrs. Osler has been much better. Yesterday she had a bad attack again—it seems, as Fowler says, a genuine bronchial asthma following the whooping-cough. Revere is so happy—he has just had the delightful experience of sending his cricket ball through a window pane. I hope you will find weather like this at Trouville. . . .

To W. S. Thayer. Guernsey, 15th [July]

Thanks for your nice long letter & for the 3rd year lists &c. I am glad that some of the men were conditioned & warned—'twas needed. Hamman seems an A.1. fellow. We can recommend him in Sept. tho. properly all the new nominations should come before the Trustees in June. I am very sorry Calvert has gone to Columbia. 'Twill not be for long. The conditions there are hopeless, I understand. Why the d—— did he not *wait* in St. Louis. What a bomb Flexner's engagement was! He deserves a good wife.

I had a most interesting visit in Paris & saw much that was instructive. Marie was most kind—also Raymond & Déjerine. Mr Phipps has promised another $10,000 when needed. We must take this chance to get the out-patient Dept. thoroughly remodelled, & a separate Tub. Clinic established. I dare say Mr. P. will do anything we ask. A model O-P. Dept. for the disease would be a great addition. Think over plans. The waiting-room—general, is all right, but the rooms should be remodelled and rearranged. I have written to the Trustees about it. We are in a comfortable little cottage here. I am loafing.—We have found a good sailor who takes us in a big boat three or four times a week. The weather is heavenly—the coast perfection, & the bathing just right. I am mahogany coloured. Mrs Osler still coughs & wheezes—there is a sort of asthmatic condition left—most distressing at times. She is better now.

As he says in a letter to H. V. Ogden, they had picked out 'a quiet little village close to Fermain Bay, one of the prettiest spots on the Island—an odd corner of the earth—half French, half English, with queer customs & laws & virtual independence of government'. And from other letters, to the stay-at-home 3-West-Franklin-Street neighbours, extracts may be taken:

July 17th.

I was much interested about the Harvey picture; which was a beauty, but after the positive statements from Cust & Power and the glaring discrepancy in the date I could not think of it. . . . I have bagged two 1543 Fabricas! 'Tis not a work which should be left on the shelves of a bookseller. . . . We should get up a lecture bureau & with a course on the great medical books of the world. Hippocrates, Galen, Avicenna, Vesalius, Paracelsus, Harvey &c.—all well illustrated with lantern slides and the original editions. I am struggling with the question of the *Editio Princeps* of Avicenna. . . . I am deep too in a life of Gui Patin & am interested in his tirades against polypharmacy & the Arabians Did I tell you I got Harvey's letter to Riolan—had to pay £6.6 for it. R. was Patin's great friend & they both scoff at Harvey's discovery even as late as 1670! I shall look up the Harvey portraits. I have stirred up a dozen dealers to look for the *de Motu Cordis*. I have got the 2nd 4th & 6th editions of Garth's Dispensary—they are valuable for the notes.

. . . I am reading Kussmaul's *Docentenzeit in Heidelberg*—'tis not up to the *Jugenderinnerungen* but there are some very good pictures of his early days.

July 25th.

. . . Besides the two copies of the '43 edition of the *De Humani corporis fabrica* I have just ordered a third. We cannot have too many copies in America & no Medical Library is complete without one.[1] We are having such a nice quiet time here—the weather has been perfect. Mrs. O. is not at all well—wheezes still like the deuce, but has been better lately. To add to her discomfort an urticaria of ferocious quality has landed upon some $3\frac{1}{2}$ acres of her back. Revere is very jolly. I wish you could take a header with me about 11 this a m—high tide & about 15 feet of water off the rocks. . . .

Osler's natural courtesy made him choose for correspondence subjects with which his reader would be familiar, and the morning 'header' described to a young friend was probably no more exhilarating than his evening 'header' mentioned in a letter written at the end of this same day to Weir Mitchell, in which he says:

Reading the Ethics of Aristotle this evening in Bk. VII Chapter V I came across the statement 'there was a man again who, by reason of disease, was afraid of a cat'. He is speaking of excessive cowardice. It may interest you in connection with your inquiry into morbid dread of 'the harmless necessary cat'.

Weir Mitchell had been writing to him of a paper he was preparing on feline phobias; but the perusal during that summer of a new edition of Aristotle's 'Ethics' (A. S. Humphries, 1902) indicates possibly that the Ingersoll Lecture was on his mind. At the same time he must have been easing his conscience with some literary work, for he sent a postcard from London on the 19th of August to Francis R. Packard to the effect that in a few days he would receive for publication a paper on the 'Visceral Manifestations of the Erythema Group'. A hint of his summer's reading, too, is shown by the leading (unsigned) editorial in the *Journal of the American Medical Association* for August 22nd—a delightful and appreciative review of 'Kussmaul's Autobiography'; and on the same day the

[1] One of these copies was forwarded to the McGill Library, and having quite forgotten the fact he sent them a second copy from Rome on March 9, 1909.

London *Lancet* published an important clinical study 'On the so-called Stokes-Adams Disease',[1] in the course of which there is quoted an observation by Kussmaul in his 'Aus meiner Docentenzeit in Heidelberg'.

To Charles W. Eliot. Arts Club, 40 Dover Street, Aug. 21st.

Dear President Eliot, Your letter reached me here a few days ago. Early in May would suit me best [for the Ingersoll Lecture]. I cannot give you the exact date until I hear from Paris as to the date of the Third International Congress on Tuberculosis which I have promised to attend. With kind regards [&c]. I shall be back Sept. 23rd.

A letter of the 25th from Mrs. Osler, Hotel Granby, Harrogate, says: 'This address means that I am here for the waters and baths. I am ashamed to come home with same old cough and Dr. Osler insisted that it was aggravated by some gouty symptoms. So here I am. You would not know me—I am alone in a very dignified hotel and have assumed a British-matron dignity and tone that are quite becoming I assure you. After the freedom of Guernsey it is a bit oppressive. Revere and Miss Nichols are in Falkirk; Dr. Osler with the Schäfers in North Berwick—but joins me this p.m. We hated to leave Guernsey—it was a haven of rest and peace.' That he so joined her and was in his usual high spirits is evident from a number of his letters, one of which, written on the 29th, reads:

I had a fall in blood pressure of 125 mm. yesterday afternoon. In an antiquariat's here I was pulling over some old books (while Mrs. O was looking at china &c) and on a chair near at hand were two fine quartos, very finely bound, one the History of the Strawberry Hill & the other, Walpole's Noble Authors, the two £1.15.0! I jumped on them thinking of Sister Kate & Pius IX—but alas the Delilah in charge knocked me over by saying that she had just sold them—not an hour before, to Sir Tristram??—Shandy I suppose—damn him!! I was disgusted. But to-day I saw at York [with Dr. G. A. Auden] the very forceps which smashed Tristram's Nose & looked at many things about Dr. Burton, the original Dr. Slop.[2]

---

[1] In all probability this was prepared for the annual meeting of the B.M.A. in Swansea, July 28–31, which he failed to attend.

[2] At the December meeting of the Johns Hopkins Historical Club he gave a paper on Dr. John Burton. Osler delighted in Laurence Sterne's book

Mrs. Osler is drinking the sulphur water & looks like Persephone— She seems all right again. Many thanks for the Shelley items. I saw that the Adonais had brought out a record price. I have subscribed at Sotheby's for the catalogues of next year so we can cable for Mrs. Osler when she wishes to make us a present. She gave me yesterday the Bronte girls' poems,—a delightful little volume. . . . Tommy is in Edinboro with Miss Nichols. I go to Norwich on Monday & then we go to Mr Phipps near Inverness for a few days. . . .

Mr. Phipps for several years had taken Lord Lovat's estate, Beaufort Castle, for the summer. It is an exquisite place, reached from Inverness by skirting the south shore of the Beauly Firth, and lying in a bend of the Beauly River, celebrated for its salmon. At Beauly there was a large house-party, including an Indian prince among others, but Mr. Phipps promptly fell under Osler's spell and followed him about as though charmed. They are said to have been inseparable, while the other guests went their several ways.

To Abraham Jacobi from W. O. 40 Clarges Street, London, 11th [Sept.]

Please delight the heart of an ardent admirer of yours, Dr. G. A. Auden of York, Eng. by sending him your photograph. He has a tough old caricature of you from some paper above his mantelpiece and I told him that I would write and ask you to send a good one. I hope that you have had a good summer and that Mrs. Jacobi is, at any rate, not worse. After three weeks in Paris, I joined Mrs. Osler at Guernsey where she had taken a cottage by the sea. For nearly eight weeks we rested & fished & bathed and had a most pleasant holiday. We have now returned from Scotland to pack up our things and get ready for the homeward trip on the 10th. I hope you got Kussmaul's 'Aus meiner Docentenzeit'. I asked to have it sent to you in July. 'Tis not up to the Jugenderinnerungen, but there are several good bits. I have got some treasures—an editio princeps of Celsus 1478, the most important.

---

and all its ramifications, especially in the fact that 'Dr. Ferriar the distinguished Manchester physician has exposed the plagiarisms of "Tristram Shandy" in the "Illustrations of Sterne"'—plagiarisms from another Burton, the 'anatomist' of Melancholy; and in a later article ('Men and Books: No. XXII:' *Canadian Medical Association Journal*, July 1913, iii. 612–13) Osler came to the defence of 'Dr. Slop', that is of Dr. John Burton of York, who was 'not only a distinguished physician but the author of a celebrated work, still an authority, on the antiquities of Yorkshire'.

To George Dock. 1 West Franklin Street, 25th [Sept.]

Your letter of the 22nd only reached me at noon to-day just after my return. We had a delightful trip back, five fine days out of seven. Revere and Mrs. Osler enjoyed it so much. The latter is better tho she wheezes occasionally, particularly if she has been exposed to the wind. She spent two weeks at Harrogate—horrorgate she calls it. The sulphur did her good I think. We went to Scotland for ten days, part of the time with the Phipps—of the Phila. Phipps Institute for Tuberculosis. He has twice sent his boys to consult me & this summer, as perhaps I told you, sent me most unexpectedly $10,000 to be used in the Tuberculosis work of the Hospital & has promised an additional $10,000 when called for. Such a man deserved encouragement so we visited him & found the whole family most delightful. I have returned laden with treasures for the Med. Chir. & our J. H. H. Library—a few good things for 1 W. Franklin. The day before I left I picked up the 3rd Ed. of the G. H. Cane (Munk's Edition) which had belonged to either Risden Bennett or B. W. Richardson. It is illustrated with 110 engravings, &c. What edition of the G. H. Cane have you? I am trying to '*sweat out*' an address on 'The Master Word in Medicine' (work, of course) for Toronto next week. The opening of some new buildings. I hope you are in good form. Love to Mrs. Dock & the chicks.

'The Master-Word in Medicine',[1] one of his more finished addresses, was being 'sweated out' in preparation for a festival to be held in Toronto on October 1st. There was to be a double function, for not only were the new medical laboratories for physiology and pathology to be dedicated, but, in addition to this, the amalgamation after years of rivalry of the faculties of medicine of Toronto and Trinity Universities was to be celebrated. The address, inaugural of the new laboratories, was given in the afternoon by Professor C. S. Sherrington, then of Liverpool, in the amphitheatre of the building; and in the evening, in the large auditorium of the gymnasium before the assembled students, came Osler's lecture introductory to the session, on the time-worn subject of the student's duty to his college, himself, and the public. As would be expected, 'from a native of this province and an old student of this school' he paid a tribute to his former teachers—to Bovell in particular; and after a reference to his fellow-student Dick Zimmerman—'how he would have rejoiced to see this

[1] Reprinted as No. XVIII in 'Aequanimitas and other Addresses'.

day!'—he went on to speak indirectly of himself in the following way:

It seems a bounden duty on such an occasion to be honest and frank, so I propose to tell you the secret of life as I have seen the game played, and as I have tried to play it myself. You remember in one of the 'Jungle Stories', that when Mowgli wished to be avenged on the villagers he could only get the help of Hathi and his sons by sending them the master-word. This I propose to give you in the hope, yes, the full assurance, that some of you at least will lay hold upon it to your profit. Though a little one, the master-word looms large in meaning. It is the open sesame to every portal, the great equalizer in the world, the true philosopher's stone which transmutes all the base metal of humanity into gold. The stupid man among you it will make bright, the bright man brilliant, and the brilliant student steady. With the magic word in your heart all things are possible, and without it all study is vanity and vexation. The miracles of life are with it; the blind see by touch, the deaf hear with eyes, the dumb speak with fingers. To the youth it brings hope, to the middle-aged confidence, to the aged repose. True balm of hurt minds, in its presence the heart of the sorrowful is lightened and consoled. It is directly responsible for all advances in medicine during the past twenty-five centuries. Laying hold upon it, Hippocrates made observation and science the warp and woof of our art. Galen so read its meaning that fifteen centuries stopped thinking, and slept until awakened by the *De Fabrica* of Vesalius, which is the very incarnation of the master-word. With its inspiration Harvey gave an impulse to a larger circulation than he wot of, an impulse which we feel to-day. Hunter sounded all its heights and depths, and stands out in our history as one of the great exemplars of its virtues. With it Virchow smote the rock and the waters of progress gushed out; while in the hands of Pasteur it proved a very talisman to open to us a new heaven in medicine and a new earth in surgery. Not only has it been the touchstone of progress, but it is the measure of success in everyday life. Not a man before you but is beholden to it for his position here, while he who addresses you has that honour directly in consequence of having had it graven on his heart when he was as you are to-day. And the Master-Word is *Work*, a little one, as I have said, but fraught with momentous consequences if you can but write it on the tables of your heart, and bind it upon your forehead. But there is a serious difficulty in getting you to understand the paramount importance of the work-habit as part of your organization. You are not far from the Tom Sawyer stage with its philosophy that 'work consists of whatever a body is obliged to do, and play consists of whatever a body is not obliged to do'.

That he should have drawn upon Kipling and Mark Twain for his allusions indicates in all probability what was being read to Revere, just as do the references to mythology in the following passage devoted to one of the several sources of 'that foul fiend worry':

> Another potent cause of worry is an idolatry by which many of you will be sore let and hindered. The mistress of your studies should be the heavenly Aphrodite, the motherless daughter of Uranus. Give her your whole heart and she will be your protectress and friend. A jealous creature, brooking no second, if she finds you trifling and coquetting with her rival, the younger, early Aphrodite, daughter of Zeus and Dione, she will whistle you off, and let you down the wind, to be a prey, perhaps to the examiners, certainly to the worm regret. In plainer language, put your affections in cold storage for a few years, and you will take them out ripened, perhaps a little mellow, but certainly less subject to those frequent changes which perplex so many young men. Only a grand passion, an all-absorbing devotion to the elder goddess, can save the man with a congenital tendency to philandering, the flighty Lydgate who sports with Celia and Dorothea, and upon whom the judgement ultimately falls in a basil-plant of a wife like Rosamond.

But as he went on to elaborate his theme he lightened it everywhere by innumerable allusions from the medley of his own favourites, old and new:

> If you wish to learn of the miseries of scholars in order to avoid them, read Part 1, Section 2, Member 3, Sub-section XV, of that immortal work, the 'Anatomy of Melancholy', but I am here to warn you against these evils, and to entreat you to form good habits in your student days.

And not only Burton but, from his memory or commonplace-book, the 'Religio', the Bible, Milton's 'Areopagitica', 'Pilgrim's Progress', 'Middlemarch', and the Breakfast Table Series are all called upon; and John Locke, Plutarch, Carlyle, Shakespeare, Marcus Aurelius, and the Rev. John Ward; St. Chrysostom, Montaigne, Jowett, Grosseteste—and, of course, the recently visited Tristram Shandy. But there is no need further to analyse the construction of the essay. He urged the students to 'get a relish for the good company of the race by daily intercourse with some of the great minds of all ages'; for 'many of you', he said, 'will need a strong leaven to raise you above the level of the dough in which it will be your lot to labour.'

A conscientious pursuit of Plato's ideal perfection may teach you the three great lessons of life. You may learn to consume your own smoke. The atmosphere of life is darkened by the murmurings and whimperings of men and women over the non-essentials, the trifles, that are inevitably incident to the hurly-burly of the day's routine. Things cannot always go your way. Learn to accept in silence the minor aggravations, cultivate the gift of taciturnity and consume your own smoke with an extra draught of hard work, so that those about you may not be annoyed with the dust and soot of your complaints. More than any other the practitioner of medicine may illustrate the second great lesson, that we are here not to get all we can out of life for ourselves, but to try to make the lives of others happier. This is the essence of the oft-repeated admonition of Christ: 'He that findeth his life shall lose it, and he that loseth his life for my sake shall find it'; on which hard saying if the children of this generation would lay hold, there would be less misery and discontent in the world. It is not possible for anyone to have better opportunities to live this lesson than you will enjoy. The practice of medicine is an art, not a trade; a calling, not a business; a calling in which your heart will be exercised equally with your head. Often the best part of your work will have nothing to do with potions and powders, but with the exercise of an influence of the strong upon the weak, of the righteous upon the wicked, the wise upon the foolish. To you as the trusted family counsellor the father will come with his anxieties, the mother with her hidden griefs, the daughter with her trials, and the son with his follies. Fully one-third of the work you do will be entered in other books than yours. Courage and cheerfulness will not only carry you over the rough places of life, but will enable you to bring comfort and help to the weak-hearted, and will console you in the sad hours when, like Uncle Toby, you have 'to whistle that you may not weep'.

This must suffice. Any student incapable of being uplifted by an exhortation of this kind is beyond the pale.

One of his old Montreal friends was ill at this time, James Stewart; and it took little more than the knowledge of this to send him flying off as though Baltimore and Montreal were next door, to give some comfort and encouragement. Hence a note of October 15th to F. J. Shepherd, which says: 'Peterson seems to be off his base about my wandering about homeless in Montreal. I purposely took my things up to the Royal Victoria, so that I could see Stewart early. I hope to be up at Christmas time.' And on the same day he wrote to C. N. B. Camac: 'Glad you like the little Stevenson. I was in New York last Sunday passing through from Montreal but I had to hurry to catch a train. I have been much driven since I got home from abroad.'

During all this time, in Maryland as well as in other parts of the country, the tuberculosis crusade was being energetically waged, and many unrelated groups of people were planning to hold congresses. In Baltimore the movement was on foot for a tuberculosis exhibition to aid further in the education of the public. This in part explains the following letter to Dr. S. A. Knopf, who had sent for Osler's criticism a document [1] regarding the forthcoming congresses over which there was likely to be a great deal of confusion unless some authoritative group of people took the matter in hand:

Nov. 25, 1903.

Dear Dr. Knopf,—Excellent in every way! There is not a word to alter, and I have nothing to suggest. It hits the nail fairly and squarely on the head. I feel that we should organize a national committee which should be composed of good men from each state. That we could do during the Baltimore meeting. The *Maryland Medical Journal* is the one in which the letter should be published.

Osler had promised to give one of a series of semi-public lectures arranged for by Dr. Flick under the auspices of the Henry Phipps Institute. The first had been given by Trudeau in October and Osler's lecture was scheduled for December 3rd. On the day before, he wrote to his friend Musser:

I was awfully sorry I could not be with you all last night, but I had not my Phipps address written, and I took cold on Sunday, so I thought it was better to stay at home. You asked me about something with reference to our work here. Personally I think the only good thing I have ever done in connection with tuberculosis (though I have written a good many papers) is the article in my text-book, which Pepper always said was the best thing I had ever written. Of our recent work at the hospital, the Laennec Society

[1] 'American and International Congresses on Tuberculosis and Tuberculosis Exhibits for the Years 1904 and 1905.' *American Medicine* ('Letter to Editor'), Dec. 5, 1903, vi. 891–2.

certainly stimulated a great deal of interest, and our hospital and dispensary records have, I think, in the matter of tuberculosis improved very much since. We have started a very good special library of tuberculosis, and this year Mr. Phipps has given us twenty-thousand dollars to have a special out-patient dispensary for our tuberculosis cases, &c.

The lecture, given on December 3rd in the auditorium of Witherspoon Hall, was entitled 'The Home in its Relation to the Tuberculosis Problem',[1] and he began in this fashion:

In its most important aspects the problem of tuberculosis is a home problem. In an immense proportion of all cases the scene of the drama is the home; on its stage the acts are played, whether to the happy issue of a recovery, or to the dark ending of a tragedy, so commonplace as to have dulled our appreciation of its magnitude. In more than 400 homes of this country there are lamentations and woe tonight; husbands for their wives, wives for their husbands, parents for their children, children for their parents. A mere repetition of yesterday's calamities! and if the ears of your hearts are opened you can hear, as I speak, the beating of the wings of the angels of death hastening to the 400 appointed for tomorrow. That this appalling sacrifice of life is in large part unnecessary, that it can be diminished, that there is hope even for the poor consumptive—this represents a revulsion of feeling from an attitude of oriental fatalism which is a triumph of modern medicine. . . . The present crusade against tuberculosis, which is destined to achieve results we little dream of, has three specific objects: first, educational—the instruction of the profession and the instruction of the people; second, preventive—the promotion of measures which will check the progress of the disease in the community; third, curative—the study of methods by which the progress of the disease in individuals may be arrested or healed. The three are of equal importance, and the first and the second closely related and interdependent. The educational aspects of the problem are fundamental. Nothing can be done without the intelligent co-operation of the general practitioners and of the community, and it is a wise action on the part of the Phipps Institute to take up actively this part of the work, and to spread a sound knowledge by lecture courses and by publications.

In the further course of the address he stated that the three pieces of work, of the first rank, so far accomplished in this country were: that of Trudeau in the Adirondacks,

[1] *Medical News*, N.Y., Dec. 12, 1903, and elsewhere.

on the value of sanatoria; of Biggs in New York City, on organization; and of Flick, the Director of the Phipps Institute, in demonstrating the relation of the home to the propagation of the disease, for there 'it is practically born and bred'. He said little about his own part in all this, though the story of the work at the Hopkins during the preceding four years—from the time the sum of money was given by two ladies!—is fully retold, with an account of the home conditions of the consumptives visited by the women medical students, to whom in sequence, by this time, Miss Elizabeth Blauvelt and Miss Esther Rosencrantz had been added.

This address, given in a draughty public hall, served to lay him low for a few days with what he calls his 'periodical *Schnupfen*', in consequence of which he was unable to attend the Janeway dinner in New York. 'Colds' were apparently epidemic in Philadelphia, where some one else was housed with one on the very day of the lecture:

To W. O. from S. Weir Mitchell. 1524 Walnut Street, Phila. 3rd Dec. 1903.

Dear Osler,—I am having just enough of a cold to claim the privilege of a day at home. Hinc illae lachrymae a[t]ramenti, which is I suspect equal to the damn-dog latin of Harvey over which I am more than puzzled. I think a commentary on his Lecture notes would tax the wits of the most ingeniously learned. See p. 7 for one puzzle. Salamon 'Eccles[s] 19. 28'—what on earth has it to do with 'waddle like a puffin'. There is scarce a page without its problem. I wrote you of the lecture, to be adjourned until Jany. I have to thank you for Beaumont which I like very much & if I measured thanks—not so much for the Canada address ['The Master Word'] or rather the first part, the last I find as Harvey says full of Admiry. In quotings on p. 23 I should like to have whispered (see book) from the German Bible. Sufficient unto the day are—not the evil—but the *cares* of the day. The good word about faith and science ['the ordeal of every student of this generation who sooner or later tries to mix the waters of science with the oil of faith'] made me like you more and more. I please myself with yr. phrase of the light that beats upon our homes [hearth] & curses with publicity. But Addison grunted over it, and clever men in his day had their home at Inns & Clubs. I have Beaumont's own copy somewhere of that little classic. Yr. ever friend.

A letter, postmarked December 7, to C. F. Martin shows

that one of his old Montreal colleagues was in ill-health. It reads:

Dear Martin, So sorry to hear of poor Blackader. What a sad time he is having—Please ask Campbell or Murray—one of the florists, to send him a fine bunch of roses & let me have the memo. What an anomalous condition. . . . Love to Bill—tell him I am just off to Milwaukee to put a bung in Mr Pabst. Yours ever, W. O. I will look after your endocarditic honeymooner!

It was his first visit to Milwaukee, where his former house-mate H. V. Ogden had called him for a consultation, and he was given a busy day, ending with a special meeting of the Milwaukee Medical Society, when he made an informal address on medical libraries. Incidentally there were many people to see, one of whom had been the source of much correspondence, and on parting, Osler said: 'Well, I'll have to call you *Ogden's* alkaptonuric friend and *my* ochronotic friend', much to the gentleman's amusement.

To Archibald Garrod from W. O. Dec. 18, 1903.

Thanks for your kindness about the *Lancet* proof.[1] I have just returned from Milwaukee, where I saw Ogden's case. He will send you the full notes. The ochronosis is well marked in the ears and beginning in the sclerotics. It is interesting, too, that he has slight pigmentation, brownish in colour, of the conjunctivae. My old patient returned to town the other day, and I looked him over with the greatest interest. Since I last saw him all the ligamentous tissues about the knuckles and the tendons have become of a steel-grey colour. When he makes a fist the knuckles are bluish-grey and the joints of the fingers also. The staining of the sclerotics has become much more marked. A very remarkable point, by the way, about Ogden's case is that he has the same curious gait as the Jackson brothers—a stoop at the hips, with a curious swinging of the arms. With kind regards and greetings for Christmas and the New Year.

By this time preparations were actively under way for the coming tuberculosis exhibition; and early in December he writes to Parfitt, who since his recovery had been in charge of a successful sanatorium: 'I do hope you and Elliott will send something representing your work for our exhibit. I am looking after the literary side of it, and hope to have

[1] Osler's paper on 'Ochronosis; the pigmentation of cartilages, sclerotics, and skin in alkaptonuria', was published in the *Lancet*, Lond., Jan. 2, 1904.

a most interesting bibliographical display.' And on the 15th to J. G. Adami:

> As you may have heard, we are to have a tuberculosis exhibition here during the last week in January, and are arranging for a series of talks each afternoon. I am instructed by the Committee to ask you to take the hour on Friday, the 29th, at five o'clock. The exhibition will be in McCoy Hall, and the subject of the lecture is of course left to you, either semi-popular, in which case we would invite the public, or strictly professional, in which case we would invite the physicians and medical students of the city.

As an interlude to all this about alkaptonuria and tuberculosis it is pleasant to picture him at home on the Saturday evening of December 26th, his clinical clerks gone for the holidays, reading a Christmas gift of a new edition of Sir Thomas Browne, from which are transcribed into his commonplace-book a page or two of quotations, among them a Golden Rule of Confucius which he soon uses in a paper—'It is a wise rule to take the world as we find it; not always to leave it so.' And still pleasanter to picture him at play with Revere, now well over his whooping-cough but not yet recovered from his violent attack of mythology. The nursery, indeed, was hung with pictures of mythological heroes, and every late afternoon when he and his father were not 'cutting up', having a pillow-fight, or playing with toy trains, sprawled on the nursery floor, the two would be making up imaginary tales from the legends of the ancient heroes. Thus it is that Ulysses *en route* to Montreal sends a birthday card, postmarked 'New York, December 27, 6.30 p.m.', on which was written:

Many happy returns of The Day
to the small Telemachus
Care of Mistress
Penelope
from old Ulysses
on the Island of Aegia

So the last days of the year find him in Montreal giving a paper before the Medico-Chirurgical Society which in the '70's he had done so much to activate and of which H. S. Birkett at this time was President. Shortly before, the Montreal correspondent of the *Canada Lancet*, Dr. Malcolm

Mackay, whom he had never met, had sent him a note which brought in reply a postcard saying: 'Yes, I will give you an abstract. I shall not have my paper ready but shall give a "talk" on our experience here with aneurysm of the abdominal aorta.' A small matter; but Dr. Mackay adds that 'after the meeting there was a reception when I was introduced by Dr. C. F. Martin; and although Dr. Osler had shaken hands with over 200 physicians that night, as soon as he heard "Dr. Mackay" he said: "Oh yes, *Malcolm* Mackay. I will give you my notes before I leave."' There is no difficulty in accounting for Osler's popularity among the profession. At this particular time, a fund for the purpose having been quietly raised among the McGill graduates, he sat for a portrait to commemorate his connexion with the University. It was stated in the notice, sent out by William Gardner asking for five-dollar subscriptions, that 'any amount in excess of that required for the picture will be expended in such a manner as Dr. Osler shall designate'; and the notice ended, 'It is worth the subscription to see what he will do with it.'

CHAPTER XXIII

1904

THE OXFORD CALL

It was to be a hectic spring—and year. It began with rumours of Oxford. But this threat of having his equanimity again disturbed, as in the Edinburgh episode, became obscured by the smoke of the Baltimore fire; by the ensuing rescue of the hospital and school from their financial embarrassment; by the establishment of the National Tuberculosis Association; by the Ingersoll Lecture, and much else besides.

Sir John Burdon Sanderson's intention to resign from the Regius Professorship had become known late in the preceding year, and there had been a good deal of agitation in regard to his successor. During his twenty years in Oxford, Sanderson had done much to advance 'the claim of Medical Science to be regarded as a University study', and he and his colleagues, chiefly Francis Gotch, J. S. Haldane, and Arthur Thomson, being fearful of losing ground already gained, were desirous that James Ritchie, the pathologist of their own group, should continue the tradition. The London graduates, on the other hand, fearful that the earlier efforts of Acland to instil a new spirit into Oxford Medicine were not being continued, expressed themselves as strongly in favour of a clinician, preferably an Oxonian, and a number of eligible candidates were proposed—Church, Payne, Sharkey, Herringham, Schorstein, and Theodore Acland being prominently mentioned.

Who first suggested Osler's name is not certain. There are several who claim the honour. More than one may have voiced the idea. But it is certain that Sir William Broadbent mentioned the possibility to Mr. (now Sir) Herbert Warren, who wrote to Osler on New Year's Day expressing the hope that he might consider some day coming to take up his residence in Oxford. Rumours of this must have reached other ears, in view of the following letter:

From S. Weir Mitchell to W. O. 1524 Walnut Street, Philadelphia,
13th Jan. 1904.

My dear Regius,—'My Son, verify your quotations'—or clarify them. You say yr. Fracas[s] is at the end of Examen Poeticum—3rd part of Miscel[s] Poems 1693—Edited by Dryden. Did he edit himself or Tate or Fracastorius—No such edition can I find in the Brit. Mus. Catl. or Watts. An interesting Memoir of Fracastorius is by Rev. W. P. Greswell 1801. He gives a long quotation fr. the Syphilis Poems—his own translation?—G. as unlike Tate as possible. I find no miscel[y] of date 1693—and if Dryden filched Tate or re-translated, you may find out. However it is an ill wind etc. It sent me to Johnson's Life of Dryden—where I found that D's first poem was on the death by Small Pox of Lord Hastings—His *pustules* he describes as 'rose-buds and—gems' etc. at last as stars, so that finally—being semiconfluent I presume

> 'No comet need foretell his change drew on (*sic*)
> Whose corpse might seem a constellation.'

Is it to be found, that Poem? And this for you—

> 'Oxford to him a dearer name shall be
> Than his own Mother University.'

This is all until we meet—on 27. I have some very fair hash-trash stewing. Yrs, [&c.] Remsen writes me of a dinner—and that, between us, I crave less than a bit of talk with you—over books.

Meanwhile the Oxford graduates had held a meeting in London, on January 5th, and voiced their opinion in *The Times* that 'the Regius Professorship of Medicine should be held by a physician who is representative of Medicine in its widest sense', a statement carrying the intimation that a science-candidate would not receive their support. Boiled down—and it took some heat—the question was, whether the Regius should be an active teacher in the Oxford group who devoted themselves almost entirely to preclinical studies; or whether he should be a man chosen because of his wider professional influence, who could be a link between Oxford and her medical graduates in London. Both sides felt themselves in the right. Pamphlets were circulated. The recommendations of the London group were answered in turn by a printed letter from those in Oxford.

But even the clinicians were in a quandary, for where could a man be found willing to forgo, as some one said, 'the financial rewards to which his abilities entitled him, for a pittance of £400 a year with a position to keep up and a high-sounding title?' The President of the College of Physicians became involved; the Vice-Chancellor was waited upon by delegates from London; it was even feared that Mr. Balfour might take the matter out of the hands of the contending parties and present an entirely independent nomination for ratification by the Crown. Many of the people concerned were Osler's friends, and of the controversy he must have been aware through the British journals, but if he had at that time any intimation, except from the President of Magdalen's note, that his name had even been considered, he at least made no mention of the fact. Indeed, other more engrossing things were happening in Baltimore.

The Tuberculosis Exhibition was held in McCoy Hall the last week in January. It had involved an immense deal of preparation on Osler's part, for he had been made Chairman of the Committee on Organization. But Welch and Osler were endowed with the administrative and social qualities which ensured the success of any such gathering which had their support. It is to be remembered that as an outcome, in part, of Osler's castigation of the Mayor a commission had been appointed by Act of Assembly in 1902 for the purpose of studying the prevalence of tuberculosis in Maryland and its effect on the economic welfare of the State. The exhibition was planned to display the results of the commission's investigations in such a way as to make a powerful appeal to the public mind.

It was a well-timed meeting. Though the antituberculosis movement was gaining momentum, nation-wide propaganda regarding the curability of the disease was needed. To be sure, ever since the time when Brehmer first established an open-air sanatorium for phthisical patients in the Waldenburg Mountains twenty years before the discovery of the tubercle bacillus, people here and there had agitated such a campaign. Its germ lay in the old Climatological Society; the community had learned through Robert Louis Stevenson about Trudeau and the cottages in the Adirondacks; Flick's work in Philadelphia was becoming widely known—indeed as far back as 1898 he had suggested the formation of a national society; A. C. Klebs had organized the tuberculosis workers in Chicago, and there were many other earnest individuals scattered throughout the country who were similarly engaged.

From a purely local standpoint the exhibition, as a popular demonstration not only of the sources and extent but also of the curability of tuberculosis, was successful beyond expectation. But the meeting had a national character as well, for it brought together the leaders of the crusade from all sides. As had been suggested by Osler in his letter of November 25th to S. A. Knopf, advantage was taken of the occasion to urge the formation of a national society of those interested in tuberculosis, in order to harmonize, if possible, certain groups of little-known people who independently had been soliciting support, lay and political, for conflicting congresses. One of them, under the leadership of Dr. Daniel Lewis, was laying plans for an international congress to be held in Washington in April, in spite of the fact that an international *Bureau Central*, an outgrowth of the Berlin and London congresses, had decided on Paris for the 1904 biennial meeting. Another, which had already received government backing through the activity of its lay-leader, Mr. Clarke Bell of the Medico-Legal Society of New York, was to be held in connexion with the St. Louis Exposition in the coming October. Neither of these movements had received the approval or support of the leaders in the profession.

Consequently, on the last day of the meeting a conference of the better-known physicians who were interested in the study of tuberculosis was held in McCoy Hall. William H. Welch, who presided, was authorized to appoint a committee, 'to consider the conditions existing with regard to the proposed Tuberculosis Congress and other national anti-tuberculosis associations in the United States; also to consider the formation of a National Committee to represent this country at the International Congress at Paris.' In accordance with this motion, Welch appointed Osler, Trudeau, Theobald Smith, Adami, Vincent Bowditch, Knopf, Ravenel, Klebs, E. G. Janeway, H. B. Jacobs, Bracken, Flick, and Biggs. It was therefore representative of the best minds in the profession; and this committee, as will be seen, met a month later in New York to take action upon the matters they had been appointed to discuss. Though much more might well be said of the Exhibition itself, it must suffice to call attention to the collection of valuable works illustrating the history of tuberculosis which Osler had taken such pains to gather together. Brief mention of this occurs in the following undated note to Chadwick in Boston:

> Yes, I give the Ingersoll Lecture in May, the 18th, Science and Immortality. Eliot says I am a *specialist* in the subject. So glad the Fletcher fund is completed. What of the frame—is it also settled, fin? Thanks for the pamphlet and in advance for the books. Our exhibit of the literature on Tuberculosis has been most interesting. Have you a 1543 de Fabrica of Vesalius? Yours W. O.

On Sunday morning, February 7th, Osler had gone to Washington to see Senator Hanna, who had recently been taken ill with typhoid fever. He got back in the late afternoon to find the business section of Baltimore in flames. He has laconically written in his account-book: 'Fire began at 11 a.m. Hurst Building—raged until Monday eve. It reached to within two blocks of 1 W. Franklin St and we were all ready to pack up.' It was a close call. There were guests as usual not only at No. 1 but at No. 3 West Franklin Street, and in the afternoon every one gathered in the Oslers' dining-room, where through the southern windows the conflagration could be seen approaching. That Osler, usually imperturbable, was nervous, was evident from the way he twiddled his watch-chain and exceeded his allotted number of cigarettes through the anxious afternoon and evening. A policeman finally came to the door and said the block between Mulberry and Saratoga Streets near by was about to be blown up and that it was time they got ready to leave. Brands were already falling on the roofs in the neighbourhood. A wagon was secured; some precious books were put in trunks; some china picked out; some linen; some clothes. The faithful but agitated black servants cooked an oyster supper and served coffee; Revere was awakened and dressed, and, just as the family was about to leave, the high wind which had been blowing from the south all day shifted and turned the further progress of the conflagration to the south and east. By 2 a.m. they were notified that there was no further danger.

From this devastating fire Baltimore reacted courageously, and a newer and better-built city soon emerged, but for a time many individuals and institutions were hard hit. Among them was the Johns Hopkins Hospital, whose major properties from which rentals were returned now lay in ruins in the wake of the fire. Of all this there is little reference in his letters—except a word, after some days, to let Trudeau know that 'we are doing the Phoenix trick here'. And later in the month to F. C. Shattuck in Boston:

I was perfectly delighted with the Gentle Reader. I have been much entertained. We have so many friends in common that I almost feel as if I knew the author. We had a devil of a time here with the fire. We shall be out about $400,000 at the hospital, but I daresay all will turn out well, and we are not worrying specially.

It was not in Osler's make-up to worry, even though at this time he had been carrying an extra load owing to Mr. Hanna's illness, which required almost daily visits to Washington. Nor was he one to occupy himself by sticking coloured pins in maps to follow the progress of the Russo-Japanese War, which had begun on the day of the Baltimore fire. He hated wars. But there was one episode with which he was concerned later in that month, of sufficient historic interest to deserve the telling. The Canal Treaty with Panama was ratified by the Senate on February 23rd by an overwhelming vote, and Roosevelt was to appoint without loss of time the seven members of the Isthmian Canal Commission—an army officer, a naval officer, and five engineers. He was promptly waited upon by a delegation of physicians, whose spokesman, Dr. Welch, tells the story as follows:

The visit to President Roosevelt relating to Panama Canal affairs was to press upon him the importance of making Gorgas a member of the commission, the creation of which had been authorized shortly before by Congressional action. The members of this delegation represented various organizations such as the A. M. A., the New

York Academy of Medicine, the Philadelphia College of Physicians, etc. An appointment had been made with the President at the White House at 12 noon. I was selected to be the spokesman. We passed through a room crowded with persons waiting to see the President, and I felt that he must begrudge every minute we occupied, especially as what I had to say I had previously communicated to him by letter, and I knew that Leonard Wood had already urged upon him all that I could say and more. I did not occupy more than ten minutes. Curiously enough I cannot remember who else was present in the delegation or whether anyone else spoke, but if Osler and Keen were there they probably did. . . . When we finished presenting our argument, which altogether could not have lasted more than fifteen minutes, President Roosevelt began talking to us and continued for at least twenty minutes, in a very interesting, dramatic and amazingly outspoken fashion. He told us that he did not frame the law enacted by Congress, and it did not meet his ideas of what the situation demanded. He would have preferred a single director, who should select engineers, sanitarians and other experts. Instead of that, he had to pick out seven members to make up a commission and the law provided that no less than five of these should be engineers, without one word about a doctor or a sanitarian. 'How can I under these circumstances', he said, 'put a doctor on the commission?' He said that he fully appreciated the importance of what we had told him, and he asked me to go at once to General Davis and tell him all about Gorgas and the importance of the sanitary side of the work. He sat down and dictated the letter to Davis. I wonder if Osler did not go with me to see Davis? I think that he must have done so. . . .

The upshot was that Gorgas, then only a Major in spite of the record behind him of having rid Havana of yellow fever, went to Panama as a subordinate sanitary officer—not as a commissioner with powers of independent action. The old scandal of 'a life given for every tie' in building the Panama railway was likely to be repeated. When Gorgas demanded screens he was told that shovels were what was needed, and there is many an unnecessary tombstone dating from the early days in the Canal Zone in consequence. All manner of difficulties were put in his way. Indeed, an effort was finally made to have him removed altogether, and it was not until Roosevelt's personal visit to the canal a year or two later that he fully realized for what Welch, Osler, and the others had been appealing. Not until then was Gorgas made a member of the commission, and the President wrote to his former Secretary of War, Elihu Root, saying that if there were only more unselfish and public-spirited men in the country like Welch and Osler willing to advise him, his executive life would be simplified.

As already stated, the probability that the Baltimore fire might seriously curtail the work of the hospital did not appear to disturb Osler's equanimity. There were possible ways out, and remembering a certain letter of March 4, 1902, telling how his Text-book had so interested certain people with large funds at their disposal that an Institute for Medical Research had been founded, he ventured to write to Mr. Gates to learn whether John D. Rockefeller might be induced to come to the aid of the Hopkins in its embarrassed condition. In response, Mr. Rockefeller sent to Baltimore his personal representative in his benefactions, Starr J. Murphy, who made a survey of the hospital and an accurate calculation of its losses, with which information he returned to New York. Meanwhile, Osler sent the following characteristic note to the President of the Hospital Board:

7. iii. 04.

Dear Judge Harlan, In case we do not get a supplementary endowment for the Hospital I shall be very glad to place my salary ($5,000) for ten years at the disposal of the Trustees to be used in maintaining our publications. Please say nothing of it outside of the Committee. Sincerely yours, &c.

The purport of Mr. Murphy's visit must have leaked out, if one may judge from a letter to Mr. H. M. Hanna written the same day. Mr. Hanna was a brother of the Senator and an equally remarkable man, with whom Osler had come in contact even before the Senator's fatal illness. He was a friend of many doctors: indeed, had leanings towards the profession which in his father's footsteps he had once intended to follow. He was himself a great benefactor of Medicine in his own community at Cleveland, where he had been a former business associate of John D. Rockefeller and Oliver H. Payne, both of whom he had influenced in their benefactions in the same direction. 'Mel' Hanna, as he was known among his intimates, passed his winters in

Georgia, where he was accustomed to go about with Osler's 'Practice' under his arm prescribing for the negroes on his plantation who might be ill. Hence Osler's title:

To H. M. Hanna from W. O. 7. iii. '04.

Dear Dr. Hanna, I do hope the 'Sun' may be right. We have no news so far. Mr. Rockefeller has sent for full information as to our funds &c. We shall be 'out' about $60,000 a year. It is interesting to note the spirit of loyalty shown by the Doctors & Nurses. There have been many offers of salaries on the part of officials of the Hospital & many nurses have offered to come back & take wards for 3 to 12 mos, without any pay. With kind regards Sincerely yours, Wm OSLER. Thanks all the same for your kind letter & for your congratulations to Mr. Rockefeller.

Betweentimes, the hospital life went on as before: classes continued; Ehrlich came and gave the first of the Herter Lectures series on the new subject of physical chemistry; H. B. Jacobs, one of the 'latch-keyers' of 3 West Franklin Street, got married; Flexner was called to the new Rockefeller Institute; new patients came and went; even old ones were not forgotten. Whenever the memory of some one passed into Osler's mind, off went a note or a postcard:

11/3/04.

Dear Mrs. Curtis, We have come to the conclusion that it is time you returned to Ward C. *We* means your entire staff including several of the men on the Surgical side. I am sure your storage batteries need re-charging & six weeks—say April 15 to June 14—would be a most favourable time. Dr McCrae was never in better form & Dr. Howard has an additional experience which would be most invaluable in your case. At present he is devoted to a St Louis widow stowed in Ward B. under my guardianship! Someone showed me a photograph of a lady said to be you with two chicks, but there was a mistake. 'Twas an elder sister of the chicks I know! I hope you keep in good form, but if you feel the slightest inkling of relapse—return—there is danger in delay. Yours (on behalf of the staff) most sincerely, Wm OSLER.

Or in place of a note or a postcard it would be flowers, a book—even a barrel of apples to Pierre Marie, who declares they are the best in the world: 'Quel admirable pays que celui où les pommes et les hommes sont aussi excellents!' What happened as the outcome of Mr. Murphy's survey is well known. Early in April came a letter from John D.

Rockefeller, jr., to Osler, stating that 'in view of the high work which the hospital and medical school are doing in medical instruction and research, including the training of nurses, which work he understands will otherwise be materially curtailed because of losses, my father will give $500,000 to Johns Hopkins Hospital.' To this Osler replied:

Friday eve.

Dear Mr. Rockefeller, Your letter brought joy to us all, not only to those of us immediately connected with the work of the Hospital, but to all the citizens. Indeed to a larger circle, as shown by the letters & telegrams which we have received, it has given the liveliest satisfaction. Please express to your father my sense of the deep appreciation of his generosity With kind regards, [&c.]

While all this was going on, the muddle among the tuberculosis experts had come to a head. Into this Osler, as Chairman of the recently appointed committee, had been unwillingly drawn. It would appear that he was in favour of joining forces with the Lewis faction; to this Dr. Flick was utterly opposed, and threatened to withdraw the support of the group at the Phipps Institute unless an entirely new and third organization was formed. The committee which had been appointed by Welch at the Baltimore conference was brought together, on February 27th, at a dinner given by Osler in New York. They agreed upon a number of delegates who should represent the various groups of people and institutions interested in tuberculosis, and adjourned to meet again a month later. Subsequently, Dr. Flick suggested that this next meeting, one of actual organization, be held in Philadelphia on March 28th, on which date Maragliano, an Italian, was to give one of the series of addresses arranged by the Phipps Institute. A vast deal of correspondence passed. The position taken by Welch and Osler is evident from their letters to Dr. Flick:

I do not see at all [Osler wrote, March 18th], if the organization of the Lewis Congress is practically handed over to us, what possible reason you could have for keeping out. A third organization is out of the question, and enough good leaven can be inserted into the present dough to make a really good loaf. What would you propose as an alternative? We ought to have the matter pretty definitely settled among us before the meeting, or there will be no end of confusion.

And Welch a few days later wrote:

> I understand your position with reference to the Bell and Lewis Congresses. The Bell affair is absolutely out of any consideration. The question is whether the Lewis Society is as bad as you think it is. I confess that I do not know much about it, but it has the support of men who will have to be reckoned with on account of their official positions as for other reasons in a National Crusade against Tuberculosis, and whom it would not be desirable to alienate. The organization seems to be almost inchoate, and probably could be moulded into any desired form by those who took hold of it. It is too bad that there should have arisen such a muddle, and possibly the best course may be to let the troubled waters settle before the leading men in the profession take any positive course of action. I feel that men like you and Trudeau who have given strength and direction to the antituberculosis movement in this country should have the main say in determining what it is best to do under these circumstances.

At the last moment Maragliano cabled that because of ill-health he would be unable to appear. Nevertheless the meeting was held, with Osler in the chair, and sixty-five of the most eminent tuberculosis workers in the country in attendance. After some heated discussion, the motion made by Dr. Flick, that a United States Society for the Study of Tuberculosis be organized, was carried. Though it was contrary to his judgement, as would appear, Osler submitted with good grace to his defeat and, as Chairman, appointed a committee of five, consisting of Trudeau, Biggs, Flick, Welch, and Sternberg, to prepare a constitution. This committee met a month later in New York, when a board of directors was chosen; these gentlemen in turn met on June 6th at Atlantic City, where Trudeau was enthusiastically elected the first President of the new society, with Osler and Biggs as Vice-Presidents; and Osler was also made Chairman of the International Committee empowered to represent the society in accordance with the constitution of the International Central Bureau.

As the Baltimore years rolled on he had become more and more overwhelmed with strictly professional work, and in this spring of 1904 it had almost reached the breaking-point. Recognized from Hudson Bay to the Gulf, from Nova Scotia to California, as the doctor's doctor, even though he might curtail the number of ordinary professional consultations this could not be done when some member of a physician's immediate family was concerned. Love of his profession meant love of his professional kind, and the afternoon was rare indeed that some doctor from somewhere, ill himself, or with an ailing child or mother or wife, was not in his consulting-room—what is more, at tea or at his hospitable table, or both. Much of his treatment was psychotherapeutic, and though he thoroughly despised the chicanery of psychoanalysis his personality was such that he could effectively administer at a single session common-sense advice which was usually followed. 'She has been worried and apprehensive [he wrote to a patient's doctor] over the possibility of a third operation on her stomach. I have urged her to take more food, to live out-of-doors, and to keep her mind out of her bread-basket.' And this to a neurasthenic doctor: 'It is very satisfactory to feel that you have got a good grip on your grey cortex. Go slowly and attend to your work, live a godly life, and avoid mining shares. I doubt if quinine could have very much influence.'

To C. F. Martin of Montreal. Sunday.

Dear Martin, I shall twist my Fraülein's neck! She is a daughter of the Philistines. I suppose she *thōt* (Lord Strathcona's usage, to be adopted by the Dept. of Eng. at McGill so Pr. Pet. [Principal Peterson] informs me!) you were in the Ass. of Am. Phy. list. I am sending them with my own hand, with inscription &c. so your forgiveness I know is assured. Is your name up for A A P? I asked Stewart about it. I hope Billy Francis is working well. He knows more about Astrophel & Stella than amyotrophic lateral sclerosis. I have not sent your bill yet to those Cincinnati people. I will enclose it with mine—they are well to do, but the poor soul is 'in the dust'. Yours, &c., Wm OSLER. Love to Hamlet. Campbell H. is a great success. Working like a Trojan.

To John H. Musser. 1/5/04.

Dear J. H., How the deuce do you find time to make such good revisions? I have just been reading the section on Blood pressure in your New Edition. Many thanks for it. 'Tis a bully book & a great credit to you. I have been swamped with work lately—& the wards are surcharged—we reached a high water mark in the private rooms—30 this week. Nine cases of pernicious anaemia in the house since March 1st & three cases outside—'Tis epidemic! Hope to see you in Washington next week. Yours W. O.

Indeed, his being so swamped had much to do with a momentous decision soon to be made. With all this pressure upon him the date of the Ingersoll Lecture was approaching, and though he had been making notes and giving thought to it during the preceding months there had been scant time for the sort of preparation the subject, once entered upon, really deserved. He, indeed, had agonized over it perhaps more than any of his previous addresses and it was rewritten and redrafted many times. The following letter to the Dean written at this time not only mentions his expected absence but dwells upon other matters which give an idea of the meagre salaries of clinical teachers of twenty years ago:

To W. H. Howell from W. O. Baltimore, May 14, 1904.

I have to go to Boston next Wednesday, to give the lecture on 'Science and Immortality' which Welch has so kindly written for me. There are one or two things which I wish you would bring up at the Faculty Meeting:

In the first place, Futcher who is Associate Professor of Medicine and does a great deal of work, and good work too, has a beggarly salary for that position: $300. Do you not think it could be increased to some decent rate? He does a great deal of teaching, and he ought to get at least $700; but whatever the Committee thinks.

Secondly, if there is no objection I should like to have some of my Instructors in Medicine lifted to the rank of Associates: Rufus I. Cole, Thomas R. Brown and L. P. Hamburger. They have been doing good work for some years.

Thirdly, would you please talk to Abel about McCrae and the question of practical therapeutics. McCrae leaves the house this year. He is a very valuable man, a good teacher, fond of materia medica and therapeutics, and could, I think, add greatly to the strength of the section if he could be appointed on the therapeutical side in clinical therapeutics, either as an Associate Professor or whatever Abel thinks, and take charge of systematic instruction in the third and fourth year in out-patient and ward therapeutics. It is a weak point in our teaching which I am sure he could strengthen with great advantage. We need not pay him much salary at first. I should think five or six hundred dollars a year would be sufficient...

There is hardly any place but Harvard that could have been left a bequest of $5,000, the income to be devoted to an annual lecture on 'The Immortality of Man'. Given such a bequest, there is hardly any place but Harvard, under a president like Charles W. Eliot, which could have kept such a lectureship going. Osler's predecessors in the Ingersoll Lectureship series had been George A. Gordon, William James, Benjamin Ide Wheeler, Josiah Royce, and John Fiske—a theologian, a philosopher, a philologist, a psychologist, a historian. How Osler was captured as the sixth lecturer has been told.

As Welch had said in refusing the lectureship, 'science has nothing to do with immortality'; and after Osler's lecture Mr. Eliot expressed himself as greatly disappointed, for instead of hearing a scientific discourse on the subject, if there could be such a thing, he had listened merely to a brilliant and charming essay. Indeed, the lecturer in an early paragraph had shifted the burden on to the shoulders of his 'lifelong mentor':

> One of my colleagues, hearing that I was to give this lecture, said to me: 'What do you know about immortality? You will say a few pleasant things, and quote the "Religio Medici", but there will be nothing certain.' In truth, with his wonted felicity, my lifelong mentor, Sir Thomas Browne, has put the problem very well when he said: 'A dialogue between two infants in the womb concerning the state of this world might handsomely illustrate our ignorance of the next, whereof methinks, we yet discourse in Plato's denne—the cave of transitive shadows—and are but embryon philosophers.'

The only portion of the address that met with Mr. Eliot's genuine approval was the brief reference to the study Osler had made of the last sensations of the dying. For the head nurses in the wards had taken down at his request, for some time, the exact words of dying patients. 'The great majority gave no sign one way or the other: like their birth their death was a sleep and a forgetting.' Raised in a rectory, destined in his early days for the ministry, conversant as few men of his time with Holy Writ, a thorough-going Christian, to stand before a lay audience and discuss with frankness, clear sanity, and kindliness of spirit whether 'mankind's conquest of nature has made the individual more or less hopeful of a life beyond the grave' must have been an ordeal. Some said afterwards that he offended neither side; others that he offended both. But as to the brilliant quality of the essay there could be no doubt. The

Athenaeum, in a review of the series as a whole, referred to them as superb examples of the art of lecturing, but added that, of the six, Osler's was 'the most common-sense and at the same time the most literary'. He made as a framework the triple classification of mankind into the Laodiceans who accept a belief in immortality, yet live their lives uninfluenced by it; the Gallionians who put the supernatural altogether out of their lives; and the Teresians with whom this faith is the controlling influence. In his conclusion he thus addressed himself to the young men in the audience:

As perplexity of soul will be your lot and portion, accept the situation with a good grace. The hopes and fears which make us men are inseparable, and this wine-press of Doubt each one of you must tread alone. It is a trouble from which no man may deliver his brother or make agreement with another for him. Better that your spirit's bark be driven far from the shore—far from the trembling throng whose sails were never to the tempest given—than that you should tie it up to rot at some Lethean wharf. On the question before us wide and far your hearts will range from those early days when matins and evensong, evensong and matins, sang the larger hope of humanity into your young souls. In certain of you the changes and chances of the years ahead will reduce this to a vague sense of eternal continuity, with which, as Walter Pater says, none of us wholly part. In a very few it will be begotten again to the lively hope of the Teresians; while a majority will retain the sabbatical interest of the Laodicean, as little able to appreciate the fervid enthusiasm of the one as the cold philosophy of the other. Some of you will wander through all phases, to come at last, I trust, to the opinion of Cicero, who had rather be mistaken with Plato than be in the right with those who deny alto gether the life after death: and this is my own *confessio fidei*.

It was not a particularly well-delivered address. Osler did not shine in this regard, and though dignified, was without oratorical bearing on a platform. On this occasion his wife, who sitting with her mother and among her own people was a distinctly agitated member of the audience, is said to have remarked that she 'wished Willie would not rub the calf of his leg with his other foot to stir up his ideas'. But even if this were true, probably no one else observed it. At an informal reception after the lecture President Eliot mentioned in the presence of Mrs. Revere that her son-in-law seemed to have a great reluctance to come and live among his relatives, whereupon Osler quickly replied that it was Mrs. Osler who objected. What for a year or more had been lurking in the President's mind is explained by the following letter:

To F. C. Shattuck from President Eliot. Harvard University, May 23, 1904.

The Corporation would like very much to get Dr. Osler of Johns Hopkins to spend one year at Harvard—that is, from October 1st to June 1st or July 1st—on the endowed professorship of hygiene which is waiting to be filled. The professorship has been established for the benefit of the students in Cambridge and not as a Medical School professorship. The incumbent is supposed to advise and generally befriend the students in Cambridge, to give some lectures but not many, to act as a consulting physician among them on occasion, but not ordinarily to practise among them or to give stated instruction either in Cambridge or at the Medical School. He would be free to do any hospital work which seemed to him desirable, and to act as a consultant anywhere.

The duties of this professorship are really to be invented; and that is a strong reason, in the minds of the Corporation, for getting Dr. Osler to hold the Chair for a year. When he was in Cambridge to give the Ingersoll Lecture I talked with him on the subject, but found that on account of his great interest in developing clinical instruction he would bring himself with difficulty to leave even for eight or nine months his opportunities at the Johns Hopkins Hospital. . . . It occurred to me, after I had talked with him, that he had some hesitation about coming to Boston temporarily with freedom to act as consulting physician, lest he might interfere with the practice of some Boston physician. Could you not relieve him entirely of this apprehension, and therefore persuade him to undertake this peculiar and interesting job as a pioneer and inventor? . . .

He would have been an ideal person for such a free-lance position, the duties of which were 'to be invented'. What he subsequently made out of his position in Oxford was just what Mr. Eliot felt was needed at Harvard. And before leaving this account of the Ingersoll Lecture it may be said that the honorarium thereof was donated to the Boston Medical Library for the purchase of some much-needed show-cases in which a few of the bibliographical treasures Chadwick was gathering might be laid out for display in the O. W. Holmes reading-room.

Dear Musser, Just back from Boston. I leave on Tuesday next. I have promised to go to the country next Sunday, a patient of Guitéras & an old patient of yours from Havana is here. Guitéras wishes you to see him also. He came last eve. I have not yet seen him. Will let you know & if you come down arrange to spend the night. Your address is A.1. Get it into the hands of the Hospital Managers. Have your secretary make out a list. They are the people to attack. Yours, W. O.

It was Musser's year as President of the American Medical Association and he must have submitted his address on 'Some Aspects of Medical Education' for Osler's criticism. It was indeed on Osler's favourite theme: that every hospital should function as a school. The meeting, which was held in Atlantic City, June 7–10, brought out what was then regarded as a record attendance of over 2,000 members. On the preceding afternoon, of Monday, June the 6th, Osler presided as usual at the meeting of medical librarians, and as a body they dined as his guests at the Hotel Traymore that evening. On the same day the delegates of the new Association for the Study and Prevention of Tuberculosis met as appointed, with Osler again in the chair. Of this meeting the following incident is recalled by W. H. Bergtold of Denver:

Among many topics relating to the function and scope of the new organization, mention was made of the spread of the disease among the blacks, and the question had been raised of including coloured people in the membership. To this a Southern physician made answer, repeatedly referring to the black race as 'niggers'. When it came time to close the discussion, Osler made appropriate remarks on the various matters which had been brought up, and in alluding to the admission of coloured members he was obliged to refer to the physician who had used the term 'nigger'. Not knowing, or having forgotten, this gentleman's name he hesitated just a second, and then quickly said with his kind smile and characteristic good humour: 'Oh, you know. I mean my melanotic friend,' which brought down the house, the Southern physician included.

The story of the Regius Professorship, interrupted by the Baltimore fire, may now be resumed. The impasse was broken when two names, those of Sir Patrick Manson and Dr. Osler, had finally been suggested to the Prime Minister as eligible candidates outside of the University circle; and Balfour must at once have written to Burdon Sanderson, who had been away on a long vacation because of ill-health, Professor Thomson meanwhile acting as his deputy.

Sanderson apparently had never considered his old pupil as a possible successor, and Osler's earlier refusal to stand for the Edinburgh position was supposed to be due to his unwillingness to comply with the traditional regulations concerning testimonials. This, however, for a Crown appointment was not required, and no sooner was his name mentioned to Sanderson than he clapped his hand to his forehead and said, 'That 's it—the very man!'

To W. O. from Sir John Burdon Sanderson. Oxford,
June 8, 1904.

Dear Professor,—You are no doubt aware that I am on the point of vacating the Regius Professorship of Medicine here. The appointment of my successor is in the hands of the Prime Minister (Mr. Balfour) who in this matter acts independently of the University. He appears at present to be unable to decide on the proper course to be taken. My colleagues and I have placed before him our opinion in favour of appointing our 'Reader in Pathology' who is also Director of the Pathological Laboratory, he being in our judgement a man of higher scientific position than any one *to be had in the United Kingdom* at present. It appears, however, that certain objections have been suggested to Mr. Balfour which from a statesman's point of view have value, however groundless they may seem to us.

This being the position of matters, it has seemed desirable to communicate to the Minister our hope that if, for the reasons referred to, he is unable to take the course we suggested several months ago, he should as the next best course ask some distinguished representative of the science of Medicine, outside of this University, to consent to occupy the position. I now write to ask you whether we may venture to entertain the hope that you might be induced to accept the position if it were offered to you.

I think I should add that my only reason for resigning my post is that declining health and strength make me unable to do the work efficiently. As you will see from the paper sent by this post the work is very light. The Regius Professor need not reside more than one-third of the year, so that he can, if he likes, avail himself of the proximity of London for any work or purpose that may require his presence.

I understand that you are to be in Oxford at the meeting of the B. M. Association. Will you and Mrs. Osler be our guests? You would find my house conveniently situated for the business of the meeting. I would have written sooner but I have been ill and have only lately found myself in a position to make any arrangements.

The story may be continued by the following account

supplied by Lady Osler, who at this juncture was visiting her mother:

As we never paid any attention to birthdays, I was surprised to hear that W. O. would arrive at Canton, Sunday morning, June 19, 1904, to be with me on my birthday. Revere and I were then on our way to Murray Bay where we had taken a cottage for the summer. Ned Revere drove Revere and me to meet the early train from Boston. A twinkle in W. O.'s eye made me feel something unusual was in the air. He sat on the back seat with me. Directly we started he thrust a letter into my hand and placed his finger on his lips to signify I must not exclaim. It was Sir John Burdon Sanderson's letter suggesting his appointment as his successor to the Regius Professorship at Oxford. As I read the letter I felt a tremendous weight lifted from my shoulders as I had become very anxious about the danger of his keeping on at the pace he had been going for several years in Baltimore. When we reached the house, Mother was on the verandah and there was no moment for explanation. Immediately after breakfast we went into the garden alone, and I said: 'Thank Heaven, relief has come; but unfortunately the telegraph-office is closed here on Sunday and we cannot cable your willingness to be a candidate.' He jokingly reproached me for my readiness to leave America, and returned to Baltimore on the night of the 20th, sending the cable as he passed through Boston, telling Sir John he would consider it, and discuss the matter when he reached Oxford.

Sir J. Burdon Sanderson from W. O. 1 West Franklin Street, [Tuesday June] 21st.

Dear Sir John,—I feel highly flattered that my name should be mentioned in connection with the Chair. I am sorry that so good a man as Ritchie should be passed over. There are so many things to be considered that I cabled you asking if an immediate decision was wanted or whether I could confer with you upon the question in Oxford. In many ways I should like to be considered a candidate. While very happy here and with splendid facilities, probably unequalled in English-speaking countries, I am over-worked and find it increasingly hard to serve the public and carry on my teaching. I have been in harness actively for thirty years, and have been looking forward to the time when I could ease myself of some of the burdens I carry at present. With the income from my book we have a comfortable competency, so that I am in a measure independent. My only doubt relates to the somewhat relative duties of the Chair. I am interested in clinical teaching, am fond of it and have acquired some degree of aptitude for bedside work which gives me a certain value in the profession. I should miss sadly the daily contact with the students, unless I could arrange for clinical work in London. On the other hand, I have a mass of unfinished literary material on hand which the academic leisure of a new place would enable me to complete. Thanks for your kind invitation. Mrs. Osler does not accompany me. I have already accepted an offer from the Dean of Christ Church. . . .

The following note written the same day to Lafleur intimates in a brief sentence what is on his mind:

Dear L. So glad to hear that you had a good rest & a profitable trip. I am working hard this spring—good p.g. class & have stood the work very well considering that it is my 30th consecutive session. 'Tis time to quit! I go to Boston on Tuesday to get the LL.D. at Harvard. Then on to Montreal on Wednesday eve. Look out for me Thursday. I shall lunch with you D V & take the boat to Quebec in the eve. McCrae goes out of the house in July. He, C—— & I sail July 16th for a short run. Mrs. O was afraid to risk the damp &c after her sad experience last summer with the asthma. Yours ever, W. O.

On June 30th, the day after his LL.D. was conferred at the Harvard Commencement, a long session of the Executive Committee of the Tuberculosis Association was held in Boston; and from there he went on to spend a fortnight at Murray Bay, whence issued a shower of hand-written notes on various subjects, some of which tell of trout-fishing with 'Isaac Walton', who is very happy; whereas matters in which he had become involved are mentioned in others:

To Miss Charlton. Caribou Cottage, Pointe-à-Pic. [undated]

I was sorry that you left so soon, as there were many things I wished to talk to you about. I hated to trouble you on the holiday but it was my only day in town [Montreal] and I had to arrange about the photographing of some of the old familiar specimens. I shall ask you to send a few books. I wish you would look among your duplicate Amer. Jr. of the Med. Sciences for the Jan. 1902 no. with a paper by Dr. Delafield on Treatment of Pleurisy. I would like it very much. We all missed you so much at the Librarians' Meeting. Everyone asked after you, &c.

To Ex-President Gilman. 7th [July]

Thanks for your note received here to-day—& for the additions, which pleased me greatly. I am publishing this summer a little volume ['Aequanimitas &c.'] of collected addresses—for the boys!—and I have dedicated it to you—without your knowledge and consent! You will not mind I know. With love to Mrs. Gilman, Sincerely yours, &c. I sail for England next week—short trip, as Mrs Osler and the boy are here.

To Professor Russell H. Chittenden. 9th [July]

I have undertaken to edit a System of Medicine for Lea Bros, & I write to ask if you will not contribute a section of 75 pp. to Vol I on Metabolism & Nutrition. General considerations—Disturbances in disease—over & under nutrition &c. You have the matter so well in hand that it should not be much trouble and a presentation of the question from the modern standpoint would be very helpful. Would you send me a line to the University Club, New York, before Friday as I am sailing on Saturday. Lea Bros. pay at the rate of $4. a page. With kind regards to Mrs. Chittenden.

Not long before this time there had been started at Trudeau's Sanitarium a semi-popular journal to encourage the open-air treatment of tuberculosis. This had come to Osler's attention the month before, when he wrote the first of these two characteristic notes to the anonymous editor; and now, though busy with other matters, he found time to send them something for publication:

To Lawrason Brown:

I enclose five dollars for five subscriptions to the *Outdoor Life*, the addresses to which they are to be sent being given below.

1. Dr. Wm. Osler, 1 W. Franklin St., Baltimore.
2. Library of the Med. & Chir. Faculty, 747 N. Eutaw St.
3. Miss Adelaide Proctor, 47 Green St., Cumberland, Md.
4. Mrs. John J. Gibson, Room 1220, N.Y. Life Bldg., Chicago.
5. To someone who you think would enjoy it.

To the Same: Pointe-à-Pic, P.Q. vii. 11. 04.

I enclose you a little memo of Fracastorius on the contagiousness of Phthisis which may be of interest enough to put in your useful paper. It was nice to see Trudeau looking so well. I leave for England on Saturday the 16th by the Campania from New York. I hope you will have a good summer—do not overwork. You must get a good holiday in Europe. Wm Osler.

To judge from the following letter, on his way through Montreal he must have seen with C. F. Martin a patient with an obscure malady, and he had evidently passed his afternoon before sailing at the New York Academy of Medicine in search of information regarding it:

To C. F. Martin: University Club, New York.
Friday [July 15].

I have been looking up the Hughlings Jackson triad to-day & have not been able to find a very good account. Bruce in Gibson's text-book is the best. An Italian article has all the cases, but the reference is at home. I would like very much to refer to Judge B——'s case when I publish my paper. Would you ask Roddick if I could have a photo of the tongue protruded &, if possible in the mouth too. The lip points in different directions in the two positions, & could you see if the left side of the palate is paralysed—it usually is. If the Judge could stand a camera on the back of his neck also—to show the atrophy of the upper Trapezius 'twould be pleasant. Let him mask the upper face when the tongue is photographed. Send me a memo of the cost of the photo. I wish you were coming with us. I have been beguiled into editing a 7 (! ! !) volume System of Medicine, (McCrae to do the dirty work) & shall need your help. What would you like to write—think & say. Yours ever, W. O.

Early the following morning he sailed with his two young friends—the three occupying the same cabin. The night before, they had dined unwisely and too well at the University Club, and Osler for a few days was somewhat stricken —below decks. On being offered the assistance of a paregoric tablet he inserted the minute object not in his mouth but in a crevice under McCrae's upper berth, where he could contemplate it as though it were Digby's Powder of Sympathy. And so he was cured. His habits aboard ship were interesting. His first act was to fill to overflowing the rack in his berth with the books and papers he intended to use. Always the first awake, he stayed in his bunk all morning reading and writing for some four or five hours, and there was plenty for him to do, as his paper for the British Medical Association had to be put together. By noon he would appear on deck, free from care, the liveliest person aboard; and soon the half-dozen doctors on the passenger list, together with Francis Verdon, the ship's surgeon, were organized into the 'North Atlantic Medical Society' which met every afternoon at tea-time, and held its final meeting on July 22nd, when a fictitious programme of papers was presented, with amusing jibes on the various members.

Any one who would keep on Osler's trail during a first

day in London must needs have good staying qualities. It is recalled that on this occasion, having been roused at 4 a.m. in the Mersey for an early landing, and having reached London by the boat train at noon, nothing would do but that the remnants of the N. A. Medical Society should go out to Haslemere and visit Jonathan Hutchinson. This was done, a delightful afternoon and evening being spent there, but when at midnight they got back to town the eldest member of the 'society', Dr. James Tyson, handed in his resignation. The pace was too much for him. The next day, a day of shopping and sight-seeing, was even more strenuous. It began with the White Star Office; to Brown, Shipley's; to the tailor's in Savile Row, where it took about ten minutes to order and be measured for four suits of clothes; to the Ulster House ditto for overcoats; to the College of Physicians; to Sotheby's auction rooms in Wellington Street; to Maggs Brothers, &c.—to account for the morning alone. It was, of course, done in one of the picturesque old hansom cabs long since vanished from the London streets. That evening, on dining with H. D. Rolleston, he casually remarked: 'Do you think I'm sufficiently senile to become Regius Professor at Oxford?'—a remark which so misled Rolleston that when told later that Osler would accept, he emphatically denied it.

During the Oxford meeting of the British Medical Association, Osler, at least in the eyes of his two young companions, occupied the centre of the stage, and it was not long before they heard to their dismay some rumours of the pressure that was being brought to bear upon him to accept the Regius Professorship. On the evening of the 26th, in the Sheldonian Theatre, came Dr. Collier's presidential address on the 'Growth and Development of the Oxford Medical School'—a timely subject. The customary vote of thanks was moved by Clifford Allbutt, and Osler in seconding it spoke most effectively in regard not only to traditions and ideals, but to the necessity of combining them with common sense. Though an impromptu speech, his familiarity with Oxford traditions and Oxford medical worthies was shown by his pointing out that John Locke should have been included among the long list from

Roger Bacon to Henry Acland whom Dr. Collier had mentioned.

On the following afternoon, before a brilliant assemblage again in the Sheldonian, the Doctor of Science degree was conferred in Convocation upon Allbutt, Sir William Macewen, Jonathan Hutchinson, Sir Patrick Manson, and one or two more, with Osler the last; he receiving an unexpected and prolonged ovation which brought an unusual colour even to his dark skin. It was a busy and exciting week, with the usual festivities: a soirée at the Museum, a concert in the garden of St. John's, a garden-party at Blenheim and another at Warwick Castle, excursions on the river and elsewhere, in addition to the scientific sessions, at one of which he gave his paper, written on the steamer, on the Treatment of Pleurisy; and at the annual dinner in Christ Church Hall he must reply to a toast—'the Guests'.

In spite of the fact that he had often said his ideal of life would be to live within an hour of the British Museum and to have *The Times* on his breakfast-table, he had difficulty in coming to a decision, and so wrote to his wife. She got his letter at Murray Bay one Sunday morning, routed out Madame Rousseau at the telegraph-office and cabled: 'DO NOT PROCRASTINATE ACCEPT AT ONCE.' This message he showed to his anxious young friends, though it was folded over, with only the 'do not procrastinate' portion visible, so that they were left uncertain until the return home whether 'accept' or 'refuse' was the next word.

Osler meanwhile had gone to North Berwick for a visit with Schäfer, leaving an impression on Oxford which is indicated by the following letter, written by the President of Magdalen to the Prime Minister the day after the B. M. A. adjourned:

Magdalen College, Oxford, July 31, 1904.

. . . What I have to say is this. Dr. Osler has been here this last week. I had some little talk with him. I found that the idea of his coming had been mooted to him by Sir John Burdon Sanderson. He gave me the impression that if he were offered the post he would take it. And if he did come I believe he would really practically unite parties as no one else could. Over and above this I understand Sir Victor Horsley would approve this appointment. But I have in particular one very strong and interesting piece of evidence. Sir William Broadbent who is of course a man of special eminence and standing and has the advantage of being quite outside our schools and their interests (and prejudices) was as it happened staying here as my guest, last week. He told me he thought this appointment of Dr. Osler would be a magnificent one for us and full of advantage for the cause of medical education and science in this country and would be recognized and welcomed as such by the medical world generally.

Further than this, I could not but be struck by the very good reception and welcome which Dr. Osler received both when he spoke on several occasions and when he came up for his honorary degree at the Theatre. His speeches, too, impressed me very much. He is a philosophic and cultivated man, a student and lover of Locke and Burton and so far the kind of man whom Oxford generally, I believe, would welcome. It would also, I think, be a very interesting and pleasing thing from the Imperial point of view just now to appoint a Professor to Oxford who is a Canadian by birth and a Professor in the United States. I might say more, but will not trouble you with a still longer letter. If you have not yet decided to prefer Dr. Osler perhaps you will let these considerations have what weight in your own exhaustive and deliberate estimate you think they are entitled to. . . . With apologies for writing so much—I hope not more than the situation deserves—I have the honour to be, Yours very faithfully,

T. Herbert Warren (P. of M.)

Balfour's letter asking him to take the Chair reached Osler on August 4th, the day before he sailed on the *Cedric* for home, and he accepted with the request that the fact be not made known for a fortnight. He said no word of his decision to the survivor of his two companions, until landing, though the fact that the writing-room steward, long before the end of the voyage, ran out of U.S.A. postage-stamps, indicated that something unusual was being communicated to countless people by an olive-complexioned man who sat in the corner and industriously scribbled for several hours each day—notes like the following:

To W. S. Thayer: S.S. *Cedric*, Aug. 6th.

You will be surprised when I tell you that I have accepted the Chair of Medicine at Oxford ;—to leave next Spring ! 'Tis a serious step, but I have considered it well from all points. I am on the down grade, the pace of the last three winters has been such that I knew

I was riding for a fall. Better to get out decently in time, & leave while there is still a little elasticity in the rubber. It will be an awful wrench to part with all you dear boys, but I shall only cut off 4 years as I had firmly decided to chuck everything at 60. We can have a last good winter's work together, I hope, before I lapse into a quiet academic life. Mrs Osler is strongly in favour of the move, which is a mercy. The offer or suggestion came last spring from Sanderson, the present occupant. I told him I would decide when I came over. Balfour formally offered me the post—'tis a crown appointment—yesterday, & I accepted. Love to Sister Susan. Yours ever, W. O.

This was the general tenor of the notes. Most of the recipients have kept them. His mother was told that 'it will be much better for Revere in every way & I will have a quieter life. We can come out every year & I dare say see more of you than we have done of late'. To Weir Mitchell he wrote: 'Just twenty years ago you & Mrs. Mitchell were important factors in inducing me to come to Philadelphia and you have been ever since a guide & friend. To you then one of the first I must tell of another change in my life.' To his colleague Halsted, that he is tired of the rushing life and that the peace and repose of the old university appeals to him, for he has been heading down hill and the pace has told. 'The worst will be parting from my old colleagues', he added. 'No man ever had better, & I hate to think that I should be the first to break the happy circle.' And to Dock, the day before landing:

. . . Sanderson, who is an old friend and teacher, has been urging it strongly, and I looked over the ground during the Association week. I shall be able to work over a lot of my material—Typhoid, Aneurysm, heart, &c which has been accumulating hopelessly. I go through to Pointe a pic, Quebec, from New York. Shall you go to St. Louis? Let me know, as we might go from Chicago together. . . .

Even after he landed and joined his family at Murray Bay, his shower of explanatory notes continued; and soon letters like the following began to pour in upon him when people learned where he was:

From S. Weir Mitchell to W. O. Bar Harbour, Maine.
14th August, 1904.

I read your letter with very mingled feelings—pained because your great example—so various in its values is to be lost to the profession—pleased because of what Oxford will gain in an untrammelled, clear-headed American physician. Yes, American—you will let me insist on that. I think you are wisely counselled to go. Twice in the last year I was on the point of writing to ask you to consider whether you were not being worked beyond your strength. Selfishly speaking I am filled with the most honest regret. One by one the older men who shared with me the fates of war and the contests of peace, have died. I have picked up new friends—the younger ones, men and women—and among the best, you—and is it twenty years indeed? When I read your letter to my wife, she said isn't it splendid? And I—isn't it sorrowful?—for of course this does take you out of my life, and at 74 the arithmetic of opportunity is easily summed up and made out. We shall see you I fear but rarely, and very soon you will be saying raily for really and H's will be lost all over the house, and you will say Gawd foı God, as is Oxford as she is spoke—Do be careful of your English. I am chaffing you to keep from saying more of the personal loss to me. As to Jn. Hopkins—perhaps you do not know that the Med. School at J. H. is or was Wm. Osler. Are we not to see you before you go? My news is small. I have a novel done, and am made an Honorary something of the French Académie.

His own notes were to the effect that his act was one of preservation. For the daily grind of a consulting practice into which he had become drawn was growing worse from year to year, with less and less time for teaching and clinical work. The new post he insisted was chiefly ornamental, though he hoped to make it useful and would at least find congenial work to do; that he had had his day and it had been a good one, but a younger man could do better—one who does not 'trade largely as we pre-seniles have to do on our past reputation'. Such a letter he wrote, among others, to Flexner on September 1st, with this postscript:

PS. What do you know of 'healed splits' of the intima in connection with dissecting aneurysm & rupture of the aorta and healed dissecting aneurysm? Have you had any cases of the latter? I am working at my aneurysm material.

To Dr. Maude Abbott from W. O. Pointe-à-Pic, P. Q. Sept. 5.

It is awfully good of you to send all those abstracts & the books. It was exactly what I wanted. I will return the books in person next week. I can then look over the other references which you have given. The subject is one of really great interest. Remind me, please, to go over the aneurysm cases in my post-mortem notes. There are 29 or 30 of them. *No. 180* I see is a perforation of pulmonary artery. I enclose you a list on a slip which please keep for me. . . . PS. Your letter & the translation of Thoma just arrived. Thank you so much. Do not mind about the others. I have been going over the Eppinger paper carefully. Thoma supplements it splendidly. I remember its appearance, but I had forgotten how good it was. I shall be glad to look over your paper—'The Museum in Medical Teaching' would be a good title. A good deal has been written I think in English journals—look in Neale's Medical Digest under Museum & under teaching.

To Joseph H. Pratt from W. O. Pointe-à-Pic, Sept. 6th.

Thanks for your kind note & the slips. Very glad of the reference in the Gazette des Hôpitaux. Somebody told me of a study in progress on the strength of the Aorta, but I have forgotten who it was. I wish you would look in the Harvard Museum if there are any specimens of rupture of the Aorta, or of splits of the intima. I am to edit for Lea Brothers a new system of medicine. I shall get only the younger men to contribute. Give me a few hints from Boston: (1) what would you like to write? (2) send me a list of the younger fellows & the special work they have been doing. Cabot will take the blood section. I suppose there could be nobody better than McCollom for Diphtheria and Scarlet Fever. One of Councilman's men should do the pathology. . .

Working at his aneurysm material and scarcely a fortnight passed! Nevertheless his wife writes to one of the 'latch-keyers' that he 'is looking very well and really having a holiday except for stacks of mail. We leave here on the 14th for Toronto, spending a day in Montreal, and I shall stay there while he is in St. Louis.'[1]

To Edward Milburn from W. O. Pointe-à-Pic, 9th.

Dear Ned, I was on the point of writing to you when your letter came. Mrs Hinneman has told me of your sorrow & trouble about your son—how terribly sad for you all. And your account is not very satisfactory. Though the early cases with haemorrhages often start very badly & later the disease is arrested. I hope you are keeping him in the 'open' in these fine days. While he has fever he should be flat on his back but the *continuous* out of door life seems so good for the digestion & for the fever. Who is your doctor? Why not let him write me a description of the case? I might be able to be of help. I do not leave until next Spring. It will give

[1] The International Congress of Arts and Sciences was held in connexion with the St. Louis Universal Exposition, Sept. 19–25, under the presidency of Simon Newcomb the astronomer.

me a change I much need of a quieter life. Do let me hear how the boy gets on. I shall be in Baltimore on the 24th.

His old schoolboy friend, one of the triumvirate of 'Barrie's Bad Boys', will be recognized; and hardly a week passed without some word of counsel or encouragement until the end came two months later, when he wrote:

Dear Ned, How heart-breaking to part from your dear boy—& an only son! I feared all along from the symptoms that it was one of these acute types for which there is rarely any hope. Better so perhaps than a slow lingering two or three years of illness with all its illusive hopes & anxious dreads. Do give my love & heartfelt sympathy to your wife & the girls. They will be unconsolable, poor things! Affectionately yours, W. O.

And on the last day of his four weeks at Pointe-à-Pic he wrote to W. S. Thayer:

Dear T. I have been so overwhelmed with correspondence that I have neglected to answer your nice letter of the 28th. . . . I am so glad to hear that the Dispensary rooms are nearly ready. What a comfort it will be to have plenty of room. I doubt very much the wisdom of taking the men from the wards. So far as I know it is never successful—they always regard the work as extra & neglect one or the other. There should be enough good young fellows, who have time enough in their waiting years. The difficulty with such men as Brown & Hamburger is a serious one—they are so good & so busy. I am sure the St. Louis address will be A.1. Send me word to Fischel, where you are. F's address is—see the Trans Ass. I have forgotten it. Thanks for the papers. The typhoid heart & arteries sequelae has I see been widely noticed. I have been deep in Aneurysm literature, & have gone thro. Thoma's five papers & Eppinger's colossal arbeit. I have spent a couple of mornings with Dr Maude Abbott at the McGill Museum going over my old specimens. . . .

They left the comparative seclusion of Murray Bay on the 14th and returned to the noisy world in whose press since the middle of August his name had been much head-lined. A week later from Dundas Mrs. Osler wrote of their eagerness to get back to Baltimore, and added: 'I am already weary of the triumphal procession through Canada of the Regius Professor and his family; do pray ask all his friends to make it easy for him: he will find it hard to say adieu.' There is no gainsaying that his decision was considered as a great blow to the Johns Hopkins. How his colleagues felt is evident from their letters to him. ‘If talents, self-sacrifice and high devotion to the good of the profession deserve any reward you certainly have earned the promotion’, wrote one of them. ‘But what are we to do here in the hospital and medical school and in the community at large, where you have done so much and are likely to leave so much still to do that nobody can do so well? The success of the hospital and medical school has been largely your achievement and you have done the most to bind together the different departments and to establish a high standard of professional work.’

Outpourings of this sort from his professional colleagues were natural enough and to be expected; but no one could have foreseen what effect his decision would have upon the community at large, among whom as an unnaturalized citizen he had resided for a short fifteen years. There was an actual wail of regret mingled with the congratulations from press, pulpit, and public on all sides. Whether he would have been able to make up his mind in favour of Oxford had he attempted to do so while in Baltimore may be doubted. He was now in for such a back-breaking autumn, winter, and spring as made the preceding ones lazy in comparison. For to his customary activities was added not only the painful duty of severing his American contacts—and such a man is not let go easily by his admirers—but also the need of picking up some threads of the complicated life ahead of him in Oxford. There were many duties in connexion with the new post—the ‘R. P. M.’—in which he had to receive instruction. The Vice-Chancellor had written during the autumn that among other things he was *ex officio* Senior Examiner for Degrees in Medicine, so a substitute must be provided; and further:

I may add a few words as to the formalities of becoming a member of the University. With our curious double system it is necessary, or at least desirable, to be a member of one of the Colleges. May I say, in case you have not yet fixed upon a College, that it would be a special pleasure to me and, I venture to say, to all the Fellows of Oriel, if I might put your name on the books of the College? The next step is matriculation, or becoming a member of the University. This follows immediately upon being admitted to a college.

Then Convocation passes a decree conferring the Degree of Doctor of Medicine. You are then a member of Convocation with the vote and all rights and privileges. . . .

There had been other proposals, and he was strongly drawn towards Magdalen, which was Sanderson's college and to which 'that delightful man Walter Raleigh has just been elected'. With all this, he found time to help other people with their personal projects:

To Dr. Maude Abbott from W. O. Sept. 1904.

The report is most encouraging. The stenographer will be a great help. I wonder how you got through so much writing. I think it would be quite feasible to get the necessary money for the printing by private subscription. Let me try what I can do. I will write to the members of the Faculty—and some others. It would be one of the very best advertisements of the School. I will try to look up R. J. B. Howard's notes to-day. I have been simply swamped with work since my return. I wish I could get free for a year. I return the notes as they may be needed. . . .

On October 5th exercises were held to commemorate the opening of the much-needed new clinical amphitheatre in which Osler was to carry on his teaching for only a few months longer. There were many guests, and addresses were made by Louis A. Stimson of New York, by Clifford Allbutt, Osler's 'brother Regius' from Cambridge, who happened to be in the country, by Abraham Jacobi, by ex-President Gilman, by Welch, and others. In the afternoon the audience reassembled to unveil the tablet in memory of Jesse Lazear of the Yellow Fever Commission. Osler presided, and before introducing the chief speaker, James Carroll, who with Lazear had shared in Walter Reed's epochal experiments, he spoke feelingly as follows:

It has been well said that Milton's poem 'Lycidas' touches the high-water mark of all poetry. This is true not only because the poem appeals to us by its intrinsic merit and worth, but because it touches that chord in each one of us which responds to the personal loss of some young man to whom we had become attached. Those of us who have got on in years mourn many young fellows whom we have seen stricken by our sides. We have had in this hospital fortunately only a few such losses. We have lost on the medical side Meredith Reese, Oppenheim and Ochsner; and we have also lost a man of rare worth, in whose memory we meet to-day, whose story will be told you by Dr. Carroll and Dr. Thayer: Jesse William Lazear, a Baltimore boy, a Hopkins graduate of the Academic Department, a graduate of Columbia University in Medicine and a resident physician of this hospital, the first man to take charge of our clinical laboratory, who, in Cuba, sacrificed his life in the cause of humanity. . . .

Beset as he was at all times, and particularly at this period, by representatives of the press, few of them ever got by the faithful Morris at the door, and when they did by feigning an appointment, the interview was brief. A reporter had broken in upon him one day to get his comment upon a cable dispatch published that morning in the *New York Herald* regarding a new cure for pneumonia (an electrical solution of gold and silver) discovered by a Professor Robin of Paris. Osler is reported to have read the clipping, to have folded it carefully and to have remarked on returning it: 'You can say that New York Herald medicine, especially the Paris variety, is discredited by the medical profession.' But there were times when, cornered by a reporter, his M'Connachie got the better of him, as it did in connexion with Jacobi's visit to attend the ceremonies of the 5th. Jacobi, a small man of frail physique despite his leonine head and shock of hair, was a guest at 1 West Franklin Street and the house was besieged by reporters, one of whom Osler finally saw. The press that evening contained a long account of Professor Jacobi's athletic prowess, for though he was incidentally a children's specialist he was chiefly known as a pole-vaulter and high jumper, in which events he held the record of the New York Athletic Association, &c. For this and similar pranks Osler was to be severely penalized in a few months' time.

Early in October his Ingersoll Lecture[1] was ready for distribution, and the first of the many reprintings and editions of the 'Aequanimitas' volume, dedicated to D. C. Gilman, had been issued both in England and America. Both of these publications were widely reviewed, and though the twelve collected addresses rescued from the oblivion of professional journals had been written for 'medical students, nurses, and practitioners of medicine',

[1] Published by Houghton, Mifflin & Co.

they proved to contain 'a deep mine of golden counsel' equally suited for others. A series of lay sermons they are, and, as one reviewer[1] said: 'It would be well for society in general if all the sermons preached from the pulpits in Christendom showed the lofty feeling for all that is good and true, the genial wisdom and the energizing quality of these discourses.' They showed not only lofty feelings but a sense of humour and a love of good literature; appended to the volume was a list of ten items constituting a 'bedside library for medical students', who were advised not to rest satisfied with their professional training but to get the education, if not of a scholar, at least of a gentleman. The list began, of course, with the Scriptures and Shakespeare, and ended with the 'Breakfast Table' series.

To Mrs. Gurney Curtis from W. O. Oct. 10, 1904.

Your name has been on the list to send that wretched [Ingersoll] Lecture to for weeks, but I have not had your address, and Miss Humpton has not been able to get it. This morning your letter comes, and I at once send you off the lecture with the greatest pleasure. I know you are a Teresian—in disguise. Dr. McCrae has left the hospital, but Dr. Howard is still faithful and good. I hope you have had a good summer. Please come into the hospital for a few weeks at least before I leave. Make it this time a *biceps tendon* so that you will be able to walk about.

Sincerely yours, &c.

With all his multiplying obligations he did not relinquish his old ones nor fail in his customary regular attendance at meetings. This was ingrained, and particularly when there was up-hill work to be done he was to be counted on. The Executive Committee of the National Association for the Study and Prevention of Tuberculosis, to give a single example, held frequent meetings—in New York on October 18th and again on November 16th, in Philadelphia on December 1st, in New York again January 9th, and so on;

[1] Another wrote: 'We have made a rough calculation that there are 650 examples of the *quotatio recta* in the less than 400 small octavo pages of good-sized type; while as for the examples of the *quotatio obliqua*—the "tags" and reminiscences of browsings among well-loved books, the words and phrases that in a flash bring to mind the inspirations of great men, and what our fathers in literature have declared unto us—their name is legion: they are not to be counted.'

and as Trudeau's health rarely permitted him to be present Osler was usually in the chair.

The two-hundredth anniversary of John Locke's death was observed by a large gathering at McCoy Hall on October 28th, and he entered enthusiastically into the preparations for the occasion—indeed did most of the preliminary work—made one of the several afternoon addresses, his topic being 'Locke as Physician'—and in the evening gave a large dinner at the Maryland Club for which he had prepared a special John Locke menu with many appropriate quotations from the philosopher's writings. So he delighted to take trouble; and one may be sure that at the corner of West Franklin Street no opportunity was lost to celebrate other anniversaries, one of them on the 5th of November, when Revere had his chance at 'gunpowder, treason, and plot', and more than the usual explosions occurred in the cellar, accompanied by hair-raising groans disseminated through the house by way of the furnace pipes.

To the Pres. of Magdalen from W. O. Nov. 10.

Dear Mr. Warren,—I am glad you liked the lecture—not an easy subject to handle. I will ask Constable & Co. to send a copy to Lord Tennyson. 'In Memoriam' has always been to me a great sermon on Immortality. You will get in a week or two a volume of addresses, some of which may interest you. I have accepted a Professorial Studentship at Christ Church. I had left the matter in Sir John's hands, as I had had invitations from Oriel and Lincoln and New. I hope I have not made a *faux pas* in accepting at Christ Church, but I had no time for consultation with anyone as I only had the letter on the 8th and the election is on the 16th, so I had to cable. . . .

To George Dock from W. O. Nov. 10.

What fools these publishers make of us! I do not see the slightest objection to your transposing verbs and adjectives and a few prepositions and making the one stone kill two birds. Is there anything that you would like better than the group of diseases associated with internal secretion? I think we shall cut the thymus out of that section and put it with the lymphatics, as it is uncertain whether it has any internal secretion. It would be a pretty full section with the suprarenals and the thyroid, including Graves' disease. Would you prefer to take disease of the lungs? That would come in Volume III, and we should want it earlier. Let me know, please, at once. Thanks for the note. I am trying to make a new book of the old quiz-compend, rewriting a number of the important sections and rearranging the whole thing. Send me the reference to the recent work showing the possibility of disinfecting diphtheritic throats. Sincerely yours, &c.

Evidently he was in for the triennial revision of the Text-book, which came at this inopportune time. There were other things enough, besides, as the following letters indicate.

To J. George Adami. Nov. 17, '04.

Miss Abbott has sent me the estimates for printing &c for the Museum Catalogue. We need $1000—possibly 1200 as it would be very nice to give her some recognition when the volume appears. I would like to raise the fund if possible [which he did: J. G. A.]. Let me know as soon as convenient the names of 15 or 20 business men who are interested in the College, to whom I might write. I will attack the doctors too. Who is the Treasurer of the faculty now—or to whom should cheques be made payable? I will start with the enclosed [the largest contribution of all: J. G. A.], which please turn over to the proper person. Love to L. M. C. and the chicks.

To George W. Norris. Nov. 22.

Thanks for your papers with which I am very pleased, not only for the evidence of good work they show, but for the memory of your father and grandfather. The tuberculous endocarditis paper is most interesting and will be very useful, as I have just been going over all of our material on the subject. Could you not come down some evening and give us a little talk at our Laennec Society? I send you our programme, and you will see the sort of work we are trying to do. We have rather a short programme for the 27th. Perhaps you will have some brief communication which would do for that day, or perhaps it would be better to give us a longer one at one of the early meetings next year. By the way, as you have been going over the post-mortems at the Philadelphia Hospital, have you any statistics on aneurysm?

To A. C. Klebs. Nov. 23.

. . . At the meeting of the Board of Directors it was quite evident that, with the exception of our President, Dr. Trudeau, none of us had done much (either to get money or members for our National Association). If it is to be a great success, we must individually try to get as many members in and out of the profession, and urge our wealthy friends to help with liberal contributions. Mrs. Colby, the assistant Secretary, will furnish you with a circular before long, which you could enclose to your correspondents. The sub-committee in charge of the arrangements for the annual meeting meets within the next ten days. Do let me have any suggestions. . . . Do find out who the good young fellows are, working at tuberculosis in Chicago. We must catch the *workers* to make the affair go. . . .

To Dr. Lewellys F. Barker. xi. 27. 04.

In a weak moment I consented to edit for Lea Bros a new System of Medicine. McCrae will do all the rough work as assistant editor. I would like you to chip in with your pen—a good introductory section to the Nervous System—like one of Cohnheim's chapters —would suit you—& me. Anything else? Throw an eye on the question of classification of the Diseases of the N. S. for such a system. What modifications would you suggest in that given in my text-book. I am sweating away at a new edition—am almost rewriting the Infectious diseases and knocking many of the other sections to splinters—I am tired of the sequence of paragraphs! I hope all goes well with Mrs. B. & the twins.

A short two years before this time there had been buried in the solid granite of the Matoppos a remarkable Englishman whose work by no means ended at his death. To judge from the following letter the Rhodes bequest had been drawn upon to help endow the Chair of Pathology so as to hold Ritchie in Oxford. For, though some of the colleges might be rich, the university itself had scant funds, as Osler was to learn:

To Professor Arthur Thomson from W. O. 28th [Nov.]

Thanks for yours of the 16th. I am delighted to hear that the Rhodes fund has contributed £200 a year. I have been in correspondence with Parkin the Secretary, who sent me Rhodes' will with its interesting Medico-Chirurgical aspiration—not likely to be realized in our day. So sorry to have you bothered with my letters. I hope to be able to fix a date for my departure before very long. My two associates would do the work at the school very well. I am really tied by a heavy literary venture for which I had signed the contract in June—a new System of Medicine—and the publishers would not let me free. I must arrange the details before leaving tho it is very slow work, assigning the articles, and making all the plans for a seven volume work. Fortunately McCrae will see to the proof reading &c on this side. I hope to be able to get away in May at the latest. I think it would be best if we took a furnished house for a few months. Mrs. Osler has been put by friends in communication with 'Brooks'. Let me know should you hear of anything. I would like to be in the outskirts, though I suppose for consultation work I should not be too far away. I was delighted to hear of my election to Christ Church.

Osler's feeling about clubs in general has been mentioned. He was not gastronomically inclined, despite the tuneless chant which a stodgy pudding usually evoked. But clubs sought him—even dinner clubs, and there were many more to follow. The next letter is from his old friend of London days in the '70's :

Sir George Savage to W. O. 3 Henrietta St., Cavendish Sq., Nov. 30, 1904.

Dear Osler,—I now write in a semi-official position. I happen to be Secretary to what is called 'The College Club'. I enclose a list of members, it is very old and very exclusive. Its chief objects being meetings for dinner, which meetings are held on the last Mondays of about seven months in the year. Of course the few Fellows residing out of London cannot be expected to dine regularly but would always be welcome. I write thus privately, as you are to come to reside with us, to ask if you would be inclined to become a member if you were unanimously elected? I shall be glad to hear from you on this point early, though our next meeting will not be till the end of January.

About this time, too, a club of Washington and Baltimore book-lovers was started, the Stultifera Navis Club, which until Osler left in the spring, met with enthusiasm once a month and then died. It seemed lifeless in his absence. Alfred Parsons, Herbert Putnam, and Worthington Ford of the Congressional Library; William H. Buckler, J. H. Hollander, W. S. Thayer, Robert Garrett and a few others from Baltimore, were members. And there was another, the Charaka Club, composed largely of New York doctors who were bibliophiles, and though he did not often attend, perhaps for that very reason pressure was brought to bear on him to come to a meeting arranged in his honour. It was then that he read his paper on Fracastorius, about whom he had been in correspondence with Weir Mitchell earlier in the year, some products of his reading having already gone to Lawrason Brown for his Saranac journal. The essay thus begins :

Upon few pictures in literature do we dwell with greater pleasure than that of Catullus returning to his home near Verona, wearied with the pleasures of the Capital, sick at heart after the death of his much beloved brother, and still, we may fancy, aching with the pangs of misprized love; but at the sight of 'Paeninsularum Sirmio, insularumque ocella ', he breaks out into joyful song and all his cares vanish.

Fifteen centuries later another ' Bard of Sirmio ' sang the joys of the Lago di Garda, ' mid Caphian hills ', and while we cannot claim for Fracastor a place beside his immortal townsman, he occupies a distinguished position in our annals as the author of the most successful medical poem ever written, and as the man from whom we date our first accurate knowledge of the processes of infection and contagion. . . .

To Mr. Henry Phipps from W. O. Dec. 23rd, 1904.

Many thanks for your kind remembrance, which I appreciate very much. I have asked Blakiston & Co. Phila. to send you a volume of addresses which I have just published. They are a bit *medicated* as Oliver Wendell Holmes would say, but you have mingled enough with doctors to understand them. I am just off to Boston for Xmas. We hope to open the Tuberculosis dispensary in January. Could you come down? What date would be most convenient for you. With kind remembrances to Mrs Phipps & your family.

Christmas was passed with Mrs. Osler's sister in Jamaica Plain, and the last few days of the year with his own people in Canada. There he was heavily subjected. In Toronto he opened on the 29th the new Library of the Ontario Academy of Medicine, towards the erection of which he had himself contributed a generous sum and many volumes. The next day he was tendered a public luncheon by the Canadian Club, his sensible and amusing remarks on this occasion, entitled ' The Anglo-American Relations of Canada ', being widely quoted in the Canadian papers. And the year ends with a note enclosing his usual Christmas gift to his old friend of Barrie days :

xii. 31. 04.

Dear Ned, You must have had a very sad Xmas—with your poor boy away. I wish I could have seen you while I was in Toronto this week, but I was up to my ears in engagements. We do not leave until May. I shall be in Toronto in April. I wish we could meet then. With love to all at home & best wishes for the new year, Ever yours, Wm Osler.

CHAPTER XXIV

1905
THREE VALEDICTORY ADDRESSES

During the few months that remained Osler had his hands full. Besides, he was very much in the public eye, in demand on all sides, the centre of interest wherever he might appear. This was not only embarrassing for a man accustomed to go about unknown and unmolested, but placed him in a situation, in those fallen times of journalism, when a slip or an imagined slip on his part was likely to be pounced upon by a feline press. There was written some years later an article entitled 'The Confessions of a Yellow-journalist', in which the forgotten author cited Admiral George Dewey and Dr. William Osler as the two best-known examples of persons who in his time had been victimized for the purpose of 'copy'—popular idols one day, held up to scorn and ridicule the next, and for so long as discussion would keep the topic alive. Not all the press participated. There were some notable exceptions, and even *Life* made ample amends for some things it had once said. According to its editor it was 'a dull time, when no other lively news was obtainable. The President had said or done nothing surprising for a week or two, Congress was in the doldrums, newspaper readers were yawning a little, and along came Dr. Osler and filled a gap.' A man with less philosophy in his make-up, less charitableness towards his fellows, and with a less well-bridled tongue than his might not have lived it down.

The Johns Hopkins University celebrates its own birthday with that of the 'Father of his Country' on February 22nd, and it was inevitable that this year the ceremonies in connexion with the event should resolve themselves into an outburst of tributes to the greatly beloved man who was soon to leave. For the occasion Osler had prepared with even more than his usual pains a farewell address which in an ill-starred moment, having Anthony Trollope's little-read novel of the same name in mind, he entitled 'The Fixed

Period '. Indeed, his interruptions had been so many and so unavoidable that, on or about the 20th, he had fled in despair to New York, where, in the seclusion of the library of the University Club, the address was put in its final form. On his return he did what for him was an unusual thing: before the assembled 'latch-keyers' at tea the next afternoon he read the address aloud, and no one of his hearers even suspected the brink he was standing upon. Only a single criticism was made, and that by his wife, who remarked: 'I'm not sure, Willie, that I exactly like what you said about "the old ladies in cap and fichu"'—a sentence he promptly amended.

The 21st was a very busy day given over to the formal opening of the Phipps Dispensary. It was the culmination of his efforts in the local fight against tuberculosis, which had begun six years before when, conscious of the unsatisfactory treatment of pulmonary consumption as practised in the out-patient clinic, he had finally appointed one of the students as a domiciliary visitor who was to follow these patients to their homes and to report upon their living conditions. There was no place in the world where social and academic functions were more happily combined than in hospitable Baltimore in those days. Many guests had been invited: Mr. Henry Phipps himself was present; Hermann Biggs of New York gave the principal address; there were others, by Osler, by Welch, and by H. B. Jacobs; and one of those famous Maryland Club dinners followed. It was all very simple, very dignified; and Mr. Phipps glowed with pleasure at the cordiality of his reception, for he was made the central figure.

The next day, the 22nd, was throughout an Osler day. Such an unrestrained outpouring of appreciation for what he had done, of regret at his departure; such a demonstration of love and affection on the part of students, alumni, faculty, and community few teachers have ever received. Most men would have to live after death to know how others really regard them, but it fell to Osler's lot several times in his life to have paid to him in public the embarrassing tributes usually reserved for obituary notices. The university had never seen such a gathering of alumni. McCoy Hall was packed to the window-sills. Osler was the centre of the stage, at fifty-five with not a grey hair in his head, surrounded by his devoted friends of the past and present faculty, several of them, like Basil Gildersleeve, already beyond the allotted threescore years and ten. Suppressing his emotion, but with unwonted colour in his cheeks, he read his valedictory:

> . . . Who can understand [he said] another man's motives? Does he always understand his own? This much I may say in explanation—not in palliation. After years of hard work, at the very time when a man's energies begin to flag, and when he feels the need of more leisure, the conditions and surroundings that have made him what he is and that have moulded his character and abilities into something useful in the community—these very circumstances ensure an ever-increasing demand upon them; and when the call of the East comes, which in one form or another is heard by all of us, and which grows louder as we grow older, the call may come like the summons to Elijah, and not alone the ploughing of the day, but the work of a life, friends, relatives, even father and mother, are left, to take up new work in a new field. Or, happier far, if the call comes, as it did to Puran Das in Kipling's story, not to new labours, but to a life 'private, unactive, calm, contemplative'.

And he went on to discuss the several problems of university life suggested by his departure—the dangers of staying too long in one place; the beneficial effects upon faculties of changes in personnel; the advantages of a peripatetic life particularly for young men; the fixed period for the teacher, either of time of service or of age, rather than an appointment *ad vitam aut culpam*:

> I have two fixed ideas [he said] well known to my friends, harmless obsessions with which I sometimes bore them, but which have a direct bearing on this important problem. The first is the comparative uselessness of men above forty years of age. This may seem shocking, and yet read aright the world's history bears out the statement. Take the sum of human achievement in action, in science, in art, in literature—subtract the work of the men above forty, and while we should miss great treasures, even priceless treasures, we would practically be where we are to-day. It is difficult to name a great and far-reaching conquest of the mind which has not been given to the world by a man on whose back the sun was still shining. The effective, moving, vitalizing work of the world is done between the ages of twenty-five and forty—these fifteen

golden years of plenty, the anabolic or constructive period, in which there is always a balance in the mental bank and the credit is still good. In the science and art of medicine, young or comparatively young men have made every advance of the first rank. Vesalius, Harvey, Hunter, Bichat, Laennec, Virchow, Lister, Koch—the green years were yet upon their heads when their epoch-making studies were made. To modify an old saying, a man is sane morally at thirty, rich mentally at forty, wise spiritually at fifty—or never. . . .

My second fixed idea is the uselessness of men above sixty years of age, and the incalculable benefit it would be in commercial, political, and in professional life if, as a matter of course, men stopped work at this age. In his 'Biathanatos' Donne tells us that by the laws of certain wise states sexagenarii were precipitated from a bridge, and in Rome men of that age were not admitted to the suffrage and they were called *Depontani* because the way to the senate was *per pontem*, and they from age were not permitted to come thither. In that charming novel, 'The Fixed Period', Anthony Trollope discusses the practical advantages in modern life of a return to this ancient usage, and the plot hinges upon the admirable scheme of a college into which at sixty men retired for a year of contemplation before a peaceful departure by chloroform. That incalculable benefits might follow such a scheme is apparent to anyone who, like myself, is nearing the limit, and who has made a careful study of the calamities which may befall men during the seventh and eighth decades. Still more when he contemplates the many evils which they perpetuate unconsciously, and with impunity. As it can be maintained that all the great advances have come from men under forty, so the history of the world shows that a very large proportion of the evils may be traced to the sexagenarians—nearly all the great mistakes politically and socially, all of the worst poems, most of the bad pictures, a majority of the bad novels, not a few of the bad sermons and speeches. It is not to be denied that occasionally there is a sexagenarian whose mind, as Cicero remarks, stands out of reach of the body's decay. Such a one has learned the secret of Hermippus, that ancient Roman who feeling that the silver cord was loosening, cut himself clear from all companions of his own age and betook himself to the company of young men, mingling with their games and studies, and so lived to the age of 153, *puerorum halitu refocillatus et educatus*. And there is truth in the story, since it is only those who live with the young who maintain a fresh outlook on the new problems of the world. The teacher's life should have three periods, study until twenty-five, investigation until forty, profession until sixty, at which age I would have him retired on a double allowance. Whether Anthony Trollope's suggestion of a college and chloroform should be carried out or not I have become a little dubious, as my own time is getting so short.

From this he went on to the second part of the address, which dealt with what the Johns Hopkins foundation had already done and might still do for Medicine ; and he told wherein lay his chief pride—in the reintroduction of the old-fashioned method of practical instruction. 'I desire', he said, 'no other epitaph than the statement that I taught medical students in the wards, as I regard this as by far the most useful and important work I have been called upon to do.' At the close, Dr. Welch, in a few moving words presented him, 'the chief ornament of our Medical Faculty', to President Remsen as the single candidate of the year for an honorary degree, and the university LL.D. was conferred. It was a memorable occasion.

That evening the lighter side of Baltimore broke loose, and at the alumni gathering, which had swelled to unparalleled proportions, there were lively speeches made and poems read and jests passed, many of them at his expense, as was possible in those days in view of the intimacy between Hopkins teachers and students. Under it all there lay, however, the deep feeling well expressed in an editorial in that evening's paper, which said in part :

> In making his last appearance at a public function of the Johns Hopkins University as a member of its faculty, Dr. Osler accomplished the remarkable feat of making an address which, both in its entertaining and semi-humorous part and in its retrospective and fully serious part, so fastened his hearers' interest as to divert their attention from the thought which would otherwise have been predominant in their minds—the thought of the loss the university and this community are about to sustain in his departure. No ingenuity of argument can diminish the feeling of what is the keenest part of that loss ; for while much may be said for the good that can come to a university from a change of professors, from the infusion of new blood, it remains an unescapable fact that there are some personalities that play a part which is unique, and for which no equivalent can be found by any formula. It is not simply by the estimate of his tangible and measurable services that the value of the presence of such a man as Osler is to be judged ; and when the delight of listening to his address was over, the first thought that came to many a mind was that the man who made the address is a man whose loss it is impossible for this community to think of without the most acute regret.

The storm did not break until the next day, when it was

headlined throughout the country that OSLER RECOMMENDS CHLOROFORM AT SIXTY ; and for days and weeks there followed pages of discussion, with cartoons and comments, caustic, abusive, and worse, with only an occasional word in his behalf lost in the uproar. Day by day there were columns of letters contributed by newspaper readers, none of whom in all probability had read the innocent paragraphs said half in jest which have been quoted above ; until to 'Oslerize' became a byword for mirth and opprobrium. Knowing nothing of the whimsical reference to Trollope's novel, interposed to mask his own pain at parting, nor of the rather pathetic allusion to his own advancing years, the public at large felt that it was the heartless view of a cold scientist who would condemn man as a productive machine. Few of these things could he have seen, for news clippings were sedulously kept from him, even the abusive and threatening letters which by the wagon-load poured into 1 West Franklin Street from all over the country never reached him, but were consigned to the basket by a devoted secretary.

He gave the famous address [writes ex-President Remsen] at my request, though I had no idea what he was going to say. I presided on the occasion of its delivery, and it never occurred to me that he was getting into hot water. It went to boiling in a few days, and in spots it was super-heated. I happened to meet him with Mrs. Osler one morning when the temperature was high, and she said : 'I am escorting the shattered idol home from church.'

It required no great degree of intelligence to distinguish between the serious and the jocular in what Osler had said, and if rightly read certainly no one's feelings, even were he past life's meridian, should have been ruffled in the slightest. It was regrettable that so admirable an address, the significance of which could hardly be over-estimated as an authoritative expression of opinion on matters relating to medical teaching, should, because of paucity of other news or some motive equally trivial, have been brought to the public eye in such ridiculous guise. Efforts were made in vain to get him to refute his statement ; and though there can be no question but that he was sorely hurt, he went on his way with a smile, and with his characteristic gesture waved off in after-years the many playful allusions to chloroforming which were subsequently made in his presence. He broke his silence on only one or two occasions: one of them was two years later when in Oxford he penned the preface of the second edition of his 'Aequanimitas':

> To this edition [he wrote] I have added the three valedictory addresses delivered before leaving America. One of these—'The Fixed Period'—demands a word of explanation. 'To interpose a little ease', to relieve a situation of singular sadness in parting from my dear colleagues of the Johns Hopkins University, I jokingly suggested for the relief of a senile professoriate an extension of Anthony Trollope's plan mentioned in his novel 'The Fixed Period'. To one who had all his life been devoted to old men, it was not a little distressing to be placarded in a world-wide way as their sworn enemy, and to every man over sixty whose spirit I may have thus unwittingly bruised, I tender my heartfelt regrets. Let me add, however, that the discussion which followed my remarks has not changed, but has rather strengthened my belief that the real work of life is done before the fortieth year and that after the sixtieth year it would be best for the world and best for ourselves if men rested from their labours.

Though he loved young people more, and felt that the future lay in their hands, his love for the aged was scarcely less. Few men during their lives had gone out of their way farther and more often to pay them tribute. By inheritance he should grow happily old himself; his mother was soon to see her ninety-ninth spring, and one need not go far to find record of his real feeling. Not many months after this trying time, at a complimentary dinner given in Providence, Rhode Island, in honour of Dr. J. W. C. Ely on his eighty-fifth birthday, there was read an unsolicited tribute which Osler had written for the occasion [1] on the art of growing old gracefully. It ended in this way: 'You remember one evening at dinner that I taxed you with having written sonnets. It was my dulness that made me suggest it. I should have known better. You have written man's best poem which your friends know by heart and which will remain as a precious memory long after you have crossed the bar.' For such generous acts as this, many old people knew and loved Osler, and heeded not the views

[1] *Providence Medical Journal*, April 10, 1906.

popularly ascribed to him. One of them, indeed, who sat on the platform on the 22nd of February, whose life has also been a poem, and who, too, has made sonnets in days since his eyes began to fail, composed this, fourteen years later, for what proved to be Osler's last birthday:

William the Fowler, Guillaume l'Oiseleur!
I love to call him thus and when I scan
The counterfeit presentment of the man,
I feel his net, I hear his arrows whir.
Make at the homely surname no demur,
Nor on a nomination lay a ban
With which a line of sovran lords began,—
Henry the Fowler was first Emperor.

Asclepius was Apollo's chosen son,
But to that son he never lent his bow,
Nor did Hephaestus teach to forge his net;
Both secrets hath Imperial Osler won.
His winged words straight to their quarry go.
All hearts are holden by his meshes yet.

And this same greatly honoured gentleman, Dean of the classical world, now in his ninety-third year,[1] has this to say of the 'Fixed Period' episode:

My relations with Osler were friendly but not close. From the beginning of our acquaintance I fell under the spell of his personality, and though not one of those who stood nearest to him, I yield to few in my affection for the man, and my admiration for his rare gifts. . . . As in the case of such wonderful men, such complex natures ever claimed a clearer understanding than is possible by the average acquaintance, and so I fancied that I understood him better than some of those who worshipped him. His famous speech which made some of the auditors grieve for me, did not cause me a flutter. In 1905 I sat opposite to him at the Christ Church gaudy, and in reply to a light remark about his McCoy Hall performance, he said: 'The way of the jester is hard.' I know that he always maintained that he was in earnest, when he propounded his Thesis, but the whole matter is an old story to one who knows that the antique floruit was forty. One of my favourite poets commends turning the fair side outward—but in Osler's case it is hard to say which is the fairer, the jest or earnest.

---

[1] Basil Lanneau Gildersleeve, Professor of Greek, Johns Hopkins University 1876–1915, D.Litt. both of Oxford and Cambridge in 1905, died not many months after these paragraphs were written.

That Osler was able to touch upon the episode with an apparently light heart is shown in his contemporary letters, of which these are samples :

Wednesday.

Dear Mr. Phipps, Thanks for your kind note. I am glad to see that you have got back safely. I hope Mrs. Phipps is much improved by the trip. The Times Editorial[1] is very much to the point. What a tempest my innocent & jocose remarks raised! Such a torrent of abuse & misunderstanding began to flow in that I took my old Master, Plato's advice & crept under the shelter of a wall until the storm blew over—working hard and reading nothing about it. I shall be in New York next week on my way to Montreal & shall call if you are to be in town. . . .

March 2.

Dear Pratt, Thanks for your letter & for the references. They are most interesting. We shall expect you to stay here on Monday. I hope you are hurrying, as the years are flying and you will soon be forty. Sincerely yours.

On the Monday referred to, the 16th, there was a symposium at the Johns Hopkins Medical Society on the subject of blood platelets, at which Osler gave a *résumé* of the history of the subject, and there were papers by George T. Kemp, of Champagne, Illinois, and J. H. Pratt, of Boston, who was 'soon to be forty'. Kemp, who had been studying blood platelets on the top of Pike's Peak, found them to contain haemoglobin, and in the discussion Osler remarked that he had seen a good many blood platelets but none that blushed.

To Professor Arthur Thomson from W. O. March 3rd.

Many thanks for your kindness in the matter of the house. I think we have settled upon the Max Müller one for June & July which will give us time to look about. I am sorry to hear that Sanderson has not been so well. I hope my re-hashed Anthony Trollope joke of chloroform at 60 years has not been taken seriously by the English papers. The Yellow Journals here have raised a deuce of a row over it & over my jests about men of 40 & men of 60. I have had a very hard time of it, but the tempest is subsiding. With many thanks for your trouble, Sincerely yours, [&c.] PS. I am glad to hear that the money is coming in for the pathology professorship. Have

---

[1] To this effect: 'It is no small feat to have deluded into seriousness a nation of humorists'.

Mount Stephen and Strathcona been asked? I might be able to do something with them.

On March 4th in New York a dinner of the Charaka Club was held in his honour, each guest being presented with a bronze plaque of him struck from the Vernon medallion and bearing on its reverse, 'The Charaka Club to Dr. William Osler, medico illustri, literarum cultori, socio gratissimo'. He was subjected to undue banter regarding 'Oslerization', which he bore cheerfully enough. Gracious! Why should he not. Had not Sir Thomas Browne written 'that piece of serene wisdom', 'The Religio Medici', at thirty? And at the end, Weir Mitchell read a charming poem, 'Books and the Man', a few stanzas of which may be recalled:[1]

Show me his friends and I the man shall know;
This wiser turn a larger wisdom lends:
Show me the books he loves and I shall know
The man far better than through mortal friends.

Do you perchance recall when first we met—
And gaily winged with thought the flying night
And won with ease the friendship of the mind,—
I like to call it friendship at first sight.

And then you found with us a second home,
And, in the practice of life's happiest art,
You little guessed how readily you won
The added friendship of the open heart.

And now a score of years has fled away
In noble service of life's highest ends,
And my glad capture of a London night
Disputes with me a continent of friends.

During all this, when not struggling over the Text-book revision or being called upon in the last hour for important consultations, he had been sitting, when time allowed, for a bust to remain in Gilman Hall; for two subscription portraits, one to hang in the Medical and Chirurgical Faculty, and another for the University of Pennsylvania; and Miss Garrett was arranging with Mr. John S. Sargent for a group picture of the four senior professors, to be presented

[1] There is a brief account of this gathering in the *British Medical Journal*, April 1, 1905, i. 728.

to the Johns Hopkins. Then there were at least three important addresses still to prepare, and in the midst of it all he notes laconically in his account-book opposite March 14–22: 'Influenza in bed. Fever 4 days, pains in joints & back. Coryza, larynx, bron.'

As usual he went to Atlantic City to recuperate, and put up at one of the more obscure hotels, probably registering under an assumed name if not that of E. Y. Davis; but he was back on April 3rd, and wrote to A. C. Klebs of Chicago: 'Yes I am going to sail incog, but I do not mind telling you we are going by the White Star Line, Cedric, on May 19th. It would be delightful if you could join us.'

To L. F. Barker from W. O. Wednesday [April 5]

I have not had a moment free since yesterday morning to send you a line of congratulation. Everyone here is much pleased, & I think the way the announcement has been made has softened the disappointment to Thayer. You will get a very hearty welcome from Faculty & students, & you have so many friends in the profession here that it will be like coming home. I hope you will be able to come on before I leave as there are many things to talk over & arrange. The work of the clinic has grown enormously & the teaching has increased to a serious degree—the classes being larger this year than we have ever had & next year the wards will be crowded. The private work, so important for the hospital also grows & takes much time of the 1st & 2nd assistant. In a way it is a burden but it is most essential to foster for the income it brings to the Hospital. The heavy work of it must be thrown on the assistants—the chief cannot possibly do more than give general direction. Of course Thayer, Futcher & McCrae make a very strong trio. I do hope Mac will stay—he is very strong as a teacher & full of sense. Futcher is a saint, you know him well. Cole the 1st assistant is a fine fellow. Emerson & Howard could not be better & Boggs who has the bacteriology is A.1. The new clin. room & your new rooms—a private one & two private laboratories will be most convenient. Much remains in the way of organization for higher lines of work—& this you can do. If you could come a couple of days before the Meeting in Washington it would be nice or when you can. . . .

The next week he was in the south for consultations—in Columbus, Georgia, in Savannah, in Richmond; and the following note to F. J. Shepherd tells of subsequent peregrinations:

I am to be in Montreal on Friday the 14th and shall come up by the Delaware & Hudson from New York. I have arranged with Roddick that I am to talk to the students at 12 o'clock and have the dinner in the evening. I shall have to leave on Saturday morning for Toronto to say good-bye there. I am, as you may suppose, rushed to death. I shall come directly to your house. Love to Cecil.

The usual Monday medical meeting of April 7th finds him in attendance, taking part with W. G. MacCallum and Rufus Cole in a symposium on Bronchiectasis as though there was nothing out of the ordinary to occupy his mind. He even finds time to write a commendatory review for the *American Journal of the Medical Sciences* of H. D. Rolleston's recent volume on 'Diseases of the Liver'—or at least E. Y. D. found time, for it was signed with these initials.

On April 11th, a few days before he left to pay his farewells in Montreal, a last meeting of the Stultifera Navis Club was held, and as a parting gift he was given a magnificent copy of 'La Henriade' bound by Padeloup and inscribed with a presentation verse from Voltaire to his friend J. B. Silva, physician to Louis XV—a proper gift to one who always acted himself on the principle that a true bibliophile has a keen pleasure in seeing an important document in its proper place—not necessarily in his own library. To the existing inscription in the volume, W. H. Buckler had added the following lines:

Your messmates in the Ship of Fools
Drink to your health and offer you
This product of the pen and tools
Of Voltaire and of Padeloup.

A famous leech received it then,
And now once more it feels content
Because in you it finds again
An owner no less eminent.

In Montreal on the 14th, as he had written to Shepherd, he gave the second of his three valedictories, which was intended as a farewell to his former students, Canadian and American.[1] By this time one might know whereof he would speak, and when the address came to be published

[1] The address appears to have done double duty and to have been given also at the University of Pennsylvania some time during the month.

there was prefixed to it from the Sermon on the Mount: 'Take therefore no thought for the morrow: for the morrow shall take thought for the things of itself.' 'The Student Life' it was entitled, and from start to finish it is an intimate though unconscious betrayal of Osler himself and the things for which he had stood since those early days in Weston when he first became aflame with a desire for knowledge:

Almost everything has been renewed [he said] in the science and in the art of medicine, but all through the long centuries there has been no variableness or shadow of change in the essential features of the life which is our contemplation and our care. The sick love-child of Israel's sweet singer, the plague-stricken hopes of the great Athenian statesman, Elpenor, bereft of his beloved Artemidora, and 'Tully's daughter mourned so tenderly', are not of any age or any race—they are here with us to-day, with the Hamlets, the Ophelias and the Lears. Amid an eternal heritage of sorrow and suffering our work is laid, and this eternal note of sadness would be insupportable if the daily tragedies were not relieved by the spectacle of the heroism and devotion displayed by the actors. Nothing will sustain you more potently than the power to recognize in your humdrum routine, as perhaps it may be thought, the true poetry of life—the poetry of the commonplace, of the ordinary man, of the plain, toil-worn woman, with their loves and their joys, their sorrows and their griefs. The comedy, too, of life will be spread before you, and nobody laughs more often than the doctor at the pranks Puck plays upon the Titanias and the Bottoms among his patients. The humorous side is really almost as frequently turned towards him as the tragic. Lift up one hand to heaven and thank your stars if they have given you the proper sense to enable you to appreciate the inconceivably droll situations in which we catch our fellow creatures. Unhappily, this is one of the free gifts of the gods, unevenly distributed, not bestowed on all, or on all in equal proportions. In undue measure it is not without risk, and in any case in the doctor it is better appreciated by the eye than expressed on the tongue. Hilarity and good humour, a breezy cheerfulness, a nature 'sloping towards the sunny side', as Lowell has it, help enormously both in the study and in the practice of medicine. To many of a sombre and sour disposition it is hard to maintain good spirits amid the trials and tribulations of the day, and yet it is an unpardonable mistake to go about among patients with a long face.

Quotations do not suffice. It is an address to be read and re-read, not only by every doctor young and old but by those in any way interested in doctors, better by far than his other two valedictories.[1] 'Of the well-stocked rooms', he said, 'which it should be the ambition of every young doctor to have in his house, the library, the laboratory, and the nursery—books, balances, and bairns—as he may not achieve all three I would urge him to start at any rate with the books and the balances.' And there followed advice on reading, on an avocation, on a 'quinquennial brain-dusting', with a picture of the type of doctor needed in the country districts—that best product of our profession. At the close came some most touching paragraphs of the long line of students whom he had taught and loved and who had died prematurely—mentally, morally, or bodily—the many young men whom he had loved and lost.

What happened at the undergraduates' banquet in the afternoon, where he again spoke, may be easily imagined; and later he met with his old friends of the 'Medico-Chi.' and read a further paper on Aneurysm which smacks of his activities of the '70's, while he was the boy-professor at McGill. On leaving Montreal he paid a flying visit to Toronto to say good-bye to his mother, and her parting admonition to her youngest son was: 'Remember, Willie, the shutters in England will rattle as they do in America.' Rattling shutters, like idle tongues, are common to all places and get on the nerves: human nature is much the same everywhere. Was ever a lecture on patience, charity, and tolerance better epitomized than in these few parting words of Ellen Pickton Osler, then nearing her century-mark?

In the account of those last few years in Baltimore, little has been said of the Medical and Chirurgical Faculty, in whose behalf he had continued so assiduously to labour. Its library had for the second time outgrown the quarters provided for it and a movement was on foot to raise money by popular subscription for a building suitable for a real academy of medicine, which was to bear Osler's name. How this larger project fell through after his 'Fixed Period' address, because of the many subscriptions which were withdrawn, need not be related, though it may be

[1] Reprinted in 'Aequanimitas [&c.]', 2nd edition, 1906, as No. xx; also, in part, by Christopher Morley in his selection of 'Modern Essays'. N.Y., Harcourt, Brace & Co., 1921.

said that the main assembly-room of the new building when finally erected was called Osler Hall. It was before this society at their annual meeting that he gave on April 26th the third of his valedictories as a farewell to the medical profession of the United States.

He drew upon the Litany for his title[1]; and to judge from the manuscript, still preserved, from which he read, it must have been an after-thought, as titles so often are. Wanting a title the address as originally typewritten became much interlined with script before its delivery, and still more before its publication; and when he came to add the title he started to write 'by James Bovell' instead of 'by William Osler', but checked himself.

> ... Century after century from the altars of Christendom this most beautiful of all prayers [the petition of the Litany] has risen from lips of men and women, from the loyal souls who have refused to recognize its hopelessness, with the war-drums ever sounding in their ears. The desire for unity, the wish for peace, the longing for concord, deeply implanted in the human heart, have stirred the most powerful emotions of the race, and have been responsible for some of its noblest actions. It is but a sentiment, you may say: but is not the world ruled by feeling and by passion? What but a strong sentiment baptized this nation in blood; and what but sentiment, the deep-rooted affection for country which is so firmly implanted in the hearts of all Americans, gives to these states to-day, unity, peace and concord? As with the nations at large, so with the nation in particular; as with people, so with individuals; and as with our profession, so with its members, this fine old prayer for unity, peace and concord, if in our hearts as well on our lips, may help us to realize its aspirations. What some of its lessons may be to us will be the subject of my address.

They were the same old truths which he hammered home in new guise; the welding together of the profession to promote unity by interstate reciprocity, by consolidation of rival medical schools, by opening the door to the homoeopathists; before peace can be attained the physician, like the Christian, must overcome the three great foes—ignorance which is sin, apathy which is the world, and vice which is the devil—and he prophetically added that 'perhaps in

[1] 'Unity, Peace, and Concord.' Reprinted in 'Aequanimitas [&c.]', 2nd edition, as No. XXI.

a few years our civilization may be put on trial and it will not be without benefit . . . if it arouses communities from an apathy which permits mediaeval conditions to prevail without a protest '. Finally he spoke of the ways of promoting concord in the profession by friendly intercourse, by avoiding the vice of uncharitableness, ' which Christ and the Apostles lashed more unsparingly than any other ', and by listening to no wagging tongues: and he ended by very happily appropriating the verses of Deut. xxx. 11–14 to a word unknown to their writer:

It may be that in the hurry and bustle of a busy life I have given offence to some—who can avoid it? Unwittingly I may have shot an arrow o'er the house and hurt a brother—if so, I am sorry, and I ask his pardon. So far as I can read my heart I leave you in charity with all. I have striven with none, not, as Walter Savage Landor says, because none was worth the strife, but because I have had a deep conviction of the hatefulness of strife, of its uselessness, of its disastrous effects, and a still deeper conviction of the blessings that come with unity, peace and concord. And I would give to each of you, my brothers—you who hear me now, and to you who may elsewhere read my words—to you who do our greatest work labouring incessantly for small rewards in towns and country places—to you the more favoured ones who have special fields of work—to you teachers and professors and scientific workers—to one and all, throughout the length and breadth of the land—I give a single word as my parting commandment:

' It is not hidden from thee, neither is it far off. It is not in heaven, that thou shouldest say, Who shall go up for us to heaven, and bring it unto us, that we may hear it, and do it? Neither is it beyond the sea, that thou shouldest say, Who shall go over the sea for us, and bring it unto us, that we may hear it, and do it? But the word is very nigh unto thee, in thy mouth, and in thy heart, that thou mayest do it '—CHARITY.

Naturally at the meeting Osler was the chief centre of interest, but he had ways of his own of dodging personal tributes; so at a session of the assembled Delegates, recourse was had to another method, and a telegram was sent to his mother asking her to share the sentiments of the Medical and Chirurgical Faculty in parting with her son, and congratulating her, first, on his distinguished career, ' but most on the innate qualities which have endeared him to his associates in Maryland.' To this came a reply from

83 Wellesley Street, Toronto, signed 'Jennette Osler', stating that Mrs. Osler, unable, because of her great age, to write, had asked her to express her heartfelt thanks for the messages which had given great pleasure: 'more especially in the expression of affection and appreciation called forth by the personal qualities of her son, since these are in her eyes more precious than all his honours.'

A year or two before this time, a medical club of a distinctly new order had been started by a group of surgeons, to the first meeting of which, held in Baltimore, Osler had been invited. Struck by this novel organization, which had equally great possibilities for the physicians, he was instrumental in launching a similar society, which came to be called the Interurban Clinical Club, and which held its first meeting in Baltimore on April 28–29 of this year. One of the purposes of these clubs, which have since been widely copied, is to introduce objective rather than subjective methods of conveying information; and at this first meeting of the Interurban Club the Johns Hopkins medical clinic, its teaching methods, its research problems, and so on, were fully paraded. Those who made up the programme naturally called upon Osler for several of its events. Accordingly the guests attended one of his celebrated Saturday-noon amphitheatre clinics for the third- and fourth-year students; he also held an out-patient clinic for them, and made, for what was to be practically the last time at the Hopkins, one of his famous ward visits—for perhaps the last time, too, he was host at the Maryland Club for a large dinner that evening.

One episode of this ward visit has been recalled. The new club having brought to Baltimore a group of the younger leaders of the profession, more than the usual queue of students followed him into the ward, crowding around the bedside where he stopped. 'Whose case is this?' said Osler. 'Mine, sir,' replied the fourth-year clerk stepping forward. 'Well, Mr. Freeman, what is the first thing you would do in examining this patient?' With some trepidation Mr. F. chanced: 'Take the history, sir.' 'No, that's already been done; what next?' Mr. F., thinking to make a hit, replied: 'Inspect the patient.' 'Not yet', said

Osler; 'what before that?' Mr. F. gives it up. 'Well, the first thing to do is to ask Dr. Lambert to stand out of the light.'

Plans meanwhile were being laid in England for Osler's reception, as the following letter from J. Burdon Sanderson indicates:

Oxford, May 2/05.

My dear Osler,—By the time you receive this I shall be performing my last duty as Reg. Professor—that of presenting for the Degree of D.M. a very able candidate, Mr. Turnbull. The only other matter that I shall have to concern myself with is the bidding farewell to the old men in the Almshouse at Ewelme. This I will do as soon as we get anything like summer weather. Just now Oxford looks very beautiful when the sun shines but we have as yet had very little of this enjoyment. In a month we hope to have the pleasure of welcoming you and Mrs. Osler. I am anxious to engage you for Friday, June 9, when we think of asking all and sundry to Magdalen College Hall. There will no doubt be other plans for entertaining you but I dare say none of the same kind. I am very glad to hear that you have arranged to occupy Prof. Max Müller's house during the summer. Our plan will be to see as much of the summer as we can. During our long life we have scarcely seen anything of England during the months that it is most beautiful—June and July. Freedom to enjoy the long days may be some compensation for many drawbacks.

On the day this letter of welcome was written in Oxford a great subscription dinner was held at the Waldorf-Astoria in New York to bid Osler farewell. At this dinner, organized by a committee of eighty who represented the leaders of the profession of Canada and the United States, there were some five-hundred participants from all over the continent. His old Philadelphia friend James Tyson presided; F. J. Shepherd spoke of Osler in Montreal, J. C. Wilson of Osler in Philadelphia, Welch of Osler in Baltimore, and Abraham Jacobi 'of the author and physician', till the victim writhed in his seat. Finally, in introducing Weir Mitchell, Tyson said 'the oldest and youngest authorities on old age are to be brought into intimate communion'; and Dr. Mitchell, with some appropriate, amusing, and affectionate phrases presented Osler with Logan's translation of the 'De Senectute', printed by Benjamin Franklin in 1744. Osler followed, though to age and the 'Fixed Period' he made no allusion. He spoke intimately of the happiness of his life—happiness which had come to him in many forms—in his friends; in his profession; in the public among whom he had worked both in Canada and the land of his adoption; in his home. With evident depth of feeling lightened only once with the usual touch of humour, he said just the right things about his affiliations with the profession and with his students, about his ambitions, and lastly, at the end, about his ideals:

> I have three personal ideals. One, to do the day's work well and not to bother about tomorrow. It has been urged that this is not a satisfactory ideal. It is; and there is not one which the student can carry with him into practice with greater effect. To it, more than to anything else, I owe whatever success I have had—to this power of settling down to the day's work and trying to do it well to the best of one's ability, and letting the future take care of itself.
>
> The second ideal has been to act the Golden Rule, as far as in me lay, towards my professional brethren and towards the patients committed to my care.
>
> And the third has been to cultivate such a measure of equanimity as would enable me to bear success with humility, the affection of my friends without pride, and to be ready when the day of sorrow and grief came to meet it with the courage befitting a man.
>
> What the future has in store for me, I cannot tell—you cannot tell. Nor do I much care, so long as I carry with me, as I shall, the memory of the past you have given me. Nothing can take that away.
>
> I have made mistakes, but they have been mistakes of the head not of the heart. I can truly say, and I take upon myself to witness, that in my sojourn with you—
>
> I have loved no darkness,
> Sophisticated no truth,
> Nursed no delusion,
> Allowed no fear.

To these his parting words, when published later on, he prefixed the line from Tennyson's 'Ulysses': 'I am a part of all that I have met.' Almost never did Osler betray his deeper feelings by any show of sentiment. His friends were well aware of this; it is a subject touched upon in a letter from Trudeau written only a few days after this dinner which he could not attend. Osler had sent for him to read a charming book by Stephen Paget—opportunely, Trudeau says, for it came at a time when he was low in mind from a relapse which had kept him for two months confined to his room and porch :

. . . I enjoyed ' Confessio Medici ' immensely [he adds] but it seems to me the author might easily write his name William Osler so much in it is so like you. The chapters about ' retirement ' pleased me most as they naturally appeal to me most. Velox and Prudens each struggling against disability in their own way are real and pathetic types. The book gives the student with startling clearness, the main features of the doctor's life, its achievements, and disappointments, and what it says about the possibilities of the professor of medicine it says admirably, but does it say all ? Are there no other ideals than efficiency and success ? I know you hate sentiment, but with some of us sentiment stands for a good deal and is a real factor in the problems of life : it is often the very spirit of that mysterious ' ego ' which governs our actions and shapes our lives after certain ideals, and to my mind *no field* offers such possibilities for the development of high ideals as does the medical profession. Excuse my rattling on in this way. I hope I may see you at the Congress if I am better by that time.

On Sunday the 15th Osler wrote his last notes from the corner of Franklin Street, and with a small handbag he left on the following morning for the meeting in Washington, leaving the bustle of packing-cases behind him, and escaping the sly remark that ' Willie's motto may well be *aequanimitas* because he always flees when things like this are going on '. He was not seen again by his family till they met for dinner three days later in New York. Meanwhile in these three days, the old Hoffman house, for seventy-five years a landmark in Baltimore, was emptied of its contents, and she who had been matron thereof for thirteen years, with the reaction of a New England housekeeper, finally introduced a battalion of scrubwomen who scoured it from attic to cellar—this, despite the fact that its demolition to make way for an ugly apartment-house was to begin early the next morning. Furniture, books, china, pictures, and memorabilia of all sorts not destined for Oxford, had been given away to people who would treasure them. The huge sideboard, for example, relic of the senior Gross and known as ' the grandstand ', a familiar sight to the legions of people who had broken bread at the table before it, went to the dining-room at the J. H. H. ; one of the ' latch-keyers ' inherited his desk, another his book-cases, another his favourite chair; and to another went a set of the first twenty *Atlantic Monthlies* with 'St. Robert' Winthrop canonized in a vignette on the back of the familiar old black-cloth covers. On the fly-leaf of vol. i, 1858, containing 'The Autocrat', the following lines had been inscribed: 'This set came from Phila with the Widow Gross when she undertook the care & education of one Egerton Yorrick Davis to whom the volumes were a daily comfort at breakfast at 1 West Franklin St. Baltimore'; and finally, as the curtain fell on the Wednesday, some one unscrewed and took away the unpretentious 'Dr. Osler' door-plate, behind which for all these years the faithful Morris had stood to welcome many a patient and many a friend.

Trudeau fortunately was well enough to attend the meetings in Washington—indeed, he was President that year of two societies Osler had helped to found—of the Association of Physicians, and of a younger society as well. He thus speaks of the occasion in his autobiography:

> When the National Association for the Study and Prevention of Tuberculosis, in which Dr. Osler was so prominent, was formed, I met him regularly at the early committee meetings, and it was no doubt greatly through his influence that I was elected the first president of this splendid national movement against tuberculosis. It was another red-letter day in my life when, at the first meeting of this National Association, in Washington on May 18, 1905, I stood on the platform with Dr. Osler and Dr. Hermann M. Biggs and addressed the great, earnest body of physicians and laymen before me.

The 'Physicians' met on the 16th and 17th, and in his presidential address on the opening day, Trudeau very feelingly spoke of Osler's departure in the usual terms: 'brilliant attainments', 'indefatigable energy', 'genial disposition', 'striking personality', and so on, adding that 'after he has left us his heart will by no means be the only one to show "cardiac cicatrices"'—an allusion to something Osler had said in a recent address. Osler probably was writing 'James Bovell' on a pad while this eulogy was delivered, and later took part in the discussion of some of the scientific papers as though his work in America was just beginning instead of ending.

And so it was with the meeting of the N. A. S. P. T., to

which Trudeau referred—a red-letter day when not only he but Osler and Biggs as Vice-Presidents all gave addresses. Osler particularly stressed the further education of both public and patient, saying that 'no greater mistake is possible in the treatment of tuberculosis than to keep from the patient in its early stages the full knowledge of its existence'—a radical point of view for those days. A long programme of scientific papers followed, and thus this very successful and important society was launched. With it from the outset Osler had had much to do, and now he must begin all over again in a similar campaign of education in Oxfordshire.

He had somehow during this time finished the revision for the 6th edition of his Text-book, and in the preface dated May 17th [1] and therefore possibly penned in Washington, he says 'so many sections have been rewritten and so many alterations made that in many respects this is a new book'.[2] This done, and leaving it with W. W. Francis to see through the press, he fled to New York. In his account-book, sometime or other, he subsequently wrote the following brief note:

Sailed from New York on the Cedric on the 19th almost dead! Arrived in Oxford Saturday evening [May 27th], went directly to Mrs. Max Müller's house 7 Norham Gardens which we had taken furnished. I was blue as indigo for the first two or three days. I was thoroughly worn out and it was six weeks or more before I felt myself.

---

[1] To show the necessity of these constant revisions it may be noted that on this very day, May 17th, a paper by Schaudinn and Hoffmann was read before the Berlin Medical Society, modestly announcing the discovery of the *Spirochaete pallida* as the cause of syphilis—a discovery almost as important as that made by Koch twenty-three years before, of the tubercle bacillus.

[2] It was this (6th) edition that provoked the amusing doggerel poem signed 'S. S.'—'The Student's Guide to Osler' that appeared in the *Guy's Hospital Gazette* for Oct. 2, 1907, ii. 240. 'S. S.' was a brilliant Cambridge and Guy's man, H. O. Brockhouse, who died in 1917.

END OF VOLUME I

PRINTED IN ENGLAND
AT THE OXFORD UNIVERSITY PRESS